W9-CMI-771

Merry Xmas Vigilos

2000

Frank Seeley

Stompin' Tom Connors

STOMPIN' TOM
and
The Connors Tone

VIKING

VIKING
Published by the Penguin Group
Penguin Books Canada Ltd, 10 Alcorn Avenue, Toronto, Ontario, Canada
M4V 3B2
Penguin Books Ltd, 27 Wrights Lane, London W8 5TZ, England
Penguin Putnam Inc., 375 Hudson Street, New York, New York 10014, U.S.A.
Penguin Books Australia Ltd, Ringwood, Victoria, Australia
Penguin Books (NZ) Ltd, cnr Rosedale and Airborne Roads, Auckland
1310, New Zealand

Penguin Books Ltd, Registered Offices: Harmondsworth, Middlesex,
England

First published 2000
10 9 8 7 6 5 4 3 2

Printed and bound in Canada on acid free paper ∞

Canadian Cataloguing in Publication Data

Connors, Stompin' Tom, 1936–
    Stompin' Tom

Contents: v.2. Stompin' Tom and the Connors tone.
ISBN 0-670-86488-9 (v.2)

1. Connors, Stompin' Tom, 1936–   . 2. Country
musicians - Canada - Biography. I. Title.

ML420.C743A3 1995   782.42164'2'092   C95-930694-3 rev.

Song lyrics copyright © Crown-Vetch Music Limited.

Visit Stompin' Tom's web site at **www.StompinTom.com**
Visit Penguin Canada's web site at **www.penguin.ca**

With gratitude,
I hereby dedicate this portion
of my autobiography
to my wife, Lena.
Without her assistance, support,
patience and devotion, this
work might not have been do-able.

Contents

Introduction   xi

The Big "Harrumph"   1

More Ups and Downs   6

My Pick-up Truck, "The Boot"   21

Well Suited for Business   30

Landing the Horseshoe   33

Flat Tires and Mufferaws   45

Bud the Spud on P.E.I.   56

My Return to Skinners Pond   64

Billboards and Toying Around   72

Newfies and Huskies   79

Wheeling, a Nickel and Doc   85

The Parade and the Pandemonium   93

All Prepared and No Play   102

Hassles, Lawyers and Companies   109

My First Juno Award   121

Hats, Beer and Recordings   132

Touring Ireland and England   149

My First Road Manager   166

Touring the Prairies   174

Massey Hall and Filming the Tour   186

Stompin' Tom with Hank and Wilf   196

From Skinners Pond to "The Mags"   205

British Columbia and the
    Northwest Territories   218

The Marten Hartwell Story   229

From the Horseshoe to "the Movies"   234

Mayor Crombie and the CNE   243

To Newfoundland and the Maritimes   255

Wedding Plans and Touring West   268

We're "Trading Hearts" Today   281

Our Extended Honeymoon   288

"Stompin' Tom's Canada" TV Series   303

One Out, One In and One Down   318

Clearing Trees and Beards   323

Buying a House and Building a Dam   328

Double "C" Resorts and Juno Theories   337

Tom Jr., the First Six Months   344

Junos, Gumboots and Calendars   351

I'll Give Up Music for One Year   362

Meeting "Mr. Trouble"   371

"Everything's All Right" with Peter   379

Quitting the Music for Good   385

Skinners Pond Vigilantes?   390

Feeling the Pinch   397

What Better Community Service...?   400

Fate Had Another Plan   407

The Fox Is in the Hen House   415

Driving "On Top of the World"   420

The Connors Tone Rejected   434

Discoveries, Birthdays and Games   439

To Assist Canadian Talent   449

Two Bombshells   459

More Tricks of the Trade   466

Dealing with Dean   475

Planning "the Comeback"   481

Stompin' Tom Returns   494

Awards, Tours and Videos   503

In Sixteen Overseas Countries   512

"The Hockey Song" Reborn   532

Lifetime Award for the Doctor?   538

The Cup, the Flag and the Key   542

Books, "Whacks" and Awards   547

A Book Launch for the Record   552

My Sixtieth Birthday Award   560

The Order of Canada Medal   568

A New Bridge for Bud the Spud   576

"Man of the Land" Tour '98   583

Everyone Sang at Maple Leaf Gardens   594

Winding Down for Another Start   601

My Last Twentieth-Century Tour   604

SOCAN Awards and Gretzky Scores   618

Lights Out at Lulu's   624

The Doctor Concludes   629

Appendix   637

Selected Discography   643

Introduction

The first thing I'd like to do is thank everybody for making my first book, *Before the Fame,* a number one bestseller. This was beyond my wildest dreams. It surprised not only me, but everyone in the industry.

The feedback letters to the book publisher and me were overwhelming. Most people said how they really enjoyed the no-frills, honest and straightforward way in which I told my story. Some even said it was the best book they ever read. Wow! I just don't know how to handle that one. But anyway, this book is written in exactly the same way. A spade is still a spade, so why call it something it isn't?

I guess if I'd been cut out to be an author in the first place, though, I might have had this book finished several years ago. But as writing doesn't come all that easy to me, I have a tendency to let a lot of other things come first. Anyway, at long last, I finally finished the work I started out to do away back in 1978.

Now, as one will gather, the title of this book has a lot to do with the word "tone." Music has tone, muscles have tone, voices have tone, colour has tone, and so does the predominating disposition of every thinking human being. It's something like one's demeanour, or the manner of spirit in which one behaves or carries himself through life. The tone of one's character, you might say.

So what this autobiography attempts to do is convey the

tone of one man's life from the beginning to the present.
This is something my music alone has not been able to do.
Therefore this book and the preceding one, both written
by my own hand, are a necessity for those who wish to
understand where Stompin' Tom's life and music and
other dealings fit within the framework of this great and
wonderful country.

So in the attempt to expand the meaning of the word
"tone" to cover a lot more than just Stompin' Tom and his
music, I have decided to call this book, *Stompin' Tom and the
Connors Tone*. This title appropriately describes the way, the
manner and the spirit in which I usually set out to accomplish things. Just an all-encompassing word that includes the
motives, methods, attitudes and aspirations of a private person by the name of Tom Connors.

As the Tone of Stompin' Tom may be found on recordings and in concert halls, the Tone behind the image may
only be found within the pages of this autobiography.

Tom Connors
February 29, 2000

Stompin' Tom

and

The Connors Tone

The Big "Harrumph"

IT WAS SATURDAY, August 19, 1967. The afternoon was overcast as I drove from my friends the Chapmans in Etobicoke to Rock Hill Park, near Shelbourne, Ontario, where I was scheduled to appear that night on the Hank Snow Show. Reg and Muriel were going to arrive later with another couple to take in the show but I had to be there early to receive my instructions and to find out what position I would have in the line-up of entertainers.

To say I was nervous about the prospects of playing on the same stage as Hank Snow would be an understatement. He had been one of my biggest country music idols all my life, and even though he had put the run to me at his ranch in Madison, Tennessee, and slammed the door of his dressing room in my face one time in an Edmonton arena, I still thought the world of his picking and singing and somehow hoped that sharing the stage with him would give me a much better impression of the man and that things could be different. But, as they say, "Just keep on hoping." The dream was never to be.

The stage at Rock Hill Park was on a barge anchored close to the shore of a small lake. It was built something like a houseboat. The stage faced the benches on the shore and had two large ramps, one on each side, extending from the stage to the beach. Backstage was a large shared dressing room; the whole barge was covered with a roof which

1

extended well out over the front of the stage.

About an hour before show time, it started to rain a little and we all headed for the dressing room to tune and retune our instruments (a job that can be very difficult on a rainy day). Before long, Hank's band, the Rainbow Ranch Boys, had also joined us and began ding-ding-dinging in an effort to keep everything in tune. They were very friendly to the rest of us and chatted quite freely about all things musicians talk about—until Hank himself arrived. At which time you could notice a marked change in the atmosphere. Hank didn't speak to anyone except his own boys and outside of a little shuffling around, the room was nearly silent.

After Hank was in the room for a while and appeared to be finished with the series of short exchanges he had had with his boys, he came over and stood near the wall, not too far from where I was standing. Although it was hard to see past the glitter of his rhinestone suit, I cautiously resolved to break the ice and finally meet the man. The least I could do, I thought, was to tell him how much I'd always loved his music and that I knew practically every one of his songs.

Then, as I turned slightly and took a step towards him, saying, "Hi, Mr. Snow, I've always been a great fan of yours . . ." he gave me a loud disheartening "Harrumph," pushed me slightly, and walked over to where his rhythm guitar player was standing.

The slight certainly didn't go unnoticed by the rest of the musicians in the room but they all just stood there looking a little bit embarrassed, to say nothing of myself and the way I felt. But there was more.

Hank then reached down and took his guitar out of its case. Without even strapping it on, he gave it one quick strum and pushed the edge of it into the midsection of his rhythm player and loudly proclaimed, "I thought I told you to tune this thing." Though the rest of us agreed later that Hank's guitar sounded perfectly in tune, his red-faced rhythm player nevertheless took it, gave it a strum, turned one tuning key a little, and asked Hank if he thought that would be "all right now?" Hank grunted something, took the guitar back, turned the same key a couple of times, and then put it back in its case.

"Wow," I thought, "I sure wouldn't want to be working for him." (A sentiment also expressed by some of the others later.)

Counting myself, doing a single act, there were three groups performing before Hank came on that night and my spot was in second place. I was supposed to do three numbers but due to the fact that it had started to rain a little heavier, I was asked to drop a number to speed the show up a little. Besides, everyone was there to see Hank, and the weather being what it was, people were beginning to be a little agitated.

As soon as I sang "Sudbury Saturday Night" and "The Ketchup Song" the crowd were already asking for Hank, and by the time the next act came out the rain was getting so bad some people were going to their cars or coming up the ramps onto the stage to get in under the roof where it was dry. The last band didn't seem to mind this, and as the stage was very large, they even encouraged more people to come up out of the rain, which was now coming down in bucketfuls.

Another clap of thunder and a flash of lightning and everyone who couldn't get on the stage immediately went to their cars, leaving the benches completely empty.

Then came Hank on the stage with the Rainbow Ranch Boys. Quickly stepping up to the mike, he demanded to know where all the security people were and why the crowd had been allowed on the stage. "The show stops right here," he declared, "until all these people are back in their seats. And if they don't want to listen from their seats, they can listen from their cars but there won't be a performance from me until this stage is cleared."

With a defiant look at everybody standing on the stage, he calmly waited till everyone faced the sheets of pouring rain and made their way, not to their seats, but to their cars, from where the majority quickly vacated the premises in the middle of his first song.

By this time I had spotted Reg and Muriel and their company and quickly made my way down one of the ramps to join them in their car. And although Muriel rolled down the window to hear Hank sing "My Mother," a song she had grown to love as a kid, she said she was never so disappointed in her life about the lack of concern that her hero, the great and wonderful Hank Snow, displayed towards his fans on such a dreadfully stormy night.

After a very short show of six or seven numbers, performed before an audience of less than ten cars of real die-hard fans, Hank and his boys were whisked away to a party at some unknown location. A party to which the rest of the entertainers and I had been previously invited, but we were later taken to another place instead. Here we were given our paycheques, a cob of corn, a couple of beers, and were asked to perform for a bunch of people we had never met.

Had I known this beforehand I would have simply gone home to Etobicoke with Reg and Muriel when the rain stopped and got them to mail my cheque to me later. But, as it was, I didn't arrive home until about three o'clock in the morning.

The first thing I did was get my sofa bed ready in the basement, go to the fridge and get a beer, and just sit and think about the show that I and everyone else had thought would prove to be the biggest break I could ever have up until then. The only conclusion I could arrive at, however, was that everything had been a complete disappointment. And the only resolve I made before going to sleep was that "if the only chance I ever get to make it in the music business has to come by way of thinking as much of myself as Hank Snow appears to think of himself, then I and the music business have nothing in common, and the powers that be who think otherwise can take their 'opportunity of a big break' and shove it. For on this point, I can in no way compromise."

One bright spot to this story, however, came the next day when Reg informed me that somewhere in the midst of the last evening's turmoil, just as Hank was being whisked away during a brief let-up in the downpour, he had rushed up to Hank, and said, "How are ya doin' Hank? I remember you from your days in New Brunswick. How about signing your name on this record I just bought?" Hank had smiled obligingly and given Reg his autograph.

Though at first I thought Reg was joking, I had to believe

him after I actually saw Hank's signature. It must have been the only one he gave that night. And given the mood he was in, it still remains a mystery to me as to why he gave it to Reg. Could it be because he and Reg are exactly the same height? And does Hank have a penchant for short people and an aversion to tall ones? Whatever the answer, I told Reg he was quite fortunate and the subject soon changed to other things.

More Ups and Downs

ONE OF REG'S NEIGHBOURS had heard that a night club down on the Queensway was holding a country jamboree on the following Saturday night, and as I had nowhere to play between now and then I gave them a call, went down to see the owner and got myself hired. It didn't pay much but I played the gig anyway as I always attached a great deal of importance to public exposure. I also took a few copies of my new album with me, but I didn't get the opportunity to sell any. The following day, Sunday, August 27, I headed out for my return gig at the Seacliffe Hotel in Leamington.

Upon driving through London, in southwestern Ontario, I dug up the address of an agent by the name of Rice, and although it was a Sunday afternoon, I went to his home to see him. He said he had never booked a single act before but because he was so impressed that I had an album he booked me for a week in mid-September in the old hotel in Stratford. This suited me just fine as I proceeded on my way to Leamington.

As I set up my equipment that night at the Seacliffe, the night-man came around with a beer and began to chat. "Since you were here the last time, Tom, the whole town has been a-buzz about that song you wrote about ketchup and potatoes. And I have no doubt that you'll have this place hoppin' for the next couple of weeks."

"Well, I'm glad to hear they liked it," I said, as I went

about testing my PA system, little realizing how true his words would prove to be.

When I came into the lounge to start my show on Monday night the place was packed. There were about twenty requests for "The Ketchup Song" and not one for anything else. Naturally, I sang it, and then told them the story about the plastic ketchup bottle I dropped from the plane in Wawa. The place went crazy and stayed that way for the next two weeks. And even without "The Ketchup Song" on my new album, they bought lots of copies by the time I left.

While I was there I took a drive one day to Kingsville to visit the Jack Miner's Bird Sanctuary and wrote a song called "When the Geese Come Back to Kingsville," but I lost the words not long after. I've always promised myself to rewrite the song but just never got around to it.

Another day, after listening to a country DJ on a radio station from Detroit, Michigan, I decided to take a copy of my new album *Northlands' Own*, across the border to see if he might play a selection or two from it. After calling and making an appointment to see him, I headed for Detroit. But when I got to the customs office at the border, my troubles began.

Although I told the officer the nature of my visit and that I would not be staying in the States for more than an hour, he wouldn't let me in with all those boxes of albums without paying the duty. Then I found out that if I paid the duty I would have to pay it again at the Canadian customs upon my return. What was I to do?

I had to drive back half a mile, go into the bus terminal and rent about ten luggage compartments and fill each one of them with records. With such a long way to carry each heavy box, it not only took me more than an hour but I was damn well tired by the time I drove back up to the customs office. When I finally appeared with one album to show the officer, he decided to search my vehicle to see what else I might have.

When at last he let me through, I drove directly to the radio station, but the DJ I was to meet had long gone. I was given the address of his home but to find it would have taken too long and I would have had more problems at the

customs office for overstaying my time limit. I therefore left
my album with someone else at the station and headed back
to the border. After loading up with all my records again at
the bus terminal, I started back to Leamington, arriving just
in time to do my show.

Although I listened to the DJ every day after that, I never
heard one mention of me or the album, so I just chalked it
up as one more bad experience.

I also did a brief interview with one of the reporters from
the local Leamington newspaper about "The Ketchup Song"
before I left town but whether it ever got printed I don't
know. I was then off to Stratford.

I didn't do too well in Stratford, being completely
unknown, and try as I might I couldn't seem to write a song
about the place. All I could do was think of Shakespeare,
and to write and sing and stomp my foot to a country song
about Shakespeare in an old run-down hotel just didn't
seem to ring my bell. "Achin' for a Beer with Shakespeare"?
No, I don't think so.

Anyway, when the boss paid me off on Saturday night, he
also paid me an interesting compliment. "One thing I can
say about you is that you might make a lot of noise with your
foot on the stage but you're really good with the customers
and not *overly good.*" When I asked him what he meant by
that, he told me, "The guy that was here last week asked to
run up a bar tab. When I came to pay him last Saturday, he
had bought so many drinks for the customers, for the band
and himself, that I not only didn't owe him any money but
he had to promise me he'd come back and play for me for
two more weeks for nothing just to settle his bar bill."

I laughed and said, "That wouldn't happen to be 'So and
So' would it?" He said, "Yeah, that's the guy. Do you know
him?" I said, "Well, let's just say in this business you run into
a lot of interesting characters and this guy is certainly one of
them." With that, I immediately jumped in my station wagon
and headed back to the Chapmans' in Etobicoke.

Arriving around three or four o'clock on Sunday morning, I quietly let myself into the house, went straight to bed
and didn't wake up till twelve or one o'clock in the afternoon. Then as I filled up on "goulash," one of my favourite

meals of macaroni and hamburg meat which Muriel quite often cooked, she informed me that my Toronto agent had called with a return engagement for two weeks in Barrie and then a double billing with another single act by the name of Vic Heluin back in Kirkland Lake at the Franklin Hotel.

This was good news, as it not only gave me a full month's work but it tied in very nicely with some other dates I already had booked for later on in the fall. It also gave me a chance to once again see my old bartender buddy, Gaet Lepine, if he was still managing the Franklin.

My first week in Barrie went over well and to make the second week even better I was able to land a guest shot on the "Alphie Fromangie Show" on the local television station. Alphie and his band were quite well known because of his weekly program and they played for a lot of dances throughout the area. It was funny the afternoon I arrived at the station to do the taping. Alphie and the boys accepted me quite readily but when the producer and others saw me carting a large piece of plywood onto the set they didn't know what in hell was about to take place.

They had their mike already set up for me to sing into, and when I slapped the board down in front of it someone in the control room was very audibly heard through the monitors to say, "Now, what in the name of jeezes does he think he's going to do with that?" The boys all started to laugh but nobody else seemed to think it was very funny. With the monitors now shut off and nobody but the studio director with his headphones able to hear what was being said, he sure got some funny looks on his face as he continued to listen. Finally, he took the headphones off and said, "They want to know what the plywood is for?" "For stompin' on," I said, and proceeded to give the board four or five heavy whacks with my boot. "Is that really necessary?" he asked, shaking his head. "It sure is," I said. "I can't really do my thing without it." With that, he marched off to the control room for a conference while the boys in the band continued to look very amused.

After a few minutes they called Alphie into the room and from what I was able to learn from him later, they wanted to know where in the f--- he "dug this guy up from, anyway?

Does he sing at all or just bang hell out of the board?" They also wanted to know if he had a couple more of his own numbers ready that he could do so they wouldn't have to use me. When he told them that he didn't and that he was taking medication for his sore throat as it was, they decided to proceed with this "wild man" as scheduled and take their chances, albeit reluctantly.

When the conference was over and the show was finally taped, everyone seemed to be quite happy with the results. But as I was leaving with my guitar and my board safely tucked under my arm, I could plainly see from the corner of my eye that some of them were still shaking their heads.

The show was aired during that first weekend and through the next week a lot of people who watched it said they thought it was great. A number of months later I found out the station ran the show a couple more times, so I guess in the end they too must have figured it wasn't really all that bad after all.

I hadn't sold nearly as many copies of my album in Barrie as I was about to sell in Kirkland Lake. Most of the songs it contained were about the north, and especially "Movin' on to Rouyn," which mentioned Kirkland several times.

When I got there on Sunday night, Gaet was hanging around the bar awaiting my arrival. Although he managed the place, he sometimes entertained on the stage himself and understood the value of a good PA system; since I'd been there last, he had acquired a whole stage full of excellent equipment. This meant I didn't have any setting up to do, so we immediately got into the beer and settled down for a long night's chat.

We talked about the night I left in the middle of the big snowstorm and wondered how in hell I ever made it. "You sure had a lot of nerve," he said. "But in a way, it was a good thing you went when you did. The roads around here were closed for two days after that and nothing moved."

Sitting with us and taking it all in was the other single act, Vic Heluin, who was just getting started in the business and was going to be playing during my breaks for continuous entertainment. At first he was looking at me like I was some kind of a big star or something, what with having an album and all, but I soon assured him that I was just a struggling musician the same as himself, and this broke the barrier that quite often prevents people from becoming friends while still having to compete with one another in front of the same audience.

For the next two weeks we got along fine, complimenting each other on our stage performances at night and chumming around together in the daytime when Gaet was too busy to join us.

At other times Gaet and I would go and shoot some snooker in the pool room, a game at which we were pretty well evenly matched, or sit up at night and play table hockey, at which I always got massacred. We also talked a lot about songwriting and other aspects of the music business. Gaet always liked writing and singing so much that he eventually went on the road entertaining for a while, sometimes as a single and sometimes with a group. Unfortunately, the combined problems of trying to keep up the hectic pace and the difficulty of holding on to good musicians soon got him down and he had to quit.

I suspect that Vic Heluin must have quit also, for on the last night in Kirkland we exchanged autographed photos, shook hands and wished each other well. And that's the last time I ever heard of him.

The next two weeks were spent doing a return engagement at John Daley's Hotel in Swisha, Quebec, and then with the prospects of having an idle week before returning to Peterborough, I called my agent to see if he had anything. If not, I thought of just driving around to see what I might pick up on my own.

As it was, the agent said he had a gig in a rundown hotel near Dovercourt and Bloor, in the city of Toronto, if I wanted to consider it. He said it was only for two nights on that following weekend and if I thought it was worthwhile to drive down and set up for it, he would have the contract there for me to sign when I arrived.

I decided to take it, even though the money was only scale. I always wanted to break into the Toronto market and one never knew just when some little gig might lead to something bigger. But, alas, not this time.

When I arrived on Friday the boss wasn't around and nobody knew anything about any contract. When I called the agent, he assured me he had delivered it so I might as well set up and play and he was sure when the boss arrived he'd know all about it.

Well, although it was against my better judgment, that's what I did. But the boss didn't show up that night. The next day the boss didn't show up either. But I was told not to worry. The boss had phoned in with instructions to go on playing. He had the contract and would be in later on that night to settle everything up with me. I didn't like the smell of it all, but being half-way through the commitment, I decided to comply.

At the end of my last set, just as I was beginning to take down my equipment, the boss arrived from out of nowhere and called me into the office. He told me he had forgotten the contract at home and passed me $40 for my trouble, saying that was the amount he thought was on the contract.

I had been in these situations before. And as I thought of the safety of my equipment, I just took the money and said nothing. Then when I finally got everything packed away in my station wagon I went back in on the pretext of having forgotten something. When I got to his office door, I rushed in. He was still counting money, and as I spied a hundred-dollar bill lying on the desk by itself, I grabbed it and ran. By the time he got around to alert anyone else about what had just happened, I was long gone. I didn't think he'd call the police as I only took what belonged to me, and as far as I know, he didn't.

I didn't bother to drive out to Reg and Muriel's in Etobicoke that night but opted instead to grab a cheap motel room somewhere in Scarborough as I would have to drive to Peterborough in the morning.

Before going to sleep that night, as I thought about what I had done, I wondered if I shouldn't have just let it go by and then gone to the musicians' union about it later. But then I remembered another incident which happened to me around 1960 at a tavern on Yonge Street near Wellesley Street, in Toronto.

I had secured a union contract for two weeks for myself

as leader and two other musicians. Richard Scrapnick from New Toronto, who had once been a victim of polio, was the drummer, I played the rhythm and sang, and a girl singer, whose name I now forget, played the bass. I seem to recall that the entire contract came to $500 with half to be paid after the show on each Saturday night.

There were at least three or four copies of the contract. One for myself, one for the owner of the tavern, and the rest went to the union office. Again, everything went well until Saturday night when the owner called me into his office to get paid.

As he invited me to sit at the desk across from him he pushed three little piles of money containing ten-dollar bills towards me and a cheque for $250 with no signature on it. "Here's your money," he said. "Just sign the cheque on the back and we'll consider it cashed." As I picked up the pen, I decided to quickly spread a couple of the piles of money and discovered they each contained exactly $50.

"There's no more than $150 here," I said. "The contract calls for $250, so where's the rest?" "Come on now," he said. "You're not going to try to be difficult with me, are you?" When I asked him what he meant, he accused me of being naïve and became very irate about it. He said it was obvious I hadn't played the hotel circuit very long and explained to me that the manner in which I was getting paid was the way it worked everywhere. "Everybody signs the cheque to please the union and then accepts the going rate. That way everybody's happy."

"Well, I'm not happy," I said, "and I'm not signing the cheque for anything less than $250, and if there's anything else I don't understand, which is not covered by our contract, I'll find out about it at the musicians' union office first thing on Monday morning."

"Listen, you stupid son of a bitch, that's not going to get you anywhere. We have a hotel association and I'll have your name blackballed all over town. You'll never get another job in Toronto, so why don't you smarten up, take your money, and don't be such a crybaby?"

I didn't listen to the rest of what he had to say; I just walked out and slammed the door, leaving him, the cheque, the money, and everything else just sitting on the table. When the band asked me what happened I just told them we didn't get paid and I was going to the union first thing on Monday.

On Monday morning, bright and early, I walked into the union office, and after waiting for over an hour I was finally given an audience with three union executives who looked more like three hoods from Al Capone's gang than musicians' representatives. They took me to a dingy-looking office where they all lit up cigars; one of them was sitting backwards on a small wooden chair, another was standing, and the other one was half lying on a big leather office chair with his feet resting on the desk. Two of them wore fedoras pulled down over their eyes, and the way they just kept glaring at me I felt like someone who was about to get the "third degree."

When I finally told them my story, they looked at each other knowingly, with a few hmm-hmmm's and ah-hah's, and told me to go back to the tavern and start playing tonight as if nothing had happened and they would "certainly look after the rest." What that meant I didn't know, but they sure gave me the impression that "someone" was about to receive a very hard time. Little did I know that "someone" was going to be me and the band.

We weren't on the stage ten minutes that night when four or five guys came storming in through the side door, walked over to the stage, and started pulling out our cords and ordering us off the stage immediately. When I asked for an explanation they merely said they were from the union and their orders were to prevent any union musicians from playing in this establishment until further notice. Before we knew what was happening, we found ourselves out in the alley with our instruments, cases, speakers, mikes and wires all in one big heap. There we were, left to sort things out, make a phone call to have someone come and pick us up (as none of us had our own transportation), and wait for the union to call us about any further developments. This they never did, of course, so after a couple of days I called them.

After getting the run-around for a while, I finally got hold of someone who knew something about the matter. I was told the tavern was now officially blacklisted and would never again be allowed to hire union musicians until they made restitution and paid the full amount of my contract even though I had not played for the whole two weeks. And what about me and the band? We'd get paid when the union received the money from the tavern.

Well, four or five years later I learned the tavern was employing union musicians and had been fully reinstated. After several phone calls from up north, I finally got talking to Gurney Titmarsh, the union's current president, and was told the union had lost their copy of my contract, but if I still had mine they would see what they could do. Well, with all the thumbing and bumming around I had done since 1960, I had lost my copy somewhere so that was that, and neither I nor the others have ever gotten paid (even to this day).

So as I thought of this incident and its final outcome while sitting on my bed that night in 1967, you can readily see why I didn't place much hope in going to the union over this recent matter. I merely felt justified about what I'd done, butted out my cigarette, and went to sleep.

The following morning of November 5, I set out for Peterborough. On my way through Oshawa I remembered I had an address for my old singing buddy Bud Roberts, so I decided to look him up and pay him a short visit if he was in town.

After I found the place and knocked on the door, Bud answered and before long we were into a big conversation about music. He said he had met someone who wanted to put out an album for him and as he didn't have enough songs written for it, he wondered if I might write him a song or two. The album wouldn't be recorded till sometime in the next year so that would give me lots of time to think about it. I of course said I'd be delighted to, as long as he made sure I got the proper credits for it on the album. With this being agreed upon, I was soon on my way to Peterborough again.

For the next two weeks in Peterborough everyone turned out again and brought their friends to see the guy they had named Stompin' Tom. It was getting to be like a family reunion. There was hardly anybody that I didn't know on a first-name basis and practically everybody was inviting me home for a Sunday dinner.

The second week I was there I ran into an old rock and roll DJ friend of mine by the name of Scott Alexander, whom I had met in Timmins. He asked me to write a short rock song for him with his name mentioned in it a couple of times, which I did. He liked it so well he got me to put it on tape for him, but whether he ever got to play it on radio I don't know.

On the last day I was there I got to thinking about writing a song about Prince Edward Island and all the potatoes they grow down there. Then I thought about Bud Roberts and the song he wanted me to write. Also remembering that Bud had once told me he used to drive a truck down in New Brunswick, it wasn't long before I realized that "Bud" rhymed with "spud," and before the afternoon was out I had scribbled on paper the words that would eventually become my best-known song. My signature song. "Bud the Spud."

My next gig was to be at the Thunderbird Motor Hotel in Brampton, Ontario, and as I would be driving through Oshawa to get there, I thought I'd drop in again to see Bud, if he was home, and tell him about the new song I had written for him to record. When I got there, Bud was just arriving home from playing a gig somewhere himself so we went into the house together, and I took out the scrap of paper and began singing him the song.

I was a little disappointed that he didn't appear to be all that impressed with the song, but I put it on tape for him anyhow, wished him good luck and left.

That evening I set up my gear in the basement lounge at the Thunderbird Motor Hotel in Brampton. My agent had booked the room for me some time ago and I had been looking forward to playing there. However, when I jumped on the stage for the first time on Monday night, I was in for a surprise.

The place was already about half full and I could tell right away by the accent of most of the beer-drinking customers that they were Newfoundlanders. This I welcomed. But what happened next caught me completely off guard.

A fairly pretty-looking girl wearing a long coat and sitting by herself in the front seat by the wall had not escaped my notice, but I no sooner started stompin' my foot like crazy to one of my fast songs when she flipped off the coat to reveal that she was wearing nothing underneath but a skimpy little bra and an even skimpier little G-string.

In another second she was beside me on the stage, dancing, shaking and gyrating as if this Wilf Carter style of a yodelling cowboy song was the greatest dance music she had ever heard. Immediately, everyone started to laugh. And just kept on laughing.

Now, I had played before in front of lumberjacks, miners, trappers, brawlers and drunks, in some of the damnedest shooting galleries you could ever shake a stick at, and through it all I was always able to maintain my control and composure. But on this occasion this smiling whirling dervish had me completely confused.

Not knowing whether the audience was laughing at me or at her, or at the combination of both of us, I stopped in the middle of a high yodel and asked her, "Can you please tell me, what in the name of Joseph and jeezes it is that you think you're doing here anyway?"

"Oh," she said, "I'm gonna be your go-go dancer this week." I said, "You're gonna *what*?" She said, "I'm gonna be your go-go dancer. Do you sing anything by the Beatles? I like the Beatles the best." "No, I don't," I said. "And I don't need any goddam go-go dancer to help me sing what I do sing. Now go back to your seat and sit down."

"I can't do that," she said. "I was hired here to dance for the entertainer, and that's what I'm going to do."

"Well, if that's what you're going to do, you can just keep right on doing it," I said, "but you'll have to do it without music, 'cause I won't be here to play it."

With that, I put my guitar in its case and walked off the stage, leaving her standing there.

By now, the audience had taken all this in, and believing they were in the middle of the first act of a comedy show, they were sitting on the edge of their chairs roaring and laughing and looking as if they could hardly wait for the next episode.

I took off up the stairs, three at a time, and stormed into

the boss's office and told him in no uncertain terms that no go-go girl was mentioned in my contract and I'd be damned if I was going to play and sing for one. "Either she goes or I go, right now," I said, "and I don't care what you do."

"Okay, okay," he said, "slow down. You stay and she goes. Most bands I bring in here appreciate the fact that I have a go-go girl available to dance for them as an added attraction. But if you don't want her, that's fine. The whole thing is optional. Now go on down and have yourself a beer and simmer down while I try to clear this thing up."

Once I realized the whole thing was a misunderstanding I felt a lot better and finally went down to have a beer and find the courage to get back on the stage. But not one second, of course, before I was absolutely sure my little Miss Go-Go was Gone, Gone, GONE!

For the rest of the night the beer went down pretty fast and I tried to put on one of my best shows ever, just to try to make up for the strange beginning. But in the end I began to realize that nobody else seemed to be in the least bit annoyed about the affair, so I soon put the whole thing behind me and acted as if it had never happened.

By the end of the week, I had gotten along so good with the Newfies I was going up on stage and making them laugh by telling them the very same Newfie jokes they had just told me during the break. They also cleaned me right out of albums and told the boss he'd better get me back as soon as possible or they'd quit drinking there every night.

When Saturday night came, the boss called me into his office and we signed another contract, only this time the gig would be for two weeks instead of one, and he assured me, "Next time, Tom, there won't be any go-go girls."

The next day I headed back to the Chapmans' in Etobicoke, which was no more than a thirty-minute drive. I hadn't seen them now for about three months, and as I had the whole next week off, I was looking forward to having a nice visit before heading out to Sudbury. Besides, I wanted to see my record company owner to find out when he wanted to record my second album, which I intended to call *On Tragedy Trail*. And I also needed to purchase another couple hundred copies of *Northlands' Own* before heading up north.

While visiting the owner, I signed another bunch of songs to him for his publishing company. These not only included the songs that would go on the new album, but some of the new songs I had just written, including "Bud the Spud." While I was there, the owner had a letter for me from my old hitch-hiking buddy, Steve Foote. Steve had come up to Ontario from New Brunswick recently, and had come across my album at Sam the Record Man's store and from the address on the album he decided to write me a note. As he was now living in Britt, Ontario, I decided to pop in to see him on my way to Sudbury.

Back at the Chapmans, one day about half-way through the week, Reg and I got to talking. Muriel was out for the afternoon doing her part-time job, and it occurred to Reg and me that she sometimes mentioned how she used to play the accordion at one time, and that she'd give anything to own one again. "Well, why don't you buy her one for Christmas?" I asked.

"In the first place, Tom, I can't afford a half decent one, and in the second place, I wouldn't know a good accordion from a bad one anyway."

I told him to jump in the station wagon and we'd take a run down to Church Street in Toronto where there were lots of pawn shops, and if we could find a real good one for a bargain I'd split the cost with him.

About the third pawn shop we went into, we spotted several real good-looking piano accordions sitting on a shelf and we bought the best one they had. Although I couldn't play an accordion, I could sure tell whether it was in tune or not, and this one was in excellent shape. It actually looked brand new.

I think they wanted around $100 for it, but after we dickered with them for a while we eventually got it for $85. In no time we were back home again, and by the time Muriel came home to supper, there it was sitting on the living-room table.

"Where did that come from?" she wanted to know, as she lightly touched it while her eyes became as big as saucers. "Who does it belong to?" "It belongs to you, dearie," said Reg, looking like the cat that swallowed the canary. "Tom and I bought it for you this afternoon down in Toronto."

"Come on now, Reg, you're just trying to pull my leg," she said, as she looked at me in disbelief. "Is that right, Tom?" When I told her it was and wished her a merry Christmas, she decided she'd better sit down before she fell down; for the next hour or so she couldn't keep her hands off it. At first she found it a little heavy, but was firmly resolved that that would be the least of her worries.

For the next couple of days, Reg would find many occasions to wink at me when he knew Muriel was within earshot and say, "Well, I don't know, Tom, I think we made a mistake getting Muriel that accordion. I notice there's not much work being done around here any more." And when Muriel would say something like "Ahh . . . shush up, Reg, I'm only trying out a couple of new chords and I'll be with you in a minute," he'd just look at me and laugh.

Anyway, before I knew it, it was Sunday again and I was heading out to Sudbury. I said goodbye to Reg and Muriel and their kids, and later that afternoon I pulled into Britt, Ontario, and went to the house where Steve was living.

It turned out that he and his girlfriend, Ginni, were staying with another couple who owned the house—Ralph Sharpe, and I seem to remember that his wife's name was Dora.

It was Dora who let me in, and when Steve spotted me from the living room, he ran to the kitchen to shake my hand while Ginni, who by now had heard so much about me, made a rather ungirlish spread-eagle jump towards me, and if I hadn't caught her the two of us would have landed in a strange-looking heap somewhere in the corner.

As everybody laughed, we were soon all introduced to one another, and the conversation began. It was almost four years now since I'd last seen Steve, and there was just no way we could talk about all the things that had happened to us from then till now. I only had a couple of hours to visit, so we just filled each other in on the important stuff and then I had to go. But I promised to call in again as soon as I came back this way, which I figured wouldn't be more than a couple of months.

That night I set up my equipment at the Brock-Dan in Sudbury.

My Pick-up Truck, "The Boot"

Now, it's at this time I think I'd better take stock of what I'm writing. In the last book, *Before the Fame*, I described things as they took place, almost on a weekly basis. And so far, in this book, I've started out doing the same thing.

Well, it just occurred to me that if I continue doing things this way, it will take another five hundred pages just to describe all the hotels and night clubs and the significant things that may have happened in each one of them before I even get to the most important parts of my career as Stompin' Tom.

Though I will have to slow down to give what I consider to be important detail from time to time, I will try from now on to avoid the routine of telling stories that may seem to the reader to have far too many similarities to something else they may have previously read.

In pursuing this course, I will have to apologize right now to some of the people who may have been instrumental in one way or another towards the furthering of my career and who may not receive an honourable mention. Having said this, I will now continue.

For the next three weeks the Laurentian University students came out in droves, and though Rudy, the owner of the Brock-Dan, offered to almost double my salary to stay over for Christmas and New Year's, I was already contracted to the Royal Hotel in Sault Ste. Marie.

After a hell of a good time in the "Soo," I was off again to Wawa. And by the last week of January 1968, for which I had no booking, I was slowly heading back to Toronto.

I say "slowly" because I stopped for a day here and there to see some friends, which I normally didn't get a chance to do, and of course I got to see Steve and Ginni again, back in Britt, before I finally landed in Toronto.

With just enough time to stock up with records again, I was off to a return gig in Collingwood and for the next month or so I just roamed around, either looking for new places to play or calling my agent to see what he might have. I played a week in Galt, one in Kingston and another in Penetang, and then I wound up doing a return gig in Pembroke, where readers of the first book will remember that I didn't do so well.

It wasn't the same this time, however. I didn't have Gordon Lightfoot playing across the street from me, and although I was only hired for one week, they held me over for another.

It was here also that Sweet Daddy Siki, the famous wrestler, who was also a well-known country and western entertainer at the time, came to pay me a visit. Unknown to me, he had picked up one of my albums in Toronto, where he lived, and had become a fan of the kind of songs I was writing, and when he heard I was playing in the same town as he was, he came over to take in one of my sets and brought his band along with him.

Having such a celebrity as Sweet Daddy sitting in the audience and clapping for every song certainly went a long way to enhance the esteem of any small-town performer. I know it certainly gained me a few notches of respect from the hotel's customers each time they learned he had been there.

I think it was the last week in March or the first week in April 1968 that I finished up in Pembroke. A couple of good friends of mine from Peterborough, Merv and Irene Marshall, had heard I was playing there and drove up to catch my last Saturday night's show. (A distance of nearly two hundred miles.) And the way things worked out, I was glad they did.

When the show was over, they stayed at the hotel for the night, and as I would be travelling to Toronto by way of Peterborough to record my second album on the following day, they waited for me and we headed out together.

Not more than thirty miles from town, I blew the motor out of my station wagon and Merv wound up towing me back to Pembroke. By a stroke of luck we stopped in at an auto wrecker's and the guy just happened to know where he could immediately obtain a Dodge slant-six motor to replace my own, and by six or seven o'clock that same night we were all back on the road again.

Around midnight we arrived at the Marshalls' house in Peterborough and quickly got into the beer. Although it had been a long day, we sat up and talked for two or three hours before hitting the sack, and about noon the following day I was off to Toronto.

With no bookings now for the next little while, I bunked down at the Chapmans' and began to wonder just how long the motor I had put in my station wagon was going to last.

One day as I was driving by the Dodge dealers, I spotted the new pick-up trucks that were lined up on the lot and decided to drop in for a better look. While I was there I got to thinking about the last visit I had had with Steve in Britt, and how much I had liked the plywood box that Ralph Sharpe had built for the back of his truck that he used for delivering the mail.

If I had one of these new trucks with the same kind of box on the back I could not only carry all my records and equipment, I thought, but I could also have a bunk and a little table where I could sleep and eat and save myself a good deal of money that I now had to spend on motel rooms and restaurants while I was on the road and looking for work.

The more I thought about the idea the better I liked it. So that evening I phoned Ralph to find out if he would build me a box like his if I bought the truck. When he assured me he would, but that he would also have to see the truck to take precise measurements, I went down the next day and traded my station wagon in on a brand-new all-white pick-up.

The day after that I drove it to Britt so Ralph could take

the measurements and get the details about how I wanted the inside to look, where I wanted the folding bunk, the table and the light fixtures, etc., and then I went back to Toronto to record my second album.

Several days later I was back to Britt and tickled pink to find out the box that Ralph had made fit the back of the pick-up perfectly and I was now standing and looking at the first structure I had ever been able to call "home."

The door at the back was regular house-door size, outfitted with a good dead-bolt lock and a window of plexiglass protected on the outside by a strong metal wire mesh. On the inside, the ceiling was about six foot four inches high, which gave me lots of clearance when I walked around with my hat on, and the bunk folded down from one side to just the right height for me to sit on when I was using the table, which folded down from the opposite wall.

I paid Ralph the money he wanted, along with a good-sized tip, and I must have thanked him a dozen times before heading back to Toronto.

Steve and Ginni were no longer living with the Sharpes at this time but had left me an address in Hamilton where I could contact them. And this I would be doing very shortly as I had another idea for my new home that I soon hoped would become a reality. First I had to paint it up just right with my name on it and a big picture of a guitar on both sides, and after I accomplished that I wanted Steve to paint a big working man's boot on each door of the cab. While I felt I could handle the painting of the box, I knew that only Steve could draw the kind of boot I wanted to see on my doors.

Though I can't seem to remember the exact date, I won't be too far off to say it was somewhere close to the first of May 1968. And when I drove up Firestone Road in Etobicoke and pulled into the Chapmans' driveway, everyone on the street was out looking and wondering who in the hell was pulling into Reggie's place now. I guess they thought I was selling fish or something. The way the unpainted box was shaped, it gave the overall appearance that a very large boot was just sliding its way up the street.

By the time I got out of the truck, there were already

several neighbours gathered around, and of course when they saw it was me they certainly had lots of questions to ask. When they found out the new truck was mine they said it was beautiful. "But what in the hell did you have to go and spoil the look of it for, by putting that crazy-looking box on it?"

"You ain't seen nothin' yet," I told them, "just wait till I get it all painted up. It's gonna be the talk of the town before I'm through. And by the time I get back this way again, sometime in July, you'll know what I mean."

After spending the next couple of days buying paint supplies I had to go on the road again. First I went back to the Thunderbird in Brampton for a couple of weeks where I managed to get the time to put the first coat of red paint on the box, and then during my next week off I went down to Hamilton to see Steve and Ginni. While I was there I got Steve to draw and paint the work boots on the doors, and then I went to Peterborough, Brockville and Renfrew.

By now, it was the first or second week of July, and due to a lot of rain and dampness over the last month I still didn't have all the painting completed. But now the weather was excellent, and with the next couple of weeks off, I decided to drive down to Picton, Ontario, where I knew the Chapmans and several of their friends were spending their holidays camping there. I resolved to finish the job.

By the time it was all done, it looked a lot like a Christmas tree, only in the shape of a boot. The box was fire-engine red and the guitar and all the lettering were a combination of blue, black and bright yellow. The truck itself of course was white and the whole thing was indeed a sight to behold. From that day on, whenever I spoke of her I referred to her simply as "The Boot."

The hotel owners thought she was the "cat's meow" and whenever I played their clubs they wanted her parked right in front of the place. And if nothing else, she was certainly a great conversation piece.

The only drawback I had with her, at first, was that I used to forget how high she was. One day while driving in downtown Toronto, I was looking for a place to park. Not being able to find one on the street, I pulled into a parking lot and drove up beside the attendant's cubicle and stopped.

The little Italian guy inside the hut began to wave his arms furiously as a signal to wave me off. When I finally got the idea that he didn't allow trucks of any kind in his lot, I got a little peeved, shoved her in gear and took off. Just as I did, the top of my box caught the edge of his overhanging roof and spun the cubicle right off its moorings with him in it. When I looked in my rear-view mirror to see what I hit, I could see the thing had been turned around to face a different direction and was still tottering back and forth. I figured this was no time to stop and ask questions so I decided to get the hell out of there. I could still see him shaking his fists through the window of the hut as I turned onto the street and very quickly got my ass out of there. I later figured he must have been too shook up to get my licence number because I never heard a word about it after. But from then on I tried to be just a little more careful. You never know what could be in your way.

For the rest of that summer of '68 I just kept making the rounds to some return engagements and managed to pick up a couple of new ones, one in Kemptville and the other in Carleton Place, both in the Ottawa Valley, and then towards the fall I ran into a drought. During the months of October and November, I just couldn't seem to land anything and the rest of my return gigs would not start again till sometime in January.

Most of my time was spent at the Chapmans', playing at a few parties and occasionally appearing at the odd jamboree, one of them being at the Locarno Ball Room on Danforth Avenue, Toronto, and another one at the Hayloft near Markham.

The first time I went to the Hayloft, I arrived kind of late and not knowing exactly what was going on, I submitted my name for the line-up of those who would be playing on stage, and after everyone had performed, they announced that I had won the "contest" and called me back on the stage to sing another song and present me with a hundred dollars. Not knowing I was even in a contest, I gladly went up and sang "Bud the Spud," collected the hundred dollars and went back to my seat.

Upon learning from someone sitting at my table that this

had been an "amateur contest" and realizing that I was a professional musician, although nobody around there knew it or had even heard of me for that matter, I decided to go up and give the money back. When everybody learned the truth and the three top prizes were finally redistributed to the three rightful winners, the audience gave me a standing ovation for coming forward as I did and bought me beer for the rest of the night for being honest.

While this didn't do my pocket-book any good at the time, it sure gained me a lot of future fans who came out to my shows whenever they heard I was playing somewhere within driving distance.

In mentioning the song "Bud the Spud" here, it reminded me that I had just recently started to sing it. When I had written it for Bud Roberts about a year before, I had expected he was going to sing it and record it. I had just learned about a month or so before, however, that Bud had indeed recorded the album but the song "Bud the Spud" was not on it. This left me somewhat disappointed so I started singing the song myself, and because of the favourable reaction I was getting from the audiences, I also became resolved to record it the first chance I got.

I hadn't seen Bud for about a year, and one evening in November I got a call from a DJ in Cobourg, Ontario, asking me if I'd drive down that night to play on a show he was putting on. He realized it was very short notice but explained that while he had expected several bands to perform, a couple of them had cancelled at the last minute, leaving him stuck. He said he'd like me to go on first if I could possibly make it.

The show was due to start at 8:00 P.M., I was seventy-five miles away, it was now about 5:30, so I thought I'd better get started. I jumped in the Boot and drove about twenty miles to the other side of Toronto when I realized I'd left my guitar at the Chapmans' and had to drive all the way back to get it. Reg met me at the door with it, tossed it in on the seat beside me, and without a second to lose I was on my way again.

When I walked in the door of the hall in Cobourg it was two minutes to show time, and without having a chance to go to the dressing room to see who else was going to be in the show, I was escorted immediately to the stage.

"Hi," I said, "my name is Stompin' Tom. Sorry I'm late, but I just wrote a song. I hope you like it." Then I started: "It's Bud the Spud, from the bright red mud, rollin' down the highway smilin'. The spuds are big on the back of Bud's rig, they're from Prince Edward Island. They're from Prince Edward Island."

There must have been a lot of east-coasters in the crowd because the whole house went wild and continued to do so as I kept belting out one song after another. When I finally let them know that I was about to sing my last number someone shouted, "Give us that potato song again," and about fifty or sixty of the others began shouting the same thing. So away I went again on "Bud the Spud" and left the stage to a standing ovation.

As I walked to the door of the dressing room, who was coming out but Bud Roberts. "Hi, how the hell are you, Bud? I didn't know you were playing here tonight," I said. But Bud only grunted something and made his way to the microphone.

For the next half hour I thought Bud and his band had done a great job, and when he came off the stage I was just about to tell him so when he said, "Well, you're some kind of a nice guy, aren't you? What kind of a dirty trick was that supposed to be?" Not having the foggiest idea what he was talking about, I said, "What do you mean?"

"What do I mean?" he said. "I mean, I thought you wrote 'Bud the Spud' for me. And here you are out there singing it. What gives?"

Well, this kind of threw me for a loop, so I started talking back to him in the same tone of voice as he was using. "Now, just a minute, Bud. I may have written the song for you to record, but I didn't 'give' it to you. Besides, you didn't think enough of it to record it anyway, so what are you so all fired up about?"

"I was saving it for my next album," he said, "but now I don't know if I want to record it or not." With that, he just started to walk away as I came back with, "Well, if you don't want to record the damn thing, don't bother. But I think it's a damn good song and one of these days I'll record it myself." At this point he was walking towards the other end of the room and I don't know whether he heard me or not.

That was the last time Bud and I saw each other for a while, but we did eventually get to solve our differences and over a period of time we once again became the best of friends. We don't now talk about it much, but I still think he kind of wishes that he had recorded "Bud the Spud" first.

Well Suited for Business

O N ANOTHER NIGHT IN LATE November of 1968 I was feeling a bit down in the dumps. My cash flow was dwindling and as I contemplated spending Christmas with the Chapmans, I wondered how I was going to afford to buy a few presents for everybody, especially the kids.

Before I knew it, I was expressing my concern about why it was that, no matter how hard I tried, I could never seem to land a half decent job in downtown Toronto. There were several adults in the kitchen, including a couple of the neighbours, and someone suggested that it might be because of the way I was always presenting myself. "You're always approaching these people in jeans, looking like a farmer," they said. "But when you're in the big city you should probably do like the rest of us when we have to go looking for a job. If you had a suit and a nice white shirt and tie, you could probably be a lot more successful."

"By God, that's right, Tom," Reggie agreed, "and didn't I see you in a suit in one of those pictures you brought down from Timmins? The one you had taken with Prime Minister Pearson? Have you still got it?"

"Yes, it's somewhere in my old suitcase, Reg," I assured him. "But there's no way I'm taking it out. After all, I'm a country and western singer and I don't intend to walk around looking like some kind of a city slicker. Besides, it's probably so wrinkled and yellowed by now, it would no doubt fall apart by the time I got it out of the suitcase."

Well, if you knew Reg Chapman, you'd probably know what I mean when I say he wouldn't take no for an answer. I argued back and forth with him for the next half hour and in the end I had to go and dig the suit out, just so they could "have a good look at it."

In another few minutes Muriel was saying, "Oh, there's nothing wrong with this suit, Tom. I'll wash and bleach the shirt tonight and press the suit and tie in the morning and have everything ready for you to wear by tomorrow evening."

Well, to cut a long story short, there I was. And with Reg and Muriel and about four others arguing against me, I couldn't win. And the following evening they decked me out in this ginky-looking suit, complete with cufflinks and the lit-tle brimless hat that went with it and sent me off to down-town Toronto to look for a job.

At that time the Edison Hotel on Yonge Street was a well-known country bar, and when I pulled up beside the place and stepped out of the Boot looking like the ambassador of France, everybody, including the hippies, just stopped and stared.

In a few minutes I was giving my spiel to a Mr. Clements, who must have been quite impressed with my suit, because he told me to go and get my guitar, get up on stage for twenty minutes or so, and show him what I could do. If he liked what he saw, he said he'd hire me for a week.

I guess he thought, by the look of me, I was going to sound like Engelbert Humperdinck or someone like that. But when I marched in with my flat-top guitar and slapped an old hunk of plywood on the stage and proceeded to kick the shit out of it, I could see he wasn't too impressed.

By the time I got to a song called "The Mule Skinner Blues," where I quack like a duck and yodel at the same time, the crowd were in stitches from laughing as Mr. Clements just walked to his office and slammed the door.

When I was finally done the audition, I went up to the bar and waited for the good word. When at last he re-emerged from the office I asked him, "Well, how did I do? Do I get the job?" "Get the f--- away from me," he said. "You stink, stink,

STINK. Do you understand what I'm trying to tell you? You S-T-I-N-K! Now get the f--- out of here." With that, he made a sign to the bouncer and took off back into his office.

Before you could say the time of the day, I found myself pushed out the door on Yonge Street with my guitar, my board and my brimless little hat thrown out behind me. As I scrambled through the onlookers to retrieve my guitar and the board, someone kicked my hat up the street a couple of times and just walked away laughing.

By the time the ambassador of France got back into the Boot he felt more like Charlie Chaplin when he played the Little Hobo. When I finally got to the Gardiner Expressway I was passing everybody and five minutes later, wouldn't you just know it, a cop pulled me over and gave me a ticket. By the time I got home, I was fit to be tied.

Off came the suit, the shirt and the tie, and everything went into the garbage. After three or four quick bottles of beer I finally simmered down and came upstairs where Reg and Muriel were waiting to hear the good news.

When I told them what had happened, Muriel was quite sympathetic. But Reg, always the one to see the funny side of everything, just sat there for the most part and laughed.

"Well, laugh all you want to, Reg," I said, "but that's the last goddamned time you'll ever see me dressed up in a suit." That only made him laugh all the more, until he fixed himself his favourite onion sandwich and took off to the bedroom. After saying good night to Muriel, I went downstairs, sat and had a couple more beers and finally went off to sleep.

Landing the Horseshoe

ON THE TWENTY-EIGHTH or twenty-ninth of November, I got my courage up again and decided to go down to Toronto and try the Horseshoe Tavern, only this time minus the suit. I really didn't have much faith in landing a job there because the Horseshoe was known all over Canada. Everybody who was a country fan and who landed in Toronto for any reason, either by plane, car, bus or train, for any length of time, sooner or later wound up paying a visit to the Horseshoe. The owner's name was Jack Star and he had kept the place "country" through thick and thin now for over twenty years and the club had a great reputation. There was hardly a weekend that the place wasn't packed, due mainly to the fact that he would always bring in a big-name act from Nashville, Tennessee, to play on Friday and Saturday night. So it was with a great deal of trepidation that I walked into the Horseshoe this day and asked to see Mr. Star, especially after my experience at the Edison.

When Jack finally arrived on the scene, I was pleasantly surprised to find that he was a very quiet, congenial man, even though he had the demeanour of a person who knew his business very well.

He made me feel at ease, and I began telling him what I had done, where I had been up until now, and just how much I wanted a chance to play his club to see how well I could fare.

"Well," he said, "I'm trying out a new house band next week, and if you want to come in and see if they can back you up, I'll give you the opportunity to see what you can do. Bring your contract in before you start on Monday night and I'll sign you on for a week."

Hardly believing my ears, I beat my way back home to the Chapmans' and that's all I talked about for the whole weekend. On Monday at around four o'clock in the afternoon, I arrived at the Horseshoe and just sat there for the next five hours until show time at 9 P.M. The only interruption to my thoughts was when Jack Star came over to my table and asked me if I had my contract ready. He hardly looked at it at all, signed it, and gave it back to me. He then shook my hand and said, "You must really want to play here. I've been watching you sit there for the last three or four hours and I don't think you took your eyes off the stage once."

When he left, I thought to myself, "If he only knew just how much I want to play here. Oh! How much do I want to play here! There's just no words I can find to describe it." I would have played there for nothing had he asked me to.

Pretty soon the band came in and set up their gear and after we were all introduced the crowd began to flow in and the music started. The band was to play for half an hour and then call me up for half an hour and then we'd break for half an hour. This system would repeat itself three times during the night and then we'd quit at one o'clock in the morning.

"This gig is going to be a snap for me," I thought, because every place I had ever played up until now, I had to carry the whole ball all by myself. I usually had to start at 8 P.M. instead of 9, and do four one-hour sets with only a fifteen-minute break after each hour before I was through for the night at one o'clock. Here I would only have to play for an hour and a half during the whole night. "But, no matter what happens, I'm gonna give it my best shot," I said to myself. And I did.

From the time I dropped my board on the stage and started to sing, I never looked back. At first the boys in the band found it hard to keep time with me, but as soon as they realized my left heel was always coming down on the off beat rather than the down beat, they quickly understood what was going on and started to have almost as much fun watching me as did the audience. Even the waiters who had been there for twenty years or more were seen from time to time to just be standing there wondering how in the hell I could stand on one foot for so long and go through the antics that I did without falling down.

Then with the benefit of having a whole hour off, from the time I left the stage till the time I got back on again, I consumed a beer at every table, talked to everyone, sold them a record, and did so much public relations that before the night was over I was standing by the door, calling everybody by their first names and thanking them for coming.

By the end of that first week, a lot of people had come back to see the show again on the weekend, and even though there was no Nashville star scheduled that week and the place wasn't really packed, I managed to get another contract signed before I left; this time it wasn't for just one week, but three.

This all took place about the first week of December in 1968. It gave me the extra money I needed to buy Christmas presents for everybody, but the best Christmas present of all was the one I got. And that was my opportunity to play the Horseshoe Tavern in Toronto for the first time.

After Christmas I was on the road again playing the circuit of hotels I had built up over the last few years and 1969 would prove to be the first year I could be booked steady any time I wanted. There were even times I had to refuse some jobs in order to get a little break.

I think it was around February when I returned to the Horseshoe and the first week I played there it was with a different house band. Jack Star had apparently been trying out different bands until he was happy enough with one to keep it on steady.

From my very first night on the stage, I could see the guys in this band were either very jealous of me or they just didn't appreciate what it was that I was trying to do. I was singing my own songs, of course, and doing absolutely nothing from the current hit parade. This they didn't seem to understand.

For the whole week they didn't talk to me and just kept

screwing up my songs whenever they could in an effort to discourage me and get me to quit. During each break they'd just go to a back table and sit by themselves while I was always associating with the people. And practically every table I went to, they'd tell me how the band kept sneering, laughing and pointing at me behind my back in an effort to get the audience to do the same thing. Unfortunately for them, their little scheme wasn't working. I just ignored the whole thing, did the best I could under the circumstances, and kept right on with my public relations.

At the end of the matinée on Saturday, Jack Star called me into his office and asked me how I liked this band and how we were getting along.

Knowing how tough it sometimes was for musicians to get work, and not wanting to lessen their chances of keeping their jobs in any way, I told Jack that while they did seem to be a little standoffish towards me, it was probably due to shyness, and while they hadn't quite caught on to my music yet, they would probably get used to me and do a lot better job next week.

"Well, Tom," he says, "that's all very decent of you, but you don't have to give me any crap. These guys have been into my office three times this week trying to get me to let you go. They said you can't keep steady rhythm, you're annoying the customers, and your foot is driving them crazy."

As I tried to defend myself against these allegations, Jack interrupted me and said, "Don't worry yourself about it. I've been keeping tabs on the whole situation, and after tonight you won't have to work with these guys any more. I'm keeping you and letting them go. Now how did you like the last band you played here with?"

When I told him I thought they were excellent and that we had all got along very well, he told me he had them on standby and assured me they'd be playing for me the following week and anytime I played the Horseshoe thereafter. He smiled and shook my hand and said, "The people really like you, Tom. Now go and get 'em."

That night the band continued their hassles to the very end, and only after they went to the office to get their pay and came back out with their walking ticket did they finally wipe those stupid grins off their faces. They were a sad-looking group as they packed up their gear and took off.

The next day being Sunday, I was scheduled for a TV interview on the "Bill Bessie Show." Anyone playing in the local clubs was welcome to come down from time to time to plug their records, if they had any, and talk about the place they were playing. Each entertainer would talk to Bill for about ten minutes and the show only ran from noon till half past twelve.

The show was being aired live, and just as I finished my interview the phone rang and Bill said, "Here, it's for you." I couldn't imagine who would be calling me at the TV station, as I hadn't told anybody I was going to be there.

When I said, "Hello?" this young woman's voice greeted me and asked me if I had ever lived in Skinners Pond, Prince Edward Island. When I told her I had, she said, "Well, I'm Marlene. My father and mother are Mr. and Mrs. Russell Aylward from Skinners Pond. I just now saw you on TV and wondered if you could possibly be my long-lost brother. Do you by any chance remember me?"

"Why, of course I do," I said. And without much more ado, I copied down her address, and within the hour I was knocking at her door. Things were a little uneasy at first, but after chatting for a little while we soon got over our clumsiness. It had been fifteen years since I had last seen her in Skinners Pond and we certainly had a lot of things to talk about. She told me that old Bill and Susan, Russell's mother and father, had died soon after I had left for the last time, and as I had made no contact with home, everybody wondered where I was, and whatever happened to me. When I tried to explain to her the reason I left in the first place, nothing seemed to register. When I told her about the extreme difficulties I had in trying to get along with Cora, she just couldn't seem to empathize with or in any way relate to the kinds of psychological and emotional trauma I had to go through every time I either thought about the woman or even heard the mention of her name. (The reader will be reminded at this point of how I described in my first book the way in which Cora, our stepmother, had shown nothing

but favouritism towards Marlene and an extreme dislike for
me. And because of this, the reader may now understand
why it was, at this time, that Marlene would find it so difficult
to empathize, not ever having known the feeling of being
shunned.)

Marlene now had two children, Gwen and Robbie, and
later on she had another little girl, Sandra. She introduced
me to her husband, Willard, who worked for Ontario Hydro,
when he came home later that afternoon. Then after supper
the conversation continued again between the three of us
until late in the evening, with Willard expressing the doubts
he'd had over the years about Marlene ever having a brother
at all. She used to tell him to always be on the alert for a
Tommy Messer (which was the surname I went by as a child
in Skinners Pond), but of course there had long since been
no such person. Willard began to wonder sometimes if Marlene wasn't suffering from some kind of delusion, and was
now finally relieved to know that she hadn't lost her marbles
after all.

By the time I left that night I had agreed to come back
and visit them occasionally, and they said they'd come down
to see me play at the Horseshoe as soon as they could.

On Monday night the band I had first played with at the
Horseshoe were just setting up as I arrived and I went over
to greet them. They said they had just seen the Clint East-
wood movie, *The Good, the Bad and the Ugly* and decided that
was what they were going to call their band. I asked them
which one of them was the "Ugly" and they all pointed at
each other. The band was a trio, composed of Mickey
Andrews on steel and Randy MacDonald on bass (both from
Cape Breton), and Gerry Hall on lead (from Newfoundland). These boys now became the Horseshoe's steady house
band for the next few years, right up until Jack Star finally
sold the place in the mid-1970s.

The next two weeks went as smooth as glass with the boys
catching on to my every move. We worked very well together
and I soon became determined to use them as my backup
whenever the opportunity arose to record my next album.

In those days, the Horseshoe Tavern could seat between
300 and 350 people and by my third week the boys and I had

her packed, even before the Nashville guest arrived on Saturday. Although most of the customers were from Newfoundland or the Maritimes, there were always lots of people from Ontario and western Canada. As well as stopping to chat at every table, I would often hold short conversations with people right from the stage, especially if I hadn't seen them in there before. I would introduce them to the people sitting at the next table and before you knew it they were pulling their tables together and acting as if they had known each other all their lives. This encouraged people to be more friendly towards one another and made them feel like we were all just one big happy family. This also made the job of the waiters much easier and reduced the incidents of trouble to practically nil.

The only small bit of disappointment there might have been was usually felt by those people who had travelled from a long distance to see me and because of my continuous table-hopping, they'd only get to have one or two beers with me the whole night long. But once I explained how necessary I believed this sort of public relations was for furthering my career, they seemed to understand perfectly and wished me well. They knew then that I wasn't avoiding them purposely.

The following is a short list of the Nashville entertainers I remember who made guest appearances at the Horseshoe during all the times I played there, between 1968 and the mid '70s. Some of them were guests more than once. Carl and Pearl Butler; Bob Luman; Grandpa Jones; Stonewall Jackson; Doc and Chickie Williams; The Stoneman Family; Lucille Star and Bob Reagan; Kitty Wells's son, Bobby Wright; Ferlin Husky; Bill Dudley; Willie Nelson; Waylon Jennings; Faron Young; Conway Twitty; and a few others whose names escape me at the moment.

Also during these years of '68 and '69 I had occasion to sing a few songs at Ann Dunn's after-hours club on Dovercourt Road and also at Aunt Bea's after-hours club on Spadina. This last place I went to more often as Bea was friends with Jack Star and the entertainers who played the Horseshoe were more or less obligated to go there.

After playing a week in Galt, Ontario, I was back in

Toronto just in time to attend the wedding of Reg and Muriel's daughter, Linda, on the first of March. Then I went back on the road for a while to attend to my northern circuit. And never going anywhere, of course, without a good supply of albums.

By this time I was getting some air play on some of the smaller radio stations up north, especially for "Sudbury Saturday Night." But not in Sudbury. With the lyrics being "The girls are out to bingo and the boys are gettin' stinko, and we think no more of INCO on a Sudbury Saturday Night," the local stations refused to play it. I guess they were afraid of the reaction they might get from INCO, the International Nickel Company, which employed most of the people in the area and who was no doubt a large sponsor for a lot of their programming. The university students and the working-class people just loved it, but all the mucky-mucks figured the song would give the town a bad name. And these are the people who pull the strings. There was even one occasion when the local newspaper, upon receiving the weekly ad for who was playing at the Brock-Dan, printed my name as STAMPIN' TIN CANNER instead of STOMPIN' TOM CONNORS. (Just an honest mistake, I presume.)

At any rate, by about the second week in May 1969, I was back in the Horseshoe Tavern for another five weeks which eventually became ten. This time I was placing two or three free books of matches on each table every night before the show as an added courtesy. As it was too expensive to have my name printed on the outside of the covers, I had a rubber stamp made and gave Reg and Muriel's kids a few bucks to stamp them all for me. The design on the stamp was the same as the picture of the guitar on the sides of my truck and the words read: HOMETOWN SONGS BY STOMPIN' TOM. Altogether, I must have doled out about nine or ten thousand books of matches during the full ten weeks I was there. They not only provided a convenience, but a lot of people just took them home for souvenirs. This was also another method of promoting myself in a rather inexpensive way.

Another method I used in smaller towns was to post a number of signs on telephone poles where I figured a lot of people would be walking. This I would do late at night when there was nobody around. Then on the following day, I would park where I could see one or two of them and watch the people's reaction. The signs would have a very large black question mark on them and in the middle of the question mark would be the following words, which started out very large and then got progressively smaller until they could hardly be seen: GUESS WHO'S NOW PLAYING at the (name of local hotel, which would be typed on a very small piece of paper and then glued on the sign in the appropriate place), and under that again, I would scribble a tiny signature which was impossible to decipher.

I used to get a great kick out of watching someone approach the sign and try to read it as they walked by. Just as they were past the pole and still hadn't got the entire message, their curiosity would be aroused enough to make them want to walk back to find out what was really being said. First they would look around to see if anyone was watching them, in case it was some kind of a trick, and then they'd venture back to read the whole thing. All they'd get, of course, was the name of the hotel. And not being able to make out the signature, they would have to phone the place to find out who was playing there. The hotel owners would always think the uncommon number of extra phone calls were coming from fans of mine who were just making sure I was playing there so they could come down to see me. This didn't hurt my image any, and it sure helped to spread my name around. The only time this little scheme didn't work was when a cop would spot me tacking the signs up in the wee hours of the morning and tell me to stop. Some towns had a bylaw which prohibited the posting of bills.

On the first Sunday evening after playing my first week back at the Horseshoe, I again went out to the Locarno Ball Room on the Danforth and sang several songs at their jamboree. This would now be about the third time in the last year that I played there. After receiving two or three ovations for my performance, I just went home, not thinking any more about it.

On the following Friday night, a delegation of people from the Locarno showed up at the Horseshoe, and just as I finished my first set, two or three of them came marching up on the stage carrying a very important-looking trophy. One of the men was the manager of the Locarno, who immediately introduced me to another man, a Bob Dalton, who he then described as being the Country Music Ambassador for the Toronto area. Mr. Dalton then made a short speech over the microphone in which he paid tribute to the "most outstanding performer at the Locarno's country and western show for the year of 1969." He then turned to me and shook my hand with congratulations, and gave me the trophy. Being quite surprised, I really didn't know what to say other than thank you, and as the audience clapped, I left the stage. Some photographer had also snapped a few pictures which later appeared in a Toronto magazine called *Country Music News Roundup.*

By the end of my third week at the "Shoe," the place was beginning to be just as packed on the week-nights as it was on Saturdays. This was when Jack Star approached me and asked what other booking commitments I had lined up when my five weeks were done at the Horseshoe. He said that he was prepared to double my wages and that I could stay as long as I wanted. As this meant I'd now be making twice as much at the "Shoe" as anywhere else, I cancelled a couple of smaller venues and wound up working for Jack for an additional five weeks. This stretch of ten straight weeks for a single featured performer would now become the official record of endurance, and lasted until the place was sold in the mid '70s.

Two other records I still hold from the old Horseshoe are for the most people and the biggest turnover in any one week, and the most people and biggest turnover on any Saturday. This last record, for Saturdays, was previously held by Stonewall Jackson. And the night it was broken, the only performers were myself and the Good, the Bad and the Ugly, and the people were lined up three and four deep, halfway down the block.

It was during this ten-week stay at the Horseshoe Tavern that a young man from Canadian Music Sales walked in one night, sat and listened to a couple of sets and then invited me to join him for a beer. He said his name was Jury Krytiuk, that he was from Melfort, Saskatchewan, and that he had just been appointed head of CMS's small record label, Dominion Records. He told me he liked what I was doing and wondered what the status was between me and my current record label and publishing company. When I told him things weren't going so hot, he gave me his card and asked me to come and see him at his office on the following afternoon.

The next day as I walked in, Jury—pronounced Yury—introduced me to his boss, Sinclair Lowe, gave me a tour of the premises and then we sat down to talk. After I told him about my poor record distribution, my complete lack of royalties and my inability to get hold of the owner, even at the best of times, he advised me as to the best way to go about getting out of my present predicament. When that was done, he assured me, he wanted to sign me up with Dominion Records and release a series of albums.

I immediately wrote a letter to the guy, by registered mail, informing him that because he had not lived up to our contracts, I was demanding my songs back from his publishing company. Also because of the lack of any royalties on record sales and the fact that I had given him money to pay for the studio production of the masters, I wanted them back as well.

In a very short time I was informed by a new person, a man I did not know, that it was he who now owned my songs and my masters. And because he had purchased these in good faith I would have to buy everything from him. The price tag for my masters was $1,000 and the publishing rights to about forty songs came to about $2,000. Though I could only scrape up about half of the amount at the time, I was able to get Mr. Lowe of Canadian Music Sales to advance me the rest, which would have to be deducted from my first royalties once I started recording for Dominion.

I now placed my songs with Time Being Music, the BMI counterpart of Crown-Vetch Music Ltd. which was a Canadian Association of Publishers, Authors and Composers publishing company owned by Doc Williams of Wheeling, West Virginia, Sinclair Lowe and Jury Krytiuk. An RCA Victor studio date was set up for me to record my first Dominion album in late August of 1969. By the time this date arrived,

however, I was in the process of switching over from being a
BMI writer to becoming a CAPAC writer, and as a consequence, my songs had to be transferred from the Time
Being catalogue to that of Crown-Vetch Music Ltd. But this
is getting a little ahead of my story.

Flat Tires and Mufferaws

DUE TO MY LONG STAY AT the Horseshoe, I had now rented a cheap room at the Edgewater Hotel in Sunnyside at the west end of Toronto. This was only about five minutes' drive from the "Shoe" and made it a lot easier to get back and forth to work than having to drive away out to the Chapmans' in Etobicoke. With the news that was breaking about a new record deal with Dominion, however, I was still making the occasional trip to see Reg and Muriel to keep them abreast of all the latest developments. It was on one of these occasions that I arrived at their house around four o'clock on a Sunday morning. I had been out partying after the show that Saturday night and decided to go to the Chapmans', use my key to get in and go to sleep, and tell them the latest news on the following day.

As I parked in the driveway and stepped out of the Boot, I spotted young Wayne Chapman's bicycle leaning up against the house. Feeling my oats a little, and not having ridden a bicycle in a little while, I decided to hop on and take a little ride. It wasn't that far down to the corner of the street and back and besides, I thought the different form of exercise would do me good.

Once I'd wobbled out the driveway and down the street, I began to realize the bike was really awkward to pedal and rather hard to control. It wasn't till I got to the corner that I realized I was riding on two flat tires.

As I made a little more than a 360-degree turn in the intersection, I thought I'd better hop off and just walk the bike home. And that's when I spotted them, and they spotted me. There were two cops up the street sitting in a parked cruiser with nothing else to do this time of the morning but chase clumsy-looking cowboys on flat-tired bicycles.

They turned their lights on, but I pretended I didn't see them. I figured I could pedal that old bike back up the street a lot faster than I could run with it, and hopefully make it into the Chapmans' driveway before they caught me.

I was about thirty feet from the driveway, and still pumpin' 'er for all she was worth, when the cruiser drove up alongside and the cop shouted, "Pull over."

Just then I struck a loose rock and pretty near went over the handlebars. When I finally got 'er under control, the cops jumped out and one of them, while taking a long suspicious look at my cowboy hat, asked me where I thought I was going.

Trying to sound casual, between all the huffing and puffing, I said, "Oh, I just came home a few moments ago, and because it was such a nice night I thought I'd go for a little bicycle ride."

"At four o'clock in the morning with two flat tires?" he said. "Not a very likely story. Do you live around here?"

"Yes," I said, "right over there in that house across the street. That's my truck in the driveway." After taking one long look at the Boot, then a look at the other cop, and another long look at me, with the hat and the bicycle, he said, "This is getting more ridiculous by the minute. What's your name?" When I told him "Stompin' Tom," the other cop started to laugh. "Well, listen, Stompin' Tom," he said, "we'll just take a walk over and see if you really live there or not. And bring that silly lookin' contraption you call a bicycle along with you."

When I finally leaned the bike up against the house and opened the door with my key, I could see at long last they were beginning to believe me.

When they read the sign on the truck which said I was a stage performer, they asked me where I was playing. When I told them the Horseshoe Tavern in Toronto, they said they'd have to come down and see me sometime. As they walked away, I heaved a big sigh, closed the door behind me, and quietly went to bed. Needless to say, that Sunday afternoon, I had a lot more to tell Reg and Muriel about than just the record news.

The following week, Reg and Muriel got to meet my sister, Marlene, and her husband, Willard, for the first time when, coincidentally, both parties walked into the Horseshoe on the same night. After I got around to making the introductions, they pulled their tables together and got along famously for the rest of the evening. This meeting was the first of many as the next few years began to unfold.

By about the end of the second week of July 1969, my ten-week stay at the Horseshoe came to a close. Not because I couldn't have stayed longer, but because I had other engagements which had to be fulfilled. The first one was to be in Kirkland Lake.

During my stay in Kirkland, an old friend of mine, John Farrington, from the *Timmins Daily Press* happened to be in town to cover another story, and while he was there he decided to do a piece on me. Upon learning what I had been doing in the three years since I left Timmins, he took some pictures and promised not only that he'd get the story printed in the *Daily Press*, but also that he would submit it to a number of other newspapers. (In August of that year, a condensed version of the Farrington story, along with a picture, appeared in the weekend magazine section of one of the large Toronto papers: just the kind of publicity an entertainer needs when he's trying to make a name for himself. I must have read it over ten times when I first saw it.)

I also made a quick trip to Timmins myself one afternoon at this time, to make a brief appearance on CFCL-TV, but I don't seem to remember much of the details.

After leaving Kirkland Lake, I was back playing Renfrew and Carleton Place, in the Ottawa Valley. And it was here one night, after one of my shows, that I heard a most unusual word for the very first time. I was invited out to an old farmhouse to sing some songs and listen to some good old-fashioned fiddle music. And by the time I arrived, the party was in full swing.

As I carefully picked my way across the kitchen to an empty chair on the far side, I couldn't help but notice a very old gentleman sitting on a woodbox, tucked half-way in behind the stove. As he clapped his hands and tapped his feet, you could tell he was enjoying himself.

After a couple of hours, when the singing and dancing tapered off, a few of the boys began to tell some jokes mixed in with a lot of tall stories. This is when the old man began to utter that strange and wonderful word. Each and every time an already tall tale became taller, and was exaggerated to the point of being absolutely incredible, the old fella would laugh out loud and say, "Now that was a mufferaw, if I ever heard one," or he might just slap his knees and shout, "Hurraw for mufferaw. Give us another one."

It must have been about four o'clock in the morning by the time the crowd thinned out, and as the old fella looked like he was about to turn in, I decided to ask him just exactly what he meant each time he called something a "MUFFERAW."

"You must be new around these parts if you don't know what a mufferaw is," he said. But when he saw how fascinated I was by the word, he began to tell me a story that, for him, had begun when he was a child, some seventy or seventy-five years ago.

"My grandfather," he said, "used to tell me stories about the time he worked on the cargo rafts with a big French-Canadian lumberjack by the name of John Joe Mufferaw. The French used to call him 'Bon Jean' and the English-speaking Canadians called him 'Big Joe.' His last name, in French, was not exactly 'Mufferaw,' but something very similar.

"When the new settlers from Ireland and Scotland were given land grants here in the Valley, their trunks and luggage and sometimes a cow or a pig would accompany them on the long trek up the river from Montreal. These voyages were usually made on large rafts either poled or paddled by a crew of very stouthearted lads, known mainly for their strength and bravery. And it was on one of these rafts that Big Joe Mufferaw acted as the foreman and one year hired my grandfather to work as one of the members of his crew.

"Now, just as often as not, these new settlers were

shunned by the ones who settled in previous years—they figured they could grab more land by keeping the newcomers away from grants that rightfully belonged to them. This they would accomplish by forming gangs of men who would intimidate the new settlers, prevent them from coming ashore, and force them to just squat on some less valuable land farther up the river. And this is where the rafters came in, usually led by Big Joe Mufferaw."

At this point, the old man lit his pipe one more time, and I could see he had become as anxious to tell me the rest of the story as I was to listen. He continued, "You see, son, it was the responsibility of the rafters to make sure the new settlers always arrived safely on their land. And the fights that ensued between the rafters and the shore gangs were often very long and fierce, sometimes lasting through the day and half the night. It was often said that Big Joe himself was so formidable he could take on several men at a time and either beat them to a pulp or put the run to them. Because of this, and the fact that so many hoods and bullies were out to get him, he gained more of a reputation for fighting than he did for his more noble attributes of being fair, honest and kindhearted.

"Even while he lived, he was such an interesting fellow that no matter where people gathered the conversation would invariably turn to the latest and greatest deeds of their protector and hero, the incomparable Big Joe Mufferaw. And after he died, a lot of these true stories became so exaggerated they soon entered into that region known as the marvellous and the incredible. Before long, it became fashionable for people to just make up their own Mufferaw stories to dupe the credulous or just to have a little fun and laughs."

As the old man now got up from the box to stretch his legs before going to bed, he said, "As a matter of fact, my grandfather was the last man on earth to ever see Big Joe. That was the day he hopped on his big old pet bullfrog and jumped over the rainbow. And that, my boy, is what the old folks called a 'real' mufferaw."

As I chuckled a little to be polite, I made some remark about how I thought that maybe some of these Mufferaw

stories might have come down to us by way of the legends of
Paul Bunyan. I hardly got the words out of my mouth when
he hit me with this bombshell:

"That's where you're wrong, young fella. It's just the
other way around. John Joe Mufferaw really lived right here
in the Ottawa Valley, in the mid-nineteenth century, and
Paul Bunyan never existed at all. It was the French-Canadian
lumberjacks who used to go working in the American lumber camps who carried the stories of Bon Jean far and wide;
by the turn of the century, when the Yankees were looking
for a good way to enhance the sale of their lumber products
they 'borrowed' the Mufferaw stories of Bon Jean and published them in a series of booklets called *The Bunyan Legends*.
The word 'Bunyan' itself was merely an anglicized corruption of the two French words, 'Bon Jean,' and the first name,
Paul, was added later. Even Bon Jean's big bullfrog became
Bunyan's big blue ox and the Ottawa Valley's own Mississippi
River, which was always mentioned in the Mufferaw stories,
was now said to be none other than the Mississippi which
flows through the United States."

With that, the old man said goodnight, and I headed
back to the hotel. He had certainly given me a lot to think
about, and before I went to bed I was resolved to find out
more about this Big Joe Mufferaw and maybe even write a
song with a few good "mufferaws" of my own.

A couple of days later, when I happened to be in Ottawa,
I decided to pay a little visit to one of the libraries and sure
enough, I came across some entries in an encyclopedia and
even a few newspaper clippings from the last century which
verified that a huge French-Canadian lumberjack by the
name of Joseph Montferrand had not only lived, but had
indeed been a man of great strength and valour. Even before
he died in the 1860s, his skills as a woodsman, a raftsman, a
fighter and a superb athlete were all legendary. The English
word "Mufferaw" was a corruption of his last name, Montferrand; and like the old fella told me, from the time Big Joe
died, he never really died. He only went to live in that land
of "the 'marvellous' and the 'incredible.'" And that's just
somewhere on the other side of the rainbow.

And what about Paul Bunyan? Where is he now? Well,

until July 24 of 1910, when a James MacGillivary published
the name in the *Detroit News Tribune,* Paul Bunyan never
existed, and still doesn't. But what about his great and wonderful "legend," you ask? And I'm glad you did ask. Because
that, my friend, is just another "mufferaw."

After jotting down a few notes and driving back to
Carleton Place, a town situated on the Mississippi River and
not too far from the mouth of Mississippi Lake, I walked into
the Mississippi Hotel where I was playing and immediately
wrote a verse to the song I was composing, called "Big Joe
Mufferaw."

> *They say Big Joe used to get real wet*
> *From cuttin' down timber and workin' up a sweat;*
> *And as everyone'll tell ye, 'round Carleton Place,*
> *The Mississippi dripped off Big Joe's face.*
> *Heave Hi, Heave Hi Ho. The best man in Ottawa*
> *Was Mufferaw Joe. Mufferaw Joe.*

That's the only verse I got to write in Carleton Place, and two
days later, on a Sunday afternoon, I was setting up my gear
in Kemptville, at the Kemptville Hotel.

Later on that afternoon, I remembered that Reg and
Muriel would once again be holidaying down near Picton,
Ontario, and according to my road map it was only 120 miles
from Kemptville, so I decided to drive down and join them
for the evening.

While looking at the road map and still half thinking
about Joe Mufferaw and some of the things the old man had
told me, I noticed the little town of Mattawa, situated about
180 miles farther on up the Ottawa River from the town of
Ottawa itself.

Realizing that Mattawa rhymed with Ottawa and at the
same time visualizing Big Joe paddling his raft up the river,
the exaggeration (or the mufferaw) that I needed for the
chorus of my song was not long coming to mind. The following words were composed on my way to Picton.

> *Big Joe Mufferaw paddled into Mattawa*
> *All the way from Ottawa, in just one day. Hey, Hey.*

On the River Ottawa, the best man we ever saw
Was Big Joe Mufferaw, the old folks say.
Come and listen and I'll tell ya what the old folks
     say.
They say, Heave Hi, Heave Hi Ho. The best man in
     Ottawa
Was Mufferaw Joe. Mufferaw Joe.

It was late afternoon when I arrived in Picton and immediately drove down to the campsite. Someone there told me
that Reg and his brother, Ray, had met some bartender by
the name of Zacharius on the previous day who had invited
the whole gang out to his farm for a Sunday evening barbe-
cue, followed by a little party. Obtaining some vague directions, I set out to find the place.

About an hour later I finally spotted a farmhouse with
two dilapidated old barns and a crowd of familiar-looking
people milling around outside. As soon as they spotted the
Boot, they all started waving, so I knew I was at the right
place and just proceeded up the driveway.

It was now dusk, that part of the evening when you can't
always spot such things as overhanging clotheslines nearly as
good as you can in broad daylight. And when I decided to
drive around the house and park in the back, guess what
happened.

You're right! The high box on my truck caught the
clothes line wire that was strung between the house and one
of the dilapidated old barns, and before I could stop I heard
a very loud creaking noise followed by a terrible, thunderous CRASH!

As I jumped out and walked around to the back end of
the Boot to see what had happened, everybody was just
standing there, staring, with their mouths open. The far end
of the clothes line had pulled away one of the props that was
holding up the slanty old barn and the whole goddamn
thing came crashing down. All you could see now was a great
big pile of twisty old beams and boards and one hell of a
huge cloud of rising dust.

As I stood there gaping, not knowing what the hell to say
or do, this Zacharius fella walked over to me and started to

laugh. He shook my hand and said, "You must be Stompin' Tom. Reg, here, has been telling me a lot about you in the last couple of days. He said you were quite an unusual fellow, but he didn't say anything about the unconventional way you have of introducing yourself. Do you do this sort of thing very often?"

When I saw how lightly he seemed to be taking the matter, I started to apologize. "Holy jeezes," I said. "I'm terribly sorry for all this, and I really don't know what the hell to say."

"Don't say anything," he said. "You did me a favour. I've been wanting to tear that old barn down for a couple of years now, and I just kept putting it off. It's a good thing you came along when you did, the damn thing might have fallen down someday with me in it."

By now, everyone was laughing, and when someone passed me a bottle of beer and a hamburger, I started to laugh, too. For the rest of the night everyone sat around joking about it and listening to Mr. Zacharius and me, as we played fiddle and guitar together and sang up a storm. Someone suggested that I should write a song about the time I pulled the old barn down, and to this I agreed. But I never got around to it. But, who knows? Maybe I'll write one yet, sometime.

It was somewhere around three or four o'clock in the morning when I finally said goodnight to Mr. Zacharius, and as there was no room in the house, I crawled in the back of the old Boot and went to sleep. The next day I bade farewell to everyone and headed back to Kemptville.

Along about Wednesday or Thursday I came up with a couple more verses for the Big Joe Mufferaw song.

> Now, they say Big Joe had an old pet frog;
> Bigger than a horse and he barked like a dog.
> And the only thing quicker than a train upon a
>   track
> Was Big Joe ridin' on the Bull Frog's back.
> Heave Hi, Heave Hi Ho. The best man in Ottawa
> Was Mufferaw Joe. Mufferaw Joe.

Now, Joe had to portage from the Gatineau, down,
To see a little girl he had in Kemptville town.
He was back and forth so many times to see that gal,
The path he wore became the Rideau Canal.
Heave Hi, Heave Hi Ho. The best man in Ottawa
Was Mufferaw Joe. Mufferaw Joe.

This was all I had to the song by the time I left Kemptville, and it wasn't until January or February of 1970 that another verse came to me.

Now, they say Big Joe put out a forest fire
Halfway between Renfrew and old Arnprior.
He was fifty miles away, down around Smith's Falls,
But he drowned out the fire with five spit-balls.
Heave Hi, Heave Hi Ho. The best man in Ottawa
Was Mufferaw Joe. Mufferaw Joe.

As these verses are spoken fairly fast, I felt the song was still too short. Then sometime in the spring of 1970, I met a guy from the Ottawa Valley by the name of Bernie Badore. Bernie was also very interested in the Joe Mufferaw legends and had even created a few of his own. Our meeting was brief, and during the five or ten minutes we spoke, we had no time to compare notes. I don't know whether I told him I was in the process of writing a song, but I did accept a small pamphlet from him which contained a few Mufferaw stories. I would later regret doing this.

One of the stories in the pamphlet which I found especially interesting was the one where Joe Mufferaw had to swim both ways in a lake one day to catch a bass that was cross-eyed. I didn't know whether this was a Badore creation or just one of the ongoing oral traditions he may have picked up somewhere. At any rate, I decided to incorporate the anecdote into one of my own song poems and build an even greater exaggeration around it. It appears here, in the second line of the following verse.

He jumped in the Calabogie Lake real fast,
And he swam both ways to catch a cross-eyed bass.

But he threw it on the ground and said, "I can't eat
    that."
So he covered it over with Mount St. Pat.
Heave Hi, Heave Hi Ho. The best man in Ottawa
Was Mufferaw Joe. Mufferaw Joe.

On the strength of the second line of this verse Mr. Badore accused me of plagiarizing his work, and in a letter from his lawyer, which came to me after the song was recorded, he demanded just compensation. Then, upon receiving a letter from my lawyer, he decided to drop the whole matter. And is it any wonder? The following is the last verse of the song.

Now, they say Big Joe drank a bucket o' gin,
Then he beat the livin' tar out of 29 men;
And high on the ceiling of a Pembroke pub
There's 29 boot marks and they're signed: "With
    Love."
Heave Hi, Heave Hi Ho. The best man in Ottawa
Was Mufferaw Joe. Mufferaw Joe.

Bud the Spud on P.E.I.

A ND NOW, AS I'M A LITTLE ahead of my story, I must go back to August 10, 1969. That was the Sunday I left Kemptville and headed back to Toronto, and later on that week I had an appointment that was going to change the complexion of my career forever. The place of the appointment was the RCA Victor Studios and the number one item on the agenda was the recording of "Bud the Spud."

The engineer was George Semkew. When I came marching in with a big slab of plywood and plunked it down in front of the microphone, he did a double take. "What are you going to do with that?" he wanted to know.

"That's my 'drum' and I intend to stomp my foot on it." I must have given him that look that said, "Listen, I've been talked out of using the boot and the board on my first two albums, and there's no way I'll be talked out of it this time," because he never asked me again.

Once the Good, the Bad and the Ugly arrived, we were set to go. It took almost as long to hook us all up to the soundboard as it did to record the album. The boys knew the material from backing me up so many times in the Horseshoe that they played without hardly thinking about what they were doing.

There were fourteen songs on the album and by early evening, when two of the boys had to leave because of other commitments, we already had eleven down. Only Randy

MacDonald stayed to play the bass for me as I put down the other three numbers. The whole album was done in one day and mixed on the next. From there it went into production, with the first single to be "Bud the Spud" on the "A" side, and "The Old Atlantic Shore" on the reverse. The album, the single and an eight-track tape were all released on Dominion within two or three weeks. I don't remember the exact date but I do remember the anxiety of waiting to hear what the results would be.

As I mentioned before, I had recently become a CAPAC writer. (People in the music industry will understand that BMI and CAPAC were two music performance societies which collected moneys for the music being used by radio, television, concert halls, etc., on behalf of their respective writers. They have since amalgamated and are now known as the Society of Composers, Authors & Music Publishers of Canada [SOCAN], the one organization to which all Canadian writers now belong.)

The reason I switched to CAPAC was because I felt that BMI was not being completely above-board with me. After I'd been with them for five years, each of the statements I received was for the very same amount of money, exactly $50. And this was in payment for the radio play I was allegedly receiving for one song only, entitled "The Northern Gentleman." This I could not understand, because I was out on the road most of the time with my radio tuned in to every station that played country music and not once did I hear it. On the contrary, I quite often heard "Sudbury Saturday Night" and on occasion I would hear two or three of the other songs. Even the DJ's I would visit in order to try to get more airplay never once mentioned "The Northern Gentleman." They were always interested in some other song.

On numerous occasions, while in Toronto, I would go down to BMI to see if I could get an explanation for this enigma, but each time I came out of the building I was no wiser. The man I usually talked to was Whitey Haynes, an elderly gentleman who loved eating oranges and talking about everything that always had nothing to do with what I was there to find out about. He'd start off by asking you if you wanted an orange, and after five minutes of listening to him tell you how good they were for your health, he would ask you how things were "down home." He wanted to know if the weather was just as severe as it was the last time he was in your neck of the woods, and whether they still made the moonshine as strong as they did the last time he had a drink of it. This took another ten minutes, and by the time he asked you where you were playing, how well you were doing, and when you thought you might be recording your next album, there was only five minutes left to the half hour of precious time he took out of his busy schedule just to talk to you. He would then get up from his chair, walk over to the waste basket, deposit his orange peels and tell you how great it was that you took the time to come in, and that he hoped you'd come and see him the next time you were in town, especially if you had any problems.

I must say, he was a very congenial old gentleman, but he was also very well versed in the art of telling you everything you didn't want to know.

In contrast to all this, I had the occasion to visit the CAPAC office one day with Jury Krytiuk, of Dominion Records and Crown-Vetch Music Publishing. We weren't in the office five minutes before they were showing us their computer monitoring system and the number of times certain songs were being played by the users of their music.

As the thousands of songs flipped by on the screen of just one of their computers, I happened to see the title, "Sudbury Saturday Night," and began to ask a few questions. "This is not our song," I was told, "but if it was, we would certainly be paying money on it because it has been showing up every once in a while." Then it was explained to me that both CAPAC and BMI monitored each other's music but they only collected and distributed money on behalf of their own writers.

As I left the CAPAC office it occurred to me that if "Sudbury Saturday Night" was being registered on the CAPAC computers it was also being registered on those at BMI, so why was I not getting paid for the song? And why did it seem like I was always getting the runaround?

When, through sheer determination, I went back to BMI one day and asked to see my song tallies on their computers,

I was indignantly informed that "nobody gets to see our computers" and "that information is highly confidential."

Another time when I asked, I was told I would have to go to the main office in New Jersey to obtain the information I was seeking, as they were the only ones who had the authority to give it to me.

All this prompted me to ask Jury, who was about to take a business trip to New Jersey, to pop in to BMI for me while he was down there and find out exactly what their computers had registered. When Jury got back, he told me they wouldn't give him the time of day and upon his arrival back in Toronto, someone from BMI Canada phoned and told him that he had absolutely no business making inquiries at the New Jersey office and that they were quite upset about the whole affair.

So for these reasons and a few others, which would require even more detail, I notified BMI that I was quitting and going to CAPAC.

On the day I went down to sign off, I was offered an "advance" of money with which to finance my forthcoming album if I decided to remain a BMI writer, but by now my confidence in the society had eroded too far. Saying very little, I quickly signed the severance papers and left the building. The following day I became a member of CAPAC.

One day during the week, after I recorded "Bud the Spud," Jury Krytiuk told me that Doc Williams was up from the States and because he was part owner of Crown-Vetch Music, the company that would be publishing my songs from now on, he might be interested in taking me on a tour with him. After all, such a venture would be mutually beneficial.

Of course, I agreed, and a couple of days later Jury and I took off in the Boot to a little town somewhere west of Toronto where Doc and his wife, Chickie, were visiting some Canadian friends of theirs who lived on a farm.

After the introductions I sang a few songs as a sort of audition, and although Doc said he liked the songs, he remained noncommittal about touring and just said he would consider it sometime. (That "sometime" would become a reality the following spring.)

My next couple of weeks were spent at the Thunderbird

in Brampton and by the time I was ready to go back to Peterborough, Jury called me and said he just received the first
batch of *Bud the Spud* albums and I could drop in to Dominion Records any time and pick some up. This I did, pronto,
and headed out for Peterborough with a load of about two
hundred. By the end of the second week, I was calling Jury
and asking him if he would drive up to Peterborough and
bring a couple hundred more. I still had another week to go
and these things were selling like hotcakes.

Jury arrived on Saturday night with two hundred more
albums and was very surprised when I not only paid him for
the first two hundred, but also paid him in advance for the
two hundred he had just brought in. "I sure wish everyone
did business like you, Tom," he said. "Most of the people in
this business ask for sixty to ninety days to pay and then you
have to run after them for it most of the time."

"Well," I said, "thanks for the compliment, but that's just
the way I am. I don't believe in owing anybody anything, if
I can possibly help it. I'd rather do without something than
go in debt for it, and the longer we work together the more
aware you'll become of the fact."

When I asked him about the "Bud the Spud" single, he
told me that all the radio stations in Canada had been
serviced with it for about two weeks now, but he still had no
word that anyone was playing it.

The next day, Jury went back to Toronto, and I arrived
back the following Sunday. I called Jury at his home from
the Chapmans' and asked him if he had any more records.
"I've only got about a dozen left," I said. "What in the hell
are you doing with them," he said, "giving them away? Come
on down to the warehouse and I'll meet you there. It's
Sunday, but I have a key to the place, and I'm sure I can
scrounge up another hundred or so." Before he hung up the
phone, he said, "And by the way, there's some guy at one of
the radio stations in Halifax playing "Bud the Spud, but
there's no action from anywhere else. I'll tell you more
about it down at the warehouse."

Jury had the records ready for me when I arrived. He
told me the name of the radio station and the guy who
was playing "Bud the Spud," but (shame on me) I can't

remember his name today. All I know is that he may have been confined to a wheelchair at the time. (Maybe if he reads this, he'll jot me a note?)

For the next couple of weeks I played in Chatsworth, Ontario, where the close proximity allowed me to again pay a visit to my friends in Port Elgin and Southampton. They also came out to see me play, and good old Jimmy Fordham bought about thirty albums of *Bud the Spud*, which he assured me he'd sell to his friends before the month was out. (Poor Jimmy is now deceased. He left us in 1995, but while living he was one of the best promoters I ever had.)

During my second week in Chatsworth, I again received a call from Jury. He told me that a couple more radio stations on the east coast were now playing "Bud the Spud" and some club owner in Charlottetown, P.E.I., was "hot to trot" to get me down there to play in his lounge. Apparently, the Charlottetown radio station, CFCY, which initially had no intention of playing the song, was now being so bombarded with requests they had to start playing it several times a day.

This, of course, was great news. I told Jury to go ahead and book the room for me, and as long as the fee was large enough to compensate me for making such a long trip I was ready to go immediately. (Besides, I was thinking to myself about the many times my sister Marlene had recently coaxed me to go back to P.E.I. and pay a visit to Skinners Pond to see my step-parents. So I thought with this opportunity to play in Charlottetown, I'd have a little time on the Island to think about it and maybe take a drive down to see them.)

About a week or so later, I arrived in Charlottetown with a truckful of records and ready to play.

The owner was a little short balding man of Lebanese descent, and even as he introduced himself as Johnny Reid, I somehow got the feeling that we had met somewhere before. Even his manner and the way he spoke reminded me of some incident in the past, but I just couldn't seem to put my finger on it. His wife, Judy, was a very charming blonde lady who also worked in the club at night, and if there was one undeniable trait that both she and her husband Johnny had, it was their great sense of humour, coupled with a very quick wit and an incredible gift of the gab.

With Johnny advertising in the paper and on the radio that people could come to the Prince Edward Lounge to hear Stompin' Tom, the guy who wrote "Bud the Spud," and the song being played every day, the crowds were very good every night and by the weekend the place was pretty well packed. I was selling records hand over fist, and when everybody learned I was brought up in Skinners Pond I was treated like family, even though I wasn't born on the Island. This made me feel really welcome on P.E.I. for the first time, and as the days passed I thought perhaps that maybe I should go back to Skinners Pond once more and at least say hello to Russell and Cora. For the moment, though, this would have to wait. I'll finish my job at the Prince Edward Lounge first, I thought, and then I'll go before I return to Ontario.

Johnny and Judy were very good to me, and when the patrons went home each night after the show, they'd often buy me a couple of beers and we'd just sit down and chat for a while.

It was during one of these chats that Johnny happened to mention that, along with running a dining room on his premises, he also had the catering contract to provide the meals for the inmates of the Charlottetown Jail.

Whoops! That was the word that rang the bell. "That's the goddamn place I met you," I said. "I knew it had to be somewhere. Weren't you thrown in there one night yourself about eight or ten years ago? You were wearing a light blue suit and you created such a commotion they had to throw you out again."

"Well, Jesus Christ," he said, "yes, I was in there. And them bastards tried to hold me on a bootlegging charge and I told them they could never make it stick, and they didn't. But how the hell did you know? Don't tell me you were one of those bums that were locked up in the cell that night?"

As I nodded in affirmation we both started to laugh like hell and outdo each other by both talking at the same time while Judy just looked at one of us and then the other, not knowing what in blazes was going on.

After we simmered down a little bit, I said, "I knew goddamn well, Johnny, the minute I walked in here that I knew

you from somewhere, but I just couldn't remember where."
"Well, you know," he said, "I felt the same way, but thinking
it was impossible, I just put the whole thing out of my head.
But now I remember, you were that long streak of misery
who offered me the cigarette, and I told you I didn't smoke."

"Yes," I said, "and you were that short streak of distur-
bance we locked ourselves in the cell to get away from. You
were threatening to sue the cops, the city, the mayor, the
government and everyone else on the Island before they did
us all a favour and threw you out."

"And I did sue the city," he said, "and I won the goddamn
case. How in the hell do you think I got the money to buy
this place?"

By the time I heard the whole story it must have been
four o'clock in the morning. Judy was half asleep, I was
finishing my ninth or tenth free beer since closing time, and
Johnny was muttering something about going home and
what a small world he thought it was.

At that stage, we all said goodnight and headed for the
"koo-kaloosh," which is down-east talk for "going to bed."

My Return to Skinners Pond

M Y FIRST SUNDAY ON THE Island was spent down at Beach Point, near Murray Harbour. Before I left Southampton, Ontario, my friend Ira Osborne gave me the address of his brother Joe, who lived at Beach Point, and asked me to pay him a visit when I was on the Island.

Joe and his wife, Gerty, received me very well and over the ensuing years we became good friends. They both liked country music and that afternoon and evening Joe had me around everywhere. We were down at the harbour where I met a lot of guys I had often heard Ira speak about and everywhere I went, of course, I had to play "Bud the Spud" for everybody. Ira also had two other brothers, Bud and Reg, who Joe introduced to me that evening. They came over to Joe's to hear a little music but left early as they had to go fishing the next day. It was quite late when I got up to go that night, and with Joe and Gerty assuring me that they would be in to catch my show some evening, I headed back to Charlottetown.

My second week at the Prince Edward Lounge was even greater than the first. I made a lot of new friends, and when I was leaving, Johnny thanked me for the good job I had done and assured me that he'd have me back just as soon as I was available. All I had to do was let him know.

Just after supper that evening, and for the first time in fourteen years, I came around the corner at the top of Josey

Edmond's hill and there, just ahead of me, lay the seaside valley district of Skinners Pond.

As I drove along the road I could see quite a few houses that had been built since I was there last. They were all painted in different colours, and even the old houses that I could still recognize were all nicely decorated. This was quite a contrast from the old standard whitewash that covered nearly every building the last time I was home. Back then, I used to know the names of everybody in Skinners Pond, but now as I passed a number of mailboxes I could see a lot of names that were totally unfamiliar to me. Perhaps I could get to know them all some day, depending on how things were going to work out with Russell and Cora.

As I drove by the one-room Skinners Pond School it looked pretty dilapidated, although I could tell by the signs, such as the wear and tear from little feet upon the schoolyard grass, that it was still being used.

When I pulled into our old driveway, I noticed there was only one barn now standing where there used to be two, and a woodshed beside the house where there had never been one before. As I parked the old Boot beside the back door I could hear my heart pounding, and as I knocked I could only wonder.

It was Russell who opened the door and in delighted surprise, he said, "Well, for God's sake, Tommy boy! Come in, come in. We heard you were on the Island and wondered if you'd drop by and see us." As we stood in the porch still shaking hands he called to Cora. "Look who's here, Cora, it's Tommy. Tommy's come back to see us." Soon I was in the kitchen, and after a short embrace, Cora said, "Welcome home. Are you hungry? Can I get you something to eat?" "No thanks," I said. "I ate on the way up from Charlottetown. But if Russell's got any of that good old home-made beer, I wouldn't mind a bottle of that." I winked at Russell, and he said, "Well, you're right in luck, Tom, I just happen to have a few bottles left from the last batch I made about a month ago and it just seems to keep gettin' better every day." While he went to get us a couple of bottles, Cora asked me how Marlene and Willard were doing in Toronto, how the kids were, and even how Steve Foote was doing these days. She remembered Steve, of course, from his being with me the last time I was home.

I told her everyone was fine. Russell appeared with the beer and asked me how I was doing (a question I noticed that Cora didn't ask), and how things were going with "the potato song." He said he caught it once or twice on the radio.

"It's going pretty good down here," I said, "but I don't think they're playing it in Ontario or out west yet. It takes a while sometimes for a song to catch on everywhere. But I hope it does; I've been waiting a long time now for something to happen."

I asked him if he had a record player in the house and when he said there was an old one of Marlene's around, I went out to the truck and brought in a couple copies of "Bud the Spud" and a copy of each of the other two albums. It took a little while to get the old machine to work but it eventually scratched out a few numbers as we talked.

They said Marlene had told them how she discovered me one day on television and invited me down to her house and how she and Willard then came to see me a few times at the Horseshoe. They also said that Marlene was after them to close up the house and come up to Toronto for the winter but they didn't know whether they would go. I told them I thought they should, as the weather was milder up there and the change would probably do them good. At this, they said, "Oh, well, at least we're thinking about it."

Another addition to the old house was a new three-piece bathroom, complete with hot and cold running water, just at the head of the stairs in the spot where my old bed used to be. This they were very proud of. And of course they had every right to be. They had lived a long time without that very handy convenience.

As the night wore on, I brought my guitar in and sang a few of the old songs as well as some of the new ones I'd written, and when I suggested it was getting late and I'd soon have to go, Russell wouldn't hear of it. Then Cora spoke up and said, "You can sleep in the little room for the night, Tom, the bed is all made up in there." Then Russell said, "You can stay here any time for as long as you like, Tom, and you're always welcome to come back whenever you want. We haven't seen you in fourteen or fifteen years and I was hoping you might be able to stay around for a few days. When do you have to go back to Ontario?"

"Well, I have to start playing Peterborough again on Monday, the tenth, so I do have to be back this weekend to prepare for that. But I wouldn't mind staying around for a couple of days and maybe do a little visiting, if that's all right with you?"

"That's perfectly all right. We'd be very glad to have you," he said, as we both looked at Cora in time to catch her nod of agreement. "Besides," he added, "I'm sure Margaret and Jordan, Anthony and Freda, and quite a few others would be glad to see you after all this time. We'll give them a call tomorrow and tell them you're home."

At this point, Cora got up and poured herself a glass of water and said she was going to bed. As I said goodnight to her, she asked Russell if he was coming upstairs but Russell said he thought he'd stay and talk to me for a while longer and he'd be coming up a little later.

Russell and I had another beer as he told me about all that had happened since I was home last. He told me about the passing of his mother and father and about the other old people who were now either dead or still living. And when I inquired about old Josey Arsenault, as to whether he was dead or alive, he chuckled a little and said, "Old Josey is a lot more alive than he is dead, that's for sure. He just turned eighty-four a couple of weeks ago, and he's been down on the shore all summer gathering Irish moss and wheeling it home, up through all that heavy sand, in an old wheelbarrow." "Does he like to party as much as ever?" I asked.

"Party?" he said. "Josey? You can't keep Josey away from a party. They try not to let him know when one is taking place, but he finds out somehow. And if he can't find someone to take him there, he walks. He still takes his mouth-organ with him, and when he starts to sing and dance you can't shut him up. Not only that, he's usually the last one to go home, especially if there's still any drinks left around."

"I'll have to drop in and pay him a visit before I go back," I said. "And maybe I'll get him to sing me 'The Man Behind.' I wonder if he still remembers it?"

"He not only remembers it," Russell said, "but he's probably added another forty verses to it since the last time you heard it. If you ask him to sing that, you'd better take a bottle with you and be prepared to stay for a few hours."

After telling me about my old school chums, where they got to and who they married, Russell started to get a bit tired and decided to go to bed. He asked me if I was coming but I explained to him how it was in the music business, how I never get to bed before three or maybe four o'clock in the morning because of having to sing every night till 1 A.M. "It usually takes me two or three hours after that just to wind down," I said. "So I hope you don't mind if I just sit here at the table and reminisce for a while before I turn in?"

"Not at all," he said. "But you know what it's like around here. We're all used to going to bed pretty early, and it's already way past my bedtime. So just help yourself to another beer if you want one, and if you get hungry, there's lots of food in the pantry. Don't worry about having to get up early in the morning. Just sleep as long as you like, and I'll see you sometime tomorrow."

After thanking him and saying goodnight, I just sat there for a couple of hours listening to the old clock tick, sometimes thinking of the past and sometimes wondering what effect my being here would eventually have on the future. I found myself feeling sorry for Russell and Cora because they had no family now, except for Marlene who was living in Toronto, and they'd probably have to end their days here alone with no one to look after them. Then I thought of how Cora had persistently driven me away from them, and I somehow concluded that if all this were not meant to be, it just wouldn't be happening. With that, I sauntered up the stairs to the little room and went to bed.

I no sooner got up the next day and finished having a bite to eat when someone was at the door looking for me. It was a delegation of church members from Tignish who had heard I was up in Skinners Pond, and they wanted to know if I would entertain some evening at the parish hall. It seems they had had a small fire or something and their organ had been destroyed, and they were looking for a way to raise money to buy a new one. They said the hall would seat about two hundred people and they were sure that, on the strength of my potato song alone, I could pack the place for them. They would charge about $2.50 a person and split the proceeds with me after the show.

I said, "It'll have to be no later than Friday night, because I have to drive back to Toronto on the weekend. And if you can have a couple of your people available to sell albums for me during the show, I'll do it. But I also get to keep all the money from the record sales."

"That'll be just fine, Mr. Connors," they agreed. "We'll get the word out right away, and we'll see you at seven o'clock on Friday night."

I spent the next three or four days visiting people I hadn't seen in a long time, and during the evenings we had visitors come to the house to chat or play some cards, or just sit and listen to me sing and play the guitar for a while. They sure did like that "Bud the Spud," and when I told everybody I'd be putting on a show at the Tignish parish hall, they said they wouldn't miss it for the world.

When Friday night came, I arrived early at the hall to set up my gear and then waited till about 6:45 P.M. when they opened the doors. They had jammed in about 230 seats and by five minutes to seven they were all occupied. At seven o'clock they were still selling tickets to anyone who would stand anywhere they could find room, and with the aisles and the doorway packed to the point of people falling over one another, I walked out on the stage and began:

> *It's Bud the Spud, from the bright red mud,*
> *Rollin' down the highway, smilin';*
> *The spuds are big on the back of Bud's rig,*
> *They're from Prince Edward Island.*
> *They're from Prince Edward Island.*

At that point, I thought they were going to tear the place down. And they almost did before the song was over. I don't know how anybody heard the songs I was singing; they were making so much noise, I couldn't even hear myself. At the end of the first set of about an hour, I sang "Bud the Spud" again and took a break.

Nobody could get through the crowd to either buy a record or sell one, and everybody just kept yelling for me to come back out on stage. I took about ten minutes off, in which time I guzzled a beer down, and then I came back for another hour. After two or three encores of "Bud the Spud," during which the crowd just kept on standing, I finally had to walk off the stage and not come back, even though the calling, the clapping, and the hollering and hooting continued until everyone finally left the place.

On the way out the door, every third person must have bought an album, because out of the hundred I brought in for them to sell, there were only two or three left. The albums sold so well that, when we came to settle up, I told them they could keep my half of the gate to help buy the organ and wished them luck in their efforts to obtain the rest of the money needed. This gave them about $750 more than they had before, and after everyone thanked me several times, I headed back to Skinners Pond.

A gang of people was waiting for me at the house, and after telling me how much they liked the concert, we all had a couple of beers and called it a night.

The next day I said goodbye to Russell and Cora, jumped in the Boot and headed back to Ontario.

On arriving in Peterborough around 6 P.M. on Sunday, I was met by a couple of representatives of a church youth group. They'd been waiting for me so they could ask me to come and sing a few songs at their youth meeting. They said it would begin at seven o'clock that evening. I said I was rather tired after the long drive, but after they told me they only needed me and my guitar and I wouldn't have to set up or anything, I decided to go. But only for half an hour, I said, because I had to get right back to the hotel to set up my equipment.

The meeting was taking place in the basement of the George Street United Church and when I got there I was met by a Reverend Snell and a reporter from the *Examiner* newspaper. It wasn't often, he said, that a tavern singer would come and entertain at a church meeting. I agreed, and especially not after driving for about eight hours just to get here, I assured him.

After I sang a few songs and said I had to go, the group gave me a big round of applause, and about Thursday that week, the paper carried an article, calling it an "unusual affair."

For the rest of that week and all the next, the patrons at the old King George Hotel had a good time chiding me about the incident, and I even got a few requests to sing "The Old Rugged Cross." But it was all done in good humour so I just laughed it off and went on with my regular program.

The last Saturday night at The King's I developed strep throat and had a hard time getting through the night. The ailment is something like laryngitis, and when you get it you can hardly talk, never mind sing. I had gone to the drugstore that afternoon and got some kind of throat spray but it didn't seem to help much at all.

I was some glad when the night was over, and when I finally got my gear packed, I went straight to bed. The next day as I left Peterborough, I took my jolly old time. I had a whole week off now before having to play the Horseshoe in Toronto, and I sure felt like the rest was going to do me good.

Billboards and Toying Around

BACK IN TORONTO, I RENTED a cheap motel room west of the city on Lakeshore Boulevard near the Humber River. Then I went to visit Marlene to tell her how things had gone in Skinners Pond. She told me she'd been on the phone and knew all about it. She also said Russell and Cora had decided to come up to Ontario and hopefully would spend the winter after all; she said my visit had somehow helped to convince them to make the trip.

The next day I went to see the Chapmans and after that I went down to Canadian Music Sales and Dominion Records to have a couple of meetings with Jury.

While I was there he told me they had just released my first two albums, *Northlands' Own* and *On Tragedy Trail,* on Dominion, and were planning to have me back in the studio to record another new one sometime in the early part of 1970. In preparation for this I signed up another twelve songs with Crown-Vetch Music and told Jury I was ready to go any time he was. I then packed another two or three hundred albums in my truck and went back to my motel. The following week, starting December 1, 1969, I was back playing the Horseshoe.

My first night, everything went fairly normal until about 11:30 when I was on my second break. While sitting and chatting at a table with a few customers, a guy walked by, passed me a beer and said, "I saw your name going up on a

billboard today; looks like you're really becoming famous."
"Yeah! I know," I said, "what's the joke?" When he said it was
no joke, I asked him where he saw it. "Not too far from
where I live, in Scarborough," he said. But when I asked him
what it said he could only remember seeing my name as he
drove by and that was all, so I just put it down to mistaken
identity and let it go at that.

The following night, just before going on stage, the boys
in the band came up to me looking rather excited. "Hey
Tom, we just seen your name on a billboard two minutes
ago. Who put that up?"

"What the hell are you talking about?" I asked. "A billboard? Where?"

"Right here on Queen Street, about a block or so east of
the Horseshoe."

"Come on," I said. "Some guy mentioned something last
night about a billboard in Scarborough with my name on it.
Are you guys trying to play some kind of a trick on me
or what?"

"No way," they said. "Don't you know about it? It's just
down the street. We'll take you down to see it right after the
first set."

"Yeah! Okay," I said. "I'll go along with your little joke.
Now let's get some music going."

By the end of the first set I was heading towards one of
the tables where someone had just bought me a beer when
the guys asked me if I was coming to see the billboard.
"Look!" I said, pointing my finger towards my eye. "I might
be Irish, but you won't see no green in there."

"For Chrissake, Tom, we're telling you the truth. There's
a billboard down the street with your name on it in great big
letters and it says something about you stamping your feet.
Come on, we'll drive you down and show you."

Just then, a couple sitting at another table got into the
conversation. "Yeah, we seen one on the way in tonight.
What's it all about anyway?"

Well, that was it. "Okay," I said, "let's go down and see
what the hell this is all about."

As we drove down Queen Street, dodging in and out of the
busy traffic, one of the guys said, "There it is, right over there."

"Where?" I said. "I can't see anything."

"It's right back there," he said. "You can't see it very good driving this way. We'll turn around and drive back. Then you'll see it for sure. It's in a big parking lot back there."

As soon as we turned around and drove back, sure enough, there it was. A great big billboard facing east on Queen Street blazed out four very large words: STAMP OUT STOMPIN' TOM. The first two words were in black and the second two were in fire-engine red, and all were printed on a plain white background. The billboard itself was about thirty feet long by about twelve feet high and stood about ten feet off the ground.

As we drove into the parking lot, I jumped out and just stood there gaping. "Who in the hell put that there?" I asked. "And what in the hell is it all supposed to mean, anyway? Did Jack Star put it up? And if so, why would he want me stamped out? Let's go back and talk to Jack and see what he knows about it."

"Well, one thing about it, Tom, it can't do you any harm," offered one of the boys, as we drove back to the club. "All publicity, they say, is good publicity."

"Yeah, but how many of these damn signs are out there?" I said. "A guy last night said there was one in Scarborough and two people tonight said they saw one some place else. I sure don't mind publicity, but I don't want the whole city of Toronto trying to stamp me out like I was some kind of a plague or something."

When I described the sign to Jack Star in his office, he assured me that he hadn't put it up and didn't have a clue as to who did. He certainly appeared rather bemused about the whole thing and said he'd make sure to have a look at it himself on the following day.

By the end of that first week practically everyone who came into the Horseshoe had a story about seeing a STAMP OUT STOMPIN' TOM billboard throughout Toronto in one location or another. Each time a new location was described to me I'd go and check it out on the following afternoon. And after several days I encountered at least nineteen different signs, all saying the same thing. One day I even called the sign company and asked who was responsible for putting them up. But the only answer I could get was "We're sorry, but the party who paid to have the signs put up wishes to remain anonymous."

Altogether, the signs were up for about six weeks, until about the middle of January 1970, and by this time they were not only the talk of the town, but the word had spread clear down to the east coast.

By this time, a reporter for *Canadian Panorama* magazine came by to interview me about the signs. He wanted to know if I had put them up. When I assured him that I hadn't, he went to interview somebody at the E.L. Ruddy sign company. According to an article which was published in *Panorama* in late January 1970 with a picture of me standing in front of one of the billboards, the result of that interview went something like this: On or about the beginning of December someone walked into the sign company with a fistful of bills, paid to have a number of the billboards printed and erected for a month, and without leaving a name, had a receipt made out to cash, and walked out just as cool as you please. The rest remains a mystery.

At the same time, a spokesman for *Panorama* in Summerside, P.E.I., was quoted as saying that the speculation on the Island was that "because Tom's song 'Bud the Spud' was drawing so much attention to the potatoes from Prince Edward Island, the signs had to be put up by some disgruntled Idaho potato grower."

By the end of it all, the theories were just getting bigger and bigger. Some of the ones I was hearing ranged all the way from "It must have been your former record company who didn't like the idea of your leaving them" to "It had to be John Lennon of the Beatles, who had just paid a visit to Toronto and couldn't stand your kind of music." One story even had it that the *Toronto Star* had put up the signs, because "if Stompin' Tom keeps on stompin' the hell out of those boards, there won't be enough wood left in the country to make a newspaper."

Anyway, when all was said and done, the boys in the band were right. The publicity didn't hurt me at all. Even Bob Dalton, who was the chief executive of the Irwin Toy company at the time, came to see me at the Horseshoe one night with a prototype of a new doll he was planning to manufacture. The doll looked like a hippie in a protest march. It had hair down to its waist and covering its entire face, which was then mounted by a huge set of sunglasses. In its right hand it carried a large placard, which read: STAMP OUT STOMPIN' TOM. Had they been for sale that night, he could have sold twenty or thirty of them right there. At any rate, he invited me down to his company so he could show me around and have a little chat, whenever I could find the time. He later told me they sold a few hundred of the dolls while the billboards were still up and for a short time after, and then they were discontinued. (I still have one as a keepsake.)

It was kind of funny the day I went down to see Bob. I walked up to the receptionist's desk and asked to see Bob Dalton. When the receptionist looked at me and saw that I wasn't dressed in a suit, she said that Mr. Dalton was a very busy man and she didn't think that he'd be able to see me today. When I gave her my name and asked her to check and find out if Mr. Dalton would see me or not, she told me to take a seat and wait till she located him on her intercom.

As she seemed to be taking her good old time, I didn't bother to sit down but just wandered down the hall a little ways. When I happened to come upon the personnel office I was struck with one of my oddball ideas. I walked up to the counter and asked the girl if I could talk to someone responsible for hiring help.

In a second or two I was talking to the personnel manager, who assured me the company was not interested in hiring anyone at the moment. When I asked him if I could fill out an application and told him I'd come back regularly to check for any new job openings, he looked me up and down and said that wouldn't be necessary, as "We just won't have a job available for someone of your limited capacity and experience."

"Well, just give me the application," I said, "and I'll sign my name on it so you'll know me the next time I come around looking for a job. I used to whittle knives and guns and stuff out of wood, when I was a kid, and if I try real hard I'm sure I can learn to make some of your nice toys."

As he passed me an application form and I appeared to

struggle with the writing of my signature, I could see from the corner of my eye the sly wink he gave to his secretary. The kind of wink that said, "If this character ever comes in here again, don't even let him in the door." Pretending not to notice, I put the pen down, thanked him very, very much and swaggered out.

As soon as I got to the receptionist's desk it was plain to see she was displaying a more personable attitude. Smiling, she said, "Mr. Dalton will see you immediately, Mr. Connors." After opening the door for me, she showed me to an elevator and gave me the directions to Bob's office. In less than five minutes we were both sitting there with our feet up on the desk, having a beer, as I told him what I had done down in the personnel office.

I can still hear Bob chuckle as he said, "You son of a gun, Tom. You've always got something up your sleeve. It's no wonder I go to see you at the Horseshoe Tavern so much. No one ever seems to know what you're going to come up with next."

Just then, as we were talking, the intercom buzzed, and guess who it was? You're right. The personnel manager. And he wanted to know if it was all right for him to come up and ask a question or two about some small business matter.

Bob winked at me and gave him the okay, saying, "This should be good. I'm going to play along with your little prank for a while till we see what happens."

When the tap came on the door and Bob said, "Come in," I wish you could have seen the guy's face when he saw me sitting there, big as life, with my feet up on Bob's desk and sipping away on his beer. But the worst was yet to come.

"I want you to meet our new vice-president," Bob said. "This is Tom Connors, who is an expert in the field of management/employee relationships, and he comes to us from Parker Brothers Incorporated with the highest recommendations. From now on you'll be taking advice and direction directly from Mr. Connors, who has been telling me, incidentally, that some of the first changes he'd like to make will have to do with you and your staff and the way you've been running your office."

By the time Bob told the guy to sit down, he looked

like he was ready to fall down. Then Bob started to laugh. "I didn't mean to rattle you, Frank, but this is that Stompin' Tom guy I've been telling you about. He's one of the greatest entertainers I've seen in a long while. You'll have to come down to the Horseshoe with me to see him some night. Then you'll have an idea of how he was able to come into your office today and make you believe he wanted a job."

Frank was looking a lot more relieved now and even managed to smile a couple of times as he received the answers to his questions and left. But I can't imagine what he must have told his secretary about that dumb-looking character she was supposed to bar from his office when he returned.

Newfies and Huskies

As I MENTIONED BEFORE, Russell and Cora had come up to Ontario just before Christmas and were staying with my sister Marlene and her husband, Willard. I paid them all a couple of visits over Christmas and they all came down to see me at the Horseshoe a couple of times. Except for the parish hall in Tignish where I performed alone on stage, this was the first time they had ever seen me interact with a large audience. They couldn't seem to grasp the fact that all these people had actually come out to "spend all that money in a tavern" just to see and hear that same orphan kid who used to yodel at the cows in Skinners Pond. I think the reason they always kept looking around was because they were half expecting the star to arrive at any moment now. And when the star didn't show up, they had to conclude that I must have been it. A rather hard thing to comprehend at first perhaps, but as the night wore on and I got the audience to acknowledge them with a big round of applause, they began to appear more comfortable, more pleased, and perhaps even a little bit proud.

After all, when a person from small-town Canada found himself sitting in the Horseshoe Tavern in Toronto for the first time there was a whole lot of things he would have to consider. This was Canada's Mecca of Country Music. This was our equivalent of the Grand Ole Opry in Nashville. This was the place where the country music fan felt the same

79

as a hockey fan would feel on entering the Montreal Forum. This was where you could see the pictures of all those stars you had heard singing on the radio since you were a kid. And they all played on this very same stage at one time or another. This place was magic. This place had so much depth of character that even the mere walking on its stage seemed to humble the most prominent.

As an entertainer, if you played on the stage of the Horse-shoe Tavern you were already a star. You may not have been an international superstar, but you had already reached that first plateau. And all you needed now was that first big hit record. And that, of course, depends a lot on your ability to either write or find the song that suits you to a T and that the majority of your listeners will always love to hear you sing. And now you only have one more requirement. And this one can be crucial. Ninety-nine per cent of all recording artists must have media exposure, especially on radio, before their song can be considered a big hit.

Depending on the amount of airplay a song receives, and where, an artist could have a regional hit, a national hit or an international hit. But it doesn't matter how good you are, or how good your song is; if for some reason radio stations will not play your song, you'll never have a hit. And on this particular subject I consider myself to be somewhat of an expert. As my story progresses, my readers may begin to understand why.

Although "Bud the Spud" was now getting played on the east coast, mainly due to public demand, I still hadn't met anybody who had heard it on the radio in Ontario. So every time I was near a country radio station I would take the album in, try to have an on-air chat with one of the DJs, and ask him if he might give it a spin or two. Most promised to do so, but few ever did. Some even said they'd never heard of the song before and wondered why my record company had never serviced them with the album.

This of course flew in the face of what Dominion Records was telling me. They assured me many times that "Bud the Spud," both the album and the single, had been shipped to every country music station in Canada. And a lot of them, they said, had been serviced twice—my first two albums included.

With this kind of a contradiction facing me, it was hard to tell who was lying. And if both the record company and the DJs were telling me the truth, then who was keeping my records away from the DJs who said they would like to play them?

As this dilemma would go on for years, I'll keep referring to it from time to time as my story unfolds.

In the meantime, while playing the Horseshoe, I spoke to Jack Star about the problem. I told him I'd been to CFGM, the station which serviced the Toronto area, on numerous occasions and wondered why I wasn't getting played. As Jack was regularly advertising his club on CFGM he was of the opinion that the station played the recordings of all the acts that performed for him. If I wasn't getting played, he said, he certainly wanted to know the reason why, and he'd be looking into it right away.

From that time on, the odd person who came into the club would tell me they heard "Bud the Spud" or one of my other songs on CFGM but only around two or three o'clock in the morning and never in the daytime. And then only while I was playing at the Horseshoe. If I was out of town, they heard nothing. (These were people who kept their dials on CFGM twenty-four hours a day.)

This was always hard to understand. Whenever an American act was booked into the "Shoe," even if he was only going to be there for Saturday night, you would hear his records being played all through the day and night for at least a week before he even arrived in Toronto.

One would expect with all this build-up that these acts would have no trouble at all in outdrawing me, but such was not the case. Even though the people couldn't hear my records on radio, they came to know me and to really identify with the kind of music I was putting out. I was developing a faithful following. Once a person came to see me perform for the first time, they always came back many times over, and a lot of them several times a week.

Apart from the songs, I think it may have been because of my down-to-earth, no-flairs-and-no-airs approach to country music itself. I was always one with the people I was singing to and never aloof with anybody.

While most other Canadian acts up till then were trying

their best to imitate their American counterparts, even to the point of copying their accents, I came on stage with a new kind of confidence. I came on stage as "Stompin' Tom from Skinners Pond." Like it or lump it. "And when them nice Nashville fellas start singing my songs, I'll start singing theirs."

The foregoing blip is in no way meant to be boastful. It's just the plain bare facts.

I remember one Saturday night when Ferlin Husky came on the stage to do his first set. Before he started to sing, he decided to tell a Newfie joke. The only problem was that, being an American, he didn't understand that you just don't tell Newfie jokes to Newfoundlanders with a condescending attitude. And you could plainly see that he had one.

He was no more than half-way through the joke when a Newoundlander who had been sitting right in front of him about two tables back started stomping his feet and hollering for "Stompin' Tom."

I will admit he may have had one too many, but I don't think Ferlin Husky was justified in saying what he did. He stopped in the middle of his joke, pointed at the Newfie and demanded that he be immediately removed. He then went into some tirade about just coming from Los Angeles where people had a lot more respect for his calibre of talent than did the type of riff-raff that was being allowed into this dive since the last time he played here.

Then without finishing his joke, he made some remark about not wanting to hear any more boot-banging and started singing one of his better known songs.

Well, during what ensued, it was hard not to feel a bit sorry for him even though I felt he had it coming to him.

Another guy started stomping his feet. Then two or three more. And within a matter of seconds the whole damn place was stompin' just as loud as they could and hollerin', "We want Stompin' Tom, bring on Stompin' Tom."

As Ferlin tried to keep on singing, the crowd just got worse. Three-quarters of the people were now standing up and the stompin' was going on from wall to wall. As Ferlin quit in the middle of one song and quickly started another it was plain to see the crowd would have none of it. The waiters and the bouncers couldn't do a thing and just opted to move towards the stage in an effort to protect him in case of personal injury.

Finally, after getting his words all mixed up, he stopped. And immediately there was a big round of applause. When he grabbed the mike and started to say something, the stompin' began all over again. Only louder. This time he stormed off the stage, completely rattled, and went to the dressing room. For a while the applause continued till the boys went back onstage.

During the very last set of the night when the people had pretty well settled down, he came out, and without saying a word, he sang a few songs and left.

Later on that night at Aunt Bea's after-hours club, he came into Bea's upstairs apartment where we were all sitting around having a drink. It was plain to see that he'd had quite a few by then himself. He started to light into me for a few minutes and blame me for what had happened, but I just ignored him and went on talking to the others. When he saw he was getting nowhere, he left. And that's the last time I laid eyes on Ferlin Husky.

There's one thing I learned from it all, though. And that was: It sure don't pay to think that your you-know-what don't stink.

It was also around this time that I was trying to get Jack Star to give my buddy Steve Foote a chance to play the Horseshoe. Steve started entertaining in some of the smaller towns of Ontario, under the name of "Stevedore Steve," in 1969. And by September of that year I had convinced Jury and Dominion Records that they should do an album with him. To this they agreed, on the condition that I pay the full shot for everything and that the resulting master recording would belong to me. It was kind of like saying, "If you think so much of your buddy's talent, then put your money where your mouth is." Which I did. I signed an agreement stating, in the event that I didn't pay, they would have the right to deduct the payment from my future royalties. I then arranged to have Jury meet with Steve and set a recording date for sometime in October of '69, and I think the whole tab came to just under $3,000.

I knew Steve didn't have any money at the time, and because I didn't want him feeling obligated or indebted to me, I never told him about the special arrangement or that it was me, and not Dominion, who had been responsible for enabling him to record his first album. I wanted him to think that Dominion was recording him strictly on the strength of his own merits.

At any rate, Steve now had an album, entitled *Songs of the Stevedore*. And this was one of the selling points I used to get Jack Star interested in having him play at the "Shoe." Once Jack agreed to give him a try, I sent Jury around to see him about signing a contract, and the rest was up to Steve.

I know he eventually got to play there, but just how well he did I don't know, as I was always out of town when it happened. Upon my return, however, a few of the tavern's steady patrons would often have a favourable comment.

Sometime around the middle of January 1970, I finished up at the Horseshoe and during the following week I went into the studio and recorded another five albums. This would be a five-album box set, not of my own writing, but a sixty-song collection of old-time favourites. This would be the first of two such collections, totalling 120 songs in all. The second set was recorded the following year. There was eventually a sampler album released for each of the five-album sets. This brought the total of all the albums in this particular project to twelve. The names of the two sampler albums were *Pistol Packin' Mama* and *Bringing Them Back*.

During February of 1970 I was out on the smaller town hotel circuit again and by the first week of March I was back in Toronto, where Jury was planning a trip to Wheeling, West Virginia.

Wheeling, a Nickel and Doc

A S EVERY LONGTIME COUNTRY MUSIC FAN will know, the radio station WWVA in Wheeling used to broadcast live country music every night from early in the evening until about six o'clock in the morning. It was a very powerful station and could be heard by listeners from Ontario to Newfoundland. Every time a country artist drove through Wheeling, they would always stop at the station to promote their new record, sing a couple of songs and talk about where they would be playing next. Then of course there was the very popular "Saturday Night Jamboree." Practically everyone I knew would be sure to listen to that, because most of their favourite singers would be performing live and singing their latest hits.

On more than one occasion I thought of what a great benefit it might be to my career if I could do a guest shot on this Wheeling jamboree. Think of the exposure and the prestige it might bring, especially if I got to sing a few of my songs about Canada.

Well, here was Jury talking about a trip to Wheeling to visit with Doc Williams (who lived there), and here I was with a bit of time on my hands and nothing better to do than to go with him—only on the condition, of course, that he could somehow arrange for me to appear on "Saturday Night Jamboree."

I don't know how he swung it (maybe through Doc

Williams?), but the following day he told me it was all arranged. It didn't pay much but I would get the opportunity to sing half a dozen of my songs on the jamboree and also get to do an on-the-air interview just before it started.

"Wow! That's great!" I said. "I'll bet this will be the first time in history that the folks back home will get to hear so many songs about Canada over an American radio station. When do we leave?"

"We'll drive down on Thursday," he said. "See Doc Williams on Friday, do the jamboree on Saturday night, and leave for home on Sunday afternoon."

As I was talking to him on the phone from Reg Chapman's house, I said, "Just hang on for a minute." Then, turning to Reg, who happened to be walking by, I said, "Hey, Reg. How would you like to go to Wheeling, West Virginia, this weekend? And don't take all day to answer. I'm going down on Thursday to appear on the 'Saturday Night Jamboree' and Jury wants to know how many hotel rooms to book. We'll be coming back on Sunday."

"Well, I'd like to go," Reggie said, "but I don't know if I can get the time off at work and I'm not sure if I can afford . . ." and on and on he went. I didn't bother to listen to the rest of his answer, so speaking into the phone, I said, "Book three rooms, Jury. Reg is coming with us. And I'll pay for any of the extra charges."

As I was leaving Reg's to go back to my motel, he was still saying, "Well, I don't know, Tom, I don't think I should let you pay for all this, and besides . . . blah, blah, blah, blah . . ." He was still saying the same thing when we came to pick him up on Thursday, and he didn't stop until the three of us arrived in Wheeling later that night.

The following day Jury had his meeting with Doc Williams while Reg and I browsed around his store for the most part, and later on we rested up at the hotel, had a few beers and turned in early. The next day, being Saturday, we had a lot of running around to do and a lot of people to meet. One of the people was a guy by the name of Raymond Couture. A lot of the older folks may remember Raymond because he played in Hal Lone Pine's band all through the Maritimes in the 1940s. He was originally from New

Brunswick, but went to live in the States in the 1950s.

On his word of honour he told us that it was he, and not Lone Pine, who wrote the song "Prince Edward Island Is Heaven to Me." Although Lone Pine's name is on the song for writing it, he bought the song from Raymond the night it was written "for a bottle of whiskey." Raymond, who was an alcoholic at the time, had written the song while he was drunk and gladly signed the rights to the song over to Hal to obtain another drink. He also told us of other songs he had written and lost in a similar manner. I think "Lipstick on Your Collar" was one of them, but I can't remember the rest.

That evening I got to do my interview over WWVA, say hello to all the people up in Canada, and talk a little about my career up to the present time. The interviewer got quite a charge out of how I got the name of "Stompin' Tom" and wanted to know whether I had to register my "board" as a musical instrument when I came across the border.

As soon as the interview was over, I had to line up behind the curtain and wait for my cue to walk on stage. I was about the third act on and when I plunked my board down in front of the mike, the audience didn't know what to think. It was a controlled audience, and when the emcee announced it was "Stompin' Tom from Canada" the applause light went on and everybody just did what they were supposed to do. But it was plain to see they didn't know why they were doing it.

As I ripped into "Bud the Spud" and "The Ketchup Song" it became obvious that the guy controlling the applause button didn't know what the hell he was doing. He had the audience clapping at all the wrong times, which made it awkward for both me and them. Finally, by the time I got into "Sudbury Saturday Night," the crowd started to get the feel of what I was all about and just ignored the applause signs altogether. They started clapping their hands and banging their feet spontaneously and even came out with a whistle or two. And that, of course, was just what I wanted them to do.

Next I sang "Luke's Guitar," followed by "Goodbye Rubberhead, So Long Boob." And by the time I finished off with my wild version of "The Mule-Skinner Blues" they were falling in the aisles from laughing so hard. Like the feller from 'ome once said, "Dey couldn't even breed b'y, from da tears rollin' down der legs." That's when I picked up my board, blew the sawdust at them, hollered "Thank you" and walked off the stage.

By now the people were standing up and clapping so hard the emcee had to call me back out to take a couple of bows just to quiet them down. As soon as I was in behind the curtain again another guy with a tape recorder whisked me off to another room where several people were waiting to do another interview.

I don't know what uses were ever made of the interview, but with several tape recorders rolling I just answered their questions till Jury came and got me out of there. Then we left.

"Holy Jumpin's, Tom," Reg was saying on the way back to the hotel. "You sure gave them a good one that time. I thought one old fella there was gonna shit himself, he was laughing so hard. I'll bet he's gonna have a few nightmares tonight."

With that statement Reg and I sat around rehashing the events of the evening over a few beers, while Jury went back to what always seemed to be his favourite pastime: yakking on the phone.

So far, the trip had been very enjoyable. Reg was having a great time, I got to play on the Wheeling jamboree, and Jury met a lot of new contacts and got a lot of business done. The only unfortunate incident occurred on the Sunday, just before we left for home.

We had gone into a restaurant for something to eat. I forget what the boys had, but when my breaded veal cutlets came and I cut the edge off this flat thing that resembled a leather change-purse (or more exactly like a flattened-out bull's bag), there was no meat in it, just the empty pouch.

As I turned it towards the boys and held the end open for them to see there was absolutely nothing in it, they took to laughing.

Had I been real hungry I might have complained, but seeing the humour in the whole thing I just ate up the vegetables, ordered another beer and left the no-veal breaded cutlet lying on the plate.

When the waitress came with the bill, it was $20.30 for

all of us. And as I looked to see how much American money I had left in my pocket, I counted $45.30: two twenties, a five, a quarter and a nickel.

Shoving one of the twenties back in my pocket and placing the five-dollar bill on the table for a tip, I picked up the cheque and headed for the cashier with what I thought was the exact amount of money to pay the bill, $20.30.

As I placed the twenty, the quarter and the nickel on the counter and pushed it towards the guy on the cash, he looked at it, looked at me, and then picked up the nickel and said, "What's this?"

As I was half turned around to walk out, the question kind of took me by surprise. "It's a nickel," I said. "Why?"

As he tossed the nickel toward me on the counter, he said, "That's no nickel. Where did you find that? In a Cracker Jack box?"

Seeing now that I had made a mistake by giving him a Canadian nickel and realizing I had no other change in my pocket, I began to pursue the matter a little further. Besides, I didn't particularly like the tone of his last comment.

"I'm down here on a visit from Canada," I said, "and I can assure you that this is a genuine Canadian nickel. It's worth exactly five cents, the same as your American nickel is worth, and if you care to check it out at the bank you'll probably find out that it's even worth a little more than your nickel is worth right now." (The Canadian dollar at the time was around a dollar and five cents American.)

"I don't care what it is or where it's from," he said. "You can't pay for a meal in this restaurant with that kind of money. So as far as I'm concerned you still owe me a nickel."

When I told him I had no other change, other than an American twenty-dollar bill, I thought he'd just say okay, and tell me to forget it. But no way. He demanded the twenty-dollar bill, changed it, and gave me back $19.95 with the added comment, "You can't buy food to run a restaurant with phony nickels."

"Well, the amount of meat you put in your veal cutlets wasn't worth a goddamn nickel," I said, as I walked towards the table where the boys and I had been sitting. And just as the waitress was about to pick up the five-dollar tip, I snatched it out of her hand and said, "Excuse me, I'm from Canada. And if you want to know what this is all about, ask that son-of-a-bitch up there behind the cash." I then tossed the Canadian nickel on the table and walked out.

When I got outside the boys wanted to know what the hell that was all about. "Oh, just some asshole," I said, "trying to turn a good day into a bad one." As we headed back to Canada I told them the rest of the story.

Although I didn't think it was very funny when it happened, there's never been a time since then, upon hearing the words "Wheeling, West Virginia," that Reg Chapman doesn't tell everyone about "Stompin' Tom and the Bull's Bag Affair." And of course, to hear Reg tell it, it's nothing short of being a chuckle in itself.

During the week of March 8, 1970, I hung around my motel room writing songs in preparation for the new album I was about to record in April. Harking back to my days at sea I wrote "The Coal Boat Song" and "Sable Island." Then thinking of my days out west I wrote "Roll On Saskatchewan," and this reminded me of a good song I once heard on a jukebox in Edmonton, Alberta. It was written by Keray Reagan and was called "Poor, Poor Farmer." I really liked the song and because I knew it hadn't received very wide distribution I decided to include it on my forthcoming album. As the words, however, only described the plight of the western farmer, I altered them slightly to include other types of farmers in order to give the song a much greater appeal. (Although this move was directly responsible for the fact that the song was eventually recorded by a group from Ireland and became a big hit in that country, I was told that Keray Reagan had trouble with the slight alterations.)

In the next two or three weeks I did a short stint at the Horseshoe Tavern and then recorded my new album about the second week of April. As I now had my song about Joe Mufferaw completed, I decided to call the album "Stompin' Tom Meets Big Joe Mufferaw."

The next week or two found me back at the Royal Hotel in Sault Ste. Marie where I found the local DJ, Don Ramsay, having a field day playing Stompin' Tom records, especially the Algoma Central song. When I told him in an interview that I had just re-recorded it with a band on my new album, he asked me to get him a copy as soon as it came out and he'd be sure to play it, even more than the first version which was done with only me and my guitar.

He also told me he played "Bud the Spud" in the daytime once in a while. This was the first time ever that I had heard about "Bud the Spud" being played over the radio in the daytime in Ontario. I later heard that it had been played in Timmins and in a small station in Ajax, but that was about all there was up until that time.

Don was also at the Royal Hotel the night I got a phone call from Jury, telling me that he had just heard from Doc Williams. He said that Doc was about to do a tour of the Maritimes and if I was available he'd like to take me along. He would guarantee me ten or twelve dates and pay me $100 a show.

I couldn't wait to announce the good news over the microphone and Don Ramsay was the first to congratulate me when I came down off the stage.

In a few days I was back in Toronto loading the old Boot up with records and heading out to the east coast.

I remember how proud I was the first time I saw my name on a Doc Williams poster. THE DOC WILLIAMS SHOW, it read. Featuring DOC & CHICKIE WILLIAMS, the Comedian SMOKEY PLEACHER, and the New Sensation, STOMPIN' TOM CONNORS. And in small letters under my name, "Singer of Bud the Spud."

The only problem was, in the first couple of New Brunswick towns we played I wasn't drawing the extra crowd to the shows that Doc was expecting. The people who did come were going wild when I sang "Bud the Spud" but somehow I wasn't getting any new people in the door.

After playing Woodstock and heading out to Fredericton, I suggested to Doc that the problem might be because everyone down here seemed to know the song "Bud the Spud" but nobody knew the name of the guy singing it. (A longstanding habit of Canadian DJs was to give American artists a real big build-up before playing their recordings and say nothing while playing a Canadian. Most of the time they wouldn't even mention the artist's name.)

I suggested that he have his posters changed to read: The Sensational BUD THE SPUD, in large letters, and in small letters underneath, "Sung by Stompin' Tom Connors." And as soon as he did that, there was a helluva big change. We had the places packed every night. Doc even took me to the radio stations, thereafter, to have the DJs talk to me and mention my name. It was funny in a couple of places because the DJs couldn't even pronounce it. They stumbled all over it, saying "Tompin' Stom" or "Compin' Stom Tonnors" instead of saying "And here's Stompin' Tom Connors to sing 'Bud the Spud.'" It was obvious that, even though they may have been playing the record, they certainly hadn't been mentioning the name of the artist.

By the time the tour was over, we had played several towns in New Brunswick, several on mainland Nova Scotia, two or three in Cape Breton, and a couple on P.E.I.

Our last date was in Antigonish, N.S., around the fifteenth of May. Doc paid me off, we thanked each other for a very successful tour before he headed back to the States, and I went to Pictou where I was able to pick up an extra $200 for playing at the race-track on a Saturday afternoon.

I remember it was teeming down rain that day as I walked through the mud to get to the small stage they had erected for me across the raceway near the finishing post.

What had started out to be a fair-sized crowd soon vacated the bleachers and dwindled down to only a handful by the time I was done singing. I was supposed to perform for an hour but after forty-five minutes of getting totally soaked, the guy called me in and paid me anyway. The next day I took the ferry over to P.E.I.

I figured I might as well go and pay another visit to Skinners Pond as Russell and Cora were back from Ontario by now and I had a few days on my hands before having to perform at Holland College in Charlottetown on the following Friday night.

The Parade and the
Pandemonium

WHILE IN SKINNERS POND I thought I'd phone Jury in Toronto to let him know where I was and he said he'd been calling all over the place, looking for me. He said the CBC show called "Countrytime," out of Halifax, wanted to know if I would tape a couple of guest appearances this coming Saturday and Sunday. Then, starting Monday, Johnny Reid wanted me to play his Prince Edward Lounge again for a couple of weeks.

I said I'd be delighted to do both gigs, but because I was playing in Charlottetown on Friday night I expressed doubts about being able to drive to Halifax on Saturday in time for the TV rehearsals.

About an hour later Jury called me back and said I could fly from Charlottetown to Halifax and back and the CBC would reimburse me for the cost. They would also put me up in a hotel for Saturday and Sunday nights while I was in Halifax. On the following Monday, I could fly back to Charlottetown and start playing the Prince Edward Lounge that night.

With everything now arranged, I stayed in Skinners Pond until Friday, played the Holland College in Charlottetown that night, and drove my truck to the airport the next morning and flew to Halifax.

During rehearsals that day I got to meet Vic Mullen, leader of the band called The Hickorys. (It was they who would be backing me up.) I also met The Chaparells, who would also be performing as guests, and of course the famous Myrna Lorrie. Myrna was being hired to co-host the show with Vic Mullen at the time. The producer of the show was Cy True.

The rehearsals came off without a hitch and the next day we taped both shows in front of a live audience. I sang "Bud the Spud" and "The Ketchup Song" on the first show, and "Big Joe Mufferaw" and "Sudbury Saturday Night" on the second. Although I didn't get to see the shows when they were later broadcast, a few people told me they went over very well.

On Monday morning, June 1, 1970, I flew back to Charlottetown. As I got off the plane with my guitar and my small overnight bag and started walking across the tarmac towards the airport building, I began to sense that something was wrong.

Standing in front of the doors to the building were eight or ten men all dressed in dark suits. They looked a lot like those undercover agents one might see in the movies—not unlike the FBI or perhaps a few members of the Mafia. And as soon as they saw me coming, they started walking towards me.

What in the hell did I do now, I thought to myself. They're all looking at me and it's plain to see that I'm the one they're after. The next thing I know they got me surrounded, and while two of them took my guitar and my overnight bag from me, another guy started shaking my hand.

"Welcome home to Prince Edward Island," he said. "We're all members of the provincial government and we're here to officially welcome you home to the Island and to express our deep thanks for all you have done for our province since you wrote and recorded your 'Bud the Spud' song. Because of that we've sold more Prince Edward Island potatoes this year than we have in any previous year in the entire history of the Island. We'd therefore like to honour you with a parade through the streets of Charlottetown. So if you would like to just come with us we'd like to get started. The people of Charlottetown are waiting."

Just then a guy came driving out on the tarmac with a big truckload of spuds and stopped right beside us. Someone told me to climb up on the load while another guy passed me my guitar and before I knew it I was following the parade. In front of me was a float with a big loudspeaker continuously blaring out the music of "Bud the Spud" and just behind me came Jury, driving the Boot.

The whole thing had been planned and set up at the instigation of Johnny Reid, and the House Members took it from there. When Jury heard what was happening he didn't want to miss it so he flew down for the occasion, and here he was now, blowing the horn of the old Boot along with the other dozen or so vehicles.

The whole thing was meant to be a surprise, and it sure was. The people on the streets were clapping and quite a few of them were waving out the windows. And I, of course, was waving right back at everybody. The whole parade eventually ended up in front of the Provincial Legislature building where I got down from the truckload of potatoes long enough to be presented with a "Gold Spud" by the Honourable Dan MacDonald, the Minister of Agriculture. After the speeches, during which a number of pictures were taken, I climbed back aboard the load of potatoes and was driven to the Prince Edward Lounge where Johnny Reid was already doing a brisk business, even though it was only around two o'clock in the afternoon.

It seemed like everyone wanted to shake my hand and buy me a beer while Johnny related the details of how he thought up the idea of the parade in the first place and how he was able to get the House Members to co-operate.

When I told him I thought they were plainclothes policemen and that they were going to arrest me for something, I thought he would never stop laughing. "That's what I should have done," he said. "I should have had you locked up for good, you big Skinners Pond hippie."

Of course, he only meant it as a joke. Throwing mild insults at a person was always Johnny's way of showing someone that he liked them. There was one afternoon later on that week, though, that I thought for a moment he was going to have me locked up.

He'd been having some problems with one of his customers and when the guy wouldn't leave, he decided to call the police. While he was waiting for the police to arrive, the guy just slipped out the back door.

In the meantime, I walked into the club and before I had a chance to sit down Johnny and I began to indulge in a little horseplay. We grabbed hold of each other and were just in the middle of a friendly tussle when two policemen walked in the front door. When Johnny saw them he hollered, "Here he is, take him. Take him down and lock him up for a while and cool him off."

Before I knew it, the cops had me half-way out the door before Johnny told them the difference. Even then they weren't sure whether they should let me go until Johnny explained that I was Stompin' Tom, the entertainer, and that the guy who had been giving him all the trouble had left the club just before they arrived.

When the cops finally let me go, Johnny took to laughing. And from that day till this, every time it's mentioned, he laughs.

At any rate, I spent a great two weeks there. The house was packed every night and on the weekends the people were lined up around the block. Johnny was a great guy to work for and even after I started touring and playing the much larger venues, he and Jack Star at the Horseshoe were the only two night clubs I would do. Johnny and I eventually became great friends and remain so to this very day.

They say, "Along with good things there always has to be a 'little bad.'" After such a great two weeks in Charlottetown, the bad thing occurred on Saturday night after my show at Johnny's was over.

During the matinée that afternoon, a DJ from CFCY radio station came into the club and asked me if I'd do an interview on the air with him that night. The guy was from Newfoundland and had just recently been hired by CFCY, and because he was the junior man at the station, the late-night hours and the less attractive time slots were all given to him.

Anyhow, when my show was over that night, I arrived at

the radio station about 1:30 or 2 A.M., and after he let me in we went to the record library to pick up the *Bud the Spud* album and then to the control room where he was going to interview me over the air.

As we sat down close to the microphone, he took the album out of the jacket to place it on the turntable so he could have it cued up and ready to play at the touch of a button anytime during the conversation.

He had previously told me he would play several of my songs as we chatted, but alas, this was not to be. As he took the record out of the jacket he gasped, "Oh, my God! What's happened to this?"

It was plain to see that someone had taken a utility knife or some other sharp instrument and made several deep gouges across all the selections on both sides of the album, rendering them unplayable. The only selection not ruined by the gouges was "Bud the Spud." And there was a little piece of paper taped to the record which read "The only selection suitable for play on this album is 'Bud the Spud.'"

The guy was completely stunned. He didn't know what to do and began to apologize profusely. I could see plainly that it wasn't his fault and I told him not to worry about it. "I'm here now," I said, "and I'll do the interview, anyway. Just because someone higher up at the station doesn't like Stompin' Tom doesn't have anything to do with you." He then played "Bud the Spud," we chatted for about twenty minutes, and then he played it again.

The poor fellow was still apologizing as I left the station but there was nothing either one of us could do about the situation. The only thing I could think about on my way back to the motel was how very unlikely it would be that I would ever receive any airplay in the future from CFCY as long as Mr. Record Gouger continued to be employed by the station. I never did find out exactly who he was but I certainly had a pretty good idea.

On my way back to Ontario I blew the motor out of my truck and was delayed in Montreal for several days. The truck was still under warranty but the labour and the time spent at the motel set me back a few hundred dollars. I later traded the truck in for a new one of the same model when I got back to Toronto. This enabled me to just take the box off the old truck and put it on the new one. The fit was perfect and the truck was the same colour so nobody ever knew the difference.

Also back in Toronto, I learned that "Big Joe Mufferaw" had recently been registered as number one on the chart of the *RPM* trade magazine. I thought this was rather odd, however, because with all the driving around I was doing, I hadn't heard it on the radio anywhere. Even for the next six weeks, as I drove around Ontario, I still didn't hear it. So I put it down to the possibility that maybe they were playing it out west.

One of my gigs that July was back in Carleton Place where I had begun to write the song. Needless to say, it really went over well with the people who came to hear it at the Mississippi Hotel, but when I took it in to Ottawa and asked Ted Daigle, the local country DJ to play it, he never did. At least not during the two or three weeks that I was still in his listening area. And nobody I met ever said they heard the song either, even though they often wondered why they hadn't.

During this period, I played Leamington and Sudbury again. And while in Sudbury, I wrote and recorded a commercial for DuHammel and Dewar, a small company that sold tires. They later told me they tripled their business because of it, and the following year they paid me for the use of it again.

By the first of August I got word that they wanted me down on Prince Edward Island again to perform for two nights at the Kennedy Coliseum in Charlottetown. The dates would be the sixth and seventh. I would be backed up by Vic Mullen and the Hickorys of CBC-TV's "Countrytime" and a girl singer by the name of Sue Watts would also be making a guest appearance. (I would later find out that Sue was the daughter of Charlie Aylward, the fiddle player who, in turn, was the brother of my stepfather, Russell Aylward, from Skinners Pond. She was now married and living in Halifax.)

Anne Murray and Gene MacLellan (of "Snowbird" fame) would also be playing the Coliseum on Saturday, the eighth. These were known as Country Days at the time and always preceded Old Home Week which began on the tenth of August.

As I was only going to be in Charlottetown for a few days

I decided to fly down. Johnny Reid offered to give me the loan of his station wagon while I was in town, and if I wanted to, I could play at his club that Saturday night, as I didn't have to be back in Toronto till Monday.

The co-ordinator of the shows at the Coliseum was a former CBC producer by the name of Charlie McCoy. And when I arrived I told him I had never played in a place this large before, and that I was a little nervous.

"Listen, Tom," he said, "don't worry about a thing. Whether you know it or not, you've become the biggest attraction Prince Edward Island has seen in a long time. The Coliseum can hold about five thousand people, and for the first time in a long while she's gonna be packed. And word has it that the same thing will happen again tomorrow night. That's five thousand people who are coming here to mainly see you. They think you've become a big star. They believe that one of their own has finally made it to the big time! So I want you to go out there and show them that you're really the person they want you to be. Don't let them down and don't disappoint them."

I had never heard this kind of talk before, nor did I ever consider this point of view. Although at first it was a little bit shocking, it all sounded so positive that I immediately felt the adrenalin pumping. A surge of confidence, unaccompanied by the sense of guilt I might otherwise have experienced in a similar circumstance, had now come over me. And along with it came a certain willingness to follow any direction that might be given by the person responsible for it. I now listened intently as he continued:

"Because your fans see you as one of them, Tom, I want you to appear from out of their midst. After the show gets started I want to sneak you around behind the audience and sit you in a seat towards the back. You won't have your hat or your guitar so nobody will recognize you. And as soon as you're called to come out on stage I'll have someone pass you your hat and guitar and you can then proceed towards the stage by walking up the centre aisle. By that time I'll have all the spotlights on you, and you can just take your time, saying hi to everyone and shaking the people's hands as you pass."

As he finished telling me the plan he asked me how I felt about it. "Ingenious," I said. "But what if I get mobbed?"

"The people will be too surprised for that," he said, "and if you walk fast enough without lingering too long in one spot, you'll be all right. Besides, I'll have a couple of guys following you just in case."

I shook his hand, told him I liked his idea very much, thanked him for the little pep talk he gave me, and wandered away to think about it a little more.

I never wanted to give anyone the impression that I was in any way above them and was always afraid to show too much self-confidence in case it was mistaken for self-importance. But now, after Charlie's pep talk, I was beginning to see things a little differently. He had somehow given me the answer to my problem without knowing it. And my fear of showing self-confidence had a lot to do with the way I identified with people around me. Until now, I didn't think it was possible to show a great deal of self-confidence without alienating myself from the very people with whom I wished to identify. But now I began to understand that the confidence I felt could only be in direct proportion to the confidence I had in the people around me. The higher I regarded others, the higher would become my self-regard, knowing I was one of them. And this makes the confidence mutual and acceptable without alienation. The same goes for importance. No one would resent your feelings of self-importance if they were certain those same feelings extended towards them and everyone else with whom you came in contact. In short, there was nothing wrong with feeling a great deal of self-confidence or even self-importance for that matter, as long as it was being extended to and proportionately shared by others, with equal pride. That way, when you rise, everyone rises with you. And that was what happened that night.

When Sue Watts was done singing and Vic Mullen called for Stompin' Tom, I walked down the centre aisle, hugged a lot of people and shook their hands, and while the spotlights were flashing everywhere, I went up on the stage and figuratively took the audience of five thousand people up with me.

The standing ovation was indescribable and the din was completely deafening. And as I just stood there waiting to sing I couldn't help but think about the Prodigal Son and how he must have felt on the day of his homecoming.

When the crowd finally settled down a little and most of them began to take their seats, I figured it was just about time to let 'er go. "It's Bud the Spud from the bright red mud, rollin' down the highway smilin'." And before I got to the end of the first line everybody was standing again with another ovation that lasted till long after I finished the song and halfway through the next one. The whole place was just pandemonium. I don't think anyone heard the songs I was singing. They just kept getting up and sitting down throughout the whole performance.

The next day the newspaper said there were 5,000 people and 4,999 of them were banging their feet. And the very same thing happened on the following night with the exception that Sue and the Hickorys had to cut their show in half at the insistence of the audience who kept demanding to see Stompin' Tom.

I really felt sorry for them but there wasn't a thing I could do. I later remember overhearing Sue Watts telling someone in the dressing room that she couldn't believe what she was seeing. "If Tom had shit on the stage," she said, "everyone would have fought for the chance to clean it up. The whole thing was incredible."

I told the band members how I felt about everything but they just shook my hand and told me to forget about it. They were really a swell group of people.

The following night I played to a packed house in the Prince Edward Lounge and on Sunday afternoon I again borrowed Johnny Reid's station wagon and drove down to the Confederation Centre where a meeting of the Paraplegic Association was taking place. After singing for thirty minutes or so to the members of this very appreciative group, I signed autographs, took pictures and chatted for a while. When the meeting was over, I took Johnny's station wagon back to him, and the next day he drove me to the airport. All in all, it had been a very busy visit, but also a very exciting one.

All Prepared and No Play

A RRIVING IN TORONTO, I learned that Canadian Music Sales had just published my first songbook entitled *Stompin' Tom Connors' Song Folio No. 1*. The cover was yellow and it contained both the lyrics and musical notes to seventeen songs. Even though I knew them all off by heart, I must have read them twenty times. I just couldn't get over having my own song folio.

By the end of that week, around August 14, I went into the studio again and recorded a Christmas album which was to be released for the coming December 1970, and during the next two weeks I was in Galt, Ontario, playing at the Iroquois Hotel.

By this time I was getting a little spoiled. After playing with Doc Williams for a hundred dollars a night and then doing one-nighters on my own for triple that amount, I started asking myself why I should play for a whole week in these small hotels for the same amount. Although I always enjoyed having the time to sit and drink a beer or two with the hotel customers, it wasn't making economic sense. But doing one-nighters enabled me to get known throughout the country a lot faster. And this, of course, was my ultimate goal.

I used to feel really bad sometimes for some of the people in the hotels who had become such loyal Stompin' Tom fans that they often couldn't wait till I got back to play in their home town again. As I said before, some of these people would drive as far as two hundred miles or more to catch another one of my shows, even though it might have been only last week that I played their local hotel. And why I mainly felt bad was because these same people were always asking me when I'd be "going to the States," and telling me how disappointed they would be when I became a "big Nashville star" and they couldn't just drop around and see me any more.

It seemed that no matter how often or how hard I tried to convince them that I had no intention of ever going to Nashville or any other place in the States, they just wouldn't buy it. "You might say that now," they would reason, "but when the time comes you'll be gone like all the rest. They all say they're staying in Canada, but as soon as the right offer comes, they soon disappear."

"Well, I'm sorry you don't understand me," I would argue. "But I'm just not like one of the rest. There's enough Americans singing songs about the States now, and they certainly don't need any more Canadians, who don't know a damn thing about that country, to go down there and sing about it for them. I think Canadians should be singing about the country they've got, instead of running off to sing the praises of another. And whether you believe me or not, that's exactly what I intend to do."

After hearing that kind of a statement most people would drop the subject. But it was plain to see by the look on most of their faces they had heard the story before, and they weren't going to hold their breath waiting for it to come true. (Oops! Did I hear someone ask whether these people are still loyal Stompin' Tom fans today? Even after twenty-five or thirty years? Why, of course they are. Loyalty runs both ways, you know.)

From Galt, I headed out for the east coast again to do another series of one-nighters. These were mainly in school auditoriums in P.E.I. and Nova Scotia, and one at the University of P.E.I. in Charlottetown.

This time I took along an old friend, Vernon Acorn, who was unemployed at the time and offered to come along for company and to help me sell some records for a small commission. We were only gone for a couple of weeks, during which we got to spend a day or so in Skinners Pond, and then we were back in Ontario. Vernon then left me in Toronto where I loaded up with more records and headed out for Penetang.

In the back of my mind I was planning to get a small band together and start doing one-nighters on a steady basis. But first I had to play all the small-town hotels I had previously booked. When that was done, I had no intention of booking any more. That is, with the exception of Johnny Reid's place in Charlottetown and the Horseshoe Tavern in Toronto. (These places were larger and paid a good deal more money.)

So for the rest of September and the most part of October of 1970 I played Carleton Place and Kemptville in the Ottawa Valley and the Brock-Dan in Sudbury, and that would be the last of my smaller engagements.

By Monday, October 26 of that year I was back in Toronto for another two weeks at the Horseshoe Tavern, and it was on the following Friday night, October 30, that I recorded my *Live at the Horseshoe* album.

By about five or six o'clock that evening the large RCA studio/sound truck arrived and parked in the alley behind the Horseshoe. George Semkew would be the engineer, and by the time the evening patrons arrived all the cables, mikes and speakers had been brought in through the back door and properly placed. The control room, of course, was in the truck.

At 8:45 it was explained to the audience that we were doing a live album and everybody should react to the music in their "usual manner." Unfortunately, this didn't happen. By nine o'clock everyone was still completely sober, uncomfortably nervous and uncommonly subdued. They had all come here to have fun, let their hair down and just be themselves. But with all these sober and business-like people walking among them they just couldn't seem to get fully into it. As a matter of fact, it wasn't until the recording people moved their equipment out that the place finally came alive. And when it did, everybody sure made up for lost time.

At any rate, we did the album, and later had to

supplement some of the crowd reaction in places where it was sometimes inaudible. This takes away from the genuineness of a live album, but when the cost of doing it all over again was considered, the record company decided to go with what we had.

I certainly expressed my disappointment about the whole project and promised myself it would never happen again. So that was the first and last live album I ever recorded.

The album itself contained only six of my own compositions. There was one by Dick Nolan, one by Gordon Lightfoot, and the rest were an assortment of songs by other writers. Songs that I altered in various ways to suit my own style and thereby render them more fitting to a Stompin' Tom audience. The scheme always worked, except for the night I wanted it to work the most. And that was the night of the live album. I guess things just seem to happen that way, sometimes. Like Murphy's Law, which states that "if anything can go wrong, it will." And that reminds me of something else that went wrong that following Sunday.

On Saturday night, an old friend of mine by the name of Lenny Brown, from New Toronto, dropped in to the "Shoe" and asked me to come and visit him sometime. As I hadn't seen him for eight or nine years, I asked him where he was now living and told him I'd pay him a visit on the following afternoon.

Knowing that Lenny was always good for a party, I pulled up in front of his house around suppertime the next day, grabbed my guitar and 24 beers out of the back of the truck, and carried them up the steps of his front veranda.

As the door was open and I could see there was no one in the living room, I thought I'd sneak in and surprise him. As I tiptoed over to the sofa, I could hear voices from the kitchen so I figured they were just sitting down to have supper.

After quietly taking my guitar out of its case and opening three or four beers, which I set on the coffee table, I took a big slug out of one of the bottles and then, Wham! I hit them with my big surprise.

Almost at the top of my lungs, I shouted, "Yippee!!!" Then banging on my guitar as loud as I could, I began to sing "It's Bud the Spud, from the bright red mud, Rollin' down the highway . . ." and that's all the words that would come out of me as two men and two women that I never laid eyes on before came rushing into the living room.

As one of the men shouted, "Who in the name o' jeezes do you think you are, anyway? And get your goddam carcass the hell off my sofa," I soon realized I was in the wrong house.

Like an octopus with eight broken arms, I quickly fumbled and bumbled my guitar and the open beers back in their cases, spilling some as I went, and stuttering something about Lenny Brown and why he wasn't living there.

"There's no goddamn Lenny Brown living here," the guy shouted. "So pick up your junk and get your ass the hell out of here before I call the police."

As I stumbled my way out the door and onto the street I could still hear them asking each other "just what in hell this damn world was coming to, anyway" and "the nerve of some people, just walking into your house without knocking and expecting to have a party."

As soon as the door slammed, I set my guitar and my case of beer down on the sidewalk and looked at the piece of paper that Lenny had given me. And while I was being gawked at by several curious neighbours, I discovered the address said number 11 instead of 17.

I then went to number 11 and very politely knocked on the door, and sure enough it was Lenny Brown's place.

Of course, there's no need to describe the reaction I got from everybody when I told them about the big surprise I had just given Lenny in the house up the street. Needless to say, my surprise for Lenny was the biggest surprise I ever got. And you can bet your sweet ass I never tried that one again.

On about Wednesday, the fourth of November, Jury came into the Horseshoe and told me that some guy by the name of Howard Cable, from up around Gravenhurst, was looking for someone to write a song about snowmobiles and winter carnivals. If he found the right song he would pay to have it recorded on a single for the Summus label and also pay for the writing of it. All rights to the song, however, would remain with the singer and/or the songwriter.

I said it sounded like a pretty good deal and I'd see what

I could do. By Friday I had the song written, I put it on a small cassette tape and gave it to Jury to see what Mr. Cable thought about it. He said it was excellent and he wanted to record it that Sunday afternoon. It seems there was something big coming up in the Muskoka area and if he could get the record out in time, he figured it would sell in fairly large quantities. So "Snowmobile Song," as I called it, was recorded on that Sunday and was released a couple of weeks later. I also heard it sold like hot cakes in the Muskokas and was even played on five or six of the smaller northern radio stations. The major radio stations, however, wouldn't touch it at all. They were still coming up with old slogans, such as "We're sorry, but it just doesn't fit our format" or "It wasn't recorded in Nashville, so the production doesn't quite meet our standards."

By now I was getting so used to hearing these same excuses that I began to feel there must be some other reason why they didn't want to play me, but I never could figure out just what it was. After all, by the end of 1970, I had eleven albums and nearly twenty singles on the market, and still I was getting no major radio play.

Right from the beginning I knew there was something wrong, and I was determined that I wasn't going to let anyone convince me that I would have to go and record my songs in Nashville just to find out what it was. I knew at the time that RCA Victor's sound studio had brand-new state-of-the-art equipment and there was no reason why Canadian radio should not play an artist who was spending thousands of dollars to record there.

I also knew of other artists, at the time, who had taken this wonderful advice and gone to Nashville to record an album. Then after spending all their hard-earned money in the States they came back, only to find that Canadian radio stations now had other excuses for not playing them.

(Today as I sit here writing these words I'm still wondering why the major radio stations in Canada who play country music have consistently refused to play Stompin' Tom records. If I count the first records I ever made in 1965 to the records I'm recording now for Capitol EMI, I have released exactly forty-five albums with at least twenty-three of them still currently available and selling well in the market-place. These twenty-three albums contain the hundreds of songs I have written in the last thirty-five years since I officially entered the music business. I have also released countless singles from this massive amount of material which people still clamour to buy, and it strikes me as nothing less than absolutely astounding to know that none of the major radio stations, in the country to which I have loyally dedicated this work, can find even one song from a whole lifetime of writing that they can ever play without defiling their precious format. It seems to me that if Canadian radio has continued to make one statement to Stompin' Tom over all these years, it's simply been that every American and every American song they've ever played over the last thirty-one years, no matter how bad it may have been, was still more deserving of air time over Canadian radio than anything Stompin' Tom has ever written, sung or produced. And as far as we're concerned, it will always be that way.)

This last paragraph, in parentheses, is in no way meant to include all program directors, DJs and other personnel from all the radio stations in Canada. As I said before, there have been some radio stations, mainly the smaller ones, who have played my music from the start. And to these I owe a debt of gratitude. But when I speak of Canadian radio I'm usually talking about the big network radio stations who can make you or break you in the music business, depending on whether they play you. I personally believe, at least up until this writing, that most if not all of these stations have wanted to break me. But all I've been able to do until now is theorize about what their motivations might be.

As my story goes on, I'll speak more about the feasibility of these theories and the events and circumstances which led up to my believing in them. And now back to November of 1970.

Hassles, Lawyers and Companies

ON NOVEMBER 12 I again flew down to Halifax to tape another couple of "Countrytime" shows for CBC television. Upon my return, Jury showed me a copy of the *Canadian Composer* magazine, with which I had just recently done an interview. This was published by CAPAC (of which organization I was now a member); there I was, with my picture on the cover of a magazine for the first time.

After discussing the article at length, the subject now turned to business, and more specifically, Jury's concern about his future with Dominion Records and Canadian Music Sales.

He'd been with the firm now for about two years and was only making $100 per week. He felt he was worth more but his request for a raise had recently been denied. So he was now contemplating the possibility of leaving and going to work for someone else, or trying to find a way to start up on his own. (I believe he also said his chances to advance in the company were being blocked by another employee.)

He was only twenty-one, but on top of his two years' experience with Dominion, he had been very active in the field of music throughout his teens in Saskatchewan and again while he attended the University of Manitoba.

Most of his part-time jobs had been with record distributors, music stores and publishing houses, and ever since I met him, he always seemed to have his head in a book which dealt with some aspect of the music business.

Because of this background, and the fact that he had a great deal of ambition, along with the vision and the confidence one needs in order to achieve one's goals, I immediately began to realize how important a man like this could be to me if we were in business together.

Because I felt I was so different from other entertainers, I knew I should be with a record company that wasn't afraid to step out and try some new ideas. I had to be with a company that would not only listen to my input, but would also act upon it. And where was such a company to be found? Absolutely nowhere. Unless, of course, I started my own. And if I did that, I would have to hire someone to run it, while I was on the road pursuing my career as Stompin' Tom.

And who would I get to run such a company? Well, it would have to be somebody who knew a great deal more about the music business than I did. And if my ears were not deceiving me, I was presently talking to the man I was looking for.

While Jury was still pondering his job options, I interrupted his thoughts. "Why don't you just start up your own record company?" I asked.

"On a hundred dollars a week I can't even afford to start up my own car," he said. "Even the one I'm driving belongs to the company I work for."

"Well, listen," I said, "I've got a few thousand dollars in the bank, and I'm interested in starting a company, but I don't have the time or the expertise to run it. So if you're interested, why don't you find out what it will cost to rent the needed space, incorporate and finance the day-to-day operations, at least until the company is able to survive on its own, and if it's within my financial capabilities, I'll put up the money for a 51 per cent share. Then after the company is considered viable, any wages you take will have to come from your 49 per cent. After a reasonable length of time, if we can't seem to make a go of it, I'll be out of pocket for the money and you'll have to go working for someone else."

After talking it over for a while we brought our little meeting to an end, and a few days later we got together for some number crunching. The cost was a little more than I anticipated, but "nothing ventured, nothing gained," so we shook hands and agreed on the terms as I've just described them, and by the end of the next week Jury gave a month's notice to Canadian Music Sales that he was quitting.

We got a lawyer to draw up the necessary papers and by January 1, 1971, we were officially in business. We rented a four-room apartment over a bakery shop on Bathurst Street in Toronto and called our company Boot Records.

At first we only needed one room for an office, so we both moved in and used the extra space for a kitchen and two bedrooms. This also marked the first time in my life that I was going to have my own permanent address, and no more sleeping in cheap motels (and sometimes in the truck).

At this point I'm just a little ahead of my story and I must go back to the first of December, in 1970.

A couple of friends of mine had been listening to an after-midnight country show on CFGM radio and heard the DJ make a rather derogatory remark in connection with my name.

Well, it was one thing for them to not be giving me any airplay, I thought, but to be running me down was quite another, so I decided to call the station to find out exactly what was said. (I knew that radio stations were required to keep tape recordings of everything they broadcast.)

Upon being told that I couldn't obtain that information without the aid of a lawyer, I immediately got one for the job. A day or so later, when we listened to a transcript of the tape recording, we found it to be quite distorted. Especially in the very spot where the DJ mentioned my name. In fact, it was so distorted you couldn't make out anything the DJ had said. So with nothing more than a few distorted words to go on, I didn't pursue the matter any further. But it did arouse my suspicion that maybe something had been said after all and somehow that spot on the tape was mutilated.

Another thing around Toronto that was becoming very bothersome to me was the way the cops were always pulling me over late at night for absolutely no reason at all. I guess I could have put up with it if that's all it had amounted to.

But every time they stopped me, they wanted to look in the back of the truck and by the time they were done rummaging around, my clothes and my records and other personal belongings were strewn around everywhere.

Sometimes this would happen three or four nights in a row and on a couple of occasions it happened twice on the same night. I began to think that maybe the cops didn't like the way I had the old Boot painted up or something. Maybe they didn't like my colour scheme? Maybe this, and maybe that.

At any rate, I was coming home from my sister's house in West Hill one Sunday night around 1 A.M., and I guess I had about thirty or forty miles to drive to get to where my motel was, on the opposite side of Toronto near the Humber.

Just as I made my turn onto the ramp at Morningside to take the 401 highway back home, a policeman on a motorcycle shot up alongside and signalled for me to pull over. As I came to a stop, I was hoping he didn't want to look in the back of my truck because tonight, for some reason, I just wasn't in the right kind of mood. But, of course, it just wasn't meant to be.

I opened the door as he came walking up, and the first words he said were "What are you carrying in the back of your truck?"

"Just a few records and some other odds and ends," I said. "Why?"

"Open it up," he said, "and let's have a look."

"No sir," I said, quite firmly. "If I opened that truck once for you guys in the last two weeks, I must have opened it a dozen times. And I'm not going to open it any more. If you want to see what's in there you'll have to go and get a search warrant."

With that, he tried to open the back door, but finding it locked he asked me where the key was.

"It's in my pocket," I said, "and that's where it's going to stay."

"Let me see your licence," he demanded. And after taking down what information he wanted, he said, "Be on your way." He then walked back to his motorcycle and I got in and started up the Boot and drove back to my motel.

I suppose I wasn't in my room five minutes when I heard a commotion outside and within seconds there was a heavy knock on my door. As I opened it, there were three or four huge policemen standing there and the whole parking lot was crawling with many more. There were five police cars in all, two unmarked and three cruisers, along with three motorcycles and a paddy wagon. With several police radios blaring at the same time, I couldn't help thinking that someone must have robbed a bank or murdered somebody. I couldn't imagine them sending an army of this size to talk to a fellow just because he didn't want to open the back of his truck for the umpteenth time. But sure enough, that's what they were there for.

First they wanted to know if I was Tom Charles Connors and if I owned the truck that was now parked in front of my door. Then they wanted to know where I worked and if the address on my driver's licence was the place of my permanent residence.

I told them they should know all this information by the amount of reports that must have been passed in to headquarters by the various policemen who stopped me in the last two or three weeks. But to save them the time to check it all out, I would be happy to tell them one more time.

After checking my birth certificate, my vehicle ownership, and my insurance card, they asked me why the permanent residence marked on my driver's licence was at some motel in Sudbury, and didn't I know the Motor Vehicles Department required by law that I keep them apprised of any change of address within six days after changing it.

"I know that," I said. "And I've explained it all to you fellas a dozen times before. I don't have a permanent home, and to comply with the Highway Traffic Act, I must have changed my address at least twenty times in the last couple of years. Just come over here and I'll show you."

I led them to the door on the passenger side of the truck, opened it up, and dug out at least fifteen or twenty driver's licences from the glove compartment with my name on them. I had them secured with an elastic band and each one had the address of a different hotel in a different town where I had played. And somewhere in the middle of the

pile I pulled out the one that had the address of the Sunshine Motel at which I was now staying.

"I'm a travelling musician without a home," I explained.
"And sometimes when I have no place to play and I can't
afford to stay at motels, I sleep in the back of my truck. But
it just so happens that tonight I'll be starting to play the
Horseshoe Tavern in downtown Toronto."

"Only one of these licences can be valid by law," the
policeman said. "And you'll have to get rid of the rest."

"Which one is valid?" I asked. "And which ones will I
throw away, given the fact that I'll no doubt be playing in
these other towns in the near future and will no longer be
staying here?

As he only shook his head and didn't answer me, I
returned the licences to the glove compartment and said,
"Now, if there's nothing else I can do for you boys, it's three
o'clock in the morning and I'd like to get some sleep."

"Not so fast," he said. "You refused to allow an officer of
the law to see what you were carrying in the back of your
truck. Now if you'll be kind enough to open it so we can
have a look, we'll be on our way."

"As I told the policeman in West Hill, you people have
been hassling me every night by rummaging through the
back of my truck and sometimes twice in the same night,
and I'm getting sick and tired of it. Nobody yet has found
anything in there that I'm not legally entitled to possess, and
I think I have the right to be left alone with my own private
belongings as long as I'm not bothering anybody. Unless you
have a court order to go in there, I'm not granting you
access. So here's my hands, you can put the cuffs on me, tell
me what the charge is, arrest me for it and take me in. But
I'm not letting anybody in the back of my truck."

"Just give us the key then and we'll take a look by ourselves."

When I told him "No dice," he said they could get a crow-
bar and smash the door in if they wanted to. "Now you
wouldn't want us to do that, would you?"

"Just go ahead and do it," I said. "And I'll make damn
sure you'll pay for all the damages. I'll sue the whole damn
police department if I have to for compensation, because

there's absolutely nothing in there that would interest the police. And you can find that out by asking the cops who insisted on looking in there so many times before."

He walked away for a couple of minutes, called to someone on the radio and within five minutes or so another important-looking car pulled in to join the rest. Immediately the door opened and out stepped an older policeman with fancy rope hanging from his shoulder and all kinds of ribbons on his uniform. From this point on it was he who did most of the talking.

"If you have nothing in the back of your truck to hide from the police, why would you object to us having a look?" he asked. "After all, your refusal to let us have a look has aroused our suspicions that you must be hiding something."

"I'm refusing because your officers have looked in there many times before and found nothing. You therefore have no reason to suspect that I have anything in there tonight. And if you do, your suspicions can't be totally grounded on my refusal to open the door. I have a perfect right to protect my personal property from snoopers. So if you suspect that I'm in any way breaking the law, you better tell me what the charge is and arrest me. Then if you break into my truck and find nothing, I will not only sue you for the damages but also for false arrest."

With an approach that was marked with a lot less severity, he asked me why I was so belligerent and unco-operative with the police.

I said, "Just look around you. There must be nine or ten police vehicles with twenty or thirty cops prowling around, and with everybody awake and peeking out through their curtains to find out what kind of a major crime I've committed, how else would you expect a decent person to act? Don't you think you might also be a bit riled if it happened to you?"

With that, he made a sign to the officer standing beside him, who went and dismissed more than half the vehicles along with the policemen who attended them. He said he could keep me there all day if he wanted to, until he was able to get some results, but he didn't want to do that. "Now what will it take," he asked, "to get you to open that truck?"

First I told him that I would like to get in touch with a lawyer to find out just how long he could keep me there before I had to open it, and secondly, I would like to have a paper signed by him to show that he had inspected my truck and found nothing, if that were indeed to be the result of the search.

"You go and call your lawyer," he said, "and I'll think about the paper while you're gone."

As there was no switchboard operator to give me a phone connection from my room at that time of the morning, which was now about four o'clock, I had to walk up to the office and bang on the door till the owner opened it and gave me a phone line to the outside.

The only lawyer I could think of was a guy I used to shoot pool with the odd time in New Toronto. He was known to do the odd favour for some of the boys whenever they got themselves in trouble, so I looked him up in the phone book and called him at home.

Given the hour of the morning, he was not just a little bit annoyed at me for waking him up, even though I apologized at some length for doing so.

When I told him my problem he just said, "Ah, for chrissake! Is that all you woke me up for? If there's nothing in the goddamn truck, just let them take a look and be done with it."

"But it's a matter of principle," I said. "They've been hassling me for some time now and . . ." There was no need to say any more. The phone clicked at the other end and I was talking to myself. As I was trying to figure out what to do about the police, the owner was raving about my giving his business a bad name and told me he wanted me to move.

"Okay, okay," I said, as I walked out and slammed the door.

When I got back to my room, I found the police had ransacked the place and the older fellow wanted to know what my lawyer had said.

I told him he said that I didn't have to let them take a look, but because it was getting so late and I'd just been thrown out of my room, I decided to open the truck for them, providing I got the signed piece of paper that I wanted.

"Okay," he said. "Open the door so we can see whether or not I can sign your piece of paper."

When I opened the door it was plain to see I hadn't been suspected of hiding anything from them in the first place. Only one policeman went in, shone his flashlight around a couple of times, and came back out. And for the first time ever, they didn't even disturb anything. I don't know whether they had radioed in to headquarters to verify the number of times I'd previously been searched, but when the older fellow got into his car and I asked for the piece of paper, he just smiled and drove off.

I thought of a few choice words I would have liked to call him, but by now he was gone and so were all the rest of them. I went to my room where I packed up all my junk, threw it in the truck and booked myself into the motel next door. With the sun now shining in the window I finally went to sleep. And I guess the odd thing about the whole experience was, even though I never did get my signed piece of paper, I never got stopped by the police for the purpose of wanting to search my truck again, either. "Knock on wood."

The date was now December 14, 1970, when I again started to play the Horseshoe. I was there on January 2, 1971, when Jury and I moved in together on Bathurst Street to begin our new business of Boot Records, and I didn't leave until January 23 of that year.

As I played the "Shoe" at night and discussed business with Jury in the daytime, we decided our company was going to have a look and a policy that were strictly Canadian. If we believed in Canadian talent, we were going to do more than just say so. We were going to put the know-how and the money we had right where our mouths were. We were going to give Canadians the benefit of the doubt and put as many as we could on record. And even though we were later accused of being strictly a country label it wasn't true. Our policy was to record Canadian talent, no matter what kind of music they played. And that's what we did.

The reader should also be reminded that it was during this time that the Canadian Radio-television and Telecommunications Commission (CRTC) ruled that all Canadian radio stations would now have to work towards the goal of making sure that thirty per cent of all the music they played was Canadian. (Before this ruling, the airing of Canadian records over Canadian radio was a rarity.)

This caused an uproar among the major Canadian music broadcasters who said there was no way they could meet such a quota and continued having meetings with the government in order to have the percentage reduced. As opposing factions sought to gain support, at least one major chain of radio stations began to send threatening letters to those they suspected of being strong supporters of the new ruling. And Boot Records was one of their targets.

During our first few weeks of business, we received two of these letters. And they both clearly implied that if our company did not immediately drop its support of the new content rulings, our records would never be played by any of their associated radio stations. History would show that we never dropped our support, and also that these radio stations lived up to their threat. And with a vengeance.

Another side agreement that I made with Jury, and one to which he was readily compliant, was that I didn't want our true business relationship to become public knowledge. I didn't want anyone to know that I had the last word in any dispute, by virtue of my 51 per cent of the company. In this way it would always appear that Jury was not only running everything as the owner and chief executive, but also that I could continue to preserve my image as the "down-to-earth country boy" that I knew was necessary to maintain the affinity it took so long to establish between Stompin' Tom and his fans. It seemed to me that if word got out across the country that Stompin' Tom was really a "bigwig owner" of a record company, and not just a simple artist recording for the label, he would soon find himself alienated from the common people he was singing about. This, in turn, would not only be detrimental to Tom, the artist, but also to the company whose very existence depended on the sale of his records. At least for the short term.

Another point to consider in order to understand the relationship between Jury and me is that while Jury knew a great deal about record companies and song publishing, he knew very little about artist management and nothing at all about instruments or the actual writing, composing and playing of music.

This meant that I continued to manage my own career in spite of what everyone else thought. The arrangement we had was that Jury would claim to be my manager and act as the sole negotiator for all my bookings and appearances, and I would verify the claim by telling all prospective talent buyers who approached me that they would have to talk to my manager and then I'd send them to Jury. This gave me plenty of time to consider each offer in private with Jury and tell him how I wanted the deal to go, in terms of money, conditions and other requirements. Jury would then get back to the guy and finalize the negotiations. All media, publicity and promotion were handled in the same way. Even my fellow artists (well over a hundred) who eventually came to record for Boot Records always believed Jury was my personal manager and planned my whole career. They were even known from time to time to make comments about how lucky I was that I had Jury for a manager, because without him I wouldn't be able to go anywhere.

This type of comment would often hurt my pride a little, and certainly lessened the impact of the advice I would sometimes give them in order to help their careers. And this was all due to the fact that they always gave Jury the credit for everything I had accomplished.

I couldn't tell anyone the difference, however (not even my buddy, Steve), because I knew if the word got out it would not only raise me a notch above the ranks of my fellow entertainers because of my own accomplishments, but it would also mean that I would have to negotiate directly with everybody without always having the time it often takes to properly think things over. The long and the short of it all is that I reasoned, and I think rightly, that I could maintain friendships and get along easier with everybody if I were thought of as someone who just got lucky instead of someone they'd have to call "boss." One can always gain more insight into people by being one of them than he can by being above them.

So while Jury now drew his wages from our new company, he also gave himself that raise he'd been looking for from

Dominion. And along with the commissions I began to pay him for acting as my intermediary (or quasi-manager), he began to do quite well for himself. It was plain to see in the months that followed that he was also pleased with the respect and prestige that came from the perception that he was not only the boss of his own successful company, but also the brains behind the rapidly rising popularity of Stompin' Tom.

As I had previously only leased my masters of "Bud the Spud" and other songs to Dominion, and therefore owned them all, I now began to negotiate (through Jury) to have them transferred to Boot Records as the lease time on each master expired. Then as each transferral date came due, I merely signed a more lucrative lease deal with my own company. And by the time a year or so had passed, all previous recordings, along with a number of new ones, were on the Boot label.

My First Juno Award

Still back in January of 1971, I decided to put the word out that I was looking to form a band. Although experience told me that I was capable of handling any size audience by myself, I thought if I just had a trio they would help to round out my sound a little more and make the stages I played on look a little less empty. Besides, I was planning to do tours of all one-nighters from now on and with all the extra travelling that would entail, I thought I'd enjoy the added company.

For the first couple of afternoons, as I sat in our living room (turned into an office) and auditioned the musicians who came by, I didn't meet anyone I felt I could be absolutely sure of. I was looking for a bass player and a lead guitar player and while most of the guys could certainly play my music, they didn't give me the feeling that I could count on them out on the road somewhere.

On the third afternoon a short stubby guy with a beard came walking in and asked me if this was the place to come and audition for Stompin' Tom. He had just read my notice on the bulletin board down at the musicians' union office and decided to come around for a tryout.

"Yeah, this is the place," I said. "What's your name? Would you like a beer?"

As soon as I mentioned beer, he smiled and said, "Sure, I'd love a beer. Thanks. My name is Gary Empey."

As I watched him down half the bottle on the first swig, I laughed a little, and said, "Gary EMPTY! Eh? Is that what you said your name was?"

"No," he said with a smile that told me he knew exactly what I was up to. "It's Gary Empey. Ee, em, pee, ee, wye. And just like this bottle, there's no T in it."

As we both laughed, I thought to myself, If this guy's bass playing only comes to half of what his good nature and quick wit comes to, I'm going to hire him.

Just as he sat down and started tuning his bass, who walks in but Billy Lewis. I knew Billy from the night he played lead for me in the Horseshoe Tavern. Gerry Hall, the lead player for the Good, the Bad and the Ugly, was sick that night and Billy was brought in to substitute. I hadn't seen him now for a few weeks, but as he had heard that I was looking to hire a guitar player and because I had told him how pleased I had been with his playing, he decided to come and pay me a visit. (Billy Lewis was a twin brother to Bobby Lewis, who was then playing bass for the very popular Carleton Show Band. And Billy once told me it was either him or his brother Bobby that was from Cape Breton, but he couldn't remember which.)

After giving Billy a beer and introducing him to Gary, I could see during the tune-up that they liked each other right away. And because I had already heard what Billy could do, I knew I was going to hire him. All I was really waiting for now was to hear what Gary could do.

I think it was somewhere in the third or fourth number that I said, "Well, that's it, boys, you're hired. And every other number we play from now on is a rehearsal for the road."

We then sat down and discussed the pay, the conditions, the rules of the road, the dress code and everything else that came to anyone's mind.

"This Saturday will be my last night playing the Horseshoe for this time around," I told them. "And the next time I play there, it'll be you guys backing me up. In the meantime I'll be expecting you to rehearse with me a few times next week, starting Monday night, the twenty-fifth of January. And by late next week we should be on the road."

The next day I had a meeting with Jury and told him I

now had a band and I wanted him to do two things: one was to rent me a new car and the other was to book a couple of small venues, not too far from Toronto, so I could break the boys in to life on the road, on the following weekend.

During the time the boys and I were preparing to do our mini-tour, Jury was busy looking for bands he felt were ready to record and who also had the material to do so. We were looking for people who had their own original songs. There wasn't much point in putting artists on the label who were only interested in playing the music from Nashville. The kind they were always hearing on the radio. Who, after all, would want to buy a Canadian copycat, singing a song that had already been made a hit by an American artist? Wouldn't it be better to buy the original? And wouldn't it also be better to buy Canadian if it too were original? At least we thought so.

So while Jury was negotiating with a group he knew from Saskatchewan by the name of Humphrey & the Dumptrucks and several others, I gave him a list of the artists that I was considering for the label. And the first one to pop into my mind, of course, was Stevedore Steve.

As my story goes along, I will no doubt be mentioning a lot of the artists who eventually recorded for Boot Records. But for now, suffice it to say that Humphrey & the Dumptrucks, Stevedore Steve and Stompin' Tom were the first three artists on the label, and in that order.

My first three jobs with Bill Lewis and Gary Empey were on Friday, Saturday and Sunday, January 29, 30 and 31, 1971, in Bracebridge, Huntsville and Gravenhurst, Ontario. I was driving a new Pontiac I had rented and Bill Lewis drove the Boot with all the equipment. Gary just took turns riding with me and sometimes with Bill.

The first three shows hardly paid expenses but they gave us the opportunity to warm up to each other and for the boys to familiarize themselves with their new duties. In those days we had no roadies, as they are now called, and indeed we couldn't afford them, so we all chipped in to set up and tear down, load and unload the truck, sell pictures and records, do interviews and sign autographs, and always be on hand for anything else that might pop up unexpectedly.

The deal I worked out with the boys was, instead of paying them for each show they worked, they were hired on a yearly basis and drew a paycheque every week, whether they worked or not. This gave them roughly three months off per year, with most of it being in the summer when they could enjoy it more, and still be able to draw a regular paycheque while vacationing, if that's what they chose to do.

By the first of February we were back in Toronto. Jury had a tour of one-night concerts lined up on the east coast and a two-week stand at Johnny Reid's in Charlottetown to start things off.

Knowing that record sales would be fairly brisk at concerts and the truck was now full of equipment and had no room to carry anything else, I decided to rent a U-Haul trailer and tow it behind the car. We filled the trailer with amps and column speakers and carried the records and the instruments, etc., in the Boot.

We left for the east coast on Saturday, the sixth of February, and started playing Johnny's Prince Edward Lounge on Monday the eighth.

The following night was my birthday, and for the whole night Johnny was selling a new drink he had just invented for the occasion. I don't know what the liquor content was, but when he brought the first two or three of them over to a table and everyone got to see the huge amount of smoke rising to the ceiling from them, the whole house wanted one. (He later told me the effect was caused by using dry ice.)

He also had a huge glass that held exactly twelve pints of beer. He filled that with Moosehead and put a little Happy Birthday sticker on it and gave it to me, saying, "Here now. Take that, you big Skinners Pond hippie, and get your ass up there and sing and don't let me hear anything else out of you for the rest of the night."

Well, I might have been able to drain the glass if it hadn't been for everyone pouring more drinks in it every time I passed by their table. And by the end of the night it was still as full as it had been in the first place. Except now, it was three-quarters full of just about every kind of liquor there was.

Sometime before midnight (the time when my birthday

was actually supposed to have taken place), Johnny's wife, Judy, had the cook bring a huge birthday cake into the lounge and everybody had a piece. By the time everyone finished wishing me Happy Birthday the night was over and I was still sitting at the bar trying to finish my drink.

Johnny came over and said, "What the hell is wrong with you, anyway? I give you a glass of beer for your birthday and you're not man enough to drink it."

"Well, thank you very much," I said. "You gave me a glass of beer and I'm gonna sit right here till I finish the goddamn thing. And I don't care if it takes me till Hallowe'en. So get the hell out of here and leave me alone."

"Well, Hallowe'en is just over now," he said. "So take off that funny-looking mask and drink up."

I don't know what I said next, but we spent the next couple of hours matching wits until I finally finished my glass of whatever it was and headed up to bed. (Johnny had a three-room apartment over the lounge at that time that he threw in for me and the boys to use as part of the deal.)

It was also on one of these first few nights that I played Johnny's, and I can't be sure whether it happened on the night of my birthday or not, but as I was coming up from Johnny's office which was downstairs below the lounge, I met one of his new waitresses coming down the steps. She was bringing something down to Johnny when I met her half-way on the stairs. As I looked up and saw the great shape of this good-looking, well-endowed beauty, my attention was particularly drawn to the exceptional size of her now bouncing boobs.

Without a crystal ball and having absolutely no idea whatever that this girl was going to be my future wife, I looked right at her boobs and said, "Where did you get those, at Eaton's or Simpsons?"

If she hadn't had her hands full she might have taken a swipe at me, but as it was she just said, "That's for me to know and you to find out, Cowboy."

A little while later, when she reappeared from downstairs, I asked her if she'd like to come out with me sometime. "I'll think about it," she said. And the next evening when I asked her again, she said she was still thinking about it.

By Saturday night I finally got her to agree to come out
to dinner with me on Sunday. When I asked her if I could
pick her up somewhere, she said she'd just meet me at the
club and we could go from there.

When Sunday afternoon came and she didn't show up,
I tried to get her phone number and address from Judy but
she wouldn't give it to me, saying she would try to get hold
of her and find out what happened and let me know. A little
later, when Judy said she hadn't been able to get in touch
with her, I decided to go to the bootlegger's with the boys
and just forget about the whole matter. And so ended the
week of my first encounters with little Miss Lena Kathleen
Joyce Welsh, who, incidentally, hailed from the Magdalene
Islands, Quebec, in the Gulf of St. Lawrence.

When the boys and I came back to the apartment later
that night we realized we only had a couple of bottles of beer
left, so we sent Billy back to the bootlegger's to get a case.
The bootlegger was only a couple of doors away, down
through one of the alleys, but it must have been two hours
before Billy got back.

He had apparently gone to the bootlegger, bought a
dozen beers and then gone to a phone booth to call his
brother Bobby in Toronto. He wanted to tell Bobby how his
new job with Stompin' Tom was going and in the course of
a two-hour conversation, just sat there on the floor of the
booth and drank the whole case of beer. When that was gone
he went back to the bootlegger's and bought another half
dozen bottles which they gave to him in a paper bag. On his
way home he slipped on the ice in the alley, fell down and
broke the paper bag, along with a couple of beers, and now
we could hear him coming up the steps. He was singing
some kind of a Cape Breton Gaelic song and dropping
another beer bottle on the stairs for every third or fourth
step he took.

By the time he staggered in the door he had one bottle
of beer left, and passing it over to me with a great big smile
on his face, he said, "Here's your beer, Tom." To Gary, he
said, "I forgot to bring yours." With that, he just leaned on
his bedroom door, went through it as it opened, and fell on
the bed. And that's where he stayed till the next day.

In the meantime, Gary and I went down the stairs and outside and retrieved as many of the unbroken bottles as we could and finished them off. And that was the last time we ever sent Billy Lewis for beer. He wasn't in too good shape for playing that Monday night, but he certainly didn't get very much sympathy from Gary and me.

After my first set that night, I was sitting at the bar when Lena Welsh comes walking by. "I'm sorry for what happened yesterday," she said. "But I got tied up and couldn't make it."

"Well, you could have phoned me," I said. "But in the meantime, just forget about that. The offer is still open, you know. Can I drive you home after work?"

To this, she agreed. And after that we saw each other as often as time would allow. We used to go for long drives in the afternoons, do a lot of talking, and one day I even took her up to Skinners Pond to meet Russell and Cora and a few of the neighbours who had once been my school chums.

By the end of my second week, although we hadn't got too serious, we nevertheless agreed that we'd like to see each other again. We exchanged phone numbers and promised to call one another when I got back to Toronto. And that's about where we'd have to leave it till I got back to Johnny's. It sure wasn't much to go on, but the circumstances of my being on tour all the time couldn't lead to very much more. But as Fate has its ways and as time would tell, there was certainly going to be one hell of a lot more.

Before that last week at Johnny's was finished, I received a call from Jury in Toronto. The Juno Awards were going to be held that following Monday and he wanted me to fly up to be there. I was not only nominated in the country category but Jury felt that I might just win and wanted me to be there in case I did.

So that Sunday, February 21, 1971, I told the boys to drive the vehicles to Saint John, New Brunswick, where our first concert date was to take place, and I'd meet them there at the airport the following Tuesday night. I then flew from Charlottetown to Toronto.

The next night Jury and I arrived at the hall where the Juno Awards celebration was to take place (I think it was the St. Lawrence Hall, but I'm not sure). And while other people were arriving in limousines, Jury and I drove up in a taxi. Jury had a nice rented suit on and I was dressed in my normal stage gear—black hat, boots, vest, etc.

After we got inside, there was a large ballroom where everyone was offered a couple of drinks before the show started, and as everyone had heard by now that "Jury had started his own record company" they were all congratulating him and wishing him well. There were very few of these types who spoke to me. (I guess they figured that poor Jury just had to drag someone along to his first appearance at an awards show on behalf of his new company, and I was the best specimen he could find at the moment. I also didn't fail to notice that it was always after they looked me up and down that they expressed the hope that Jury would do "a lot better in the future.")

Needless to say, once the show got started, there were a lot of these people who were just as surprised as I was that I was called on the stage to receive the Juno Award for best country artist of 1970.

The big question that seemed to be floating around was "How did this guy rate getting a Juno when we've never even heard him on the radio?" And to tell you the truth, I was wondering the same thing. I was doing more travelling than probably anyone in the country, and with my ear to country stations everywhere I might have heard "Bud the Spud" played a couple of times on the east coast and "Sudbury Saturday Night," "Big Joe Mufferaw" and "The Ketchup Song" once or twice in Ontario. And like I said before, these plays nearly always came from the smaller town stations. The major stations were playing a lot of other artists, especially Americans, but never any Stompin' Tom. So why was I receiving a Juno? And why, for that matter, had a couple of my songs been charted in *RPM* magazine as being among the top ten?

When I posed these questions to Jury, his answers seemed to go like this: The voting for the awards didn't all just have to do with radio play. A lot had to do with record sales. And if my record sales were in great enough numbers to offset the amount of air play received by others who might not be selling as well, then the voters would have to give me the nod. And besides, the TV ratings for the shows that I had appeared on were known to have risen considerably because of those appearances. The *RPM* charts, he said, were undoubtedly subject to some of the same influence.

This answer sounded quite reasonable to me at the time because I knew I had two albums approaching "Gold," which was based on sales of $100,000 or more, while retailing from $1.98 to $2.25, and I also knew through the grapevine that no other Canadian country artists were even approaching those figures. (Word throughout the industry, at the time, was that even Tommy Hunter with the popularity of his weekly television show could in no way come close to the number of sales I was enjoying. And it was Tommy, incidentally, who had won the top country award for the one or two years previous to my winning the Juno. I should also mention that in order to become eligible for these awards, my record company always had to submit my sales figures to the sponsor of the awards, *RPM* magazine, for verification.)

While I've always been an advocate of the principle that all awards should be given and received fairly, I also believe that all awards should be perceived by all to have been given and received fairly. And while Jury's answer seemed to deal adequately with the question as to why it was possible for me to receive a Juno without the expected radio play, it didn't answer one of the so-called street questions that was being asked at the time, and is indeed still being asked, more than twenty-five years later. This question has several parts and should, I feel, be directed to each of the trade magazines who, in turn, should honestly answer it for the benefit of not only the entire industry, but also for the concerned "man on the street." (Though it's presently unknown to me at this writing, if any of the trades have adequately dealt with this question, I feel their answer should be reprinted from time to time as a reminder to everyone that all are being dealt with fairly. Especially during the periods of award presentations.)

The question is: To what degree or extent does a trade magazine's chart position of any given song depend upon any one or all of the following?

1. The actual amount of radio airplay it's getting regionally, nationally or internationally.
2. The actual volume of record sales chalked up regionally, nationally or internationally.
3. The actual amount of trade magazine space bought by anyone who might have an interest in the song's promotion regionally, nationally or internationally.
4. The actual amount of interest the trade magazine itself might have in enlisting the services or other favours of anyone associated with the song regionally, nationally or internationally.
5. The actual amount of interest the trade magazine might have in the song itself, or in its artist, promoter, producer, recording company or publisher, etc., by way of having a personal investment in any one of these.

The asking of the foregoing questions should not in any way be considered as an insult to anyone. They have been asked for many years now by concerned people who might have their faith restored in the legitimacy of song charts everywhere if they were given a credible answer.

As anyone in the music business will tell you, it doesn't feel very good to have someone make the statement or even insinuate that your song is high on the hit parade or on the charts only because its position was bought and paid for. It's high time this cynicism was put to rest before it's allowed to destroy the credibility of a lot of honest people. (On the other hand, if there's anyone out there engaging in these sorts of practices, it behooves us all to weed them out of the industry. I'll have more on this subject later.)

The morning after receiving the Juno I taped a television show for the CBC. I forget now which one it was, but I think it was one of their talk shows. Then in the afternoon I flew back to the east coast.

The boys came to meet me at the airport in Saint John, New Brunswick, and when I told them about winning the Juno Award for best country male vocalist, they shook my hand and asked me when the party was going to start. "As soon as we get in town," I said. And it was a good thing we didn't have to work the following day because we hit just about every drinking place we could find before the rising sun told us it must be time to turn in.

We had run into a few buddies I had known from the days when I was bummin' around, and when they had heard "Bud the Spud" and saw me on TV a couple of times they couldn't get over how far I had come in the last year or so. And now, when they heard I had just won the Juno, they could hardly believe it. They wanted to see it and touch it. But I had to tell them I left it in Toronto, and all I had was a Polaroid photo which had been taken by Jury as I brought it down from the stage during the presentations. In hindsight it was probably a good thing I hadn't brought it with me or I might have left it at one of the bootleggers' places that night.

Hats, Beer and Recordings

O N WEDNESDAY, THE TWENTY-FOURTH, we only had a couple of beers and went to bed early. And on the twenty-fifth we made preparations to play at the Saint John Vocational School.

The gig that night was to be in the same auditorium where I had sat many years previous when I attended school there. I had even entered an amateur contest there on the same stage at one time, though I hadn't won any of the prizes.

After we got our equipment set up, I took the boys for a walk along one of the corridors and showed them where my old classroom was. I would like to have gone in for a couple of minutes but the door was locked and the caretaker wasn't around to open it.

When we got around to the front lobby, I drew their attention to the large mural up over the front doors of the auditorium. The mural was a depiction of all the sports activities that went on at the school. And when the art department had been commissioned to paint the mural many years ago, it was I who had posed for all the male characters now seen holding their footballs, hockey sticks, basketballs and various other sports equipment. (The faces, however, had all been mercifully modified to give each character a semblance of good looks.) There! I said it before you did.

Although we didn't quite fill the auditorium that night we nevertheless received a very rousing welcome. At first I felt a little apprehensive as I wondered what some of the people might be thinking. I wondered if some of my old school chums might be there and thinking, "Who in the hell does he think he is now, coming back here pretending to be a big star or something," but as soon as I walked out on stage and sang my first song, my jitters all disappeared. Somewhere in the midst of the applause a few of the younger people started stomping their feet, and by the end of the second song the party was on.

During the course of the show I was able to spot a lot of familiar faces of people I used to know and quite a few of them later stayed to have a chat during the autograph signing. One of my former teachers, Audrey Shehan, also stopped by for an autograph and expressed her delight that I seemed to be doing so well, and offered her best wishes for my continued success. I thought this was very nice of her, in light of the fact that I hadn't exactly been one of her best behaved students.

The following day we headed out towards Newcastle, N.B., and right from the minute we arrived we started to have some problems.

Most of our concerts in those days were booked in advance by contacting the different service clubs in a particular town and then coming in under the sponsorship of the one we felt could do the best job of promoting the show as well as providing the best possible facilities for the most reasonable percentage of the take.

The sponsor we decided to go with in Newcastle was the Royal Canadian Legion. But even this I couldn't be sure of at the time, because I'd lost the piece of paper containing the name and phone number of the person I was supposed to contact. So the only thing to do, I thought, was stop someone on the street and ask them if they knew what place Stompin' Tom would be playing at. If I knew that, I could maybe go there and find out from somebody just who it was that was bringing us in.

The first pedestrian I spotted was a guy running along the sidewalk, so I told Gary Empey who was sitting on the passenger side to roll down his window and ask the guy where we were playing.

"Hey, buddy. Where 'bouts in town is Stompin' Tom playing?" Gary shouted. As the guy just then veered off to run down some alleyway, he shouted back, "He's at the place."

When I asked Gary what the guy had said, and where it was that we were playing, he just looked at me, shrugged his shoulders and said, "We're playing at 'the place.'"

"What place?" I wanted to know.

"I don't know," Gary said. "I only heard him say something about 'the place' and that was all. You'd better pull over so I can ask somebody else."

Just then I had to stop for a red light and Gary asked several young people who were standing on the corner. "Could you tell me where Stompin' Tom is playing?"

"Oh, Stompin' Tom?" one of them said. "I think he's playing at the place, but I'm not sure."

Then one of the others got into the act and said, "Yeah, that's where he's playing. I saw his name somewhere on a poster that said he was playing at the place."

"Yeah, I know he's playing at the place," Gary said. "But what place is he playing at?"

By this time the light had turned green, everybody on the corner was laughing, and I began to think that because Billy Lewis was following right behind us in the Boot with my name all over it, these kids were just playing some kind of a trick on us. After all, it probably did look a little suspicious to them. Here was a couple of guys wanting to know where Stompin' Tom was playing, and the Stompin' Tom truck was right behind them. Why in the hell wouldn't they just go back and ask the guy who was driving the truck?

As I pulled around the corner of a side street where there was a lot less traffic, I stopped beside two old ladies who seemed to be out for a stroll.

After Gary poked his head out the window and asked them several questions, he quickly pulled it in again and almost took the handle off the door trying to wind the window back up.

"Well, what did they tell you?" I asked. "Do you know where we're playing?"

Gary just looked at me with a glare.

"Yes, I know where we're playin'," he shouted. "We're

playin' at the f-----' place. That's all they know and that's all I know. So don't ask me any more foolish questions."

"Did you ask them where we could find the place?" I said.

"No, I didn't. And I'm not going to," he said. "And if you want to know anything more about the goddamn place, you'll have to go and ask them yourself."

After pulling up beside the old girls again, I decided to get out and have a talk with them.

When I explained to them who I was and the problem I was having, they soon made me understand what all the confusion was about. I got back in the car and explained it to Gary.

"You see, Gary, it's like this," I said. "In the first place, 'The Place' is the place where we're playing, because 'The Place' is really the name of the place. And that's why we couldn't find the place by the name of 'The Place' in the first place."

For the next five minutes, Gary thought I was putting him on until I actually drove into The Place. And that's what the place was called.

In the meantime, Billy had been on the CB car radio the whole time (which didn't help much) and was just as confused as the rest of us. And of course the first question he had to ask Gary when he got out of the truck was, "Hey buddy, you wouldn't happen to know where Stompin' Tom is playin', would ya?"

When he didn't get an answer, he asked him again. Then again, and again, until finally he pestered him so much they both wound up in a playful wrestling match. And that's where they were when I came out of the building with the information I needed. We went to our designated motel where we had a few beers and just joked around for the rest of the evening.

The next afternoon when we got to The Place, we found out what kind of a place The Place really was.

The makeshift stage was no more than a few sheets of plywood nailed to a series of sawhorses. And when I got up and gave it two or three stomps, the whole thing wobbled so much it damn near fell down. But this would only be the beginning of our problems.

This was the first concert tour the boys and I were on together, and also the first big test of our patience and desire to carry on. As it turned out, we were all willing and able to meet each challenge as it presented itself, and in the course of the next few years there were certainly going to be a lot of them. And some even worse than we were having now.

With a hammer and a few spikes and nails, we got the stage so that I could at least stomp on it, providing I stood directly above one of the sturdier sawhorses, and then we set up the equipment for a sound check.

Acoustically, the room was terrible. No matter where we placed our speakers, the sound bounce just kept getting worse. We found a few old curtains in a storeroom and hung them up, but the effort was futile.

Next we had to line up all the chairs that had been strewn around everywhere after some function that had been held the night before, and by the time we cleaned ourselves up and got our stage clothes on, the people who were supposed to look after the door arrived at the same time as the crowd did.

As there was no place for us to go and hide, we just stood around and waited for the place to fill up. And the moment it did, we carefully made our way onto the stage and let 'er rip.

As the audience mostly consisted of burly and rugged-looking men who reminded me of the lumberjack and fishermen types, I purposely selected the kinds of songs I thought would suit their preference. And after the first few numbers, their heavy applause and loud whistling let me know I had made the right decision.

From my vantage point, however, I could also see that a bunch of the boys were really beginning to feel their oats. The bottles were being passed around a little too frequently, and just as I began to finish our first set with "Sudbury Saturday Night" all hell broke loose. I don't know how the fight started, but there it was. And I wasn't going to stop singing now for hell nor money. Drawing from good sound advice and past experience, I indicated to the boys that we were going to remain on stage and immediately went back to singing.

As we tried to maintain our balance every time somebody bumped against the stage, and managed to duck the odd chair and flying bottle, I must have gone through "Sudbury Saturday Night" at least half a dozen times before the cops arrived and carried out the casualties.

With the music and the stompin' still going strong, it didn't take long to once again get the audience's attention. And without taking a break at all, we just performed the entire two-and-a-half-hour show as if nothing had ever happened, then thanked everybody and left the stage to sign autographs for all who might want one.

A lot of people, especially the women, thanked us for continuing with our music, thereby holding most of the crowd's attention and keeping them in their seats. Had we not done this there might well have been a great panic rush towards the door and a lot of people might have been injured, especially the kids and the older folks. (While the boys admitted later that we had done the right thing, for a few minutes there they thought I was crazy.)

About half an hour before the show was over, while we were still on the stage, about thirty or more Legion members came in and stood at the back of the hall. They all had their Legion jackets on and after the show they told us they had all just come down from the Legion hall to invite us back to some sort of a celebration that was still going on.

It was now about 11:30 P.M., which really wasn't late for a Saturday night, but because we were so dog-tired from all the work we had to do since about three o'clock that afternoon with no let-up, I tried to politely refuse.

When that didn't work, I tried to take advantage of one of their long-standing rules, which disallowed "the wearing of hats in the Legion."

"Whenever I'm on tour," I said, "the long-established dress code of Stompin' Tom is that he must always wear a black cowboy hat while appearing anywhere in public. And while I respect your law that forbids the wearing of hats, you can maybe understand how it sometimes prevents me from entering the Legion, especially when I'm in town as Stompin' Tom, on official business."

Just as I thought they'd have no comeback for my answer,

they were all quick to assure me that the no-hat rule in Newcastle was practically obsolete and really nothing to be concerned about. They assured me that if I came along they'd explain my hat problem on the way in the door and after that, I'd be sitting with thirty-five of them, plus a dozen or more of their friends who were still at the Legion, and if anyone made any funny comments they wouldn't be long looking after the situation.

"Well, I don't know," I said. "I don't want to get anybody in trouble, and besides the boys and I are tired and we got a long road tomorrow."

"Come on," they said. "We thought Stompin' Tom was a better man than that. Don't be such a spoilsport." And after a little more arm-twisting, I finally decided to go.

About five minutes later we were at the door of the Legion where they spoke to someone inside and before we knew it, we were all sitting at a number of tables along one side of the room. Billy and Gary and I were allowed to sit with our backs against the wall and well surrounded by the the gang that brought us in. So for the short run, at least, I began to feel well protected and not just a little bit thirsty.

The place was now packed solid, and with the waiters being so busy, we had to wait a little while before anyone came to serve us.

Finally, when someone did come, it was one of the waiters who hadn't yet been informed about the permission we had received at the door about wearing the black cowboy hat.

Before bothering to take our beer order, the first thing he did was point a very authoritative-looking finger at me and say, "Hey, you! Are you ignorant or something? Take that stupid-looking hat off. Don't you know you're in the Legion?"

Before I could say anything, a couple of the guys who brought us in began to tell him that I was Stompin' Tom and that it was all right for me to wear my hat. But because he was the very impatient type he didn't bother to wait for the rest of the answer. He just walked away, saying the whole table was "cut off" until I got rid of the cowboy hat.

I don't know where he went or who he told that I wouldn't take the hat off, but within thirty seconds he was back with four or five helpers who immediately got into a big argument with practically all those Legion members who brought us in.

It wasn't any time before the word got around the crowded room that some asshole didn't want to take his hat off, and now there were just as many from the opposite side of the hall who wanted it off as there were from our side insisting that it was going to stay on.

Sensing that it was too late now for me to either take the hat off or leave it on, I told the boys we'd better get the hell out of there before the fight started and while we still had the chance. Unfortunately, I didn't say the words fast enough. The whole house was in an uproar. All the women had somehow managed to make their way to the far end of the hall and all the men from the opposite side of the room, who far outnumbered the ones on our side, were trying to fight their way through to get at me.

In one desperate attempt to make my escape, I jumped on a table and made one hell of a leap towards the back door. Unfortunately, as I came down out of the air there were too many hands grabbing for me, and before I knew it, about six or seven big burly men carried me over their heads and threw me right out the back door.

The only trouble was, the back door of the building wasn't on the same level as the one we had entered from the street. All the buildings were built on the side of a hill, and all had steps from the back entrance leading down to the alley below.

It was a good thing there was lots of snow on the ground, because when they threw me out the back door, I cleared the railing and fell about ten or twelve feet into a big fluffy snowbank.

As I squirmed around to get my bearings, I heard a very loud "Aahhhh!" and out came Billy Lewis, who landed right beside me. And in less than another minute, all three of us found ourselves in the snowbank wondering what in the hell happened to us.

Just when I figured I'd probably seen the last of my hat, the door at the top of the stairs opened again, and down she came. It took me a little while to get 'er in shape but soon I had 'er back on my head and we were walking up the street to where I'd parked the car. None of us were hurt very much. Just shook up a little. But what a helluva last couple of days it had been. We hadn't asked for any of this, but we got it anyway. And that wasn't even going to be the end of it.

Somehow my name always got mentioned every time people remembered the brawls that happened in Newcastle that night, and along with the association, I must have received at least part of the blame. Although nobody ever told me the reason, none of the town's service clubs ever wanted to book me again. And it wasn't until twenty-two years later, in 1993, that I was able to make a successful return. But that, as they say, is just how it goes sometimes in the music business.

The following day, on Sunday, the twenty-eighth of February, 1971, we headed out for Tignish, Prince Edward Island, and played the parish hall on Monday, the first of March.

Jury had arrived on the Island from Toronto that afternoon and after renting a car in Charlottetown, he drove the hundred miles up to see us. He also brought the Juno Award with him and all that night we kept it on display at the overcrowded hall. During the intermission, Clifford Bernard, the chairman of the Village Commission, presented me with a maple wood carving of Prince Edward Island along with a desk set (not knowing I didn't have a desk to put it on), and seizing upon the opportunity, a couple of the local politicians also got into the act by making a pitch for votes during their welcoming speeches.

After the intermission, as I started my show again, I thanked everybody, including the DJ from CJRW in Summerside who had been giving me a few spins on the radio station, and immediately went into my "Song of the Irish Moss." This threw everybody for a loop, because gathering the Irish moss from the ocean is one of their big industries on that end of the Island, and everybody was taken by complete surprise. I hadn't told anybody I had just recently written the song, and after dedicating it to the whole audience of 1,300 or more (including the four or five hundred we piped the music to outside), I just started singing the song.

When I was through, I told everybody it was my intention to record the song on my next album and expressed the hope that they'd all be looking for it when it came out sometime during the summer.

Amid the standing ovations and the deafening applause, they made me sing the song several times again, and when the show was over I must have signed autographs on pictures and records for over two and a half hours. By the time we all got back to the farmhouse in Skinners Pond, which was only seven miles from Tignish, I was completely exhausted. Two of Russell's home brews later, I hit the sack and never got up till noon the next day.

Being on tour, however, I wasn't able to stay around home for very long, and that evening we headed out for Charlottetown where we rented a motel room for the night.

We then went down to Johnny Reid's for a few jars where I got to see Lena Welsh again after work and the next evening we played our first gymnasium, at the high school in St. Peters. Needless to say, the acoustics were terrible, and people could hardly make out any of the words of the songs, not to mention anything about the jumble of music. It was more of an irritation than anything else, and during the autograph signing they sure let us know about it. After that, I got after Jury, and told him not to book us into any more gymnasiums if it was at all possible. Playing gymnasiums is one sure way of ruining your reputation among people who pay their money to hear the music, and not to sit there all night and be vexed.

The following night we played Montague and by Sunday we were up in Alberton. We then left the Island to play Amherst, Nova Scotia. And by Wednesday the tenth, we had a late afternoon/evening gig to do at Dalhousie University in Halifax.

This gig turned out to be a real disaster. We didn't know until we got there to set up that they wanted us to play in two places at the same time. One was a large cafeteria downstairs and the other was some kind of a boardroom upstairs.

We had to plug our amps and PA system in on the one stage and after playing for twenty minutes we had to unplug everything and carry the whole works, including our instruments, up a very narrow flight of steps, plug everything in again and start playing on the other stage. When our twenty-minute show was over upstairs, we had to unplug and do the same thing all over again downstairs.

Our contract had called for twenty minutes on and ten minutes off during every half hour for two hours. We didn't know we would have to spend our ten minutes off lugging equipment like furniture movers up and down stairs. And after stomping my foot for twenty minutes and then lugging all that equipment, I found myself all out of puff long before I even got to start each performance.

While this alone might have been bad enough, we encountered an even greater problem. All the students, both upstairs and down, had been drinking pretty good even before we arrived. And by the time we got around to doing our second performance in each place, everyone was getting pretty rowdy.

First, the guys in the cafeteria began to poke fun at us, especially me, and then they started shaking their beer bottles and allowing the contents, which were now under pressure, to spew all over the stage and mainly on us. This they found to be very funny and continued their little game until our twenty minutes was up and we got the hell out of there.

By the time we got our gear upstairs again and commenced to do our last show, the boys in the boardroom had decided they could do my show even better than I could. So a group of them came up on the stage, took over the microphone and started to sing, leaving me and the boys just standing there.

By the time they screwed up three or four songs, stomped their feet a dozen times, and left our equipment in complete disarray, they thought they'd better go down and have a beer and leave the rest of the entertaining to us.

Unfortunately, we weren't going to get off that easy. There was more to come. Just as we got things straightened out and I got back to singing, a group of our "friends" from downstairs showed up, and the beer spewing began all over again. Soon they had the upstairs group doing it, and when I decided to bring the show to a halt, the whole fracas just got worse.

As we tried to get our equipment together everybody was up tramping all over the stage, spilling and spewing beer everywhere, and making it practically impossible for us to do anything.

I would have liked to complain about the treatment we got right from the start. But the guy who booked us in had only stayed around long enough to show us where we had to play and then disappeared. He left us in the middle of this din with absolutely no one to turn to in case there was any trouble. I might have even quit and packed up earlier but I didn't know my way out of the building. And the people we were playing to were certainly in no condition to offer any assistance.

By the time the room cleared out and the guy who brought us in came around to pay us, our clothes and our amps, our instruments and everything else were reeking with beer, and I had a hard time to contain myself when I explained to him what had taken place.

Although he apologized and appeared to be genuinely sorry for what had happened, he said he found it hard to believe that all these "nice guys" would do such a thing.

This didn't help us much. It was going to take nearly all the money we made for the gig just to clean up our clothes and put our equipment back in order.

At any rate, he did help us to lug some of our gear out to the truck, where he shook my hand and wished me a safe journey back to Ontario.

We finished our tour in Lindsay, Ontario, where we played for the Horsemen's Association on Saturday, March 13. After that we went home to Toronto and took five days off before playing the Sportsmen's Show at the CNE grounds from March 19 to 28, 1971.

This was a gig where we got up on stage at the beginning of each hour, sang three or four songs until we drew a crowd around, and then a pretty girl would get up with us and give her promotional spiel for one of the car companies. I'd then sing one more song and we were all through for another hour. These performances took place from mid-afternoon until about eight o'clock of each evening. It wasn't the kind of gig I was crazy about but the pay was good and it allowed

us to play for a lot of people to whom we might not otherwise have gained exposure.

When the Sportsmen's Show was finished on the twenty-
eighth of March, I decided to take the next six weeks off
to record six more albums. Five of them were to be of
traditional songs packaged in a sixty-song, five-album box
set, and the other one was to be an original with all of my
own compositions.

The original album was to be called *My Stompin' Grounds,*
and while I already had a number of songs written for it, I
also had a lot of good ideas that I was anxious to write about.

One of the songs I really wanted to write was a tribute to
one of my personal heroes, Wilf Carter, and another one was
about some of the things I saw and did during the years
I worked in the tobacco fields around Tillsonburg, in southern Ontario.

I already had eleven albums on the market, and if I could
succeed in getting the next six recorded in the allotted time,
I would have seventeen by May tenth, the day I was to start
playing at the Horseshoe again. I remember everyone saying
they thought the project was impossible, and they even had
me wondering sometimes if I hadn't bit off more than I
could chew. But I nevertheless set up the goal, so I intended
to give it my best shot.

Jury, in the meantime, had been scouting around everywhere for bands he felt were good enough to record, and on
one of his outings he came across an Irish group by the
name of Brannigan's Boys. They were only a trio but Jury
thought that I should go down with him to a bar called the
Camelot, where they were playing, and see what I thought.

The leader of the band who did most of the singing was
Joe Brannigan (whose real name was Noel Gogarty), and
though he didn't play an instrument at all, he had such stage
presence that he had the audience eating out of his hand.
And the other two guys, Glen Reid and John Spence, played
the banjo and guitar so well they seemed like four guys up
there instead of two.

As the reader may know, Irish bands were quite popular
at the time, and these three guys were exceptional. I was not
only impressed and told Jury to go ahead and record them,

but I wanted to have a talk with them myself. I especially thought that Glen Reid and John Spence would provide a nice touch to the music on the albums I was planning to record. And as it all turned out later, my thoughts proved to be right.

Meanwhile, I found out that Joe Brannigan loved to play chess, and incidentally so did Gary Empey, and as chess had always been one of my favourite games, we started to see a great deal of each other and we soon became great friends.

In a lot of ways Joe and I were quite similar. We both liked to poke fun at each other, make "federal cases" out of the smallest arguments just to outdo one another, and find the greatest amusement in getting other people to think we were almost at the point of fighting with each other, when in reality the total opposite was true. I think it had a lot to do with the Irish blarney that we both seemed to have in great abundance.

We also seemed to have the same degree of stubbornness. And we found that out one night while we were having a card game at my sister Marlene's house.

We were all down in the basement, and when the game was over we were all supposed to go upstairs to have a lunch before leaving for home.

Well, as Joe and I got into one of our fun-arguments about which of us had the most endurance, some guy by the name of Gerald Taylor, who was a natural-born shit-disturber from the east coast, gave us a proposition we couldn't refuse, just before he went upstairs.

"With all the endurance you fellers have," he said, "the first guy to come upstairs for lunch will prove that the other guy has more endurance to stay away from food than he has."

Well, that was it. Neither one of us wanted to be the first guy to go upstairs. That would prove that one of us was a wimp, and neither one of us wanted that to happen.

After taking about half an hour to convince each other that this was all silly, we agreed to go to the top of the stairs and both put our foot on the top step at the same time. That way neither one of us would be the wimp, and both of us would have the last laugh on Gerald Taylor.

The only problem was, when we got to the top of the stairs we both tried to force the other fella to put his foot down first. Now we didn't trust each other, and for the next hour the crowd was divided into camps, each betting on which one of us was the wimp.

I believe we would still be there if Marlene's husband, Willard, hadn't gone out the front door and sneaked in the side door right behind us, and pushed us both up the stairs at the same time.

Of course, we still argued later about which one of us landed on the kitchen floor first. But as that was now too hard to prove, the subject just went to the back burner till we couldn't find anything else to argue about.

Another time, after playing chess all night at our Boot Records apartment, Joe was in the process of losing another game so he just decided to get up from the table and go home.

As we lived over a bakery shop, there was a long flight of stairs at the end of the hall which led down to the front door at street level.

As Joe got to the bottom of the stairs and before he got the door open, we started to slag one another to see who was going to get the last good word in before he went home.

Just for the fun of it, to see if I could scare him into opening the door and taking off much faster than he intended, I grabbed one of the car tires I had lined up along the hall and threatened to roll it down the steps at him.

As he figured I wouldn't throw it anyway, he took up a valiant stance with his chest sticking out and said something about not being scared of anything; not of me, the tires, or "even the goddamn truckload of potatoes they might have come off of."

Just as he said that the tire slipped out of my hands and went rolling down the stairs.

Well, you talk about a guy changing his attitude in record speed? He went all the way from being a hero to a coward in less than a nanosecond. He fumbled for the lock on the door, and just as he got it opened he went flying out on the street with the tire right behind him. I don't know how he ever managed to get out of the way, but as he did the tire went speeding across the street and plopped itself down on the far side.

I'm not sure what the passing drivers were thinking but they were certainly giving Joe some awful dirty looks.

As I looked at his long bearded face and walked across the street to get my tire, I couldn't stop laughing. And even now, as I think about it, I can still hear him castigating me in that deep, gruffy Irish brogue of his, as he kept calling me a "crazy fooking Canadian bawstard."

He still doesn't believe my story today, about the tire just slipping out of my hands. And though we're the best of friends, he still doesn't trust me around stairways.

By the last of April 1971, we had the sixty songs recorded for the five-album box set and I had all the songs written for the new "original album" that I was about to record during the first week of May. So far everything was right on schedule, and I even found the time somehow to tape a television show for the CBC called "Here Comes the Sun."

I'd also been talking to Lena Welsh on the phone from Prince Edward Island a few times, and the latest word was that she was coming up to visit her sister, Pauline, who was now living in Toronto. She eventually arrived by train on the fourth or fifth of May, and I immediately invited her down to the studio to see what went on at one of my recording sessions.

When she came in and saw all the school kids lined up in front of microphones, she couldn't imagine what was going on. At the time, we were recording one of my newly written songs called "Name the Capitals," and as I called out the name of each of the ten Canadian provinces the kids would shout the name of its capital city. It was a real fun song and everybody was having a good time.

Later on that night we finished the album by recording the last three or four songs. One of them was the song from which came the title of the album, "My Stompin' Grounds," and the very last one, which I had just finished writing, and nobody had yet heard, was "Tillsonburg," with its now famous line, "My back still aches when I hear that word." This one had everybody smiling at most of the lyrics, and after recording a total of seventy-two songs altogether, it gave us all a great note to end on.

By the end of that week we had most of the mixing done and put the finishing touches on it during a couple of afternoons the following week, while I was playing each night at the Horseshoe.

With so much going on, I didn't get much time with Lena. But I did manage to take her out to dinner once or twice, and she came down to the Horseshoe to see me as often as she could. From there we went up to my apartment a few times. But it really wasn't until my gig was done at the "Shoe" that we were able to see each other practically every day.

Touring Ireland and England

B Y THIS TIME JURY HAD made some contacts with a couple of booking agents from England and Ireland. And because my recording of "Poor, Poor Farmer" had generated a lot of interest over there, they were very anxious to book me on a tour of those countries.

We were scheduled to leave around the first of June, and by this time Lena had gotten herself a job and decided to stay in Toronto. Her brother, Ted, was also in Toronto. So she found herself an apartment not too far from where he lived, on Eglinton Avenue.

One of the first things that struck me when the boys and I arrived in Ireland was the preponderance of Irish music we were hearing on Irish radio stations. Without a doubt they had to be playing their own recording artists at least 70 per cent of the time. And the remaining 30 per cent was foreign, i.e., British, American and others.

Coming from a country like Canada, this presented a great mystery to me. I couldn't figure out, for instance, why we had to fight like hell in Canada to pass a law to get our radio stations to even play Canadians, and then only to the extent of 30 per cent of the time, while here in Ireland the stations were playing their own talent 70 per cent of the time and they didn't even have regulations. Nor did they seem to need them.

What was going on? I asked myself. And how did this

come to be? After all, we were a much richer country than Ireland and in the eyes of the world, we were a lot more progressive. Ireland had an internal war going on which was straining their already weak economy, and yet, with a population of only three million as compared to twenty-seven million in Canada, they were away ahead of us when it came to having pride and respect for their own arts and culture and the continued preservation of same.

While it's true that a lot of people were leaving Ireland to obtain employment in other parts of the world, the same wasn't true of their recording artists. And most of the ones I was meeting were doing far better than I was at the time.

In contrast to this, it wasn't people seeking work who were moving out of Canada in large numbers. It was our actors, singers, writers, musicians and producers, and many other people in the professions that were moving out. And while I can't speak for them all, I know that our own Canadian radio stations were continually encouraging our musical artists to record in the United States rather than here at home. The implication was that nothing recorded in Canada was good enough to qualify for airplay. And yet the equipment in our studios at the time was, and still is for that matter, state of the art, and every bit as good as, if not better than, what was being used south of the border.

So with writers and singers being denied airplay in their own country, they were flocking to the United States in great numbers, leaving Canada much poorer, culturally, because of it. And at this writing, the trend has never stopped. It has only gotten worse.

Is it any wonder, then, that the three million people of Ireland (and most other countries, including the United States and Great Britain) don't seem to have a problem identifying with who they are and where their roots are? And it shouldn't come as any surprise that Canadians do.

All other countries in the world see nothing wrong with allowing their singers to extol the merits of their own homeland. In fact they encourage it. But in Canada they don't. In fact most of our radio stations belittle it and laugh at it.

The result of this is that most of our Canadian children, getting up in the morning and going to school, are humming and whistling the lyrics and melodies of songs that not only don't remind them of who they are as Canadians, but continually bombard their minds with the notion that their opportunities in life are far greater in a foreign country, where people are proud enough to sing about themselves, than they are in a land they perceive as being dull.

Most kids like exciting music and are naturally attracted to its source. If the source or the content of a song is not in Canada or can't readily be identified with, related to or associated in some way with the lives and aspirations of the Canadian people, then the radio stations who play such songs, and indeed the singers who sing them, can only be likened to the Pied Piper of Hamelin. The only difference seems to be that while they get paid for luring the children away, the rats get paid no attention.

As an entertainer myself, the foregoing is in no way meant to imply that I would rather live in Ireland or any other country. But what it does mean is that Canada deserves a lot more respect from its people than it has been getting. This country has been giving wealth and freedom to us and to all those who have come to our shores, and while we may not be able to give her back the wealth, the least we can do is use some of our freedom to write and sing and broadcast the fact that we love her, and that we're not ashamed to tell it to the world.

That doesn't mean we have to shove it down people's throats. It only means that we have to show that we are a nation among nations and a people with a sense of belonging. Canada doesn't deserve to be a ship without a gallant captain and a loyal crew, or for that matter, a lost whale without a sense of direction. What Canada does deserve is a crew of people who know exactly who and what they are and where the hell they're going, instead of a self-serving bunch of scallywags who punch holes in their own lifeboat every time they see a mirage.

While that's enough on the subject for now, you can bet your boots I'll be back to it later.

In the meantime, our tour of Ireland was headquartered in the city of Dublin and the towns we played were all in the south. They were Wexford, Waterford, Kilkenny, Clonmel and Cork. Then on to Limerick, Ennis, Galway and Athlone. We played twice in Dublin: once before leaving on the tour and once when it was done.

All our gigs were of the cabaret type, which means we only played for half an hour or so while the local dance bands took their breaks. And because some of the towns were only twenty or thirty miles apart we were sometimes able to do two cabarets on the same night.

Both in Dublin and in Cork we appeared as guests on a couple of TV musical/variety shows and the rest of the time we were on our own.

We had rented a car for touring and in the afternoons we did quite a bit of travelling around. (With the steering wheel being on the opposite side of the car, the boys didn't do much driving. They preferred, instead, to sit around and laugh like a couple of fools while I made all the mistakes.)

We got to go through a lot of old castles, including the one at Blarney, where we all got to kiss the famous Blarney Stone. This is reputed to have been the stone that Jesus leaned on to pray in the Garden of Gethsemane, and it was later taken to Ireland during the first century A.D. by Joseph of Arimathea. Then in the early part of the sixteenth century, when the English king, Henry the Eighth, desired to possess it as a symbol of his sovereign right to thwart certain edicts of the Pope, it was allegedly cut in two pieces, with one half sent to Scotland to become known as the Stone of Scone, and the other half to be strategically placed among the many other stones that were to be used in the construction of the bulwark at the top of Blarney Castle.

The legend has it that the Stone of Scone was later found by one of the English sovereigns, who took it from Scotland and placed it in a specially built compartment under his throne, the same throne upon which the Queen of England sits today. The stone was returned to Scotland in 1996, piped across the border with great ceremony, I seem to recall. But by the time the other half of the stone, the Blarney, was discovered, its importance as a religious symbol had significantly dropped, and so did the desire to possess it.

It nevertheless remains as a tourist attraction at the top of Blarney Castle, where you have to have somebody hold on to your ankles as you bend over backwards and are lowered into a bottomless hole in order to kiss it. Not to worry though. After a few mishaps, they've now installed a grating just below the stone to prevent people from falling out of sight. (In the event that your most trusted friend happens to let go of your ankles? Oops! Sorry about that, old pal. But here, just bend over and we'll try it again.) At any rate, the kissing of the Blarney Stone is supposed to endow those who are worthy with the gift of eloquence.

Before leaving Ireland for England we had a few days around Dublin to go sightseeing. And because the traffic was always so heavy on the city's many narrow streets, we decided to do what many other people were doing and that is, to rent a motorcycle.

For some reason having to do with insurance, the rental company wouldn't assume any liability for the bikes they rented to foreigners. But if we bought them outright and brought them back in good shape they'd buy them back from us for the price we paid for them, minus the amount they would have charged us had we rented them. They of course wanted their payment up front, and after dickering back and forth for an hour or so we eventually bought two small motorcycles we felt were within our means and away we went.

My bike was a little red Honda, and because the boys would have to double up, their bike was a Kawasaki of a little bigger size with a bit more power.

The guy at the rental place also told us to beware of bike thieves as there were a lot of them around Dublin. So after we drove around all that afternoon I decided to ask the guy at the Belvedere Hotel where we were staying if we could keep our bikes overnight in the compound they had for such purposes around at the back of the building.

After gaining the necessary permission I locked my bike in for the night and told Bill and Gary they should do the same. "Ahh! To hell with it," they said. And they just left the Kawasaki leaning up against the lamppost in front of the hotel.

The next morning about eleven o'clock I noticed it was still there, so I went and got my bike out of the compound and parked it just behind theirs, in preparation for taking off for the rest of the day, as soon as we had something to eat.

All during breakfast I had to listen to Bill and Gary tell me I shouldn't be so paranoid about getting my bike stolen. And when we went out on the street to start up and get going, my goddamn Honda was nowhere to be seen. The Kawasaki was still sitting there as pretty as you please and my bike was gone.

While the boys were having a chuckle over my hard luck, I called the police and went down to the station to give them a description of what the bike looked like, and for the time being that's all I could do. They told me there were dozens of bikes being stolen every day and I'd just have to wait to see if mine would turn up.

In the meantime, I wasn't going to just sit around. I got the map of Ireland out and asked the boys if they wanted to tour the whole country in the car with me for the next two or three days. They said they wouldn't mind if I was just going to stay within the twenty-six counties of the Irish Republic, but when I mentioned going to the six counties of Northern Ireland they balked. They said with all the trouble going on up there they didn't want any part of it.

I tried to tell them that this might be the only opportunity they'd ever have to see all of Ireland but it didn't seem to matter. So I just filled the car up with gas and went by myself.

It's only about a hundred miles from Dublin to Belfast in Northern Ireland, but when I was just ten or fifteen miles from Belfast I had to come to a complete stop. There was a continuous line of traffic from where I was to the city.

It seems that someone had blown up one of the buildings at the checkpoint where I had crossed the border not more than twenty minutes ago, and the army was now out in full force, checking every car heading into Belfast.

There were armoured trucks and other military vehicles everywhere, and the soldiers with loaded rifles and fixed bayonets were ordering everybody out of their cars and searching everything. And they weren't being very polite as they went about it.

As they came to me, I was ordered out of my car with my hands in the air and told to drape myself over the side of the roof. Then while three or four soldiers searched me and practically turned the car upside down, one of them stood about ten feet behind me with his gun pointing directly at me the whole time.

I remember thinking to myself that this guy can't be any more than eighteen or nineteen years old. And with his young fingers pressing against the trigger of his automatic rifle, I was sure hoping nothing would happen to startle him. Because if it did, there was one Stompin' Tom that wasn't going to be stompin' around any more.

Finally, after checking all my papers, they ordered me back into my car and told me to stay there. They moved on to the next vehicle behind me and went through the same routine. And there were soldiers all along the line of traffic doing the same thing.

After about an hour, the cars began to move very slowly, and about six o'clock that evening I arrived in Belfast.

The first thing I wanted to do after that ordeal was to park the car and make my way to the nearest pub. And when I found one and walked inside, although the place was full, everyone fell mysteriously silent. I guess they smelled "stranger" all over me and were certainly giving me the eye.

The only seat I could see that was available was a stool at the end of the bar, so I sat down there and ordered a bottle of Harp beer. (This was about the only kind I liked in Ireland.)

When the bartender took my money and gave me change without even saying a word I began to feel uneasy and unwanted. The atmosphere in here was like no other pub I'd ever been into. It felt like something pretty scary had just happened or was about to happen, and I quickly decided I didn't want to be around when it did.

It only took me two or three guzzles to drain the bottle and I was gone. That place was like a morgue and everybody in there reminded me of a bunch of zombies from an entirely different dimension. Some kind of a time warp in which I certainly had no desire to remain.

After driving five or six miles out of town in a northerly

direction, I came to a motor hotel called the Chimney Corner in Newtownabbey. There I got a nice comfortable room, had a few beers and went to bed. Sometime during the night I woke up from a nightmare. Some zombie dressed in a soldier's uniform was chasing me with a knife. But other than that everything was okay. The following morning I got up fairly early, had a good breakfast and headed out for a long day's drive.

First I drove to Londonderry, crossed back over into the Republic of Ireland, visited Letterkenny and stopped for a beer in the town of Donegal. From there I drove down to Sligo, Galway, Ennis and Limerick, and then spent the night in a small hotel in Tralee.

I had travelled a distance of about 355 miles that day, and the next morning I drove out to Dingle and back to Tralee, a distance of about sixty miles on the round trip over a fairly bumpy road. Had the road been in better shape I would have driven the extra ten or twelve miles out to Dunquin just so I could say I had been to the town that is situated on Ireland's most westerly point.

After leaving Tralee I had a beer in Killarney, another one in Tipperary and then headed back to Dublin. The whole trip took me about two and a half days and I travelled approximately 750 miles. I saw a lot of very beautiful countryside and only wish I'd had more time so I could have stopped more often to take in some of Ireland's rich history and very famous landmarks.

Upon arriving back in Dublin there was a message from the police waiting for me at the hotel desk. They had found my motorcycle and wanted me to come down to the station to pick it up.

When I got there it was covered with mud, the back wheel was out of line, half of the front fender was torn off and the handlebars were all crooked. I did manage to drive it to a garage, however, where they were able to straighten it out temporarily, and that night I again locked it in the compound at the back of the hotel.

Late the following afternoon we were supposed to fly to London, England, so we planned to take our bikes and sell them back to the rental company earlier that day.

The first thing I did that morning when I woke up was to take my bike out for one last ride. After all, it was four days now since I'd bought it, and I'd only had one ride on it.

After scooting around town for about half an hour I decided to go into a little restaurant for a ham sandwich to take out. I parked the motorcycle right outside the restaurant window where I could keep my eye on it while I waited by the cash register for my sandwich to be made.

When the guy came with the sandwich and I took my eyes off the bike long enough to pay him, I looked around, and wouldn't you just know it, the goddamn thing was gone again.

I rushed out the door just in time to see some son of a bitch jump on it and head down the street. I hollered at the top of my lungs at the guy but he didn't even turn around. He just blew the horn a couple of times and left me standing there looking back and forth, first at him and then at the ham sandwich that had fallen out of the wrapper and was now lying on the sidewalk.

As I was only two or three blocks from the hotel I decided the walk back might do me good. I didn't bother to get another sandwich, as I wasn't hungry any more. And it's a good thing somebody didn't stop to ask me for anything, because I might have hauled off and ploughed them one. I just kept asking myself, "Why me? What the hell did I do to deserve this?" The boys had driven their motorcycle around everywhere and left it parked in the damnedest places for the last four days and not one thief even bothered to look at it. And here I was, being so careful, and had mine stolen twice.

As I got back to the hotel the boys were standing in the doorway. Not knowing what had happened, Billy asked me one of his usual smart-ass questions. "Hey, Tom. Whatcha doin' walkin'? Where's your bike? Someone steal it again on ya?"

I didn't bother to answer. But when they followed me into the hotel lobby and heard me make another phone call to the police about my bike being stolen again, they turned into a couple of laughing hyenas.

When I told the police I was leaving Ireland later that day

and that I wouldn't be back, they asked me for my Canadian address so they could get in touch with me if they located it. And as long as I would pay the cost they'd ship it over to me.

I told them I thought that would be very nice of them, said thank you, and later that day we flew over to London.

(About a month later, when we were back in Canada, I got a notice in the mail from the Dublin police saying they had found my bike and wanted me to phone them to make arrangements for transporting it over to Canada. When I asked them to crate it up and find out how much it would all cost, they told me the crate wouldn't be necessary, and that they could just leave it "in the bag." When I asked them what they meant by leaving it "in the bag," they told me it was all apart when they found it and they just picked up the pieces and threw them in a bag. They couldn't even be sure if all the pieces were there, or indeed, if all the pieces in the bag belonged to the same motorcycle. So after hearing that, I just told them to keep the goddamn thing and hung up.)

Upon arriving in London we settled into the Ker-Robert Hotel, not too far from Heathrow Airport, and waited for our contact to meet us there.

Once we found out what our schedule would be, there was no need for me to rent a car. Most of our gigs were going to be in the greater London area and the guy that brought us in was the son of a big brewing company owner and he had engaged one of the taxi companies to take us wherever we needed to go.

The string of night spots that we were to play in were also owned by the brewing company, so everything we did seemed to be tied in somehow with the same outfit. And the only other town we got to play in besides London was Southampton.

The largest and most famous night club that we played in was the Nashville Room, which had a reputation somewhat similar to that of the Horseshoe Tavern in Toronto, but it was only about half the size.

Although they treated us very well they also kept us very busy. I think we only had about three nights off during the whole time we were in England and that didn't give us any time to travel anywhere.

I think the most memorable thing for me about playing in these clubs was the comments I continually kept getting from all the customers. They just couldn't seem to get over the fact that I was singing so many songs about Canada. Some had never heard a Canadian song before and others said they learned more about Canada from listening to me sing for an hour than they had from any of the books they had read about it.

This made me quite proud that I was able to promote my country to others in this way. Unfortunately, I didn't have any records overseas with me or I would have been able to sell quite a few of them, in both Ireland and England.

On one of our nights off, in London, while the boys decided to just sit around their room and watch the "telly" (the TV), I thought I'd go out and have a few beers at one of the pubs down around Soho. I wasn't out very long before I ran into a bit of trouble.

The pub I was in had a long bar, at which there were no stools, and a number of tables which were presently occupied. So after ordering a beer I walked down to the end of the bar and parked myself in the corner, just under the television set.

Just as I ordered my second beer the Johnny Carson show came on the telly. It was a re-run of a show I had watched just before leaving Canada, and the special guest was none other than Anne Murray. She would be singing a couple of songs, but first she would be interviewed by Johnny. And one of the questions I remembered him asking her was what part of Canada she was from, and when she told him Nova Scotia he wanted to know how to get there. She told him to travel a couple thousand miles north until he met a Mountie, who would be able to give him further directions.

While all this seemed innocent enough at the time, I had no idea what kind of a problem it was going to create tonight.

What happened was that the Americans had edited the program before it ever left the States, and now as it was being aired in England there was no mention at all that Anne was from Canada. That part was cut out altogether, leaving the impression that she was an American from the United States.

I guess I could have lived with the fact that I was the only one in the pub who knew the difference, but just as the program started, something else happened.

About four or five hefty-looking Americans came swaggering into the pub, came down to the end of the bar where I was, and rudely pushed up against me as they ordered their beer.

Well, as I was at the very end of the bar with the wall beside me, I would have liked to say something, but with four or five of them standing there I figured I'd better just let the incident pass.

As I ordered another beer, the American next to me heard my accent and asked me what part of the States I was from. And when I told him I wasn't from the States, he said I'd have to be from there because I sure as hell didn't sound like all these "limeys" around here.

As I politely asked him if he and the boys might like to move down a little, as I was being crowded into the corner, I told him I was a Canadian from the province of Prince Edward Island.

"Where in the hell is that?" he asked. "Is that on the map or just some dirt in one of the wrinkles?"

While he and his partners had a good laugh, I just took a sip of my beer and didn't bother to answer.

By now, Anne Murray had started to sing. But the Americans were talking so loud I doubt if anyone could hear her anyway.

Then one of them said, "Hey, Canuckey! What do you think of the gal on TV? I'll bet you guys got nothing up in Canada that can sing as good as her. Or do you have anybody that can sing up there at all?"

Well, that was when I'd have given anything for that little piece about Anne being from Nova Scotia to have been left in the program. But it wasn't, so I decided to tell them myself.

"For your information," I said, "the 'gal' you're talking about is from Canada. Her name is Anne Murray. And it just so happens that she's from Nova Scotia, which is not more than fifty miles from where I live."

"Bullshit!" was the loud answer that came back. "Anne

Murray's from down around Boston somewhere." Then another one said she was from Tennessee. And on it went.

In the meantime, they began to crowd me so much I hardly had any room left between the wall and the guy next to me for my arms to even reach in to the bar for a drink of my beer.

As there was absolutely no doubt that these guys were trying to push me away from the bar altogether, I made one last effort to force my way back in between the guy and the corner. And with my back to the wall I managed to get my foot up to somewhere around his midsection and gave him one hell of a shove towards the rest of them.

As each guy bumped against the other, in a domino effect, the beer along the bar spilled everywhere. In less than a second they were all after me. I managed to hit one fellow a couple of times, then another fella hit me. When I knew I was about to get massacred, I jumped in over the bar and began pounding on one guy who had a hold on the tail end of what was left of my shirt.

Then something pretty wonderful happened. All the English guys who had been sitting rather quietly at their tables immediately jumped to their feet, grabbed the four or five Americans, and tossed every one of them right out through the door and onto the street. They then came back and told me to sit right up on the bar where they laughed and joked and bought me all the beer I could drink for the rest of the night. They told me that from where they were sitting they could see everything that was going on, and they didn't blame me one bit for what I did. But they said, "There's one thing we do know, and that is that you Canadians sure have a lot of guts."

When I finally got home that night, I hardly remember getting out of the taxi. I somehow meandered up the stairs to my hotel room, flaked out on the bed, and went right to sleep. Sometime around noon the next day, I was awakened by some loud knocking and someone slipped a newspaper under my door. Though my eyes were still a bit bleary, I jumped right out of bed when I read the huge headlines. I grabbed the newspaper, which was called the *London Gleaner*, and blazoned all over half of the front page was: STOMPIN'

TOM CONNORS APPEARS NAKED ON A WEST END STREET.

The only thing was that when I went to look for the rest of the story, it was nowhere to be found in the paper. I then knew those two hombres I had brought overseas with me were up to no good. Upon further examination of the paper I could see it was a fake. I later found out the boys had it printed up in a novelty shop and slid it under my door for a lark. But as I had never heard of such a thing until that day, it certainly woke me up with a helluva jolt.

Later on that day, when we had moved to another hotel, I had gone to the desk to get all the keys to our separate rooms. And as I was walking along one of the halls, the cleaning lady was making up one of the rooms. As I noticed she had dropped the key near the open door, I just picked it up and kept on walking.

When I got to the rear of the building where the boys were waiting, instead of handing Bill the key to his proper room, I gave him the key to the room the cleaning lady had been making up.

Billy would often go to sleep for an hour or so in the afternoon, and today was one of those days when he planned to do just that. By the time he got to the room, the cleaning lady was gone so he just went in. And before too long he was fast asleep. That is, until a short time later, when someone came in and rented the room that was supposed to be vacant.

By this time I had told Gary what was going on. So every time we heard the least commotion in the hall, we'd poke our heads out the door to see what was happening, and if the room was being rented.

Sure enough, and before too long, a man and woman came down the hall with the desk clerk. And with a brand-new key, they just opened the door and walked in.

Not wanting to miss anything, Gary and I began to casually stroll down the hall, hoping to get there just in time to catch all the fun.

First we heard a roar and a rumble, then a short argument, followed by an apology from Billy who soon came bounding out the door, still half asleep. And with his guitar in one hand and his clothes hanging from the suitcase in the other, it didn't take him too long to figure out what had happened.

By the time we helped him carry his stuff to the right room he popped himself a beer and started laughing right along with the rest of us.

Another thing I took particular notice of in England, and even more so in Ireland, was the fact that most radio stations that I listened to were playing just as many domestic "covers" of the foreign hits as they were playing the original artists.

By way of example, when an artist or group that is domiciled in England or Ireland makes a recording of a song that is currently a hit by, say Johnny Cash, Willie Nelson, Waylon Jennings or Garth Brooks, the home-grown artist will receive just as much airplay for the song as would the foreign original.

This of course enabled the domestics to compete right along with the stars for any good song that might have been written or recorded anywhere in the world. And the listeners didn't have to listen to the same voice on the same song all the time. If they didn't especially like the song being done by one group, they could always listen to one or two others. Instead of "one song, one voice," there was plenty of variety, and radio listeners as well as record buyers had multiple choices of the different versions.

This was also true when the foreign stars came into their countries to do concert tours. Their version of a particular song was not the only version familiar to everybody, and their concert was not the only one at which it could be heard.

This also prevented foreigners from charging the extravagant prices they do for people to hear their particular star singing their particular song. Because the domestic artists were being heard on radio just as often as the foreigners their concerts were just as popular, with attendance being just as good and quite often even better. (Something which kept the money circulating within their own economy.) And like I said before, all the artists that I met overseas were at that time doing far better than I was. While my potential market at home in Canada was twenty-seven million, the Irish artist's market was about three million. But

because of the far greater exposure they received from the
media, and especially radio, they were all driving around in
Cadillacs and limos, sporting the greatest outfits, and playing with the latest kinds of equipment that I couldn't even
afford.

This didn't make me jealous in any way. I wished them all
the more power, and realized how much their country, their
people, their government and their media were supporting
them. And it made me wonder how much more proud of
our artists my own country could be if our people, government and media were following the same policy.

Our people could then have the choice of hearing any
current song by any current artist on any radio station, TV
station or at any concert hall they wished to tune in to or
attend, instead of having to go out to some local bar to hear
the totally unfamiliar voices of bands they don't know, trying
to sing over the top of loud boisterous talking and the tin-
kling of glasses.

This would also enable some of our more talented artists
to get the hell out of some of these joints and make some
decent money for a change, while performing in a less hos-
tile environment to a more supportive audience.

It has always been my contention that if our Canadian
artists had received the kind of support to which I have been
referring, there would have been far less of them in the
United States today. But such is not the case, and the drain
on our country is much worse now than it has ever been.
Although many people continue to ask why, we haven't done
one single thing in the last twenty-five years that would
encourage our talent to stay here instead of going elsewhere. And, given our current complacent attitudes, it
doesn't look to me as if anything will ever be done. I guess,
in our case, the old saying seems to be true: we probably
won't miss the water till the well runs dry.

Incidentally, there were a couple of groups from Ireland
who had recorded my version of "Poor, Poor Farmer" and
were getting a lot more airplay on it than I was getting. So
much more, in fact, that it was their recordings that made
the song an overseas hit instead of mine. But as I say, this
didn't bother me near as much as knowing that they were

getting more airplay in their country than I was getting in mine. They'd been introduced to the song by hearing my recording of it, then went ahead and recorded it themselves and made it a hit. So I can't help wondering if I too might have had a hit with it if Canadian radio stations would have only played it here at home. At any rate, this was all just a part of learning what it was that Canadians had to go through as the price to pay for believing in their own country.

My First Road Manager

B Y THE END OF JUNE 1971, the boys and I arrived back in Canada, and immediately began to prepare for a concert at the arena in Huntsville, Ontario.

Up until now we had handled everything between the three of us but it was getting harder and harder all the time. So while we were overseas, Jury had hired a guy to help around the office, and upon our return he was to join us on tour as our new road manager.

His name was Dick Ivansic, and his duties were to go ahead of us to each town, tack up posters, see that the venues were in order, book our rooms, visit the media and a whole mishmash of other things. Then on the night of the concert he would sell tickets, records, pictures, etc., and always make sure we had plenty of these things in stock.

He was also about six foot, three inches tall, with a very loud intimidating voice that went along with his already gruff demeanour. And while this would prove to be a great asset whenever we ran into people who didn't want to pay us our contracted amount, he sometimes scared hell out of people who hadn't done anything wrong in the first place. This used to annoy me from time to time, but I mostly over-looked it because he was always on the ball and did such a good job for us. After about a year, however, his forceful behaviour just seemed to get a little worse, and after I spoke to him several times about it, I had to let him go.

In the meantime, everything worked out great in Huntsville. We played there on July 2 to a packed house and with Dick's help, taking a lot of the worry off my mind, I wasn't as tired as I usually was before going onstage. As a result, I seemed to have a lot more energy to put into the show. Both Bill and Gary began to get along with Dick right off the bat, and even though he wasn't the most jovial guy in the world, they managed to make him laugh a few times.

The following night we were back in Toronto. And for the next week, with the exception of Wednesday the seventh, when we had to go and tape two programs for "The Don Messer Show" on CBC, I got to see Lena Welsh again and take her out a few times. She was now working in a small boutique at the West End Mall, and had her own apartment on Eglinton Avenue, near Caledonia Road.

That following Saturday we played the Mariposa Folk Festival on Toronto Island and then we lit out to eastern Ontario, where we played for a couple of weeks during the Summer Festival at Perth. It was here that I met Freddy Dixon, who had written a song I liked so well that I later recorded it on one of my albums. It was a historical song about the last fatal duel that had ever occurred in Canada. And the surviving combatant, who was a lawyer, later went on to become the judge who presided over the famous Black Donnelly murder trials in London, Ontario. (Freddy also wrote a tribute song to me which I hope to mention a little bit later.)

By July 28 we were in Florenceville, N.B., and then with George Hamilton in Fredericton. After playing Summerside, Charlottetown and Montague on P.E.I. we did shows in Bathurst and Campbellton, New Brunswick, and by August 8 we were back in Ontario.

We then played a stock car race-track in Cargill where the stage was made on the top of an old hay wagon. And as I reached up for one of the boards to pull myself up on the wagon, the board came off and I landed on the ground on my back. I hurt myself quite badly but I did the show anyway. Every time I stomped my foot the pain was excruciating so I tried to keep it down to a minimum. I could see the people weren't all that pleased that I wasn't living up to my reputation as "Stompin' Tom" but there was little I could do about it. It sure wasn't one of my better shows but then it didn't pay much either. And with all the stock cars roaring around there was half an inch of dust all over our clothes and equipment, not to mention how much I had to breathe in and swallow while singing. As I limped off the field I met a few of my friends from Southampton, but all in all, it just hadn't been a very good day.

The next day we played Walkerton and then we were off to Peterborough to perform at their exhibition. The stage again was out on the race-track, and with so much noise and commotion the people on the grandstand weren't hearing us very well. Then just before we were finished, the local DJ, Sean Eyre, sneaked in behind us with a live rooster and let him fly all over the stage. (He later told me that some of my staunchest fans called in to his radio program and gave him hell for pulling such a prank, declaring it was done in very poor taste. He readily agreed and duly apologized.)

After Peterborough we went back to Toronto where we took a couple of weeks off. Our next gig would not be until September 1 in Tillsonburg and we were getting all kinds of good news from that area about the new "Tillsonburg" single that had just been released.

A Dave Smith, who was a country DJ at CFRS radio in Simcoe, Ontario, was quoted in the newspapers and trade magazines as saying that "Tillsonburg checked in at an impressive No. 5" during the first week, "and it has to be the most requested song in the history of CFRS as we've received literally hundreds of requests for this song."

Jury, at Boot Records, was beside himself. He was on the phone continually with our distributors, who wanted to know what in hell was going on. They had never seen the like of this kind of demand for a record in any given area before. Not only the record stores, but every store in Tillsonburg wanted to have them for sale.

The day we arrived in town it was unbelievable. Every second store up and down the main drag had a record player going with a speaker outside, and "Tillsonburg" was playing everywhere.

In the afternoon, one of the bigger stores had requested

that I come in for a little while to sign some of these albums that were selling like hot cakes. But when I got there I couldn't get near the store at all. As soon as I got out of my car I was swamped right there on the street. I must have stood there signing autographs for a good two hours before I had to go and get ready for my show.

We were playing at the Strand Theatre. And when I arrived Dick Ivansic introduced me to the owner. The first thing that struck me about the fellow was how much he stuttered. I wondered how he could conduct his business at all because I couldn't understand one word he said.

At any rate, the show went off magnificently. Everybody had come to hear "Tillsonburg" and that's what we gave them, at least four or five times during the whole show. Then there were more autographs. They wanted them on records, pictures, scraps of paper, on their clothes, arms and legs and everywhere imaginable.

It seemed that everybody must have heard the song a great many times in the last two or three weeks because they all knew the words off by heart, and they just wanted to keep on singing it.

By the time the last autograph seeker had left, Dick and the boys had everything packed and were waiting for me out at the back of the building. When Dick saw me coming out the back door and knew that everything was all right he just took off in the old Boot. And when he did, the owner of the theatre came out the back door to say goodbye and thank me for the great show. I was amazed to find that he didn't even stutter once. He spoke in perfect English without the slightest hint that he had stuttered at all. So I decided to ask him about the sudden change.

He told me he had stuttered as a kid, but after some special training he had gotten over it. At least he thought so. He hadn't stuttered for over twenty-five years until earlier that afternoon when Dick Ivansic arrived on the scene. When Dick, with his intimidating voice, started to order him around, he just totally lost control of himself and hadn't been able to talk right since. And just now, at this moment, when he saw Dick drive away he immediately got his confidence back and was able to speak perfectly.

The boys and I got quite a chuckle out of this, and of course he just laughed right along with us. He said he was quite worried all evening about whether he'd ever be able to speak properly again, and now he was quite happy to have his voice back.

As we left I shook his hand and promised him I'd make sure when we got the chance to come back that Dick would tone himself down a little and try to exercise a little more consideration. He said he'd appreciate that, and he was glad to be back to normal. I gave him a copy of the words to the song "Tillsonburg" and took off back to Toronto.

Reprinted here are those words:

TILLSONBURG

1.

While away down Southern Ontario
I never had a nickel or a dime to show.
A fella beeped up in an automobile;
He said, "You wanna work in the tobacco fields,
Of Tillsonburg?" Tillsonburg!
My back still aches when I hear that word.

2.

He said, "I'll only give you seven bucks a day
But if you're any good, you'll get a raise in pay.
Your bed's all ready on the bunk-house floor;
If it gets a little chilly you can close the door."
Tillsonburg! It was Tillsonburg.
My back still aches when I hear that word.

3.

Well, I'm feeling in the morning anything but fine.
The farmer said, "I'm gonna teach you how to 'prime'."
He said, "You'll have to don a pair of oil-skin pants
If you want to work in the tobacco plants
Of Tillsonburg." Tillsonburg!
My back still aches when I hear that word.

4.

We landed in a field that was long and wide
With one old horse and five more guys.
I asked him where to find the cigarette trees;
When he said, "Bend over" I was ready to leave
Tillsonburg. Tillsonburg!
My back still aches when I hear that word.

5.

He said to pick just the bottom leaves
And don't start crawlin' on your hands and knees
Prime your row, 'cause you'll get no pay
For standin' there pickin' at your nose all day
'Round Tillsonburg. Tillsonburg!
My back still aches when I hear that word.

6.

With a broken back from bendin' over there,
I was wet right through to the underwear.
And it was stuck to my skin like glue
From the nicotine tar and the morning dew
Of Tillsonburg. Tillsonburg!
My back still aches when I hear that word.

7.

The nearest river was two miles from
The place they were waitin' for the "boat" to come.
When I heard some talk about "makin' the kill" [kiln]
I was down the highway and over the hill
From Tillsonburg. Tillsonburg!
My back still aches when I hear that word.

8.

Now, there's one thing you can always bet,
If I never smoke another cigarette.
I might get taken in a lot of deals,
But I won't go workin' the tobacco fields
Of Tillsonburg. Tillsonburg!
My back still aches when I hear that word.

On September 3, 1971, we played the Brockville Civic Auditorium, and the next night, Saturday, we played the Trent Valley Jamboree in the Belleville Collegiate Auditorium. Among the other entertainers that night were Bunt Lewis and the Country Showmen from Uxbridge and Kent Brockwell from Peterborough. The show was emceed by Dick Lovering and Harold Tomkins from radio station CJBQ in Belleville and the place was really packed.

Jack McCaughen and Ken Stapley, both from the Canadian Country Music Association, were also on hand. And to my surprise at half-time, they announced that I was the winner of the No. 1 Country Singer Award for the Year of 1971.

(A few years later, when another musical organization by the name of ACME decided to change their name to the Canadian Country Music Association, they didn't even recognize my award. I don't know how it all came about. Maybe ACME bought the name or something, because they still operate under Canadian Country Music Association. At any rate, you'd think that if they took over the old CCMA the least they could do is recognize the former award winners and not pretend they just don't exist. I'm sure there must be a lot more of them out there besides me with one of those plaques still hanging on their wall.)

On September 5, we played the Kingston Speedway and then we went back to Toronto to tape the "Tommy Hunter Show." And the following Monday, on the thirteenth, we found ourselves back in the Horseshoe.

By the end of the month we recorded another album, this one entitled *Love and Laughter* (now changed to *Stompin' Tom and the Moon Man Newfie*). This album was the seventh one recorded in 1971 and counting the compilation just released by Dominion Records, *The Best of Stompin' Tom*, I now had nineteen albums out on the market.

From the third of October to the ninth we did a mini-tour of my old original stompin' grounds up north. We played Cochrane, Timmins, Kirkland Lake, New Liskeard and Kapuskasing, in that order.

In Timmins, we played the MacIntyre Arena, and it was good to see so many people there that I had once met in the old Maple Leaf Hotel where I first started out in 1964. I played all the songs I used to sing for them when I was just a bum and brought my Juno Award along for all to see. And I made it quite clear to everyone that without their initial support and encouragement I probably would have been still sleeping under park benches.

Just as my second show was to begin, I was presented with a hand-carved replica of my stompin' board. It was presented by Henry Kelneck, the famous "big band leader" from Timmins, who was known all through the north, even long before I arrived on the scene. The board had a boot carved on it and said "To Stompin' Tom Connors from all the members of the Timmins Musicians' Association" (of which I was still a member at that time) and wished me continued success in the future.

The mayor of Timmins, Leo Del Villano, then came on stage and presented me with a set of cufflinks mounted with the town's logo. And he was followed by Bill Ferrier, the MPP for Cochrane South, who gave me a zinc plaque on behalf of the riding, and also a citation from the Mount Joy United Church where I had once done some singing.

I was really quite moved by the whole thing and I expressed as much in a short thank-you speech before I began my second set of northern songs.

Incidentally, Henry Kelneck, the big band leader mentioned above, eventually became the subject of one of my songs recorded in 1995. It was co-written by myself and Gaet Lepine (the bartender from the old Maple Leaf Hotel) and is entitled "Polka Playin' Henry."

On Saturday night we finished the tour in Kapuskasing where we packed the old Royal Theatre with a lot of people who came out specifically to hear the "Reesor Crossing Tragedy," the song I had gotten into so much trouble about at the Radio Hotel in 1965 (described in *Before the Fame*).

On this night the show went over quite well, however, and except for a little skirmish out by the front door there was no trouble at all.

Touring the Prairies

AFTER KAP, WE HAD TO RUSH back to Toronto; Jury wanted me and the boys to drive down to Nashville where he wanted us to play at the DJ Convention.

I wasn't all that excited about it, but when he told me a lot of Canadian DJs who hadn't yet seen me perform would be there to take in the show, I agreed to go. After all, I still wasn't hearing my music being played with any regularity and thought if this might do it, I'd better give it a try.

By the way, it was the news about this one trip to Nashville that later caused most of my detractors from radio and other branches of the media to declare that "the only reason Stompin' Tom doesn't go to Nashville to succeed like all the rest is because he has already been there and bombed out. And the only place he can ever succeed with his crude, simplistic songs is among the small town types in the backwoods of Canada."

These are the kinds of statements that surfaced later and only served to fortify some of the disparaging opinions already unjustifiably held by a number of radio people who had no intention of playing Stompin' Tom's music in the first place.

The true circumstances surrounding this trip to Nashville were these: we got to Nashville on the evening of the fourteenth of October, 1971. The following day, on Friday, we found out there were to be two shows on two different nights. The first one was to take place that very night in the smallest of the two concert halls, and the second, which was to be the extravaganza, was to take place the following night, on Saturday.

This second show was of course to be the main event. It would take place in a plush, soft-seat auditorium and be well attended by anyone who was considered to be a somebody in the music business. The first show, on the other hand, was to be attended by the so-called regulars. Just your ordinary beer-drinking crowd. And the stage was set up in a large meeting hall with movable-type chairs, where the acoustics were not unlike those found in a school gymnasium. The rumours had it that this first show was to be an "informal jamboree where anyone could come for free if they wanted to." The only trouble was, hardly anyone came. And I can't say as I blame them.

Each act only got to do one or two numbers and the sound was terrible. At the beginning, the house was about one-quarter full, and by the time I got on the stage half of them were already gone and the other half were holding their hands over one or both of their ears. Such was this wonderful "musical showcase" that I don't think there was one DJ in the whole place. At least I didn't run into any.

Of the ten or twelve groups that took their turns scrambling up on the stage to do their couple of numbers, I had never heard of one of them.

The only time I met someone I'd heard of was when I went outside where they were serving beer from off the back of a two-ton truck. As I bought myself a beer, I started talking to the fellow beside me and was surprised to learn that I was having a beer with Tom T. Hall. Pretty soon I bought him one and he reciprocated by buying me another.

He was a very down-to-earth type of fellow, one of the regular guys who talked a straight line. He was just wandering around with his guitar, singing the odd song here and there, with no axe to grind and looking for some new song ideas.

He had seen me up on stage and asked me what in hell I came all the way down from Canada to sing in a dive like that for. He wanted to know why I wasn't playing on the main event that was to take place the following night.

When I told him that was rather impossible, as I had to leave in the morning to drive to Calgary, Alberta, and be there for Tuesday, a distance of two thousand miles, he understood.

"That means you're gonna have to drive over six hundred miles a day for the next three days," he said. "No wonder you can't stay around for the big show tomorrow night." He wanted to know what was going on in Calgary that I couldn't postpone.

I told him I was booked as one of the two opening acts for Bill Anderson at the Jubilee Auditorium there, and that the other opening act was Ray Griff. He told me he had played there one time, and after talking some more about all things Canadian, including Canadian Club whisky and Canadian women, we each went our way and never saw each other again.

I certainly had occasion to recall the moments I spoke with him again, however. In the spring of the following year his new album contained a song called "Canadian Club and Canadian Women." And in one of the lines he says, "I was up in Canada where I met Tom and he taught me how to stomp." I thought that was sure nice of him, to say the least. (Thank you, Tom T. Hall.)

The following day, on Saturday, the sixteenth of October, the boys and I left Nashville for Calgary, while Jury stayed on for a few days and later flew back to Toronto. To sum up this wonderful occasion of the first and last time I ever played in "Music City," U.S.A., I can only say that if my detractors still want to insist that Stompin' Tom "bombed in Nashville," then why in hell didn't they also describe the details and the circumstances under which it happened? They can't. That's why. And the reason why they can't is because there wasn't even one of them there to see it. They knew I was going to be there but they didn't even come by to lend moral support for one of their own. They were too busy being wined and dined by the Americans. And in the end, if somebody bombed, it was them as well as me. For the degree of respect we hope to receive from our hosts in a foreign country is in direct proportion to the degree of respect we show that we have for one another. If one of us falls, we all fall. And no

Canadian can ever look good by trying to make another Canadian look bad, and if he tries to, he should never be sent abroad to represent our country in the first place.

In the meantime, the boys and I passed through the states of Tennessee, Kentucky, Illinois and Missouri. And then through Iowa to South and North Dakota before entering Canada at a place near Estevan, Saskatchewan.

I seem to recall the distance was close to 2,100 miles by the time we reached Calgary on Tuesday afternoon. I had done most of the driving, and all we did was stop for gas and a sandwich or two to take out along the way. We had averaged about seven hundred miles a day, so after three solid days of just sitting in the one spot we felt pretty cramped. The first thing we wanted to do when we arrived at the motel was to take a long walk.

Of course our road manager, Dick, was already on the scene. He had driven the Boot from Kapuskasing to Calgary, and after stopping to visit radio stations and tack up posters in some of the towns we were booked to play in, he dropped our equipment off at the Jubilee Auditorium and then met us at the motel.

As soon as we had our little walk and got cleaned up a bit we were off to the venue. This was going to be our first time playing out west and I wanted everything to work smoothly. So arriving early at the building to set up was just one of the precautions I felt to be quite necessary.

Another thing I always liked to do was meet the people in the other bands that were going to be on the show. I always liked to ask them a few things about themselves so that when I made reference to them during my performance I could say something that was true about them as well as complimentary.

I had met Ray Griff and a few of the other musicians and everything seemed to be going along quite well. That is until I met Bill Anderson himself.

I had been in my dressing room for a few moments and hadn't noticed him come onstage. As I came out from behind one of the back curtains, I spied him sitting on the top of a small table right near one of the wings, so I decided to go over and make his acquaintance. (I don't know what it is about some of these big stars, but some of them sure love themselves.)

As I walked up to him with my outstretched hand and a smile on my face, I said, "Hi Bill. I'm Stompin' Tom, and it's a great pleasure to be working with you tonight. I hear the tickets have all been sold and we're going to have a packed house."

I didn't quite get the last sentence out. And without even extending his arm to receive my handshake, he looked me up and down and said in a very matter of fact sort of a way, "You're not going to be doing any of my songs on your portion of the show, are you?"

After my initial surprise, I looked him in the eye for a moment. And then, after seeing that he was entirely serious, I pulled my hand away and said, "Why, hell no! Not unless you intend doing some of *my songs* on your portion." And with that I walked away leaving him with a very odd look on his face. I went back to the dressing room, had a beer with the boys and waited for Ray Griff and his band to open the show.

By the time Ray's set was over, the boys and I were standing in the wings, waiting to be called onstage. Then I watched him do something I had never seen done before.

Anticipating the audience were going to call him back for another song when he left the stage, he sang his last song, thanked everybody, and instead of going to his dressing room he just stood in front of me at the edge of the curtain and waited for his band to generate a standing ovation.

The way everything was happening, I thought he was taking a hell of a chance. From where I stood, it didn't look to me like he was going to get called back at all. While one of his boys set up a microphone for him in front of the piano, another guy kept prompting the audience by clapping his hands and indicating Ray would come back and do another song if they'd only show they wanted him with some strong applause.

Like me, I think the audience was somewhat confused. They thought Ray's set was over and were now expecting to see Stompin' Tom.

Finally, when the band member was able to generate

what I would call a rather mild applause, Ray went running back out on the stage making elaborately gracious bows as if the audience had just torn the house down to get him back, and then went over to the piano and started singing.

Now Ray Griff is a very talented singer-songwriter and a highly polished performer. And had the audience decided not to respond to the prompting at all, it would have been a shame for him to have had to deal with that kind of embarrassment. I noticed the next night, at the Jubilee Auditorium in Edmonton, he decided to omit that little trick from the end of his program. And although he didn't receive a standing ovation, he at least got to do all the songs he previously planned on doing.

Other than these couple of small hitches, the shows with Ray Griff and Bill Anderson went over very well. I was especially pleased with the way the Alberta people received me and the boys. Although "Bud the Spud" had now been out for a couple of years, most westerners were just now beginning to hear it the odd time on radio. (So much for magazine charts that had declared it a national radio hit in Canada.) Some of the people I signed autographs for were telling me they had never heard the song until that night when I sang it on stage.

After the Jubilee Auditoriums, we moved to Saskatchewan and played the Centennial Auditorium in Saskatoon and the Arts Centre in Regina. Then Dick and the boys and I struck out on a small-town tour throughout the west. Before we were through, we had played in a lot of places that even I didn't know existed. Just take a look at some of these names in Saskatchewan alone: Melville, Esterhazy, Kamsack, Canora, Wynyard, Eston, Kindersley, Biggar, Luceland, Kerrobert, Gull Lake, Maple Creek, Glaslyn and Cut Knife. And that's just to name a few. Most of these places were off the beaten track and the people around those little towns had never even heard of Stompin' Tom.

In one town, if it hadn't been for the people from the Indian reserve there wouldn't have been anybody at the show. In another, they all thought Stompin' Tom was a wrestler and came to the show expecting to see a wrestling match (and there almost was one when they found out we

were only going to play music). In another town, we didn't
get paid. And in still another, nobody showed up at all.

The buildings we played in were usually old run-down
theatres, arenas and community centres. Dick would always
go out three or four days ahead of us, buy some ads on the
small radio stations that could reach the area we were playing in, and then go to the little places and tack posters on
everything from trees and telephone poles to church doors
and out-houses. Then he'd have to be in town the night of
the show to sell records and pictures and collect the money.
If there was any. He was indeed a busy man.

Upon entering most of these buildings, the boys and I
would first of all have to clean things up. Some of these
buildings hadn't had a show of any kind in them for years.
We'd have to clean out the debris, sweep the floors, set up
the chairs, and if there was a stage at all we would have to
straighten it out as best we could.

I especially remember the stage in Glaslyn and some of
the trouble we had with the old curtain. It was a drop-curtain
which had to be raised and lowered by an old frayed rope
which ran through a series of pulleys to a wooden winch with
a handle which had to be cranked by hand. That was my job.

The curtain itself had been made of some kind of very
heavy paper which was ripped down the middle and only
half of it remained. And the plan was for the boys to go out
on stage first and stand behind the remaining half and start
playing the music as I raised the curtain. They would then
casually move out towards the centre of the stage once the
curtain was up.

The only trouble was, the curtain was terribly heavy, and
I was having one hell of a time trying to wind it up. It had a
long heavy wooden pole tied all across the bottom of it to
give it the weight it needed to draw the curtain down when
the time came to lower it.

Well, the boys started the music all right, but when I got
the curtain up to about the height of their shoulders, the
damn thing got stuck and didn't want to go up any further.
I then had to lower it a little ways and start raising it again.
For about five minutes all the audience could see was the
boys' knees, then their shoulders, and then only their knees

again as I kept the curtain going up and down in my struggle to get it unsnagged.

As the boys kept bending over to smile at the audience
underneath the curtain, I was getting into more of a panic
as the minutes ticked on. My arms were aching by the time I
got the damn thing up. Then just as I secured the crank so
it wouldn't move, the rope broke, and down came the
wooden pole with the curtain and all. Everything hit the
stage floor with a hell of a crash. There were heaps of twisted
paper with ropes, poles and pulleys lying everywhere. The
dust from the old boards of the stage went rising in the air
to meet the rest of the pieces of crap that were falling from
the ceiling, and neither the audience nor the boys could see
one another for about ten minutes.

Finally, while everybody laughed at us, we got most of the
junk pushed off to one side of the stage and started playing.
There was no running water in the building and our sweaty
faces looked worse than our messy clothes as we kept rubbing them with our dirty hands. But, as they say, the show
must go on, and it did.

We didn't fare much better in the small towns of Alberta
or Manitoba than we did in Saskatchewan. And by the end
of November 1971, we left the west, and after doing a show
in Dryden, Ontario, where we also found time to be in their
Santa Claus parade on the first of December, we finally
headed back to Toronto.

When we tallied everything up by subtracting the total
expenses from the total earnings, my first western tour net-
ted me exactly sixty-seven cents. I didn't consider this to be
a disappointment, however. Because without the help of any
major radio play for my records I had to get known somehow. And this was the only way I knew of to make it happen.
I still had to pay my dues, so to speak.

I got to play my songs for a lot of people and wound up
getting my records in a lot of homes. After that my record
company sold a lot more of my records by mail to people
who now wanted to hear the rest of my product. I know it's
a long slow procedure and requires a lot of patience, but I
had learned by now that if I wanted to be successful in the
Canadian music business there was no point in waiting for

someone else to make it happen for me. I was going to have to do it by myself and I would have to stick to it. Any money I made would have to be poured back into making myself known in ever-widening circles.

To my knowledge, there had never been anyone before my time who had made it in Canada without first going to the United States (with the possible exception of Don Messer, who wasn't a singer), and I really had no reason to believe it could be done. But I was sure going to give it my best shot.

I instinctively knew that most people tend to admire and support the honest efforts of the little guy who struggles to succeed in spite of his obvious disadvantages. It seems to somewhat encourage us all when we see some little guy make it for a change. It kind of adds a little more hope to the possibility that our own personal goals can also be accomplished. So because of this I thought that if I could become a major success in Canada maybe a lot more entertainers would be encouraged to stay here and do the same thing. At least I was hoping that would happen. After all, it seems a shame that such a prosperous country as Canada should always have to carry the reputation that we're a nation that spurns our own young and aspiring talent. How can we ever consider ourselves as being cultured when the very music we listen to (among other things) has to first be acceptable to and receive the approval of a foreign country—namely, the United States? And that even applies to the music that is composed in Canada by Canadians. For if the composition doesn't sound "Statesy" enough, it will never get to see the light of day. It will never get played on our major radio stations. And that's because the musical formats they follow either originate in the United States or must first be approved by that country.

Have you ever wondered why most of the Canadian artists you hear singing on radio sound so much like their American counterparts? Why do they all sound like southerners? Why do we never hear singers on radio with a Newfoundland accent? Or a French-Canadian accent? If the Americans are not ashamed of their President Kennedy style Massachusetts accents and their Texan and other southern state drawls, why should we be ashamed of hearing accents unique to the different regions of Canada?

We not only don't hear singers on the radio who sound typically Canadian, but we very seldom hear one of them singing songs about their own country. Is this because they don't want to? Or is it because they know they won't get their record played on radio if it contains such material?

And lastly, why is it that singers and songs that sound identifiably and unmistakably Canadian get belittled and laughed at by so many music business executives and especially those in the big commercial radio business? Is it because those same Canadian singers and songs are also being laughed at by the Americans? And that our so-called leaders in these fields are merely clones, dummies and yes-men who don't have the pride or the backbone to stick up for themselves, let alone music that is truly Canadian?

Enough questions for now. But it is my intention to deal with these and to ask many more before this book is finished.

When I arrived in Toronto, I also learned that a magazine called the *Last Post* had published an eight-page interview I had with one of their writers by the name of Mark Starowicz. This was really great news to me as it was the first time anybody had asked me so many in-depth questions about who I was, where I came from, what my music was all about, and what my intentions were concerning the future. This gave people a greater insight into Stompin' Tom and from that point on many other writers began quoting from the same article. I had been introduced to Mark at the Horseshoe Tavern by a couple of mutual friends, Tom and Cathy Gallant from New Brunswick, and from the "Shoe" we went up to Mark's place and taped the interview over a few beers until about four or five o'clock in the morning. The article also contained some very good pictures and the whole thing was very well done. I didn't get to see Mark after that to thank him for his timely and much-needed boost. So thanks a million, Mark, wherever you are.

It was now the first week of December 1971. And in reviewing some of my pages for the year, I realize I mustn't leave out one of the most important contributors to the success of our publishing side of the business.

Just before we started Boot Records, Jury had met a very
bright young man by the name of Mark Altman, and the two
of them had done a few projects together. Mark was still
going to university and wouldn't have his degree until June
of '71. After that he planned to come with Jury and me to
start out our new publishing company. This one was to be
called Morning Music, and if Mark agreed to come aboard,
we would cut him in for 25 per cent of the company.

Sometime in June or July, Mark came on the regular pay-
roll and immediately began to show his worth. He was very
good at keeping all the publishing company's books in
order, which was something Jury was never much good
at, and had an astonishing ear for music. (You could bounce
a ball on the floor and Mark could tell you what note
the sound of it had made.) Music was one of the subjects
Mark had majored in, and while neither Jury nor I could
write musical notes, Mark was writing scores for symphony
orchestras.

So with Mark now on board we put Crown-Vetch and
some other minor publishing companies all under the
Morning Music umbrella and gave him the responsibility of
managing our whole publishing department. While Jury did
most of the travelling to make the necessary contacts (which
was really his forte), Mark was in charge of keeping everything in order at home base.

And speaking of home base, there were so many people
running in and out of our apartment by this time, Jury and
I decided we'd have to move out to make more room for
business offices. We began to look for a house to rent. By the
end of January 1972, we leased one in the north part of
Toronto, not more than three or four miles from Bathurst
Street where our business was located. Our new house was at
240 Searle Avenue.

I had given Bill Lewis and Gary Empey the months of
December and January off while I wrote some songs and
moved to our new place, but I saw them quite often as they
hung around Boot Records a lot and helped out with things
around the office. They also attended our house warming
and several other parties we threw from time to time.

Also during these couple of months Lena and I had a temporary falling out, mainly due to the fact that I was either on the road or just too damned busy to see her most of the time. I had spent Christmas at my friends the Chapmans' house, and Lena had gone to her brother Ted's. After I moved into the house on Searle Avenue, however, we got things patched up and began seeing each other again.

Massey Hall and Filming
the Tour

O N JANUARY 1, 1972, OUR Boot Records Company was one year old so Jury and I had to have a series of meetings with our accountant and our lawyer. Although my own records were selling in quite large numbers, most of the other acts that we had recorded to date were not selling nearly as well. The word was that if the company was going to survive I would have to pour more money into it. So instead of taking the royalties from my own sales which were due to me I told Jury to take the money to pay some of our bills. The amount, I agreed, could be paid back to me when the company was able to do so, and we drew up an agreement to that effect.

This deal, of course, remained unknown to the rest of my fellow Boot recording artists, a good number of whom were even getting their musicians and studio time paid for by our company, and they thought Jury was just the most wonderful guy in the world for doing it. It just wasn't being done by anyone anywhere else.

In effect, I was taking all the monetary risks to keep the company afloat so there would always be an open door to come to, for all those with talent but no money to develop it. That was my only motive. After all, hadn't I travelled this country up and down for years, seeking the opportunity to record my songs when no such open door could be found?

It wasn't like I was sinking my very last penny into the company and leaving myself dangerously broke, however. That would have really been stupid. Besides, if the company turned out to be very successful, not only the artists stood to gain, but I also stood to gain substantially. If the company failed, however, I would be the big loser, but not to the extent that I was going to allow myself to be ruined. I had learned a lot, the hard way. And just because it was in me to want to help others didn't mean I thought they would come running to my aid if and when it was me who was down. I knew better than that. I just wanted to share with others some of the opportunity the God of Fate had steered my way. (Not an opportunity I thought I necessarily deserved, but just one that was freely given.)

Two more items of note that happened in 1971 were, first, the fact that I was able to become a one-third owner of the Crown-Vetch Music Publishing Company. This happened when T. St. Clair Lowe of Canadian Music Sales announced his retirement and was selling off all his holdings. By buying his one-third share I was now a partner with Jury and Doc Williams, who each held one-third respectively. And with 38 per cent of Morning Music Limited I was now officially in the music publishing business along with recording. The other shares in Morning Music were Jury, 37 per cent, and Mark Altman, 25.

All this ownership, of course, was only on paper. The companies weren't making enough to pay everybody's wages and I was covering the shortfall. My payment was supposed to come by way of dividends at the end of each year. But what if the companies couldn't make it? What if they were unable to survive? Well, there just wouldn't be any dividends and Mr. Stompin' Tom would have to work a little harder, play a lot more concerts, and kiss the business goodbye, along with the investments.

So by the end of January 1972, that was pretty much the predicament I found myself in when I agreed to forfeit my royalties to keep the company going. After all, Jury and Mark couldn't live on air and neither could our secretary, Janet O'Brien, who was very efficient but was also aware that she was worth a lot more than we were paying her.

The second item of note that happened around September of 1971 was that Jury's father, Mikolaj Krytiuk, who was a Ukrainian Orthodox Catholic priest, decided he'd like to move from Melfort, Saskatchawan, to Ontario. When his transfer to a parish in Sudbury came through, he wanted to buy a house in that city and bring Anna, Jury's mother, and Peter and Mary, Jury's brother and sister, there to live as well.

The only problem was, he didn't have the money to buy the new house and make the move without selling or mortgaging his house in Saskatchewan. And this he was having a hard time doing, given the fact it all had to be done on such short notice and he didn't want to let the house go for an amount far lower than its true value. And this is where I came in.

I had never met the man before and I had no desire to own a house in Melfort, Saskatchewan, but as a favour to Jury I was able to come up with the necessary funds and wound up holding a first mortgage on the house and property. Mikolaj then bought the new house and moved his family to Sudbury.

And by February of 1972 he again was able to get another parish transfer to Toronto. He commuted to Sudbury for a while and after a few months he sold both his houses, paid me back the money for the mortgage, and bought another house in Toronto.

The whole family lived with Jury and me for a month or so, until they could move into their own house, and Jury's father came to work for us at Boot Records on a part-time basis thereafter.

While all this was putting quite a strain on my personal finances I really didn't mind because it was nice to see a family get together again that might not have been able to otherwise. Both Mikolaj and Anna thanked me very much for the favour and it wasn't too long after that Jury moved into the new house to live with them as well.

And now back to January of 1972.

The fan mail was still pouring in from Tillsonburg, the song was still selling like crazy, and everybody wanted us back to do another concert. So on the twenty-eighth of the

month, the boys and I headed out. First we played Tillsonburg to a sold-out crowd and then we went to Simcoe and
did the same thing. All I can say is, those people who live
down in the tobacco belt of Ontario sure liked that song.
They couldn't get enough of it. In Tillsonburg alone, the
record had sold almost twelve thousand by now (in a period
of about six months), and the town's whole population was
only six thousand. Truly amazing.

Now it was back again to Toronto for the real big test. Up
until now I had only played the Horseshoe Tavern, which
seated around three hundred people, but I had always been
convinced that I could take on a much larger venue. And
even though it scared me sometimes to think about it, I was
determined that one day I would get to play in no less a
venue than the great Massey Hall.

I heard the place could seat just under three thousand
people when packed, and on February 4 I was planning to
see what kind of a dent I could put in that magical number.

The ads had been out now for a couple of weeks and
everybody in the music business was saying that "Stompin'
Tom must be crazy. He might be able to pack some places
away out in small-town Canada, or maybe even a few booze
halls like the Horseshoe Tavern, but he's out of his mind if
he thinks he can draw people into such a prestigious landmark as the world-famous Massey Hall, especially with his
kind of a cornball show." Everybody figured I was commit-
ting suicide in whatever musical career I'd been able to sustain up until now, because if nobody came to the show I'd
wind up being a laughing stock. After all, this was the big city
of Toronto, not Charlottetown, Prince Edward Island. And
Massey Hall was a venue which demanded nothing but the
finest, and nothing short of the best of what the world had
to offer. "And along comes Stompin' Tom. Ha ha ha. Who in
the hell does he think he is anyhow?"

One of the guys we worked with to book Massey Hall in
the first place, and on a percentage basis, was Richard
Flohill. Richard was a freelance writer for a number of magazines and also had a good deal of experience in booking
acts for Mariposa and other large venues in the Toronto
area. He seemed to have a fairly bubbly and outgoing

personality which always picked you up when you got worried about things, but it also made you wonder at times if he wasn't just a little over-confident. And if so, this could spell disaster, from the point of view that maybe the timing wasn't right or perhaps the whole venture may have been just a little premature.

At any rate, Richard got us a write-up in a couple of magazines, I did a bunch of interviews with newspapers and anyone else who wanted to talk to me, and everyone at our Boot Records office, including their relatives, distributed pamphlets under windshield wipers, in parking lots, supermarkets, hotel lobbies, grocery stores, and everywhere people might be expected to pick them up. Nobody, at least from our side, wanted to see this show flop, so everyone just worked like a bunch of beavers.

On the afternoon of February 4, while we were setting up our equipment in the hall, we were paid a visit by a television filmmaker by the name of Mike Maltby. He was freelancing for the CBC and was hoping to get a scoop for one of their weekend shows that usually came on after the 11 P.M. news.

Along with clips of the Massey Hall concert, he wanted to follow me around on tour for a week or so. When I gave him the okay and told him I'd be leaving for a tour of the Maritimes in a couple of days, he was delighted, and agreed to meet us in Amherst, Nova Scotia, on the night of my birthday on February 9.

Finally, when our lighting and sound check was done, we all headed for the dressing room where the boys were about to dig into the food they had ordered in for supper. As eating was something I never did before a show, I just watched them gorge themselves as usual and opened myself a beer.

About an hour or so later Jury came running back to the dressing room. "Tom!" he exclaimed. "Guess what? There's people coming! They're actually coming! There's a big line of them out on the street waiting for the doors to open."

I told him that was great news and maybe he should run right out and talk to them to make sure none of them got away. About every five minutes after that he was back giving me another head count. And by showtime he was all smiles and chuckles. "We did it, Tom! We did it! There's over 2,800 people in here and they're still drifting in." I don't ever remember him being so excited before that time or after. This was his really big moment, to say nothing of my own. But now it was time for me to find out whether I could make this "big city audience" feel justified in coming and spending their money here in the first place.

The answer to this concern wasn't long coming. When the curtain went up and the chorus of "Bud the Spud from the bright red mud" filled the air, and the sound of a hard, solid boot pounding down on a stomping board rang out from wall to wall, I could tell by the reaction from the audience that the illustrious reputation of the great Massey Hall would never be quite the same again. I guess there are those who would say the old shrine was desecrated. When the whistles and catcalls from a Stompin' Tom audience finally died down that night, I don't think the old hall ever figured out what really happened to her. She had never seen this kind of a crowd before, and neither did a lot of these people have previous cause to come here before. It was like some kind of a revolution had taken place. The little man got to dine at the big man's table, and even got to choose his own style of entertainment.

The show turned out to be a complete success. And even the critics had to erase some of the venom from their previously written lines. The disaster they predicted never happened. The world didn't come to an end, Massey Hall was still standing, Stompin' Tom had proven he could play in the big leagues, and the pride of the common man was slightly elevated because of it all.

The following day there were more interviews and even an invitation by Elwood Glover for me to come down and have a chat with him on his currently popular "Luncheon Date" program which was nationally televised on the CBC.

On Sunday the sixth of February, Dick and I and the boys headed out for the east coast and on the ninth we were playing in Amherst, Nova Scotia. The local radio station was getting good response from playing my records there and decided to sponsor my show. A couple of the DJs, one of them being Paul Kennedy, went out and bought me a birthday cake and presented it to me that night on stage. I thought that was very decent of them, and the audience just "ate the whole thing up." (I just couldn't resist that one.)

In the meantime, we had met Mike Maltby again with his couple of assistants and the TV cameras were trained on us for most of the show. The following day I went up to the radio station and did an interview with the DJs and taped a couple of plugs for their individual programs and then the boys and I headed out for Truro with the TV cameras filming us for most of the way. Sometimes Mike and one of his cameras would get right in my car with me and tape an interview as I drove along.

At the motel in Truro I got a message that Jury wanted me to call him as soon as I got in town. When I phoned him, he told me that *My Stompin' Grounds* album which had only been out now for seven months had gone "Gold." This is the album that contained the song "Tillsonburg," and after checking his figures a dozen times he submitted them to *RPM* magazine for verification and I was now going to get a front-cover story for the accomplishment.

Back in those days, as I mentioned, to be entitled to receive a Gold Album Award an artist had to have sales of $100,000 or more at retail level in Canada. And in the country music category, no Canadian artist had ever achieved this level of sales for a record before. The *RPM* magazine article dated February 12, 1972, put it this way:

"His *My Stompin' Grounds* album has now chalked up sales in excess of $100,000 at retail level—*the first Canadian country artist to ever accomplish this feat.* Boot [Records] was so excited by this *first,* they put together a Gold Disc Award for Tom." (The italics here are my own. Because several years later another Canadian country artist also received a Gold Album Award and in *Maclean's* magazine it was claimed that "this was the first." And although Jury wrote them several letters, it wasn't until a couple of issues later that they finally printed a very small inconspicuous retraction. And even with that, the words that were chosen were not exactly in the very best of taste. It sounded as if it had been printed very reluctantly and the writer in no way wanted to give credit where credit was due. Or for that matter, take back the credit from where credit wasn't due. At any rate, before the year of

1972 was over I had a total of three verified gold albums: *My Stompin' Grounds* on Boot Records; *Bud the Spud* on Dominion Records in April; and *Live at the Horseshoe* on Dominion in December. And for even further verification, *RPM* magazine presented me with their own special Gold Leaf Award.)

On February 10 we played the Cobequid Centre in Truro and on the following day we drove to the P.E.I. ferry at Cape Tormentine, N.B.

On Saturday night the camera crew filmed us performing at the Prince Edward Lounge in Charlottetown, and after the show that night they even caught us at one of the bootleggers' during the wee hours of the morning. This I quickly put a stop to as Lena's sister, Pauline, and her husband, Gerald, were sitting beside us, and they weren't too fussy about having their faces televised across the nation from, of all places, some bootlegging joint in Charlottetown. (Although the filming immediately stopped, a small clip of this incident did eventually find its way onto the ultimate broadcast.)

The next afternoon, Sunday the thirteenth, we all went up to Skinners Pond to film the old house and a bit of the surrounding area. The one scene we did from North Cape, where I was looking out over the ice-bound Northumberland Strait, reminded me very much of the time in previous years when Steve Foote and I stood in the very same location as I tried to make up my mind whether I would ever bother again to return to Skinners Pond, even for a short visit.

After a few more minutes, we drove back to the house where they filmed Russell and Cora and me having supper together. Cora was in one of her very rare delightful moods and even managed to smile for the camera a couple of times, while Russell was his usual ordinary self and just took everything in stride.

As soon as the interviews were over, we all headed back to Charlottetown where, on the following night, we taped another show at Johnny Reid's.

On Tuesday of that week we took the ferry again from Borden to Cape Tormentine and headed back into Nova Scotia. These ferry crossings, by the way, are very picturesque in the wintertime. The Abegweit car ferry is a powerful ice-breaker and quite often has to make some very interesting manoeuvres as she encounters the ice clumpets of varying degrees of thickness. Watching all this can be fascinating and can often result in some interesting film footage. (And so can some of the antics that the boys and I went through out on deck during this one particular voyage.)

After filming a show in Antigonish and also a question and answer session with a gymnasium full of high school students the next day, we finally said goodbye to Mike Maltby and his crew, wished them all well with their project and headed out for Cape Breton Island.

We then played in Bill Lewis's home town of Whitney Pier, met his dad and mother and spent a very nice evening at their house. Billy's father, Archie, as it turned out, was a very good singer and guitar player. He especially liked singing the old Hank Williams songs and did an excellent job of them. I had to laugh a little, though, as Billy's mother was always trying to keep Archie away from the beer. She had most of it hidden in the washing machine and wouldn't tell him where it was. I think he had a bottle of something hidden upstairs though, because after every third or fourth song he'd go up and come down again and sound even better after each trip.

From Whitney Pier we went to Cheticamp and Port Hawksbury and then back to the mainland of Nova Scotia. There we played New Glasgow, and after Dick rolled the Boot on its side by slipping off the slushy road, we finally arrived in Halifax to do a concert and tape two more shows for "Countrytime" before going on to New Brunswick.

Between February 25 and March 3, we wound up our east-coast tour by playing Mount Allison University in Sackville, a high school auditorium in St. Stephen, the Composite School in Woodstock, and finally the Cormier High School in Edmunston.

Somewhere on this tour of the Maritimes (I forget just what town it was), Jury had called to inform me that I had won another Juno Award. This was my second, and my sister Marlene had gone to the presentation and accepted it for me.

This had sure been a great piece of news with which to conclude my east-coast tour. As soon as I arrived back in Toronto on March 6, we all had ourselves a little celebration. We invited everybody who was by now in any way associated with Boot Records and practically raised the roof off 240 Searle Avenue.

After all, winning the second Juno Award was like an assurance to all of us that the first one hadn't been a fluke. We all began to realize that one Boot recording artist had really arrived, and now it was time to concentrate our efforts on having others do so as well.

Stompin' Tom with
Hank and Wilf

BY THE SPRING OF 1972 we had started a budget label
called Cynda. And between the two labels, Cynda and
Boot, we must have had over a dozen artists signed up or in
the process of doing so. Some of the artists we already had
albums on were the following:

Humphrey & the Dumptrucks, two albums; Stevedore
Steve, three albums (this includes the first album I got
Dominion Records to release); Bud Roberts, one album; Roy
Payne, one album; Larry McKee, two albums; The Wolftones,
two albums; The Brannigan Boys, one album: and myself,
with two albums (of my own writing). Some of the artists we
were then negotiating with, and who eventually came aboard,
were Kent Brockwell, Sullivan, Angus Walker, East Wind, Con
Archer, Clare Adlam, Chris Scott, Joyce Simone, Brent
Williams, Sean Dunphy, Gaet Lepine, Julie Lynn, and Par
Three. There were even more prospects at this time and I will
try to remember them as they came on the label.

Most of the artists mentioned above were in the traditional folk or country field, but you must remember this was
only the spring of 1972 and as yet, we had only been in business for a little over a year. Ultimately our roster of well over
a hundred artists provided our labels with music from practically every genre.

From the classical guitar stylings of Liona Boyd to the songs and chants of the Inuit from places as remote as Northern Yukon, Baffin Island and Greenland, we considered nothing untouchable, unapproachable or without merit. From Stan Rogers to the Canadian Brass, from Rita MacNeil to the Emeralds, from the tribal music of Africa to the polkas of Walter Ostanek, and from Stompin' Tom to the reggae music we were first to bring into Canada from Jamaica, we had them all. And we were never afraid to try something new. We had dinner music, dance music, mood music, funny music, exercise music, old-time fiddle music and traditional music from just about every corner of the world. And it was played by every kind of orchestra, from jug band to symphony. This is what Boot Records eventually became in its heyday. Then after about sixteen years it abruptly folded. (I will deal with these events as I come to them.)

On March 9, 1972, the boys and I did a guest appearance on Ian Tyson's television show for the CTV network, and then on the eighteenth a concert at Guelph University. We took the month of April off to rest up and write some more songs.

On March 25, the *Toronto Star's Canadian* magazine gave me a great cover story by Dick Brown, who had interviewed me at Massey Hall, and *Maclean's* magazine was preparing a story which eventually came out in August. By now, it seemed like everybody had to have their little piece of Stompin' Tom, and with only a couple of small problems, I didn't mind the attention they were giving me a damn bit. I didn't like the way I was being misquoted sometimes; I didn't like the out-and-out mistakes that sometimes got printed; and I didn't like the fact that my true relationship with Boot Records had somehow leaked out. I had always wanted to be known as just an artist on the label and not really an owner. At least the true percentages hadn't come out, so I guess most people who read the articles probably figured I had merely bought a few shares and left it at that.

Sometime during the month of April, Jury came across my list of about 250 fan-club members and decided to re-activate the club. It had been started in Timmins by myself and Jim Etherington of Schumacher while I still played at the Maple Leaf Hotel. Jim was the president and kept it going till about 1971 when he gave it up to attend university in Windsor, Ontario. Jury asked my sister, Marlene, if she wanted to take over the duties as president and for the next several years it was active until Marlene also had to give it up. Nearly a thousand members were then given notices that the club was shutting down and it hasn't been in operation since. Although a few people during the late '80s and early '90s expressed interest in starting the club up again, I decided against it, mainly because I was afraid it would start up for a while and then have to shut down again, and that wouldn't be fair to my fans. The longevity of fan clubs is very unpredictable. People seem to want to run them for a while and then for some reason or another they lose interest and give them up. I feel that it's better not to have a fan club at all than to have one that is folding all the time.

On May 8, 1972, the boys and I again started playing the Horseshoe Tavern for a week. Jack Star would have had us there for as long as we wanted to stay but with the demand across the country growing as it was, we had to be on the go. One afternoon, however, while playing the Horseshoe, I was involved with a documentary film by a fellow named Ed Moodie who was attending York University. He was doing a thesis on filmmaking and asked me if I could help him out by being the subject of his film project. I later learned the documentary helped him attain his diploma. I thought that was great and, obviously, so did he.

Towards the end of the same week, a fellow by the name of Jock Ferguson, from the CBC, came by and asked me if I would be interested in writing a theme song for a television show called "Marketplace" which was to make its debut in the coming fall season. He said they already had a number of submissions but if I could write a song overnight and give it to him the following day he would see that it received due consideration along with the rest.

That was on a Friday night. And on Saturday night, when he arrived back at the Horseshoe, I had the song completed and gave him a tape recording of it along with a lyric sheet.

I was later informed the song had won over the rest and

by August 3, 1972, the CBC had sent me a contract to come into the studio to film and record it.

Needless to say, I was delighted, and for the next several years "Marketplace" became one of the most popular shows to be seen on Sunday night television. And of course there I was each Sunday singing the theme song. It was called "The Consumer." The only problem was, a lot of people who watched the show every week thought I was there live and wrote me letters asking me if I only had the one shirt to wear. They were, of course, seeing the same shirt every Sunday. (Ho hum! You just can't win.)

While all this was going on, Jury was busy contacting the handlers of Hank Snow to get a tour going with Hank, myself and Wilf Carter. The first three shows were to be in Portland and Bangor, Maine, then Boston, Massachusetts. These first three shows were to include only Hank and myself, and upon arriving back in Canada we were to be joined by Wilf Carter for a series of dates in Ontario and Quebec.

I really welcomed the Boston date because I knew there were a lot of Prince Edward Islanders and other Maritimers living in that city and figured if I could play there with Hank it would be a good stepping stone for me to tour further into the States with my Canadian songs.

Unfortunately, on our way down through the States on the seventeenth of May '72 we were informed that Hank had cancelled and Boston and Bangor would not take Stompin' Tom by himself because they were afraid I wasn't known well enough. As a result of this, we had to make some quick changes in our plans. We played Portland by ourselves and were lucky that everyone at least broke even. That was on the nineteenth of May. Then Jury quickly got us a booking in Caribou, Maine, near the New Brunswick border where a lot of Americans had heard of me through their close proximity to and association with Canadians. Given the short notice and all, we did surprisingly well in Caribou and immediately headed back to Ontario where we had to do a show in Windsor on the twenty-fifth and Chatham on the twenty-seventh.

Then, on June 1, in Thunder Bay, I finally got to play on

the same stage as Wilf Carter. Wilf would be backed up by a real fine group of musicians who were well known at the time. They were known as the Ziebert Brothers and had a style not unlike the Sons of the Pioneers. They were very easy to get along with, and for the rest of the tour we all developed a real friendly relationship.

When I first saw Wilf, I felt a little intimidated by his long-standing reputation and his huge stature. But within two minutes of talking with the man, I came to realize that this was the real genuine article. With his big friendly smile, he immediately won the hearts of everyone he spoke with. He began to talk and tell stories to you as if he had known you for years. Although you could see by the look of him that had been through a lot of hard times and certainly wouldn't take any shit if it were thrown his way, he made you feel warm and welcome to be around him and that he would surely give you the benefit of the doubt in any dispute about your integrity. He also looked like a man you'd be wise not to cross, however. And stories I later heard about a few unfortunate fellows who did decide to cross him all seem to bear this out.

Backstage and around the dressing room, Wilf Carter was just one of the boys, but the minute he walked on the stage with his guitar and big white cowboy hat the crowd became electrified. Here was the granddaddy of all the singing cowboys, the great Canadian troubadour who so many of them had grown up listening to, and the first man to ever put Canadian placenames on the country music map of the world. This was "Montana Slim." This was Wilf Carter, the original "Singing Cowboy" himself. And behind the curtain, as I watched him perform for the first time, I shed a bit of a tear, and told myself, "This is the kind of a man I want to emulate."

For the rest of the tour Wilf was a superb person to be around. He was always helpful and co-operative. There were even a couple of times when we were short on dressing-room space and Wilf would say, "Don't worry about it, boys. You fellows take the dressing room and I'll just grab a stool or something and sit back in the shadows behind the curtains somewhere, and when you want me just give me a shout, and don't you worry about a thing." That was Wilf Carter. And a lot of today's performers could certainly take a few lessons from such a man, instead of believing they are God's gift to the people.

On June 4 we all arrived in Peterborough, Ontario. And here at the Memorial Gardens we finally met up with Hank Snow and his Rainbow Ranch Boys.

After me and my guys (The Rovin' Cowboys, as they were known by now), and Wilf Carter and the Ziebert Brothers all finally got set up for the show, we retired to our dressing rooms to wait until Hank and his boys arrived.

Upon their arrival, my guys wanted to go out on stage to meet them as they were setting up.

I was a little reluctant about this because of the memories I had of the last few times I had been shunned by Hank while trying to meet him. But after waiting a few minutes, I decided to go out and make my presence known.

As I entered the stage area, Hank was walking toward me on his way to the dressing rooms. As our eyes met I tried to look as casual as I could, and raising my hand in a slight wave, I said, "Hi, Hank," and gave a little smile. I was hoping maybe to strike up a little conversation. But again, it wasn't to be. He just walked by as if I wasn't there.

Well, I thought to myself, this is the last time I'll ever go out of my way to meet the Great Hank Snow. (And to this day, though I still very much admire the great songs and music he gave us over so many years, to say the least, I think he was one of the most unsociable and disgruntled people I ever met.)

The promoters of these shows of Hank, Wilf and myself had previously agreed that we each take our turn to open and close the show in each of the towns we played on the tour. And tonight in Peterborough, Wilf was to open the show, Hank was to go on second and I was to close.

With the people of Peterborough being such great country fans, the arena didn't take long to fill up and with a packed house we were soon on our way. The Zieberts did about three numbers and brought Wilf on to thunderous applause and it stayed that way till his set was over. Then came Hank and the applause continued. That is, up until he seemed to overstay his welcome. By the time he was ten to fifteen minutes into my portion of the show, the applause from the audience had not only diminished but most of the people had started stompin' their feet.

Hank finally got the message that he wasn't the only one the fans had come to see and he quickly but grudgingly left the stage, giving me a nice dirty look as he went.

With my allotted time onstage now having been curtailed as it was, I had to tell my guitar player, Billy Lewis, to forget about singing the one or two songs he usually did before calling me on stage and just walked out without the regular introduction and started singing.

As this was the largest venue I had ever played in Peterborough since the days of the old King George Hotel, I guess my old fans and friends were really glad to see me on such a prestigious show. From the minute I opened my mouth to sing, I was honoured with a standing ovation. And for the rest of my set, I just sang whatever songs were shouted up from the audience instead of the line-up of numbers I had originally planned.

After the show Wilf and I signed autographs and tried to make appropriate excuses for Hank's not being there. And while this left some people a little disappointed, most said they had a wonderful time. I only learned later that Hank left the venue immediately after his set was over and didn't even stay to hear one of my songs. Well, gosh! This was sure going to be a real friendly tour!

Later on that night I had occasion to talk to Wilf and I asked him, "What seems to be wrong with Hank, anyway?" And when I told him about the experiences I had with Hank before, he just said, "Oh, don't let it bother you, Tom. He's always like that." "Well, it's kind of too bad," I said. "He's such a great talent and all." "Yeah," Wilf said, "but he knows it a lot better than you do." With that I dropped the subject and never mentioned it again.

The next few shows took us to Sault Ste. Marie, Sudbury, North Bay, Timmins, Hamilton, London and Brantford.

In North Bay I again had some words with Dick, my road manager, concerning his arrogance with some of the people. And as this was now becoming more frequent and he didn't want to heed my advice, I decided I'd have to let him go. I immediately notified Jury in Toronto who, by the end of June, was able to come up with a new road manager. His name was Wayne Hughes. He was originally from Montreal but was now living in Toronto.

Also, just after the London show, we were informed that Hank was again going to cancel out on a few shows and we probably wouldn't see him again till we got to Montreal.

Somehow the promoters were able to get the Kitty Wells Show, which was currently touring Ontario, to join our tour in Hank's place for a few dates which fell between their own committed engagements. This enabled the promoters to continue advertising us as a show with three headliners.

On the Kitty Wells Show was Kitty herself, with her husband, Johnny Wright (of Johnny and Jack fame), and her son, Bobby Wright. This made for a well rounded-out country package. And while a few people may have been a little disappointed not seeing Hank, the shows remained a huge success.

The towns yet to be played on this tour were Cornwall, Kingston, Ottawa, Oshawa, Kitchener, Smith's Falls, Orillia, Montreal and Hepworth. Kitty and/or Wilf were with me on six or seven of these and the rest I did alone.

Hank was back again with Wilf and me for the big Montreal show. This took place in the Paul Sauvé arena (I think it's in Rosemount), where our half French and half English audience nearly went wild for Hank and Wilf. They were extremely popular in Montreal at the time and though I wasn't, due to the lack of airplay, I managed to hold my own.

It was funny to hear the emcee, who was from the local radio station and didn't even know my name, introduce me to the audience as "Mr. Stomper." He even stumbled over the name a couple of times before getting it right. I'm not sure how he fared when he again tried saying it in French, but the delighted crowd sure got the message when I finally put my left foot down.

As well as singing songs for all the provinces, I also sang several I had written about Quebec. And along with the two or three French-language songs I had learned over the years, I was doing just great.

After the show we signed autographs and even Hank

joined us for a short while. But one of the things I especially remember is the fact that every Stompin' Tom record we had there that night got sold and people were still asking for more. And of course everyone was asking me that same old question I've had to answer a million times before and ever since, "Hey, Tom. Why don't we ever get to hear you on radio?" And all I've ever been able to answer is "I don't know. I guess you'll just have to ask them."

Before leaving for Toronto the next day, while talking to Jury on the phone, he told me my song "The Moon Man Newfie" was number one on *RPM* magazine's country music chart. "Wow!" I said, "that's great! But it's also very odd. I've had my radio tuned in to every country station for the last month from Thunder Bay to Montreal and from Sudbury to London and I have yet to hear it once. I've also visited several radio stations along the way and nobody even mentioned it. But I'll keep my ears open on the way to Toronto. I'm bound to hear it somewhere, now that it's number one."

Needless to say, I never heard it on the way to Toronto. And all through the months of July, August and September, which took me from Charlottetown, Prince Edward Island, to Nanaimo, Vancouver Island, in British Columbia, I still never heard it even once. Not bad for a number one hit, eh? And Jury wasn't wrong, either. I still have the clipping from the trade magazine. (Incidentally, the song "The Bridge Came Tumbling Down" went to number two in July of that year and I only heard it once.) I suppose some could say that, coincidentally, I may not have been listening in at the right times.

Back in Toronto, I dismissed the boys and told them to take the month of July off and I would see them on the first of August.

From Skinners Pond to "The Mags"

Lena had asked me for a long time now to come home to the Magdalene Islands with her to meet her folks on Entry Island, and because I had some business I wanted to attend to in Skinners Pond, I thought this would be a good time to do both. So after doing a thirty-minute documentary film for York University we packed up the car and drove to Prince Edward Island.

During our visit in Skinners Pond, I made arrangements with Russell to buy the old farm from him. First, of course, he would have to talk it over with Cora. And although she had said many years before that I "would never own this farm" she consented to the sale.

The arrangement was that I would have the whole farm surveyed, and a small lot upon which the house was situated would be severed from the rest so they would continue to live there. This, of course, they would not sell. Nor did I want them to.

After having the property appraised and because I secretly wanted to help them out in their old age, I wound up giving them three times more for it than it was currently worth and also threw in a brand-new car to seal off the deal. This all came as a great surprise and they were delighted, to say the least.

I also got a surprise out of the deal. In having the deed searched by the lawyer I found that the property upon which

the Skinners Pond School sat, which was just at the corner of
the Aylward farm, had never been deeded off the original
property. And although the school had been built there
over a hundred years previously, the taxes on the land
had always been paid by the Aylwards. This meant the school
property was now being transferred into my name. And
when the government announced to the district that year
that the school would have to be abandoned and the
children would have to be bussed to a larger regional school,
the old building went up for sale to anyone who wanted to
haul it away.

There were no takers for such an old building and this is
how it fell into my hands. And with Prince Edward Island's
Centennial coming up the following year, 1973, I immediately made plans to restore the old school to its original
state. And by June 1973, there she stood, just as pretty as the
day she was built. Only this time she had a foundation and
all. Even the blackboard and all the original double-seat
desks were restored. The old pot-bellied stove was all shined
up and stood in the middle of the floor complete with poker,
shovel and coal scuttle. The only thing missing was the
teacher and the students. And to help compensate for that,
a lot of the older folks in the district were good enough to
donate some class pictures of days gone by which were hung
nicely around the walls.

Outside, the school was painted white with green trim
and all around the school yard was a nice wooden fence
painted the same. And at the far end of the schoolyard was
a brand-new outhouse with two doors, one marked "Boys"
and the other one "Girls." This too was white trimmed with
green and set the whole place off nicely. You might say it
gave the whole setting that "still in use" look.

As a final touch to all of this I had a stone cairn erected
near the road just inside the fence. The words on the plaque
read as follows:

SKINNERS POND SCHOOL NO. 19

This is the oldest known one-room schoolhouse
on Prince Edward Island, still standing where it

was originally built in the early nineteenth century, by the people who first settled in the district of Skinners Pond.

Stompin' Tom Connors, one of Canada's well-known folksong composers, who came here as an orphan and lived on the Aylward farm for several of his boyhood years in the 1940s, attended school in this building.

It has been Tom's wish that this school should be preserved as an historical landmark for his friends, the people of Skinners Pond, as a part of their contribution towards the Prince Edward Island centennial year celebrations.

Here, in 1973, this stone is erected in memory of the builders, the teachers and the students, living or deceased, who have left a part of themselves within the walls of this building, affectionately known as the Skinners Pond School.

Unfortunately for all, this storybook setting of an old-time wooden school was not to last very long. The vandalism of a few local hooligans soon took its toll and in a few short years the old school was back to looking the way it always had. Pretty sad and decrepit.

I will catch up on this part of my story later but now I must return to July of 1972.

After visiting a few friends in Skinners Pond and having a few card games of Auction 45s (a favourite game down home), Lena and I left for Charlottetown, where we stopped in to see her sister Pauline and our friends Johnny and Judy, owners of the Prince Edward Lounge, and the next day we were off to "The Mags," which is just the short form for saying the Magdalene Islands, Quebec.

I had previously written and recorded the song "The Isles of Magdalene" mainly going by everything Lena had told me about them and now I was going to get the chance to see just how accurate the song was.

We left the car at the Charlottetown airport and in less
than half an hour we were circling the Mags. It was a nice
clear afternoon and far off over the Gulf of St. Lawrence to
our right I could see a land mass in a southeasterly direction.
This I knew must be Cape Breton. And as we circled, I could
see glimpses of the many small islands below us which
went to make up the archipelago known collectively as
the Magdalenes.

I could also see that most of these islands were connected
by long narrow sand dunes which in places seemed to partially surround the lapping waters of the gulf and capture
some of it into long picturesque lagoons. The capes, which
were bright red, as those on Prince Edward Island, provided
a beautiful contrast as they reached up to meet the rich dark
green grass that flowed down into the fields on the other
side. This place was indeed as beautiful as Lena had said
it was.

Upon landing, we found everyone at the little airport to
be very kind and co-operative. And though Lena and I
couldn't speak French very well, we managed to secure a taxi
to drive us to one of the other islands where we were to meet
the small fishing boat which would take us to Entry, the
island where Lena was from.

As I said before, most of the islands are connected by
sand dunes and these provide a sort of causeway for the
main highway that runs from island to island. The only two
islands that remain unconnected are Brion Island, which is
twenty miles or so away from the rest and remains unin-
habited, and Entry Island, some seven miles out from
Amherst, the island from which we would soon set sail on
the fishing boat.

Our taxi driver was French but could speak a little English
and between the three of us we were able to communicate
sufficiently to understand each other. When Lena told him
who her dad was, he remembered meeting him a few times
and this broke the ice and enabled us to carry on some interesting conversations. The drive, after all, would take us an
hour or more, and who wants to sit around in a cab saying
nothing when you're in such a strange but beautiful place.

The largest town we passed through was called Grindstone. It was the capital of all the islands and the centre of most of the commerce. It had several hotels and motels which catered to mostly francophone tourists from the mainland of Quebec, to which the islands belonged, and a few restaurants and bars along with your normal shops and grocery stores. The large car ferries docked here—the one from Gaspé, Quebec, and the other from Prince Edward Island. The overall population in 1972 was roughly 16,000 with 85 per cent of these being French and 15 per cent Irish and Scotch. The latter were mostly concentrated in Grosse Ile and on Entry Island.

Finally, we arrived on Amherst Island and drove out onto the wharf. I paid the cabbie, who by now was talking and smiling like an old friend, and there, walking towards us to help us with our luggage, were Lena's two brothers, Ted and Pete. Ted was the younger brother whom I had met in Toronto and who had recently moved back home with his wife, Cathy, who was also from Entry Island, and their young daughters, Tracey and Trudy.

Ted introduced me to Pete and also to the fellow who owned the fishing boat, Cecil Aitkens, and within a few minutes we were aboard and sailing out of the harbour.

With a light breeze and the late afternoon sun glistening over the water, the seven-mile voyage proved to be just exactly what the doctor ordered.

One of the boys passed me a nice cool bottle of beer, and after Lena had a small sip I just "put 'er away" and reached for another one.

A couple of miles out we passed by a couple of other boats jigging for mackerel. From the distance they waved their hands to say hello and we, of course, did the same. Such is the custom among fishermen, whether they know each other or not.

With my arm around Lena and gazing out over the bow of the boat towards Entry, I said, "You know something, Babe? When I was only sixteen I sailed by these islands on a coal boat, and while looking through a pair of binoculars, I wondered what sort of people would live away out here in the middle of the Gulf of St. Lawrence. Not only was I not dreaming that someday I would come out here to find out, but also that someday I might come here and fall in love with one of their beautiful daughters." With that, I kissed her till it occurred to me that I'd better tear myself away before one or both of her brothers came and threw me overboard.

As we came around the breakwater and pulled into the little harbour, Cecil cut the motors so we could drift close beside the wharf till we came to a suitable place to tie up.

"Who are all these people?" I asked Lena. There must have been a couple hundred of them lined up along the top of the wharf. "Oh, they're just my relatives and the people of Entry coming out to get a good look at you. They've seen you on TV and you're a big star to them, you know." "Wow! I'll have to be on my best behaviour," I said, as I stepped on the dock and tripped over the nearest suitcase. Everybody snickered and so did I, as my attention for a second quickly focused on "the Man upstairs." "You certainly have a great way of letting people know that these so-called big stars are not one bit better or smarter than they are, don't you? Thanks for helping me let them know that."

I shook hands with practically everyone there and tried to remember the names of every one of Lena's relatives. There must have been fifty of them alone. I especially remember Lena's dad, whose name was Peter. He was a man I presumed to be in his early seventies, around five-foot-six with a slight build. He tottered on his feet a little, due to some kind of foot trouble, and was quite hard of hearing. His long, narrow, weather-beaten face was covered with the most beautiful and mischievous grin I had ever seen. As he walked up to me and gave me a vice-grip handshake, he said, "Welcome home to Entry, Tom. Where 'bouts on Prince Edward Island are you from, anyway?" "Skinners Pond," I said. And due to his lack of good hearing, from that time on he always referred to it as "Kinner Pon."

After all the handshakes and autographs, we were ushered into an old pick-up truck full of suitcases and boxes and rumbled up the worst damned old pot-hole filled road I'd ever seen or been on. But apart from this the island was beautiful. The whole island was about the size of the district of Skinners Pond, back home, and I was told its dimensions were approximately two and a quarter miles in diameter and the circumference would be seven miles if one were to sail around it.

There were several huge grassy hills surrounding another one of a monstrous size. This latter was known appropriately as "Big Hill." And on all of these hills, using a pair of binoculars, you could see cattle grazing everywhere. It wasn't uncommon to see a horse and cart moving slowly up or down the roads from time to time (this was no place to test the endurance of a Cadillac), and the pace of life itself ran along at about the same speed.

About three-quarters of the population here were freckled, especially the men and children, and most of these had reddish hair. The other 25 per cent were of various other complexions, and all had an outgoing, pleasant and humorous demeanour. And I, of course, was taken in by all of them.

When we reached the house, Lena's mom was standing in the doorway looking excited but also a little nervous. Lena jumped out of the truck and hugged her for a couple of minutes and after she wiped a tear or two from her eyes I also gave her a hug and told her how glad I was to meet her. (She wasn't a very talkative woman, so Lena must have got it from her dad. Just kidding, of course, but Lena's gonna kill me when she reads this.) Her mom's name was Lottie and I couldn't get over how much they resembled each other. I could also see how close they were and figured they had a lot to talk about so I just excused myself and went to help the boys bring in the luggage.

With a bunch of the neighbours standing around watching all of this, one young fella spotted my guitar case and said, "Hey, Tom. Ya gonna sing 'Bud the Spud' fer us tonight?" "Well, either tonight or tomorrow night," I said. "After we've had a bit of a talk we'll decide all that later." "Okay," he said, "I'll be right over just as soon as I hear all the stompin' goin' on." I laughed at that one and carried my guitar on into the house.

Shortly after that, Lena's dad arrived back from the wharf and pretty soon we were all sitting down to supper. Lena had told her mom that I just loved all kinds of fish and there before me was a great big feed of mackerel and cod.

There were Lena and me, her dad and mom, her brothers
Pete and Ted, and Ted's wife, Cathy, with the two kids who
sat in, and I was busy gorging myself until Ted happened to
mention that he and another fella were going to bring in
some lobsters for later on. Well, that did it. I had been planning on having two plates of supper but I quickly decided to
only have one. Lobsters were my favourite and I was going to
make damn sure I had lots of room later to get my full share.
One has to think ahead about these things, you know.

After supper we chatted a lot and I guess Lena's dad must
have asked me a million questions. He also told me a million
stories about his earlier life. Everything from when he had
to go fishing in a home-made dory to the time the Diefenbaker government invited him up to Quebec City as a Conservative delegate. He told me how the rum-running ships
used to store some of their booze on Entry Island during the
U.S. days of prohibition and how he ran the first store on
Entry out of his house. He explained to me how the mail
used to come to Entry in the old days by a barrel set afloat
on the other side of the channel. Sometimes the barrel
arrived and sometimes it didn't. He remembered once when
one of the mail barrels was picked up on the beach in Prince
Edward Island over a hundred miles away and didn't arrive
back on the Mags until the following year when the post
office on Amherst Island once again set it adrift towards
Entry. And to cap off all these wonderful stories, he showed
me the medal he received from the Canadian government
after the war for the role he played in sighting enemy sub-
marines and other sea and air traffic.

One more story I was particularly interested in was about
a small horse called Farmer who was born on Entry Island
back in the early 1920s. The horse had been driven across
the channel on the natural ice bridge that usually forms in
the winter, and was lost that night in a poker game. The man
who won him drove him home to Grosse Ile on the opposite
end of the Mags, a distance of about sixty-five miles
from Amherst.

The following spring the horse ran away from his new
master and wandered along the shores and sand dunes,
avoiding capture several times until he found himself back

on Amherst Island. From here he wandered out along the arm of sand jutting out towards the channel between Entry and Amherst islands, called Sandy Hook, and from here he swam the rest of the way home, a distance of about three miles over very choppy water. Although the new owner wanted the horse back after he discovered his whereabouts, the people of Entry would not part with him again.

I later checked this story with many people and they all came up with the same answer. The story was true. (A number of years later I wrote a poem about this horse, telling a lot more detail than I have here. I set it to music, the song is called "A Horse Called Farmer" and is now recorded on an album of mine entitled *Dr. Stompin' Tom . . . Eh?*

This story is unique in that you may very often hear accounts of cats and dogs returning home over great distances after being lost for long periods of time, but never a horse. Wow!

A couple of hours after supper someone asked me to get the guitar out and play a couple of songs. This I did until the couple of songs turned out to be several dozen. I just perched myself on a chair in one corner of the kitchen and let 'er go.

It was almost as if half of Entry Island were standing outside the door and when the first note was struck, in they came. When they couldn't pile any more in the kitchen, they stood in the doorway or looked in through the open windows. A more enthusiastic audience I never had.

After I sang about fifteen or twenty songs I received another surprise; Lena's mom came out of the other room with a fiddle in her hand and proceeded to play a snappy little jig. Well, I soon found the key she was in and away we went. I didn't recognize what tune it was but it sure sounded great. We must have played a half-dozen tunes or more before she got a little tired and from there on I just continued on alone. Wherever anyone could find a spot on the kitchen floor to give a little step, they did. And if the lobsters hadn't come around twelve o'clock I'm quite sure we'd have been going all night. But as soon as the lobsters were all gone (with a good share of them in my belly), we had another bottle of beer and soon retired. (Most of the guests had gone home as soon as the lobsters arrived.)

The next morning when I got up, Lena's dad was sitting in the kitchen alone drinking a cup of tea and asked me if I wanted one. I said sure, but when he poured it out of the pot I wished I hadn't. You talk about a strong cup of tea. This tea was like molasses. He must have boiled a half pound of tea leaves in the pot for an hour. And when I put the spoon in the cup, the damn thing almost stood up by itself. After a few minutes, when he saw I hadn't taken any more than one small sip, he asked me, "What's the matter, Tom. Don't you like King Cole tea?" I said, "Yeah, but it's a little too weak. I think I'll just have a bottle of beer instead." And as I took one out of the box, he laughed and said, "I don't know about you young fellers these days but one good strong cup of Ol' King Cole is better than five pints of beer any day." He gave me a big wink, downed the rest of his tea and walked outside. I don't know whether he was trying to tell me he had something a lot more powerful than beer in the pot or not, but whatever it was, it was some vile and I didn't want any part of it.

For the rest of that day, Lena took me around to visit a lot more of her relatives, especially the older ones who couldn't get out much, and that evening I met her other sister, Amy, and her husband, Foster. Amy also played the fiddle and Foster ran a lighthouse over on Caribou Island, Nova Scotia. They had arrived home on vacation that day and had just come in on the local ferry. They invited me to drop in to see them any time I happened to be touring in their area, and in the years to come both Lena and I did just that on numerous occasions.

As a matter of fact, it was on one of these occasions that Foster presented me with one of his hand-carved replicas of the world-famous schooner, the *Bluenose*. As one might expect, lighthouse keepers quite often have lots of time on their hands and Foster, being no exception, had taken up the hobby of creating miniature models of all the old sailing vessels along with a variety of fishing boats. He became so good at it after a while that he often entered his models in competition throughout Nova Scotia where he won the first-place ribbon at least a couple of times.

I think he said the model of the *Bluenose* that he made for me took him over five hundred hours. When I think of how tedious a job this must be, even if he put in as much as four hours a day it still would have taken him over four months to complete such a task. But there it is, and it's a beautiful treasure. Thank you, Foster.

During the next few days on Entry, Lena and I went for long walks all over the island and along the beaches. We even climbed to the top of Big Hill and surveyed the surrounding area. It was absolutely breathtaking. Big Hill is the highest point anywhere on the Magdalene Islands and you can see everywhere—just about every isle of the Mags, and just about every wave of the Gulf, and all from this little piece of a lost paradise out under the boundless blue sky.

It was thrilling; it was awesome; and yet it was also sad. For tomorrow we'd be leaving, after handshakes and hugs, a few quiet tears and a wistful goodbye.

The following morning we boarded the small local cargo ferry which was operated by a French fellow from Amherst by the name of Roland Renaud and waved a fond farewell to all the folks on Entry.

We had a great time, met a lot of nice people, had a few parties, I got my lobsters, fresh cod, mackerel and herring, and Lena got to see her family, friends and all her old schoolmates. (And of course, being a fisherman's daughter, I think she also got to show off her new "catch.")

After watching the people and the houses fade from sight over the stern of the little ferry, we turned to face the bow and began to contemplate the future.

The folks had requested me to sing "The Isles of Magdalene" so many times that I was now inspired to write a song specifically for the people of Entry Island and resolved to include it on my next album, which had to be recorded as soon as I got back to Toronto.

The idea had first passed my mind while standing on Big Hill with Lena but now the whole thing was gnawing at me. I remembered how Lena's dad had told me there had only been thirteen separate families who originally settled on Entry and all the people living there today are their descendants, bearing one or another of these old family surnames.

I still had the piece of paper in my pocket upon which these names had been scribbled and by the time we docked in Amherst I had all the names rearranged into a good rhyming order, and by the time our taxi dropped us off at a small hotel in Grindstone, I had most of the song finished.

I had described the little island fairly well, I thought, and to add even a little more mystery to it than it already had, I purposely left out the name "Entry," so as to arouse the interest and curiosity of those who love to discover by themselves and thereafter visit some of the world's most exotic places. The name of the song is simply "Where Would I Be?" and it's recorded on the album entitled, *Stompin' Tom and the Hockey Song.* (Some of you may already have it.)

The reason we stopped in Grindstone is because while I was there I wanted to rent a car and quickly drive to the other end of the Mags so I could at least say I'd seen them all. When I mentioned car rental to the old guy who ran the hotel, he said, "Don't bother. Take mine."

I was flabbergasted, to say the least. I offered to pay him but again he said, "No way. Just go and have a good time and fill 'er up again with gas when you get back." He then passed me the keys and walked away. His name was Manuel LeBlanc. A bilingual Frenchman with a heart of gold. And it's these kinds of people who still keep this country a great place to live. He didn't know me from Adam, yet treated me like a brother.

For the rest of that afternoon we took in lots of beautiful scenery, stopped in to see a few people in Grosse Ile and Old Harry who Lena was related to, and then drove to the harbour at Grande Entrée. This was as far as the highway could take us, and after stopping to browse around for a few minutes, we headed back to our hotel in Grindstone. All in all, we must have put 150 miles on Manuel's car. And the next morning as we prepared to take our taxi to the airport, I paid for our room and gave the lady whom I presumed to be Manuel's wife, $30 for the use of his car. She didn't want to take it, but I insisted, telling her we had such a great time that this was the least I could do.

Less than an hour and a half later we were back at the Charlottetown airport waiting for our luggage. Once in the car, we drove to Lena's sister Pauline's house to tell her how everyone was on Entry, what a swell time we had, and of course, my plans to record the new song as soon as we got back.

That night we stayed at a nearby motel as Pauline's house was rather small and with her and her husband Gerald and the two girls, Cindy and Patsy, they didn't have much room. And the next day, July 27, we headed back to Toronto.

On August 1, I was interviewed on the Elwood Glover show called "Luncheon Date," broadcast live at noon across the country from the Four Seasons Hotel in downtown Toronto. Elwood always asked some very in-depth questions to his guests and always seemed to get the best out of them. This made his show very popular and interesting and at the same time provided a great opportunity for recording artists and many others to promote and publicize their records and tours, etc., across Canada. His background music for the show at the time was Sonny Caulfield and his orchestra who, later on, recorded one of my songs on a single for Boot Records entitled "We're Trading Hearts."

British Columbia and the Northwest Territories

From the second of August to the fifth, in 1972, me and the boys, Bill and Gary, went into the studio to record the Hockey Song album. Other musicians on the set were Freddy McKenna, a multi-instrumentalist, mainly known for his many appearances on CBC television's "Countrytime" show and "Singalong Jubilee"; Glen Reid, from the band known as The Brannigan Boys and who also made numerous appearances on "Singalong Jubilee"; and John Devlin, who was a member of The Brannigan Boys as well.

Along with "The Hockey Song" I also recorded "Where Would I Be?", the one I had just written about Entry Island, and eleven more, including "The Consumer," which was soon to be aired on CBC's Sunday night television program, "Marketplace."

Immediately after this recording, I took all the same boys up to the CBC studios where we again recorded "The Consumer" song on film and also had the opportunity of meeting Joan Watson and George Finstad, who were about to be the hosts of "Marketplace."

Oops! I guess I forgot to mention before that while we played in Hepworth, Ontario, at the end of June, Jury and Bill Lewis blew the motor out of the old Boot on their way back to Toronto after the show. And while Lena and I were down home in July, Jury had bought a van for us to take on tour. And now that we were ready to go again, we only had one problem. Peter Krytiuk, Jury's younger brother, just tore the side off the new van by slamming into a guardrail on the 401 highway. This took place on the weekend and we were booked to play Thompson, Manitoba, on the following Saturday, August 12. As Thompson is one hell of a long drive, and here it was Monday and the van wasn't fixed yet, we decided to pack up what we could in a couple of cars and a small trailer and head for Thompson, leaving Wayne Hughes behind till the van was fixed—he'd meet us in Thompson later.

As it turned out, the van was ready to go the day after we left and Wayne was only one day behind us. We arrived in Thompson late on Friday night, and late on Saturday afternoon, just in time to set up for the show, Wayne arrived with the van. He was dog-tired so I told him to go and catch a couple of hours' sleep while the rest of us tended to the setup.

Just before Wayne arrived, something else that struck me funny also happened. When me and the boys got to the arena, there was a car with three or four important-looking gentlemen sitting there waiting for us. And as the boys walked into the arena these men summoned me over and started walking towards me.

They said they were from the mayor's office and they had come to welcome me to Thompson. They gave me a couple of pins and souvenirs and while I was thanking them for their thoughtfulness, I guess they thought they had softened me up enough for this gem:

"We sure like your song 'Sudbury Saturday,' Tom, and we would like to ask you a small favour?" Thinking they were going to request it or something, I said, "Sure. I'll be glad to oblige."

They proceeded: "Well, this being an INCO town, nice and quiet, you understand, and knowing how considerate you've always been in not wanting to stir things up and all, we would appreciate it if you *wouldn't* sing that song tonight."

"Just a minute," I said. "Do I understand you gentlemen correctly? You're asking me to *not* sing 'Sudbury Saturday

Night' on my show tonight?"

"That's right, Tom. You know how sensitive our—?" I didn't wait to hear the rest.

"Look, boys," I said. "This is a free country, even in Thompson, Manitoba. And if the INCO workers or anyone else in this town want to hear 'Sudbury Saturday Night' then this is the night they're going to hear it." And with that, I took one of the guys' hands, plunked the trinkets back into it and marched myself into the building.

I never saw any of them again. And ironically, the first song the audience shouted out for me to do that night, and even before I stepped up to the microphone, was "Sudbury Saturday Night." I sang it immediately, and several times more before the show was over. There was absolutely no trouble at all, and the crowd loved it. And that was the record we sold the most of that night.

When I told the boys about the incident a little later, they wanted to know, "Where were those guys from, anyway? The nineteenth century?"

From Thompson, Manitoba, we drove to Vancouver where we taped two television shows before commencing our tour of B.C. First we were guests on the "Irish Rovers" show and then "The Juliette Show," both on the CBC. We understood these would be aired later, but we never saw them, due to playing concerts on the nights they were shown.

Maclean's magazine also had a huge article on Stompin' Tom in it in August 1972. This was a reprint of the article written for the *Atlantic Advocate* by Alden Nowlan which had appeared earlier that year. Alden had been visiting Halifax with his son and attended my concert on February 23. It was at this time that he came to my hotel room and conducted the interview. I especially remember how surprised he was when I mentioned something I had read in Homer's *Iliad* concerning the "winged words" from the gods. When he asked me where I got that phrase from, I kiddingly said, "Skinners Pond University." He laughed.

There was also another full-page ad in *RPM* magazine that month and I remember one of the boys saying, "With all the money Jury's spending on ads lately, I guess you'll soon have another number one hit, eh Tom?" At this, I just shrugged and told him to eff off.

Our tour of British Columbia officially started in New Westminster that year and from there we went to Nanaimo, on Vancouver Island. We then played Campbell River and crossed again to the mainland to play Powell River. From there, it was back to the island again to catch a ferry to Prince Rupert, where the western end of B.C.'s northern east–west highway begins. I must say that this ferry route is one of the most scenic I've ever been on. The ferry wends its way in and out of so many channels and between so many forested islands that you can't help but feel you are really the first person here, just as the early discoverers felt so many years ago. It's absolutely fascinating.

It was while I was in Prince Rupert that I went to the radio station, as I often had occasion to do when the time allowed, and asked the country DJ if he was playing my records and especially the song about the bridge disaster in Vancouver as it had recently gone to number two on the charts. He said he hadn't because he never received one, but he was playing "Bud the Spud" and a few others. When I asked him about my previous number one hit, "The Moon Man Newfie," he said he'd never heard of it, but he'd certainly play it if only he had it.

It wasn't hard to believe that he'd been playing some Stompin' Tom records, at least lately, due to the fact that we were buying ads for the show that was scheduled for that very night. But for the rest of the year I couldn't be sure. I knew his station had received the records we spoke of because I happened to have a list of stations they were sent to, and his station was on the list.

At any rate, I went out to my car and found the album that contained the song "The Bridge Came Tumbling Down" and took it in to him. He thanked me profusely and said he would be sure to play it from now on, as well as other cuts from the same album. I thanked him very much and said if I didn't see him at the show tonight I probably wouldn't be able to in the morning, as we had a very busy schedule and had to hit the road fairly early.

I didn't see him at the show that night and the next morning, even though we were pressed for time, I decided to go to the station to thank him one more time and say goodbye. (Sort of good public relations, if you know what I mean.)

There was no one at the front desk so I just wandered along the hall till I came to the room where we had had our conversation the day before. And there in the wastebasket just inside the door, not a foot from where we'd been talking, was the album I had just given him. It had been bent over and snapped in two, still inside the jacket with the cellophane unopened.

"That son-of-a-bitch," I said to myself, as I stepped back into the hall. Just then a side door at the end of the hall opened and there he stood for a split second. He spotted me and quickly went out the back door. By the time I got to the door, he was getting into his car and he drove away like a bat out of hell. I retraced my steps, went out the front door and got into my car. I called the boys on the CB radio and said, "Let's get the hell out of here before I kill someone." We drove to Kitimat and played the next gig before I told them what had happened.

I'm not sure whether we played Terrace or Vanderhoof on this first tour of northern B.C., but I know that Smithers, Burns Lake and Prince George were definitely included.

From there we left Highway 16 altogether and went south to Quesnel on Highway 97. We played there and continued south to Williams Lake and then on to 100 Mile House. The thing I remember most about 100 Mile House is that the population at the time was only about two hundred and we had over eight hundred at the concert. Wherever they came from I don't know, but having four times as many people at a show as there are in town must be some kind of a record, for sure.

We now doubled back, going north again on 97, through Prince George and on up to Dawson Creek. Here we did two shows before going on up to Fort St. John, on the Alcan Highway. (Alaska–Canadian, and sometimes referred to as just the Alaska Highway. I have a song on one of my albums about this highway called the "Alcan Run.") Farther on up the Alcan we played Fort Nelson and again we turned around and doubled back. And by the first of October we

crossed the B.C./Alberta border and played Grande Prairie
that night.

Now for those who think, wow, this sure seems like one
hell of a lot of driving, this tour was not over by a long shot.

We then headed straight north through Peace River
country and right on up to the Northwest Territories. This
was the second of October and the snow was already flying.
On the afternoon of October 4, we landed in Hay River on
the south shore of Great Slave Lake, a distance of about 530
miles, and over half of this on secondary roads, not to mention the couple of snowstorms we encountered. We played
Hay River that night and the next day we drove through the
Wood Buffalo Park to Fort Smith, a distance of two hundred
miles of straight woods with nothing in between. The only
time we stopped was to take some pictures of a number of
very tame buffalo that were just walking along the side of the
road. You could walk right up to them and they wouldn't
even move.

The next morning after playing Fort Smith, we all got
quite a chuckle just before we left. There was a drunken
Indian guy slouched down on the front steps of the bar next
door and trying his best to go to sleep. Unfortunately (or
fortunately) for him his little white dog kept licking his face
as if to say, come on, we got to go home. First the guy would
be slouched over in one direction and after being licked and
slurped on that side he'd come to, just long enough to wipe
his face a little and then, in an effort to get away from the
dog, he'd slouch over to the other side, only to have the dog
walk around to that side and start slurping on his face again.
This went on for quite a while till the dog got frustrated. He
then ran around the corner of the building and came back
with two other Indian guys who picked the first feller up and
guided him home. This was all being supervised by the little
dog who was now barking happily and wagging his tail. I still
laugh every time I think of this.

Our next stop was still 260 miles north of where we were
(the way the crow flies), but another 520 miles the way we
had to go. We were heading for Yellowknife on the far
northern shore of Great Slave Lake. And unfortunately, we
couldn't just cross over the lake, we had to drive around it.

We doubled back through Wood Buffalo Park passing just a little south of Hay River and then headed out on No. 3 to Fort Providence on the north side of the Mackenzie River. We arrived there late at night after fighting our way through another snowstorm and that's where we stayed.

As we gassed up the next morning and the guy took a look at our Ontario licence plates, he said, "You greenhorns ain't gonna tackle that road to Yellowknife today, are you? It's 150 miles to the next gas station and if you go off the road there won't likely be anyone coming by to help you." When I assured him that I was no greenhorn and that I'd made it through a lot worse roads than these, he looked at me kind of funny and said, "You wouldn't happen to be Stompin' Tom, would you?" When I told him I was, he said that he'd seen me on TV and heard my records on the radio a few times. He also had an uncle or a brother who had met me while I was playing the Maple Leaf Hotel in Timmins a while back and he wanted to know if I could give him a couple of autographs. "No problem," I said, as I dug a couple of small pictures out from the back seat. "You gonna be at the Yellowknife show?" I asked. "I will now," he said. And as he thanked me I said, "I'll see you there then." He was still waving as I drove away.

The road ahead wasn't quite as bad as we had anticipated, and by one o'clock in the afternoon we arrived in Rae Edzo with only about sixty miles left to go. The weather had turned colder, but the road was good and we arrived in Yellowknife about an hour later.

The motel we booked into was really not a motel at all but a series of trailer homes with a different number on each door; each trailer was equipped with a stove and fridge and plenty of dishes for the purpose of private housekeeping. These types of lodgings are quite common throughout the far north, as they are easy to move from place to place whenever the job moves.

As soon as we got settled down, one of the boys went to buy some groceries and decided to do some cooking of his own for a change. And while this was going on I went to look up a fellow by the name of Leo Treeshin, who was one of the people responsible for bringing in the show.

Leo was from Mattawa, Ontario, and had come to Yellow-knife to follow the construction boom several years before. Ever since he heard the song "Big Joe Mufferaw" he had been a Stompin' Tom fan and had just recently contacted Jury to see if he could get me booked in the north.

I found Leo to be an extremely nice guy who couldn't do enough to help a fellow, but today he was terribly busy and unfortunately we didn't have much time to talk. At any rate, the show went on that night without a hitch. We had a great crowd of people from everywhere in Canada. And those were just the kind of people I was singing about.

This audience was composed of people from Newfound-land to Vancouver Island, and they'd all come here to follow their dream of finding a better way to live than the dog-eat-dog rat race of the larger cities. It was a little colder here but hearts were a whole lot warmer. And I could say this about practically all the people living in the north. I don't know what it is, maybe adversity, maybe the weather, or maybe just a oneness with the land, but it seems that all people who go north expecting to stay for just a little while eventually wind up making it their home for a long while. In the end I guess it just might be the inner knowing that you're living among people who really do care. At least that was my impression from the people who attended these northern concerts and who obtained autographs after the shows.

Our next gig was to be in Peace River, almost eight hundred miles from Yellowknife. Away down in the "sunny south," as one fellow described it, even though it was still 340 miles north of Edmonton, Alberta.

Anyhow, we headed out to cross the Mackenzie again and across the 60th parallel. Just into Alberta we hit another snowstorm and Wayne Hughes hit a patch of ice under the snow and careened the new van into the left-hand ditch, rolling it over on its left side into a huge snowbank. As I'm usually driving ahead, leading the troupe, I wouldn't have noticed he went missing except the boys in the rear vehicle called me on the CB.

By the time I got back, Billy Lewis, who never missed an opportunity to film something with his movie camera, was sitting on the top of the right-hand side of the overturned van looking down through the open window of the passenger side, and with his camera cocked and rolling, he was hollering, "Smile, Wayne, smile." (Such was the distorted sense of humour of my indescribable Cape Breton guitar player. Poor Wayne could have been dead as far as Billy cared; all he wanted was his pictures.)

"Get that camera the hell down out of there," I shouted, "and help get this door open so Wayne can get out."

"Do I have to, Boss?" he said, with that crazy look that always had Gary Empey rolling around in stitches. I didn't want to let them know it, but I almost laughed myself as I thought what a useless pair of fuckin' assholes I had to get stranded with, especially in the middle of nowhere.

A couple of minutes later, pale-faced, dishevelled and all shook up, Wayne crawled out from the top of the van mumbling something, but otherwise in pretty good shape considering what he'd just been through.

"How do you feel now?" Billy asked. As if Wayne had just come out of a steam bath or something. I can't remember the answer Wayne gave but "you son-of-a-bitch" was part of it. By now, we were all laughing and throwing snowballs at each other.

The snow was still falling; there was no wind, and the only sound that broke the silence was a lot of crazy laughter and the snapping of beer caps.

With absolutely no traffic up here, I decided to take a drive down the road to see if I could find someone to help us get out of the ditch. We hadn't come upon a house or any kind of dwelling for the last fifty miles or so, and when I took off I didn't know how far I'd have to go for help or how long it would take me.

About five or six miles down the road, there was a building on my left with a lot of heavy equipment around. The kind they use in road construction. The place looked really desolate, but after I drove by I thought I'd better turn around and check it out anyway.

After trying the front door and then walking around to the back, I saw a pick-up still running and a guy inside the building. I told him what my problem was and he said not to worry and he'd come up the road with me to see what he could do. I expected him to follow me in his pick-up but when I looked around behind me, there he was coming along with a big road grader.

Once at the scene, he went right to work. He took out some heavy ropes and chains (the van was in about sixty feet off the road) and placed a big hook on the frame. After another hook was attached to the grader he jumped in, pulled up the slack, and gently brought the van back onto her wheels again. He placed the hook in the front and said, "Okay, if one of you boys will just get in and steer we'll have your van out of there in no time."

One quick look around told me none of them wanted the job so I went over and jumped in. There was at least a foot of snow on the level and as much as three or four feet in the drifts. When I felt the tow rope tighten, I just grabbed the wheel and braced myself.

He couldn't pull me straight out of the ditch, of course, but had to drag me along for several hundred feet while I kept steering and inching myself slowly but surely towards the road.

Every time he dragged me through a large drift, I couldn't see a damn thing. And with the van hitting rocks and bumps under the snow, the pitches and jumps I was taking almost rolled me over again a couple of times. When I finally got close to the hard snowbank the ploughs had made, the van took one hell of a jump and a tumble, and after hitting my head several times on the ceiling, eureka, I found myself back on the road.

As I emerged from the van, in a lot worse shape than Wayne was in, I offered to pay the guy for his trouble, but once again, as in the Magdalene Islands, the payment was refused. "Well, the least I can do is give you a couple of my tapes," I said. And as he casually rumbled down the road the boys and I proceeded to straighten out the contents of the van. The snow had been heavy enough to cushion its fall and except for one or two little scratches the van looked as if nothing had ever happened.

Some three hundred miles or so later we played Peace River and then drove down to Edmonton, a distance of another three hundred miles, and guested on the Tommy

Banks television show as well as doing a concert in one of the arenas. And by the fifteenth or sixteenth of October we played Calgary and at last we were on the home stretch.

On the way back we only did two or three more concerts, which sort of broke up the monotony of the long drive, and by the last week in October of 1972 we were back in Toronto.

The distance I had driven so far this year was over 16,200 miles and before the year was out, I still had to drive to Prince Edward Island and back, which would add another 2,000 miles. This would eventually bring the number of miles to 18,200. There may be some truck drivers who drive these kinds of distances, and that's the job they get paid for. But an entertainer must do this on top of his regular job if he ever intends to make it in the music business.

Back in Toronto the boys and I took a few days off before doing a few gigs just outside of town, not more than a hundred miles from Toronto, and then I gave them the rest of the month of November off.

The Marten Hartwell Story

IT WAS DURING THIS TIME, while I was writing some new songs for my next album, that the Marten Hartwell story broke. It was on the news everywhere, how Hartwell, the pilot of a light plane, had left Cambridge Bay in the Northwest Territories with three passengers on the evening of November 8, and was supposed to arrive in Yellowknife later that night, but never did.

The story at the time had it that Mr. Hartwell was approached by a federal government nurse, asking him to convey a couple of her patients to the Yellowknife hospital for some emergency attention that couldn't be provided in Cambridge Bay. One patient was an Inuit lady who was having some kind of complications with her pregnancy and the other was a young Inuit boy by the name of Davey Kootook who was suffering from a bad case of appendicitis.

It later came out that Mr. Hartwell was reluctant to fly that day because of a bad weather forecast predicting a storm, but due to the urgency of the situation he decided to take the chance.

The flying distance would have been approximately five hundred miles but after they were up for an hour or so the storm seemed to sneak up on them and somehow they became disoriented. It was now after dark and though there was a signal station near their half-way mark at Lake Contwoyta, they somehow missed it completely.

The speculation at the time was that maybe Hartwell's flight instruments jammed in some way but, at any rate, instead of continuing to fly in a south-southwesterly direction towards Yellowknife, he began to fly in a more west-by-southwesterly direction which took him some two hundred miles off his course, and sometime during that night in the middle of a blinding snowstorm the plane came down and crashed near Lake Hotah, some seventy-five miles south of Echo Bay on the Great Bear Lake.

The Inuit woman and the nurse seemed to have been killed upon impact while Mr. Hartwell and the boy survived, only to face several weeks of extreme cold, more snow, and the terrible thoughts of dying from starvation.

While Hartwell couldn't move around too much, due to the fact that he had sustained two badly broken ankles, he stayed near the crash site and kept his battery-operated signalling device beeping for help while the boy went searching for firewood and whatever forms of lichen he could find to make a little soup. According to Hartwell, the boy did this every day until he finally succumbed to the pain and the effects of his acute appendicitis and died.

Hartwell had somehow survived a few days longer until his beeper signal grew faint but was finally heard at the last minute by the search and rescue planes that had been circling the area almost continuously for a whole month. To the relief of the whole country, Marten Hartwell was rescued on December 9, 1972, but many were also saddened to hear that all the others had perished.

While this story was gripping the whole nation I was busy writing the song, and by the time the outcome was known I finished the last verse and immediately went into the studio to record it on a single. It was released to the radio stations about a week later. And they played it.

But, alas, they didn't play it for too long. After a more thorough examination of the crash site, it was discovered that, towards the end and just after Davey Kootook died, Mr. Hartwell had partaken of an unspecified quantity of frozen human flesh. To this he allegedly admitted, stating he believed at the time that if he had not done so he would not have survived.

It now became an open and closed case. While some people asked themselves what they might have done if faced with the same set of circumstances, others just closed the door, refusing to believe that Mr. Hartwell was anything other than an out-and-out cannibal.

It is my belief that the radio immediately sided with the latter position and as quickly as they had begun to play "The Marten Hartwell Story," they just as quickly snapped it off the air.

This was rather unfortunate for everyone, I thought, as the song mentioned nothing about the eating of flesh but concentrated more on the heroism of Davey Kootook. Although he was a mere lad of thirteen years old, he unselfishly shared what little food he could find and assisted the disabled pilot for as long as he could withstand his own suffering. An exemplary human being who certainly deserves to be sung about. "Had it not been for Davey's help, right from the beginning," said Hartwell, "there's just no way I could have made it."

For what may or may not have been one small error committed by a lone man despairing for his life somewhere in the cruel vastness of the Northwest Territories, the good deeds of another great Canadian hero were soon swept under the rug and just as quickly forgotten.

The writing of the song was finished on December 12, 1972, and it was recorded the next day as a single. Although the play stopped abruptly, it was eventually included on my next album entitled *To It and At It,* and the same album went on to win a Juno Award for best album of the year in 1974. Here are the words:

THE MARTEN HARTWELL STORY

CHORUS:
Lost up in no man's land of the Northwest
    Territories,
They were lost up in no man's land, The Marten
    Hartwell Story.

1.

*On November the eighth of seventy-two, north of the
    Arctic Circle,*
*A plane took off from Cambridge Bay and the pilot's
    name was Hartwell,*
*He had to make it to Yellowknife although the night
    was stormin',*
*To save the lives of an Eskimo boy and a pregnant
    Eskimo woman.*

2.

*Oh Mr. Hartwell, said the nurse, I pray that you
    will guide us,*
*To save this woman with her child and the boy with
    appendicitis;*
*But the wind it blew and the storm it grew and the
    signal of Contwoyta,*
*They missed by miles and flying wild they crashed
    beside Lake Hotah.*

REPEAT CHORUS

3.

*Now Judy Hill the federal nurse, she never lived to
    waken,*
*And the life of the mother and her child were both
    soon after taken;*
*But the pilot woke to find himself and the Eskimo boy
    were livin',*
*Left in pain beside the plane to search the skies of
    heaven.*

4.

Day by day the pilot lay with both his ankles broken,
*And it took the lad everything he had to keep the fire
    stoken;*
*While in the sky, too far away, the rescue teams were
    seekin',*
*A signal wave that might be traced to Hartwell's
    radio beacon.*

REPEAT CHORUS

5.

*After nineteen days the aerial search was said to be
    completed,*
*But someone cried "They're still alive," and the
    search must be repeated;*
*And the day the "beep" was finally heard is a day
    we'll all remember,*
*The man was found safe and sound on the ninth
    day of December.*

6.

*Hartwell said he should have died at thirty-five
    below zero,*
*And the reason Hartwell did survive, the boy had
    died a hero;*
*He brought me food when I couldn't move, while he
    himself grew feeble,*
*Yes, Davey Kootook died a saint and a credit to his
    people.*
*Davey Kootook died a saint and a credit to his
    people.*

REPEAT CHORUS then fade . . .
*The Marten Hartwell Story, the Marten Hartwell
    Story, the Marten Hartwell Story.*

From the Horseshoe to "the Movies"

A S I SIT HERE REVIEWING my thoughts for 1972 I realize
I left out a couple of things. As well as touring and doing
other guest shots on TV I also found time to appear on the
"Pierre Berton Show." He interviewed me once in the spring
and another time around the first of August. This latter show
was aired sometime in September while I was on tour out
west. I enjoyed these interviews very much, not only because
Pierre is a very informed and proud Canadian but he also
shows great interest and empathy towards the person being
interviewed. Although I was too busy to see the airing of
either one of these shows, those who did see them assured me
that both the questions and answers were very enlightening.

I also performed on Ian Tyson's television show in the
latter part of November or the first of December. I was also
told at the time that this particular show would also be aired
in fifty-six American markets.

It was also during the month of November that three of
my albums, namely, *Northlands Zone, On Tragedy Trail* and
Bud the Spud had run their contractual course with Dominion Records and were now re-released immediately on our
own label, Boot Records. The *Bud the Spud* album also came
accompanied with another gold album for sales of over
another $100,000 just in the past eleven months. This

234

marked the second gold for *Bud the Spud* since its release in the fall of 1969. (This would have been a platinum record had there been such a thing in those days.)

Now, in December of '72, from the fourth to the ninth, the boys and I were once again in the Horseshoe Tavern. And all this week Jack Star, the owner, was celebrating the bar's silver anniversary. It had been twenty-five years since he opened the "Shoe" and was proud to proclaim that in all that time the entertainment had been nothing but straight good old country music. And that, of course, was exactly what his thousands of loyal patrons had always come to hear.

Along with banners flying and hundreds of well-wishers coming and going all week, I continued singing the "Horseshoe Hotel Song" several times every night. This was one of the songs included on the *Live* album I had recorded in the Horseshoe a year or so previous and it was sure getting a real workout on an occasion as special as this.

On Saturday night the place was just hoppin'. And with the stage all decorated with wreaths and flowers, we invited Jack on the stage to receive his well-deserved accolades, to take a few pictures and give a little speech.

With members of the press in attendance, Jack told about the time he bought the building and how he'd missed by only one day obtaining the very first liquor licence ever awarded in the city of Toronto, and how he'd always been so partial to country music and to all those people who continually came to his bar over the years to hear it.

He reminisced about some of the good times and some of the bad, and named some of the great country stars who had frequently performed on the Horseshoe stage, both from Nashville and elsewhere, and then out of a clear blue sky, he came out with this:

"But, ladies and gentlemen, of all the great entertainers that ever played on this stage, the one that jingled my till the most, the one who broke all previous attendance records and set new ones, the guy who came from nowhere and surprised all of us, and the guy we love because he sings all those songs that make us proud to be Canadian is none other than this young man standing right here: Stompin' Tom Connors."

With that, I thought the crowd would take the roof off the joint. And while I waved and took a slight bow towards the audience, Jack reached into a box he was carrying and pulled out a gold album of *Live at the Horseshoe* and passed it to me, saying, "This is one you never expected, Tom, and Jury and all the gang from Dominion Records and Boot Records asked me if I'd present it to you, and I'm more than happy to do so. And whatever you do, Tom, just keep on stompin'."

At the mention of the word, that's what everyone started to do—stomp. And as I tried to say thank you to everyone who had bought the record and helped to make the gold album possible, several people were dumping some pretty stiff drinks into my water jug that I usually have on stage and some of it was falling into the flowers.

The press took a couple of pictures of Jack and me with the gold album propped in front of us, and after we answered a few questions, we left the stage.

I had a short set to do later, and after wishing everybody a forthcoming Merry Christmas, we all drank up and departed.

When we were in the car Lena said to me, "Wow! That's the fourth gold album you got this year. What are you going to do with them all?"

"Melt them all down and make a wedding ring," I said. With that, she just snuggled up close and remained that way till we got home.

Lena and I were now living together on Searle Avenue. Jury's mom and dad had bought their new house in Toronto and along with Jury's younger brother and sister, Peter and Mary, they had moved out of the house on Searle some weeks ago. And with Jury spending most of his nights with his family, it pretty well left me in this large house alone.

Lena was working in another part of the city and maintaining her own apartment but it didn't seem to make very good sense to keep both places going, so we just decided to drop one and move in together.

At this point I was notified that the premier of Prince Edward Island, Alex Campbell, wished to bestow upon me the honour of being the Island's goodwill ambassador on

December 31, New Year's Eve. And on New Year's Day of 1973, the first day of the Island's Centennial Year, I was to be presented to Canada's governor general, Roland Michener, as the Island's official ambassador.

I decided I should go down to P.E.I. to accept this honour, and I thought it might also be a good opportunity to spend Christmas with Russell and Cora in Skinners Pond. So without much ado, we packed up the car and away we went.

We picked up most of our Christmas presents on our way down and arrived in Skinners Pond around the nineteenth of December. The school by now had been raised on its new foundation and the outside was pretty well completed. They were working on the inside and were expecting to be finished by the end of January.

In the meantime we spent a fairly quiet but enjoyable Christmas. We had a small tree, and the old farm cooking, of course, was scrumptious. We stayed about eleven days, did a little visiting, played and sang a few songs for some of the neighbours and just relaxed or played cards now and again till it was time to go.

A couple of times just after Christmas we had rain, which took a lot of the snow away, and by the time we arrived in Charlottetown the roads and the streets were bare.

On the night of the thirty-first there were throngs of people outside Government House and in between a couple of the many speeches, they had me sing some of my songs about Prince Edward Island, which I did with just my own guitar accompaniment from the outside balcony. After this the premier presented me with the goodwill ambassador scroll.

About an hour later, Lena and I were invited to some sort of a "get-acquainted" party at the Confederation Centre where we were officially introduced to all the dignitaries of government and everyone else who might have been a somebody.

It was here we were joined by Jury, who had flown down for the occasion and though he was a little late, he was still on time for the New Year's Centennial Party and Ball which we were now about to attend in the next room. Jury, who never seemed to want to miss one of these formal parties, was dressed in a big tuxedo. Lena was wearing a long gown.

And yours truly was dressed to the nines (black shirt and jeans, black leather vest, black cowboy boots, and all very nicely topped off with a big black cowboy hat). Urbane, suave, debonair, wouldn't you say?

I only had one dance with Lena and then Jury took over the post while I spent my time talking with people and "tipping" glasses of champagne. (Or was it "tippling" glasses of champagne? I just forget.)

At midnight, amid the din of laughter, buzzers and horns, Lena and I danced the New Year in and sang "Happy Birthday" to Prince Edward Island. Shortly after that we left to go down to the Prince Edward Lounge and wish Happy New Year to our friends Johnny and Judy.

We were supposed to have met the governor general that night but due to bad weather conditions en route from Ottawa his plane was delayed. I met him the next morning, however, at his New Year's levee, where we also took some pictures.

We then went to Lena's sister Pauline's house for a short visit and drove back to Toronto. Jury took the plane.

Most of January '73 was pretty slow. Other than writing a few songs and being visited for a few days by Stevedore Steve and his wife, Gini, we went out to a few clubs and tried to catch up on what our friends were doing.

Jury and everybody else at the office were busy preparing again for a Massey Hall concert, on January 20, and I was deciding whether I would have guests on the show this time. As I knew it would be great exposure for some of our Boot artists, I decided to include Bud Roberts, vocalist; Delmer Dorey, accordionist; Clare Adlam, fiddler; Kent Brockwell, vocalist; and Stevedore Steve. Unfortunately for Steve, he was already booked for the date but the others were free and they jumped at the opportunity.

The show went on as scheduled with a lot less tension than the last time and the crowd seemed to enjoy the variety, although the papers later said they interviewed a number of people who said they would have liked to see more of Stompin' Tom. (You can't win 'em all.)

Among the dignitaries present that night and sitting right near the front was Toronto's newly elected mayor,

David Crombie. As I recognized him and also remembered reading how he was advocating the preservation of Massey Hall while others wanted to tear it down, I acknowledged him to the crowd and gave him my support for his cause. As David stood up to take a bow, the applause of the audience indicated their overall approval.

It later came out in the papers that David had once worked in the tobacco fields of Tillsonburg as I had done, and had always been an avid country music fan. He also had several Stompin' Tom records and played them frequently, even in the mayor's office at city hall.

Incidentally, when Toronto's new city hall was completed a little later on that year, David sent me his personal invitation to be his first official guest in the new mayor's office. I accepted of course, and in front of several press and television cameras he welcomed me to city hall, where we exchanged gifts. He gave me a beautiful picture book on the history of Toronto and I gave him a complete set of my albums. He laughed as I signalled to one of my boys outside the door to bring him in a large seventy-five pound bag of Prince Edward Island table potatoes. As I plunked my ass down on the mayor's chair and looked at him from behind the huge desk, I said, "Not a bad setup you got here, Davey. I wouldn't mind having a job like this myself." "Well," he said, "if you teach me how to play the guitar and stomp my foot I'll make you an even trade." We both laughed, and as I left I said I'd have to give his offer some serious thought.

A few days after the Massey Hall concert, the boys and I flew down to Halifax to videotape a couple more CBC "Countrytime" shows with Myrna Lorrie, Vic Mullen and the Hickorys. Two of the other guests on these shows were Donna Moon and the Chapperells. Of the four songs I sang on these two shows, one of them was the "Marten Hartwell Story," but the other three have now slipped my mind.

Back in Toronto I got wind of a Prince Edward Island songwriting competition that was going on. They wanted all songwriters to submit a song for P.E.I.'s Centennial Year and it had to be written in plenty of time to have it recorded before the first of July, the day Her Majesty, the Queen, was scheduled to visit Charlottetown. That's when I wrote

"Prince Edward Island, Happy Birthday." I submitted it but I never heard back from the committee. They must have thought it was a real dud to not even bother to send back a thank-you note for the submission. I later recorded the song anyway and sang it everywhere for the rest of the year.

In the early part of February I did a phone-in show called "Cross Country Check-up" on CBC radio out of Montreal. The interviewer was Pierre Pascau. And once he opened the lines I was answering questions posed by people from coast to coast in Canada. Most wanted to know how many sheets of plywood I stomped through in a year, how many heels I had to replace on my cowboy boots, and everything from what Irish moss is used for to when I had my breakfast last. But everybody was friendly and wished me well in my endeavour to keep singing songs about Canada. The interview lasted about an hour.

On February 9, Lena invited all our friends to the house to celebrate my thirty-seventh birthday and the house was packed. Most of the guests were musicians so you can imagine what kind of a shindig it really was. Everybody sang and danced till daybreak, and all those who were too far gone just flaked out on one of the extra beds or crashed on the floor. The next day as all the stragglers left, me and Joe Gogarty (Brannigan) were still up. What doing? Playing chess, of course.

On the sixteenth of the month I made another appearance on the "Tommy Hunter Show" and on the twenty-third Lena and I got officially engaged.

We figured that after all, if we were going to live together we might as well tie the knot. We had known each other for over a year and a half now and all the "little arrows" seemed to point towards complete compatibility. So-o-o! I got that gal a ring, and we set the big date for November 2, 1973. By then my summer tour would be over and our honeymoon could be freely planned without the usual time constraints.

The following day, Saturday, we went to visit my friends, the Fordham, Osborne and Ens families, in Port Elgin and Southampton, Ontario. I think this was the first time they had ever met Lena, and when they heard of our engagement I had to take a little razzing, especially from Ira Osborne and

Pete Ens. They remembered that I had said a number of years before that there was no way that I'd ever get married and there wasn't a woman born that could ever tie me down. Well, now they were making me eat the words and they were gloating. It was all in good humour, of course, and soon the razzing subsided. Lena got along real well with Olive, Liz and Irene, and promised to make sure they'd all be invited to the wedding.

As soon as we got back and opened the door of the house the phone was ringing. It was Jury. "Where have you been the last three days?" he said. "I've been trying to get you everywhere. We've got to talk immediately. There's a movie company out of Montreal who are extremely interested in making you a movie star, so stay home, I'm coming over right away."

When I told Lena what Jury said, she got all excited. "Wow! That's great. You're gonna be a big movie star. Maybe we'll even go to Hollywood." "Oh, I don't know about that," I said. "I think I'd just as soon stay home, look out the window, and watch the cows fly by."

In less than fifteen minutes Jury was at the door babbling a mile a minute. I told him to come in and sit down, have a beer, and start all over again. I couldn't understand a damn word he said.

When he finally calmed down and got everything out straight, it sounded like everything was quite legitimate and all the movie company was waiting for was an answer from Jury as to whether I'd be interested. And if so, their representatives could be in Toronto within a couple of days to hold meetings and discuss the details.

"Well," I said, "it really sounds too good to be true but there's no harm in having a meeting. By doing this we can at least find out what they're up to."

The following morning Jury called them up and told them I was interested. The meetings took place on the following weekend, the second and third of March.

Through the course of the meetings, it was revealed that D.A.L. Productions, a subsidiary of Cinepix of Montreal, wanted to film three movies on Stompin' Tom, not just one. The first one was to be a full-length country music musical featuring myself and my songs, which would be filmed in the middle of May and released in the late summer or early fall. The second would be filmed and released the following year, in 1974, and the third in 1975. The latter two movies would portray me in a more serious role, playing myself in situations not uncommon to things that happened during my career. All three movies would be full-length feature films and Boot Records, our publishing companies, and myself would always retain the rights to release all soundtracks.

The filming of the second and third movies, however, was to be conditional. The sooner they made their money back on the first movie, the sooner the second would go into production, and if I would keep my fee down to a bare bones minimum, this would help to insure the filming of the second from which I would receive a much higher fee as well as recouping my previous shortfall.

While this sounded fair at the time, especially to a guy with a certain number of "stars in his eyes," I agreed to the deal on a slight condition of my own: that I could appoint Jury as a co-producer to insure that I would not be portrayed or filmed in such a way that might be unreasonable to me.

Within the next couple of days the contract was drawn up and in the presence of our respective counsel we signed the agreement on the seventh of March, 1973. The photos and the story were then released to the press.

The other Boot recording artists selected to appear as guests in the film were Sharon Lowness, Bobby Lalonde, Joey Tardif, Chris Scott, Kent Brockwell, and my two long-standing band members, Billy Lewis and Gary Empey. All the inside filming was done on the stage of Toronto's Horse-shoe Tavern and the movie was to be called "Across This Land, with Stompin' Tom Connors." There would also be a tribute song composed in my honour by Freddy Dixon and sung by him at the end of the film, though he never appeared on camera.

As a piece of trivia, it may be noted that this movie would mark the first time a full-length musical had ever been produced in Canada. It was filmed in May, and the première was attended by Lena and me with our entire wedding entourage on November 2 at the Imperial Theatre in downtown Toronto. This all took place in 1973.

Mayor Crombie and the CNE

On March 8, the day after the movie contract was signed, the boys and I flew up to Moosonee, on James Bay, and did two concerts, one on the ninth and one on the tenth. This was almost like another homecoming to me as many of these people had heard me on radio when I had my half-hour program on CKGB in Timmins some eight or nine years before. They used to listen to my program faithfully and bought a lot of my records by mail. They had never seen me or attended one of my concerts, but on this occasion they seemed to have made up their minds that they weren't going to miss this one big opportunity. They came out in droves.

Everybody from the area came to the show on the first night and everybody from the area came to the show on the second night. I've never seen anything quite like it. Two identical audiences attending two identical shows.

They wanted to hear the newer songs but they also wanted to hear all the older songs I used to sing live on the radio. They especially loved the songs with a story, and my song about "May, the Millwright's Daughter," which mentions a guy who worked in Moosonee, was continuously requested. Before we left town on Sunday morning, I don't think there was one person who didn't buy a new album or at least get an autograph on an old one. Some of these good folks also gave me a few little personal gifts before leaving, which I still have.

243

Back in Toronto on the twelfth of the month, I received my third Juno Award. It was presented to me at the Inn on the Park by none other than the mayor, David Crombie, who was lauded for having given the best speech of the night. In part, he said: "My father once told me the only difference between politics and the theatre is that the theatre knows when it's absurd." And, "People have said that Stompin' Tom's music is not culture. But I say that it's real."

As I accepted the award and thanked everybody, I couldn't help but think to myself, "With fans like David Crombie, the people's choice for mayor of Toronto, standing on a stage in front of national television cameras and proclaiming to all of Canada that he endorses Stompin' Tom, one of my long-term objectives is finally being met." Namely, to try and prove that a simple and friendless orphan kid with nothing can come from nowhere, and be accepted and respected as an equal individual among all people of all ranks living anywhere. It just takes a lot of good old-fashioned, honest determination to find out the results are well worth the effort.

What detractors call impossibilities, I call possible, probable facts.

Right after the Junos I did several short films of the documentary type for some independent producers whose names escape me at the present. The most important of these, however, was a short movie called *Catch the Sun*, which was filmed one afternoon at the Horseshoe Tavern, while I was singing "Algoma Central No. 69." The movie was mainly a documentary about the beautiful Agawa Canyon in northern Ontario through which the Algoma Central Railway runs. And as I was the only one who had a song about the area, they wanted me to perform it in the film.

The thing I remember most about the shooting of my portion of the film was the huge camera they were using. I had never in my life seen one like this; it was gigantic. It was something new at the time, and I kid you not, the cameraman first stepped up onto a chair and then crawled right into the camera and disappeared.

It was explained to me that this camera was very unique in that it was able to film things in gigantic proportions. And they weren't just kidding.

When Lena and I were later invited to Ontario Place to see the film, we were taken into a specially built theatre called the Cinesphere. And here, the screen took up the entire space of one of the walls which was itself extremely large.

The movie began with sound only. And was it a sound! It nearly terrified everybody. It was so loud it seemed to be coming at you from everywhere. And what was it? It was the heavy stomp, STOMP, STOMPING of my left cowboy boot on a huge piece of plywood which everyone could now see covering the whole wall. Even the splinters and wood chips coming off the board were the size of logs that seemed to be flying towards everyone.

I won't describe any more, as this is not the place for it, but if you can imagine Big Joe Mufferaw as I've depicted him in my song, this is exactly what I looked like when I finally appeared on the screen. The whole movie was truly fantastic, and it played every day in the same place all summer. Even the Queen went to see it when she was in Toronto and said it was one of the highlights of her visit.

Meanwhile, back in March, something else was beginning to brew, and it wasn't just another small pot of tea. It was more like the overalls that were thrown into "Mrs. Murphy's Chowder" (an old Irish song). And it just kept simmering and stinking everything up for the next year and a half. Most of the media began referring to it as the ongoing trial of "Stompin' Tom versus the Canadian National Exhibition," but I preferred calling it "The CNE versus Itself."

The whole thing seems to have started in January '73 when Jury and Barco Media, the CNE's official booking agency, began discussing the possibilities of booking Stompin' Tom at the Grandstand of the CNE. As Jury was booking me for a late summer tour he needed to know what date the CNE wanted so he could keep it free and not have me double-booked in another place. (If you don't book at least six months ahead, the venues get taken by someone else, and you find when the time comes, your act is out of work. And you don't want to be booked in two places on the same date and get sued for not showing up at one of them.)

There was never any problem or any doubt about whether it would be the Grandstand at which I would perform, it was always the date that kept everything at a stalemate. First, Labour Day was proposed and then it was another day, then back to Labour Day again. This went on and off and on again from January till the end of March. This was a long time for Jury to wait and not be able to book any shows during the three weeks or so that the Exhibition was to take place. In fact he lost several good paying venues during that time frame just because Barco or the CNE was keeping him on the hook.

Finally, by the end of March or the first of April, Jury received confirmation that the date would be Labour Day, the third of September, and the money offered was $3,500. And for this money his act, Stompin' Tom Connors, would have to provide a much more elaborate sound system than I had to adequately cover the large area, a lot more lighting than I usually carried, and at least two or three more backup musicians. All these extras were required because I would also have to back up an unnamed guest who would be appearing sometime during my show.

Now, this is where I enter the picture for the first time. In considering all my extra costs against the $3,500 offered, I came up with the conclusion that I would only break even at best, but I decided I would do the show anyway. This was because the CNE Grandstand was such a coveted venue to play for all Canadians, and to play there even once would show all my critics everywhere that I had been equal to the task of overcoming the last great hurdle. It would show them once and for all that I had really made it to the big leagues.

There was only one thing left for me to know before signing such an agreement, and that was: Who was the guest I was going to back up? I needed to know this so me and the boys could rehearse the material in plenty of time before the actual performance.

Upon learning my guest would be the American black country music artist, Charlie Pride, I was delighted. The boys and I already knew most of his material from frequently playing it in jam sessions and besides, this would be a good opportunity to introduce him to one of our own black country artists, on the Boot label, by the name of Brent Williams, who was a big fan of Charlie's.

As Fate would have it, and just before the ink was put to the paper, in walks Jury with a photocopy of a signed contract. "What do you think of this?" he said.

There before my eyes he laid a true copy of Charlie Pride's agreement to play as a single performer on the CNE Grandstand on Labour Day.

When I asked Jury, "Where in the hell did you get this?" he said, "From a friend I once did a favour for, who now works in one of the offices where these things are often left lying around."

As I read down the page the requirements were simply stated: "Artist will sing six songs only, accompanied by adequate musicians provided by host employer or his designate."

Then my eyes nearly popped out of my head as I read, "Price Agreed Upon: $35,000.00 to be paid in U.S. currency." There was a sentence below this which stated that Mr. Pride would also be receiving a "percentage of the Gate" (the exact figure now escapes me), with travel expenses paid.

After several seconds I looked at Jury, who was waiting for my bewildered reaction.

"Thirty-five thousand dollars to sing six songs!" I shouted, "What in the name o' jeezes is goin' on here? This can't be true. You playin' some kinda games with me or somethin'?"

"No way," he said. "What you see here is the gospel. I've been negotiating with these people for three months now and all I've been able to squeeze out of them was $3,500, max. Barco Media assures me that the CNE execs have never heard of you, and for an 'unknown' to get the chance to be seen on the Grandstand stage with Charlie Pride would be a great boost to his career. And that's all they were prepared to say."

"Oh, yeah?" I said. "Well, you go and tell them bastards to shove it right up their royal American arseholes. And that's all I got to say."

Jury knew I was entirely right, but he asked me if I wanted him to go back and ask for more.

"I don't give a damn," I said. "That's up to you. But if you do, it better be one hell of a lot more. There's no way I'm gonna let Charlie Pride, or anyone else, receive over ten times more money than I'm getting, while I do ten times the work, carry all the expenses and take all the risks, just to hustle my own ass down there to break even."

Jury agreed. And the next day, after finding out they wouldn't come up with any more money, he rejected the whole thing out of hand.

It was now that the CNE came up with another twist. They had another stage on the grounds they called the Bandshell, which was a lot smaller and a whole lot less prestigious. They would let me play there, they said, and still give me the same amount of money. The only difference would be that they would have to change the date to August 17, which again, would be a far less important day than Labour Day on September 3.

Though Jury still didn't have me booked anywhere during the whole time the Exhibition was on, due to the fact they couldn't make up their minds about dates, I decided to reject the whole thing. And my reasons were the following:

No. 1. For the last three years, consecutively, I'd been voted number one Canadian Country Music Artist and I had the three Juno Awards to prove it.

No. 2. The different branches of the media, throughout Canada, had covered this fact quite well.

No. 3. Though Charlie Pride was also well known in this country, due to the tremendous amount of airplay his records received on Canadian radio, in his country, the U.S., he had only received one Grammy Award up to this time.

No. 4. If the winning of one Grammy Award by an American is equivalent to the winning of three Juno Awards by a Canadian, and if the American Grammy winner is entitled to receive over $35,000 for singing six songs at the Canadian National Exhibition, then why shouldn't the Canadian Juno winner be entitled to the same amount for singing thirty songs on the same stage at the same venue? Especially, when his expenses are greater and his show is all about *exhibiting Canadian nationalism?*

No. 5. Even to expect Canada's Triple-Crown Country

Music Artist to accept, never mind play, an engagement on a less prominent stage, such as the Bandshell, where his status as a performer is perceived by the public to be considerably inferior to that of his American counterpart presently playing on the nation's number one Grandstand, is, to say the very least, highly insulting. Not just to the artist, or even to the industry's award giving committee, but to all Canadians, everywhere.

No. 6. The CNE, which is arguably the largest show in Canada, should be primarily exhibiting what its name "The Canadian National Exhibition" would suggest. And one of those exhibits should definitely be Canada's musical talent. And while it may be all right to relegate some of this lesser-known talent to the smaller stages, the award winners and "well knowns" should be given their place on a stage befitting their nationally recognized eminence. This would mean that Canadians, and all who visit this country, would be treated to a lot more Canadian headliners on the Grandstand of the CNE. And a goal of 60 per cent should not be considered unrealistic.

No. 7. The eyes of the people who run the CNE seem to be on every country in the world except Canada when it comes to musical talent. They don't seem to have any interest in reading their own newspapers or at least inquiring once in a while as to what is going on in the industry. And this is why they didn't seem to have a clue as to who I was, where I came from or what my accomplishments were. And once they were informed, they didn't give a damn anyway. I was just a nuisance and hardly worth the bother.

Now, just around the time that Jury was negotiating for a Stompin' Tom date at the CNE a young lady by the name of Carol Jamieson appeared one day at the Boot Records office looking for Stompin' Tom. She represented a certain tobacco company who wanted to know if I'd do a TV commercial promoting their brand of cigarettes.

Jury said he didn't think that I would because the cigarettes in question were not the brand I smoked. She wanted to know what difference that would make, and Jury told her, "Well, you just don't know Tom. But I'll take your proposal to him, anyway, and let you know tomorrow."

After seeing the proposal which, incidentally, was worth a good buck, I turned it down on the grounds that Jury had just given.

The next day when Jury had given her my answer, she declared that in all the time she'd ever been in the business of approaching people to do commercials, she'd never heard of anyone who would turn down an opportunity to make good money just because they didn't use the product.

With her curiosity heightened, she said she wanted to meet such a person, and she kept bugging Jury until, a couple of days later he called me, and I told him to send her over to the house.

Lena and I had just recently moved from Searle Avenue, and the meeting with Carol Jamieson took place at our new house on Bedford Park Avenue, not more than two blocks from the Boot Records office.

After we talked, Carol went back to see Jury and told him she was so impressed with my views that she wouldn't mind working for such a person. And this is how Jury came to hire her, at first on a part-time basis, to be a publicist for both Stompin' Tom and the record company.

Carol hadn't been with us for more than a week or two when I turned down the offer to play the CNE. And when she heard my reasons for doing so, she agreed that my decision was very honourable. She also told me, at the time, that she was a member of a small dedicated group of people called the Society for the Recognition of Canadian Talent, and that the president of the group was a City of Toronto alderman by the name of Ben Nobleman, and it just so happened that Mr. Nobleman was also a member of the Metro Toronto Council Executive Committee to whom the CNE Board of Directors was answerable.

It was now part of Carol's job, as my publicist, to advise me as to how the media and the public might react when the word got out that I had turned down the CNE's offer. "They'll no doubt want to know the reasons why."

"Well, just to make it short and sweet," I said, "tell them I declined the offer in protest of the way Canadian entertainers are being treated by the CNE and that I was angry at the Board of Directors for taking so long to give me a date, due to the fact that most, if not all of them, didn't even know who I was, let alone what I did."

I told her I didn't want to release the whole story in detail because I didn't want to stir up a bigger can of worms. I was already disliked by radio for being in favour of the 30 per cent government content regulations and I didn't relish the thought of seriously jeopardizing my chances of ever playing the CNE again, or any of the other Canadian exhibitions for that matter. After all, a guy does have to work.

(It's interesting to note that, from that time, I have never been able to obtain one booking at any of the major Canadian exhibitions. I guess this is what happens to all the honest guys who dare to stick their necks out.)

From the day Carol released my above statement to the press, and a photocopy to alderman Ben Nobleman, the shit began to hit the fan.

The members of the Metro Toronto Council, including Mayor David Crombie and Alderman Ben Nobleman, wanted to know what was going on. And this prompted the CNE Board of Directors to issue a press statement which, along with other things, subtly intimated that my refusal to play the CNE could have had more to do with the fact that I discovered I'd have to share the stage with a black man than it did with anything else.

What now began to look to me like the beginning of a smear campaign quickly prompted me to retaliate with all the pertinent facts, including the money amounts and all the reasons for my refusal, as I have just related them.

I also had more to add to the statement. But by the time the press editors were done chopping it all up, it began to look like several different stories in several different papers. (Conserving space, you know, for more important issues. And besides, a lot of the words that got printed were sometimes not even my own.)

At any rate, my second press release now became a catalyst for all the debates and policy changes that occurred thereafter.

Ben Nobleman submitted a resolution to the Metro Council calling for the CNE to increase the number of its Grandstand headliners to 60 per cent Canadian (the same as television at the time), a resolution that passed but did not subsequently become binding on the CNE, and for that reason they never did come close to reaching the goal, even though they said they would try.

There were petitions circulating among the people at the time and one from the doorstep of city hall alone had garnered more than two thousand names. All these people were in favour of the 60 per cent Canadian headliner quota for the Grandstand, and thousands of letters were written to the editors of newspapers with copies sent to the CNE Board of Directors, demanding the same.

The only major voices speaking out against the resolution were those of a number of radio commentators. This was understandable, since most radio stations had been fighting for over two years now to have the CRTC's imposition of a 30 per cent Canadian content ruling on them reduced or done away with altogether. As a matter of fact, at this writing, they're still fighting it. And remember that back in early 1971, when Boot Records was just opening its doors, we received not one but two letters from major Toronto radio stations suggesting to us that if we, or our company, should endorse this newly proposed CRTC 30 per cent Canadian content ruling, we might as well expect that our records would never be played on their station, ever. And to my knowledge, they've always kept their word.

Now, in answer to all the heat the CNE Board of Directors were taking, one of their statements to the press, given by their general manager, David Garrick, assured everyone that they were presently employing at least 90 to 95 per cent Canadian performers. This, of course, left the impression that it would be ridiculous to impose a 60 per cent Canadian content ruling on the CNE, which was already doing a lot more than its share to promote Canadian talent.

This balloon came crashing down, however, when Mr. Nobleman's rebuttal appeared in the papers the following day. He stated that his facts, which were taken from the CNE financial reports themselves, indicated that while it might be true that the Exhibition employed up to 95 per cent Canadian talent, only 5 to 10 per cent of the payout in dollars was going to them, while 90 to 95 per cent of the payout was going to the other 5 or 10 per cent of the talent, which was foreign and/or American.

And so the controversy raged on for the rest of the summer and into the following year, with the CNE stating there weren't enough performers in Canada, at least of high enough calibre, who were popular enough to draw any kind of a respectable crowd to a venue the size of the Grandstand. This was, in turn, rebutted by the argument that if the CNE and other venues were to spend even half the money on Canadian talent that they did in promoting American and other foreign acts, the Canadians would outdraw their foreign counterparts anytime. Witness the high percentage of big-name Canadian actors and performers in the United States who were forced to go there because the opportunity and promotional money had just never been made available here.

When Mr. Nobleman later proposed to set up a committee that would seek out, screen and recruit the calibre of talent capable of meeting the drawing power requirements of the venue, the CNE made a counter-proposal declaring that such a committee would be more competent if it were set up by themselves. And this they promised to do. As a matter of fact, I was sitting on the panel while these proposals were being discussed and at the same time being locally televised. (Alas! Why do some things never change?)

So to any of my readers who may not have known what all the hullabaloo was about at the time, you have just heard my interpretation of what was happening. And if anyone should know, it's me, because I was right smack-dab in the middle of it.

I will leave this subject now, before it gets too boring. But before I do, there's still one more small incident I feel I must relate. So here it is, for what it might be worth.

While all this controversy concerning myself and the Exhibition was going on, I was driving down the 401 highway one afternoon, just thinking about what kind of trouble I might have got myself into for speaking out about a policy I perceived to be wrong and unfair. I knew the CNE was big and powerful and as a pawn in this big chess game, there was no way I was going to gain, one way or the other.

If the 60 per cent Canadian content quota were to be imposed on the CNE, I would look like the culprit to be shunned by them for stirring up all this shit in the first place; if the quota was eventually swept under the rug and forgotten about, I would still be remembered and shunned for the same reasons. I was in a no-win situation. Even if I were lauded by my fellow performers for bringing about some long-awaited changes from which they could eventually benefit, it sure wouldn't put any extra money in my pocket.

With my car radio tuned to CFGM, the country radio station at the time, I was just in the mental process of trying to justify my stand by thinking, "Well, if nobody speaks up, and nobody has till now, the plight of all Canadian talent will always remain as deplorable as it is. But the honourable thing to do in this situation is to sacrifice at least some of one's personal goals when it looks like there might be a chance to help increase the advantage of others."

Just then my thoughts were interrupted by the radio announcer who was about to interview Anne Murray. His second or third question to Anne was: "What do you think of Stompin' Tom's stand against the CNE and the proposed 60 per cent Canadian content regulation both he and the city wish to impose on their Grandstand performances?" The answer I heard was certainly not what I expected. The gist of what she said was that I was all wet and away out in left field on this one. And the CNE was doing just fine the way it was. When I heard this, I very nearly drove off the road.

One possible motivation for her saying this quickly dawned on me, however. This was a time when radio was fulfilling its 30 per cent Canadian content regulations by only playing Anne and a handful of others to the point of saturation. So why should she stick out her neck and jeopardize her own favoured position?

To Newfoundland and the Maritimes

AROUND THIS TIME, BILLY Lewis, my guitar player, had written a very nice song called "Sleepy Country Roads." We recorded it on April 10, and released it to radio later on that month. Unfortunately, it didn't receive much airplay and Billy didn't bother recording again. Too bad, because he had a very nice voice and the single was well done.

During the first week of May, I attended the grand opening of a big Muntz store in Toronto. They specialized in very high quality stereo equipment and awarded me with one of their sets for my participation.

During the same week I recorded a couple of radio jingles, one for the United Way and the other for the Prince Edward Island Department of Tourism. This latter jingle was one I wrote, and was played so often down east that the phone number, which was incorporated within the lyrics, is still quite vividly remembered by thousands of people, one of whom is the great blues singer Holly Cole, who once stated she still couldn't get it out of her mind. The jingle was called "Dial an Island" and the number was 800-565-7421. (The "1" was not required at the time.)

In the second week of May I recorded the album entitled *To It and At It* which included "The Marten Hartwell Story" and "The Don Messer Story." (Don had just recently passed away and was greatly missed by all of Canada.) The musicians on this album, incidentally, included several members of the Toronto Symphony Orchestra and the album went on to capture the Juno Award as best album of the year in 1973.

For the rest of the month of May, I was busy filming the movie, *Across This Land, with Stompin' Tom Connors.* The inside shots were done at the Horseshoe Tavern in Toronto and the outside shots were done at several other locations.

By June 1, I was on tour again. First in Ontario, at Leamington, Sarnia, London, Pembroke, Brockville and Belleville, and then to Sherbrooke and a couple of other towns in Quebec. We then went to New Brunswick and played St. Stephen, Saint John, Newcastle, Dalhousie, Moncton and Fredericton.

It was while we were in Saint John that my dad came out to the show. I hadn't seen him for a few years, and after the concert we spent the rest of the night talking. He was down on his luck and after giving him a couple hundred dollars I told him that if he came to Toronto I could get him a job working at Boot Records as soon as this present leg of the tour was over. Sometime around the end of July, he arrived in Toronto and Jury gave him a job.

Meanwhile, on June 24, the boys and I left our vehicles in Charlottetown and flew to Toronto to do a concert at Ontario Place. In contrast to the three months it took to obtain a concert date at the CNE, the Ontario Place date had been negotiated within a few hours. This fact was mentioned in the newspapers several times while the CNE controversy was still being hotly debated. And the venue, which seated some six thousand people, was filled to its capacity.

I was also scheduled to meet the Queen earlier that morning when she arrived at Queen's Park, but due to her late arrival and a heavy itinerary, our meeting was cancelled, even though I was there at the scene.

On the evening of June 25 we flew back to Charlottetown. But due to the great amount of fog, the plane was not able to land, so we turned back and landed in Moncton, New Brunswick, instead. We had to rent a car there and drive to the Island.

On our way to catch the last ferry which was to cross at

1 A.M., we were hitting some pretty heavy fog patches. Wayne Hughes was driving, and sometime just after midnight, a big black horse loomed up out of the fog and we struck it.

I was sitting on the passenger side in the front seat as Wayne veered to the left to miss the horse, but it struck the right side of the car and went right up over the top, breaking the windshield and spraying glass everywhere throughout the vehicle. The horse landed over the ditch and the fence on the right-hand side of the road and the car was now heading for the left side.

In a fit of panic, Wayne jumped out from behind the wheel and started running up the road while the car was still in motion. Although I was still half-dazed from the impact, I saw that we were headed for the left-hand ditch and I darted down on the floor to get my hand on the brake pedal. This stopped the car just as it was about to plunge over the edge of the road and drop down what we later estimated to be a fifteen-foot embankment.

I reached up, shut off the motor, pressed down on the emergency brake and crawled out on the pavement. By this time Billy and Gary were out of the back seat and we all looked down to see where we almost landed. I hollered some wild curse words at Wayne and told him to get his ass back here and take a look at the spot where he almost killed us.

After giving him a blast of shit, I got into the car and backed it up from off the left side of the road where it might get hit by the oncoming traffic and parked it on the right-hand shoulder. Then we all went over into the field to see what had happened to the horse, but it was dead.

We went up the road a little piece to a house where we intended to phone the police to report the accident. After knocking on the door and waking the people, we found out the horse belonged to their young son, who was now awake and crying when he learned his horse was dead.

We all felt terrible, of course, but there was nothing we could do about it. When the police arrived, it was soon established that the horse should not have been on the road in the first place. And with the fog and all, we couldn't be faulted for the accident. After I compensated the man for the loss of his horse, we hurriedly drove to Cape Tormentine and by the skin of our teeth we managed to catch the last ferry of the night.

When we reached the Island, we drove to Charlottetown and picked up our vehicles. And while Wayne and the boys dropped the damaged car off at the rental depot, I drove down to Lena's sister Pauline's place and related the whole story, as Lena picked the tiny pieces of glass out of my clothes, my hair and my skin. When this was done, we drove back to the motel where the boys were still awake, and after having a beer or two and discussing the events of the evening, we finally retired at about five o'clock in the morning.

On the next two days we played Souris and Kensington, P.E.I., and on June 29, 1973, we were in Skinners Pond to play a few songs and officially open the newly renovated Skinners Pond School to the public as a historical site. Practically everyone from Skinners Pond was there, along with a few of the local politicians and dignitaries. The premier of the province was invited for the unveiling of the plaque, but due to his attending to the arrival of the Queen in Charlottetown he couldn't make it.

A scholarship was also set up that day to be awarded to any high school student from Skinners Pond who might be graduating each year. This was to come from any money donated by the visiting public and given to the student to help them pay for their tuition should they enroll in any institution of higher learning.

During the next three or four years, three or four local students obtained a substantial grant. Then the school became so badly damaged by some of the local hoodlums that the money from the fund had to go towards constant repairs. This was rather unfortunate, as some of the students began looking forward to the help made possible by these yearly grants.

On July 1, Canada Day, we were all back in Charlottetown where I was again invited to meet the Queen. About an hour before this was to happen, Lena and I were standing in the huge crowd in front of Government House when I decided I'd go over to the television booth to say hello to Lloyd Robertson, who was then covering the daily events for the CBC. And while I was talking to Lloyd, there was a small commotion in the midst of the crowd, and just about in the spot where I had left Lena standing.

As I hurried back to see what had happened, I found Lena had fallen down in the midst of the crowd and was now lying prone on the grassy lawn. She had fainted.

As I picked her up and started carrying her towards some first aid people I saw from a distance, she started coming to and wanted to stand up, saying she now felt okay. The early afternoon sun had been very hot that day and the closeness of the crowd must have caused her to pass out. When she finally felt strong enough to walk by herself, we slowly made our way to the flower gardens where I was soon to be introduced to Her Majesty, Queen Elizabeth, and her husband, Prince Philip.

After we walked through the garden for about ten minutes, the Royal Couple made their appearance. They soon began to stroll about, shaking hands and chatting with each person individually. (The only people permitted in this garden were those with special invitations.)

As the Royal Couple approached the spot where I was standing I removed my hat and extended my hand to receive first that of Her Royal Highness and then Prince Philip. They congratulated me for the work I was doing and the awards I had received for the writing and singing of so many songs about Canada. The meeting was very friendly and cordial until the Prince thought of something which had occurred several days previous when he and Her Highness were in Toronto. Alluding to me and the movie they had seen at Cinesphere in Ontario Place, he asked the premier, Alex Campbell, if he had ever seen it. When Alex said he hadn't, both the Prince and the Queen began telling him how astounded they were to hear and see such a large boot come stomping down on that giant piece of plywood. We all laughed when the Prince stretched out his arms in emphasis while describing "the size of those big woodchips that made us both duck down as they came flying towards us."

After a little more chit-chat and a quick press photo, the Royal Couple moved on, as they had a lot more people to meet and talk with. I donned my hat and went to join Lena in another part of the garden. The photo that was taken was not from a very good angle but it does show the Queen, the Prince, the premier and myself as we chatted among the people. I later got Jury to obtain a copy for me.

I almost forgot to mention that on June 30, the day before Canada Day, I headlined a concert at Victoria Park, in Charlottetown, where the audience was estimated to be eleven thousand. This was the largest crowd I had performed for up until this time. The Queen was also invited to this one, but again, due to a very hectic schedule, she couldn't make it.

On July 2 and 3 we played Tignish and Montague, on P.E.I., and then moved out to Newfoundland. This would be my first tour to that province and I was really looking forward to it.

By now, Lena was on the road steady with us, helping out with the sales of records, tapes and song books, along with pictures, bumper stickers and other souvenirs.

The Newfoundland shows all took place between July 7 and July 19 and included Port Aux Basques, Corner Brook, Gander, and two nights in St. John's, before going to Bonavista, Grand Falls, Mary's Town and Stephenville.

The big song they wanted to hear me sing in Newfoundland was, of course, "The Moon Man Newfie."

While sitting in a bar one afternoon and hearing it on the jukebox I asked one of the waiters if the song got played very often. "Played?" he said. "The needle's been wearin' on that groove so often you can sometimes hear the song on the other side playin'." Here's the words:

THE MOON MAN NEWFIE

1.

Codfish Dan from Newfoundland, he dreamt that he had three wishes;
He took Mars and all the stars and he turned them into big fishes.
He said the sky was much too dry and he made a wavy motion,
And the moon, like a boat, began to float upon the starry ocean.

CHORUS:
*And you might think it's goofie, but the Man in the
   Moon is a Newfie*
*And he's sailin' on to Glory away in the Golden
   Dory.*

2.

*One night he strayed to the Milky Way to cast his
   nets upon it;*
*When he spied the tail of what he thought was a
   whale, he harpooned Haley's Comet.*
*He never had a pot for the fish that he caught, so he
   had to use the Big Dipper;*
*And the sun, by Jove, was a very good stove for
   cookin' up smelts and kippers.*

REPEAT CHORUS

3.

*Now, the northern lights that seem so bright, like
   nothin' could be grander;*
*Well, they're just waves of the moon-boat made by the
   Newfoundland Commander.*
*And don't you sigh and say "Oh, My! What gross
   exaggerations."*
*'Cause he'll tell you the dream was true when
   Codfish Dan awakens.*

CHORUS:
*And you might think it's goofie, but the Man in the
   Moon is a Newfie;*
*And he's sailin' on to Glory away in the Golden
   Dory.*
Sailin' on to Glory away in the Golden Dory.

Printed by permission. Crown-Vetch Music Ltd.

In Corner Brook I got to see my old buddy, Lucky Jim Frost, whom you may remember as one of my old hitch-hiking companions, spoken of in my previous book. Jim was now married to a Newfoundland girl by the name of Minnie, and their family consisted of three or four lovely girls. Over a few beers he told me he was in the carpet-laying business and was doing all right. We talked a lot about the old days and he wanted to know how Steve was. I told him Steve was now calling himself "Stevedore Steve" and had three albums out on Boot Records. After yackin' and singin' and pickin' for most of one night and all the next afternoon we bade farewell to one another and promised to write once in a while.

As we travelled from town to town, the food just seemed to get better. I was a big fish lover and found no trouble eating it every day. There was everything from seal flippers and cod tongues to fish and brewis and salmon. We also managed to have a couple of moose steaks and a Jig's Dinner (salt pork hocks, boiled vegetables, etc.), and always washing it all down with a few pints of Dominion.

One of the down sides to the tour was that we would have had more people attend our concerts had our prices been a little cheaper. But this all happened through no fault of our own. The agent who brought us in set the prices long before we got there. And while we think of $3.50 a head as being nothing at all today, it was considered quite a bit in the Newfoundland of 1973. It meant that some people could come to the shows and other people just couldn't afford it. Each town we went to the people were saying the same thing: that they had a lot of friends who would like to have come to the show but the prices were just too steep.

The following few lines are typical of the apology I placed in each local paper before leaving town the day following each concert.

AN APOLOGY FROM
STOMPIN' TOM CONNORS

To the people of St. John's and surrounding areas. I wish to apologize for the high price of admission to my show. The price was solely determined by the agent who brought me into Newfoundland. I was totally unaware of the high price until I arrived in the province.

I assure you that in the future when I return to play this area the admission price will be much more reasonable. Please accept my humble apologies. Sincerely, Stompin' Tom Connors.

(The next time I did a tour of Newfoundland, two years later, there wasn't one adult ticket above $2.50 and this time all kids under fourteen got in for a buck. These shows were all booked by ourselves with the tickets being sold by local service clubs.)

It was after the show in Bonavista that my road manager and I had a major disagreement concerning some of his duties and early the next morning, to my surprise, he taxied to Gander and took a plane back to Ontario. I called Jury right away and he immediately flew down to conduct the business for the rest of the tour.

At this point we only had Mary's Town and Stephenville yet to play in Newfoundland and then we were back aboard the *William Carson* ferry to play Sydney, on Cape Breton Island. Here, Billy Lewis got to go home to "The Pier" to see his folks for a one-day visit and then we were off to Halifax to play on the twenty-fourth and twenty-fifth of July.

It was while we were in Halifax that Jury told me that Sam the Record Man (Sam Sniderman) was in town opening up a new record store and that he would like very much to see me make an appearance for the occasion.

Arriving in the store in the afternoon I signed a few autographs and took some pictures with Sam in front of a very nice Stompin' Tom display which he had previously set up, and then he came up with a surprise of his own. He and Jury had somehow been in cahoots and managed to have Sam bring a gold album down from Toronto, and this was what he now presented to me.

This gold album was for *Big Joe Mufferaw* and marked the fifth gold album to date.

By July 27 we had played Shelburne, then Yarmouth, Digby and Berwick. It was a radio music director who brought us in for these last three shows. And after we played the towns, he refused to pay us from the money he collected.

Everything went well in Yarmouth and Berwick as far as the performances were concerned, but when we arrived to set up in Digby, we noticed a very strong smell throughout the arena we were supposed to play in. It was soon discovered to be an ammonia leak from one of the pipes, and some of the town officials were called in to make a determination as to whether the arena was fit to play in or not. The mayor of the town advised us that to be on the safe side we should move the show to a high school auditorium just down the street. This we did and arranged for someone to stay at the arena to advise the people when they showed up that the concert would take place at the high school.

Well, it happened that the guy bringing us in showed up after the change had to be made, and when he saw the number of people in the auditorium was not as many as he had anticipated, and that the take at the door was also less, he used the fact that we had changed buildings without his authorization as an excuse for the low attendance and refused to pay what he owed us.

After two years of chasing him from Nova Scotia to P.E.I. through lawyers' letters attempting to collect our money, all we were getting was a number of NSF cheques. And the last I heard from Jury in late 1975 was that the money still wasn't paid. And I really don't think it ever was. (I tell this story, just as one of many, to warn the young groups getting started to be cautious and try to get at least half your money up front and the rest of it on the night you do the concert. These gigs were all on union contracts but in the end it didn't seem to make any difference.)

One more question that occurred to me while all this was going on was how much this situation was going to interfere with any radio play my records might (or might not) get at the stations where this guy was subsequently being employed. We knew he moved as program director to several stations during the two and a half years we were chasing him for our money, and it's my bet that he wasn't using any of his influence to make sure Stompin' Tom was being played on any of them.

But what are you supposed to do, I thought; allow him to get away without paying, just because he's a program director? Sometimes it's a hard decision to make, given the possible consequences to your own career, but if nobody dares to hold him down to his moral and legal responsibilities the chances of him doing the same thing to others is greatly magnified.

Our last two concerts in Nova Scotia that summer were in Amherst and Antigonish, before returning to P.E.I. to do a couple at the Birchwood High School, in Charlottetown. The rest of that week, from the eighth to the eleventh of August, we were back at Johnny Reid's in the Prince Edward Lounge.

It was at this time that Lena and I asked Johnny to be best man at our forthcoming wedding, and Judy, Johnny's wife, one of the bridesmaids. We also asked Pauline, Lena's sister, to be the maid of honour, and her husband, Gerald, to be one of the groomsmen. We later asked my sister Marlene and her husband, Willard, to also join the wedding party as an additional bridesmaid and groomsman. We were pleased they all assented, but for the present, we only knew the date we had set and that the wedding would take place somewhere in Ontario, but we'd have to wait till we got back home to plan the exact location. We didn't even know who we were going to get to marry us, or if the wedding was going to be large, medium or small. We only hoped to let everybody know within a couple of weeks.

It was also at this time, while I was playing the Prince Edward Lounge, that I was surprised to see a good buddy of mine come walking through the aisles towards the stage. It was none other than Richard Hatfield, the premier of New Brunswick.

Dick was an avid country music fan who attended most of my shows whenever I chanced to play in his area. And during the past year or so there had been more than one occasion when Lena and I had gotten together with Dick and his girlfriend, Libby Burnham.

We were quite the foursome: Stompin' Tom and the premier of New Brunswick, struttin' our girls down the streets of Fredericton, saying hello and cracking jokes with everyone we met till the wee hours of the morning. Then after closing the bars and restaurants, we'd hop into that mighty fine Bricklin of his and, after a nightcap at the motel, we'd bid goodnight to a couple of swell friends, promising to do the same thing again sometime.

Well, here he was again tonight, prancing towards the stage where I was singing. "Lend me your stompin' board, Tom," he said. "I can't explain now, 'cause I'm in a hurry. But I'll bring it back a little later."

I wouldn't have given the board to just anyone. But, to Dick Hatfield—why not? It was all banged up with a couple of holes in it and I would soon have to start stompin' on another one anyway.

Unknown to me at the time, there was a premiers' conference being held in Charlottetown and Dick had slipped out for a few minutes to get my board. And for what reason? Not I, but God only knew.

Within the hour, and returning all out of puff, came the smiling face of Richard Hatfield with two or three other premiers trailing behind him. Into the crowded lounge he came, found his way up to the stage once more and laughingly presented me with my stompin' board. Only now, it was autographed by each of the ten Canadian premiers. "You always seem to be signing your name for everyone else, Tom," he said. "So here's a few names I thought you might like to have."

As the audience showed their approval by applauding, we snapped a few pictures of Dick and myself and the other premiers, and then sat down for a chat over a couple of beers.

It was here I first made a small mention to Dick and the others about what was going on between myself and the CNE. They wanted to hear more but I had to return to the stage, and they had to leave the club before I finished my set. (I later had Jury draught a letter explaining the full problem in more detail.)

It might be interesting to note that, some seven months later, on the fifteenth day of February 1974, the president of the CNE sent the following letter to The Hon. Richard R. Hatfield, Premier of the Province of New Brunswick. And I quote:

Dear Sir: I am very pleased to inform you that at the Inaugural Meeting of our Board of

Directors, held on February 8th, 1974, you were unanimously elected an Honorary Director of the Canadian National Exhibition Association for the current year.

A copy of our Annual Report covering our activities for 1973 is enclosed.

It is our sincere hope that you will honour us with your acceptance of this appointment.

Yours very truly, Douglas V. Palmer, President.

In a letter dated March 1, 1974, Richard Hatfield sent Mr. Palmer the following answer. And again I quote:

Dear Mr. Palmer: Thank you for your letter advising that I have been elected an honorary director of the Canadian National Exhibition.

It is with regret that I write to say I do not wish to accept. As you know, I take exception to the policy of the Canadian National Exhibition in not giving top billing to Canadian talent. Until this unfortunate attitude changes, I must decline.

Sincerely, Richard Hatfield.

As anyone can see by these letters, Dick Hatfield was indeed a people's premier, just as I have always claimed to be a people's entertainer. And a lot of the common people of New Brunswick who had the pleasure of meeting their premier can still recall how it probably took place a lot more often while he walked through a bar on a hot summer's afternoon and bought them a cold beer than it did in the hallowed but stuffy halls of Parliament.

He sympathized with the plight of the underdog, and in my books, that's what makes the man. It's not often you meet a man who takes his concern for the other fellow more seriously than the enhancement of his own self-aggrandizement. But that's the Richard Hatfield I knew. And although more letters were sent to him by the CNE, trying to get him to change his mind about the offer, he steadfastly refused, citing the grounds just given.

Wedding Plans and
Touring West

On August 14 of 1973, our tour of the Maritimes ended in Alberton, P.E.I., and then we headed back to Ontario.

After a couple of days' rest, and while Lena and I were planning the details of our wedding, Jury comes knocking on the door. I immediately knew something was up by the way he tried to look thoughtful even though he was being bothered by something he had on his mind.

After he prodded us for a few minutes about our wedding plans, I said, "Okay! Out with it, Jury. What the hell is on your mind?" "Well," he said, "it's like this . . ." and he proceeded to tell us that a short discussion had been held by Carol Jamieson, himself and Drew Crossan, the producer of the Elwood Glover show. And in the course of the conversation our wedding had come up, and someone mentioned (I never did find out who) that with all the fans Stompin' Tom had, he would almost have to be married on television to accommodate them all. And before the discussion was over, everyone agreed, and Jury was elected to ask Tom and Lena what they thought about the idea.

"Get the hell out of here. I don't like the idea at all," I said. And Jury left. Then after thinking it over for several hours, while trying to decide who we were going to invite to the wedding and who we were going to leave out, the problem was becoming unsolvable. "Maybe Jury had the right idea after all," we thought, and soon we began to consider it seriously. We could invite most of our family and our immediate friends to the actual wedding place, and the friends we couldn't invite would be able to see the ceremony on television, along with all the rest of the people we'd met throughout Canada.

There were still some hitches, however, and I decided to call Jury back to the house to discuss them.

Neither Lena nor I had seen the wedding of Tiny Tim on the "Johnny Carson Show" a couple of years previous in the States, but word had it that it had been quite a farce. "It had been anything but solemn and respectful," so we heard, and we certainly didn't want our wedding winding up the same way. So when Jury got back to the house, we explained our position to him and told him that we would agree to get married on television only if it was promised that the ceremony would be conducted in strict accordance with all the highest standards.

After another day or so, Jury came back with Carol and assured us that the CBC would respect all our wishes. And if we agreed, the wedding would take place at noon, November 2, 1973, on "Luncheon Date." To this we agreed, and immediately set out to find a minister who might be willing to conduct a nondenominational service. Within a few days, a gentleman by the name of Reverend Bev Leslie, from the Christian (Disciples of Christ) Church, called the CBC and offered to perform the required ceremony.

We provided Carol Jamieson with the huge list of names and she sent out all the invitations. She also looked after most of the wedding arrangements and became the chief liaison between the CBC and ourselves.

All that seemed to be required now was to make the official announcement. But wouldn't you just know it? One of the local country radio stations did the honour for us. One day while Lena and I were visiting the station they plunked flowers and champagne in our hands and snapped a picture. The next day the whole story, including photo, appeared in the local papers. Where the radio station got the scoop in the first place is anybody's guess.

Marlene and Willard now threw a shower for us on or about August 25, during which we received some very weird parcels and packages. The presents I opened up, because my name was on them, were all delicate things meant for Lena. And the things she received with her name on them were obviously meant for me. This trick, of course, prompted a great deal of laughter, as we both had to have our pictures taken sitting in a corner, unwrapping and holding up an item or two of each other's rather suggestive looking underwear.

While all this was going on, it was getting very cramped over at the Boot Records office. We were expanding by leaps and bounds and we had no more space for storing records, never mind room for people to work. My dad, by now, had come up from New Brunswick and Jury had given him a warehousing job. But with no place to put anything, we decided that Jury should immediately look for a much larger place.

Within a couple of days we had bought a brand-new building on Matheson Boulevard, in Mississauga. This contained a nice large glassed-in reception area at the front, which gave access to two halls with offices on either side. At the end of each hall a door led into a large warehouse which occupied approximately two-thirds of the entire building. The whole building itself contained about 4,500 square feet of floor space, and the ownership was divided between myself and Jury, 75 per cent and 25 per cent, respectively.

While Jury was preparing to move into the new building, I was trying to write a few songs. But it was becoming rather difficult because of all the interruptions. There were not only the constant questions concerning our upcoming wedding, but I was also planning another western tour. And even before this was to happen, I had to do a week at the Horseshoe Tavern between the third and the eighth of September.

It was during this week at the Horseshoe that my dad got his first taste of selling records and other souvenirs at a venue where I was playing. He seemed to be doing quite well and it was decided that, because we hadn't been able to replace Wayne Hughes as yet, we would take my dad on the road with us. The first concerts would be fairly small and this would enable him to gain the needed experience before he had to tackle the larger ones. Besides, Lena would be there, and Jury would come along to conduct the business until we could find someone qualified enough to take over that responsibility.

Between the ninth and twelfth of September, the Boot Records office was moved from the Bathurst Street address and relocated in Mississauga. And on the fourteenth we headed out for our first concert of the tour. This was to take place in Grand Valley, just a short distance from Toronto, on that very night.

I seem to remember the Mercey Brothers opening for us and, after we finished our portion of the show, the Merceys went back on stage to play for a dance while we signed a few autographs for the crowd. I also remember meeting the federal minister of arts and culture, Perrin Beatty, there that night. And although our meeting was brief, it would not be the last time we'd be engaging in conversation.

Our next concert was in Kincardine. And it was here that I had to have a word with my dad about the bottle he kept carrying around. I had told him even before he came to Ontario that I didn't want him drinking on the job. I had told Jury he was alcoholic before he was hired but I wanted to give him a chance to straighten himself out. Now here he was carrying a half-empty whisky bottle around several hours before the show.

I knew it was probably hard on him seeing myself and the boys having the odd bottle of beer throughout the day but, because of his problem with alcohol, I couldn't jeopardize the show by letting him drink, unless he was safe and sound on his night off in a motel where we could keep an eye on him. I could also see that the boys really liked my dad but I had to ask them not to encourage his drinking as he was known to quickly develop a very dirty disposition when too much alcohol was involved.

After our little talk, my dad put the bottle away and he was very efficient at the show that night. And except for the power going out all over Kincardine and delaying the second half of our show for an hour, everything else went pretty smoothly.

Next day we took the ferry from Tobermory, on the

Bruce Peninsula, to Manitoulin Island in preparation for a September 17 concert in Manitowaning. On the twentieth we played Dryden, Ontario. And on the twenty-second, Fort Francis. That's when our troubles really began.

Unknown to me, my dad had been nipping on the bottle again that afternoon. And by showtime he wasn't feeling any pain.

During the intermission of the show, while the boys and I were in the dressing room and Lena and my dad were selling records, he began to tell a few bystanders who he really was. When they wouldn't readily believe that he was my father, he became a little annoyed and asked Lena to verify his statement. When she complied and the people were convinced, this still didn't satisfy my dad, and he now began to carry the whole thing a little too far.

With everybody's attention, he grabbed a couple big handfuls of change, mixed with a few bills, and started raving about how his son was "making a lot more money than you ever thought of making."

By this time, word had quickly reached the dressing room that there was a commotion going on at the concession tables. And just before I arrived, Lena told my dad to simmer down a bit because this was no place for such conduct. And upon hearing her reprimand, he threw several handfuls of change in her face and left the building.

As Lena was obviously hurt and very near to tears, I reassured her a bit and quickly helped her straighten out her money and her tables. I went outside to see where my dad had gotten to, but he was gone. And as I was already late for my second set, I beat it backstage to get my guitar. I walked on the stage, and after apologizing to the people for all the commotion, I proceeded to finish my show.

I didn't do too many autographs that night as I was anxious to get back to the motel to see what had become of my dad and to give him a piece of my mind, if he was in any way coherent. As it turned out, he was in his room flaked out on the bed with an empty bottle beside him. So I left him there to sleep it off and went to my room where the boys were talking to Lena.

Over a couple bottles of beer, when I learned that Jury

would not be with us to drive the equipment van in the morning because he had to fly ahead to Winnipeg on some business, I proposed that one of the boys drive it while my old man straightened out in the passenger seat.

Unfortunately, by the time we all got up the next morning, my dad was gone. And so was the equipment van. I knew there was a tour schedule in the van's glove compartment and I knew my dad was aware of that. But the thing I didn't know was whether he would stay in sober enough condition to even bother looking at it. And if he didn't, he was in a part of the wilds of Canada where he had never been before and God knows where he'd wind up.

On the supposition that Jury would have alerted us if the van had been gone when he got up to take a taxi to the airport, we figured my dad might not have left too long ago. So without eating, we jumped into our vehicles and tore up the highway in hopes of catching him or reaching him on the CB radio—providing he was even listening.

For the next 130 miles we travelled north along Highway 71 with no sign or word from my dad anywhere. We turned west on Highway 17 and drove for another fifteen miles into Kenora. There it occurred to me that if my dad had turned east instead of west fifteen miles back, he might have discovered his mistake and by the time he got pointed in the right direction he would now, of course, be behind us.

On such a hunch I told the boys to wait for us at a restaurant in Kenora while Lena and I drove back to check it out. After driving fifty miles or so towards Dryden without meeting him on the road, I gave up on the idea, turned around, and drove back to Kenora.

I now had myself a real worry. Our next concert was in Brandon, Manitoba, 260 miles away, with the city of Winnipeg to drive through to get there. If my dad was ahead of us, could he find his way to Brandon? And if he was behind us, he was heading back east instead of west with a truck full of records and all our equipment. What the hell could we do besides hope?

It must have been ten or eleven o'clock that night when we pulled up to our motel in Brandon. And there as nice as you please was our van, parked up at one of the rooms. I immediately walked over and knocked. "What kept you guys?" my dad asked, as he opened the door. "Never mind that," I said. "I thought you understood before we left that all our vehicles on each tour must always stay together and travel together? And secondly, you owe Lena an apology for your actions last night while you were drinking on the job."

Taking a quick nip from his bottle, he said, "I'm used to getting up early in the morning and doing something besides standing around all goddamn day waiting for a bunch of lazies to hit the deck. And furthermore, when some broad decides to tell me how I should be doing my job, I think she should owe me an apology."

I could see now that he was on the verge of one of his dirtier moods, and there wasn't much sense talking to him any further. As I headed for the door, I said, "Look! I'm gonna forget you said that last bit. But I told you away back in New Brunswick that I would try to give you a chance. Well, I gave you a couple already. And now I'm only going to give you one more. I've worked too damned hard to gain the confidence of so many people to just stand by and let you and your bottle wreck everything for me. So if I catch you drinking on the job, even once more, you'll find yourself on a bus going home." As I opened the door to leave, I added, "And from now on, I want that van to be travelling with the rest of us."

With our next concert taking place right there in Brandon and not having to travel the next day, we didn't get up until twelve or one o'clock. When I looked out the window and saw the van missing, I assumed that my dad had just gone down town for something to eat. We usually didn't go to set up at the venue till around three-thirty or four o'clock in the afternoon so I wasn't really worried about his absence.

When three o'clock came, however, and he still wasn't back, I asked the boys what they thought. And I told them what I had said to him the night before. "Oh, don't worry about it, Tom," they said. "He probably had something to eat, then did a little shopping. And he probably went straight to the venue."

"Well, maybe," I said. "But let's go down to the venue a little early to see if he's there, just in case."

As I suspected, when we got to the venue, he was nowhere in sight. We waited until four o'clock or so and then I decided we'd better go looking for him.

We had tried to raise him on the CB but without success and figured he just didn't have it turned on, so we now took separate sections of town and went looking up and down the streets systematically.

Brandon wasn't that large at the time, but a full hour later we were still looking. As I was just entertaining the thought that he might have got mad at what I told him and decided to take the van and head back home, I spotted him parked on the side of a little suburban side street.

As I backed up and turned to go down to where he was parked, I gave the boys my location on the CB and pulled up alongside the van. When I got out to take a look, here he was slumped behind the wheel with the window open, the CB blaring and a near empty bottle sitting beside him.

When the boys arrived, I got one of them to drive my car and told him to follow me back. I pushed my dad over to the passenger side of the van, got behind the wheel and headed for the motel.

After stretching him out on the bed (I didn't have time to take his clothes off), we rushed the van back to the venue where Jury and Lena were waiting for the records and the equipment to be unloaded. It was now after six o'clock and Jury had spent the last hour trying to assure the guy who had brought us in that we would indeed show up to play the concert. Now that we had arrived Jury was breathing a lot easier and asked us where the hell we had to go to find my dad. "I'll explain it all later," I said. "But there's one thing for sure. Tomorrow, he gets his bus ticket."

The show was late getting started that night, due to our late setup and sound check, and although the people had to be kept outside waiting to get in for an extra fifteen minutes or so, they really didn't seem to mind. But all I kept thinking the whole time was that it could have been a hell of a lot worse. What if I hadn't been able to find my dad at all? What if we had no amps, speakers, mikes or lights? And how would the newspapers report what had happened to cause Stompin' Tom to be sued for not putting on his concert, even though he was in town in plenty of time to do so?

Both after the show and all the way back to the motel, I was still having visions of a police photo of a drunk man sitting behind the wheel of my van appearing on the front page of the papers the next day, under the headline: STOMPIN' TOM SHOW CANCELLED DUE TO DRUNKENNESS.

As Lena and I stepped out of my car, I could hear a commotion going on through the open door of my dad's room and, after giving her the key to our room and telling her I'd be seeing her later, I decided I'd better go and investigate.

The boys had arrived just before I did, and were now in my dad's room listening to him spout off about everybody who was ever responsible for anything he didn't like. With the look of a man possessed, he was lashing out at everybody and everything he could think of. And my appearance in the room didn't help the situation one bit.

It was obvious that, somewhere deep inside, he was being devoured by some kind of a demon none of us were qualified to contend with.

I had walked into the room with the hope of somehow making peace with him before letting him go. But the deck was stacked, and the cards were dealt, and Fate was having its way. To show anger was futile; to reason, impossible; and friendly diplomacy was met with disdain.

This man who disowned me before I was born was now fast becoming more childless. He raked my pedigree over the coals while I stood there feeling quite helpless.

When I finally couldn't take any more without hitting him, I just turned and walked out and left him there to rage on with the boys. I went over to Jury's room and told him I'd reached the end of my rope and before I got up in the morning, I wanted him gone. "Give him a couple of weeks' pay and buy him a bus ticket to Toronto or Saint John, or to wherever he wants to go, but he can't stay here."

When I got back to my own room, Lena was sleeping, so I just crawled into the extra bed. And after making peace with my real father, The Old Man Upstairs, I went to sleep.

By the time I woke up the next morning, Jury was back from the bus depot. He told me my dad wanted a bus ticket to Saint John, New Brunswick, with a stopover in Toronto, and appeared satisfied with the two weeks' extra pay. When Jury questioned him as to why he wanted the Toronto stopover, he just boarded the bus, and with a quick glance he turned around and said, "You assholes are gonna find out."

(Subsequent letters from Michael White, our lawyer in Toronto, verified that, before going on to Saint John, my dad spent a couple of weeks going around to several different agencies inquiring as to how he might be able to sue me for wrongful dismissal and a number of other things. Now, that's gratitude for you.)

On September 26 we arrived in Yorkton, Saskatchewan, and immediately went to the radio station where we met Ron Waddell, the local DJ, who had just recently run a contest on the air to find out which country artist was the most popular in his listening area. The contest was among all country artists, both American and Canadian. And out of 1,270 letters received, when all the votes were counted, the results were as follows:

The No. 1 Favourite: Stompin' Tom, with 218 votes.
The No. 2 Favourite: Charlie Pride, with 117 votes.
The No. 3 Favourite: Johnny Cash, with 116 votes.

And the rest of the votes were divided between all the other artists.

This made me think that with just sixteen more votes I would have wound up with more than Charlie and Johnny put together. And if the CNE in Toronto had taken a similar poll they wouldn't have been so quick to offer Charlie Pride $35,000 plus for playing the Grandstand while offering me a miserable $3,500 from which I'd have to pay all my own expenses.

Can anyone now wonder why I turned this offer down at the time and told the CNE to wise up and start treating Canadian talent with more respect?

I also thought at the time, and I still think today, that if Canadian radio stations would take a more positive attitude and play the records of more of our identifiably Canadian talent, as opposed to those who copy their American counterparts, they would soon realize how fast the outcome of popularity contests similar to the above would apply to a lot more of our home-grown talent everywhere. (Why in hell don't they just give it a damn good try and see? And let no one be unfair by playing the artist they prefer to win a lot more than the one they prefer to lose.)

I might add that during Country Music Month (October) of that year Ron Waddell sent the results of his radio contest to a number of American and Canadian trade magazines and (don't be surprised) very little or nothing came of it. It even seems that if you're a pro-Canadian DJ you're shunned and frowned upon.

As might be expected, we played to a packed house in Yorkton and the same thing occurred in Estevan and Weyburn. We then moved across Saskatchewan and played Medicine Hat, Alberta, on October 1.

By now, most of the people who came to our shows had already learned that Lena and I were to be wed on television and every autograph session was composed of well-wishers. Only by now they wanted autographs of both the bride and the groom.

The remaining towns to be played in on this western tour (and the last tour I would ever play as a single man, I might add) were Lethbridge, Calgary, Red Deer, Edmonton and Edson, all in Alberta. Then we went back to Saskatchewan and played Prince Albert, Melfort, Saskatoon, Regina and Wynyard. And it was here in Wynyard, Saskatchewan, that I wrote the song "We're Trading Hearts" for our wedding. This song was later sung by Sonny Caulfield on the big day, and still later recorded by Sonny on a Boot Records single because of popular demand. (Radio, of course, didn't give it much play.)

I must mention that while we were still in Alberta, I guested once again on Tommy Banks's CBC television show, and this is where I ran into an old school buddy of mine, Collin MacLean. Collin and I were both Shakespearean actors in the play *A Midsummer Night's Dream* during my brief attendance at the Saint John Vocational School in New Brunswick. He was now a scriptwriter for the Banks show and also had a radio show of his own. We'll be meeting Collin again later on in my story.

By October 22, 1973, we were back in Toronto. And due to all the hustle and bustle about the wedding, we had absolutely no time to rest up from the long drive down from Wynyard, Saskatchewan.

It seemed like Jury must have shut down the business of Boot Records and had all the staff concentrated on nothing but wedding preparations. Plane tickets had to be bought. Family members, bridesmaids and groomsmen, and other special people had to be flown in. Lobsters and several kinds of fish had to be sent in from the east coast. The meats and other kinds of food had to be looked after. And of course the wedding cake. And don't ask me who was in charge of all this because I was busy with all my own problems.

While Lena was out with Carol Jamieson looking at wedding gowns, etc., I was having meetings with Drew Crossan, the producer of Elwood Glover's show, and other members of the CBC. For a whole week before the wedding everything was going crazy.

Lena and I had to meet with Reverend Leslie a couple of times to go over the marriage vows and other spoken parts of the ceremony. Then there were the music selections that were to be played. The guests and special friends that Elwood would interview before and after the wedding. And where were all these people from out of town going to stay? Where, indeed, were Lena and I going to stay on our wedding night to hide from all the pranksters? And among all the people we knew there would certainly be lots of them.

I don't know how everything eventually came into place, but on November 1, 1973, the day before our wedding, all the bridesmaids, the groomsmen, the special guests, the minister, and everybody who had something to do with the wedding ceremony were booked into rooms at the Four Seasons Hotel in downtown Toronto where the wedding was to take place at noon the following day, November 2.

But for this day, the TV cameras all had to be set up and everybody had to rehearse. They had to know from where they would enter and to where they would walk, and where they would be standing during the ceremony. And this was making me almost as nervous as I was on the next day when we had to do the real thing.

When the rehearsal was over, we all went back to our rooms. My room was filled with guys who were passing around the drinks. And Lena, of course, had her own room where she was being attended to by all her maids and galpals.

To my knowledge, both the second and third floors of the Four Seasons Hotel were totally taken up by people involved with the wedding. And maybe there was more. And no matter where you went, there were people scurrying up and down the halls and darting from one room to another. And remember, the regular wedding guests would not appear until the following day. So this was turning into one very momentous occasion.

We're "Trading Hearts" Today

O N THE MORNING OF OUR WEDDING day, November 2, you couldn't sleep even if you wanted to. It sounded like a party was going on in the hall and someone decided to knock on my door. When I opened it, an arm came through with a bottle in it. I took the bottle and said thanks and added it to the other six or eight that were sitting on my dresser.

By the time I was up and about, with a piece of toast in one hand and a bottle of beer in the other, everyone was getting all dolled up, except me. I was going to be wearing my regular Stompin' Tom regalia while everyone else was getting into their gowns and tuxedos. "How in hell can they wear those things?" I thought. "The last time I wore even a suit I got tossed out of the Edison Hotel when the owner told me my singing stunk."

A couple more beers and I decided to wander up to the other end of the hall to where all the girls were getting their hair done. I was hoping to catch a glimpse of Lena and see how she was faring. But a group of excited females soon put the run to me and chased me back down the hall. That's when I began to think that maybe a nice secluded spot in either the Yukon or Labrador might not be a bad place to be in right now.

Next thing I knew, someone was grabbing me and leading me into a room where all those people with powder and lipstick work. You'd think by now I would have gotten used to these "dabbers," but I hated them then and I hate them now. (Not so much for who they are or what they do, but what they do to whom with what they've got.)

By about 11:45 all the guests were seated in their places. I think there were 140 to 150 of them because that's all the room could hold, given the space the cameras needed to move around. There were another three hundred guests invited but we wouldn't get to meet them until later at the reception.

Pretty soon it was twelve o'clock noon and every room in the hotel had their TV sets on and tuned into Elwood's show. The music of the Sonny Caulfield Orchestra played a few bars and the cameras gradually focused on Elwood, who introduced himself and welcomed everybody in Canada to witness the wedding of Stompin' Tom Connors from Prince Edward Island and Lena Welsh of the Magdalene Islands, Quebec.

After a brief explanation of who Lena was and what some of my accomplishments were, he drew attention to some of the more prominent people among our invited guests, such as the federal member of parliament for Egmont, Prince Edward Island, the Reverend David MacDonald; the premier of New Brunswick, Richard Hatfield (accompanied by his girlfriend, Libby); Toronto mayor David Crombie; Toronto alderman Ben Nobleman; Sam (the Record Man) Sniderman; and a few others.

He then interviewed Richard Hatfield; Billy Lewis, my guitar player; and my old buddy, Gaet Lepine, from Timmins. Both Billy and Gaet sang a song and then Sonny Caulfield sang "We're Trading Hearts," the song I wrote out west for our wedding. And then the network went to a couple of very tasteful and appropriate commercials (a prerequisite for showing the wedding on TV).

While this was going on, my best man Johnny Reid and I were ushered to our places in front of the minister's podium to a round of applause from the audience. (This was off camera, of course, but I think Johnny was a lot more nervous than I was.)

Just as I took my hat off and passed it to Johnny, the cameras switched on and the orchestra began to play

"Here Comes the Bride."

First to enter the room were my other two groomsmen, Willard Clohossey, my brother-in-law, and Gerald Hill, Lena's brother-in-law. Next came Lena's two bridesmaids, Mrs. Judy Reid and my sister, Mrs. Marlene Clohossey. They were followed by the matron of honour, Lena's sister, Mrs. Pauline Hill. And then came my beautiful bride, Lena. First she walked a short distance by herself and then, after taking her father's arm, they both approached the podium.

During the next few minutes Reverend Leslie described in detail the meaning of the sacrament of marriage, the significance of the ring and the sacredness of the vows. He then asked who was giving this woman in marriage, and when Lena's dad gave a little cough, he took it to mean "I am" and proceeded to ask us both the most important question: "Do you take . . ." etc. And when we each said "I do," he asked my best man, Johnny, for the ring.

After blessing it, he passed it to me and I put it on Lena's finger. He then gave us both his blessing and good wishes and pronounced us "man and wife."

Sonny Caulfield, with the orchestra, now began to sing the very beautiful "Whither Thou Goest, I Will Go," as Lena and I went down to mingle with the crowd and then join Elwood for a short interview. We then had a long receiving line of well-wishers who offered their congratulations to both of us. And while this was going on Jury came up to me and whispered in my ear that there was a truck outside that had just arrived from the east coast. It contained 200 24-bottle cases of Moosehead beer, straight from the Moosehead Breweries, and delivered to Lena and me for a wedding present. The only problem was, the liquor control board of Ontario regulations would not allow for beer from another province to be unloaded at the hotel. So Jury wanted to know what to do.

"Here's my house key," I said. "Send someone up with the truck and unload the whole damn works in my basement, and I'll find a way to deal with that problem later. I'm sure as hell not going to send it back to New Brunswick. And by the way, leave a couple of cases in the truck for the boys and tell them Stompin' Tom says 'Thanks.'"

Someone now led us over to the large tables where the food was displayed in preparation for everyone to help themselves. Neither Lena nor I had ever seen such an array of food choices in our lives. As we walked the length of the display tables, the first thing that caught my eye was a huge tree of lobsters. And I mean huge. They were neatly stacked side by side in circular rows, layer upon layer. The whole thing reminded me of a steep pyramid. And its height must have been four feet or more off the table, while its base had to be over three feet in diameter.

As we walked towards the far end, we passed the most sumptuous and delicious looking hams, roasts and fish assortments that one can imagine, and all these were interspersed with great bowls of scalloped potatoes and colourful, fresh salads. (I felt like stopping right there and digging in.) But just ahead of us was the grand finale.

There at the end of the table was a huge wedding cake in the shape of Prince Edward Island, decorated in such a way as to accurately depict the three counties of Prince, Queens and Kings, and to name and show the locations of practically every well-known town, including, of course, Skinners Pond. And there parked on the top of this beautiful Island cake was the symbol of Prince Edward Island itself—a huge smiling potato in the shape of a man playing the guitar. And on top of his head was a big black cowboy hat, of course.

Beside this "potato man," on another little stand, was a miniature cowboy boot encircled around the top with a frilly blue garter. Both of these items were so unique and so thoughtfully chosen they would have made wonderful souvenirs. And they did. But not for Lena and me. (Someone, that day, stole them.)

The next duty for Lena and me to perform was to cut the cake. It seemed a shame to desecrate such a beautiful piece of work, but with knife poised on Skinners Pond, and with my hand on hers, we carved our little niche out of Prince Edward Island.

Now it was time for everyone to line up with their plates and dig into this great selection of food. It was all buffet style and everyone, including the bride and groom, were expected to help themselves.

Lena and I, with an assortment of food on our plates, including lobster, made our way to the head table where the champagne was flowing like water. We had two beautifully glazed bride and bridegroom glasses with our names engraved on each, which were given to us for just this special occasion (and even after all these years it would still be nice of the person or persons whose possession they are now in to please return them.)

The first toast was proposed to us by the Reverend David MacDonald, MP for Egmont, P.E.I. Then several others followed. Each one was very touching and meaningful and very humbly received, as we sipped from the glasses I just described.

Between the clatter of silverware on plates, indicating everyone wanted to see me kiss my bride, someone was reading telegrams from different parts of the world. Most were from Canada and the United States, but some were from Ireland, England, and as far away as Australia. Just two that immediately come to mind were from Wilf Carter and Johnny Cash.

Just before leaving the account of our wedding, I will leave you with the words of the song I wrote for this memorable occasion. Although Sonny Caulfield sang it beautifully at the wedding, his recording of it has not been available for a long time. However, my own original version is still available on CD and cassette, should you be interested.

WE'RE TRADING HEARTS

1.

We're Trading Hearts today; we're going all the
*   way;*
Changing from yesterday; two people apart.
I'll love you, come what may; this holy vow we say
On this, our wedding day: We're Trading Hearts.

2.

We're Trading Hearts today; knowing the world's
*   okay;*
Walking the same highway; never to part.

*And if the skies be grey, I'll take your hand and
    say,
Will you be mine today; We're Trading Hearts.*

3.
*We're Trading Hearts today; we're going all the
    way;
Changing from yesterday; two people apart.
And if the sky be grey, I'll take your hand and say,
Will you be mine today; We're Trading Hearts.
Will you be mine today, 'cause We're Trading
    Hearts.*

After everyone had eaten and the wedding party had now changed into something more comfortable, most of our guests followed us to the Imperial Theatre where my movie *Across This Land* was coincidentally premièring. It isn't often that a new bride and groom go to a movie immediately after getting married but, as stated before, in this case the groom was the star and the movie was the first Canadian full-length musical ever. Lena and I would be embarking on our honeymoon first thing in the morning and, if we failed to see the movie now, we wouldn't get to see it again for a couple of months, for that was the length of time we'd be out of the country.

As soon as the movie was over, we jumped into the limos and headed straight for the reception where another three hundred people were waiting for us to arrive. The reception was being held in the Civic Square Commonwealth Room at the Holiday Inn, and by the time we got there, at around 10 P.M., the place was already hoppin'.

The backup music was provided by a very popular country band known as The East Wind, and the guest singers who mounted the stage one after the other were myriad. They all offered their congratulations and best wishes, interspersed with the usual jokes, mainly aimed at the groom, and some of them even gave their own renditions of a few Stompin' Tom songs, complete with foot stompin'.

Lena and I were, of course, given the floor to perform our first dance, and after that, I hardly saw her again for a while. It seemed like we were dancing with everybody. And, believe me, there were people there from every walk of life. There were politicians, doctors, lawyers, accountants and all kinds of business types, intermingling with farmers, fishermen, truckers, mechanics, painters and factory workers. And this doesn't even take in the people involved in any way with the music business. They were the producers, publishers, singers, songwriters, musicians, agents and promoters who all, in some way or another, were connected with my career or the marketing of the Stompin' Tom or other artists' records. And, of course, a few of the media types were there to cover every move.

Sometime just after midnight, Lena and I sneaked out to a waiting car and zoomed off to a secret location where my own car was hidden. From there we went to a previously booked motel out of town where our honeymoon luggage was packed and ready for the trip.

Our Extended Honeymoon

THE FOLLOWING NIGHT WE spent in Niagara Falls and from there it was a long drive to Miami, Florida, where we boarded a cruise ship called the *Southward* and sailed around the Caribbean for the next couple of weeks.

Some of the places we visited were Caracas, Venezuela, on the South American continent, and a number of islands such as Curaçao, Grenada, Barbados, Martinique, Antigua, Puerto Rico, the Dominican Republic and the Virgin Islands. Our last stop before returning to Miami was the Bahamas. We didn't take the tour bus in these places very often but opted instead to take the local taxis or just walk around by ourselves and talk to the local people.

We found that by doing this we could get a better handle on how the people actually lived and what they mostly thought about. There was no way to learn this from listening to a tour guide on a bus, travelling through the most opulent parts of towns and visiting historic sites and monuments.

We gambled a little on some of the islands—without much luck, I might add—but Lena was able to pick up a couple hundred dollars one night aboard ship, playing bingo. (Not one of my games.)

There were three or four bars and lounges on board and the music was entertaining for a while, but with nothing "country" we began to feel that two weeks was just a little too long. Once you'd seen all the acts and played all the games, the routine began to get boring. The meals were very good and we got to meet some very nice people, but we were also glad to get back to Miami and start out on the next adventure.

While in Montgomery, Alabama, we went to visit the gravesite of the late great Hank Williams, and also the museum where a number of his personal effects were displayed. And from there we drove through the states of Mississippi, Louisiana and Texas, into Mexico. This was sometime during the last week of November 1973.

We crossed into Mexico at Laredo, and for the next three days we drove pretty hard until we got to Mexico City. The first night in town we bumped into a chap by the name of Jose Castro who could speak a little English and offered to drive us around in his own car to see the local sights and amusements for as long as we decided to stay in town. His price? Ten dollars a day (U.S.), which, at the time, was approximately 120 pesos. Of course, I took him up on it, and for the next three days we went to the theatre and saw a musical extravaganza, went to a bullfight and a dog show, toured most of the city, and spent most of one day at Teotihuacan climbing up and down pyramids and walking through ancient ruins. This place is spectacular and, of course, I captured all of it on my movie camera, as I did with all other interesting places and events.

After leaving Mexico City we just took our merry old time. We hadn't booked any accommodations ahead before we left home, and so we just took our chances everywhere we went.

In Vera Cruz we were held up for five or six days while I had to have the front left fender of my car totally replaced. While I was about to go through a downtown intersection, a bus driver who decided to run a light came crashing into me. And to my surprise, when the police came, they took not only his driver's licence away, on the spot, but they also took mine. The bus driver was clearly in the wrong, but because the policeman couldn't speak a word of English, I just had to go by his hand signals. He indicated that I should leave the car right where it was and go looking for an address he wrote on a piece of paper. Lucky for us, it was just a couple of blocks down the street, and it turned out to be a government motor vehicle licensing office.

After we found one man who could speak a little English, he informed me that I would have to get a lawyer before I could get my licence back. This would take several days, so I might as well find myself some accommodations while I was waiting. Meanwhile, the normal procedure was for the police to tow my vehicle to a pound until my lawyer notified them to release it into his custody or the custody of some repair shop that he would designate. It could not be released into my custody until I got my licence back. And when would that be? Only after a "thorough police investigation" into the accident to determine the damage done to both vehicles and to what extent I might have been at fault, if any.

He gave me the address of a lawyer whose business it was to look after these things. He then bid me good day.

Lena and I walked to the lawyer's office, which was again just down the street, but unfortunately it was closed. We then walked nearly a mile and a half back along the same street to the motel we had booked for one night, just two hours ago, and managed to make them understand what had happened. I also got them to agree to rent us our room on a daily basis until we found out what was going to happen to our brand-new Chevy Caprice.

It was too late in the day to do anything else but go to our room and wait till tomorrow. I spent the rest of the night with my nose in the little book I had bought, entitled *How to Speak Spanish in 5 Minutes.*

The next day I left Lena to sit around the swimming pool while I went to see the lawyer. He also spoke a little English (and maybe even more than he let on). And as soon as I told him my problem, he said, "Fifty dollars. I fix everything." And he indicated he wanted to be paid right away. "Come back tomorrow," he said, as he walked me to the door.

When I went in the next day and asked him what was happening, he said, "Fifty dollars." And until I slapped it down he looked determined that he wasn't going to tell me anything. When I put the money down, he smiled and told me that he had notified the police and that my car was now at an auto body shop waiting to be repaired. When I asked him about my licence he told me, "This is Mexico, Señor, it takes a leetle time. Come back tomorrow."

The following day was the same thing. First comes the question and then the "Fifty dollar" answer. Every time I thought of Jose Castro, who drove us around for three days in Mexico City for $30, I couldn't help but think that this guy who called himself a lawyer was just milking me for everything he could get. After all, I had just paid him $150 (1,800 pesos) and I was still no further ahead.

The next day, instead of going to the lawyer's office, I called a cab and went to the police station. After insisting I wanted to speak with someone who understood English, I waited for half an hour or so, until some high-ranking officer appeared and took me into his office.

"Where is my car?" I wanted to know. "And why can't I get my driver's licence? The accident was not my fault. Even the bus driver can tell you that," I said. "So where is he?"

"Now, don't get excited, Señor," was the reply. "The bus driver? He is in jail. And that is where you could be if you cause any trouble. Your lawyer is looking after your car and the licence bureau will give you your licence back when and if they see fit. In Mexico, we are very thorough in what we do, so just have a little patience. Now, good day, Señor."

From the police station, I taxied over to the licence bureau, and when I found the same guy I spoke to before, he said there was nothing he could do but inform my lawyer when the status of my licence was known.

In total frustration, I walked down the couple of blocks to see my lawyer. When he was ready to see me in his office, I walked in and said, "Yeah, I know. Fifty dollars. Now what in hell can you tell me today that I didn't know yesterday?"

After scooping up the fifty dollars, he said, "Ahh! Señor, I just received some good news. You have been cleared of any fault concerning your accident and you may go down to the licence bureau tomorrow at three o'clock in the afternoon and they will give you your licence."

"Well, that's better," I said. "Now what about my car. Where is it? I would like to see it." "Oh, your car," he said. "It is quite far away and they are just beginning to repair it, but if you come back tomorrow I—" And that's where I cut him off. "Listen," I said. "I came all the way down here from Canada on my honeymoon and I don't intend to spend my entire budget coming to your office every day. If I get my licence tomorrow, my wife and I are going to rent a car and see something more in Mexico besides the inside of a motel room in Vera Cruz." With that, I left him mumbling something to himself.

At three o'clock the following afternoon I went to the licence bureau and, not being able to see the guy I spoke to before, I found myself lined up at a wicket waiting to get my licence. After another forty-five eons of time, it was my turn to present my name, my passport and other credentials to the teller. She said something to me which I didn't understand and, after looking at me as if I was stupid, she marked something on a piece of paper and passed it to me. I looked at it and immediately understood. She wanted me to pay her before she passed me my licence. The sum? Six hundred pesos. Or, to be exact, fifty dollars.

She looked at me and smiled when I paid her. But I just grabbed my licence and took off with the suspicion that the whole damn town must have been in cahoots. Just some kind of a tourist rip-off. I then grabbed a cab and went to a car rental service. All I could get was a dinky little Volkswagen Beetle, but I took it anyway, and 'round about 5:30 P.M. I arrived back at the motel.

As I drove up and jumped out, Lena was walking around looking bored as usual under the frustrating circumstances. Taking a look at the Beetle and then back at me, she said, "Is that all that's left of our car?" At least I could see she still had her sense of humour intact, so I said, "Yeah, that's all. But it's going to get us the hell out of here in the morning. They're just starting to work on the Caprice, and given the speed with which they work around here, they should be done by the time we get back from the Yucatan."

The following day we took off and spent the next three nights in Villahermosa, Campeche and Mérida. We viewed the ruins at Uxmal and climbed the pyramids in Chichén Itzá. We would then have gone on to Cancun and Cozumel, but the delay in Vera Cruz had cut our time short, so in Valladolid, just 101 miles short of our proposed destination, we turned back. The date would be somewhere around the thirteenth of December 1973.

On our way back we visited the ruins of Palenque, and from the top of the highest pyramid we entered the newly discovered, long, winding stairs down into the base of the structure. And there we viewed the beautifully carved stone that covered the huge sarcophagus which had been the burial place of some ancient mummified king. Or was he a king? In one of his books, the famous Erich Von Däniken supposed that he may have been an ancient astronaut. The being depicted on the large rectangular stone would certainly suggest that he was operating some kind of a craft, not unlike a miniature submarine or a space capsule. Both his feet and hands seemed to be controlling some kind of buttons and levers, and he seemed to be intent on going somewhere.

On about the eighteenth of December, we were back in Vera Cruz after travelling some thirteen or fourteen hundred miles in that bumpy little Volkswagen. We arrived in the evening so we booked into the same motel as we had before. And needless to say, I was ready to tear the town apart if my Caprice wasn't ready by now.

At ten o'clock sharp the next morning, I was in the lawyer's office with my fifty bucks in my hand. And when the lawyer saw me, he reached out and took the money and with a smile he said, "Ahhh! Señor Connor, she is a fine day, no? Your car, it is ready. And if you come into my office, I have the necessary papers for you to sign so you can go and pick it up."

As soon as I signed the papers, he said, "Now that will be 4,800 pesos, or four hundred dollars, Señor." I said, "Just a minute. If it's all right with you, I'll just pay the guy that fixed the car, after I see it." "Ahh! But that would be impossible, Señor," he said. "The guy who fixed your car, he is my brother, and you don't know where he lives." "I get the goddamn point," I said. "If I don't pay you, I don't get to see my car again. You guys have a real nice setup around here, don't you?"

As I peeled off the 4,800 pesos, he just smiled. He then recounted the money and passed me an address with directions to a location not more than five or six blocks away from where we were.

"And by the way, Señor Connor," he said, as he walked me to the door, "I wouldn't make too many unfounded accusations in this town if I were you. Our very honourable chief of police might not like hearing about them."

"Thanks for the advice," I said. "And by the way, is he your brother, too?" At that, he just smiled and looked up at the sky, saying, "Ahh! Señor Connor, she is a fine day, no?" I jumped in the Volkswagen and drove away, leaving him standing by the door. As I drove to the motel to get Lena, before picking my car up, I thought, "If I ever go to a foreign country again, I'll make damn sure I have proper insurance to cover this kind of thing." (Regular Canadian insurance did not cover Mexico at the time.)

After checking out of the motel and with Lena aboard, we drove to the address where my car was. I was surprised to see it was only parked in the alley behind a private dwelling. There was a small one-car garage that obviously looked like the place where my car was fixed, and as I jumped out to take a look I was expecting the worst. Actually, upon closer inspection, I was happy to see that they had done an excellent job.

As I told Lena to get in and drive the Caprice while I took the Volkswagen back to the car rental, we realized we still didn't have the keys. Just at that time a couple of burly-looking fellows came walking towards us. One had my keys dangling from his hand. He said something in Spanish which I didn't understand, but I said, "Gracias" anyway, and reached for my keys. "No, Señor," he said, "pesos, pesos," as he stuck out his other hand.

"What the hell is going on here?" I said. "I already paid the lawyer for the repair job." I then pointed in the direction of the lawyer's office. "Si, si," he kept saying, as he smiled and kept moving his head up and down, but still indicating he wanted me to put some pesos in his hand before giving me the keys.

He must want a tip or something, I thought, so I pulled some money out of my pocket and put a hundred-peso bill in his hand. He indicated that that was not enough, so I gave him another one. It was still not enough. And when I got up to six one-hundred peso bills, he smiled again and said, "Gracias, gracias," and passed me the keys.

By now, I began to see the resemblance between him and that goddam lawyer. And the amount of money I paid him came to exactly fifty dollars.

When I passed the keys to Lena, I said, "Let's get the jeezes out of this f-----' town before I go nuts." We then took the Volkswagen back and said goodbye to Vera Cruz forever, and ever, and ever.

Not counting the motel bills and the cost of the car rental, the accident cost me $750 or 9,000 pesos. And it wasn't even my fault. I kept feeling quite peeved about the whole thing until I began to think about the bus driver. By the way the laws in that town worked, he was probably still rotting in jail.

Later that night, we stayed at a hotel in Oaxaca (pronounced Waw hawka) and the following morning we went to see the famous Tree of Tule just a few miles out of town. This is a magnificently large tree whose leaves and branches cover an entire churchyard and extend over half the church itself. I estimated its trunk to be at least sixty feet around, with a diameter of approximately twenty feet. According to some authorities, it is the oldest tree in the world. And local superstition has it that the twisted faces of thirteen men who were once hung from its branches can still be seen in the gnarls of its trunk. On the other side of the church there is another tree about half the size, which is a seedling from the first and is itself considered to be eight or nine hundred years old. Judging from the appearance of the curious bystanders this famous tree was being visited by people from all over the world.

A couple of days later we pulled into Acapulco. This was the twenty-first of December, on the afternoon of Lena's birthday. We booked into the Ritz Hotel overlooking the beach and immediately upon getting unpacked she dragged me uptown for a shopping spree. There she bought several great-looking outfits which, back home, would have cost a fortune, but down there they were surprisingly reasonable. That evening we watched a floor show and later went wining

and dining under candlelight near a nice bay window
where the moon reflected beautifully on the waters of the
Acapulco harbour.

I guess I would have looked out the window more often,
but I couldn't take my eyes off Lena, who was just sitting
there looking so lovely, with her hair all done up loosely in a
Mexican style and wearing her new two-piece outfit of white
cotton and lace. As we ticked our glasses together, I'll always
remember thinking how lucky I was to be married to not
only the greatest, but also the most beautiful girl in the
world. (And she still is.)

The following day, after going for a swim and lying on the
beach for a while, I began thinking about our financial
situation and whether I would have enough money to make
it back home. The problems we had in Vera Cruz had hit me
quite hard in the pocket-book and I decided to go to a bank
and have some money transferred just in case.

When I got to the bank I found that this was a lot more
easily said than done. After finding out how complicated it
was and the number of days it was going to take, I decided
to call Jury in Toronto and find out if there might be a
quicker way.

It just so happened that a friend of Jury's who worked in
a travel agency was flying to Acapulco the following day and
she could bring the necessary funds to me upon her arrival.
This turned out great and the next day I had the money.

The following afternoon, while lying on the beach and
getting pestered by the hawkers trying to sell us everything
from clothes to jewellery, I happened to notice, a ways further down the beach, that a speedboat with a long rope was
towing a very large wing which ascended from the ground
into the air with a man attached to it. After soaring around
the harbour for about ten minutes, the speedboat brought
him back and he alighted once again on the sand.

"Let's take a walk along the beach and see what's going
on down there," I said to Lena. And in a few minutes we
were watching this thing rising and descending with a different person on each trip. They were charging people to
take them for a ride.

"I think I'll try this thing and see what it's like," I said.

Lena looked at me and said, "What! Are you crazy or some-thing?" And before she could say another word, I bought a ticket. "Get the movie camera ready," I said. "I'm going for a ride."

Pretty soon the contraption landed. After they unhar-nessed the guy, it was my turn. No sooner did they strap the harness on me when the speedboat took off and, in an instant, I was in the air. When I looked back and spotted Lena, she still had her hands over her eyes. I guess she thought that was the last she was ever going to see of her new husband. But finally, after a while, she got brave enough to look through the camera and take a few feet of film.

I'll have to admit it was a lot more bumpy up there than it appeared to be from the ground. As long as the boat beneath me sped along in a straight line I kept rising, but just as I was over a small rocky islet in the harbour, the boat decided to make a turn. And just as it did, I lost altitude, and just as it appeared that I was going to come crashing down on the rocks below, the boat again was speeding along in a straight line and I was swooped high in the air once again.

"Well, finally," I thought, "I know what it feels like to be a bird. Except I don't have any control." I could have stayed up there a little longer but the boat was now preparing to take me in for a landing. Below me was a high board fence, and they damn near brought me down astraddle of it. But at the very last second, they gave me another quick pull and there I was landing on the sand, rolling head over heels. It had been a great experience, but at the same time I was glad to get the hell out of there.

When I walked over to where Lena was, I asked her if she wanted to go up. "No way," she said. And so we walked along the beach and back to our hotel.

That evening we dined in a small restaurant where three traditionally dressed Mexican entertainers were walking from table to table playing their guitars and singing. They harmonized beautifully together and we both just loved their music. It appeared they were playing requests for tips so I summoned them over and requested "Via Con Dios" and "La Cucaracha."

I don't remember what we ate but Lena got very sick later

that night and the doctor had to be summoned to our hotel room. Perhaps it was the water. At any rate the doctor gave her something and by the next morning, she was feeling okay again. We weren't able to understand the doctor too well so we just supposed that she had a touch of Montezuma's Revenge, something that didn't effect me at all, as I was drinking Corona beer the whole time I was down there.

Other than in Acapulco it was very hard to obtain meals that were not terribly hot and spicy. Even at breakfast time, the eggs were not only spicy but also very chalky. For two people such as Lena and me, who like our food on the bland side, it was extremely difficult to get a decent meal.

While the countryside is beautiful it is also dotted with the poorest of poor dwellings. Mostly thatched-roof houses with clay floors. And it's not uncommon to see women washing clothes for ten or twelve kids by scrubbing them on the rocks by the sides of rivers.

In larger centres, such as Mexico City itself, if your hotel room happens to be higher up than five or six floors, you get a surprise when you look down from out of your window. For there below you, on hundreds of flat-roof buildings, lives the entire subculture of Mexico. Whole families live in the tiniest tarpaper shacks where pigs and chickens and other smaller animals roam freely within the confines of fences constructed around the roof's edges to keep them from falling over. They have huge tubs for collecting rainwater, I presume for washing, but what they do with their sewage, I don't know. (But their vegetable gardens seem to be thriving quite well.)

The streets are full of shabbily dressed beggars and hawkers and one gets tired after a while from giving so many handouts and buying worthless trinkets.

One day around noon, Lena and I were sitting by the window of a second-storey restaurant. While we were having lunch, we happened to notice a woman sitting on the sidewalk up next to a building on the opposite side of the street. She was wearing a huge faded blanket with a hole cut in the centre to poke her head through. This was her dress.

As we kept watching this woman, we couldn't imagine

what all the commotion was going on under her blanket. Within minutes we found out. She must have had four or five kids under there and somehow they must have gotten into a fight. First, one of them came running out from under the blanket, followed by another one who struck the first and made him cry. A third one was now standing outside the blanket observing the other two and the blanket was still moving to suggest there were still another one or two kids huddling beneath it. All these kids were stark naked.

The woman, who obviously couldn't get up and chase them around, was hollering at them to get back under the blanket. Finally they did and the woman now calmly went back to holding her hand out to the passersby.

Noticing that there weren't too many people on the street and those that did pass by were just ignoring her, I said to Lena, "You wait here. I can't stand to see that poor woman sit there all day with those kids under that blanket waiting for someone to give her enough to feed them with." I got up and walked down to the street.

Not to arouse her suspicion, I first walked away from her until I got to the intersection. I then crossed at the light and came walking down towards her on the opposite side of the street from where Lena was looking out the window. With five hundred pesos (the equivalent of about $41) scrunched up into a little ball in my hand, I approached her. As I placed the little ball of money in her hand, one of the little kids stuck his head out from under the blanket. I ruffled his hair and walked on.

By the time I got to the end of the short street, I crossed over again and started back to where Lena was still waiting in the restaurant. When I was directly across the street from the woman, I could see she was extremely excited. She was now standing up trying to organize her brood, and I have to say it was funny to see her under that huge tent trying to waddle down the street just as fast as those little feet would allow her.

Lena, of course, had been watching this whole episode from the upstairs restaurant window. And when I went up to get her she was wiping her eyes with a tissue, so I asked her what was the matter. "Oh, nothing," she said. "I just can't seem to get used to these hot spices."

Back to December 24, 1973. It seemed a bit odd, to say the least, to be lying on the sandy beach of Acapulco, taking in the sunshine on the day before Christmas. All we talked about all day was what we thought everyone else would be doing back home.

With all this hot weather and no snow there was nothing to remind us of the festive season. No Christmas shoppers, no decorations, no tree and no presents to open. What, with no turkey and dressing and no friends to have a drink with and wish Merry Christmas to, we began to look at each other and say, Yeah! What the hell are we doing here anyway? So that night we packed up, and on Christmas morning we said goodbye to Acapulco and headed for home.

On Christmas night we arrived in a small town where I went into a hotel to book our room. When that was done the desk clerk told me I could park around at the back. With Lena in the car, we drove around back and just as we opened the doors we heard one god-awful clamour and ruckus going on up near the building. As we stepped out, we saw one very large pile of rubbish and garbage piled up against the back of the hotel. And the noise and commotion was coming from a scurrying horde of rats that had been scavenging through the garbage. As Lena gave a yelp and jumped back into the car, I jumped in and turned around. And when my headlights hit the garbage heap, there must have been fifty rats that ran every which-a-way in front of us. As soon as I drove back to the front of the hotel, I went in and demanded my money back, and we drove on to the next place.

The following day, as we stopped to eat and gas up, Lena went into a small grocery store to buy a chocolate bar. After we ate and were heading back to the car, Lena decided to open the package and munch on her bar. I happened to be looking at her just as she was about to take a bite and quickly snapped the thing out of her hand. "What did you do that for?" she said. I picked the bar off the ground and showed her. The chocolate had a small break at one end, and there moving in and out of the hole were a million maggots. Needless to say, she didn't buy any more chocolate till we got back to good ol' Canada.

The next day, in Durango, Mexico, we spent the afternoon going through a small western-movie type town which was built by some film company from Hollywood. All the buildings except the saloon were movable. There was a train station next to a short piece of track which went nowhere, and several passenger coaches which went nowhere also.

Living in the saloon was a Mexican family who had been hired as caretakers and, although they were not allowed to let anyone snoop around, an American five-dollar bill soon changed their minds.

There was a general store, a church, a bank, a land office, a blacksmith and a livery stable, along with a few dwellings with little white paling fences out front. As Lena and I had the whole town to ourselves, we wandered in and out of everywhere pretending we were Marshal Matt Dillon and Miss Kitty.

That night we ate in Durango and stayed there, and the next day we were on our way. We passed through some really spectacular looking country where bands of *caballeros* (cowboys) were driving their herds from place to place, over open ranges, and sometimes right across the road in front of us. Of course, we'd have to stop until they all got by.

The grandeur and splendour of the great expanses of land that we passed through, with all their mysterious-looking mesas and unreachable-looking mountains, were absolutely breathtaking. Then we passed through what seemed to be a million miles of cactus trees growing everywhere. And although we saw no dwellings or vehicles parked anywhere along this seemingly endless road, we were occasionally reminded that we were not alone. For just when you were not expecting it, from out behind some weird-looking cactus plant would step some lone Mexican, or sometimes one accompanied by an old scrubby-looking burro. Where they would come from or where they were going is anybody's guess. And what the hell they were doing all alone away out here in this vast wilderness of wasteland, God only knows.

Our last night in Mexico was spent in Chihuahua and the next day we travelled the last 250 miles north to the Texas border, into El Paso, across the Rio Bravo (known to us as the Rio Grande).

One more point to remember for anyone who wants to drive the length and breadth of Mexico as we did: Every time you cross the border or meet a customs officer (and sometimes they can be stationed in just a little hut in the middle of nowhere), when he wants to check what you are carrying, let him. And don't forget to tip him. Because if you don't he's apt to hold you up for a couple of hours for absolutely no reason. And when he finally lets you go, he phones the guy up the road at the next checkpoint, and you can be sure you'll be held up there as well.

On our last day in northern Mexico we saw a few snow flurries but that was all. There wasn't much in West Texas, but after we left Albuquerque and Santa Fe, New Mexico, we ran into a bit more. Somewhere around Denver, Colorado, we headed into a big ice storm. And you could tell by all the cars in the ditches that the people from around there just weren't used to driving under these conditions. On one occasion when we were coming down a grade there was a long bridge ahead of us. And there on the middle of the bridge were several cars that had just been in an accident. Nothing serious yet, just fender benders, but one car was bouncing back and forth against one guard-rail and then over to the other. There was no way I could put on the brakes, 'cause if I did I'd be just another car all dinged up with the rest of them. Judging by what side of the road the bouncing car would not be on by the time I got there, while Lena was shouting "Ooo, ooo" and "Oh, oh," I managed to miss him by a hair's breadth and just kept right on going. I couldn't have stopped anyway, even if I had wanted to.

After that, there was snow all the way, and in some places lots of it. We travelled through Nebraska, Iowa, Illinois, Indiana, Ohio and Michigan, and finally crossed the border into Canada at Windsor, Ontario. The date was now the sixth of January in 1974. And on the seventh of January we were back home in Toronto. All in all we had travelled some 14,000 miles and that's just by the way the crow flies, with no bends in the road.

In late 1969 someone covered Toronto with billboards as shown above.
We still haven't found out who did it.
Canadian Panorama, 1970.

The honourable Dan MacDonald presents Stompin' Tom with a
"Golden Spud" in honour of his 1969 hit recording
"Bud the Spud," the song that brought instant acclaim to the
Prince Edward Island potato, June 1, 1970.

*Premier Richard Hatfield of New Brunswick and Premier Ed Shreyer of
Manitoba present Tom's stompin' board back to him
autographed by all ten premiers of Canada during a premier's
conference in Charlottetown, P.E.I., in the early 1970s.*

*Sam (the Record Man) Sniderman presenting Tom with one of his
many gold albums in Halifax, July 1973.*

Tom and Lena get engaged in February 1973.

*In front of onlookers, Tom gets to meet Her Majesty Queen Elizabeth II
and Prince Philip, July 1, 1973, in Charlottetown, P.E.I.
From left to right: Queen Elizabeth, Premier Alex Campbell of P.E.I.,
an unidentified woman, Prince Philip and Tom on the far right.*

JUST MARRIED
Tom, his bride Lena and the Reverend Bev Leslie (left),
November 2, 1973.

Kneeling: Tom's new bride, Lena. Standing: Lena's mother, Lottie, Tom,
Lena's father, Peter Welsh and Premier Richard Hatfield of New
Brunswick, November 2, 1973.

Tom and Lena were married on Elwood Glover's CBC television show Luncheon Date *at noon, November 2, 1973. Here Elwood interviews the newlyweds.*

Tom and Lena on their honeymoon in the Caribbean, November 1973.

The caption "A little 'Romper for the Stomper'"
appeared with this picture in newspapers across
Canada in late June 1976.

The proud Dad with Tom Jr.,
June 1976.

*In Montreal, Tom's mother, Isabel, holding
Tommy Jr., who was three years old, 1979.*

*The first big catch. Seven-year-old Tommy Jr. and Dad
at Skinners Pond, P.E.I., 1983.*

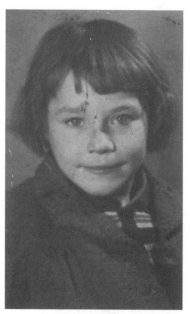

Lena at seven years old at home on Entry Island, Magdalene Islands, Quebec, 1953.

Tom Jr. (M.V.P.), 1979.

Tom and Lena crossing the Arctic Circle on the Dempster Highway in the Yukon, June 1980. The picture was snapped by Tom Jr. at four years of age.

*The first meeting of Tom and Brian
Edwards at Ann Dunn's
Matador Club in Toronto, 1989.*

*Tom performing at Toronto's
Matador Club during the
"Comeback Party" in late 1989.*

*During a news conference, Tom sends his six Junos
back to CARAS, the Canadian Academy of Recording
Arts and Sciences, March 1978.*

On tour in 1990. Stompin' Tom
is back with a vengeance.

Stompin' Tom in action,
beginning his Comeback Tour
in 1989.

Tom and Lena, taken at their house, circa 1992.

This huge Stompin' Tom mural appeared on the side of Sam the Record Man Sniderman's building, downtown Toronto, circa early 1990s.
It was painted by Bill Wrigley.

Stompin' Tom visiting Stonehenge, summer 1992.

"Put your name right here, Stompin' Tom."
(Somewhere in the wilderness of British Columbia.)

Congratulating Canada's Blue Berets in 1994
during a trip through
C.F.B. Camp Petawawa and Camp Borden, Ontario.

Tom Jr. graduates while Dad sheds a happy tear and
Mom wants to celebrate, November 1995.

Dr. Stompin' Tom.
In May 1993 Stompin' Tom receives a Doctorate
of Laws (Honoris Causa) LL.D. at
St. Thomas University, Fredericton, N.B.

One of the many line-ups for the Stompin' Tom
"Comeback Tour" in 1990.

Stompin' Tom breaking the all-time record
at Lulu's Roadhouse in Kitchener, Ontario,
for the third time in 1993.

Jean and Gaet Lepine and Tom and Lena Connors.
French frogs and Irish logs out to a liquid lunch on
Mother's Day, mid-1990s.

*The old Skinners Pond School tries to make it again
in the mid-1990s.*

*After unveiling the Stompin' Tom Award for the "Unsung Musical
Heroes" of the East Coast in Charlottetown, P.E.I., February 8, 1996.
From left: the premier of Prince Edward Island, Catherine Callbeck,
with Tom and Lena Connors.*

*Tom's sixtieth birthday party at Johnny Reid's Prince Edward Lounge
in Charlottetown, February 9, 1996.
From left: Eric McEwen (ECMA chairman), David MacMillan (EMI Records),
Tom Connors, Lena Connors, Johnny Reid and J.P. Cormier.*

Receiving the Officer's Medal of the Order of Canada from His Excellency Romeo LeBlanc, Canada's governor general, at Rideau Hall, Ottawa, November 14, 1996. From left: Lena Connors, His Excellency Romeo LeBlanc, Mrs. Diana Fowler LeBlanc and Stompin' Tom Connors.

(Photo: Sgt. Christian Coulombe)

The Connors family during the "Man of the Land" Tour '98.
From left: Tom Jr., Tom Sr. and Lena Connors.

The billboard says it all. This lighted sign remained unchanged on Guelph Street in Georgetown, Ontario, during November 1998.

On the ice at Maple Leaf Gardens. Stompin' Tom with Mark LaForme and the Formula setting up their equipment. This was the last night the Toronto Maple Leafs would ever play at the Gardens and Tom was invited to play and sing "The Hockey Song," February 13, 1999. (The finale was awesome.)

Stompin' Tom with Cynthia Good (publisher of Penguin Books Canada) and Dean Cameron (president of EMI, Canada) at the "Book and Record Launch" at Ann Dunn's Matador Club in Toronto, October 26, 1995.

(Barry Roden Photography)

"Stompin' Tom's Canada"
TV Series

WELL, HERE IT WAS THE EIGHTH of January 1974. We had just arrived back from our honeymoon yesterday and the phone was ringing. It was Jury. "Guess what, Tom? The CBC wants you to star in your own series, and they want to talk to us tomorrow."

There was no sense telling him I had just got in the door and I needed a bit of a rest to collect my marbles. So the next day I was out to a long meeting with the CBC brass and on January 10 the contract for my television series, "Stompin' Tom's Canada," was signed. I was given a choice of several producers, including Cy True of "Countrytime" fame, from Halifax, but I opted instead for Don McRae, from Edmonton, Alberta. My reasons were simple. I had gone to school with Collin MacLean. He and I had worked together as actors in Shakespearean plays and I knew that if Don McRae were producing, Collin would be helping me with the scriptwriting.

The CBC wanted twenty-six episodes in the series while I only wanted to do thirteen. My reason was that I was a firm believer that too many appearances on TV cuts drastically into one's record sales and if a person is on the screen all the time, he sells no records at all. (I still believe this.) So a compromise was struck and the number of episodes was set at twenty-one.

303

Between the twelfth of the month and the twenty-fifth, Don McRae, Collin and several of the Edmonton crew flew down to Toronto for a series of meetings. These were to find out just what my ideas for a series were and how they could be implemented. Once they found out that I wanted to travel with the crew all across the country to document all I had written in my songs, the format was set and all they had to do now was get a road crew together and start travelling.

During the days when there were no meetings, I was writing a few songs and going in and out of the studio to record some of them. One day I was on the "Tommy Hunter Show" and another I was back on "Luncheon Date" with Lena, being interviewed by Elwood Glover, who wanted to know how everything went on our honeymoon.

When my birthday on February 9 rolled around, I told everybody to come to my place for a big party. And whatever you do don't bring any booze. Remember those two hundred cases of beer I got from Moosehead Breweries on my wedding day? Well, they were still in my basement and I was just itching to get rid of some of them so I could move around. Everybody who came to the party had to drink beer. And as each person left he was given two 24s of Moosehead to take home. Like one fella said, "This is the kind of party I want to go to all the time. You come with nothing, drink to your heart's content, and leave with a forty-eight-pint 'traveller.'" I guess I must have given away at least fifty cases that night, plus all we drank. But it still didn't seem to put much of a dent into the pile. Anyhow, no worry. It sure didn't go bad. I had several more parties of a similar nature before the whole winter was out and soon the place was back to normal.

Off and on, for the next couple of months, either myself or the boys and I and Lena were flying back and forth from Toronto to Edmonton to film winter scenes for the series. While we were out there on one occasion we got a chance to finish the album I had started to record in Toronto in January. We finished it off in the Damon studios and called it *Stompin' Tom Meets Muk Tuk Annie.*

All told now, at this point in time, with *Muk Tuk Annie* included, I had eleven albums of original songs recorded, ten albums of cover songs, two compilations of the cover song albums, two albums taken from the soundtrack of the movie, and one Dominion compilation of the albums I had previously recorded for them. Altogether, this made a total of twenty-six albums released by the spring of 1974.

Also, in March of that year, I was awarded another Juno for top country male vocalist, making it four in a row for that category; and I also picked up a Juno for best album of the year, which was *To It and At It*. This made a total of five Junos won so far.

On March 23 and 24, I was back in Alberta, at a farmhouse owned by a Mr. and Mrs. Switzer. They lived in a little community called New Sweden, and they were good enough to give their home up for a couple of days while we filmed our Christmas show right in their living room and kitchen. We were looking for authenticity and we got it. The episode would be shown the following December.

Round about this time I was called upon once again to answer some inaccurate statements given to the press in and around Toronto and Ottawa concerning my refusal to play the CNE and the Central Canadian Exhibition back in January of '74. (The CCE is in Ottawa.)

First the statement concerning the Toronto CNE, released while I was in Edmonton, on March 20.

"It has come to my attention in the last few days that certain inaccurate comments have been made concerning my policies, actions and commitments, in front of the press and various politicians. For this reason I feel I must set the record straight on a couple of matters of importance to me.

"When my manager, Jury Krytiuk, was approached earlier this year, 1974, with a C.N.E. Grandstand date for me, it was turned down for the following reasons:

"One year ago, in 1973, I made a statement that I would not play at the C.N.E. Grandstand until such time as I felt that they were making every effort to further and promote Canadian Talent. I further stated that I felt that 60 percent Canadian Talent at the Grandstand was a desirable figure to aim for. I still feel this way, and to date, I do not feel that the C.N.E. has made all possible efforts to achieve this level of Canadian identity in packaging their Grandstand shows.

"However, my manager offered to assist the C.N.E. in any way possible, to produce a Canadian country show with top Canadian acts for a one night engagement at the Grandstand. To this he was told that his help was not wanted, and further told that his refusal to accept a date for Stompin' Tom would now hurt Tom's chances of *ever* playing the C.N.E.'s Grandstand in the future. And the meeting ended on that note.

"Subsequently, because the C.N.E. officials have only stated that I refused to play the C.N.E. without giving an explanation of either their position or mine, I request that your attention be given to the real story."

And now concerning the CCE in Ottawa, this statement was released to the press on the same day, March 20, 1974.

"On speaking of fairs and exhibitions, the Honourable Claude Bennett, Minister of Tourism for the Province of Ontario and a director of the Central Canadian Exhibition, in Ottawa, stated in Toronto on Friday, March 15th, at a meeting of the Grandstand attractions committee of the C.N.E. that 'Stompin' Tom Connors also turned down the Ottawa Exhibition for 1974.'

"To answer this, let me say that no such offer was ever received for me to appear at the Central Canadian Exhibition this year or any other year. In December, 1973, Mr. Bennett, along with a Mr. Quinn [an alderman], a Mr. Jones [a controller], and a couple of other directors, all journeyed to Las Vegas to engage talent for their show. Apparently, they were duped into thinking that some smooth talking U.S. agent could deliver me to them. Not so! I wish to state that I have never been represented by U.S. agents and that my services as a performer are only available by contacting my Toronto offices. This is a very well known fact, and anyone in the entertainment business should know this, and would not go seeking the services of Stompin' Tom in the U.S. of A.

"I would further like to point out that one of the reasons these fairs and exhibitions are having trouble finding Canadian Talent is that they are looking in all the wrong places. Canadian Talent is found right here in our own back yard, not in some casino in Las Vegas.

"In the future, may it please be known that either my manager or myself will be happy to confirm or deny the Stompin' Tom stories directly, so that the Hon. Mr. Bennett and others do not have to rely on third party information.

"My career has been founded on a truthful, straight forward approach to all things, and I would like to keep it that way. Thank you."

The months of April, May, June and July of 1974 were spent on the road with a CBC filming crew of no less than fifteen persons, including myself and Lena. The tour took us from Vancouver to Newfoundland and all points in between. "Stompin' Tom's Canada" was filmed for the purpose of retracing the steps I had taken in my hitch-hiking days, as described in *Before the Fame*. And to help document the songs I had written about the various places I had lived in or visited. The verification of the subject matter of these songs was also an important factor.

While there's no need to describe every incident that happened in each location along the way, it is important to let my readers know some of the problems this CBC crew had to face while travelling with Stompin' Tom.

In the first place, neither the producer nor any of the rest of the crew had ever been on the bum. They all came from respectable families so could hardly be expected to show a tramp with twenty years' experience how to be a tramp. While I would have been perfectly satisfied in a motel room out on the highway, most of the time we were booked into the best hotels right downtown.

This didn't rest too well with the CBC when it came to budget restraints. We had only been on the road a month or so when they called Don McRae, the producer, back to home base in Edmonton a couple of times to discuss the matter. In fear that they were going to take him off the project, before he flew back the third time he came to me and asked if I would give him a letter indicating my strong support and that I definitely wanted him to be the producer of my series right to the end. I don't know whether he told me all the extenuating circumstances at the time but I wrote a letter on his behalf anyway, stating I wanted him on the series no matter what. When he came back from Edmonton this time he was all smiles and wasn't bothered thereafter.

Unfortunately, for me and some of the members of the crew, once he was sure his job was secure he began to develop a "better than thou" attitude. He started becoming quite bossy at times and gave the cold shoulder to anyone who wouldn't take it.

I found myself in the rather awkward position of not being able to complain even if I wanted to, after having given him a letter to take to his superiors as proof of the high regard in which he was held by Stompin' Tom. Nevertheless, and even though a few things became somewhat testy at times, I decided to make the best of it. I guess I just came to the conclusion that he was basically a social climber and couldn't understand anyone who was not. It must be difficult for some producers to find out that they are not filming a big star after all, but really the most down to earth guy they've ever tangled with.

Like I said before, some of the hotels this guy was booking for us were really out of sight as far as I was concerned. For instance, when we got to Ottawa, we found ourselves booked for three nights in apartment-sized rooms in the Chateau Laurier, no less. And for those who may not know, this is a hotel frequented by prime ministers with big long limousines and fancy-looking chauffeurs. I later found out that the cheapest room in this place was $65 per night, and that was in 1974. It didn't take me too long to calculate that thirteen rooms for three nights at $65 would come to a nice twenty-five-hundred-dollar bill. (There would have been fifteen rooms but Don McRae and myself were booked with our wives.)

As soon as we arrived, Don informed us that we would all meet (or was it rendezvous) in the dining lounge at 7:30 P.M.

As Lena and I arrived about ten minutes late, I told her to just go on in ahead and I would join her as soon as I went to buy a package of cigarettes.

When I arrived at the door of the dining lounge and proceeded to walk in to where Lena and the others were sitting, two big arms, one from either side, stretched out in front of me. "You can't come in here without a tie on sir," one of them said. "Well, my friends are just sitting over there," I said. "And besides, I don't own a tie." "Well, we can't help that, sir," they said, as they gently but convincingly nudged me back out the door. "I'm staying in this hotel," I protested. "And I want to go in with my friends to eat."

After getting a "Sorry, sir. But those are the rules," I decided to see just how far those rules could be pushed.

Going to the desk, I filed my complaint with a rather smug-looking fellow who just said, "Sorry, sir. But I can't do anything for you. Those are the rules of our dining room, and they must be maintained."

"Well, who is the manager of this place, and where can I go to see him?"

He tried to dissuade me for a moment, but when he saw I was not going to take no for an answer, he directed me to an office away up on one of the top floors.

After retelling my complaint to two different secretaries, I was finally admitted to a swanky office with a pretty important-looking fellow sitting behind a large desk. I could see he had already been forewarned about my intent, so there was no point in wasting his time or mine.

"Sir," I said, "I don't know whether you've ever heard of me or not, but my name is Stompin' Tom Connors. And I'm in Ottawa to film a television series with a CBC crew of fifteen people. We are all booked into your hotel for three nights. And because I don't own a tie, and never have for that matter, I find my way being barred to the dining room where my wife and all the others are waiting for me to join them. Now, if I can't go into that dining room to eat, just the way I am, I will see to it that everyone that's with me immediately checks out of this hotel to go somewhere else where I can at least get something to eat. After all, if I wasn't in this hotel, none of these people would be here either."

"I get your point, Mr. Connors," he said, "and if you'll just be good enough to go down to the dining room, I will phone and clear this matter up immediately." As I said "Thank you" and turned to leave, he was already on the phone.

Five minutes later I was at the door of the dining room and you should have seen the change that came over those two pompous goons when I entered. With their forced smiles they were falling all over themselves trying to escort me to my table. As I sat down and took out a cigarette one of them lit it for me before I hardly had it in my mouth. The waiters, in black suits with white towels draped over their arms, were all around me bowing low and assuring me that they would fulfil my every wish the very instant I made it known.

I couldn't get over the looks on everyone's face, especially that of Don McRae. I can still see him with a forkful of something halfway to his open mouth, while the amazement of the moment was preventing his well-intended motions.

Without hesitating for an instant, I thought I'd better play this one to the hilt. Where would I get a better opportunity?

Taking a long drag of my holder-held cigarette, I snapped my fingers and said, "Waiter! Please bring me a large cool bottle of Black Tower and a baloney sandwich," looking at him straight in the eye, and he at me. He said, "Ahh, y-yes sir," and away he went. He was back in a flash with the bottle of wine in an ice bucket. "And w-what was that kind of sandwich you wanted again, sir?"

And now, a little louder this time, I said, "Baloney!" and spelled it, "B-A-L-O-N-E-Y, baloney. I'll have a baloney sandwich." "Yes, sir," he said again, and away he went. A moment later another dude appeared from the kitchen. Coming up to the table he whispered, "Sir. I don't think we have any baloney." "What!" I said out loud. "No baloney? Well, you better get some. And I'll have another bottle of Black Tower while you're at it."

They must have sent someone out to a grocery store down the street to get some baloney because the sandwich didn't arrive for at least a good hour and a half. By this time I was into my third bottle of Black Tower and my second package of cigarettes. I kept one guy just lighting me up and taking away the butts.

And now the grand finale. You should have seen that baloney sandwich when it finally arrived. They wheeled it out on a fancy table inside a huge silver dome surrounded with flowers and candles and several kinds of salad. Lifting the dome, they exposed this huge silver platter, the size you would serve a large turkey on, and there surrounded with every kind of pickles, cheese and peppers known to man was this daintily carved baloney sandwich. There was so much other stuff on the platter you could hardly see it.

As I reached into the middle of the platter and scooped out the sandwich pieces and placed them on the table, I knew everyone else had long since been done eating, so I just told the waiter to take the rest back to the kitchen.

After four quick bites the sandwich disappeared and so did the third bottle of Black Tower. As we all got up to leave, I looked at the line-up of waiters and, rubbing my belly, I said in a voice I'm sure everyone in the dining room could hear, "Thank you very much, boys. That was the best damn baloney sandwich I ever had. And I'll be back tomorrow night for another one."

I never did go back, of course, but opted instead to eat in a restaurant down the street where they don't have Black Tower and they don't light your cigarettes. But they sure know what you're talking about when you order a baloney sandwich.

I also noticed after that that Don McRae usually ate at a different time of the day than I did. But the rest of the crew saw the humour of the whole thing and got a great kick out of it. I think it was Collin MacLean who later made the remark, "It's too bad we weren't filming the whole thing. It would have been a great skit for the series."

Another night in Halifax, the boys and I decided we would all go out and do a little bar hoppin'. There were about ten of us, including Gary Empey, my bass player, who had joined us for about half the tour to sort of be my aide while I was busy filming and couldn't always leave to get things for myself. The producer, of course, wasn't there. He really wasn't up to such things.

Anyway, we had just left one bar to walk to another, and as we were going up this hilly street we came to an alley where myself and a few of the boys had heard the call of nature, so we all went in to check it out. The alley was pitch-black, and while some of the boys decided to finish off the half pint of beer they had snitched from the last bar, we heard a commotion from the street. A screech of tires and a number of voices hollering, "Okay, you guys, this is the police. Get your asses out here."

Quickly ditching the bottles, we found ourselves facing a number of policemen with flashlights shining directly in our eyes. After they marched us out into the lights of the street we could see several squad cars and a couple of paddy-wagons. As I opened the door of one and started to get in, one of the cops yelled at me and told me to get over here, where he was telling everybody else to get lined up. He then wanted to see everybody's identification. I can still see poor Collin MacLean. I don't think he had ever been stopped and questioned by a policeman before in his life. In fumbling through his wallet for his ID he was dropping papers all over the sidewalk. And while trying to convince the cop that he was indeed a wonderful and honourable family man, he'd bend over to pick something up off the street and, finding it wasn't his ID but just a picture, he would draw the police-man's attention to it and tell him what member of his family it was and how much the dear one thought of him and how much they were missing him at home. After doing this sev-eral times and still not finding his ID, even the cop began to get a grin on his face.

"What do you do for a living anyway?" he asked. When Collin told him he worked for the CBC and we were all out here filming "Stompin' Tom's Canada," he looked at me and said, "Ain't that right, Tom?" When I said, "Yeah, that's right Collin," the cop said, "Well, what in hell were you guys all doin' there in the alley?"

"We just went in to take a leak," I said.

"Well, the next time you guys go in an alley to take a leak make damn sure it's nowhere near a bank."

Instantly we all looked at the same time. And sure enough there it was as big as life, the Canadian Bank of Commerce.

"All right," the cop said, looking at Collin. "Pick up your papers and don't let me catch you hanging around in dark alleys again, or the next time I won't be so easy on you. Now, be about your business, all of you."

With that, we all went up to the next pub and had a few laughs mimicking Collin as he talked to the policeman.

"What do you say we all go back the same way we came, Collin?" someone asked. "To hell with you guys," he said. "There's no way I'm going within ten miles of that alley again. When I leave this joint, I'm takin' a cab." That was pretty good advice; we all took a cab home that night.

It wasn't until about a week later that I learned that on the following morning, bright and early, when Don McRae heard about what had happened the previous night, he immediately made reservations and ordered everybody to pack up and head for the airport. His intention was to abandon the rest of the shoot and leave me and Gary right where we were, in Halifax, to wonder what in the hell had happened. Fortunately for us and the whole series, not one of his crew was willing to go. And rather than go by himself, he cancelled the tickets and stayed on.

Lena had known nothing about this incident at the time as she had heard several days before that her mother was sick and she had flown home to the Magdalene Islands to be with her. The family now had taken her to the hospital, but it wasn't long after that she passed away. I would like to have attended the funeral but we had run into a few rainy days, and in trying to make up for the lost time I was needed on the set. Her mom passed away on June 27 of 1974.

By now, we were in Newfoundland where we had Dick Nolan join us for a couple of songs, "Aunt Martha's Sheep" and "God Guard Thee, Newfoundland," which were later included in the series. And during our walks and talks on camera, we discussed the very interesting history of his home province and later, he took several of us out to his house where his wife cooked us up a great big feed of fresh salmon.

The next day, while the crew were packing everything in preparation for going to P.E.I., Dick took Gary and me for a long mountainous tour of some of the lesser known villages of Newfoundland. As we intended to do some drinking along the way, we rented a cab between the three of us for the journey. Our taxi driver's name was Charlie, and as Dick and I sat in the back seat playing our guitars and singing, I think he enjoyed the trip a lot better than we did. Gary Empey in the meantime kept him in stitches by telling him all the dirty jokes he could think of.

We must have stopped in a dozen little places where Dick would jump out and introduce us to all the people and after we'd sing them a couple of songs we'd be on our way to the next place. The scenery in these places was really great but the roads into them could hardly be called roads at all.

By July 1 of '74 we were on Prince Edward Island in Skinners Pond to film the harvesting of the Irish moss for which I had written a song, and from there we went to Lena's home on Entry Island. This was our last outdoor shoot and by the fifth of July we were all back in Charlottetown. From here the CBC crew flew back to Edmonton to prepare the studio for the rest of the filming to be done in a couple of weeks.

In the meantime, Lena and I and Gary drove back to Toronto where we had a three-day gig to do at the Horseshoe Tavern from the eleventh to the thirteenth.

On Thursday the eleventh of July, the boys and I walked on the stage at about 7 P.M. to set up, and there at a table right in front of the stage, swigging away at a pitcher of draught and demanding to hear the music a full hour before starting time, was Charlie, our Newfoundland taxi driver. It hadn't been more than two weeks since we'd seen him last.

"Hey Charlie," I said. "What the hell are you doing in Toronto?" "Ah," he said. "I got tired drivin' cab down home and makin' no money, so I decided to come to Toronto and seek my fortune. I been up here for a week and a half now, and I got a new job already. When I heard you guys were going to be playing the Horseshoe I had to get my ass up here early so I could get a good seat."

"Hey, that's great, Charlie," I said. "But how did the cab company down home take it when you quit in such short notice?"

"Oh, dem guys ?" he said. "You know the three hundred dollars you guys paid me for the fare that day? Well, I just put 'er in me pocket, parked the cab at the stand and left a little note sayin' I'd be sick for a few days. And here I am."

Having a hard time keeping from laughing, I asked him about his new job. "So what are you working at now, Charlie?" When he said, "Drivin' taxi," I thought Gary was going to fall off the stage.

On July 15 the CBC flew Lena and me and the boys back

out to Edmonton where they had a nice stage built and another large room full of sets and props they felt were necessary as background for some of the songs I would be singing for the next two weeks. They also rented us a car which we hardly ever got to drive, given the heavy filming schedule they had us on.

We did two and sometimes three shows a day in front of a mixed family audience, and all the songs were later interspersed by the on-location scenes.

It had been strongly suggested to me, right from the beginning, that I should have American country stars appear as guests throughout the series. But my answer to this was always the same. "Our Canadian talent is every bit as good as the American, and it's high time we gave them the national exposure they need and deserve. So if I can't have the guests I want on this series, there won't be any series."

Once again, I was not too well liked for this attitude, but we were too far along in production for these American talent lovers to turn back now. As a result of this bit of stubbornness "Stompin' Tom's Canada" was 100 per cent Canadian. And most of the following Canadian guests might not have been on this series had I for one minute caved in and capitulated.

These guests were first, from out west Jimmy Arthur Orge, Al Oster, Medric Godrey, Alphie Myer and Russ Gurr. Then from central Canada (including Quebec), Earl Heywood, Gaet Lepine, Willy Lamothe, Kent Brockwell and Joan Watson. And thirdly, from down east, Dick Nolan, Stevedore Steve, Billy Lewis and Buddy Roberts (now known as Buddy Black). There may be one or two others that don't come to my mind right now. But most of these names had never been exposed on national television before. And due to the amount of time the Americans get on our airwaves, they've never been exposed since. Most of them just got tired waiting for the opportunity, then gave up and quit. Our country is ridden by such examples.

And one more point about these people is that they all seem to belong to a dying breed. (Or is it just because this type is not wanted anymore?) Every one of these people wrote and sang what I would refer to as "Identifiably

Canadian Songs." That is, not just songs that are written by
a Canadian about all places and things south of our border,
but songs that are about ourselves, with which we can all
identify. Songs about our land, our history and our people,
how we live, laugh, love and work in our own unique Canadian way. (Give me an ample daily dose of this kind of music
and you won't hear me complaining about having to listen
to the rest.)

On or about July 28 when the filming was all over and
ready for the editors to piece it together, we decided to have
a little going-away party. The guests had all gone home now,
and the only ones left were Lena, myself, the boys in the
band and the CBC road crew who had followed us all across
Canada. The get-together was held for only about two or
three hours in one of the large basement rooms of the CBC
building. We had a few bottles of champagne, and while we
waited for Don McRae to arrive, we decided to partake.
Knowing that Don would arrive at any moment, the atmosphere of the room was in a sort of a hushed anticipation.
Unfortunately, Don didn't arrive until about three-quarters
of our time was up. And when he did, it was to just look
around without having a drink and bid us all farewell. In
about five minutes he was back out the door. Then what? We
all just looked at each other questioningly, and then somebody said, "Hurray."

Then we all said "Hurray" and stood on our chairs and
said "Hurray" several more times. I won't speak for the rest,
but I took this to mean that the party pooper was gone. And
from then on the hush from the room was gone also. For the
last hour we had a good time and thanked each other for a
great tour, and expressed the hope that we'd do it again
sometime. As I can't now remember all their last names, I'll
acknowledge their first names and they'll each know who I
mean.

There was Don, Chris, Collin, Kasey, Alan, Vic, Sylvia,
Bill, Gary, Jim, Harvey, Roy, Tom and Dale. (Hope I didn't
leave anybody out.)

There were also a couple of great stories about the night
the guests on the show and I were having a party in my motel
room when Gaet Lepine arrived in town. Some of the things

that were said and done, including me wearing Buddy
Roberts's boots and he wearing mine around the parking
lot, were pretty funny. But as these stories are pretty long, I
won't bother to tell them here. And besides, if I tell you all
the good stories, I won't have any to tell you when we meet.

With the filming of the series "Stompin' Tom's Canada"
now complete, we flew back to Toronto on July 29, 1974, and
immediately began to prepare for the next concert tour,
which was to begin on August 1, in the city of Ottawa.

One Out, One In and One Down

I N THE MONTH OF AUGUST 1974, we just toured Ontario, some of the places being Ottawa, Minden, Ontario Place in Toronto, New Hamburg, Belleville, Oshawa, Sarnia and Port Elgin.

During this tour, Lena looked after the concession sales by herself. But by the end of the month we decided to hire another guy to help her. This was Graham Garvy, a young man of about twenty-one who was from Toronto. We then lit out again for a tour of British Columbia.

Starting in Mayerthorpe, Alberta, we headed west and played all the northern part of B.C. We then took the ferry from Prince Rupert down to Vancouver Island, in preparation for playing Vancouver City and all points east in southern British Columbia.

Just before we got to Vancouver, however, I had a rather unfortunate altercation with my guitar player, Bill Lewis. From day one, when I hired my musicians, one of the main rules to always be maintained on the road was that anybody could argue his point in any disagreement without reproach, but the minute anyone threw a punch, he could take it that he was automatically fired on the spot.

Well, it just so happened that Bill, who had a tendency to get hyper now and again, went a little too far this time and overlooked the main rule. It happened in his berth aboard the ferry. And there were only he and I present.

We had gotten into one of those no-win arguments about something rather insignificant, and as I got up to leave he suckered me and I went down with my back against the door at the end of the narrow little hall leading out of the room.

"Well, Bill," I said. "I guess you know this means you're fired." "Yeah," he said. "I know what the f--- it means. So if I'm fired I might as well finish the job," and he started kicking at me. But for him it was all in vain. I had my back up against the door in the little hall and all he could do was kick at my feet. He figured there was no way he could take me if I ever got up, so he wanted to make sure I stayed down. And I figured there was no way of getting up without getting a boot in the head. So here we were at a stand-off. Me with no way to get up and at him, and him with no way to come down and get me.

As I thought of my back to the door, which was his only way of escape, and the fact that it was about three o'clock or so in the morning, I started to laugh.

I said, "You better let me up, Bill, and take your chances with me on my feet. In the first place you've always known that I've always been reasonable with you. And you know that I would never sucker a guy, like you just did to me. Now, secondly, there's no way you can get out of this room unless I get away from the door, and there's no way I'm going to do that unless you stand at the other end of the room. And thirdly, Bill, you know what my sleeping habits are. You've seen me stay awake for two and three days at a time, while you have a hard time keeping your eyes open even now. So if you don't agree with my proposition, there's no way you're going to outlast me. And when you fall asleep I'm going to kick the shit right out of you. And by the way, it doesn't matter what you decide, you're getting fired anyway."

After about five minutes, he began to see my logic and also started to smile. As he backed to the other end of the room saying, "Well, you know I didn't mean anything, Tom, I guess I just flew off the handle a little bit," I immediately jumped to my feet.

"You're f-----' right you flew off the handle," I said, "only not just a little bit, but a whole f-----' lot. You're only lucky I'm a man of my word or I'd drop you right here for what you tried to pull." With that, I just left the room and went back to my own quarters.

All the next day my bass player, Gary, tried to get me to change my mind, but I stayed my course. After paying Bill off and giving him some extra money, I let him go. Then Gary and I finished the B.C. tour by ourselves.

Now, just so my readers don't get the wrong idea. While Bill Lewis worked for me, he always did an excellent job. I always liked him and I still do. We have since solved our differences and today he understands what I did and why I had to do it. I had no time to get another guitar player and it wasn't easy trying to finish the tour without one. Especially when you're only a trio to start with. But everyone who goes on the road with me knows up front what to expect. There are no secrets and no exceptions to the rule.

We finally finished the tour by the end of October and by November 2, 1974, Lena and I were back in Toronto to celebrate our first anniversary and rest up for a week before heading out again. I still had some shows booked in Ontario, but I didn't have a guitar player. So I told Gary to keep his eyes open around the clubs and let me know if he spotted a likely candidate.

On Tuesday night, the fifth, Gary was on the phone. "I just got home from the Gladstone Hotel," he told me, "and there's a guy playing there who sounds pretty good. The kind of style you like. Can you come down tomorrow night and see him?"

The following night, with a ball cap pulled down over my eyes, I walked into the Gladstone with Gary and found a seat at the back. By the time we got our beer, the band was just getting up on stage.

When the guitar player joined them, I did a double take. There in the distance stood almost the dead ringer for Gary. Same stature, same height, same hair style, same demeanour and even the same style of beard that Gary was always noted for.

"What the hell is this?" I said. "You tryin' to get your twin brother a job? Ain't it enough that I have to put up with one of you Empeys?" Gary just smiled and said, "Listen."

Sure enough, he was playing the plain simple runs in a

nice clear confident fashion that always appealed to me. A style reminiscent of all traditional country pickers. "Tell the waiter we want to buy him a beer and we'd like to see him at our table," I said. And in another few minutes, he arrived.

Gary spoke first: "Hi! My name is Gary Empcy and this is Stompin' Tom Connors. We'd like to talk to you about your guitar playin'."

As he told us his name was Ronny Richard (as in Rocket *Ree-shard*), I thought he was going to choke on his beer. "You're not really Stompin' Tom, are you?" he said.

"Yes, I am. And I'd be interested to know if you'd like to come and play with me and Gary here, on the road."

"I'd be honoured," he said. "I've always been a great fan of yours, but jeeze, do you think I'm good enough?"

I told him I liked what I'd heard so far and if he wanted to come to a rehearsal the following night, he could just give Gary a call tomorrow and he'd be given the directions.

The following night, after rehearsal, I hired him and that Friday I did my first gig with the "Empey Twins." (Gary always wore a tweed cap on stage, and when we got one for Ronny you couldn't tell the two of them apart.)

Our first concert was at the Woodgreen United Church Hall, in Toronto, and then we did Chatham and another town in that part of Ontario, on the tenth and eleventh of November.

Around this time I had heard that my friend Buddy Roberts (now Black) had just had a terrible car accident and he was in the intensive care ward of the Oshawa General Hospital. He had run off the road somehow and dropped some sixty feet over one of the capes onto the rocky beach of Lake Ontario. They didn't get him out of the car until some twelve hours later when he happened to be discovered by a passing motorist.

I guess he was nearly dead and pretty badly broken up by the time they got him to the hospital, and he'd been lying there now for nearly a month by the time I heard about it.

Getting Jury to cancel one of my shows in southwestern Ontario, I had him book the United Auto Workers' Hall in Oshawa and get as many other entertainers as might be

available to put on a benefit concert for Bud on the thirteenth of November.

The next day me and some of the boys who had played
the concert, including Stevedore Steve, Delmer Dorey, Lloyd
Mackey and Freddy McKenna, went to the hospital to pay
Bud a visit. He was still in pretty poor condition, but when
we presented him with the profits of the show and told him
a few jokes, he lightened up quite a bit. It seems his wife had
also left him a couple of months before and this had made
him feel quite despondent. But now, with a few friends
around him, and a few bucks to sort of help out when he got
better, he began to feel that maybe life could be a little more
worth living. We couldn't stay as long as we might have liked
to, but at least we left him in a lot better spirits than he was
in when we arrived. A couple of weeks later, it was good to
hear that he was up and about and thinking of going back to
his singing and playing.

On the fifteenth of November, Ron and Gary and I played
the Horseshoe for the weekend, and during the next week we
finished touring for the year by playing Hamilton Place, St.
Catharines and the University of Western Ontario in London.

Clearing Trees and Beards

By November 30, 1974, Lena and I and Gary, with Steve-dore Steve and his wife, Gini, were all headed out for Skinners Pond, P.E.I.

I'd been planning now for a couple of years to convert that old willow and alder tree hollow into a nice pond beside the old farmhouse. But it was going to take a lot of work. So I enlisted the help of Steve and Gary and Lena's older brother, Pete, who joined us when we got to the Island.

The day after our arrival in Skinners Pond, I took the boys out to Tignish, and there we bought axes, saws, whetstones and other equipment we were going to need for the job, and then we started to work.

For the next three weeks, we chopped, sawed, dragged, piled and burned till we had every stick of rubbish and scrub completely cleared out of the hollow. The weather was cold and the ground was swampy. But with all the whisky we drank, we hardly felt the cold—although some of us got a little wet once in a while, such as the day when Stevedore Steve fell in the brook.

While me and the boys were doing all this, Russell was kept busy bringing the booze, running for supplies and keeping the wood in the house stoves. In the kitchen, Cora, Lena and Gini kept the hearty meals coming, and the cakes, pies and bread baked. And you better believe how that kind of work can make a feller eat. Just ask Lena's brother, Pete.

He had the biggest appetite of all.

For a while there, it looked as if we were running a lumber camp. One of the neighbours had his horse down in the hollow twitching out the bigger logs and trees that we couldn't burn, while the rest of us, in checkered jackets, just whistled and hacked away with nothing else on our minds but the party we were going to have again tonight.

Even old Josey (Jerome) Arsenault, at ninety years old, made his way up to the house every second or third night, along with the rest of the guests, to listen, sing and dance along with the music.

With Steve and me taking our turns at singing to the acoustic guitars and Gary on the bass, and every once in a while old Josey on the mouth organ, we had that old house in Skinners Pond just a-shakin' like she hadn't done in years. And the next day, we'd be right back in the hollow, workin' up another appetite and looking forward to the next party.

On December 19, I phoned Hayes Paving & Excavating Company, from Alma, P.E.I., to come down and do a little survey and give me an estimate on what it would cost to build a dam at one end of the hollow from one side to the other. I knew that the small amount of water flowing in the brook would create its own pond sooner or later, and that the size of the pond would be determined by the size of the dam. And of course culverts had to be installed at strategic heights in the dam to prevent overflow and washout.

Gary had left for Toronto the day before, as most of the manual work was done, and Lena and I drove Pete down to their sister Pauline's in Freetown. (She had moved there from Charlottetown.)

Lena's dad, Peter, was also paying Pauline a visit at this time with the intention of staying over for Christmas and New Year's. So we stayed for a few hours. Then, depositing our gifts, we left again for Skinners Pond.

Steve and Gini, in the meantime, had decided to stay over with Lena and me and Russell and Cora, to spend Christmas. And of course his help came in handy over the next few days as well.

We spent a real nice country Christmas together, enjoying the tree, the sharing of gifts, and, of course, the great food the ladies all chipped in to cook. But soon the days slipped by and on about the twenty-eighth of December they left to go back to Ontario.

So now, with all the boys paid off for their work, I had to concentrate on the new job at hand. The Hayes boys had already moved in with their heavy equipment to gouge out the hollow to make it even deeper and to lay the footings for the dam. They worked away during the Christmas week and only stopped for New Year's Eve and New Year's Day of 1975. And during these two days Lena and I decided to go down to Freetown to see the new year in with her dad, her brother Pete, her sister Pauline and her husband Gerald.

They had invited quite a large crowd to the house that night, and I wound up singing for about three hours. Then about 11:30 they put on some records and we danced till way after midnight.

With 1975 now well under way, Lena and I went back to Skinners Pond the following afternoon. There was more work to be done.

For the first week or so in January, the Hayes boys worked very diligently. And even though they got the bulldozer stuck and mired down in the hollow a couple of times, with the big scraper having to take a whole day to pull him out, they were proceeding on schedule. They had the five deep holes that I wanted in the bottom of the pond already dug; but then, a snag. One day when they said they were going to be back, they didn't come back at all. I waited for two or three days and then called to ask if they had forgotten about me. The answer was "No, there'll be a man there tomorrow."

Two days later, I was calling again. Then they arrived and did a couple of days' work. And I didn't see them again for another week. Finally, I took a drive up to Alma to ask what the hell was going on, but nobody was there. So I left a message.

Next day the boss, a Mr. Dawson, came down to see me. And though I suspected he had his crew out doing a more lucrative job, he assured me that the boys would be back in a couple of days. He said one or two of them had been sick and a couple of machines had broken down.

By the first of February they had the dam nearly half-completed, but I was told they couldn't do any more until next spring when the ground was dried out.

Needless to say, I was not a little frustrated, and I wondered why I couldn't have been told this before. So with little else to do, all I could do was wait.

At least there was one thing I was able to accomplish in January before I left Skinners Pond. And that was to award the first scholarship money that came from visitors to the school during the previous year.

The award was set up to help the student from the district who had graduated from high school with the highest marks in the previous year to further pursue a degree in higher education. And if they chose not to, the award would go to the student with the next highest marks, if they chose to go higher. Once the student could prove they had been accepted by the new institution of learning, they got the money.

So on January 28, 1975, I was there to make the first scholarship presentation to ever be made to a Skinners Pond high school graduate. Her name was Pauline Keefe. And a picture of myself congratulating her and presenting her with the cheque appeared in the Prince Edward Island papers on January 30.

As this was to be an annual presentation, it continued for another two years, with cheques going to Roger Arsenault and Justine Knox. But by the year 1978, as I mentioned before, the newly renovated school had been damaged so badly by local hoodlums that the scholarship money had to go to repairs. And not only for that year but every year after. Until finally, the upkeep of the school became so impossible that potential visitors just drove by the shabby-looking place in disgust.

Anyway, I'll speak more on this later. But for now, Lena and I are just about ready to leave Skinners Pond. And on the morning of February 2, after Lena came down the stairs and wished us all "Happy Ground Hog Day," we had our last breakfast with Russell and Cora, bid them goodbye till next time and headed out to Charlottetown.

We stopped in to see our friends Johnny and Judy Reid, and from there we went to Beach Point, P.E.I., to see a couple of other friends, Joe and Gerty Osborne. Then, after spending my birthday at Joe and Gerty's, on February 9, we left Prince Edward Island and headed for Toronto.

On our way back we stopped to see several friends along the way, two of whom were Aubrey and Connie Harper of Annagance, N.B., and also Harry and Alva Atcheson of Hartland, New Brunswick. Both of these families are related to Reg and Muriel Chapman. As a matter of fact, I think Muriel was working for us at our new Boot Records office in Mississauga by now. She and Reg didn't live too far away from where we were located on Matheson Boulevard.

As soon as we got home, we threw a party at our house for all the people who worked for us, plus a number of our friends. This gave me another chance to clear some of the beer cases away from my dart board and to make a little more room in my basement. It seems kind of funny to have to say we all had to keep drinking to give ourselves more room to drink.

At one point early on in the evening I discovered some-one among the guests who I didn't know and who I was sure we didn't invite. He only looked to be about eighteen and hardly suited to be drinking with my kind of crowd. After asking, and finding out that nobody brought him or even knew him, I walked over and tapped him on the shoulder and said, "Sorry, friend, but I'm afraid I'm going to have to ask you to leave. This party is for invited guests only."

In quick answer, this little baby-faced guy turns around to me and says, "What the hell is wrong with you, Tom? Don't you recognize your own bass player when you see him?"

I almost fell on the floor, and then I started to laugh. It was Gary Empey with his beard shaved off, and I'd never seen him like that before. His face was round, soft and pale, and he had no chin. "What the hell did you do to your-self?" I said, and I couldn't stop laughing. "You better grow that hair back on your face before we go on tour again or I'm gonna have to put some lipstick on you and paint you up like a girl. Now get yourself in here with the boys, grab yourself a couple of beers, and see if you can start lookin' like a man."

Needless to say, the boys ribbed him all evening. They tickled him when they got the chance and even asked him out on a couple of dates. That's the first time to my knowl-edge that Gary Empey ever went home early from a party. Two weeks later, the beard was back on.

Buying a House and
Building a Dam

F ROM THE END OF FEBRUARY to the middle of April, I just stayed home and wrote songs.

Sometime in March I collected another Juno Award for best male country singer. This was the fifth in a row for that category, but I had an extra one for best album from the previous year. So this made a total of six altogether. And these would prove to be the last. As I recount the next couple of years, my readers will see why.

On April 8, 1975, I composed and recorded a radio jingle for the Moosehead Breweries, to be played throughout the Maritimes. And by April 20 of that year, I finished recording my new album entitled *North Atlantic Squadron*. This was my twelfth album of personally written songs, and my twenty-seventh release to date, counting all covers and compilations.

During the latter part of April, Lena and I decided that the little house on Bedford Park Avenue was just too small. Besides, it was crammed between two others with very little room outside. Both of us were originally from the country and used to the wide-open spaces. So we contacted a couple of realtors and spent the next while looking for a larger house with some land. We hoped it would be somewhere within an hour's drive of the Boot Records building in Mississauga.

Without finding what we wanted and with another tour looming in the near future, we got Jury to also go out with another realtor whenever he could spare the time. After a couple of days, this paid off. He spotted something he thought we would like and, after being introduced to the new realtor, we went out in the countryside between Brampton and Guelph to have a look.

The house wasn't ideal, but given the fact we now only had a couple of days to prepare for the tour, we decided to buy it. Besides, it had ten acres of land and lots of trees, and the driving distance to Boot Records was just right.

The deal was quickly made and our date to move in was the third of July. We immediately put the Bedford Park Avenue house up for sale, and within a week it was bought by Alice Bixler, the photographer who took the pictures at our wedding. Jury notified us about all this while we were on the road.

Our tour commenced on May 17 and lasted until the end of June. We played towns in the Ottawa Valley, then on to Montreal and a couple of other towns in Quebec. And by the end of May we were back in Ontario to do Brockville and Kingston.

I would certainly be remiss at this time if I didn't mention that we had a new member now added to our band. His name was Billy Jones and he was one hell of a fine steel player. I had hired him to play on the *North Atlantic Squadron* album with us and liked what I heard so well that I asked him to come on the road. To this he agreed and he was working out perfectly. I might add that Billy was already quite experienced before I met him, after having played with many well-known bands throughout Canada and the States.

As an added attraction on this tour, I also brought along my old buddy, Stevedore Steve, to sing a few warm-up songs before I came on stage. Steve had three albums by now on our label, and while he had a mild drawing power for the show in areas where he had previously done club work, we were intent on getting him exposed in areas where he was relatively unknown, mainly out west.

On June 1 of '75, our tour moved into Peterborough where another one of our Boot Records artists lived. Kent

Brockwell now had two albums with us, and when we called him to the stage he was greeted with tremendous applause. Although he only had 10 per cent vision, he wrote a lot of songs about his area and sang them in clubs, at fairs, church picnics and practically anywhere or any time there was a crowd assembled to listen. He always played the dobro guitar and usually threw in a yodel or two when he sang. He was also one of the few artists on our label who didn't expect the company to do everything, i.e., he sold boxes upon boxes of his own records, which he bought wholesale, and always paid his bills promptly. (Some artists wound up never paying their bills at all.)

One little story that Kent always liked to tell when the subject came around to selling records was how, on one afternoon while he was coming out of a church just after a funeral, someone wanted to know how he was doing and what he'd been up to lately. When he told them he was making records, they wanted to know if they could see one. Promptly leading about twenty people over to the trunk of his car, which was always driven by his wife, he pulled out a box of LPs and sold seventeen right there. (Now that's salesmanship for you.)

At any rate, Kent was well known, well liked and well received, especially that night on stage in Peterborough. I'm sorry to say, though, that our lovable Kent Brockwell has passed away since those days.

By the third of June, we took our show into the packed outside area of Ontario Place, in Toronto, and from there we moved on to North Bay and to all points west.

From the sixth of June to the fourteenth our Ontario shows were in North Bay, Sudbury, Sault Ste. Marie, Nipigon, Thunder Bay, Fort Francis and Kenora. In Manitoba, we hit Winnipeg, Dauphin and Flin Flon by June 20. And from there it was Prince Albert, North Battleford, Saskatoon and Regina, all in Saskatchewan. And by June 28, we were once again heading back to Toronto.

(At this point it may be timely to mention to some of my readers who may think that reading all the names of these towns in Canada is getting boring, I can only say: "Why don't you try driving to all these places sometime, and then you won't have to read about them." These places are full of very interesting people. All with a different story to tell. And if I had the time and the space, I would write about every one of them. But because I don't, I can at least do them the courtesy of naming their town and the date I was there, so they can always know I have never forgotten.)

On July 3, 4 and 5, Lena and I, with the help of Stevedore Steve, the boys in the band and my brother-in-law Willard, moved everything out of the Bedford Park Avenue house into our new home in the country. And as anyone who has ever moved from house to house over any kind of a distance can tell you, it can be hectic. You not only find out you have stuff you never knew you owned, but when you get it there, you don't know where in hell to put it. So after setting up the table and chairs, the bed, fridge and stove, and a few other necessities, we just locked the doors and took off on another tour.

By this time Jury had not only his dad working for him at Boot Records but also his sister Mary as well as his brother Peter. All told, including himself and Mark Altman, we now had about fourteen people working in the building, all contributing, in his or her own way, to recording, publishing, packaging, cataloguing and warehousing the tons of musical product that was now going in and out of our doors every day. And this, not to mention the amount of publicity and correspondence that was being handled for over a hundred artists. Although I was hardly ever there, they were also handling my tour bookings and the bookings of a few others. For a while we even had our own printing press and silkscreening outfit. This place was a regular bee's nest.

It was funny one day when I called the office looking for Jury and this woman's voice answered: "Boot Records here. Anne Murray speaking." Though I was somewhat taken aback, I just asked for Jury. And when he answered, I said, "What's goin' on down there? We must be gettin' pretty big when we even got Anne Murray answering the phone for us." He chuckled, of course, and explained that his new secretary's name was, indeed, Anne Murray. But not the singer.

Anyway, between July 9 and 13, we did concerts in Barrie, Owen Sound, Waterloo and Brantford, Ontario,

and again moved into Quebec for shows in Sherbrooke and
Quebec City. On the nineteenth, we played Edmunston,
Dalhousie and Petticodiac, New Brunswick, and then went
to Charlottetown, P.E.I., to play the Coliseum.

After a huge feed of lobsters at Johnny Reid's Prince
Edward Lounge, I dismissed the band until further notice,
and they all went back to Ontario.

Lena now flew over to the Mags to see her family for a
week and I went up to Skinners Pond. There was still a lot of
work to be done on the dam I was building and the old barn
on the property had to be completely renovated. I was also
having the whole farm surveyed to make sure all the old line
fences were exactly where they should be to prevent any possible dispute with the neighbours.

When I arrived, I found that Russell had already started
on the barn. He hired a carpenter from Miminegash named
Fred Butler and his helper, Jim Wedge. In a couple of days
the surveyors arrived, but there was still no sign of the dam
builders. I kept busy for the next few days running back and
forth with the surveyors or helping to fix the barn.

One of my neighbours with whom I was having a dispute
over the exact placement of a fence finally agreed with me
one day that wherever the surveyors determined the lines
should be, that's where the new fences should go. Unfortunately, when the survey was completed, and they went over to
his house to get his signature on the papers, he refused and
said they had surveyed it wrong. His contention now was that
the line should not have been straight in a certain spot, but
rather should have followed the little winding brook instead.

Upon hearing this I got on the phone and asked him
what had happened to our agreement. The deal was that if I
paid for the surveyor, he would agree with the outcome, and
he gave me his word over a handshake.

"Oh, that was then," he said, "but since I thought it all
over, the line should not be straight in that spot, but should
follow the brook."

"But," I said, "if the line were to follow the brook it would
be crooked as a snake, and besides, the brook comes right
down through the pond and through the centre of the dam
I'm building. Now if I hear you right, you're saying that

because the boundary between us is in the centre of my pond, you rightfully own half of everything I'm building, including the dam?"

"Now you're getting the idea," he said. "That's exactly what I mean; fifty/fifty."

"Well, Bennett," I said, "the day you get your fifty per cent of that dam, it'll be falling on your house, because I'll blow the son-of-a-bitch sky high before you get to own it. Now, you better get yourself a lawyer 'cause I'm on my way to Tignish right now, and we'll see where that fence is supposed to be."

"Suits me," he said. And we both clicked the phone down. Six months later the courts determined the survey to be entirely accurate and in total agreement with all past maps and surveys of the area. The line fence was to be straight and he had to sign the papers to that effect.

Meanwhile, back to the first week of August, I had to leave the carpenters working on the barn while I went over to the Magdalene Islands to visit for a couple of days and bring Lena back to Skinners Pond.

I took my car over on the ferry, and after visiting with Lena's family we took another whole day and drove all over the Magdalenes. We stayed in a motel in Grindstone that night and took the ferry back to P.E.I. the next morning.

In a week or two the Hayes boys finally arrived with all their equipment to finish the dam. There was a dozer, a loader, a grader, a backhoe, a tandem truck and a carry-all. And just as they got nicely started, who should arrive on the scene from Tignish but the local federal fisheries officer. I was just driving in one of our driveways when he was driving out the other.

The boys had stopped work. And when I went over to see what was going on, I was told that they had been ordered to stop and that the dam would have to be taken back out.

"All right, boys," I said. "I think I know who's responsible for this. You guys go home for now and I'll be in touch with you tomorrow. Leave all your equipment here and I'll pay for any lost time and work."

I then went to Tignish to visit the fisheries officer who tried to tell me I didn't have the right to build a dam on my own property. When I asked him if a certain one of my neighbours had anything to do with this, he flinched just enough to tell me I was right, though he never came right out and admitted it.

"Well, if you're not going to give me the okay to build my dam, I'm going to see your superiors in Charlottetown, and I'm not going to wait till tomorrow. I've got ten men with their equipment that I'm paying and will continue to pay until they can go back to work, or until I get the official word that it can't be done. And if your authority goes no further than someone you know in Skinners Pond, you might have to answer for it."

I could see that he was taking this pretty lightly, and because he knew that getting things done through the government on P.E.I. at the time was hardly worth the effort of trying, he just shrugged me off and wished me luck.

I immediately went out and jumped in my car, without even returning to Skinners Pond, and headed for Charlottetown. I got there too late to do anything about it that day, so I got a motel room. Early the next morning, I was in every government office there was in that city.

Run-around after run-around and waiting room after waiting room, about four o'clock that day I finally got to talk to the guy who could give me some answers for my problem.

Armed with an officially signed document and a promise that the Tignish fisheries officer would be apprised that my proposal to build my dam was acceptable within all federal laws and regulations at the time, I immediately phoned the Hayes people and told them to start work in the morning.

I drove back to Skinners Pond that night and the next morning, bright and early, I was waiting in Tignish for the fisheries officer to show up at his office.

When he arrived to unlock his door, he said, "Well, Tom, what can I do for you today?" I couldn't share his unfounded enthusiasm as I said, "I took a little trip to Charlottetown yesterday . . . and . . ." Just then his phone started ringing. As he sat down behind his desk to answer it, I placed the papers I got signed in Charlottetown on the desk in front of him.

As he thumbed through the several pages, all I could hear him saying on the phone was "Yes, sir. Yes, sir," as the smile began to leave his face.

After saying, "Yes, sir" for the last time, he hung up the phone and asked, "What in hell did you do in Charlottetown yesterday? I didn't even know they knew this office existed." With a very businesslike look, and without the smile, he said, "I've got to hand it to you. I've never seen anyone around here ever get things done so fast."

Knowing exactly what he meant and where the phone call had come from, I said, "Never mind that. Just give me a piece of paper with your okay on it so I can get my crew back to work. I've got things to do."

By eleven o'clock that morning I showed the Hayes boys the paper and they immediately went to work.

"How in hell did you ever swing that, Tom?" they wanted to know. "We thought you were done for sure." "Well," I said, "we'll put it this way. When you're right, you're right. As long as you never let assholes convince you of anything different."

By the nineteenth of September the dam was completed. And on Saturday, the following day, when the boys came to take all their equipment out, I had a thank you and farewell party for them. It was a nice day. We had some lobsters and a variety of other foods, and of course lots to drink. I played the guitar and sang for them, and by the time they left, whether it was the booze or the music (I don't care), they told me I was the best guy they had ever worked for.

Freddy Butler also had the barn completed by now, and it was time for me and Lena to say "So long" to the old folks and leave P.E.I. again for another little while. We'd had a few hectic spells over the summer, but we made up for it by having a few sing-song parties and card games during the evenings, sometimes at home and sometimes at the neighbour's. And the problems of each tomorrow, we left for tomorrow to work out by itself.

Before going back to Ontario to our new house, we visited Lena's other sister, Amy, and her husband, Foster, the lighthouse keeper, on Caribou Island in Nova Scotia.

It was always interesting to go to Foster's because he was not only a self-taught carpenter who could build seaworthy fishing boats and excellent cottages and houses, but like I mentioned before, he had a knack for building miniature models of all forms of sailing vessels, from the oldest to the modern. And, of course, I always enjoyed Amy's fiddle playing. That is, when you coaxed her long enough to get her going. All in all we had some great parties at their house over the years, which I hope to tell about when I get to the time.

At any rate, by the twenty-ninth of September we were finally on our way. And after making several more social calls, we arrived home in Ontario to do what all people must do when they move into a new house. We bought it the last of April, and here it was the second of October, and as we drove up the road we couldn't even find the place. But when we did, there were clothes to unpack, pictures to hang, dressers and other furniture to place, and above all, where in hell amongst all this junk sprawled out everywhere were the things we wanted to put in all the places we could no longer find to put them.

With too much of that and not enough of this, we found ourselves throwing out a lot of stuff. And because this house was a lot bigger than our last one we had to buy a lot of new furniture. Also, with having more time now to walk around the grounds to see what I actually bought, I found I had a lot more swamp land than I thought. This gave me the idea of converting some of it into a pond, which I eventually did a few years later.

Double "C" Resorts and Juno Theories

AFTER WE GOT STRAIGHTENED away and had a house-warming party, Lena and I got talking to Marlene and Willard about the possibility of them maybe moving back to P.E.I. with their kids, Gwen, Robbie and Sandy. Although Willard had a good paying job as a cable splicer for Ontario Hydro, he was getting a little bored with the work and was considering a change.

We talked about my plans to develop a tourist attraction in Skinners Pond centred on the school, with the future possibilities of creating a small golf course and trailer park, and, later on, a licensed dining room adjacent to a small Stompin' Tom museum.

Through the course of these conversations, I proposed to Willard that if he decided to go down home, I would form a partnership with him, and if he would do the work and look after the place, I would pay him a basic wage until the project itself was capable of sustaining him. Any profits thereafter would be shared on a fifty-fifty basis. I also planned eventually to donate my share of the profits to the district to help create other tourist projects in the hope that together we could all provide some employment for the young people whose idleness was contributing in no small way to a lot of the vandalism going on throughout the area.

It was also my intention to provide the money to buy the necessary equipment, supplies and materials, and the other details could be worked out as time went on.

Willard and Marlene said they would give it some thought, and that's where we left it for the time being.

On the sixteenth, seventeenth and eighteenth of October, I was back in the Horseshoe with Billy Jones, Ronny Richard and Gary. And on the twentieth we flew out to Vancouver to appear as guests on the Rolf Harris television show. It is interesting to note that not only is Rolf a great singer and entertainer, but he is also an accomplished artist. As a matter of fact, he asked me if he could paint a portrait of me while I was singing a song. I consented, and in exactly two and a half minutes (the length of the song), he was finished. I got him to sign and date it, and I took it home with me on the plane.

We did a couple of shows not too far from home, including Welland, Ontario, where our good friends the Hortons, Yvonne and Everett, invited us out to their house after the concert. The meal they put on for all of us was really spectacular. And as anyone who travels a lot can tell you, one good home-cooked meal is better than twenty you get out on the road. I might add here that I would state without hesitation that the Hortons have travelled to and attended more Stompin' Tom concerts over the years than any other family. One for the record books.

Lena and I now had a few days at home again in which to celebrate our anniversary before continuing the tour, and on that special evening I took her out to Fong's Dining Room in Georgetown, Ontario, for Chinese food.

It was, of course, November 2, 1975, a Sunday. And after we had eaten, we decided to read our fortune cookies. "You read mine and I'll read yours," Lena said, as we began to break them open. I agreed and began to read Lena's fortune first. Making it up as I went, I said, "Look around, for somebody near you who loves you." "Is that really what it says?" she asked. "Yes," I said. "Now what does mine say?"

She smiled for a moment and said, "Yours says that you're going to be a father in about seven months from now."

It took a moment for this to sink in, and finally I blurted

out, "What did you say? How do you know? When did you find out? Are you kidding me, or what?"

As I put my arm around her she assured me that it was true and she would be expecting the baby sometime around the middle of next June.

"Well, that's just wonderful, dear," I said, as I ordered a bottle of the best wine in the house, and told her how great she was at reading fortunes. Needless to say, the forthcoming arrival was at the top of our list of conversations during all that winter and through the next spring.

Lena's family physician at this time was a woman doctor by the name of Englebreck, whose office was at 101 Guelph Street in Georgetown, Ontario. But as time went on, she began to see a lady gynecologist, a Dr. Bandine, in the city of Guelph. But this gets me a little ahead of my story.

Heading out on tour again, we gave the keys of the house to Jury's father, Mikolai, who was a carpenter, to build me a work bench and a hall closet and a couple of other things while we were gone. Mikolai, as I said before, was also a priest of the Ukrainian Orthodox Catholic Church.

Although this tour still required a lot of driving, we didn't do that many concerts. We started out on the twelfth of November and arrived back home on the fourth of December, and only played Ottawa before going to New Brunswick to play Woodstock, St. Stephen and Sussex. On the twenty-sixth and twenty-seventh we did two nights in Halifax, and on the twenty-eighth and twenty-ninth we were in Antigonish and Canso, Nova Scotia, respectively. As we didn't have a road manager on this tour, Jury came along to look after the business and help Lena sell records.

While playing Canso, we were as close to Ronny Richard's home as we would ever get on a tour. So after the show that night we drove the forty miles or so to Charlos Cove, where his parents lived, and they put us up there for the night. We had a few bottles of beer and talked a lot with Ronny's dad, and the next day his mom made us all a nice meal, and again we said farewell. (A number of years later, when Lena and I were driving through that way to go and see Wilf Carter's old home town in Port Hilford, Nova Scotia, we stopped in and had another chat with the Richards. But as we were in a bit of a hurry we didn't stay too long.)

On December 4 we arrived home in Ontario and started our Christmas shopping. And for the next couple of weeks I just puttered around, fixing things and preparing our new house to live in for the oncoming winter months.

Our first Christmas in our new house in the country was just that—a Christmas in the country, with a natural tree I cut down in the woods with some handmade trimmings as well as some of the regular store-bought things. Our guests were our friends Reg and Muriel Chapman, who brought pumpkin pies to go with the turkey dinner, and after we exchanged presents we sang a few carols.

For New Year's Eve of '75/76 we all went to a party at Gerald and Bernadine Taylor's house. And there, sometime during that evening, Willard and Marlene announced to everybody that they would be moving home to Prince Edward Island, and that they were prepared to take me up on my offer concerning the project in Skinners Pond.

Within a few days I had my lawyer draw up an agreement which Willard and I both signed, and a joint account was set up in Tignish, P.E.I., under the name of "Double 'C' Resorts." The "Double 'C'" stood for "Connors & Clohossey," and the first deposit was for $10,000, which Willard or myself could draw from at any time. Willard's wages, at the time, were to be approximately $180 per week. And I think he and Marlene and the kids moved home to P.E.I. during the following week, at least by the tenth of January 1976.

From here on till the end of February, I had to isolate myself again for the purpose of writing songs. I planned to record my thirteenth album of self-penned songs by the first of March. And the only thing that disturbed me, other than having to soon pay the tax man, was the fact that I received a list of Juno nominees where I spotted my name. I was being nominated for pop artist, as well as country artist, for the year just past, 1975.

"What the hell is going on here?" I asked myself. "I'm no pop artist." I never was, and I don't ever want to be. And I certainly didn't want to be classed with artists who have previously and adamantly stated to the press that they were definitely not country artists yet allowed their names to stand as nominees in the Country category, thereby depriving the true country artists the opportunity of being nominated in their own natural slot. (Some artists will do anything for a Juno Award.)

Though at the time it didn't make me the most popular guy in the industry, I did the honourable thing and withdrew my nomination from the Pop category to allow some genuine pop artist the opportunity to be nominated in my place. And that's more than I could say about what most of the other artists of the time would do. I could name some of these artists, but due to a professional courtesy which I adhere to, I won't. But if anybody cares to review the newspaper and magazine clippings of the time, they will read in quotes the kind of disdain some of these artists felt towards country music, and one can only wonder why they would even allow themselves to be nominated in that category.

Another thing that had begun to bother me about the Junos was why the same people kept winning all the time. Some artists already had over twenty Junos and were still being nominated in several categories in the hope of winning more. It seems to me that if three successive Junos in the same category could not prove that an artist had now earned the right to be a full-fledged member in the club of those who had excelled in their field, how could twenty-three or thirty-three Junos prove it?

While the artists themselves could not be faulted for this situation, it was my proposal at the time that CARAS (the Canadian Academy of Recording Arts and Sciences) put a limit, such as three in a row, on how many Junos an artist could win in his chosen category. He could then be given a pin to show that from then on he was lifetime member in the Junos' Club of Excellence. This would have allowed more artists to be nominated in that specific category. And today, instead of having only one artist during the period with thirty-some Junos standing all alone in the Club of Excellence, we could have had ten or more members standing as equals in a club where everybody has three Junos each. To me, all the Junos ever succeeded in doing was creating one or two great big giant winners while also creating one hell of a bunch of Canadian losers.

And the trouble is, we cannot now bring all this great Canadian talent back. They have long since been discouraged and just plain quit.

Now, there is one more point I will touch on in passing, just one more proposal I made which also got swept under the rug. And that is that right from the start, there should have been a National Juno Award for all those artists who chose to work within this Canadian musical community, *and* an International Juno Award for those Canadian artists and/or others who chose to work in or out of any foreign musical community. This would have prevented those artists who seek additional help within larger and more powerful foreign musical communities from competing unfairly with their Canadian counterparts who chose to stay and work at home.

It's no secret how all people everywhere like to welcome someone home who has been away for a while. We are also glad to hear them tell us how successful they've been while working abroad. But does this mean we have to give them our local Citizen of the Year Award while someone else who stayed at home and worked their ass off for the community gets nothing? Well, I for one don't think so.

I have absolutely no qualms about rewarding and/or showing our respect to those Canadian artists who have been successful internationally. But once in that class, they should be competing for international awards only. And in no way should their names appear in a line-up of nominees competing for an award considered to be national. And the guidelines for distinction between the two should be clearly drawn.

In my opinion, most of the award systems in Canada are set up in such a way that instead of being an encouragement for talent to stay in this country, they're an encouragement to leave it. When the acclaim that one should receive for excelling in one's own country is eroded or taken away by those who have left it, the only thing one can do is follow the brain drain.

In a democratic system, if a person leaves his country because he wants to, that is entirely his free choice. But when he is forced to leave his country because circumstances will not allow him to pursue his honourable goals, well, that is another matter.

During the first week of March 1976, the boys and I went into the studio and recorded my thirteenth self-penned album, entitled *The Unpopular Stompin' Tom*. The title was merely to reflect the reaction I was receiving throughout the industry at the time for my stand against the policies of radio, the CNE, the Junos, and others, whom I thought were not giving Canadians a fair shake.

This album, though it was called *Unpopular*, was very popular in the northern part of Ontario, due to the song "Muckin' Slushers," or as it is sometimes called, "A Damn Good Song for a Miner." It's all about the town of Elliot Lake and all the guys who ever mined for uranium there. Something like a Tillsonburg of the north, if you will.

Once the recording was finished we did an extensive tour of Ontario. Starting March 5 until the middle of April we played the following towns: Simcoe, Windsor, St. Thomas, Midland, Huntsville, Elliot Lake, Wawa, Marathon, Geraldton, Hearst, Kirkland Lake, Timmins, Cochrane, New Liskeard, Cornwall, Alexandria, Smith's Falls, Arnprior, Coburg, Newmarket and Shelburne.

While I was singing about the "Muckin' Slushers" in Elliot Lake to an uproarious crowd of miners, I got word from Toronto that I hadn't won a Juno Award this year. Lena and Jury were at the show and I guess they might have been more disappointed than I was. All I could say was, "Good. Now maybe someone else will have a chance to share in the glory."

Our road manager during this tour was Chuck Goudie, from Abbotsford, British Columbia. His wife Dana Goudie also worked for us in the Boot Records office at the time, but later left us to work at Capitol (EMI) Records of Canada Ltd.

Tom Jr., the First Six Months

A S SOON AS MY TOUR WAS OVER, Lena and I drove down to P.E.I. There I dropped her off at Pauline's for two or three days where a shower was planned for her by Pauline, her other sister, Amy, and her niece, Donna, who was over to Charlottetown on a visit from the Mags.

I just continued on to Skinners Pond to see how Willard and Marlene were making out since they moved down from Ontario earlier that winter.

So far, they had been staying at Willard's father and mother's place in Nail Pond and Willard himself was complaining about all the raw wind they'd been having for the last few months. He hadn't quite gotten used to it yet after having lived in Ontario for so long. He was also hoping to buy a long house trailer as soon as he could find one available, and place it on the property in Skinners Pond.

After a couple of days, I drove to Charlottetown to get Lena. And on our way back to Skinners Pond, she told me all about her friends and relatives who were at the shower and what a great time she had.

She also informed me that it turned out to be a double shower, as Judy Reid, who was also expecting at the same time as Lena, was also present. They were both about seven months along now, and decided to make a bet as to which one of them would have their baby first. It eventually turned out that Judy won by having her baby just five days before

Lena. (You'll remember Johnny and Judy Reid as being best man and bridesmaid at our wedding.)

As Willard and I and Russell mapped out our plans for developing the Skinners Pond project, Lena was busy having a couple more showers. One at her friend Joyce Butler's place in Miminegash, which she and Cora and Marlene attended, and one which Cora and Marlene got up for her at the house, to which a lot of the ladies from around home were invited.

By the third week in May, I figured I'd better get Lena back to Ontario where she could check in with her doctor and start the final countdown. The doctor said the baby would be born around the twenty-first of June and everything was going fine and according to schedule.

On the ninth of June we got word that Judy Reid just had her baby and it was a boy. She called him John Ferris Reid and we sent flowers for the occasion. That was on a Wednesday.

On Thursday, and for the rest of the weekend, the newspapers and other media had it that the Jehovah's Witnesses proclaimed that the world was going to end just as the sun came up that following Monday morning, on June 14.

On Sunday evening of the thirteenth, while all the local J.W.s were preparing for this momentous happening, the worst thunderstorm that ever hit our area in a very long time began to gather up steam.

Also, on this night, Lena began to feel some labour pains. And as they got worse, I decided I'd better call her doctor in Guelph. Her doctor was on vacation up at her cottage, and could not be reached. Another doctor told me she might be having false labour, as the baby wasn't due for another week. But if things seemed to get any worse I could bring her in for a check-up.

Sometime around midnight, the pains were getting worse. So in the middle of a raging squall, with rain, wind and thunder and lightning coming from everywhere, I bundled Lena in the car and headed out for the Guelph General Hospital, a distance of about twenty miles.

There wasn't a car on the road that night, and it was a good thing, because I couldn't see a damn thing ahead of me as my wipers struggled to keep the torrents of rain away from my windshield.

Lena was half-crying with the periodic surges of pain. I remember thinking to myself, what if I have to deliver this baby out here on the road in the middle of a storm? And it would have to be at the end of the world, at that.

I'm not sure how we made it, but we did. At the hospital, I soon had help from a couple of interns and a nurse to get Lena up to a room where a doctor took over and told me to wait in the hall. For the next several hours I was allowed to go in and see her, periodically, and though I was holding her hand, I'm not sure she even knew I was there. She wasn't having a very easy time of it.

Around about seven o'clock in the morning I was told to leave the room for the last time. Two nurses and a doctor wheeled Lena into the delivery room and shortly after the doctor came out and walked down the hall. And that was the last I saw of him until after the baby was born.

At approximately 8:30, one of the nurses came out of the delivery room and passed me a little bundle, saying, "Mr. Connors, your new son is a healthy baby boy, at seven pounds and two ounces. He was born at twenty-three minutes past eight o'clock. You may hold him for a while, but your wife has been through a hard time and she's going to need some rest. But she's going to be fine."

I guess I held him and talked to him for ten minutes or so before the doctor finally came down the hall to check him over. They took him from me and said that I might as well go home and that everything was going to be all right. After waiting another hour or so, when I found out that Lena was still sleeping, I drove back home. The date was June 14, 1976.

The baby's name was Tom Charles (the names Lena wanted to call him), and I couldn't help noticing on the way home how brightly the sun was shining. "What a strange way for this be-laboured old world to end," I thought. "As the sun comes out right after the storm, so the world begins when a baby is born." (I never got a chance to put that in a song, but maybe I will someday.)

After arriving home I phoned a few people to let them

know the good news and then I went to bed.

Lena was in the hospital a few days, and after having a number of visitors who brought gifts and flowers, I was able to take her and Tommy home.

Our good friend Liz Osborne, from Southampton, Ontario, came down and stayed with us for a few days until Lena got on her feet. And she also brought down her baby carriage for Lena to use. Which was extremely nice of her. A lot of other people also gave us things that could be used for the new baby at the time, including a great old wooden highchair, which was given to us by Marlene. Needless to say, all such things were greatly appreciated.

Lena herself had brought an old wicker bassinette up from down home that she once slept in when she was a baby, and this was going to be Tommy's new bed until he grew out of it.

Before leaving the subject, I must mention that Tommy was delivered by a nurse by the name of Hope Schofield with her assistant, Margaret Cook, while no doctor was present. Lena's own gynecologist later sent her an apology, however, along with best wishes to her and the baby.

Next came the baby pictures. They were taken by Art Stanton, a photographer who had previously taken photos for the Boot Records album covers. And of course Jury made sure a couple of them made their way into the hands of the press. The caption under the photos which later came back in our press clippings read, "A Romper for the Stomper," which we thought was quite cute.

I was able to stay home with Lena for about six or seven weeks after Tommy was born, and then I got her dad to fly up to Ontario to be with her while I was on tour.

Chuck Goudie was once again our road manager, and during the month of August we toured the western and northern part of his province, British Columbia. During September we were back in Ontario. Here I got to slip home once in a while between shows to see how Lena, her dad and Tommy were making out.

October saw us in the Maritime provinces and Newfoundland. And it was in Newfoundland that I got to make good my promise that I would reduce the price of the tickets from $3.50 across the board (which was the price the agent who brought me in before had charged, that I couldn't do anything about), to $2.50 for adults and $1 for anyone under fourteen years of age. I might also add that during this tour of Newfoundland, I again played Mary's Town. While I was there I found out that their local Catholic church had just burned down. Immediately after my concert I called the local priest to the stage and presented him with the total receipts from the show as my donation towards the church's reconstruction.

Later that year, I got a letter of thanks from the priest, saying that because an outsider had come in and made such a large donation towards having the church rebuilt, most of the local people and merchants donated generously and the reconstruction of the church was now under way. (In the early 1980s I once more had occasion to pass through Mary's Town, just as a tourist. And the church they built was a real fine piece of architecture. I didn't know where the priest lived or I might have dropped in for a minute to say hello.)

By the last week in October I was home in Ontario again. But only for a couple of days. Just long enough to kiss Lena, hug Tommy, say hello to Lena's dad and hit the road again.

We took off for out west to play a couple of towns we missed in eastern B.C. earlier in the summer and a lot we had missed on the prairies. The Manitoba and Saskatchewan towns we played on the way out, and our last concert for the year of 1976 was played in Vegreville, Alberta. We drove back to Ontario through a couple of bad snowstorms and arrived home on the twentieth of December, in time for Lena's birthday, on the twenty-first.

For the year of 1976 I had driven twice across Canada and played approximately a hundred concerts, this, on top of writing songs and recording them on an album, and helping to get Willard and Marlene set up in Skinners Pond.

Tommy was now six months old and was, understandably, acting a little strange towards me. As many times as I would try to get him to smile, there was just no way, while Lena and her dad, of course, could get him to smile any time they wanted to. But I was going to be home for the winter, now, and that would all soon change.

As I had had all the excitement I cared to have for one year, we decided to have a nice quiet Christmas at home. There was just the four of us, but it was always exciting enough in its own way to see Tommy's eyes gleam in wonderment at the lively colours of the tree trimmings and the rattle of the paper as the presents were opened.

One funny little joke I played on Lena's dad that Christmas always gives us a chuckle every time we think of it or speak about it to the family. It happened like this:

For years and years, every Christmas, as long as anybody could remember, every time Lena's dad was asked what he might like for Christmas, his answer was always "A silver do-nothin' to hang on the end of it."

Not knowing about this, I asked him one day, before I went out shopping, what he might like for Christmas. And sure enough, he said he'd very much like to have a "silver do-nothin' to hang on the end of it."

I went to Lena to ask her what he meant, and she said she didn't know, nor did she think that anybody else did. She then told me the whole story.

Anyway, while I was out shopping and thinking about all this, I happened to walk past a toy store with a large box of plastic snow throwers sitting outside. You know, the kind that have a plastic cup built into the end of a handle that kids dip into the snowbank to fling ready-made snowballs at each other.

Well, I bought one of these, made of green plastic, and then went to the Canadian Tire store and bought a can of silver spray-paint. As soon as I arrived home, I sprayed the snow thrower with silver paint, tied a leather thong on one end, and let the whole thing dry. The following day I wrapped it in some nice Christmas paper and put it under the tree with the words "To Peter from Santa Claus."

On Christmas Day, after everybody had opened most of their presents, Lena (not knowing what was in the package) took this strange-looking object, and after reading the tag, she passed it to her dad.

Peter looked at it very curiously, and after reading the tag, he opened it. While I was trying to contain myself, he looked it all over for a couple of minutes and finally asked me in front of Lena, "What the hell is this thing anyway?"

I said, "You should know, Peter, you've been wanting one of these for years."

He still didn't catch on, and said, "How in hell could I ever want one of these when I don't even know what it is? What the hell is it anyhow?"

When I told him it was a "silver do-nothin' to hang on the end of it," I thought he would die laughing.

"Well, well, well, well, well!" he said, finally. "Are they hard to come by? My grandfather always wanted one of these and I never knew where to get him one."

With that, we all had a good laugh. And at long last we all found out where and how the expression had originated. A silver do-nothin', indeed.

For the first time in a long while, we had a very quiet New Year's Eve. We just sat and played cards and listened to the radio. And when the year 1977 finally rolled in, we wished each other Happy New Year by drinking a toast, then finished our card game and went to bed.

Junos, Gumboots and Calendars

A s '77 ROLLED IN, I HAD some extra room in my base-ment, so I decided to build myself a much-needed office. After buying a whole bunch of plywood, two-by-fours, wires, switches and nails, and with a little advice now and again from Lena's dad, I erected what I needed and went on to the next project.

While talking the previous summer, Willard and I came up with the idea of making miniature stompin' boards and selling them to tourists who came by to visit the Skinners Pond School. So with the help of Peter and Lena, I started hand-sawing little rectangular ten-inch by six-inch pieces out of large eight-by-four-feet sheets of quarter-inch plywood and gouging authentic-looking holes in them. While I did this, Lena and her dad would sand and varnish them and set them out to dry. The silkscreened lettering on them read "Stompin' Tom from Skinners Pond," and we made almost two hundred of them. Then we boxed them up in prepara-tion to take to the Island the following spring.

Upon reviewing the lists of nominees for the Juno Awards in February of '77, I expected to see some changes being made concerning artists who were being nominated in all the wrong categories. But it was just as helter skelter as it had been the previous year.

I had withdrawn my name from a category (Pop) I had no business being in, just to try and set an example as to

what one should do when he finds his music classified as
being something that it is not. But was anybody bothering to
take the direction? No. Nobody seemed to give a damn as
long as they had a chance to amass more Junos.

I couldn't help but ask myself just how principled some
of these artists really were. When they were asked by the
press what kind of an artist they were and what style or genre
of music they had chosen to pursue in their professional
vocation, they would say one thing. But when it came Juno
time, they accepted nominations in just about any old category at all, no matter how ridiculously contrary it made their
statements to the press appear. Did these people not care
who they were or what they even stood for?

I began to wonder, for example, just how some of these
artists would react if a visitor to their home, after seeing
their great line-up of Junos, were to ask, "By the way, how do
you justify having accepted all these awards for a category of
music that, according to the press, you don't even play? And
if that's the case, how many of these awards do you feel
should actually be sitting on the shelves of those who do play
that kind of music? All of them? None of them? Some of
them? Or what?"

It now becomes obvious that people who think before
they grab will never have to answer these kinds of questions.
But then again, maybe some people just don't care.

And to those who say, "Well, it was just not my fault. I was
misdirected," I can only say, "It's never too late to turn
around and begin doing things that will help prevent the system from misguiding others. Don't be afraid to speak up
when you recognize that something is wrong. Because if you
don't, the very thing that is unfair to someone else now will
be unfair to you later. And if you didn't bother to help them
when you had the chance, how can you expect them to help
you when you're down where they were? Or maybe you
expect to always be on the top. And if so, I hope for your
sake you always will be. Because the road down is always a
hell of a lot faster than the road up."

Another point that was bothering me about these nomi-
nee line-ups was the fact that a lot of these people were
either living in the States or spending all their time working

and recording there, and only coming back to Canada for one day of the year to attend the Juno Awards. And that was only because their name was included among the nominees. But what the hell were they doing for this country that even made them think they deserved a nomination? Did they think their country should be rewarding them for the fame and wealth they sought to gain for themselves, while ignoring the needs and the problems they left behind for the people back home to face? Or maybe they thought their country owed them something? Not for their contribution to it, but for the fact they did their country an immense favour just by being born here.

For the moment, that will be enough about the artists. But what about the people running the organization that allowed all this to happen? It seemed to me that all they cared about was the award show, and raking in the big bucks, while obtaining the top entertainment for cheap. What would it matter to them where or to whom the awards were going, as long as the show continued to bring in the money? And why would anyone want to change the policy of an organization whose only way of making money was by exploiting the hungry aspirations of a lot of good talent in desperate need of national recognition.

To me, it's somewhat similar to the donkey who works all day while pursuing the dangling carrot. If he ever catches up to it, it's probably plastic anyway.

And to those who said at the time, "Yes, but look at the recognition we're bringing to Canadian talent," I can only say, "The NHL hockey players also had plenty of recognition before they formed the Players' Association. They could win the Stanley Cup, they could be on TV all the time, and they could show off their NHL winner's ring. But history proves that all these things didn't make them very much money. And since when did a Juno or any other award put dollars in the pockets of our entertainers? Never. They didn't then and they still don't now."

Had there been such a thing as the Canadian Organization of Musical Entertainers (COME) back then, the Canadian Academy of Recording Arts and Sciences (CARAS) would not have been able to obtain their entertainment so cheaply. Nor would they, or any other awards group, be able to obtain it so cheaply now. (I often wonder today how many early Juno Award winners had to go back to their day jobs because their income from playing music could not sustain them. It couldn't then, nor can it now.) I plan to come back to this subject a little bit later.

During the early spring of 1977, I just relaxed at home, wrote a few songs, played a few card games with Reg Chapman's brother Ray, and his wife Lil, and watched Tommy make a mess of himself in his highchair while trying to say Mama and Dada. (By March 14, at nine months old, he was walking.)

By now, Jury was on the phone wanting to know when I wanted to go out on tour again, as the requests for bookings from all over Canada just kept pouring in.

He was quite surprised when I told him that, for the first time ever, I had decided I wouldn't go out on tour at all this summer. I had done almost a hundred dates in the previous year of '76 and I figured the country had been covered well enough to afford me the luxury of taking a year off for a change. And besides, I wanted to go down east to Skinners Pond to help Willard do some work on our mutual project.

Around the twenty-fourth of May, we headed out for P.E.I. First we took Lena's dad to Skinners Pond for his first visit to see Russell and Cora. While he was there we invited old Josey (Jerome) Arsenault, who was now ninety-two years old, to come to the house for a little sing-song and a bit of a party. It was funny to hear old Josey calling Peter, who was now seventy-seven, the "young feller" all night. But the two of them got along great, and a good time was had by all.

In a couple of days, I took Lena and Tommy and her dad to the Charlottetown airport so they could all go home to the Mags. Lena was anxious to show Tommy off to everybody as no one on Entry Island had seen him yet. They stayed there until Tommy celebrated his first birthday and then flew to Nova Scotia where they went to visit her sister Amy, on Caribou Island. From there they flew back to Charlottetown by helicopter, where I again picked them up and brought them back to Skinners Pond.

During the time they were away and for a couple of

months after they got back, Willard and I were busy building fences, planting trees, cementing stones around the old well, and painting everything we could find that looked even the least bit shabby.

It was always a little bit difficult for me to get anything done, because every time I was spotted around the house by tourists who came to visit the school, they would always call to me or come over to where I was, to have a little talk and have me sign a few autographs. This could sometimes take up a reasonable amount of time. I might just get over to the schoolyard and take a couple of pictures in front of my old truck (the Boot), and be saying goodbye to one group of people, when another group would just be driving in. And there I would be chatting away again for another fifteen or twenty minutes. It often happened that, while this was going on, Willard would have to sit waiting for me in the truck before he could do anything that required my help. It got so that after a while I used to keep my eye on the cars coming up or down the road, and if they even slowed down at the school, I would duck behind something until the coast was clear, and then we'd start back to work again.

In the evenings we played a lot of cards, either at home or at one of the neighbours', and had a few parties. The card games we mostly played were Auction 45s or 45 straight. Most everybody from down east is familiar with these games.

In September we left the Island and went to visit Reg and Muriel Chapman, who by now had moved back to New Brunswick from Ontario, and were living in a new house trailer in Annagance. I especially remember this visit because I can still see Reg and me drinking beer at the table and laughing like hell at Lena and Muriel trying to give Tommy a bath in the kitchen sink. Between laughing and crying, it was hard to tell sometimes whether he was loving it or hating it.

By the first week of September we were back home in Ontario and I was planning to record yet another album. I still had three or four more songs to write for it, so I thought I'd buckle down and start writing right away. One of the songs was "The Gumboot Cloggeroo," which eventually also became the name of my fourteenth album. Back in the old days it wasn't uncommon to see farmers or fishermen on the east coast going to a barn dance wearing rubber boots or a lower-cut gum-rubber shoe known as a "gumboot." Along with reels, jigs and waltzes, the fiddle players would often play schottisches, polkas, two-steps and clogs. This latter dance called the clog was traditionally performed by people wearing hard leather or even wooden shoes so that the clatter against the floorboards would accentuate the beat of the music, much in the same way that drums do now. A lot of people who couldn't afford the more expensive footwear, which was most of them, just did their clogging in their plain old gumboots. Thus originated the "Gumboot Cloggeroo." In this story the young fisherman's name is Jack and his girlfriend's name is Sue. This is why he has called his fishing boat the *Suzie Jack.* And, as everyone on the east coast knows, if a fisherman could bring in a thousand pounds of lobsters in one day he would indeed have "money comin' out of his stockings." Here now are the words of the song.

THE GUMBOOT CLOGGEROO

1.

Oh, we sailed away at the break of day
To pull traps, in oilskin trousers,
On the Suzie Jack, *but tonight we're back*
With a thousand pounds of lobsters.
Oh, shanty town, we're gonna tear you down;
I got me money comin' outa me stockin's.
Tonight I'm due to bushwack Sue
And take her to the "Gumboot Cloggeroo"
And we'll do a little gumboot cloggin'.

2.

Gimme fish and brewis and a quahog stew
And a bo-oo-owl o' clam chowder;
See me reach for that Newfie Screech
When they diddles up the fiddle jig louder.
Hear the French girls sing and the guitars ring
And the squeeze-box squeekity-squawkin'.
Me and my Sue (we're) gonna hoop-dee-doo;

Take her to the "Gumboot Cloggeroo"
And we'll do a little gumboot cloggin'.

3.

There's "Boots" Bernard and the rough Richards
And the girls from 'way down Tracadie.
How many Blue Nosers and Herrin' Chokers,
We just don't know exactly.
Pack 'em all in tight and we'll dance all night,
Get the old barn floor just a-rockin',
Buy a ring-dang-doo for P.E.I. Sue,
Take her to the "Gumboot Cloggeroo"
And we'll do a little gumboot cloggin'.

(Just a note on the line, "Tonight I'm due to 'bushwack' Sue." In the days when nobody could afford cars, you went courting your girl in a horse and buggy. Most of the main roads were unpaved and quite narrow. And the lovers' lanes were no more than minor bush-covered roads winding through the woods. Even on a moonlit night, while your horse was making his way, and you were snuggled up to your girl and whispering sweet nothings in her ear, you would quite often get a "wack" from an overhanging tree branch that you didn't see coming. If any of these "wacks" were severe enough you might even have a few tell-tale bruises the following day. Of course, you may have gotten a couple of slaps, too. But either way, everyone knew you were out "bushwackin'." Maybe while I'm at it, I might as well explain a few of the other terms that could be unfamiliar to anyone who is not from the east coast of Canada. Brewis, pronounced brews, as in beer, is a type of hard-tack bread soaked overnight in broth, gravy or the like, and served the next day with cod fish. Quahogs, pronounced co-hog, is just another kind of clam with a round shell and just a bit larger. A Newfie, of course, is a Newfoundlander, and Screech is the kind of liquor they are known to be very partial to. Blue Nosers are Nova Scotians and Herring Chokers are from New Brunswick. A ring-dang-doo is no more than a real sparkly engagement ring, and P.E.I., of course, stands for Prince Edward Island. So there you have it.)

Now, I'm sure that everyone has heard or read the story of Rip Van Winkle who slept for so many years that when he woke up and made his way back into town no one recognized him nor did he recognize them. He became a lost soul, disoriented, and completely out of touch because he had slept for so long.

Well, in February of this year, 1977, I had written a song as a sort of parody on this story. Instead of the subject of my song being Rip Van Winkle, the subject is Canada's prime minister, his cabinet and the Canadian Radio-television Telecommunications Commission, the CRTC. In the song I refer to them as "Ripped Off Winkle" because I felt they were being ripped off by the major radio stations, the national exhibitions and others who were discriminating against Canadian talent right in front of them while they slept. They had passed the much-needed legislation that would have helped the Canadian talent, six years previously, and then fell asleep and didn't bother to check and see whether anyone was even paying attention to it. Their law was like a barking dog with no bite. Something to be ignored.

In this song I'm trying to put myself in the shoes of any aspiring Canadian artist of the time. This is how myself and most of the rest of us felt.

RIPPED OFF WINKLE

1.

*When I was young I had an old guitar and I
    learned to sing and play
From a book I bought on how to be a "Star" written
    in the U.S.A.
And every movie that I seen had a message just for
    me
If you want to be a "Big Country Star" you go to
    Nashville, Tennessee.*

*CHORUS (repeat after each verse)
That's my song . . . . That's my song . . . .
Hey! Old "RIPPED OFF WINKLE" Can't you hear the*

bell go dong?
Hey! Old "RIPPED OFF WINKLE" Don't you know you
*   slept too long?*

2.

Well I had my hopes of being a "Star" but not for
*   selfish greed,*
I wanted my country to take the credit for me if I
*   succeed,*
And if I don't no one will know, except the ones that
*   should,*
And no one in some foreign land can ever say I was
*   no good.*

3.

So I'm a North American, "Second Class," as some
*   would judge my fate,*
But I'll keep singing about what I am and
*   Nashville, you can wait,*
The Canadian National Exhibition is where I'd
*   rather be,*
But they don't take no "Canadians" even at the CNE.

4.

I'm forty-one years old today with a message for the
*   young,*
This country has a song to sing and that song must
*   be sung;*
Do a deed that'll make your country great as a
*   favour to yourself,*
And there won't be no greener grass in a pasture
*   somewhere else.*

With only another song or two to write for this upcoming *Gumboot Cloggeroo* album, I kind of got sidetracked by an invitation I received from the president of the Canadian Club of Toronto. The invitation read, in part, that they requested my attendance at a luncheon being held at the Royal York Hotel where they wanted me to be a guest at the head table while the premier of New Brunswick, Richard

Hatfield, was addressing a group of business people. The luncheon was to take place on Monday, October 17, 1977.

Had it been anyone else, I probably would have declined. But this was Dick Hatfield, my good friend and strong supporter of greater recognition for all Canadian talent. How could I not be there?

The only thing was that, by the time I came back home, the whole change of atmosphere had snapped me out of my songwriting mood and I couldn't get back to it. The recording of the album therefore had to wait. The final recording wasn't done until March of 1978.

In the meantime, though, I began to get interested in something else. Perpetual calendars. I couldn't find one at the time that could tell me the information I wanted to know.

I was reading history and ancient works and became interested not only in the date of a specific occurrence but on what particular day of the week the date fell on. And not according to the ancient Julian calendar, which was proven to be out by ten days back in October of 1582, but according to our present calendar, known as the Gregorian calendar, which is fixed yearly at the vernal equinox.

Now if, according to our calculations, October 15 in the year of 1582 was a Friday, then October 4 in 1582 had to be a Monday, and *not* a Thursday as stated by the old Julian calendar calculations. Therefore, the Julian dates should be adjusted to synchronize with the modern dating system. This would mean that, in the Julian calendar, October 4 in 1582 would now become October 14, 1582. It could then truly be called a Thursday, and so on, as the days and years are correctly numbered backwards. All the new books on ancient history would of course have to reflect the changes of the Julian dates. But at last this long overdue adjustment would enable us to take the "kink" or the "gap" out of our perpetual calendars and allow us to quickly calculate all days of the week along with their proper dates back into time immemorial.

Because I couldn't find a perpetual calendar in 1977 which would do the calculations just described, I decided to make one. This took me a number of months. But by the spring of 1978, with only the aid of a hand calculator, I accomplished the job. I then received a copyright under the name "Everdate" and by 1980 I had over 15,000 manufactured. They were indelibly printed on durable plastic the same size as a business card for easy carrying and reference.

On December 9 of 1980, I advertised them in the *National Enquirer* as "Stompin' Tom's 3000 Year Calendar" and wound up selling quite a few of them all around the world. To see how the calendar works, you can turn to the Appendix.

For Christmas of 1977 which, incidentally, was on a Sunday, we had Lena's dad up again from the Mags. He brought Lena's older brother Pete with him, but after a few days Pete wanted to go home again. I guess he didn't care much for Ontario and got a little homesick. They both left just before New Year's. Jury also came out to the house that year and brought Tommy a few presents. And other than Ray and Lil Chapman and one or two more guests, that was about it for that festive season.

I'll Give Up Music for One Year

IN JANUARY OF 1978 I GOT right down to work on the calendar again, and by the end of February it was pretty well finished. Then it had to be copyrighted and manufactured.

I really wanted to get all this out of the way as quickly as possible, as I hadn't done a concert tour the previous year and Jury was being bombarded with requests for more Stompin' Tom appearances. Then I got my eyes on the list of the new Juno nominations. It was becoming a bigger farce than ever.

Artists of one kind of music were being nominated in categories of music they didn't even play. Artists who were living and working steadily in foreign musical communities were accepting nominations in Canada, a country in which they didn't even live anymore. And we had an awards organization that seemed to do nothing but encourage it.

It seemed to me that here we were, in Canada, through our government agencies, trying to promote our arts and culture while there were people, companies and organizations promoting the very opposite. And a lot of our talent was, unwittingly perhaps, helping them to do so.

Canadian radio, by and large, was still telling the Canadian artists that if they wanted airplay, they should go to Nashville, Tennessee, or elsewhere to do their recording, while at the same time there were at least two studios in Toronto with the most up-to-date, state-of-the-art equipment.

The major record companies in Canada were all foreign-owned. It was they who had the biggest clout when it came to promotion of their artists and influence throughout the industry. And as long as their artists won Juno awards it mattered little to them what category they won them in. They would have nominated an artist in every category if they thought they could get away with it. And what was this doing to help the Junos gain any respect?

The artists and their managers, in turn, saw the record company as a mere stepping stone towards gaining a more lucrative contract with its foreign and/or American parent. So the thinking was: the more Junos an artist could win in this country, the higher his or her profile would be while trying to gain that foreign parent contract. So what incentive was there for them to withdraw their name from a category of music they knew little or nothing about? On the contrary, in this dog-eat-dog system, it was better to forget about scruples and grab everything in sight.

Again, the Canadian Academy of Recording Arts and Sciences (CARAS) did nothing at the time to prevent all this. In fact, not only were they allowing Junos to be won by artists who had lived outside this country for a year or more, but there were people who hadn't lived in Canada for a considerable number of years who were receiving Junos. I could even name one or two Juno recipients who were not only living in the States at the time, but had become naturalized American citizens some twenty years before. Either CARAS didn't know about this or, if they did, they didn't seem to care.

And where did the public stand on all this? They just didn't know what the hell was going on.

And where did Stompin' Tom Connors stand on all this? He did the only decent thing he felt he could do—get the hell out of this bedlam before it got worse.

For two or three years now I'd been feuding over the lack of recognition for Canadian talent at the CNE and what did it get me? Blacklisted? No. There was a more "politically correct" name for it at the time, and all the exhibitions in the country must have been using it. "We just won't hire the son of a bitch." And from then till now, they never have.

So knowing what could happen to a fella if he stuck his neck out too far, I decided to just quietly withdraw my name from the Juno nominations for male country artist on the grounds that too many people were being nominated in all the wrong categories and because others who were being nominated didn't even live in this country anymore. "And until this policy changes, I will no longer stand for any nomination."

This happened on or about Monday, March 27, 1978, which was two days before the Juno Award Show was to go on television, March 29.

Had it all been kept quiet, maybe nothing more would have come of it. Jury was in the process of booking my upcoming tour for the summer, and I would have just been on my merry little way, minding my own business. But this was not to be.

Somebody in the media got wind of what I had done and cooked up the story that I had withdrawn my name from the nominations because I knew my record sales could prove that I didn't warrant the nomination.

I didn't know who concocted this lie, but it no sooner came out over the radio than I got hold of the newspapers and gave my true reasons for withdrawing my name. There was just no way I was going to let some asshole slander my good reputation. So the truth now had to come out. I also invited all those with appropriate credentials to come to our Boot Records offices to personally examine all records pertaining to my sales. My books were open, but nobody came.

It's really funny in this business. Your enemies always sit somewhere in the bush and take pot-shots at you and try to ruin your career, but they won't come out and face you with their accusations. And that's because they know they're totally unfounded and that they've just made them up.

And were the enemies satisfied now that my real reasons were out in the papers? No. There was no way they were going to let me off so easily. The new accusation the following day was that I had really withdrawn my nomination as a ploy to gain publicity for my upcoming tour, just as I had done by demanding that the CNE hire more Canadian talent to headline the Grandstand. And, after all, isn't that also why I got married on television? Strictly for publicity?

Well, by the time Friday came, two days after the Junos were televised, I had had enough. Just because I had withdrawn my name from a nomination for an award whose authenticity I could no longer believe in, the motives for everything I had done or stood for were being questioned and vilified.

"All right!" I thought. "Enough is enough. If it's a goddamn publicity stunt they're looking for then I'll give them one."

I got Jury on the phone.

"I want you to call up every television company, every radio station and every newspaper reporter that's available. And tell them that Stompin' Tom would like to meet with them at the Boot Records office at four o'clock this afternoon, March 31, 1978. And if they want to know why, just tell them that something big is about to break. Something they can fill their wires and pages with for the next couple of weeks."

He wanted to know what the hell I was up to. "You've never done anything like this before, Tom. What the hell is going on?"

"You'll find out when I get there," I said. "Just have a taxi standing by to make a quick delivery. And if you have any dates booked for me anywhere, just cancel them."

With that, I hung up the phone and hurriedly scratched out a statement on a piece of paper. I then threw on my black hat and jacket, tossed my six Junos in a box and headed for the office.

I arrived just before the media. And while they were assembling in the foyer, I took Jury into one of the back offices and explained what it was I was doing.

In a very few minutes the cameras and mikes were set up, and away I went. I walked into the foyer and over to a large desk. I took my six Junos out of the box and placed them beside each other on the desk and sat down. By this time the cameras were rolling, and so were the questions.

"What's all this about, Tom, and why are we here?"

Without hesitation, I pointed to the Junos and said, "These are the reasons why you're here. You're here to see me pack them up and send them back to where they came from—the Canadian Academy of Recording Arts and Sciences. And maybe they can give them to some more of those Juno Jumpers who live outside Canada, but like to jump back in for a Juno once a year.

"Like I said before. I have no qualms about Canadian artists who wish to tour abroad once in a while to entertain, but while they do so it should be perfectly understood that their principal place of residence is in Canada, and they are working out of the Canadian musical community. This means that they record their music in Canada, their pro-moters and managers reside in Canada, and when they go abroad, they go to represent Canada as well as themselves. Then, and only then, should they be entitled to a Juno, which rewards them not only for the honour, but also for the added wealth they bring to their country." (This would be an International Juno. And a National Juno would be provided for those not considered to be in the International category, i.e., those whose records had not yet been picked up and reproduced internationally.)

"Then," I said, "we also have the problem that CARAS does nothing about artists jumping all over the place, in and out of categories everywhere. More Juno Jumpers, within our own country, who have previously said they wouldn't have anything to do with the kind of music for which they now cheerfully line up to accept an award, which more deservedly belongs to someone else.

"So it's for these reasons that I withdrew from the nominations and told CARAS that I would no longer stand to be nominated until they adopted guidelines that were more fair to everyone.

"Now because of this pro-Canadian stand, I find my integrity is being questioned everywhere. It's been hinted that I might have lied about my record sales figures to obtain a Juno nomination. And now I'm accused of not only using the nomination withdrawal as yet another publicity stunt, along with the CNE fiasco, but it's even being suggested that I'd stoop so low as to use my own wedding to gain publicity.

"Well, I wonder what those muckrakers will try to accuse me of next? What will they say when they hear I gave all my

Juno Awards back? Will they believe in my integrity then? I don't think so. It just seems to me that they're just out to get me for rocking their boat. They want the injustices to remain just exactly as they are. Almost as if they see some gain to be made in all of this.

"Well, anyway, I'm sending these Junos back to CARAS immediately, in the taxi waiting outside. I have just stated my reasons for doing so. And to prove that these are the reasons, and the only reasons, I have instructed my manager to cancel all my bookings and I will stay away from all concert work for one year so that I can in no way take advantage of any publicity these actions may afford me. And if, at the end of a year, the Canadian Academy of Recording Arts and Sciences has corrected these outstanding flaws in their system, I would then consider re-entering my name in their list of nominees, if I were eligible, and continue to work at my career in the music business. Maybe this, if nothing else, will stop the attacks on my integrity."

At this point, I called Jury's brother Peter over, and after we placed the Junos in the box, I instructed him to take them out to the taxi and deliver them to the office of CARAS in Toronto. (I never saw them again.)

There was now a short question period and the press conference was over.

I stayed and talked with Jury for a while. He was flabbergasted, to say the least. He wanted to know what I was going to do now. And I told him I didn't know. But one thing I was going to do was keep my word. I only hoped that my action would draw attention to some of the problems so that something, at long last, could be done.

Along with the six Junos, in the same box, and also by mail, I sent CARAS the following letter, dated March 31, 1978.

To the Canadian Academy of Recording Arts and Sciences. 245 Davenport Road, Toronto, Ontario.

Gentlemen:
I am returning herewith the six Juno Awards that I once felt honoured to receive but which

I am no longer proud to have in my possession. As far as I'm concerned you can give them to the border jumpers who didn't receive an award this year and maybe you can have them presented by some American.

I feel that the Junos should be for people who are living in Canada, whose main base of business operations is in Canada, who are working toward the recognition of Canadian Talent in this country, and are trying to further the export of such talent from this country to the world, with a view to proudly showing off what we can contribute to the world market.

Until the Academy appears to comply more closely with aspirations of this kind, I will no longer stand for any nominations nor will I accept any award given.

Yours very truly, Stompin' Tom Connors.

And I signed it.

(This was the letter I had scribbled on paper before I left home and had our secretary at the office type up.)

Those Juno Awards I sent back to CARAS on March 31, 1978, were these: Country Male Vocalist (CMV) received for five years in a row: CMV for 1970 received in '71; CMV for 1971 received in '72; CMV for 1972 received in '73; CMV for 1973 received in '74; and CMV for 1974 received in '75; Add to these five the country album of the year for 1973 and you have a total of six.

Clips from the press conference and parts of my announcement were carried that night, March 31, on the national television news and by the next day the papers were full of it. Some articles said I was right and some said I was wrong, but everybody had some sort of an opinion. I was being called everything from a lunatic to a hero, and the controversy raged on for several weeks. For the first week I gave phone interviews to radio and the papers, then I stopped. The questions were becoming the same and so were my answers, so I just let them go with what they had and left it at that.

Jury wanted to know what to do about the new *Gumboot Cloggeroo* album I had recorded just before the Juno fracas. Should it be released or not? I told him he should go ahead and release it because it had a couple of songs on it pertaining to what I thought about the Junos and all the Canadian artists who were running to the States. One of those songs was "Ripped Off Winkle," already printed, and another one just recorded was called "The Singer: The Voice of the People." Jury released the album sometime in 1978, but I didn't pay much attention as I had to keep my mind off music for a whole year. I will, nevertheless, print the words of "The Singer" here, so that my readers may get some idea of just how much it meant to me to see our singers leaving our country by the dozens.

THE SINGER
(The Voice of the People)

1.

You hear every day how they're going away,
I guess they just don't understand;
The Singer is the voice of the people
And his song is the soul of our land;
So Singer, please stay and don't go away
With so many words to be said,
For a land without song can't stand very long,
When the voice of its people is dead.

2.

O Singer, you must search for your place on the
*   earth,*
While the same for your nation is true;
So lift up the soul of your country
And a place will be found here for you;
But don't go and run till your song has been sung
And the words of your soul have been said;
For a land without song can't stand very long,
When the voice of its people is dead.

3.

You may pile up your gold but the pride of your soul,
Is the small bit of hope you bestow;
On the children who come this way tomorrow
In search of the right way to go;
So Singer, sing on, like the first ray of dawn,
With your promise of day just ahead;
For the land without song can't stand very long,
When the voice of its people is dead.

(Repeat first verse)

Meeting "Mr. Trouble"

SITTING AT HOME, and just thinking things over, I wondered what the hell I was going to do with myself now. I hadn't done a concert tour since the fall of '76, over a year ago, and now I had to wait for another year. My calendar was done. There would be lots of time now to write songs. So what project could I tackle in the meantime?

"Well," I thought, "why not write a book? I'd never written a book before, but who's to say? I'll never know if I can write one if I don't try. Well, where do I start? Well, why not start at the beginning? The beginning of what? The beginning of your life, you dodo."

So, anyway, that's how I came to start writing about everything I could remember from the day I was born. And during the months of April, May and June of 1978 I wrote about the first four years of my life, which took approximately 130 full pages. Then I got discouraged. I was remembering way too much. I was now forty-two years old, and at a rate of 130 pages per every four years, I would have to write over 1,300 pages just to get to my present age. "This is a project way too big for me," I thought, "and besides, this is the end of June. The weather is nice and warm. Willard is going to need some help in Skinners Pond. And what the hell am I doing sittin' around the house trying to write an encyclopedia that no one will ever want to read anyway?"

I tucked the pages away somewhere and decided to enjoy

the summer. My interest in writing a book never returned to me again until the 1990s. The time spent on it, though, had certainly helped me to get my mind off the hassles of the music business. That was at least something accomplished. (And that was how the first 130 pages of *Before the Fame* came to be written.)

Tommy was two years old now, and on June 14 his mom got him one of those little toy motorcycles. For the next couple of weeks, until we headed out for P.E.I., he must have driven a million miles and worn half an inch of varnish off the living-room floor. He had to get his hands slapped a couple of times, too, for pulling the knobs off the television set and trying to eat them. It was funny sometimes to peek around the corner after that and watch him reach for a knob and then shake his head and pull his hand away, remembering they weren't to be touched.

Once on Prince Edward Island, I rented a nineteen-foot trailer and hauled it up to Skinners Pond for Lena and me and Tommy to live in for the next couple of months. Russell and Cora were getting old and we didn't want them to be bothered by Tommy running around the house and disturbing them.

We parked the trailer across the pond from the house, next to Willard's forty-five-foot trailer, and there we stayed until September.

Willard had built a couple of cement posts in the middle of the pond the previous fall to support a long foot-bridge that we were going to build, but unfortunately, the ice over the winter had heaved them and they were now too crooked to do anything with.

We had bought a backhoe and a front end loader the previous year. As well as doing work on the property, Willard had been using it to do work for other people, to help pay some of his wages. He graded up the two existing driveways and built a third one across the field between the old house and the schoolyard. This was to give him a short cut and ready access for any work he might have to do there.

It also came in handy when we bought a small building that used to be a store, and erected it beside the school to be used as a canteen to sell refreshments and souvenirs. The souvenirs included Stompin' Tom tapes and records, bumper stickers and pictures, and of course, the miniature stompin' boards that Lena and I and her dad had made.

While a certain amount of progress was being made, there was also a certain amount of vandalism. The old tour truck, the Boot, which was sitting in the schoolyard, had been damaged. The windshield had been stolen out of it and had to be replaced. And other things had been missing off it, such as motor parts, hub caps and anything else that was of easy access.

There was a lot of damage in the school itself, due to bullets coming in through the windows. Stove pipes, pictures and other antique fixtures which had been donated were shattered or left in shambles, to make no mention of the holes these bullets left in the walls. Outside the school, one day, I counted sixty-seven bullet holes in the shingles alone. They were all near the windows and obviously meant to go in. The trajectory of all these bullets was easily determined by the angle of their point of entry into the school. And they all came from one direction. Which of course brought me to the conclusion that a certain party would have to be very closely watched from now on.

After I was home for a couple of weeks, in an unrelated matter, I noticed a certain teenager who kept walking through one of our fields every couple of days, and I asked Willard if that was the guy I thought it was, and why he thought this guy should always be roaming through our fields.

He assured me that my identification was right, but told me I was probably getting just a little bit paranoid. He was just another fun-loving teenager who liked to roam by himself a little.

One day when I saw him walking across the fields, I dug out a pair of ten-power binoculars and decided to watch his comings and goings a little closer. He appeared to be busy doing something behind a small growth of trees. When he was done, and made his way back down through the fields, I decided I'd take a walk back there to see what he was doing.

After walking about a half mile I came to the little growth of trees, and there just beyond them was a nice little patch of something I suspected to be marijuana. I pulled a couple of plants out of the ground and put them in my pocket.

When I got back home, Willard wasn't around, so I jumped in my car and took the twenty-mile drive to Alberton. That was where the nearest RCMP detachment was located.

As soon as I got to talk to an officer, I pulled these plants out of my pocket and asked him what he thought they were. "What do you think they are?" he asked me. I said, "Wait a minute. I think you're playing games with me. Because if they're what I think they are, I don't want them growing on my property. Now what are they?"

"They're marijuana plants," he said. "Now where exactly is your property? I think we should go and have a look."

"Well, I don't know if you've ever heard of me or not," I said, "but I'm the country singer known as Stompin' Tom Connors, and my property is in Skinners Pond. I've just come home on vacation and spotted a young fella going through my fields. And when I went up to check what was going on, I found this stuff growing in the spot where I saw him puttering around from time to time . . ."

Before I had a chance to finish my story, he said, "Skinners Pond, eh? His name wouldn't happen to be So-and-so, would it?" When I told him it was, he said, "Yeah, we know him well around here. We call him Mr. Trouble. Now let's go and see the spot you're talking about."

"Well, it would be kind of foolish to drive along by the school on the shore road," I said. "That would be too obvious. So I'll take you in by the back roads. That way no one will ever know you were there."

I jumped in my car and he followed me back to the far rear of my property. We walked a good piece down through the fields until we came to the marijuana.

When we examined the spot more closely, we found an old shovel and an empty fertilizer bag. After a few minutes the Mountie looked at me. "Tom?" he asked. "Have you got any enemies around here?" "Well," I said, "I don't know. I might have one or two jealous neighbours who may not understand what I'm trying to do here, but to go so far as to say that one of them might be an avowed enemy? I don't think I've ever given anyone a just cause for that. Why?"

"Because it's a damn good thing that you discovered this and brought it in right away like you did. For if someone who didn't like you had discovered it and filed a report, I would have had to arrest you for growing an illegal substance on your property."

"That's just great," I said. "I can see the headlines in every paper across the country now. 'STOMPIN' TOM BUSTED FOR DRUGS,' when I've never even tried them, let alone grown them or trafficked in them."

After pulling the plants out of the ground, we walked back up through the fields to our cars, and just before he drove away he told me someone from the detachment would be around in a couple of days to pick Mr. Trouble up for questioning.

(A number of years later, when the very popular Richard Hatfield, premier of New Brunswick, was arrested for marijuana possession, it cost him the next provincial election and put a very black mark on his illustrious career. I, for one, believe to this day that the marijuana was planted in the outside pocket of his luggage by some of his jealous enemies. Because whenever I had occasion to be in that man's company, and there were many, he at no time even mentioned drugs of any kind, let alone took them. And while all this was happening to Richard Hatfield I couldn't help but think that this very same thing could have happened to me in Skinners Pond.)

That evening, when Lena and I discussed the matter with Willard and Marlene over in their trailer, and suggested that we put up some "No Trespassing" signs in strategic areas where damage and other unwanted deeds were taking place, they were of the opinion that maybe I was taking all this just a little bit too seriously. Instead, they suggested that I just go and have a talk with those under suspicion and maybe something could be ironed out.

While I didn't think they fully understood the gravity of the situation and the damage that a drug connection could do to a person in the public eye, I agreed to have the proposed talk.

This didn't take long. The next morning when I got up

and looked out the window of our trailer, who was making his way across the field with another teenager but just the fellow I wanted to talk to. He was headed, of course, in the direction of his marijuana patch.

As I walked over in the field and came within earshot, I called out to them. When I got up close, I asked Mr. So-and-so where he was going.

"Who wants to know?" was his reply.

"Well, I'd like to know," I said, "being as this is my land."

"And if I don't want to tell you," he said, looking rather defiantly at my hat, "what are you going to do about it, cow-boy? Shoot me with your gun?"

"No," I said, "but if you keep that kind of talk up, I'm going to have to ask you to stay away from my property."

"You're the one that better f--- off," he said. "No one wants you around here anyway. And you can take that slut with you when you go."

With that, I made for him. But the two of them took off for a short distance, and when they saw I wasn't still coming behind them, they slowed down and started bad mouthing Lena and myself with a lot more filthy words than I would care to repeat here.

The following morning a small section of one of our new fences had been torn down. Nobody saw who did it, of course, so nothing could be done but go and repair it.

That afternoon, two police cars came roaring up the shore road. Anybody in Skinners Pond could see them with their lights flashing two miles away, as they came across what we call Edgar's Hill.

If they had any intention of finding anybody they sure went about it the wrong way. After visiting a couple of houses, one being Mr. So-and-so's, and after making the kind of display one would only see in the movies, they left the district empty-handed.

Another discussion with Willard and Marlene that night ended with no firm resolve as to what could or should be done. So for the time being, things were left just the way they were. Keep building today on the hope it would still be there tomorrow. (A little naïve, under the circumstances, I would say, but I supposed that every scenario should have its right to be played out. Sometimes one must have a lot of patience in these things.)

Johnny and Judy Reid drove up from Charlottetown to pay us a visit one afternoon and my cousin Danny Aylward (of blueberry fame) was down to the Island from Ontario and stayed around for a couple of days. We had some great laughs and chats about the time we ran away together as kids, and of course I had to ask him if he still hated blueberries. (See *Before the Fame.*)

Before we left Skinners Pond, we had the canteen going good with Marlene's very popular fish burgers of different kinds, and lots of fresh potato chips along with her hot dogs, healthy hamburgers and an assortment of home-made sandwiches, both hot and cold. As well as the tourist trade, her food had also become quite popular among the locals, and for a while there she was doing a fair little business, especially during the summer months. It had to be closed down, of course, once the colder weather set in.

The canteen was also good because of the fact that, along with the school, we were able to employ a couple of the local teenage girls to help with everything. This provided them with some much needed money that was otherwise unavailable.

Tommy also loved it down there. His mom and I would sometimes take him down to the nice sandy beach at the foot of our property and let him wade around through the wavelets that rolled in on the shore. After that he would busy himself by digging in the sand until he got himself all dirty. Then after a good washoff in the clear ocean water it would be time to go home.

A nice boardwalk along the beach was also a part of our plans, along with other things. But the big question that was now entering my mind was how were we going to contend with the vandalism?

Our plans by now included a nine-hole golf course, a small ten- or twelve-unit motel, a licensed bar and dining room, a trailer park with pony rides and farm animals for the kids, and even cross-country skiing and open pond skating in the winter time.

All great dreams. But if this kind of money was going to

be spent, we would have to have some co-operation from the people of the district and a lot of protection from the law. It seemed to me, for the moment, that these necessary requirements might be hard to come by in a place as remote as Skinners Pond.

Anyway, we left it all to Willard and Marlene again for another year and headed back to Ontario.

"Everything's All Right" with Peter

WE ARRIVED AROUND THE MIDDLE of September. But we weren't home for too long when Lena's sister Pauline informed us that their dad, Peter, was now taking treatments for cancer in Charlottetown.

This, of course, didn't sit too well. After getting almost daily reports for a month that the treatments didn't seem to be doing him much good, we got Pauline to bring him up to Toronto on the plane so we could get him into the Princess Margaret Hospital, which was well known for its work in the treatment of cancer.

By the end of October they arrived and poor Peter was looking just terrible. He had lost most of his hair and he could hardly walk without help. Within a few days we were able to get a bed for him in the Princess Margaret, and after a week, he began to feel pretty good, so they released him.

We brought him home to the house around the middle of November, and for the next couple of weeks or so he seemed to be doing pretty good. He was walking better by himself and talking a lot. He even played a few games of cards. And when he and Lena, as partners, would get as far as 350 in the hole at playing Auction 45s he would just laugh and say to Lena, "Aw, it's just a card game, and as long as we're having fun everything's all right."

Tommy, who didn't know what was going on, would always wait till he saw Peter making his way to his favourite living-room chair, and he'd race him to it. And there he'd be sitting in it when his Grampy Peter got there. But foxy old Peter wouldn't allow that to last too long. He just tickled Tommy till he squirmed out of the chair and then he'd grab it for himself. Poor Tommy never did catch on.

It was in the first week of December. Pauline had already gone back to Charlottetown by now, and everything looked like it was going to be all right. Then on the evening of the ninth, Lena called me upstairs and said, "Come quick! It's Dad. There's something wrong."

When I got upstairs I knew I had to take him to the hospital right away. I didn't know what was wrong but I told Lena to call the hospital in Georgetown, Ontario, because I'd be bringing him in to Emergency right away.

As I carried him downstairs and out to the car, Lena grabbed Tommy and was ready to go by the time I got him situated in the seat. When we got to the hospital they were all ready and waiting and immediately took charge.

After signing him in, we waited around till we could see him safely in bed, and after bidding him good night around 11 P.M. we came home.

For the next three days Lena and I took turns going to see him in the afternoons and the evenings, as someone had to stay home with Tommy. When we got up on the morning of the thirteenth, the phone rang. The nurse said that we'd better come down to the hospital, as they didn't expect him to last too long.

Unfortunately, when we got there, he had already passed away. Lena, of course, was beside herself. While one of the nurses took her into another room to give her something to relax her, I took Tommy and answered any questions that had to be answered and began to make some of the preliminary arrangements for the remains to be removed from the hospital.

Three days later, on Saturday, December 16, 1978, we were on the plane with the casket, heading for Charlottetown. Then on to the Magdalene Islands. From the airport in the Mags we followed the hearse for thirty miles or so to

Amherst Island, and there we loaded the casket onto the open deck of a fishing boat. The time would have been about 9:30 at night.

The waters were exceptionally cold and rough at this time of year. And while Lena's brother Ted and I and a couple of the boys stood on deck with the casket, she and Tommy huddled down below in the fo'c's'le and listened to the hard crashing of the waves against the bow of the boat as we pounded our way over the night waters.

I went down below with her through some of the worst of the pitching and assured her that everything was going to be all right. Poor Tommy, who was only two and a half years old, didn't have a clue as to what was going on. Except for a few jars and jolts now and again, he practically slept through the most of it.

After a solid hour of battering our way against the waves and the wind, we finally came into some of the calmer waters on the lee-side of Entry Island and made our way into the little harbour.

Although the night was cold, with snow on the ground, a lot of sombre people stood on the wharf to welcome their good friend Peter home for the last time.

As soon as we got Lena and Tommy into somebody's truck and safely on their way to her old home, we unloaded the casket onto another truck and slowly drove the last half mile up to the house. The time was about fifteen minutes to eleven.

When we finally got the casket into the old living room to let some of the women of the island begin keeping their all-night vigil, as was the custom, me and some of the boys plunked ourselves down in the kitchen for a couple of well-deserved beers.

Lena and Tommy had gone next door to Ted and Cathy's house by this time, because that's where we were going to sleep. And around about 12:30 or 1 A.M. Ted and I left the old house and made our way up to meet them.

After a light supper and a cup of tea and a final bottle of beer we all went to bed.

The next day being Sunday, as we prepared for the wake, the minister walked in. Within a few minutes we learned that he wanted to conduct the funeral and burial the following day, on Monday morning. This would mean the wake would only be held one night. Although two or three nights was always common and traditional, the minister was in a big hurry to get back to his diocese, which was in Quebec City.

(The Anglican parish on Entry Island is apparently not large enough to warrant a full-time minister, so one is sent down from Quebec City periodically to administer services. He then returns home to his diocese, where other appointments are pending.)

Lena and Pauline (who was now present), her brothers and other members of the family were now becoming very agitated on account of the minister's insistence. They asked him to delay the funeral until Tuesday, but he said he had other important duties to perform elsewhere. And through all of this, his demeanour remained very pompous, authoritarian and officious, as if these unsophisticated people from this remote little island could easily be swayed by pretension of superiority.

As soon as he left Pauline said, "I'll bet he doesn't have any 'other important duties' to do at all. He just wants to get away from this little place as quick as he can, for his own personal reasons."

"Well, maybe there's one way to find out," I said. "Phone the diocese. Someone there will have a copy of his itinerary and be able to tell you where and on what date his next duties are to be performed."

"That's a good idea," she said. And after calling one of the neighbours who had a lot to do with the church, she came up with several emergency phone numbers.

At first we had some difficulty, but finally we got in touch with one of the minister's superiors. He gave Pauline the itinerary, and just as she suspected, the minister was off duty until after Christmas, as soon as his stay on Entry Island was completed. She was also told, however, that once a minister's duties were completed and he was on his own time, he was pretty well free to come and go as he liked.

At this point, I got on the phone for a few minutes and explained the unique circumstances, of how Lena and I had bundled up our baby in Toronto and managed to get the remains all the way down to this little island, only to find out the minister wanted to do a rush job on everything just so he could get off the island and back to his regular circle of friends. "If this minister is officially off duty tomorrow," I said, "is it too much to ask him to hold the funeral off for one more day, on account of the fact it would mean so much to the family and to so many other friends and relatives in such a tight-knit community? Whether he's being paid or not, couldn't he do this little favour for compassionate reasons, if not for anything else?"

At this point the voice at the other end sounded quite sympathetic and said he would have a talk with the minister. That's where the conversation ended.

About an hour later, with indignation showing all over his face, the minister arrived at the house. "You people have no right to phone my superiors . . . etc. . . . etc. . . . and if there's a way off this island tomorrow, I'm taking it." With that, he turned on his heel, bid us all a resounding "Good day," and left.

Immediately, Lena's brother Ted got on the phone and called Craig, a guy on the island who owned a light plane, and explained the situation. He then called all the fishermen who still might not have had their boats hauled up, and they all agreed. "There's nobody getting off this island until Tuesday. Not even the minister."

So the wake was held that night, and I'm sure old Peter, who had a great sense of humour, must have looked down the next day and had a great laugh to see the minister going from house to house looking for someone to take him off the island. I would like to have heard all the excuses he was given, because the ones I did hear were dandies. One fella lost the plug out of the bottom of his boat, the other fella had his rudder stolen over on Amherst Island, and the best one of all was the guy who said for some reason he could never seem to get his motor started on Mondays. (I never did get to hear why the plane couldn't fly, but rumour has it that one of the wings wouldn't flap.)

The minister appeared at the wake that night, the second in a row, and though his face was a little redder than normal he appeared none the worse for the wear. The following morning, Tuesday, he conducted a very nice service in the little church. And by twelve o'clock or so on December 19, of 1978, we lowered old Peter's casket down beside his faithful wife, Lottie, who had passed away several years before. May they both rest in peace. Peter was seventy-eight years old.

The minister flew out with Craig on the light plane just after the funeral, and Pauline, Lena and I, and Tommy flew out on the twenty-first. We stayed overnight in Charlotte-town and on the evening of the twenty-second we arrived back home in Ontario.

Needless to say, Christmas wasn't much that year. With no time to get a real tree, I hustled out to buy an imitation one that we quickly trimmed for Tommy's sake, and Lena managed to wrap a few toys.

On Christmas Day, as we sat down to eat, a rather odd thing happened. Lena began to smell a very strong scent of pipe tobacco. As I couldn't smell it, I just told her that, because her dad had always smoked a pipe, there were probably a few traces of the smell still floating around. But this she would have none of. She insisted that the smell kept getting stronger and weaker at intervals for the next twenty minutes or so, and then it was completely gone. She took this to be a sign from her dad that wherever he was, everything was all right. I don't think she smelled it again after that.

Quitting the Music for Good

As 1979 ROLLED IN, I DIDN'T have much to do, so
I began to try my hand at a bit of cabinet making. First
I made a broom cabinet for the kitchen. Then a garbage disposal cabinet which matched and fit tightly to the end of the
existing counter top. When you opened the counter-top lid
it exposed the open mouth of a regular-sized garbage bag
which was easily replaced with a new one as soon as it was full.
This was a rather unique and very practical invention and
many people complimented me on the idea. Some even
wanted the plans so they could build one for themselves.

Next I built a seven-foot-long stereo cabinet for the living
room with lots of fancy doors and shelves to store albums
and tapes, and lots of room on top for record players and
stereo equipment.

While all this was going on, I was keeping my eyes and
ears open to find out what was happening in the music business. Was the CNE employing more Canadian headliners for
the Grandstand? Were the radio stations playing more "identifiably" Canadian music? And especially, was the Canadian
Academy of Recording Arts and Sciences making any of the
recommended changes to their system? The kinds of
changes that would allow me to feel better about re-entering
the competition. Such as creating an International Juno for
those Canadians with international status, along with the
National Juno for those doing all their music within the

country. And also, were they defining the categories in such a way as to help avoid the nomination of artists in categories of music which they didn't even play?

With Jury chomping at the bit to fill all the requests for booking me across the country, we anxiously awaited the announcement of all the new nominations.

When they finally came out and I read the lists, I could see that my plea for change had been completely ignored. I had not entertained for a whole year to prove my sincerity to all doubters of my integrity. I had only asked that the system be changed to show that all awards were given out fairly so that each Juno recipient's worthiness would be absolutely beyond question, both in the eyes of the industry and in the eyes of the public at large.

So how did this make me feel about my efforts? How did this make me feel about the people I had to deal with in the industry? And how did I feel about awards, period?

For my efforts to help improve an inequitable system I was being labelled a fool by people who didn't care what they were doing as long as they could get away with it.

"Where was their conscience?" I thought. "Where was their sense of justice? And where was all this wonderful 'integrity' they were accusing me of not having?"

Had I not put my career and my income on the line for a year to prove that I was truly a conscientious dissenter and not just a blow-hard shit-disturber looking for publicity?

If my integrity was still intact after putting it up for public scrutiny, why couldn't CARAS and all the others who were involved in the Juno Awards do the same. If there's nothing wrong with what you're doing, why not show the public everything you're doing? Or is it the fear of public demand for change that prevents you from doing so?

All the public ever gets to see are the results. But they never get to understand the methods and criteria being used to determine those results. They get to see an artist win a Juno, but they never get to understand exactly why his competitors lost, or even whether the competition was run fairly.

As the newspapers of the day had attested, there were just as many people who stood for my position in all of this as there were for the other side. And maybe a lot more. So because I had allayed any doubts about my integrity for one year at my own expense, I reasoned that the least my accusers could do now was prove their own integrity, stop their mud-slinging, and have the decency to face the problem square on and show the public that they were serious about getting rid of any and all unfairness wherever it could be found.

And to those who were saying I was just a fool for going to such lengths to uphold my integrity, I can only ask, if they equate integrity with foolishness, what do they call someone who only feigns integrity and is later proven to have none? A hypocrite, maybe? Well, if they can't come up with the right name, I'm sure I can help them come up with a few.

So how did I (or how do I) feel about awards? There's nothing wrong with awards, in and of themselves. But when they have to be yet another source of unfairness to Canadian artists, in an industry that already reeks of unfairness, it's time for those with even an ounce of integrity to separate themselves from those who can't see anything wrong with its perpetuation.

And that's exactly what I did in March of 1979. I continued to stay away from them. I told Jury at the time that I could not, in all good conscience, remain part of an industry that could not look within itself to make the changes required to place itself above reproach, not only in the public eye but also to the artists who live and work within the Canadian musical community.

To remain part of an unjust organization is to contribute to it. And when the injustices finally come to light, you're just as much to blame for them as anybody else. (Though rats may jump from a sinking ship, it doesn't prevent them from drowning. And a clean, safe ship has no rats, and therefore no rat holes to cause sinking.)

And there you have it. That's why I quit playing music altogether, and the name Stompin' Tom practically disappeared from the annals of the Canadian music industry. Gone, you might say, but not quite forgotten.

For the next ten years I would be trapped between a rock and a hard place. On the one hand, my fans wanted me to continue to record and entertain. But they just didn't understand the situation. (Thousands of letters that I had to personally answer during the interim, and of which I still have copies, will attest to that.) I felt that to record and entertain would be tantamount to becoming a part of the music industry once again, at least in the eyes of the public, and therefore caving in and turning a blind eye to its injustices.

On the other hand, although I was disappointing my fans, I felt that someone had to be the champion of the truth. I had talked with plenty of entertainers right from the beginning of this mess, and all agreed that something must be done. But when asked if they were prepared to stick their neck out with me, they all declined, for one reason or another. The basis for all these reasons came down to one thing: they were afraid that if they spoke up as I had done, the same thing would happen to them that had happened to me. They would receive a black mark from the manipulators and any progress they had made up till now would soon be taken away from them. In other words, they admitted to knowing, just as I knew, that they were working within a musical community that expected them to keep their mouth shut and say nothing if they wanted to get ahead. (What a system to have to work under! Whether it's right or wrong, don't criticize. Put up with everything or be forced out. You must learn the art of kowtowing. Because talent alone will not get you there.)

So someone had to stick their neck out for the rest. If something was ever going to be done to improve the situation, somebody had to stand up and make the personal sacrifice that no one else had the courage to make. And who better qualified than me for the undertaking? I had been through a lot more adversity than most, and could probably stand up to a lot more to come.

So I became the visible candidate, the spokesman for those afraid to speak for themselves. If I won the battle or made some gains, everyone could come out and admit they were on my side right from the start. And if I lost, and ridicule drove me into total obscurity, they could always say they never knew me. There was nothing to lose; they had it either way.

I hope that now, by reading this, everyone will

understand why I stayed away from the music business for so long. Every time I had an interview with the press they cut my statements to ribbons, and what the public finally got to read was always someone else's interpretation of what I really wanted to say. So here, at long last, for bad or for worse, you have it in my own words.

Skinners Pond Vigilantes?

IN JUNE OF 1979 LENA AND I and Tommy headed out once again for Prince Edward Island. Once in Charlottetown, we made our visits to see Pauline and Johnny and Judy Reid and after putting Lena and Tommy on the plane for the Mags, I spent a couple of days with my friend Ray Goguen, just outside of Charlottetown. (You may remember Ray and Grace from when I used to stay at their place on 4th Street in New Toronto. See *Before the Fame*.) I always had a good time at Ray's, as he and I both played the guitar and sang, and there were always lots of his friends around who enjoyed the music. This was one of the places on the Island that Lena and I would always visit each time we were home, though I may have failed to mention it up till now.

Anyway, after my visit with Ray I landed in Skinners Pond. There I became enlightened about some more of the vandalism that had taken place after I left the previous summer. The most of it took place towards the end of October. Among the worst of it was one night, maybe Hallowe'en, when someone hot-wired the backhoe and front end loader and drove it into the pond. All that was sticking out was the top of the backhoe. The lawn tractor that I had bought for Russell to cut the grass was also in there somewhere beside it. They had, of course, both been pulled out by now and were back in good working order. But once again, not a soul had any idea who was responsible for all this.

The conversation with Willard and Marlene about posting "No Trespassing" signs had also, once again, got me nowhere.

I suggested that the "No Trespassing" signs read: "$300 reward for any information leading to the arrest and conviction of anyone known to have caused damage to this property or to any of its belongings."

My hope was that this reward money might get someone to come forward as a witness, so the guilty party or parties could be prosecuted.

This idea was turned down by Willard and Marlene on the grounds that, "We have to live here and you don't. These are all our neighbours and our kids have to go to school with their kids. And what would everyone think?"

This brought the "No Trespassing" sign issue to a close. "Well, what the hell are we going to do then?" I asked in frustration. "The new windshield is gone out of the truck again. The windows of the school are being smashed faster than we can replace them. Two tractors have had to be pulled out of the pond and repaired. Culverts for the dam have been plugged. The fences are being destroyed. And some son of a bitch is using this property to grow marijuana. There must be something we can do to prevent the money that's being spent here, and the work you're putting in, from all going down the drain?"

I told them I had just quit playing music, and depending on what changes would be made in the music business, if any, I had no way of knowing if I'd ever go back to entertaining again.

Although that source of my income had dried up, I told them I still had some money put away to see the day when this project could make enough money to keep itself going. But in order for this to happen, the vandalism would have to come to a stop right now.

"Everybody in this district knows how, when and by whom all this damage is being done, and not one single person will open his mouth and say anything. So I ask again, is there something, or anything, we can do? Or are we just going to sit around and let things get worse?"

After a lot of speculation composed of if's, and's and

but's, we arrived at no concrete solution, so we decided to put it away for another day.

"But on a higher note," Marlene said, "we've bought a 140-acre farm down in Nail Pond. You know, the one right next to Willard's dad's place? And we'll be expecting to move down there soon. There's a house and a barn on it, where we can raise cattle. And a big field away up back that's perfect for growing blueberries."

"That's great," I said. "I hear there's lots of money being made in the blueberry business, nowadays. And of course, you'll probably find some time to continue keeping Double 'C' Resorts going?"

"Oh, no problem there," Marlene said. "Willard will drive down every day and do what work needs to be done around here, and Robbie is getting big enough to do a lot of things around our new place. And things will work out fine."

"Well, I'm real happy you got a new place," I said. "And by the way you describe everything, it looks like things should work out great for all of us."

I was truly and genuinely happy for them, that they were able to buy a place to call home. And though I had a few misgivings about what would happen to our Double "C" Resorts agreement, I realized this was certainly no time to discuss it.

For one thing, I had offered them any one of several sites on the Skinners Pond property, at no charge, so they could build a house. And I couldn't understand why they hadn't taken me up on the offer.

The next day I drove down to Alberton to have a talk with the head Mountie who was in charge of the detachment. I related my problems about all the vandalism going on and just exactly who I thought was responsible. "Isn't there something you people can do?" I asked. "I've been trying to pour money in this area to help draw tourists to this end of the Island and to also create badly needed jobs. But if this continuous destruction to my property doesn't stop, the money is going to stop. The school I renovated three or four years ago is looking almost as bad today as the day someone wanted to make a pig barn out of it. This whole thing is insane. Why should people have to live like this? Where is the law and order?"

"Well, Tom, it's like this," he said. "We know who all the culprits are around here. But we too have our own problems. We have a very soft magistrate in Summerside, and as fast as we apprehend these hoodlums they're back out the following day calling us pigs and pelting us with eggs. They taunt us and make a mockery out of what we stand for. One night in Tignish they even upset one of our police cars with one of our young officers in it. We've complained to the province, but so far they have not given us the authority or the manpower or the co-operation to clean this mess up. Our hands are practically tied and there's really very little we can do, other than stay visible."

"Well, isn't that just great?" I said. "That doesn't give me a hell of a lot of incentive to build anything, if all I can look forward to is having it demolished while my back is turned."

"I wish there was something I could do, Tom," he said. "But you're not the only one having these troubles. And some are a lot worse. Some people are scared to leave their homes because they've seen others being threatened, and due to non-compliance, have later had their houses mysteriously burn down. Fishermen have had their lobster traps burned and one or two have had their boats sunk. The Tignish liquor store has been broken into several times and gas has been stolen everywhere, including out of cars with siphoning hoses. And every district around here has one or two of the same kind of lads as you have in Skinners Pond. And when they get together at night there's no telling what they're up to. So without co-operation in Summerside, we're just as frustrated as you are. We just do the best we can, and the most we're allowed."

After I got home that evening, I had another talk with Willard and Marlene and told them where I'd been and what I was told.

"That's all pretty well common knowledge around here," Willard said. And then he went on to tell me a few more things, including the afternoon that half the people attending a wake had the gas siphoned out of their tanks as their cars stood parked outside the funeral parlour. The thieves had apparently sneaked up through the adjacent cornfield, filled all their cans and disappeared.

I had to admit that that was a pretty funny story, but it wasn't doing anything to solve our problem. So far, since the beginning, I had spent $150,000 on this project and when you looked around, a lot of it was already in shambles.

"You know," I said, "in a lot of other places, the people wouldn't put up with this kind of living, with senior citizens being intimidated every time they step outside their door. And every time they come home from shopping they can't be sure if their homes or barns are even going to be there. And when the Mounties can't keep law and order, this kind of thing is going to spread rampantly throughout this whole end of the Island.

"If I were living here all year round, I wouldn't put up with any of this. When citizens are not safe in their own homes, and everything they worked for all their lives is being taken away from them by an unruly bunch of reprobates, it's time that something was done. Something a little more drastic than just asking these known culprits to please stay away from us and we'll be real nice to you. What I would do is form a group of secret vigilantes and have them pay a couple of the same kind of nightly visits to them as they are paying to the innocent people. A little taste of their own medicine might scare them enough to either chase them the hell out of here or cause them to at least leave people alone."

"Yes, but you don't live here," Willard said.

"No, I don't," I said, "but I'd certainly support such a group in any way I could if one were formed. Even in New York City they have vigilantes who apprehend lawbreakers and scoundrels and turn them over to the police. But at least there, the police can turn them over to someone else who will put them in the cooler for a while instead of giving them a little slap on the wrist."

"Well, I don't know anyone around here who would be willing to form a group of vigilantes," Willard said. "Everybody's afraid to even speak up and say who the culprits are, never mind forming a group of vigilantes to go after them."

"Yes, and that's exactly what the culprits are counting on," I responded. "Intimidation. If this kind of thing is not checked now, people will find themselves having to pay protection money to the very same hoodlums they fear. And to those who say, 'Well, why should I worry? Nothing's happening to me,' I can only say, 'It's just a matter of time. Because your turn is fast approaching.'"

Sometimes I wondered, during these conversations, if Willard and Marlene were not thinking that maybe it was just me. Maybe for some reason I wasn't liked by the people of the district and my presence here was not wanted. And maybe, if I would just go away, the vandalism in the district would also just quietly disappear.

This kind of thinking on their part would have been rather naïve, however, in light of the fact that we were not the only ones being victimized in the district, let alone in the countryside. I therefore put the thought out of my mind and forgot about it.

A few days later, I was taking a walk through some of our back fields, and there in a very secluded area I came upon not only a few marijuana plants, but no less than a quarter of an acre of them. There must have been a dozen empty fertilizer bags along with all the necessary hand tools required for maintaining the crop nicely hidden under some bushes.

Here's where my old tobacco-picking experience came in handy. In twenty minutes there wasn't one plant left in the field. Every one had been picked and left in a pile to rot.

I knew that some Mr. So-and-so was going to be terribly mad. But no madder than I was at Mr. So-and-so. I made my way down through the fields, well hidden by the trees and shrubs, in the same manner I had gone up. And I didn't bother to tell anybody anything until the day I left the Island. Then I told Willard.

The day after the marijuana pull, I drove to Charlottetown to meet Lena and Tommy getting off the plane from the Magdalene Islands and brought them back to Skinners Pond.

By this time, Cora had become ill and had to be hospitalized in Charlottetown for a couple of weeks. She was then tranferred to Summerside where we got to see her more often, and finally she was allowed to come home. The whole ordeal took about three weeks and it seems to have started from a dose of the flu that she had had previously, which somehow affected her middle ear. Russell, who was now seventy-five, was quite worried about it all and was glad to see her home again.

After working around with Willard a little while longer, Lena and I and Tommy left Skinners Pond and went to visit her sister Amy and Foster at the Caribou lighthouse, in Nova Scotia. From there we went to see the Harpers, and Reg and Muriel Chapman, in Annagance, New Brunswick. And by mid-September, we were back home in Ontario.

Feeling the Pinch

A FEW DAYS AFTER I GOT HOME, it was time to have a long talk with Jury. The gist of it all would be: now that I was no longer entertaining, and the money from that source had dried up, I was going to have to get some income from Boot Records. I had financed the company to get it started back in 1971, and had not received anything in return ever since. Even my royalties, over the years, had not gone to me, but were poured back into the company to make sure it was kept afloat. And while a record had been kept of all this, I hadn't received anything. I figured it was almost pay-back time.

Although our publishing companies were flourishing, Boot Records had been in the red every year since it began back in 1971, and without my personal royalties to keep it going, it probably would not have survived. And had it not survived, there were one hell of a lot of artists who would never have been recorded, whether it was on the Boot label or the Cynda label. (Most of these artists never knew at the time where the money was coming from. As far as I was concerned, Boot Records had to have the appearance of a successful company at all times. Up until now, I was surviving quite well on my concert revenue. But since December of 1976 I had not done even one concert, and I was now feeling the pinch. After all, this was September of 1979, and I was getting a little tired of dipping into my savings.)

397

Up until now, I had been doing everything I could to record and promote Canadian artists who were completely unaware of the extent of my total commitment to their cause. I didn't want anyone to feel that they were indebted to me. And I figured the less they knew, the more confident they could feel within themselves. After all, it always makes people feel good to know that they have accomplished something totally on their own. (Self-confidence, once gained, often leads to greater accomplishments.)

But now, even though Boot Records was still in the red, I was going to have to put the damper on some of our spending, in order to have my own company start contributing to my own cause.

We set up a system whereby I would receive a monthly payment, and at the same time try not to hurt the company too much. We would try to keep doing as much for the artists we had, but we would have to cut down on the taking in of new ones.

The reader might be surprised to find out some of the names of artists who either got their start with us, were recorded by us or had their record distributed by us. I will just list a few and apologize for the great many omissions.

Stevedore Steve; The Dumptrucks; Sons of Erin; Julie Lynn; Rita MacNeil; Sean Dunphy; Barbara Gryfe; Sharon Lowness; Larry McKee; The Wolftones; Bud Roberts (Black); Liona Boyd; Roy Payne; Dick Nolan; Delmer Dorey; Clare Adlam; Sonny Caulfield; Pat Lynch; Walter Ostanek; Fred Dixon; Rick Fielding; The Hoedowners; Barley Brae; Rebecca; Clint Curtis; Brent Williams; Billy Lewis; Lloyd Mackey; Mickey Andrews; The Allan Sisters; Claudette La'5'; Charley Russell; Stan Lorel; Ray Griff; Dennis LePage; Kent Brockwell; Stan Rogers; Dixie Flyers; The Emeralds; Charley MacKinnon; Mendelson Joe; Chris Scott; Ryan's Fancy; The Brannigan Boys; Gerry Doucette; Chuck Goudie; Ian Tyson; Sullivan; Joe Firth; Little John Cameron; Jim Martin; Canadian Brass; Marie Babin; Alphie Fromangie; Jack London; Gaet Lepine; The East Wind; Stu Clayton; Angus Walker; The Molly Mcguires; Eddie Coffey; Harry Hibbs; Sheila Ann; Danny Doyle; Chef Adams; Ray Smith; Joyce Seamone; Ivan Romanoff; Ted Wesley; Tom Gallant; John Ham; Chubby

Wise; Kayton Roberts; Wilf Doyle; Phil Bond; Graham Townsend; Par Three; Gabe & Peter; Digno Garcia; Bill Guest; Lee Creemo; Stompin' Tom Connors . . . oops! I better quit for now. I'm running out of breath.

What Better Community
Service...?

IT WAS ALSO AROUND THIS TIME that I began to take a closer look at why the great majority of radio stations in Canada were chafing against the Canadian Radio-television and Telecommunications Commission, the CRTC, for their ruling that radio must play 30 per cent Canadian musical content on the airwaves.

For the last nine years, all they seemed to be doing was playing the music of five or six artists to the point of saturation while ignoring the vast number of recordings of other artists that were being sent to them.

At the same time, they kept asking the CRTC to either cut back on their Canadian content ruling or drop it altogether. Because, in their view, there was "not enough talent in Canada to justify keeping it."

Because of this and other arguments they continued to mount, it sometimes looked as if they might even get their way. If they ever did, I thought, it would spell the end of what little opportunity there was left for new Canadian talent to ever be heard on the radio again. It would be a complete tragedy and must never be allowed to happen. So I wrote down some of my thoughts on the subject and sent it off to a couple of newspapers, but to my knowledge it never was printed.

The following is what I wrote at the time:

Radio Stations want the Canadian Content Rules of thirty percent changed because they claim they can tell by their requests that listeners prefer to hear American talent over Canadian. And therefore, if they play Canadian, their ratings go down and the money they receive from advertising is less. This diminishes their popularity, followed by their profits, and therefore their ability to provide maximum community service.

Well, let me try to answer this claim by making the following comparison, which will attempt to show why American talent may be more popular than Canadian.

From a cross-section of North American people, let us take 2 average five-year-old children who are both learning to sing or play an instrument. Let's say one is Canadian and the other is American and both have an equal amount of talent.

Surely, at this age, no one would say that one of these children is better than the other just because his nationality is different; that would be discrimination. But what about when they are fifteen years old; would that make a difference? How about when they are 30, or even 50? Would that make one of them better than the other? The answer, of course, still has to be "no."

Then how does it happen that American talent always gets to be played over seventy percent of the time on our radio stations, and 100 percent of the time on their own? Is it because their talent is that much better than ours? No Way!!! But we do ASSUME that it is.

That's because we, the Canadian listening public, have let our American puppet radio stations lead us down the garden path for so long

that we now unconsciously take it for granted
that American talent is better than ours, and we
don't even bother to question the validity of
this ASSUMPTION any more.

Well, let me question it now, and try to point
out to you why the radio stations are wrong,
and why we're every bit as good as we've been
led to believe the Americans are. But first, we
do have a small problem.

Remember, there is one fundamental char-
acteristic about the American people that we
must all come to realize. They are proud of
what they are and who they are, and they have
no drawbacks whatever when it comes to telling
the whole world just how great they are. This
has always been the hallmark and the "big
secret" behind their economic success. And
even though at times they do get overbearing,
one cannot afford to knock them without being
accused of getting jealous.

So, hurray for them. But what has all this got
to do with comparing five-year-olds and saving
Canadian talent? Let me explain.

The American five-year-old begins by learning to sing and play the songs written about his
own country that his proud parents and relatives taught him, and they encourage him to
continue singing them because they never
seem to tire from hearing more about themselves. This is really all quite natural, as humans
all, from time to time, engage in vanity. But this
is the catch: Are we as Canadians not allowed to
also engage in this harmless human foible?
We'll soon find out.

Now by the time this American child is 15 he
has learned and heard so many songs about his
own country on the radio that he knows his
chances of being heard are pretty good if he
ever decides to cut a record. All he has to do is
follow a simple formula which states that he

must sing what all the people want to hear.

He knows that Americans want to hear American songs on American radio because that's about all they ever request. This is how they praise each other and advertise their glory to the world. And to the extent the world believes them they remain economically successful.

Even as you now read these words thousands of people are being enticed to buy products while they listen to songs called "jingles" which tell them how great the products are. This, too, is exactly how we have come to be lured into believing that the Americans, their country, and all their achievements are so much greater than ours.

We're subtly told all these things while we listen to the songs they write, sing and record. And to the extent that we believe what the songs tell us, we tour their country to see their greatness, while in our hearts we know our money might have been better spent if we had stayed at home and toured our own. We often buy American products even though our own manufacturers may be going broke. And along with a host of other things, we seriously take their advice, and so do our radio stations who keep us listening to the "great American hits" which continue to reinforce our inferiority complex so much that every time we mention our own songs, our own country and our own talent, somebody laughs.

This is how we passively came to allow over seventy percent of our broadcast time to be taken up by the music of all the so-called "American Stars": One of whom will soon be the 15-year-old we were just talking about. He will soon be given the opportunity to sing and tell the world how great his country is, while we continue to help the American economy by buying his records instead of those produced by our own Canadian music industry.

Can you now see why it is that such great numbers of Canadians have unconsciously come to believe that American talent is "better" than ours? Whatever the Americans believe in, they encourage their talent to sing about. For this, they pay them dearly. And why shouldn't they? It greatly improves their economy while everybody in their country benefits. Even their President often takes time out to congratulate them. (There must be a lesson in here somewhere.)

Now, let's take a look at the other side of our comparison to see what happens to our Canadian 5-year-old.

Because his own parents and relatives, who have been listening to radio for a generation or two, don't know or sing any songs about their own country, how can the little fella ever be expected to learn any?

The only songs this 5-year-old will ever be encouraged to learn and sing are those he hears on the radio, which are sung by Americans telling him about their country and how great they are. And by the time he reaches 15 he will be singing so many American songs that what he really amounts to is just another talented Canadian who was subtly made over to become another American copycat. In other words, a clone.

The poor kid soon learns that Canadian people never request Canadian songs on Canadian radio because they don't know of any. And if they did, the radio stations wouldn't play them anyway. And this, of course, would be on the grounds that their listening audience prefers American music over Canadian, and they'll offer to prove it by citing the amount of requests they receive. (A paradox, or what?)

What an impossible situation we leave our young Canadian talent to face. We ask him to be proud of his country and give him no reason to be. When he writes or sings songs about Canada he's considered "hokey" and laughed at. When he sings songs like the Americans do, he's considered a copycat. And who wants to buy or hear songs that are sung by a copycat when the real thing can be obtained directly from the Americans themselves? That's why our talent goes nowhere. (Except maybe South.)

So by the time our 15-year-old turns 30, the lack of opportunity in this country has discouraged him so bad that he either quits the music business altogether or bites his Canadian lip and goes to the United States. And there, if his talent is any good at all, it will be used to sing more of those "great American songs" that those gullible Canadians are so anxious to buy, as they gather and say to each other: "I always knew he was good enough to be a 'Superstar,' but I wonder why he ever went to the States?"

The simple fact is: had he not gone to the States he would have been forced to join the ranks of so many other talented Canadians who grow old in factories or digging ditches; knowing in their hearts they were just as good as the Americans were, but for some "unknown reason" they didn't get the breaks. Someone told them there was "No Canadian Option." And someone led them to believe that if they didn't do it the American way their talent was no longer acceptable. Because, after all, "Canadians prefer to listen to American music rather than Canadian."

So this mysterious "unknown reason" is simply that everybody, to some degree, has become mentally conditioned to prefer and to buy American because it's so damn much "better than ours."

And now that this so called "unknown reason" is not so "unknown" any more, and if you
still think anything of your country at all, I
IMPLORE YOU, on behalf of all Canadian talent
everywhere, to CONTACT YOUR LOCAL RADIO
STATIONS AND INSIST THAT YOUR VERY OWN
"IDENTIFIABLY CANADIAN MUSIC" BE PLAYED
CONSISTENTLY. And that way we can finally put
a dent into this American monopoly on music
once and for all, and at the same time gain back
some of the pride we lost over the years by
believing that Canadians don't really have anything to sing about.

And one last question to radio would
be: WHAT BETTER COMMUNITY SERVICE THAN
THIS COULD YOUR RADIO STATION POSSIBLY
PROVIDE???

(Note: Because the above did not appear in any newspaper at the time, I included it in the liner notes of an album
I released eight years later, in 1987, entitled *Assist Canadian
Talent* (ACT), in which I appeared on the cover with six other
artists in order to help them gain recognition in the music
business. I hope to describe this later in a little more detail.)

Fate Had Another Plan

SOMETIME AROUND THE MIDDLE of November 1979, Russell had informed me that since Willard and Marlene had left Skinners Pond to live in their new place down in Nail Pond, the vandalism had gotten worse. With no one there now during the evenings and the nights, the hoodlums had become even braver.

They threw a whole bunch of trash and junk in the well and at night they were coming up while he and Cora were sleeping and throwing rocks at the house. On Hallowe'en night, somebody with a truck attached a long rope or more likely a chain to the new cedar-board fence all along the road in front of the property, and tore it all down. Even the cedar posts had all been ripped out.

As if that wasn't enough, a couple of nights later they had come with chainsaws and cut all the boards and posts in half so they could never be re-used or repaired. The noise had to be heard for half a mile, but not one neighbour came out to try and stop anything. And where were the police in all of this? Answering too many calls about similar complaints in other districts.

As Russell was too old now at seventy-five to be out and around through the night to deal with these hooligans, I told him I would be down as soon as I could, and in the meantime I called Willard to see what he could do. He said he'd try to keep a closer eye on the place from now on and

that he'd have a couple of the kids take turns staying at the
house with Russell and Cora at night.

For some reason, I can't seem to remember our trip driving down to P.E.I. this time, or the exact date, but I know it
was sometime around the first or second week of December.
The thing I seem to remember the most was getting there
and having a look around.

There's just no way of describing the look of what once
was an expensive, nicely painted cedar-board fence. Something like four hundred feet of it was lying in sawed-up
pieces all over the ground. Not one piece was usable. All had
to be hauled away and burned.

Two or three gates had also been smashed, and the windows in the school had all been broken again, and Willard
had them all boarded up with plywood.

I felt like crying. The place was in a shambles. About the
only thing that had no damage done to it was the land. And
if they had had a carry-all earth mover, I felt sure the land
would have been gone too.

It was all too much. "What the hell did I ever do to
deserve all this?" I asked myself. "Is this the price one has to
pay for trying to keep on the straight and narrow? And why
isn't there somebody, somewhere along this road with the
guts and the decency to come forward with the information
that would put these bastards away for a while? Or is everybody really that scared?"

There was obviously not going to be a scholarship given
away this year. The upcoming student would just have to
realize that the money would have to go to help make
repairs. And if I couldn't think of some way to stop all this
carnage, I would have to pull out altogether and forget the
whole damn thing.

When I thought about my early days in Skinners Pond
and why I had to run away from it all then, it was coming
back to haunt me now. Why was I trying to break my ass for
people who really didn't give a shit? They didn't then, they
don't now, and by the looks of it, they never will.

A couple of days before Christmas, Jury had occasion to
fly to Charlottetown on business, so he decided to rent a car
and drive up to Skinners Pond to spend Christmas with Lena

and Tommy and me, and Russell and Cora.

We opened presents together, had a nice dinner, exchanged visits with Willard and Marlene, and the vandalism was all but forgotten about. That is until the night after Boxing Day.

Jury had left early that afternoon because we heard there was a big storm coming on. And he got out just in time. By six o'clock that evening, there was already about two feet of snow down and no signs of it letting up. It finally stopped around 9, after dropping about three feet, and then the lights went out.

You don't worry so much about that on the farm, as there are always lots of oil and propane lamps around and the oil, wood and coal stove kept everybody warm. The only thing was, since hydro came in, the old hand pump was gone, and with no power, we had no water for tea. And though that didn't bother me so much, because I was drinking beer, I was elected to go outside and get a bunch of newly fallen snow to melt in a large pot to boil some water.

Around midnight, Russell and Cora had just gone up the stairs with one of the old lamps to prepare for bed, Tommy had already been sleeping now for a few hours, and Lena and I were just thinking about doing the same.

All of a sudden and from out of nowhere came the sound of four snowmobiles. They no sooner broke the silence of night when they went buzzing around the house throwing snowballs up against the windows. If you can remember how loud the first snowmobiles use to be, it might give you some idea what four of them might sound like right outside your window. It sounded like a war zone. They buzzed the house three times in succession and then took off. The whole episode took place in less than three minutes.

Three minutes was all it took me to get my heavy clothes and snow boots on and grab three or four bullets from a little drawer and load one of them in Russell's old single-shot rifle. I told everyone to stay inside.

Just as I got outside to the corner of the house, they were passing our barn and heading over the top of the dam which now provided a bridge across to one of my neighbour's fields. There they circled for three or four minutes, and just

when it looked as if all four of them were about ready to
return over the dam, they stopped to have a chat.

As I stood peeking around the corner of the house with
my gunsights directly pointing at the lead snowmobile,
I could hear them talking and laughing hilariously over the
light frosty breeze, though I couldn't make out exactly what
they were saying.

All I could think about was "You son-of-a-bitch. If you
make one attempt to come back onto my property and cross
over that dam you're gonna get one of the biggest surprises
you ever got in a long time." As a matter of fact, I just stood
there wishing he would. I could just imagine that bullet
clanging against the metal of the snowmobile or even hitting
him in the leg for that matter, and watching him go head
over heels in the snowbank as I reloaded for the next guy.

Too bad, though. Fate seemed to have another plan.
They started their motors and just as I was anticipating
pulling the trigger, they turned around and went back the
other way. Once again, they got away with doing just whatever in hell they wanted to.

When I went back in the house, everyone wanted to know
what had happened. And after I assured everybody that the
gang had left, the five of us all went to bed. Myself, I guess
I lay awake for another hour or two, just thinking about what
the hell could be done about all this. Well, I thought, at least
they hadn't broken any windows.

Next morning we were in the midst of another snowstorm and there was no possible way anybody could move. It
takes forever for the snow plough to come down the road,
and when they do, they leave a mountain of snow piled up
in front of your gate. And by the time you shovel it all out by
hand they come down the road and fill it all up again.

As the hydro had now been out for a couple of days, the
farmer on the other side of us came over and asked us if he
could draw some water from our pond for his cattle.

"No problem," I said, "providing you can find some way
to get over here with some kind of a rig to haul it with."

Later on that day they had rigged up some kind of a
make-shift snow plough on their tractor and made their
way across the field towing a wagon with a couple of large

barrels. And after they had made several trips and watered all their stock, I got talking to them for a few minutes.

I told them I would have to go back to Ontario soon, and it didn't look like I was ever going to get out on the road with all this snow. They told me there wasn't a great deal of it behind one of their barns and they might be able to make a path wide enough for a car to make it out onto the road. This would probably be sometime tomorrow, and if I was willing to try the risky venture, I was welcome.

I knew that first I would have to make it across the field to their place, then through their yard and between their barns out onto another field I knew to be quite marshy every time it thawed. And if I made it that far I could slip through a hole in the fence and out onto the road. But if I had to stop, even once, I could be there for the rest of the winter.

After thinking it over for a minute, I said, "Well, I've been over a lot of bad roads and pulled through before, so what the hell, I'll give 'er a try." The boys said they'd be over the following day to let me know as soon as the "super highway" was completed.

That night, while Lena was packing everything up, I explained to Russell what it was I was proposing to do. "Well, whatever you do," he said, "don't get stuck over there in Knox's field, because when the January 'silver thaw' comes, you'll sink right to the axles and you won't get your car out till next summer."

"I know," I said, "but if I don't try it I may be here till next summer anyway. And besides, I've got some business in Ontario that I'll have to fly up to first thing in the new year if I can't get my car out now." I really didn't want to leave them there with the possibility of being further hassled by those marauding punks but there was very little more I could do. When you can't be sure who they are or when they'll strike, you could stick around all winter and maybe nothing more would happen.

Even though Willard and Marlene were trying to do their best, and one of the kids would always try to be there for company, it was still little comfort to a couple of elderly senior citizens.

I had proposed off and on that they come to Ontario to

spend the winters with us, but until now they had declined. "Maybe next year," they would say. And that would be the end of it.

Anyway, the next day we got the word that the "super highway" was open. We packed the car, said goodbye and piled in for a very interesting ride.

The road was only as wide as the car with twists and turns every forty feet or so, and the snow was so high in most places you couldn't even see where you were going. All I kept thinking about was "No matter what, don't stop for chrissake. Because if I do, the snow is so high on both sides of the car we'll never get the doors open wide enough to get out."

Bump after bump, turn after turn, and skid after skid, we finally got to Knox's barnyard. Someone waved to us but I paid no attention and kept on driving. A quick turn into an alleyway between the two barns found me trying to skid my way out of an old manure pile and back onto the snow road which led across the swampy field to the main road. We almost stopped several times as I tried to manoeuvre a couple of hairpin turns, but as I felt the wheels going down I just gunned 'er and hoped for the best. Under the snow the ground wasn't frozen and at times it felt like we were driving over a sponge.

Not being able to see a damn thing, we finally hit a hell of a bump I presumed to be the ditch, and we bounced out onto the main road. It was a good thing that no one was coming, because we just appeared on the road from nowhere and he would have hit us for sure.

Once on the road, I pulled over and stopped so we could straighten everything out, including ourselves. And after standing up on the snow bank to wave goodbye and thank you, we proceeded down the road.

All in all, it had been one of the most precarious drives that I had ever taken. We must have brushed the sides of the snowbanks at least a dozen times, but the snow was damp and soft and just gave way to the impact, so the car came through without any scratches. Lena complained for a little while about the smell of cowshit, but after a short run through a car wash in Summerside she started smiling again.

It was after dark on New Year's Eve when we got off the ferry in New Brunswick, so we decided to get a motel room for the night. Our friends, Keith and Barb Wall lived up the road a couple of miles from the motel so we decided to pay them a surprise visit.

As we left the motel the lights went out in that part of New Brunswick, and when we got to the Walls' they were in the dark.

It was now around eight o'clock or so and a couple of their friends had arrived to see them, including Barbara's brother Delbert. But after the lights went out, it seems a few of the other guests they were expecting decided to stay home.

We nevertheless had a great time. Delbert was always the kind who could keep everybody in stitches with his jokes and stories, and while the candles burned, Keith and I played our guitars and sang the New Year in till about two in the morning. We then woke Tommy up and headed back to the motel.

The next day, it wasn't hard to understand why the lights had gone out. We hadn't driven twenty miles up the road when we ran into another snowstorm that had dumped a couple of feet of snow down on top of what they had had before.

The roads were quite bad while you could see them, but as soon as it got dark around 4:30 or so, there were cars and trucks going in the ditch everywhere.

I remember thinking, "Why does it always have to happen that, just when you want to pull in to a motel, there's not a damn one in sight for miles?" And there wasn't. We had to drive through this highway junkyard for more than an hour before we finally found a place to stay.

The following day we managed to make it to Woodstock, New Brunswick, and as if we really needed it, we ran into another big snowstorm. It seemed like there was no end to the stuff.

Although the roads were becoming really hazardous again, I kept driving for another fifteen miles or so to Hartland, New Brunswick, because we also had some friends there.

First we got ourselves a motel room again and then went to visit Harry and Alva Acheson. Harry is the guy I mentioned before who played the fiddle and had a whole farm full of kids. But great kids they were. The girls were always helping their mother do everything around the house, from cooking to sewing, and the boys were always busy doing the chores out around the barn. They were all very polite and couldn't seem to do enough for you. And the thing they seemed to like the most was music.

One of Harry's boys also played the guitar, and once Harry and I struck 'er up on the fiddle and guitar, the young fella joined right in there. This was always a great place to go and visit, 'cause we always had lots of fun and jokes. And of course me and Harry could always drink lots of beer. Now, that was important.

So after singing a bunch of songs and talking about the time he pulled me out of the snowbank, and a few other stories that kept getting more exaggerated each time they were told, it was time to say goodbye again. And the next day, Lena and I and Tommy were back on the road.

Once we hit Rivière-du-Loup, Quebec, there wasn't as much snow and the highway was clear, so in a couple more days we were home. A little exhausted, you might say, from all the hectic driving, but still healthy and all in one piece.

The Fox Is in the Hen House

In January of 1980, the big concern at the office was how Boot Records, Morning Music and Pose Distributing were all going to become computerized. The rest of the industry seemed to be getting into computers and, naturally, we didn't want to be lagging behind.

Although I was considered to be the "farmer" when it came to business decisions, when it came to the expenditure of any large amounts of money my approval always had to be sought. It wasn't my habit to run interference with the day-to-day operations of any of the companies, but when it came to the overall direction as to where these companies were going, I had to know about it and be there.

Hardly anybody knew anything about computers at that time, especially us. And mostly me. So after consulting an "expert" who was going to set us up with computers and the appropriate programs to run them, I gave my consent, and within about six months we had solidly entered the computer age.

There were a lot of glitches in the beginning, but once Mark and Jury got them ironed out, the computer became a lot more efficient than the old way of looking up files, crunching numbers, sending out statements and making out invoices.

I even got into the action by purchasing a computer from Radio Shack, along with a whole bunch of books on how to become a programmer. But by the time I spent most of the winter just to get a stick man to move his arms, and then found out I would have to buy another book to get his legs to move, I scrapped the whole idea of becoming a nerd or a geek and got back into some serious beer drinking.

Another thing that occurred around this time was that a representative of an organization called the Academy of Country Music Entertainers (ACME), which had formed a couple of years previous, had been after Jury to try to get him and our record company to sign up as members. (For those who may not know, ACME was the organization out of which the Canadian Country Music Association later developed.)

The guy making contact with Jury was a fellow by the name of Bob Cousins. And I guess he was somewhat surprised to find out that Jury would have to have my approval before signing our company up as a member. After all, in most circles, it was still thought that I was merely an artist recording for the label.

With a little persistence, Bob was soon able to persuade Jury to bring him out to the house. Then, after a pretty good sales pitch for ACME and all the benefits it could promise to its members, he again asked if we would join.

"Well, I don't know," I said. "Before signing up for anything I would first like to see the organization's letters patent, along with its constitution and by-laws. If you can obtain those for me to read over, I'll give the whole matter some serious consideration."

"I'll get them to Jury in a couple of days," he said, "and he can get them to you by the first of next week."

I told him that would be fine, and we set up a meeting for the following Sunday. "By then I will have read the papers and be prepared to give you my final answer."

I received the papers along about Monday or Tuesday, and by Thursday I got around to reading them. On Friday, I knew my answer would be an emphatic "No." This was definitely not an organization I would want to belong to.

Almost half of all the recording artists our company had at the time were country singers, writers and musicians, and if we were going to belong to any organization, I had to be certain that the interests of these artists would be first and foremost. And nothing I read in the letters patent or the constitution and by-laws of the Academy of Country Music Entertainers led me to believe that this organization was anything more than a scheme to control Canadian country entertainers to further the interests of radio.

If not, why would an organization calling itself ACME, which claims its goal is to help and promote the Canadian country entertainer, be started out by program directors and other people from radio?

And why were at least five, if not six, of its eight-member board of directors all people who held positions at radio stations?

And where a two-thirds majority vote was required to pass any motion or proposal by this board, how was anyone to believe that this organization was set up for anything else but the interests of radio? They already had over two-thirds of a majority presently sitting on the board. And to top things off, there wasn't one full-time entertainer even remotely connected to the planning and the operation of this organization.

So when our meeting on Sunday came and Mr. Cousins couldn't refute even one of these allegations, the reader shouldn't wonder why Jury and I, and the company of Boot Records, from that time on, would never have anything to do with ACME.

Why should I be against people from radio running an organization claiming to exist for the purpose of promoting and furthering the careers and the interests of Canadian entertainers? After all, isn't it the program and music directors of radio stations that entertainers look to in order to have their recorded music played and made known to the public?

Why, of course it is. But when these same people from radio have consistently lobbied the government and the Canadian Radio-television and Telecommunications Commission to do away with, or at least reduce, the 30 per cent Canadian musical content regulations because, in their own words, "there's not enough Canadian talent to justify keeping it," how can any entertainer in his right mind believe there is even one ounce of sincerity in anything radio people might say?

After all, isn't it a special part of their training to say that every product they advertise is "magnificently excellent," even though, in most cases, they wouldn't dare be caught using it themselves? Sometimes they know absolutely nothing of the product about which they speak. But they're always willing to say almost anything to please the people who pay them for saying it.

It is therefore not hard to see how some of these people could be used to convince others that something is good for them, when in fact it is not. It kind of reminds you of how politicians work, doesn't it?

We all seem to be looking for people we can count on. People who are sincere. And people who, when they tell us they know something is good for us, it is good for us. And it's not just some damn lie they told us because someone else paid them to do so.

Now, because it was well known, even back then, that Canadian radio was trying its level best to get out of its responsibility to the Canadian people (the government), and the recording artists, on whose behalf the 30 per cent content regulations were put in place, this prompted one big question. How could an organization (ACME or any other) whose board of directors had even one member from radio, never mind six, which was openly committed to the abolishment of the only guarantee the Canadian artist ever had that he might get played on radio, ever be trusted to sincerely and adequately represent the interests of the Canadian entertainer?

I remember thinking that, if this is allowed to continue, it will be the worse case of fraud ever perpetrated since the fox convinced the farmer to let him look after the hen house.

People who work for radio have only one allegiance. And that is to the radio station that pays them and provides them with a livelihood. If even one of these people is sitting on a board of an organization whose determination is to get his radio station to do something it doesn't want to do, namely, play more Canadian, there's no damn way they're going to get his vote.

And to the extent that any organization claims to represent the interests of Canadian talent, they should not, under
any circumstances, allow people from radio, or anyone else
opposed to more on-air exposure, to even get their nose
inside the door, let alone sit on the board.

Canadian entertainers should have their own organization to help them fight for the goals they wish to achieve.
And this organization should be run by themselves, for
themselves. And only in this way can they ever expect to
accomplish anything for which they can really be proud.

Maybe then they'll be able to afford to spend more
money on magazine ads promoting their own causes.
Instead of the millions they spend every year thanking DJs
who either don't read the magazines or couldn't influence
the amount of airplay an artist will get even if they did.
That's because DJs have had absolutely no say in what songs
they play for a great many years. They collect their pay for
what they're told to play. And the same thing goes for what
they say. And if they want to keep their jobs, they'll keep on
saying it.

(And like I said before: the Canadian Country Music
Association was born out of ACME with its board of directors
composed of a great many people from radio. And what are
they doing to promote our Canadian country music artists
here at home? They're not only encouraging them to go to
the States, but they're using the funds of the Canadian mem-
bership to take them there. Instead of using them to get our
own radio stations to promote them right here. Stay tuned.
There's more wonderful American music to come.)

Driving "On Top of the World"

B Y March of 1980, when I saw there were no changes of consequence in the selection of Juno Award nominees, I began to feel there never would be. So I said to Lena, "When the warm weather comes, I'm going to buy a nice big van, and you and I and Tommy are going to take a real long trip to the Yukon, the Beaufort Sea, Alaska and the western islands of British Columbia. And maybe then I can get my mind off business problems, Skinners Pond hoodlums, radio stations and everybody else who is too blind to see what a great country we could have if they'd only stop taking advantage of the other people they believe to be more stupid than they are."

So, sometime around the first of June, I managed to look over a whole bunch of vans, and finally settled on buying a Dodge Ram, which was called a stretch van at the time. Two weeks later, just after Tommy's fourth birthday, we packed up for the two-month drive to see Canada's great wilderness.

(Even while writing this, I take pause to wonder why anyone in this vast country of ours could have so narrow a concept of themselves and who they really are, that they would even take the time to contemplate a visit to another country without first getting to see and know their own. What is wrong with our government? Why haven't they seen fit to make sure that every child who was ever born on Canadian soil could and would be the first ones to know that they have been blessed by Almighty God with the Crown Jewel that sits on the top of this planet as an eternal beacon, forever flashing its hope throughout a world that has extinguished its own light by not teaching its children to acknowledge and enjoy the light they have while it's still shining?)

On Friday, June 20, 1980, we packed our new van and struck out for the Yukon. First to Sudbury, across to Sault Ste. Marie, past Thunder Bay, and on to the Manitoba border. We drove across the prairies, passing Winnipeg, Saskatoon and Edmonton. After picking up the Alcan Highway (Alaska Highway) in Dawson Creek, B.C., we started the great northern climb.

Passing Fort St. John, and spending the night in Fort Nelson, on June 30, the next day, on Canada Day, we arrived at Watson Lake, Yukon, late in the evening. This is hardly any more than a half-dozen miles over the 60th parallel. (By the way, Steamboat Mountain is quite an experience to drive over. I have a song called the "Alcan Run" on my *To It and At It* album which describes this mountain and other parts of this famous highway that one may encounter while driving to the Yukon and through to Alaska.)

From now on we started to take our time because we were already where we wanted to go. There were three seats in our van and the back two folded in such a way that you could either make a bed out of them or a table that you could sit up to for a meal. Behind the three seats there was also plenty of room for Tommy to sleep. And no matter where we found ourselves, we could just pull over on the side of the road anytime and have something to eat or go to sleep. We also brought our own folding picnic table and three folding chairs so that we could sit or eat outside anytime we wanted to. With a propane stove and lots of vittles, I figured we were prepared for anything. I even brought two spare tires instead of one because I knew we would sometimes have to drive for hundreds of miles before coming to a gas station, never mind a town. And that's why two five-gallon cans of gas always came in handy now and then.

One thing I didn't count on, though, was bringing extra headlights or a screen-guard to protect the ones I had. I went through seven of them before the trip was finally over.

I also had to replace my windshield when I got back. All this is because of the many stones that fly when somebody passes you on the gravelled roads. At that time all the roads were gravelled, even the Alcan Highway.

We spent the night in White Horse on July 2 or 3, and a couple of days later we were in Dawson City.

Now, this is the land of "The Klondike." This is "The Land of Gold." This is the land of Robert Service and all the beautifully mysterious stories he told about the great Gold Rush. The cremation of Sam McGee and the shooting of Dangerous Dan McGrew.

This is where the history of Canada in the late nineteenth century comes alive. This is the great Dawson City, where men from all over the world came to seek their fortune by staking their claims, grovelling in the dirt and panning those glittering flakes that flowed down from the mountains and into the Klondike and other beautiful rivers of that ever so mysterious land called The Yukon.

It was here in Dawson City that we stayed for several days. We walked up and down the wooden sidewalks and crossed the old clay streets where many a man fell and bit the dust because someone else was faster on the draw, and the Mounties didn't get there fast enough to prevent the shoot-out.

It was here in Dawson City, "On Top of the World," where not a hell of a lot had changed in almost a hundred years. The old saloons were still there, and so were the old codgers with gold nuggets sewn into the bands of their old wide-brimmed weather-beaten hats. Here, too, you could still see the prospectors, the sourdoughs and all the characters of western-movie fame come alive before your eyes, and all intermingled with the odd first nation Indian and Inuit. In this place the world of Halifax, Toronto and Vancouver held about the same far-off significance to the average joe as London or Paris would to the guy living in downtown Regina.

This was the world of the can-can girls at old Diamond Tooth Gerty's gambling saloon, where the blackjack tables and one-arm bandits had been in operation ever since the first pouch of gold dust was traded for a bottle of good strong hooch and the luring smile of a dance-hall dandy.

This was 1980, but they were all still there. And Lena and

I went to see every one of them, while a very gracious lady, only several doors away at the hotel where we were staying, kept an eye and an ear on Tommy as he slept.

In the daylight hours, while Lena went shopping in and out of every one of the little old quaint-looking shops, I would take Tommy out to some open lot where we could get the baseball, bat and gloves out to have a game of catch. And often we'd be joined by a couple of other little kids who happened to be wandering by. At other times we just threw the frisbee or went playing around on the swings.

For such a small town we sure found lots of interesting things to do. One day Lena and I and Tommy went into a little shop where a photographer would take your picture after you dressed up in some costume typical of the old gold rush days. And after Lena went into a little change room and came back out to have her picture taken as a dance-hall dandy, Tommy tugged on my arm and said, "Let's go, Dad. Mom's gone out the back door." He didn't recognize Lena at all, and in no way did he want anything to do with her. We still look at the picture today, think of Tommy's reaction, and have a few laughs.

After visiting a number of historic sites and old grave-yards, we went to see the old riverboat that used to sail up and down the Yukon River. And the day before we left, we paid a visit to the house where Pierre Berton was born, and just across the street we went through the old cabin where Robert Service wrote all his poems. We even sat on the lawn for an hour that afternoon and listened to a gentleman by the name of Burns recite some of Service's well-known poems from the deck of the cabin where Robert himself sat to write them. This was really a touching experience.

There was a lot more about Dawson City that I would like to tell. But I must move on to the next day when we tackled the road that would take us some five or six hundred miles still farther north from where we were. This was the Dempster Highway to Inuvik and up to the inland water reaches of the Beaufort Sea, some three hundred miles north of the Arctic Circle. (If anybody says they've driven all the highways of Canada, ask them what they thought about the "Dempster," because you can walk faster over this highway than you can drive it.)

About 150 miles north of Dawson City, we came to a little place called Ogilvie, with a population of about fifty. This was the end of what I would call any kind of a decent road. Here we gassed up in preparation for the long trip into the "Unknown."

Travelling past the Ogilvie Mountain Range, our top speed might have been around fifty mph and the slowest around fifteen. We then levelled off into an area they call the Eagle Plains. This took us right to the Arctic Circle, which is about 250 miles north of Dawson City.

Here we came to a little campsite with nobody in it but us, and we decided to spend the night. Oops! Did I say night? This was the "Land of the Midnight Sun" and they really mean it.

This was around ten or eleven o'clock P.M., and the sun was still high in the sky.

Poor Tommy was always asking, "Why do I have to go to bed now, Dad? The sun's still up."

"Well, where we are now, Tommy, at this time of year, the sun never goes down. It just stays up all the time, and the only time it ever gets dark is when you close your eyes."

"Well, can't you make it go down for just a little while, till I go to sleep?" he asked.

"No, I'm afraid not, Tommy," I told him, "because what God puts up, nobody can take it down. Now close your eyes and try to get some sleep."

I don't know whether he believed me or not, but pretty soon he was in another world.

The sun would actually dip below the horizon for an hour around 3 A.M. But by 4 A.M. it was on the rise again for another twenty-three hours. We were told that had we been in the Arctic about two weeks sooner, the sun would not have set at all for the whole twenty-four hours. (People living in more southern latitudes who are used to seeing the sun always shining in the east, south and western skies will never cease to be amazed to see the sun shining directly over the north pole.)

It seems kind of stupid to say we awakened the following morning, when in reality it was still the same day. It just never gets dark at any time so you never experience what we know to be night. But anyway, according to my watch, we awoke the following morning around nine o'clock.

During breakfast outside we had to put up with the usual guests, who always came around especially at meal time. These were the different variety of birds who would just sit on the side of your plate and chirp at you for being so mean if you didn't pass them something. You would think they were household pets because of the way they showed absolutely no fear of humans.

It was also a common occurrence to have a squirrel or some other little varmint crawl up the outside of your pant leg and hop on the picnic table and demand to be fed. After all, this was "share and share alike" country, wasn't it?

Even the larger animals, with whom we were totally unfamiliar, but had the appearance of caribou, elk and sometimes goats, would just wander up to us. Then one or two from out of the herd would walk up close enough to smell you. Then they'd give you a look and some kind of a mild bleat that seemed to indicate to the rest of the herd that while these strange-acting visitors looked rather odd and comical, they were really quite harmless, so we might as well just ignore them and maybe they'll go away by themselves after a while.

Then the odd fox would happen by. And if you were parked somewhere between him and the straight line to his next meal, he wouldn't even bother to skirt around you. He would just follow his nose, without giving you the slightest glance, and keep right on going about his much more important business of the day.

This was a veritable Eden. With beautiful mountains sitting on the distant horizon and the peace and quietness of it all, it made you feel as if you had just stepped into a postcard. You had to purposely shake yourself and think of the southern rat race for a second just to realize that you were still on the planet.

You could even bend down and drink the water running in the ditches along the road. And we often did. And although I always had my ample supply of beer, I have to admit that even the roadside water up here tasted better.

And coming from Stompin' Tom, that's saying something.

It's not a damn bit of wonder why the people of the north are so concerned about the pollution brought in by multinational corporations from the south. While the jobs may be helping the northern economy, the pollution has to be watched like a cat watches a mouse, because this is one of the last places in the world where man can meet nature one on one and be no more than just one of God's creatures. (A rather simplistic view, I suppose, to those who bow down to the "god of money." But it shouldn't be too much to ask that just a little untouched piece of this planet be preserved for those of us who still think that the gift of life in a natural and healthy environment is the only reward we need for having passed by this way.)

A couple of miles up the road we came to the last sign we would see for a long while. It read: ARCTIC CIRCLE CROSSING. Mile 253.7 of the Dempster Highway. Construction reached this far on August the 6th of 1977. It was funded by the Department of Indian and Northern Affairs and engineered by the Canadian Department of Public Works. The Contractors were made up from General Enterprises. (I later learned that the completion of this highway had been the lifelong dream of one of our illustrious prime ministers, the Honourable John Diefenbaker. He not only wanted Canada to have the first road in the world that would reach into the far northern regions of the Arctic, but he wanted it to be freely accessible to all of the people. And to my knowledge, though other countries now have private government and company roads, there is still not one accessible to the public, other than our own Dempster Highway. (I do hope, though, that it has been improved since I drove on it in July of 1980. I also believe it had only been totally completed in 1979, the year before Lena and I and Tommy arrived.)

After taking some pictures beside this very unique sign we hit the road across what could only be called "The Top of the World."

During the next 150 miles we first crossed over into the Northwest Territories, then we passed Fort McPherson, and after changing a flat tire we stopped in a little place called Arctic Red River to have the flat repaired.

Arctic Red River was a little town of about two hundred people, situated on the west bank of the great Mackenzie River just before the Mackenzie widens out to form its 150 miles of delta.

By now we were about 450 miles north of Dawson City and still heading north. But the road now had become not much more than a wagon trail, where your top speed might have been twenty mph, but most of the time you were only doing five mph. Sometimes your speedometer wasn't registering at all.

The road bed in most places was covered with some kind of shale rock that was very sharp on the edges and if you didn't take it real easy you could cut your tires to pieces in no time. There were also lots of holes, dips and dives everywhere, and all we seemed to do was jostle up and down and back and forth for the next seventy-five miles to Inuvik.

I was game for travelling the last hundred miles to Tuktoyaktuk, but I was told that the road was closed farther up the line to all traffic that didn't have four-wheel drive. So I just drove a piece and turned around and came back.

We got a hotel room in Inuvik, I think it was called the Finto, and decided to rest up for a couple of days. Again it seemed funny watching the national television news on the CBC at 11 P.M. with the bright sun shining through the window as if it were still the middle of the afternoon.

We walked around town and took in some of the various sights. One building that stuck out as being very unique was a real massive igloo. We didn't go in to see but I think it was the City Hall. The population would be about 2,500.

They had a small radio station there, so I popped in and gave them a couple of albums. They said it was very hard to get albums away up there and promised to play them regularly. I don't know if they ever did, but then we weren't in the area all that long.

Once when Lena and Tommy were browsing around, I decided to take a little hike over to the East Channel of the Mackenzie Delta whose waters intermingle with those of the Beaufort Sea, and dip my feet into it. As the Beaufort Sea is really a part of the Arctic Ocean, I just wanted to be able to say I had dipped my feet into three oceans of the world, the other two being the Atlantic and the Pacific.

Over the course of the next three days we drove the five hundred miles back again to Dawson City. On the way back we had two more flat tires all in the course of a couple of hours. And although I still had one spare left, which I was in the process of putting on, a fellow in a pick-up came by and asked me if I needed any help.

When I told him everything was all right except for wanting to get my two flat spares repaired, he said if I wanted to wait for about an hour or so, he could take them into some camp he was going to and fix them for me.

He was back in about an hour and a half with the tires looking just like new and when I offered to pay him he wouldn't take anything. I offered him a case of my beer, which he accepted without question, and throwing it on the seat of his truck, he headed back to his camp.

Once more in Dawson City, we spent another night at the Eldorado Hotel and the next day we headed west to a place called Sixty Mile.

It was here I turned off the main road and headed down a long trail that had been made a couple of years previously by my friend Stan Stempien, from Sudbury, who, along with a few buddies, now had a fair-sized goldpanning operation going. The trail we were now on would take us through the woods and over the mountains for about twenty miles into Stan's claim.

Stan played the accordion and had several albums on the Boot label under the name Stan Lorel but decided to give up the music business to go north and be a sourdough. And the previous year, while in Toronto for a visit, he had dropped into my place and told me that if I was ever in the Yukon to drop in and see him. He had given me some directions, and even though I didn't have them with me, I figured my memory was good enough to take me there. He had no idea at this time that I was anywhere near the Yukon, but here we were driving over this very precipitous trail on our way to his claim to surprise him.

I guess we'd been driving for about ten or twelve miles and we were coming down the side of this mountain when we spotted a pick-up truck ahead of us and coming our way.

The minute they spotted us, they slammed on the brakes and the two occupants jumped out with their handguns drawn and darted behind two big rocks for cover.

Not knowing what the hell was going on, I stopped the van and got out. "Hello there," I said. "Does anyone around here know Stan Stempien? He's a friend of mine and I've come all the way from Toronto to see him. I'm the guy they call Stompin' Tom."

One guy came out from behind the rock, and shoving his gun back into its holster, he shouted, "Tom! For the love o' pete, is that you? What the hell are you doing away up here?" It was Stan himself. After telling the other guy it was all right, they turned their truck around and led us back to their campsite.

As soon as we arrived and Stan introduced us to half a dozen or so of the boys, I asked him, "What's with all the guns?"

He explained they all had guns because armed bandits would quite often swoop in on your claim and take your gold. They were only ten miles from the Alaskan border and the thieves would often fly in with American helicopters, land, shoot the place up, and take all your gold back with them. And they didn't give a damn if they had to kill you for it either. With gold being over $800 an ounce, there had been more than a few left lying around dead in the last year or so. This gold mining was a serious business.

Heavily locked inside a tractor trailer they had two wash-tubs full of the stuff. It was usually Stan's job to sit inside the locked trailer with water tubs and gold pans and containers full of the gold-rich dirt which was brought to him every once in a while by the others. He would have the tedious task of sitting there all day shaking a pan and separating the gold from the rest of the dirt.

This heavily laden dirt was taken from the sieves at the bottom of a large sluice trough leaning against a very large dam they had built with two or three DC-9 bulldozers.

Behind the dam was a huge deep pond of water which had accumulated over the last couple of years due to the prevention of the flow of a small stream. While the dozers now tore the soil away from the huge banks of the canyon, a large machine with a big bucket would pick it up and drive it across the rim of the dam and dump it into the sluice so that the overflowing water could wash it down into the sieves. This took all the boulders, branches and gravel out of the dirt, leaving nothing but a bit of sandy soil at the very bottom. It was this sandy soil which contained all the gold that had to be separated by Stan.

They had three or four industrial-size ATCO trailers where everybody slept and ate and did their laundry. This was quite the operation, with practically all the conveniences of home. They had their own electricity and all the appliances to go along with it. There was a deep freeze that was well stocked and shelf upon shelf of every kind of canned goods imaginable. Everybody had his own quarters, and according to Stan, everybody was making good money and all the guys were great to work with.

A couple of Stan's partners were away on business at the time of our arrival so they had no problem putting us up. We could have stayed in our van, but they wouldn't hear of it.

We played some music and sang some songs that night (or day), and the next afternoon (or evening), Stan took us up the little river and taught us to pan for gold the old-fashioned way. You take your little hand-pick and dig a little soil out of the river bank, and put it in your pan. You then take this down to the river and fill your pan about half full of water and start shaking it.

Since gold is heavier than any of the other dirt, as you shake your pan, you try to let some of the soil and water out of it with each swish. And when all the water and soil are gone the only thing left in your pan is the gold. It sounds easy but there's quite a knack to it. It took me quite a few tries before I was able to retrieve even a couple of flakes of gold. Lena was able to catch on to it long before I was.

Tommy, of course, was more fascinated with the big machines, and one of the guys was even good enough to give him a ride on one. He also enjoyed watching that big bucket dropping all that soil from the top of the dam into the water going over the sluice. He seemed to be hypnotized by it all.

Due to the short summers in the Yukon, Stan and the boys could only work their claim for about three months. And during the rest of the year Stan was either on vacation down in Costa Rica (one of his favourite haunts), or making gold jewellery, some of which was rather exquisite.

Before we left he gave Lena a beautiful necklace and a matching set of earrings. Both the earrings and the locket on the necklace had a glass front and back to them which could be opened and closed. And within each earring and the locket he placed a few dozen flakes of gold that you could see moving back and forth through the glass as they were being worn. It was a wonderful gift that Lena would always treasure. And she still quite often wears it with pride. It's truly one of a kind.

After leaving Stan's claim, we continued to travel west, and in a short time we crossed the border into Alaska.

During the next four or five days, we drove through a lot of Alaskan towns including the cities of Fairbanks and Anchorage. As a matter of fact, we still have several motel-room keys that we forgot to turn in from this trip, one of them being the key to room 108 of the Mush Inn in Anchorage, Alaska. And a couple more from the Yukon. Namely, Inuvik and Dawson City.

After driving some 1,200 miles through Alaska and doubling back, we finally came to the Yukon border once more, only in a different spot from where we entered. The first town we hit was called Beaver Creek, which has the distinction of being the most westerly town in Canada. Here we stopped to eat and gas up and then drove another couple hundred miles to the Kluane National Park before eating again and bunking down in the van for the night.

Next day, instead of continuing on the Alcan Highway to Whitehorse, we took what is known as the Haines Cutoff and crossed the 60th parallel into the extreme northwest corner of British Columbia, near a place called Million Dollar Falls. And after another fifty miles we were back into Alaska. This was the lower part of Alaska known as the Panhandle, in the vicinity of Skagway. We now drove down to Haines and Port Chilkoot where we boarded a ferry to Juneau, the capital of Alaska.

Juneau was just a stop where all passengers had to be checked by customs officers, and then we proceeded on down through the many channels of lower Alaska until we finally crossed into Canadian waters near Dundas Island, north of Prince Rupert, in British Columbia.

We then sailed down the western channels of B.C. until we landed on the northern end of Vancouver Island and drove from one end to the other. After spending a couple of days in the beautiful city of Victoria, we took the ferry to Vancouver, where we went to see Reg and Muriel Chapman's daughter Linda. And from there we began the long drive back home.

We drove back through our gate on the tenth of September of 1980. We had been gone for two and a half months and travelled over 11,000 miles. We had a total of four flat tires and went through six or seven headlights. We had to replace the windshield and buy some more new tires. But other than that we were all in good health and all the better for the experience.

Although the following song was written some fourteen years after we made this trip, on a night when I was telling Gaet Lepine about it, I thought that its inclusion here might nevertheless be appropriate.

LONG GONE TO THE YUKON

CHORUS:
I'm Long Gone to the Yukon. Those Northern Lights
*   I want to see.*
I'm Long, Long Gone to the Yukon, boys,
'Cause the Yukon is callin' for me. Yeah, the Yukon
*   is callin' for me.*

1.
Well, brother, I just got your note this morning
And you tell me that you've found a little gold;
And before another day is dawnin'
On that long northern train I'm gonna roll.

2.
I can see a little cabin by the mountains,
And I'll soon be there to share the gold with you;
'Cause I want to live a life like Robert Service,

Old Sam McGee and Dangerous Dan McGrew.
  (To chorus)

3.

Where the wind along the river will be music,
And the midnight sun is always ridin' low;
I'll paddle my canoe along the Klondike,
And I'll pan the gold and be a sourdough.

4.

And when I pull into Dawson City Yukon,
I'll be headin' for old Diamond Gert's saloon;
I'll gamble to a honky-tonk piano,
And I'll chase the dancin' girls around the room.
  (To chorus)

5.

Well, they say that once you've heard those mystic
    voices,
From the silence of the North you can't return.
Now, I hear that lonesome timber wolf a-callin'
By the fire where I watch the bannock burn.

6.

And it won't be long before I'm pickin' nuggets.
My brother says they're lying everywhere.
And my boss is gonna want to be my butler,
'Cause when I get back I'll be a millionaire.
  (To chorus)

The Connors Tone Rejected

NOTHING MUCH HAPPENED FOR the next couple of weeks except I went out and bought a 200 cc dirt bike for driving around the property. And then one day Lena got a call from her niece in the Magdalene Islands saying that Pauline was over from Prince Edward Island to visit her and her husband, Achilles. And because Pauline would be spending her birthday at Donna and Achilles's place on the twenty-ninth of September, Donna wanted to know if there was any way Lena could fly down and give her a big surprise.

After thinking about it for a couple of days, Lena decided to go. She called Donna and told her to find some excuse to get Pauline out of the house on the afternoon of her birthday so that Achilles could pick Lena up at the airport and drive her to the house before Pauline got back.

Everything worked out like clockwork. Donna got a mutual friend of theirs, Jacques Chevarie, the captain of the *Lucy Maude Montgomery* car ferry, and his wife, Carmen, to invite Pauline over for supper. And by the time they all arrived back, Lena was at Donna's tucked away in a large box all done up with ribbons. There was of course a concealed airhole in the box so she wouldn't suffocate.

When Pauline came to the box, she thought she was getting a dishwasher or some other kind of an appliance for a birthday present. And when she opened the box, out popped Lena. "Surprise! Surprise!" I guess poor Pauline almost had heart failure. All she kept saying was "Oh my God! Oh my God! It's my sister, it's really my sister."

After all the other presents were opened, they got the guitars out and had a sing-song. (Most of Lena's relatives are all quite good singers.)

As this was a rather unusual way of making an appearance at a birthday party, I felt the small mention of it here was quite merited. Your sister doesn't always show up from hundreds of miles away completely gift wrapped.

While Lena was away for a few days, Tommy and I went for some motorcycle drives up and down the roads. I had bought him a little helmet and sat him up in front of me to give him the feeling that he was doing the driving, and as far as he was concerned he was. One day he even asked me if I wanted him to take me for another motorcycle drive. When I told him I didn't think so, not today, he looked at me rather sadly and said, "Okay, then. But if you're good, can I take you tomorrow?"

After Lena got back, it wasn't more than a couple of weeks before we finally convinced Russell and Cora that they should close down the old house in Skinners Pond for the winter and come up to Ontario and stay with us.

Down home, Willard and Marlene weren't coming around now near as often as before, due to the concentration of getting their own place in Nail Pond fixed up, buying a few cattle and working more at the blueberries. The kids came down to go swimming in the pond or at the shore and pay a visit once in a while, but the Double "C" project itself had pretty much come to a standstill. For all intents and purposes, the hoodlums had driven us out.

Russell and Cora seemed to enjoy their stay. We often had friends from down home who would pay us a visit periodically and we played a lot of cards. The local community centre was putting on jamborees and amateur contests at the time and Russell and Cora always enjoyed those.

Russell also had a great recipe for making beer. And needless to say, we not only had a batch for Christmas, but several others before the winter was out.

Reg and Muriel Chapman had also come up from New Brunswick and while they were visiting their kids they also came out to have New Year's dinner with us. That evening we all sat around telling jokes and playing some cards. This was pretty much the fare for the rest of that winter.

But although it might have been quiet in Ontario, it certainly wasn't that way in Skinners Pond.

Willard and Marlene had chosen not to tell us the bad news because they didn't want to upset Russell and Cora, but the old house had been broken into and a considerable amount of damage had been done. It was only after they got home in the spring that they had to face the grim reality.

A lot of things had been either smashed or stolen and to make matters worse, the hoodlums had cut the pipes to the oil tank outside the house and allowed the oil to spill out all over the ground. This of course cut off all fuel supply to the furnace, allowing all the waterworks in the house to freeze up and bust all the pipes.

The same thing was done to the oil tank for the school, leaving another mess over there. And this is what Russell had to face when he got back home. Needless to say, they never came to Ontario again.

It cost a bloody fortune to tear walls apart and replace water pipes and bathroom fixtures, not to mention all the rest. Some things they had had all their lives which had no value to anyone but meant the world to them had to be thrown out, never to be replaced.

I can't imagine what sort of a person could stoop so low as to even think of doing this kind of thing, never mind actually going through with it.

It was sometime towards the latter part of May 1981 when Russell and Cora went home to face all this mess. And I didn't actually find out about it until I went down home in July.

Still in the month of June, Lena's two sisters, Pauline and Amy, and her niece, Donna, came up from down east by train and stayed with us for a couple of weeks. And just after they left, I bought my first trailer. It was a nineteen-foot Prowler. And this is what we took down east with us in July.

Upon arriving in Skinners Pond and finding out what had happened the previous winter, I just threw my hands up.

After asking Willard if there was nothing at all that could

have been done to prevent all this, besides having a friendly little chat with these nice boys, I again went down to see the Mounties, and came back with even less satisfaction. All anyone seemed to have were excuses. But there wasn't a damn thing anyone could do.

I went back to Willard and told him, "I'm packing the whole damn thing in. If there's anything you want out of this, such as the backhoe and front end loader, you can buy my shares of it. And as far as the school is concerned, you can get a four-by-eight-foot sheet of plywood and paint a very large sign on it, asking, IS THIS THE WAY YOU WANT THIS PLACE TO LOOK? And mount it away up on the roof of the school where everybody can see it. And you can leave all the rest to just sit there and rot." (The sign was never put up.)

Given the value of the dollar in the 1970s, I had spent well over $150,000 (the value in today's money is anybody's guess). And all this was to help the local economy and improve the district. The real truth of the matter was, it didn't look one bit better now than it did the day I started. And not one person anywhere had even come forward with a scrap of evidence that might help to stop this ridiculously wanton destruction and the waste of so many good intentions.

For years after, I would receive dozens of letters from people who would travel by the place, and having no idea what went on there, would ask me why I hadn't done anything to make improvements, and say I should feel ashamed of myself for just sitting by and letting the place go down.

Some of these letters I answered. But after a while there got to be so many of them I couldn't take the time. And while so many people wondered, the school just sat with its windows half boarded up or broken, while the wind howled through the place with the door hanging from its hinges. A fine testimonial to the many years of work and a total waste of money.

For reasons that should be obvious by now, we didn't spend much time that summer in Skinners Pond. We were there for a week or so and then we travelled around to visit other people we hadn't seen in a long time.

There were Raymond and Grace Goguen, Johnny and

Judy Reid, Joe and Gerty Osborne, Reg and Muriel Chapman, Aubrey and Connie Harper, Steve and Gini Foote, and Gerry and Leona Marks, just to name a few. When we came back to Ontario, we visited others, such as Pete and Irene Ens, Ira and Liz Osborne, and Jim and Olive Fordham, all of Port Elgin and Southampton. We stopped in to pay my cousin Danny Aylward a visit in London, and then, at last, we pulled the trailer home. This would be around the end of September '81.

By now, it had been five years since I did a concert tour and two and a half years since I released an album, and by now I had begun to hardly think of the music industry at all. The only exception being when Jury and Mark and I had to have a meeting with accountants and lawyers and other business associates.

There were still people from all over the country wondering where I was and what I was doing, but as far as the public eye was concerned, except for my records, I had completely disappeared from the musical map. And I was starting to like it that way.

I'm sure that the major radio stations, the national exhibitions, the different awards people and the Canadian music scene in general were all glad that I had disappeared too. Nothing was being done and nobody was complaining about it. And that was just fine with them.

While I'm getting literally hundreds of letters per year through the Boot Records address, asking why they can't hear any "identifiably Canadian songs," either on the radio or during the awards shows, they're out there saying that nobody wants to hear that stuff.

The only answer I could give most people was that "if you want it, the only thing you can do is raise hell until you get it. Write letters, just as you have done with me, and call your local stations and don't give up. Tell them, if you have to, that you will not only stop buying the products they advertise, but you will also go to their sponsors and tell them the same thing. I was fighting for this for years all by myself, and now it's time for people power to take over. If they won't listen to one person, maybe they'll listen to a whole number of them. Best of luck!"

Discoveries, Birthdays and Games

DURING THE NEXT FOUR OR FIVE YEARS (1981 to '86), life began to slip into somewhat of a routine. We visited people, they visited us, we played a lot of cards and even started a regular 45 Club with several chapters. We had our own constitution and trophies that could be won each year by the person with the highest points. It was spread out across the northern regions of Toronto from Oshawa in the east to Guelph in the west at one point in time, until some people wanted to go against the constitution, and then it gradually fell apart.

The games were held every third Saturday from mid-October till the end of March, and a newsletter was published to everybody every third week with the latest point standings of each member and the goings on within each chapter. I personally felt the club could have expanded right across the whole country with chapters everywhere, had people wanted to abide by the constitution. But some just wanted to go their own way and the club soon fizzled out.

One year we took our trailer, and along with Lena's brother Ted and his wife, Cathy, we toured the Cabot Trail in Cape Breton. Then we crossed to Newfoundland, touring the whole province up to St. Anthony, and even drove as far as we could go into Labrador. Unfortunately, at the time, we couldn't go any farther than Red Bay, because there were no more roads.

We had also been to Mary's Town where we got to see the new church that I had given the big contribution to help build after the old one burned down. And then we took the ferry from Fortune to St. Pierre et Miquélon. These two islands belong to France and they're hardly more than twenty miles off the Newfoundland coast. This is a very interesting place where everything is operated under the French government. Lena and Cathy especially had a ball going in and out of all the quaint-looking shops, dragging Tommy with them wherever they went, while Ted and I visited some of the great bars.

On this same trip we visited Lena's sister Amy and her husband, Foster, on Caribou Island, Nova Scotia, and took Amy out to celebrate her birthday. Pauline was there, along with Ted and Cathy, and Cathy's father, Earl, and his wife Ethel. A couple other good friends, Allan and Gail Jankov, were also present.

After this, back in Ontario, Tommy had started school and was doing quite well. For the first three years we had put him in French immersion.

We also traded the Prowler trailer in for a twenty-three-foot Citation which we found to be a lot better trailer, quality-wise. And I also bought a larger motorcycle, a 600 cc Kawasaki.

I also took out a patent, during this time, on a board game I invented, called "Codamania." Any number of players, from one (solitaire) to eight, could play it, and it had to do with the making and breaking of codes. There was a spinning wheel and a number of code books involved. I still have the prototype and the instructions. Although I never did get the time to manufacture and market it, the few people who played the game on the original said they really enjoyed it.

In these years, we spent most Christmases at home with Tommy and a few friends who would sometimes drop by, such as Danny Aylward or my old bass player, Gary Empey. The only Christmas we spent away was the year we went to Entry Island for a couple of weeks. Here we stayed at Ted and Cathy's house and from there we visited practically everybody on the island. Christmas day itself was an uproarious one. Ted and Cathy now had three girls and a boy of their own—Tracey, Trudy, Lisa and Corey—and when Tommy got in with them, the fight over toys was on. Just after New Year's we bid them all goodbye and took off in Craig Quinn's light plane.

We only made two or three short visits to Prince Edward Island during these years to say hello to Russell and Cora, who were now living with Willard and Marlene down in Nail Pond. One of these trips was to Russell's funeral on April 30, 1984. He had had a pace-maker for the last couple of years and while he was in the Alberton hospital having it checked, he just passed out on the table and couldn't be revived. Buried at the Palmer Road Church Cemetery, he would have been eighty years old on his next birthday. Cora continued to live for another ten years.

My father by blood, Tommy Sullivan, also died during this time, in Saint John, New Brunswick. Although I was able to contribute to the cost of his funeral, I was notified late and wasn't able to attend. I think he was around sixty-four. He also had an older brother, Charles, who died a few years later, in Ottawa. (These were my two namesakes, Tom Charles, and Connors, of course, was my mother Isabel's maiden name. See *Before the Fame.*)

Now, there's one more thing of major importance, at least to me, that occurred during these years between 1981 and 1986. This was the fact that I now had the time, especially during the winters, to sit and contemplate my entire life, and to ask myself those age-old questions, like, "Who and what am I, why am I here, and what exactly is my true connection to this whole universe?" These are questions that many people ask, but not too many can or will even bother to take the time to come up with the answers for.

My answers, of course, may not be for everyone, due to a multitude of reasons. And for all I know, I may not have the number of pages in this book I will need to describe them all.

"Does that mean the reader is going to have to wait for another book to find out what all this is about?"

I don't know for sure. But at the moment, I'm trying to jam another fourteen years into this book. And at the rate I'm going, I'm not sure whether I'll have any space left to deal with some pretty serious mathematical, religious and philosophical observations.

What I'm trying to say is: if I take a few chapters now to relate all this, I may not have room here to finish the story of my life up to the year 2000. So my plan is to bring the full story up to date. And if I have the space at the end of this book, I will deal with the more serious matters. I hope I do. But if I don't, another (short) book will no doubt follow. In the meantime, I will try to put as much in this book as time and space will allow.

To give my readers just a small idea of what these matters are about, I will have to digress briefly to one of the times when I was hitch-hiking out west. (And there were many, as described in *Before the Fame*.)

I was alone on a summer's afternoon, sitting on the side of the road in the grass up next to a fence. This was somewhere just west of Thunder Bay.

I wouldn't have taken a ride at the time even if someone had stopped and said "Get in." I was thinking of absolutely nothing, when a series of vocal sounds and numbers just popped into my head from out of nowhere. Something told me that they were of great significance and I should always remember them. I hope to describe these numbers and sounds later, but for now, let's just say I tucked them away in my memory until the early 1980s. And that's when their real significance became known to me, during the long winter nights when I was doing all this contemplating.

With books on just about every subject in front of me, including mythology, philosophy and ancient scriptures from all religions, this series of numbers and sounds again popped into my head. Something was telling me that now the time had come for me to discover their real use.

As I slowly began to sound out passages that previously made no sense whatever, and applied the numbers at the same time, it was almost as if the angels were talking to me, and revealing for the first time exactly what these scriptures and other ancient writings were trying to say. (Don't worry, reader, I'm fully aware of the implications of what it is I'm saying. But it can't be said in any other way.)

This system of sounds and numbers was especially useful

for deciphering passages of the Judeo-Christian Bible, and revealing things that would astound scholars who have been studying it for thousands of years.

For example: the ratio of the circumference of a circle to its diameter, otherwise known as pi, is given in the book of Genesis and many other books throughout the Bible, along with the exact measurement of the distance around this planet of ours. (And not the flat earth that most people today think that our ancient ancestors supposed it to be.)

Through this system of numerical sounds, which, by the way, not only works in English but also in French and German (as was proven by a couple of friends of mine), and for all I know, probably works in every language of the world, one can find out through its application to the Bible alone, the speed of light, the dimensions of our Milky Way galaxy, the true meaning of the "Zero Factor," the number of one's name, the number that represents the Name of God, and even how to find the stone that has your name written on it.

These are only some of the many fascinating things that can be found in the Bible by this peculiar system. But the light it sheds on the passages of other ancient writings are staggering.

(To those who are curious about whether this system is in any way similar to *The Bible Code*, a book written by Michael Drosnin and published by Simon and Schuster in 1997, I can assure you it is not. And for this reason, if for none other, I hope I can include the proof of my claims within the pages of this book.)

Meanwhile, back to my story.

During the past five years Lena and I had met and made a lot of new friends through the 45 Club and other ways. Art and Jeanette Hawes, Eddy and Betty Hawes, Cliff and Ann Evans, Reg and Bev Landriault, and a host of others too numerous to name here.

An entertainer, singer and songwriter by the name of Wiz Bryant, from Penticton, B.C., who was presently living and playing in the local area, also used to come to the house.

We also had occasions, during this hiatus period, to have a reunion with a daughter of mine who was now married with a couple of children of her own. Her name was Carol, and her husband's name was Chris. This made me an unexpected grandfather. We also met my son, Taw, who was living in northern Ontario at the time, and who was still unmarried.

There would be yet another daughter, named Karma, whom I would meet in later years, but I will speak of all these things in due course.

On Sunday, February 9, 1986, I turned fifty years old. And while the day passed by almost like any other, Lena was planning an extra-special big party for me at the local community centre a week later, on the following Sunday. It was supposed to be a surprise, and it certainly was.

She started duping me in the middle of the week by telling me that Eddy and Betty Hawes, who lived a few roads over from us, were celebrating their twenty-fifth wedding anniversary on Sunday. And his brother Art was holding a surprise party for them at the hall.

I told Lena I would go, but I wouldn't stay very long, as I had something important that I was working on.

All the invitations had been sent out by our office in Mississauga, so when Lena and I pulled up to the community centre and I saw all the cars, I was none the wiser.

I remember saying to Lena, "Let's get parked and get inside the hall quickly before Eddy and Betty arrive. Because if they see us they'll know something's up and it will spoil the surprise for them."

As we walked up the steps and into the hall, the doors flew open and the cameras started flashing and I quickly turned around to see who was behind me. I thought it was Eddy and Betty, but there was nobody there.

The band on the stage immediately struck up the music and somewheres around 150 people started singing "Happy Birthday" to me. I was totally speechless.

There were friends there I hadn't seen in years, as well as a lot of my recent acquaintances. Lena had certainly gone all out for this one and the surprise had been perfectly well executed.

Along with entertainers I hadn't seen in a long while, who were performing on stage—Ronnie Richard, Gary Empey, Bud Roberts (Black), Freddy Northcotte, Wayne

Chapman, Wiz Bryant, Sam Leitch, Clare Adlam and Kent Brockwell—she had a group of professional cloggers who danced and did their stuff to top off this great country jamboree known as a birthday party.

Jury and everyone from Boot Records were there, along with our lawyer, Michael White, and our accountant, Dick Withey, and many more of our business associates, including Mark Altman and his wife, Pnina.

Jimmy and Olive Fordham, and others from Port Elgin/Southampton way, were there, and so were most of the people from the 45 Club.

Just some of the last names of those present were Chapman, McKinley, Gogarty, Taylor, Keefe, Steele, Buston, Andrews, Evans, Landriault, Hawes, Caves, Linstead, Nelligan, Shortill, Arsenault and Watcha McCallum. (Sorry if I left your name out.)

The birthday cake was made by my daughter Carol, and it was a beauty. A giant map of Canada with flags for every province and names of my songs written all over it. It must have taken her a couple of days to make, but it was delicious. And of course big enough for everybody to have a fair-sized piece. I later had to perform some of the songs that were written on the cake.

At one point early in the evening, someone came to me with a message saying that there was some kind of newspaper reporter outside who wanted to see me. As I went outside with the intention of telling him to get lost, I found that he was very cordial and down to earth, so I told him that he and a couple of his friends were welcome to come in and have a couple of beers, as long as he left his camera in the car.

Once I saw they had taken a seat and weren't bothering anybody, I went over and sat down and gave the guy an interview. He asked a lot of the kinds of questions that told me he was not just trying to get a story, but was also somewhat of a fan and had been following my career for a number of years. He had also been trying to contact me for some time.

I'm not sure how long he stayed or when he left the party, but I later became a fan of his and took Lena to see his band a couple of times in future years. This was Dave Bidini, leader of the great band called the Rheostatics.

In late June of 1986, we again packed our trailer and headed out for Prince Edward Island. This time we took a couple of friends with us, Art and Jeanette Hawes. Art had a new Gold Wing motorcycle, and he and Jeanette were going to follow us down.

Most of the trip was pretty much run-of-the-mill with the regular stopovers at motels, diners and gas pumps. That is until we got to New Brunswick.

It was here for a while that Tommy and Lena came up with a little game that Tommy always got a great kick out of.

Every once in a while, when we stopped and got out of the van, upon returning to it to continue our journey, Tommy, who always sat with me in the front seat, would say, "Hey, Dad? Don't leave yet. Mom's not in the van."

Lena would be crouched down somewhere in the back seat where I couldn't see her, and I'd have to take a look. This soon got to be a lot of fun. Anything to make Dad look back.

Even sometimes when Lena was sleeping in the back seat and only Tommy and I had gotten out, he would play the same trick on me when we got back in.

Upon arriving in Annagance, New Brunswick, we stopped not only for gas, but also to have something to eat in the little restaurant attached to the Irving service station. Muriel Chapman was now working here as a waitress and also as a cashier for the little variety store.

After introducing Muriel to Art and Jeanette, we had something to eat. Then after browsing around the variety store, we went out to the van and the motorcycle and proceeded to take off.

On our way out the gate Tommy made his usual statement of "Hey, Dad? Don't leave yet. Mom's not in the van."

For some reason I just wasn't in the mood for jokes at that moment and ignored him.

Two minutes later: "Hey, Dad? Where are we goin'? Mom's not in the van." As I took a look at him and saw that he seemed to have that same little smirk on his face, I said, "Yeah, I know she's not in the van; but we're going anyway."

After another couple of times doing this, I just got fed up and said, "Well, why don't you go back there and look for her, and when you find her you can let me know."

As he came back and got in the front seat, I asked him if he had found her. With the same smirk on his face, he said he couldn't find her, so I said, "Well, we'll just have to keep going without her then, won't we?" And as he didn't say any more, neither did I.

We were now approaching Magnetic Hill, and as I knew Art and Jeanette had never experienced it, I decided to stop in.

As I approached the attendant and stopped to buy the tickets, I shouted, "Magnetic Hill! Gift shop!" As there was no stir, I figured Lena had gone to sleep by now, so I proceeded down the hill. After checking the famous landscape, we continued on our way to the P.E.I. ferry.

As my friend Keith Wall lives just three miles on this side of the ferry terminal, I decided to drop in for a few minutes to say hello.

After pulling the trailer up to his door and finding no one home, nature was calling, so instead of going to the toilet in the trailer I walked over behind Keith's barn.

On my way back, although the trailer was partially blocking my view, I could see a car coming in the driveway with two people in it. When it stopped, I could only see the driver's side where this tall, light-complected fellow stepped out and waved to me. Thinking it was Keith Wall, who is also tall and light-complected, I just waved back.

As we both approached the trailer from different sides, we met each other as we came around the corner. I was surprised to find out it wasn't Keith Wall at all. It was Aubrey Harper.

Then from around the corner came Lena, who started in to giving me proper shit.

For a minute or two I thought she was just kidding. But when I asked Aubrey what the hell he was doing around these parts, he told me he had just driven Lena all the way from Annagance to try and catch up with me before I got to the P.E.I. ferry. I had indeed left her behind in the little restaurant at the service station and travelled almost a hundred miles without her.

With everybody talking at once and me trying to explain

the game I thought Tommy was playing on me, I did everything but stutter. While Lena was raking me over the coals and not believing one word, she was puffing on cigarettes two at a time, after having quit for three whole weeks. And every time I looked at Tommy, he still had that silly-looking smirk on his face. I was getting all the blame for this, and he was getting off scot-free.

Even Art and Jeanette had thought Lena was in the van, so they had no reason to honk their horn to draw my attention. That was another reason why I had paid no attention to Tommy.

It was a damn good thing we stopped at Keith Wall's when we did, or I would have driven right on to the ferry, and wouldn't have discovered Lena was missing until we were on our way to the other side. We would then have had to turn around on P.E.I. and come right back on another ferry, while an irate Lena would be waving to us from another boat in the middle of the Northumberland Strait.

Anyway, we thanked Aubrey for all his trouble and told him we'd be stopping in for a visit on our way back. We then proceeded toward the boat.

Lena was back to normal in about two or three days or so. But there was something I noticed that was always different about her after that. Whenever we stopped for anything, she was always the first one back in the van, sitting there just as pretty as you please and all ready to go when the motor started. There was no more dilly-dallying around, and no more funny little games.

To Assist Canadian Talent

FINALLY ARRIVING ON THE ISLAND, we went to see Pauline. A few years previous, she had split up with her husband and was now engaged to be married to a military man from Virden, Manitoba, who was stationed at the Canadian Forces Base in St. Eleanors, P.E.I. His name was Bill Hawes.

Of course, by the time all the introductions were made, Bill Hawes and my friend Art Hawes began a merry old conversation trying to find out how they might be related. Had one's great-grandfather gone from Ontario to Manitoba, or was it the other way around? At any rate, Pauline wanted Lena to be her bridesmaid, and the date was set to be the twenty-third of August, 1986.

After assuring them we'd be there in plenty of time for the wedding, we headed out for Willard and Marlene's place in Nail Pond.

We were only there for a day or so when Art's brother Eddie and his wife, Betty, arrived with their son, Brian. They also had their own trailer and parked it in Willard's yard for a couple of days beside ours. Art and Jeanette had rented a cabin just down the road.

The Haweses weren't able to stay for more than a few days before they had to go back to Ontario, so I showed them around as much as I could and got them a couple of good feeds of lobsters. We also had a party or two and then we bade them farewell.

After the Haweses left, Lena and I went around to say hello to old Josey Arsenault, Roy and Noreen Clohossey (Willard's father and mother), Joe and Edna Ellsworth from Palmer road, and the Butlers in Miminegash. The Perrys, Bernards, Knoxes, Doyles and Keefes from around Skinners Pond were names that were also quite frequently on our agenda.

I didn't hang around Skinners Pond too much in these days due to the bad memories I had about the school, the farm and all the damage that had been done.

In Russell's will, he had left the house and the lot that had been surveyed off the farm to Marlene. Around this time she had sold it to her three children, Gwen, Robbie and Sandra.

Saying goodbye once more to Willard and Marlene, we headed out to see Ray Goguen, who was living in Summerside. Ray was now working at the Sea Foods packing plant and could always get me a case or two of mackerel, clams and other kinds of fish that I always enjoyed now and again throughout the winter.

After spending some time with Ray and a few other friends of ours, we arrived in Charlottetown in time for Bill and Pauline's wedding. The maid of honour was Pauline's sister, Amy. And Bill's daughter, Terry, and Lena were the bridesmaids. The groom and groom's men were all dressed in their military uniforms. The wedding took place at St. Paul's Anglican Church and the reception was held at the Kirkwood banquet hall.

The following day we all met at Bill and Pauline's house in Miscouche, P.E.I., where Lena and I were introduced to Bill's mother, Louise, and his two sisters, Jean and Ruth and their husbands, Bob and Joe. Bob's last name was McKay but I forget Joe's. They had all come down from Manitoba, to see Bill and Pauline get married.

On our way back to Ontario, we stopped in to see Reg and Muriel Chapman and Aubrey and Connie Harper, and I took quite a ribbing for leaving Lena behind in the service station. (I still do today, occasionally.)

Passing through Montreal, we went to see my mother for

a day or two so she could see Tommy. We bought her a few things and then we came home.

In September, Tommy was back to school and would soon be playing hockey again. He eventually became quite good at it, winning MVP several times.

In the fall of 1986 it would be exactly ten years since I had done a concert tour and eight years since I had given back my Junos. By now I would have completely forgotten about both, but the letters over the years had still not stopped coming in. Although any little bit of airplay on radio that I might once have gotten was now totally dried up, people across the country were still asking me to return to the music scene and start making more records. Bottom line? I still wasn't interested. If the industry wasn't interested in cleaning up its act, I wasn't interested in being a part of it.

The only thing that was bothering me was the fact that I was receiving all these letters and tapes from people asking me how to make it in the music business. Some of this stuff was quite good, but radio would have no part of it if it wasn't recorded in Nashville and for a number of other foolish reasons. By now they had even started saying, "We can't play it because it's too Canadian." If you can imagine that.

Even all the Boot Records artists (over a hundred of them) were not receiving any airplay to speak of, even though Jury had caved in to a certain extent by now and had recorded some of these artists in Nashville. Radio preferred solid American and that was that. And because of this, a record company that had started out to record and promote Canadian artists was now hurting financially and couldn't afford to take on any new artists. At times Jury was coming to me to borrow substantial amounts of money just to keep the production of records flowing.

A very large part of the success of any record company is the fact that they must receive radio airplay. If radio doesn't want to play your records, nobody will hear them. If people don't hear them, they won't go to a store asking to buy them. If the store gets no request for a record, they won't bother to order it or stock it on their shelves. With no orders from the stores, the album sits on the shelves of the distributor, until he sends it back to the record company where it will eventually be destroyed.

Millions of dollars get spent each year in Canada on records destined for the garbage dumps. And all because Canadian radio won't play them.

What a waste of good money and good talent. And what a shame that it all has to be destroyed before the listening public ever gets a chance to decide whether they even like it.

Because record companies know they need radio to play their records in order to survive, they send copies of every one they produce to the stations. And when a listener phones that station to request that a record be played, and the answer he gets is, "Sorry, we'd really like to play it for you, but we don't have it," he can be sure the reason they don't have it is because they threw it out the minute they received it, and had no intention of letting the public hear it in the first place. This way they control what it is they want people to hear.

The public never gets to know the sorrowful, degrading situation that radio has forced recording companies into, when they have to go begging the stations to please play the music they know to be good, otherwise they wouldn't have spent their money on producing it in the first place.

Most of these same companies exist for the sole purpose of producing Canadian music, and they're going broke. They're falling like flies. And radio is letting them. Because without that necessary airplay the record company goes down, and so does the talent. And the Canadian people are the worse off for it.

I don't think there is one honest person in this country who can't say that, at one time or another, he hasn't heard some American music played on our Canadian radio stations that was nothing but absolute crap. And the converse is also true: there is a hell of a lot of good Canadian music being thrown out because radio has judged it to be bad, long before the public ever got to hear it. Or even had a hope to hear it.

My only answer to this would be that if we have to listen to any crap at all, why can't it be Canadian instead of American? But the truth of the matter is that a lot of the music being thrown out is a lot better than the American in the first place.

And one more thing, although I have no proof that this has ever happened. If, for any reason, a radio station wanted one record to sound not quite as good as another, they certainly have the technology to do so. Just one small touch of a dial could have the listener believing that the quality of one record was inferior to another. What the motive might be for doing something like this could be anybody's guess. But then, why Canadian radio prefers to play American music over Canadian is also anybody's guess.

So with a lot of talented artists writing to me, and a lot of others floating around the countryside, I thought I'd try to devise a plan that might help some of these people get themselves known and possibly get some airplay.

This, briefly, was the plan:

I would produce an album on which I would personally sing four songs I had written, and six other artists would each sing two songs they had written. A total of seven artists singing sixteen songs.

This would be a co-operative effort where everybody would share equally in the costs, and if the record sold, they would share equally in the profits. The manufacturer and distributor would be Boot Records Limited.

The front cover of the album (which was vinyl) would read "Stompin' Tom is back to ACT (Assist Canadian Talent)," along with a large group photo of myself in among the six other singing artists. Below the picture would be the names of all the artists prominently displayed along with the names of the songs they were singing on the album.

On the back cover the names of the artists and their songs would again be displayed along with a photo of all the musicians who played on the album. And below this photo would be all the musicians' names.

This album would also be available in cassette. An address was posted for anyone wishing to write for further information on the talent.

Inside the album jacket along with the record was a letter from me, asking the buyer to help me assist Canadian talent in the following way:

First they should listen to the album and choose the singer and the song they liked best, and then phone their local radio station and request it.

When they were told, "We don't have that record," they

were to take their own album up to the station the following day and give it to some person of importance, and have him stamp the name of the radio station as well as signing his name to a little coupon found inside the album jacket.

When this was done, he could send the coupon to the company address and receive a brand-new ACT album free of charge, along with a nice wall certificate signed by yours truly, in recognition of his help to Assist Canadian Talent.

Now, if the buyer phoned the radio station the next day to request his song, and the voice at the other end said, "We don't have that record," he could be told of a certainty that indeed he did have it, because the caller had proof that he dropped the record off at the station on the previous day. (The coupons were in duplicate. One for the record company and a copy for the buyer.)

If the radio station still refused to play the song, both the buyer and the record company had proof that the refusal was not on account of them not having the record. And furthermore, the record company could prove to the CRTC (who issue radio licences) that even though that station had the record they wouldn't play the Canadian talent on it. Even when it was being requested by their own listeners.

The letter in the jacket also urged the people with the proof to be persistent with the stations. And if they still got no results they were urged to go to the sponsors whose products were being advertised by the station. And tell them why they would no longer listen to the station and why they would not buy the products it advertised.

Radio stations might soon begin to play what the people decided they want to hear, when the sponsors pulled their ads and the money dried up.

Now, while this plan might have helped the new Canadian talent to get some airplay, it also had some other benefits.

When soliciting club work or other kinds of playing jobs, it not only enhanced a musician's chances to show he had an album out, but if that album was proof that he had indeed recorded with a major, well-known artist, it was bound to make any prospective employer look twice, and give him a little more consideration. After all, the picture on the cover would say it all.

Another point is that if the album were only bought on account of the major artist, the secondary artist would still gain the exposure he needed in people's homes. And whenever the major artist got played, so would he. This gave the otherwise local artist a national exposure.

And finally, this co-operative effort held out another benefit to other struggling artists: if any artist on this album gained enough fame and popularity, through airplay or other exposure, to warrant having his own album, and was now being considered a star in his own right, his agreement was that he, in turn, would do what Stompin' Tom had done, and first put out an album with six other struggling artists before going on to his own greater destiny.

In this way, it was hoped the plan would continue to perpetuate itself.

Now that I had a plan formulated, the next thing I did was to call a meeting of a number of struggling entertainers who had expressed the hope that some day they might be able to make it in the music business.

After explaining the plan to all, it was almost unanimously accepted, and the first six artists were selected and told to come up with two of their best songs for the album. And for those who were a little unsure of themselves, I brought them to my house and conducted a little song-writing seminar.

With a little help to some, and more to others, we finally came up with an acceptable program. And sometime around the middle of October 1986, everybody's contribution was in, and we all headed for the recording studio.

The names of the artists on this album, other than myself, were Bruce Caves, Art Hawes, Cliff Evans, Kent Brockwell, Donna Lambert and Wayne Chapman. Most of these singers also played their own accompaniment along with the following musicians who made up the local group known as Marion's Country Band. Marion Armstrong, on keyboards, was the leader. Sam Leith played fiddle, Wayne Armstrong played bass, and Earl Burt played lead. The four background singers were a group known as Manon.

I gave the master, the photos, the design and all the rest of the pertinent information to Jury. And while Boot

Records did the manufacturing, all the rest of us could do was sit around and wait.

Anticipating that radio stations wouldn't play "identifiably Canadian" songs anyway, I made sure the content of the album contained songs that ranged between no mention of Canada at all, to songs that were unmistakably Canadian. And as I knew that radio was not going to play any Stompin' Tom cuts anyway, I included the following song to try and stir up their conscience.

NO CANADIAN DREAM

1.

The music of strangers, they play in our homes,
And tell us that we don't have songs of our own,
They give us no choices and make it quite clear,
They'll play what they want us to hear.

Canadian Radio, boy, is it grand,
When you want to hear music from some other land,
They tell us to like it, and flow with the stream;
We Have NO CANADIAN DREAM.

CHORUS:
There's NO CANADIAN DREAM, my friends,
We Have NO CANADIAN DREAM;
The Radio blares and the Music declares;
We Have NO CANADIAN DREAM.

2.

We hear the American telling his son,
Of the battles he fought and the Freedoms he won,
He sings about Home and the Pride that he has,
And his son wants to be like his dad.

Canadian Radio, boy, is it grand,
When you want to hear stories from some other land,
They teach us to long for those far away scenes,
Where there's NO CANADIAN DREAM.

(Repeat chorus)

3.

No, we've got no cotton, and no Uncle Sam,
We've got no Texas and no Alabam;
From all of our singers, we don't hear a sound,
From St. John's to Vancouver Town.

We don't write letters, we don't use the phone,
We have no petitions to make our Cause known;
Even our Children don't know what it means,
To Dream A CANADIAN DREAM.

(Repeat chorus)

The ACT album was released around the first of December '86, and we all gathered at my house for a celebration party. Everyone was given a couple of boxes of records for promotional purposes and asked to go to the press in their local area and try to get a write-up in the paper. About five out of the seven of us were successful. And I considered that was pretty good for people who had never tried to do this sort of thing before.

Although the album hadn't been released soon enough to catch a lot of the Christmas shoppers, it sold in quantities sufficient to warrant a good deal of optimism. Anyway, we were all anxious to find out how our plan was going to work.

After having a big skating party around the time of my birthday, in February 1987, in which we cleared our pond, played some hockey and skated around with the kids, we began to think that maybe the plan wasn't going to work.

Then one day a couple of coupons came in, all properly signed and documented. In another day or so there were several more. This meant the albums were getting to the radio stations, and some of the songs on the album were liked by somebody well enough that they wanted to have them played on the air. This was great news, and when I told everybody, they were elated.

Some of the people even wrote a little letter telling which songs they liked the best, and because they had no idea what was going on with radio, they were more than glad to help.

The new replacement albums were promptly sent out, along with the signed Canadian Talent Promoter Certificates. The plan seemed to be working.

Two Bombshells

THEN ALONG ABOUT MARCH, a bombshell of another kind hit. I was doing some work around the house when Lena returned home from town with the mail. One of the very large envelopes was addressed to me. And it was from Mark Altman, my other partner at the office in Mississauga. And the contents were all concerning Jury.

All of these papers dealt with some very serious matters. There were letters from lawyers and their clients with whom we had business dealings threatening lawsuits of one kind or another. There were documents proving what, up until now, had only been allegations. And there were papers that showed that he had not been totally up front with me concerning some very sensitive matters, both business and personal.

The entire contents of this envelope were papers signed by Jury which dealt with matters to which I should have been made privy and wasn't.

I quickly read these papers and copied them, then jumped in my van and headed down to Mississauga.

We had a new receptionist to whom I had not yet been introduced. When she tried to stop me and ask me who I was, and what was the nature of my business, I hurriedly walked by her saying, "Just never mind. Because it won't be long before you and everybody else around here finds out."

After looking in several offices, I finally found Jury doing

459

something in the warehouse area. "Jury!" I shouted. "I want to see you in Mark's office. Right now!"

I went into Mark's office, plunked myself down, said "Hi" to him and spread the contents of the envelope out across his large coffee table.

Mark didn't say a word. He knew exactly why I was there. About thirty seconds later, in walks Jury.

"What's all this about?" he asked.

"Just have a nice seat on the sofa there, behind the coffee table," I said, "and you'll soon find out."

All I had to do was tell him to read the papers. After he quickly glanced at several, his face became red as a beet. When he looked up to see what Mark's and my expressions were, I simply asked him to verify whether the documents in front of him were true.

He said they were, and I gave him several alternatives, one of which was that he could immediately go into his own office and come back out with a signed document saying that he had resigned as president of all the companies, and that he was in total agreement with his share of the assets which were about to be determined immediately on this spot.

Without going into the other options, it's enough to say that he took the one just described, and within the next half hour, a formula suitable to the circumstances was worked out.

Jury then went to his office, typed out the necessary papers, and brought them back for Mark and myself to read.

When we were both satisfied the papers were in order, Jury signed them. And though it had been eighteen years, or more, this was the day when my long association with Jury came to an end.

The final split was that Mark Altman and I wound up with Morning Music and all its holdings. Mark's share was 40 per cent and mine was 60. And I was the president. I also wound up with Jury's half of Crown-Vetch Music, only to find out later that it owed several thousands of dollars to CAPAC (now SOCAN).

Jury wound up with 100 per cent of Boot Records and all its holdings. The only catch here was that Jury would have to move the record company out of the building. And because he owed me a substantial amount of money, he would have to leave all his masters in my possession until the debt was paid.

While all this was going on, there was also an issue concerning credit cards. But I'll just leave that one hang.

In the meantime, where did all this leave the ACT album? Temporarily in limbo.

For the sake of the talent and our co-operative agreement, I retained all the rights to the album. But I didn't have a record company. So what do you do when you have this unique kind of album, and there's not a record company anywhere that understands the concept of the work, never mind wanting to handle it?

Well, I guess you just start up your own record company again. So I did.

One of the entertainers on the ACT album who showed a lot of interest in the production, manufacture and distribution of the record was Cliff Evans. He didn't live too far from me, so I thought I'd pay him a little visit and offer him a deal.

Once the deal was accepted, we went to the lawyer's office, and before long we were partners in a newly incorporated company called ACT Records Ltd.

Sounds big and wonderful, don't it? I sure wish it was.

Starting out from scratch again, we had to have more albums and cassettes manufactured. This meant renegotiating all previous deals that Boot Records had for the album and, of course, searching around for a new distributor. And again, what distributor would want to handle only one solitary album that had a very questionable reason for its existence?

Well, there was only one answer for that. I wasn't going to start up a distribution company as well as a recording company just to supply the country with an album that had six unknown artists on it. So what was the answer?

Stompin' Tom was going to have to come back!

I knew that any distributor would take Stompin' Tom with his whole catalogue. To make it even more enticing, I would record a brand-new comeback album. With this package to offer, I would insure that the ACT album would continue to be distributed.

Poor Cliff, with no experience, now had not only one

album to get manufactured, but sixteen, counting the new one I was about to record. It was all going to cost a pile of dough, and we had to get at least a half-dozen albums into production immediately. We just had to have the product before approaching the distributor.

As if we weren't having enough problems trying to promote Canadian talent that spring, the major radio stations had gotten together to form a united front against the 30 per cent Canadian content regulations. And it looked like they were about to convince the CRTC to reduce the percentage from thirty down to fifteen. This would allow them to play 15 per cent more American than they were already playing, boosting the 70 per cent foreign content they now played up to 85 per cent.

This called for rallies to be attended, petitions to be signed, and all kinds of letters to be sent to members of parliament. And especially to the Minister of Communications.

You almost have to have eyes in the back of your head sometimes, to see just what it is that radio is trying to pull next. (How sweet it would be if listeners themselves would just take a little more time to be concerned with this immensely important issue. As Canadian radio stations can't be trusted to play Canadian music, they must be regulated. And the question is: just how much and exactly what kind of regulations will it take to ensure that our talented people who wish to stay in this country can do so? And at the same time make a decent living singing about the way of life that all Canadians can truly understand and relate to? And finally, why is it that all the Canadian talent we do hear on radio sound so damn American? Isn't it because of the fact that if they didn't, they wouldn't get played on Canadian radio in the first place?)

Without a doubt, the lesson from the above seems to be that we send our talent south of the border for one purpose only. And that is so they can finally learn to sing and play just as the Americans do. And when they get good enough at it, Canadian radio will play their records. We are discouraging originality in this country and creating a nation of copycats.

It's no wonder the people of Quebec want to separate, even though we in English Canada can't even understand the reason why.

I dare anyone to go to Quebec and tell me they didn't hear Quebec music on Quebec radio stations. Then why? And why, why, why can't we hear English Canadian music on English Canadian radio stations?

And let no one pick me up wrong. When I use the word "Canadian" in the context of songs and music, I mean "distinctively and identifiably Canadian."

There is a tremendous need in this vast country of ours for all of its people to get acquainted with each other. It's the need to know and understand the similarities and the differences in the aspirations of all our people from coast to coast to coast.

We Canadians need to be informed about who, what and where we are. That leads to greater unity, not greater divisions. It leads to the desire to help those we know instead of ignoring the problems of those we don't. And to the extent that a song is capable of doing any of these things, it should be played on all of our radio stations.

Everyone in this modern world must know by now that songs are vehicles that convey messages. And what are the messages now being conveyed to all our young people by the songs currently played on Canadian radio?

Are the children of the P.E.I. potato farmer being informed about the Toronto factory worker, the office worker, the stockbroker, or for that matter even the garbage man? And vice versa? The answer is "No." Are the children of the Montreal taxi driver being informed about the great oil fields and the people who harvest the massive amounts of grain throughout the Canadian prairies? And vice versa? The answer is "No." Are the children of the B.C. loggers, truckers, ranchers and fruit growers being informed about the lives of the Cape Breton miners, or the Newfoundland fishermen? And vice versa? The answer is "No."

Well, what exactly is it that Canadian radio bombards all our young people with, in terms of song messages?

In simple terms, they're feeding all of their listeners nothing but pap. You would think, by listening to the great majority of Canadian radio stations, that their only responsibility to the people of this country is to brainwash them into thinking that all business, cooking, working, travelling, fishing, farming and road building take place in the bedroom.

If, according to all these song messages, the only thing we do in this country is "make love, love, love" all the time, why can't we even get to know each other long enough to enjoy it? And why do westerners drive around flaunting signs on their cars that say "Let Those Eastern Bastards Freeze in the Dark"?

I'm not saying we shouldn't have songs about the eternal love triangle, or whatever, but should we have to be subjected to it night and day, "eternally"? Surely there must be something else going on in this country. Or is it because I'm really not up with the times? I haven't been down in the mines lately. But maybe my old pals are really starting to enjoy their coffee breaks in the bedroom.

But seriously, shouldn't all of our licensed radio stations be expected to intersperse their complete diet of pap with some "distinctively and identifiably Canadian" songs and music? I personally think they should. And I think our government should lift the licences of all those stations that don't.

After all, shouldn't it be seen that the Canadian people are getting something back from radio stations in return for granting them a licence to use the airwaves to line their pockets? As far as I'm concerned, the only ones who think they might be getting something back are the children who don't know any better. And these, of course, are the ones that most radio stations are catering to and trying to influence. Not to teach them anything, but only to convince them to buy the products that radio is being well paid to advertise.

I'm well aware that Canadian radio will never ever play a Stompin' Tom record on their divinely dictated playlists. But why should I worry? I never ever made it to their playlists anyway. The thing I care about mostly is that they'll never ever play any artist who even attempts to sing or sound "distinctively and identifiably Canadian." And in that respect they fail to live up to their obligation to "serve Canadian communities."

(Again, let me make myself clear. To the extent that there

may very well be certain radio stations in this country who live up to the spirit as well as the letter of the Canadian content regulations, and there may be some who do even more than the regulations require, they in no way have to take umbrage or feel offended by anything I have said about radio. It's the guilty and offending parties who know exactly what I'm talking about. And it's not only the perceptive Canadians they're offending. They're making a mockery of the whole country, and especially those of us who are unperceptive.)

More Tricks of the Trade

By LATE SUMMER OF 1987, Cliff Evans and I finally had two or three Stompin' Tom albums, as well as our *Assist Canadian Talent* album, released by our newly formed company, ACT Records Ltd. We had made a deal with a company by the name of Holborne to have them distributed.

Also, at this time, I couldn't seem to get anyone to rent the space left vacant by Boot Records when it moved out. And to expect Morning Music, which was now being run solely by Mark Altman, to shoulder a heavier burden of rent to meet the overhead was not right. So we decided to move Morning Music out to a nearby location where the rent was cheaper. And now, with no one in the building, I put it up for sale. (I had bought Jury's share from him a couple of years before.)

By the end of October of 1987 the building was sold. Cliff was manufacturing more Stompin' Tom albums for ACT Records. And I was writing new songs for the album I intended to record sometime early in the following year.

Some of these new songs were "Canada Day, Up Canada Way," "I Am the Wind," and "Lady, k.d. lang." k.d. lang, as everyone will remember, won several Juno awards in the 1980s. She was that flamboyant girl from Alberta with the great voice who jumped on the stage in a wedding dress to accept her first award. And as I thought she was a welcome change from all the years of Juno humdrum, I decided to write a song about her.

On the twenty-first of November that year a small fishing boat called the *Tammy Anne* from Entry Island, Lena's home, went down at sea with several of her relatives aboard. There were no survivors.

I was writing a song about this disaster, "The Wreck of the *Tammy Anne*," when Christmas overtook me and I had to finish it in January. So these were just some of the songs that would later be recorded on the album entitled *Stompin' Tom, Fiddle and Song*.

Lena's brother Ted and his wife, Cathy, brought their kids up to spend Christmas with us that year. They also stayed for New Year's Day, and then they went back to Entry Island. And so began the year of 1988.

In January we had another skating party or two, and by the end of February, ACT Records had several more Stompin' Tom catalogue albums manufactured.

The coupons for the ACT co-operative album started to come in again. And in greater numbers than before. The certificates and the replacement albums were again sent out, and it looked like the plan was going to work once more.

We got word from several of the people who had sent in the coupons that the small radio stations in their areas had agreed to play the talent on the album, and in fact, they did. But the real problem with the plan seemed to be that after some radio stations had accepted the album and then still refused to play it, the people who had requested their favourite song to be played were reluctant to pursue the matter any further. And because there wasn't any concerted effort mounted, the stations just ignored the plea of the callers, and the whole issue was allowed to be forgotten.

Personally, I think the plan could have worked then, and I think it could still work now. But some people either just don't have the time, won't take the time or don't actually believe they have the right to demand that radio play the kind of music its listeners want to hear, and not just play what it wants the people to hear.

While I agree that radio should have the right to introduce new music to its listeners, that new music should be local music as well as national and foreign. And the listeners should have the right to choose from out of all the newly introduced music which selections they want to hear. A radio station licence is not a licence to be a dictator. Because once they start dictating what kind of music they want you to hear, the next step could be to start dictating what kind of news they want you to hear.

As a matter of fact, when was the last time you heard a public debate on radio concerning the kinds of music they should or should not be playing? Or any of the other topics in this book, for that matter? Never! That's when. Because they consider it to be against their own best interests. So don't wait for radio to tell you what they're doing wrong. They won't. According to them, everything they're doing is right.

So, to the extent that you consider any of the points made in this book to be valid, you should write or contact your federal Minister of Communications and also the CRTC in Ottawa. And tell them exactly how you feel.

By June of 1988, it was finally time to go into the studio and record the new album, *Fiddle and Song.* This would be the first one since the *Gumboot Cloggeroo,* in 1978, ten years earlier, and my fifteenth personally written album overall.

Escarpment Sound was the studio selected, and the engineer was Brian Hewson. The location was in Acton, Ontario.

Lena also got into the act this time. We recorded one song that we quite often sang together at house parties. It was that old one made popular by Lucille Starr back in the early '60s, "The French Song." Lena was a little nervous singing her parts, but I thought it would be a nice touch for the album and also for the fans.

The photos for the cover were taken by Bruce Caves of Hornby, Ontario, and from then on the album went into Cliff's hands for ACT Records to manufacture and release for distribution to the stores along with the rest.

It must be remembered that I still had no intention of coming back to entertain. This new album of Stompin' Tom, along with the other old catalogue items, was merely an incentive for the distributor to carry the co-operative album. And we already had four or five out of the six new artists all lined up and waiting for the next such album to be recorded. We were prepared to put out a hundred such albums if we had to, in order to get the talent from all over Canada exposed. But unfortunately, as I said before, it began to look as if we could only expect the buyers to do so much, and without some sort of further incentives the plan would have to be dropped.

The Stompin' Tom albums gained the necessary distribution the co-operative album needed, but they were doing nothing to help the co-operative plan once the album was out there. So until we could think of something else to solve this dilemma, the whole co-operative program had to be put on hold. At first, this was only meant to be temporary. But as the reader will soon see, the project eventually had to be abandoned.

In July, Lena and I and Tommy again took our trailer to the east coast. And when we returned, another big pot of stew began to boil.

Mark Altman wanted to buy me out of Morning Music Limited, along with its subsidiaries around the world, in places such as Nashville, England, Ireland and Australia, as well as others.

He didn't want to give me what I considered the company to be worth, so I didn't want to sell. I was also the president, holding 60 per cent of the shares.

But Mark also had another ploy. This was an ultimatum. If I didn't accept his offer, I would now have to buy his 40 per cent, based on the amount I considered my 60 per cent to be worth. And if I did, it would present me with several big problems.

First, if I bought him out, I would have 100 per cent of a company I didn't know how to run. And, of course, he assured me that because he did know how, he would soon start his own publishing company. And because he knew all the contacts, he would soon run me out of business.

Secondly, if I didn't buy him out, or accept the amount he was willing to pay for my shares, he would start his own publishing company anyway, and would no longer be working for Morning Music. This meant I would have to find somebody I could trust to run the company no matter which way I looked at it. And Mark, of course, was free to sell his 40 per cent share of my company to anyone he liked, while his own company kept whittling away at the remainder of mine.

There were a few other minor details, but in essence, this was the predicament I perceived myself to be in as a result of his proposal.

I really didn't want to sell the company, and especially at the price being offered. But with somebody as knowledge-able as Mark, with all the company's inside information, including computer passwords, etc., planning to be my immediate competitor, I decided to get some legal advice.

When I was told that I would be able to sue in the event that he tried to take away any of the company's business for a "reasonable period" (approximately three years), I noti-fied him that I would be prepared to buy him out at the price stated, if he still chose to sell.

I figured that surely, within three years, I could either learn how to operate this business, or at least, find some trustworthy person who could.

As the only conclusion I could come to, based on Mark's offer, was that he no longer wanted to work with me and was going to start up his own company anyway, as the president and major shareholder of Morning Music, I immediately put new locks on the doors and relieved him of his duties.

Again, there were more details. But to cut a longer story short, within a few days Mark came up with another offer to buy me out. This time it was more in line with what I was ask-ing. And after a little more "nickel and diming," a deal was struck. And Mark Altman became the sole owner of Morn-ing Music Ltd. Approximate date, September 29, 1988.

For a while there, it looked like we were going to be arch enemies. But as reasonable men can always iron out their differences, we soon found that we could help each other more by working together than we could apart.

Today, we are still friends, and his publishing company administers mine.

Still in October of 1988, a lot of university campus radio stations were playing my records. They had been doing so over the years. And although their listening area was very limited, these young people were proving once again that the songs of Stompin' Tom still had appeal to the young as well as the old. Some of them were playing whole albums, never mind a song or two. They were also playing more groups which had a sound that was decidedly more Canadian. And to my ears, this was music. It didn't matter to me whether it was country, rock, pop or folk. As long as it had a distinctive sound that showed the groups were original and not trying to copy something foreign, I felt they were at least on the right track. (A little bit of fresh air.)

I had a visit from George Fox around this time, also. I found George to be a very decent, down-to-earth fellow, and we had a few beers together.

He proposed that we might join forces to write a couple of songs. But as his time was limited and we would have to get to know just what it was that each of us looked for in a song, we left it alone till a future date.

Although the future date never came, my friend Gaet Lepine and I wrote a song called "Alberta Rose," and knowing that George was from Cochrane, Alberta, I sent it to his management. But I guess he was on tour and didn't get to see it. He did, however, send Lena and me a postcard or two from a couple of places to which he travelled.

Sometime in November, a column writer for *Country Music News* magazine, Henry McGuirk, got in touch with me, wanting to do a cover story. He came to the house to take some pictures and the article appeared in two segments. One in the January 1989 issue, and the other in the February issue.

During this interview, Mr. McGuirk mentioned that an acquaintance of his who was having some business dealings with Capitol Records heard the president, Dean Cameron, say that if anyone knew how to get in touch with Stompin' Tom he'd appreciate them letting him know. According to Mr. McGuirk, Mr. Cameron also stated he would be interested in having Stompin' Tom on the label.

I took the rumour as something very amusing and we just went on with the interview. This was still in late November of 1988.

In the first part of December, Cliff Evans got a call at his house (the temporary headquarters of ACT Records, until we could find a suitable building) from Peter Gzowski's office.

Peter had been a long-time CBC radio commentator, and for the last couple of years, usually around the first of January, he would read an open letter over the air asking Stompin' Tom, wherever he might be, to finally come out of hiding and return to the business of entertaining the Canadian people. If nothing else, would I please give him a call, as he would like to interview me on his radio program.

I had actually heard one of these pleas but completely ignored it. I didn't like the American kowtowing attitudes throughout the Canadian music industry when I quit ten years ago, in 1978, and I hadn't seen anything happen since to make me change my mind about wanting to become a part of it now.

Besides, radio and other media had manipulated and twisted my words on so many occasions in the past that I didn't trust any of them.

And now, here was Peter Gzowski's office calling Cliff's house every second day, looking for an interview.

Because Cliff was inexperienced at these things, he would have to put them on hold and call me to find out what I wanted him to say. He knew I certainly didn't want them or anyone else to have my phone number.

As the media always answer one question with another question, poor Cliff was on the phone continuously. First to them, then back to me and back to them again.

Finally, Cliff said, "Why don't you give them an interview? It might do something for your cause to help Canadian talent! And at least it might do something to help me to get them the hell off my back."

"All right," I said. "I'll give Gzowski an interview. But it will have to be on my terms. I won't go to his studio, so tell him we'll have to do it at your house. And above all, tell him I want editing rights, so that if I see that an answer or two might need a bit more clarification we can go back to the question to get my answers right for a change. I'm getting sick and tired of people hearing these interviews and still not understanding what it is that I'm all about. So if I get Gzowski's word that he agrees with this I'll do the interview. And if he doesn't, just tell him and his office not to bother ever calling you again."

As it turned out, Peter agreed with the terms, and a meeting was set up at Cliff's house one afternoon between Christmas and New Year's.

Peter brought two other people with him. They came in a car and a van that carried the equipment. And after setting up, Peter and I would talk over the kitchen table while the taping machine was being controlled from Cliff's living room.

We talked for about an hour straight and when the interview was over we chatted again for a minute or two without mikes and then I asked to listen to the tape back so I could hear what was acceptable and what, if anything, I might like to do over.

"Oh!" Peter said. "I thought you wanted to edit the tape, question by question, as we talked. And if you found something wrong with one of your answers we could have immediately redone the part. But as you made no such indication, I thought you were satisfied with the way everything went down."

Peter was putting on his coat as I hurried to the living room to get the tape. But Peter's helper was long gone. And the tape, van and equipment were gone with him.

I knew immediately that Gzowski had pulled a fast one. I only had his word, his verbal agreement, and not a damn thing on paper.

As he was going out the door, I said, "Thanks one hell of a lot, Peter. And now that I know that your idea of editing rights is a hell of a lot different than mine, there's not too much I can do about it but trust your judgment when you air this thing. But I want you to know I don't like the way I've again been manipulated." With another word or two, here and there, he was soon in his car and gone.

About the first week in January 1989, he played the whole hour-long tape. And as far as I was concerned, it was one of the worst interviews I had ever done. Instead of playing the whole hour, he should have cut half of it out and only run it for a half an hour.

When you believe you have editing rights, you quite often give answers quickly and without too much thought, because you know you can always go back to clarify and correct something if you think your answer might be misunderstood by your listeners. And when you know you don't have editing rights, you think more thoroughly about the answer you are giving. You are more on your toes because you have to get it right the first time.

So after hearing the tape back for the first time on "Morningside" my overall impression was that Peter Gzowski didn't care one bit about how his listeners would interpret my answers as long as he got what he wanted. And that was to be able to say that he and only he had been capable of interviewing the great "hard-to-get" Stompin' Tom on radio. After all, it had been over twelve years since I had previously done a radio interview. And I thought a little more consideration should have been in order.

This reminded me of when the CFGM radio station heard through the grapevine that Lena and I were planning to get married. They invited me up to the station on the pretext that they were going to start playing my records. They planned on doing an interview and said that I should bring Lena along so they could introduce us to everyone and show us around the station. (This was back in 1973.)

We drove up to Richmond Hill, just outside of Toronto, and as soon as we got in the door everyone was all over us. They had flowers for Lena and champagne for me. We quickly took some pictures, they showed us around, and within the span of about fifteen minutes we were out of there.

On our drive back I said to Lena, "Boy, that was the shortest interview I ever did. I hardly said hello to the DJ and it was all over."

The next day the Toronto newspapers all carried the story that Stompin' Tom Connors and Lena Welsh were about to be married. And there above the announcement was the picture of Lena and me smiling and holding a bouquet of flowers and a large bottle of champagne.

They had played us both for a couple of fools. All they had really wanted to do was be the first to get the scoop to the newspapers, as if we didn't have the intelligence to do so ourselves. And did they play any Stompin' Tom records? Yes. Someone told me they heard one being played on the station at 2:30 A.M. And nobody heard anything since.

Dealing with Dean

Around the first of February 1989, I got a call from Henry McGuirk, asking me how I liked the story he sent to *Country Music News*. During the conversation he again mentioned that his friend who had some dealings with Capitol Records had suggested to the president, Dean Cameron, that if he still wanted to get in touch with Stompin' Tom, a friend of his (McGuirk) might be able to relay the message.

At this piece of news, Dean Cameron was supposed to have shown a great deal of enthusiasm, and said that he would like to meet me to talk about a record deal.

As this was all still nothing but rumour, I told Henry that I would like to meet this friend of his and hear what he had to say myself.

A few days later a brief meeting was held. And after hearing what the guy had to say, I gave him a message to take from me to Mr. Cameron the next time he happened to be going to Capitol Records. (This was supposed to be within the next week.)

The message was that I would meet Dean on a certain afternoon at a restaurant in Brampton, Ontario. I would be there alone at three o'clock, and we could have a private conversation. I wasn't sure that he would be there, but I had to test the validity of this rumour.

I was there at 2:45 P.M., wearing a cowboy hat so that I would be readily recognized by Dean when he walked in.

475

(I usually never make myself so obvious.)

I no sooner ordered a beer at the bar when the whole place was a-buzz. "Is that Stompin' Tom or isn't it?"

Instead of coming up and asking me directly, one guy remembered that the maintenance man who worked there had once said that he used to play with Stompin' Tom at the Horseshoe Tavern in Toronto. So if anybody would know if this guy sitting at the bar was Stompin' Tom, he would know.

Within a few minutes this guy came poking his head around the corner.

"Stampin' Tam," he shouted, in his broad Cape Breton accent. "How in the hell is she goin', b'y?"

It was Boom-boom Randy MacDonald, who used to play bass for me at the Horseshoe when he was a member of the band called The Good, the Bad and the Ugly. (They also played on the *Bud the Spud* album.)

As Randy and I were having an old-time chat over a beer at the bar, between signing autographs, in walks a hefty looking bird with a beard. He looked around for a minute or two, and when I signalled to him that I'd be right over to talk to him, he found a booth and sat down.

After telling Randy that my expected company had arrived, I took my beer and wandered over to the booth to meet this bearded gentleman. Introductions were made fast. I plunked myself down and the conversation began. And this was a conversation between two different people from two different worlds. And yet, maybe not so different.

For the first few minutes we felt a little uncomfortable with one another. I was a man who had lost all faith with people in the music industry. I really didn't want to have anything to do with them. And I figured by the time I talked for an hour or two with this guy, that he wouldn't want anything to do with me either. And that would have been just fine with me.

But things didn't work out the way I had expected. This guy didn't come off as a shiny, sophisticated, I-know-it-all, briefcase-carrying president. This guy had some real gutsy, honest-sounding points to make.

He told me he didn't just walk into the presidency of Capitol Records. He started out loading trucks off the shipping dock of the company, and then, little by little over the years, job after job and promotion after promotion, he got to be where he was today.

He had been through every department of the company and, to top it all off, he had even played in some bands as a drummer. (Heavy credentials!)

But, okay, thanks a lot. Now, what can we do for each other?

After telling me that he'd been a long-time Stompin' Tom fan, and that he thought I was doing an injustice not only to myself, but also to the rest of the people of the country by staying away, he said I should make a comeback. And he wanted Capitol Records to re-release and distribute my entire catalogue. (The price could be negotiated later.)

"This is a great offer on your part," I said. "But I don't think you're being at all realistic. What you're proposing is going to cost a great deal of money. And as a businessman, I assume you know how you are not only going to get this money back, but also know how you can realize a reasonable and fair profit.

"Now, at the risk of losing this great offer," I told him, "there is something you're going to have to understand. If you're counting on radio to play Stompin' Tom, you'd better forget you ever met me. They don't play me now, they never have, and unless some miracle happens, they never will. In my own judgment I consider myself to be a proud Canadian, but in their judgment, they consider me to be an asshole. And while it is true that I am capable of selling a lot of records without radio, don't count radio into your business equation."

"Tom," he said to me, "that's where you're wrong. A great deal has happened in the music industry since you left the scene. And radio has since come on side. They are now playing more Canadians than they ever played before."

"What kind of Canadians?" I asked. "The kind of Canadians that sound more American than the Americans do?"

After bantering this one around for a while, he really hit me with a statement that told me this conversation was quickly coming to a close. And this deal, as expected, was going to wind up as a deal of "nought."

"Tom," he says, "don't you realize that Capitol Records is a hell of a lot bigger than Boot Records ever was? And don't you know that because of it, the music we put out is naturally perceived by radio to be of a higher and more eminent quality?"

As I took this as a given, though somewhat reluctantly, I just said, "And?"

He then proceeded to "encourage" me further by telling me that a long-time radio friend of his had recently been transferred from a station in Calgary to the local country music station in Toronto. And if anybody in this country would play Stompin' Tom music, without a doubt, it would be him.

"And what is his name?" I asked.

Upon hearing the guy's name, I laughed out loud.

"You can't really be serious," I said. "Do you know that just last year this same guy, as a program director, raked a DJ over the coals, and for all I know, had him fired from a Calgary radio station for even allowing a Stompin' Tom song that was being picked up from the satellite to be partially aired from their radio transmitter? Do you know that because of this action, the radio station had two minutes of dead air, which is a 'no-no' in the business? And do you know that when my lawyer checked all this out, he was told by the station's head office that this man was dismissed for his actions? And you're going to tell me that because he's now in Toronto, he's going to be a nice guy and play Stompin' Tom records? You must be out of your mind."

I must say that at this moment I had to give Dean Cameron a hell of a lot of credit for not just throwing up his hands and saying, "It's been nice knowin' ya." But instead, with a great deal of poise, he said, "I wasn't aware of these things, Tom. But the deal is still on. And apart from your experiences with radio, if you decide to come with us, we'll at least do everything we can to change things for the better." He then gave me his card and a very private number that I could use to get hold of him if I should decide to come with Capitol Records.

During the months of February and March '89 there was beginning to be a lot of dissension in the 45 Club. Some people who didn't want to live up to its constitution were encouraging others to do the same, and as a result, the whole thing was beginning to fall apart. One chapter had broken away altogether to follow their own devices. So by April 4 of that year, I resigned as president and yes, as a member.

Cliff Evans, by now, was also becoming disenchanted with running ACT Records, and with no one on the horizon I thought immediately capable of taking over, I began to think more and more about the offer made by Dean Cameron.

On one of my days when it looked like nothing was working out right, I decided to give Dean a call. He was glad to hear from me, and after he assured me that he still wanted to handle my catalogue, I told him to send me out a contract so I could take a look at it.

After reading it and making some changes, I sent it back. They made some changes to my changes. And after it was sent back and forth several times, we found ourselves with a mutual agreement we felt we both could sign.

Our ACT Records distribution agreement with Holborne had run out by now, so I didn't bother renewing it. I just notified Holborne that ACT was no longer in business, and I would go down and pick up all the remaining unsold stock they had in their warehouse. It took another while before we finally settled up, but that's another story.

On June 1, 1989, I officially signed on with Capitol Records (EMI of Canada Ltd.). The negotiators and signers of the document were Dean Cameron, president; Trish Harris, vice-president; and, of course, yours truly.

And so began another era in the very up and down career of Stompin' Tom.

A day or so later, Lena and I were invited down to Capitol to meet everybody who would be working on the Stompin' Tom product. And because Henry McGuirk had done the cover story on me in *Country Music News*, I made sure he would be there to take pictures and get the first scoop on this unique milestone of my career.

Some of the people we met that day besides Dean Cameron and Trish Harris were Tim Trombley, Jody Michell, Eddie Colero, Steve McAuley, Peter Diemer, Al

Andruchow, Ron Scott, Olie Kornelson, Marianne Girard, Claude Prieur and Dana Goudie. Oops! Did I say Dana Goudie? (She used to work for us at Boot Records for a few years before going to Capitol. It was good to see her again.) We also met Dean's and Trish's secretaries, May Darmetko and Mary Ellen Gavin. We were also introduced to a number of other very nice people with whom I wouldn't be having a lot of contact, and therefore some of their names have since slipped my mind. (I hope I don't catch hell for this.)

One of the last duties performed for me by Cliff Evans before he signed off from ACT Records was to be my go-between for negotiating the contract with Sandra Faire, who was the producer of a CBC television special on k.d. lang. They wanted me to do a guest appearance on the show, along with Dwight Yoakam. (I had agreed to make this first public appearance in almost thirteen years because of my recent signing with Capitol. As I knew I wouldn't get any radio airplay, I figured this national TV appearance would help them to boost the sales of my records.)

The k.d. lang special was filmed in Red Deer, Alberta. Lena and I flew out on the thirteenth of June. We were treated exceptionally well, and along with meeting k.d., we also got to meet her mother and her little sister, from Consort.

Another big surprise we got in our hotel room was when my old steel guitar player, Billy Jones, walked in with a friend of his. We naturally had a few beers and chatted about old times away on into the night. With the filming completed, we flew back to Ontario on June 16.

Also in June of that year, Capitol Records celebrated their fortieth anniversary by having a huge outdoor picnic which Lena and I and Tommy attended. They had a stage set up where a number of their current artists took turns to give a short performance. Among those were Glass Tiger, Murray McLauchlan, and myself, doing a single.

After the picnic, Lena and I and Tommy again packed up our trailer and headed for the east coast.

Planning "the Comeback"

WILLARD AND MARLENE WERE NOW living in Millville, New Brunswick, and running a show cattle farm for an old fellow who spent most of his time down in the States living with his relatives. Their son Robbie was looking after their own cattle farm in Nail Pond, P.E.I.

After seeing Willard and Marlene in Millville, and our friends the Chapmans and Harpers in Annagance, we went to see Lena's sister, Pauline, the new Mrs. Bill Hawes, at their home in Miscouche, P.E.I.

As we were on our way to the Magdalene Islands by ferry, Pauline wanted to come. So a couple of days later we were in Souris, P.E.I., in the line-up waiting to get our van on the boat. (I had previously made arrangements to leave our trailer in one of the nearby motel parking lots.)

We were quite a ways back in the ferry line-up and the word came that I wouldn't be able to get my van on the boat today, but would have to wait until tomorrow.

As I knew the people in the Mags were going to be waiting for us to get off the ferry that evening, I told Lena, Pauline and Tommy to go on the boat as foot passengers and I would wait with the van to catch the next crossing the following day.

That night I parked my van beside my trailer in the motel parking lot, went into my trailer to have a beer or two, read the paper, and planned to go to bed early for a change.

Around 9 or 10 P.M. I heard a commotion outside my trailer and looked out to see a bunch of musicians arriving. Upon stepping out to see who they were, I found they were the group playing for Rita MacNeil, who was doing a concert in Souris the following night.

Although Rita had recorded her first album for me on the Boot label, I had never met her, and I thought this would be a good opportunity. Unfortunately, I was told that Rita had arrived about an hour before, and because she had been very tired, she had already gone to bed.

As I had a bottle of beer in my hand, and a couple of the boys looked very thirsty, I invited them into my trailer to have a jar. After polishing off the best part of a 24, we all decided to turn in. And on the next day I caught the *Lucy Maude Montgomery* ferry and sailed off for the Mags.

When I finally sailed into Grindstone, Lena's brother Ted was waiting for me. The fishing boat that was supposed to pick us up and take us to Entry Island would not arrive yet for another few hours, so we headed for one of the local bars.

After having a couple of beers, we got talking about music and I decided to go out to the van to get my guitar and sing a few songs.

Although everyone there, except Ted and me, was French, they enjoyed the music. Then after about an hour or so, we bid them all farewell, and headed down to where we had to meet the fishing boat. About an hour or so later we arrived on Entry Island and finished off the party we started in the Grindstone bar.

I had taken my fiddle with me this time, and a few of the boys on Entry who played had to of course try it out. (I had written a couple of my own fiddle tunes by this time, and had included them on the *Fiddle and Song* album. I'm surely no Graham Townsend on the fiddle but at least the tunes were acceptable.)

I didn't stay on Entry as long as Lena and Tommy did. I was only there for about three or four days and then went back to Souris, P.E.I., to pick up my trailer.

From there I drove up to Nail Pond to see Willard's son Robbie and find out how he was making out. His sister Gwen was the only one home, so after saying hi and talking for a few minutes, I left and went to Summerside. There I stopped in to see my friend Ray Goguen, who was going to a party that night, so I just tagged along. We played some guitar and fiddle and sang a few songs, and after getting some canned fish from him the next day, I took off for Saint John, New Brunswick.

Here I visited my two old hitch-hiking buddies Gerry Marks and Stevedore Steve Foote. I even got to see my old friend Gerry Cormier, the guy who showed me the first two chords on the guitar. And I also got to see my cousin, Ned Landry. (See *Before the Fame.*)

While visiting Stevedore Steve and his wife, Gini, I came to find out they had fallen on some really hard times. Steve had sold his guitar a year or two before and told me he would really like to start up again in the music business. He had a lot of offers, but without a guitar and no money to buy one, he was unable to take on the jobs.

He told me he had his eye on an excellent guitar but it had a price tag on it of over $2,400 and was therefore away out of his reach.

I didn't say too much then, but that night when I went back to where my trailer was parked, at Lily Lake, I wrote out a cheque for $2,500. And the next day I gave it to him. Not as a mere loan, but as a gift. (I later found out he bought a guitar for around $1,000, but as he and Gini were in straits at the time, I didn't begrudge his spending the rest of the money on other necessities.)

From Saint John, I pulled the trailer back as far as Annagance, unhooked at Reg and Muriel Chapmans', and the next day drove the van into Moncton to pick Lena and Tommy up at the airport.

After a two- or three-day visit in Annagance, we drove to Millville to see Willard and Marlene again, and then we headed back home to Ontario.

By now it was mid-August of 1989, and we no sooner got home when Capitol Records was on the phone wanting me to do a video. I had agreed to do one in my contract, and as there had been a freelance producer by the name of David Story who had previously contacted me wanting to do a Stompin' Tom documentary film, I submitted his name as a possible candidate to produce the video.

As it turned out, Capitol selected David to do the video. And while the negotiations and preparations were going on, Dean Cameron was asking me if I knew of an appropriate place where he and the company could hold a Stompin' Tom "comeback" party. A place where we could launch the release of the new album *Fiddle and Song*, and a place where the decor was just right to suit the Stompin' Tom image.

I immediately thought of Ann Dunn's Matador Club in Toronto, and when Dean sent someone down to make contact with Ann and take a look at the place, they felt it was just perfect.

So on Thursday, October 19, 1989, the official Stompin' Tom "comeback" party took place at the Matador Club. And what a party it was.

I was able to get my old lead player, Ronnie Richard, and my bass player, Gary Empey, to bring their "axes," and when we got up onstage to perform, it was just like old times. This would be my first live public performance on a stage in thirteen years, from 1976 to 1989.

My demographics hadn't changed much. There were just as many young people as there were older ones. The only thing different was the way the younger people were now dressed. The styles had changed but the audience was just as enthusiastic as before.

Gaet Lepine, my old bartender friend from Timmins, was there with his wife, Jean, along with Dave and Pat Newlands and a few of our other friends. Capitol Records had been considerate enough to provide a couple of stretch limousines which took us all to and from the party.

When me and my guys weren't on the stage, a lot of speeches were being made, including one by Dean Cameron, who said some nice things about me as he welcomed me "into the fold."

Between all this a few members from other bands got on the stage and did a little jammin'. One of these groups was Dave Bidini and the Rheostatics. (You'll remember Dave as being the journalist who crashed my fiftieth birthday party.)

That night I met a lot of the newer people who had entered the music industry since I'd been away, and they seemed to have a more pro-Canadian attitude than those of the previous decade. I took this as being a very positive sign of the times.

There was one group of people, though, who were very conspicuous by the fact that not one of their representatives was there. The people from radio. Capitol had released my first single to radio in fourteen years, entitled "I Am the Wind," which was also going to be the song featured on my upcoming video. But radio again just ignored it. And the message to Capitol Records and everyone else was clear. They're just not going to play Stompin' Tom no matter what song he sings or what company puts it out.

Now, that's what I call real determination. Or should I call it blatant discrimination? Here is an artist who obviously fits within their Canadian content guidelines, and radio says they can't find enough Canadian talent to fulfil their 30 per cent content obligations and that's why they want them reduced. Strange!

Here is an artist that one of the largest major record companies in the world has decided they like so much that they're going to spend a pile of money on him, not only to put out one record but to release his entire catalogue (at that time fifteen albums, with at least 50 per cent of each being "distinctively and identifiably Canadian,"way more than any other artist). But radio says, "Stompin' Tom doesn't fit our Canadian content format." Strange?

And finally, here is an artist whose popularity throughout Canada hasn't waned one bit, even after being out of circulation for more than a dozen years without an ounce of airplay on the commercial stations. And radio says, "He's not well enough known, and far too 'regional' to play on the air."

Well, all I know is that if a radio station in Alabama wouldn't play an artist from Tennessee because he sang a song about Texas, the American people would burn the station down. They wouldn't put up with the kinds of answers given above for five minutes. And why would that be so strange?

Among other people I met at the party that night was a young man from Peterborough, Ontario, by the name of Brian Edwards. Brian was there with his girlfriend Barb. And once we were introduced I recognized him as the same fellow who had written me a couple of letters stating that he was running a talent management agency and if I ever decided that I again wanted to do some concert work, he would like to be the one to do the bookings and handle the tour. He said he had always been a fan of mine ever since his dad had bought his first Stompin' Tom record.

After introducing Brian and Barb to Lena and Gaet and the rest of my friends, we talked some more while we had lunch. I told him that I wasn't sure yet, but now that I was with Capitol the possibility of a Stompin' Tom tour would be a lot more likely, and I would certainly consider him for the job if and when the time came.

The party must have lasted till about three in the morning, and after signing the board I had stomped on for Ann Dunn to hang on her wall, we jumped in the limos and left for home.

Sometime in November Jim Baines from *Country* magazine came to pay me a visit. We had a long talk which resulted in a cover story and I think it came out in the December 1989 or the January 1990 issue. He said he was also writing a play about Stompin' Tom, but I guess he just never got around to finishing it. He later printed an article I wrote, however, in the same magazine, called "Passport Patriots," in which I expressed my disappointment with artists who leave the Canadian musical community and return for only one day a year to accept a Juno Award that might have otherwise gone to a Canadian who was making Canada the base from which he conducted all his musical business.

I also wrote a few songs at this time. And when Gaet Lepine came down to spend Christmas and New Year's at our house, we talked about writing some new songs together. But because I pretty well had all the songs I needed for the time being, I told him to wait for the next album. Besides, I had already promised my friend Art Hawes that I would record a couple of songs on this forthcoming album that he and I had written together. Gaet understood this perfectly well. And the time did come eventually when we teamed up to co-write over a dozen songs.

Along about February of 1990, I began to seriously

consider going back on the road to do another cross-Canada tour. Nineteen seventy-six had been the last one, and that was over thirteen years ago. Was I really capable of doing such a tour? I wondered. Here I was fifty-four years old on February 9, and maybe I was over the hill and not up to the strenuous pace anymore.

Still, I figured, because the chances of radio playing my records for the public were next to zilch, the only way I could help Capitol Records to realize a profit on their investment was to get out and sing these songs to the public myself.

The more I thought about it, the more I decided to do it.

Then one day when Art Hawes was telling me that the plant where he worked would be shutting down its Canadian operations and moving to the States, leaving him and a number of others jobless, I decided to take him into my confidence.

First I told him that I was planning to do an extensive tour all across Canada the following summer. I still had a list of all the contacts from previous tours. And although some of these people might not be in the same business anymore, they could steer us to the people who were, if and when needed.

I knew that Art was pretty good with figures, as he had demonstrated on previous occasions, so I told him that in the event of such a tour, I would make him my road manager. This would entail looking after all my personal business while we were on the road.

While he expressed a great deal of interest in all of this, I told him that first we would have to consider which tour-booking agent we would get.

I thought of Brian Edwards and a couple more guys who had written me letters, but I knew they were quite small and might have trouble booking a national tour. So the first thing Art and I did was to make an appointment with a couple of big agencies in downtown Toronto.

After several meetings with these people we found out that, first, they didn't know what in hell we were even talking about. Secondly, when it was explained, they said they didn't book any more than about fifteen cities across Canada. Thirdly, they'd never heard of a Canadian performer, at least living within this country, who could do a coast-to-coast tour which took in our proposed seventy-five to eighty venues.(They all, of course, wanted to know where they were, but we had the list tucked neatly away in our pockets. This was in the event that had we not been able to find an agent that could book us, we were prepared to do the job ourselves.)

And finally, there wasn't one of them who could understand why anyone who wasn't receiving any airplay on radio would be so foolhardy as to undertake a cross-Canada tour in the first place.

Well, so much for the faith our largest talent-booking agencies had in Canadians at the time. And this was nearly fourteen years after I had proven it could be done a multitude of times.

This didn't do a hell of a lot for Art's confidence in the project either. But then that was understandable. Art had never had any experience with this kind of thing before. But little did he know that before I was through, he would have a lot more experience in this business than anybody we had talked to thus far.

After three or four days of this negative bullshit, and before finally deciding to hire the help necessary to do the job ourselves, I thought again of some of the little guys who had written me. First of all Brian Edwards.

I'll never forget the first night Brian drove from Peterborough to have a meeting at my place. And for that matter I won't forget the next two or three, either.

When he showed up with his briefcase, I directed him into my old workshop where Art and I were having a beer. I pointed to an old kitchen chair that I was fixing and told him to have a seat.

After he neatly parked his briefcase down beside him, I asked him if he wanted a beer.

As he quickly took a look around to view the axes, hammers, saws, wrenches and all the other pieces of junk around the work bench, he said, "No, I'll just pass for now and maybe have one later."

As I looked over at Art, who always wore a beard and a crooked cowboy hat, I said, "This is Art, and Art, this is

Brian." And after they acknowledged each other, I plunked myself down on an old wired-up chrome stool, and we began to talk.

Without beating around the bush, I came right to the point. "Art here is going to be my road manager," I said, as I pointed to Art, who just nodded his head in acknowledgement. "We're going to do a tour of about eighty cities and towns throughout all ten provinces, from coast to coast in Canada. And if we have the time, we'll try to do some in the Yukon and the Northwest Territories. We won't be flying anywhere, we'll just drive all the way."

Pausing here for a drink of beer and a puff of my cigarette, I again looked at Brian and continued. "Now, your job for this tour will be to book all these venues as well as the motel rooms along the way, and make sure all the TV, radio and newspaper ads are taken out at the right times to correspond with the dates of the shows." Pausing for another drink of beer, I asked, "Is there any questions at this time, or shall I proceed?"

It was here that Brian reached down to open his briefcase. And instead of pulling out the expected bunch of papers, he hauled out a bottle of Tylenols. After poppin' two or three, he gulped a couple of times, and asked me if I had a drink of water.

Quickly snappin' a cap, I passed him a beer and said, "Here, take one of these, and you won't have to take any more of those."

After taking a swig, he still wanted a drink of water, so I directed him to the nearby bathroom where a clean glass was waiting near the sink. When he finally came out with the glass in his hand, he popped another Tylenol and started pacing the floor of the workshop.

"What's the matter?" I said. "You got a headache?"

"I think so," he said, "but I'm not sure yet. It's just comin' on."

"Well, what do you think so far?" I asked, as I snapped another couple of caps for me and Art. "After all, you're the talent agent."

Still pacing the floor as if he was trying to think of something, he said, "Yeah, I know. But you just can't go into these things too fast. There's a whole lot of things that have to be considered, you know."

"Well, for a guy who wrote me several letters wanting to book me, you don't seem to be very enthusiastic now about doing so," I said.

Still pacing the floor, this called for a couple more Tylenols. Now he was pacing much faster.

As Art just sat there in his usual noncommittal way, I looked at Brian and then back at Art, rather questioningly. But all I got was a shrug of the shoulders.

Finally the pacing stopped for a moment. "Well, Tom," he said, "I'm gonna be straight with you. I had no idea in God's earth that you would be planning a tour this big. This is entirely away over my head. In the first place, I don't have the kind of contacts that would enable me to book all the places you're talking about. And in the second place there's no way I can scrounge up the money it would take as a lay-out to even begin promoting this kind of a tour, never mind handling all the other things you're talking about. Are you sure you're really serious about all this?"

With his hand on his chin, he resumed his pacing.

"I wouldn't have called you all the way down here if I wasn't serious," I said, "and I have no intention of wasting your time or mine. The tour I'm proposing is going to happen whether you're involved or not. If I have to book the goddamn thing by myself, I will. I didn't start out by asking you how much money you had. I merely told you what was going to happen. Now, if you're ready and willing to work with us, we're planning a national Canadian tour, and the minor details we can work out later. Now, speaking of contacts, here's five or six pages of them. I've worked all these venues before and drew large crowds. And next to them, you'll see the radio and newspaper contacts along with some of the motels. Now, you go home and count your money and see how much you can put up towards doing this venture, and then come back and let me know. I'll then figure out how to finance the rest."

After another Tylenol or two, he said he'd be back to see me in a couple of days. He then stopped pacing, picked up his briefcase and headed for the door.

As he was leaving, I said, "Good night, Headache— I mean, Brian." He just looked at me, smiled a little bit and left.

When I went back in the workshop to have another beer with Art, I asked him what he thought of "Headache." (I must have called him Headache Edwards for almost a year after that. It was not until our very successful Tour '90 was over that he finally relaxed and stopped poppin' the Tylenols. But I swear you can still see the path on the floor of my workshop that was worn out by the constant pacing of Headache Edwards.)

Art said he thought that maybe the guy was too much the nervous type to handle the kind of operation I was talking about, and therefore we should maybe make contact with a couple more of these smaller agents I had gotten letters from. And if they didn't work out, we'd better think of doing the project by ourselves.

I told him I knew exactly what he meant, but there was just something about ol' Headache that I liked. He seemed to be honest, even though he was understandably troubled about taking on something he wasn't sure he could handle. So for the next couple of days we just decided to wait and see what would happen.

In the meantime, as I had a few doubts as to whether Brian might be able to handle everything, I called Henry McGuirk and asked him if he would be interested in going on the road ahead of the tour to make sure all the publicity was in order well in advance of each concert date. For a week or two he seemed quite interested, but then one night, without any apparent reason, he lost interest and turned the offer down.

Brian came to the house a couple more times, and after more pacing and I'm not sure how many Tylenols (I lost count), it looked like ol' Headache was really going to come through.

We agreed on how the financing was all going to be done, and by the time he added my list of contacts to his own, it looked like the so-called impossible eighty-date tour was not only possible, but every phone call that Brian had made had brought nothing but a response of total enthusiasm.

It got so after a while that every time I talked to Brian on the phone, he was more elated than the last time.

So by the first of March, with the tour bookings under way, I decided it was high time to get a band together.

First I called Gary Empey and Ronnie Richard. They both told me they couldn't come because they now had good jobs they didn't want to leave. Next I called a few other musicians I knew, but the results were the same. Then I happened to call my old steel-player friend, Mickey Andrews, who had played with me many years ago at the Horseshoe Tavern.

Back in those days I had asked Mickey if he wanted to come on the road and play steel for me, but he had several times refused. So I didn't have any expectations that he might want to come with me now. But I thought I'd call him anyway, and maybe he could put me on to somebody.

Mickey surprised me by telling me he would like to go, but because he was playing in a band, he wouldn't go unless I took the band also.

I told him to bring the band out to my place so I could meet them and hear what they had to offer. I would then decide whether to take them all or to continue looking for someone else.

Upon their arrival at the house, Mickey introduced me to Ray Keating, who played rhythm guitar and sang, and Mary MacIntyre, who played keyboards and also sang. (There was a drummer as well, but I can't remember his name. Sorry. But as it turned out, he wouldn't become part of the tour anyway.)

After auditioning the band and finding out that Mary was also able to play some nice bass on the keyboards, I hired them, and we immediately set up some practice dates. My intention was to also use them to help in the recording of my forthcoming album.

During the first couple of weeks of April 1990, after the required rehearsals, we all went out to Brian Hewson's Escarpment Sound Studios in Acton, Ontario, and recorded the album entitled *More of the Stompin' Tom Phenomenon*.

This album contained my tribute song to Rita MacNeil, my song about a guy sitting on a stool in "J.R.'s Bar" (Johnny

Reid's Prince Edward Lounge in Charlottetown), "No Canadian Dream," about how radio plays no distinctively Canadian songs, and "Margo's Cargo," the song about the Newfie couple who bought a clock made out of nothing but cow dung. These are just a few of the fourteen songs on this, my sixteenth album of all originals.

Along about this time, I had received a letter and a tape from an old acquaintance of mine, Tom Gallant, who was now living in Nova Scotia. He was writing some songs and wanted to know if I might be interested in singing one or two. As I liked what he was doing, I invited him to come on the tour with me. And instead of me singing the songs he wrote, he could sing them himself.

This he readily agreed to do. And while we talked on the phone about all of this, he mentioned that he was acquainted with a young fellow who was a very versatile musician, able to play fiddle, mandolin, banjo, lead guitar and other instruments, and very good at them all.

This sounded like a guy who would be an asset to any country band, so I told Tom that when he came up to Ontario he should bring the young fellow with him.

They arrived just while I was mixing the *Phenomenon* album. And after hearing this young fellow, I immediately brought him into the studio to lay down a couple of fiddle tracks behind one or two of my songs.

This young fellow, who was no more than twenty years old at the time, was none other than the "Awesome" J.P. Cormier. The kid who could switch from playing lead, fiddle, banjo, mandolin or waffle-board in the same song without missing a note. (While eating a hamburger.)

Stompin' Tom Returns

Tour '90 officially started on May 3, in a high school auditorium in Owen Sound, Ontario. Although it was packed, it only seated about eight hundred. This would be the second-smallest venue we would play throughout the whole tour. A small venue was chosen on purpose, so I could get used to playing to a crowd after not doing so for fourteen years. (If the truth could ever be known, "like the fella said," "B'y, I was nearly shittin' me drawers.")

After playing Wingham the following night, and having one of the greatest feeds of fish and chips that any of us ever had, which was cooked up after the show by a Mrs. Jamieson who owned a local restaurant, we headed out for Sudbury. This was the gig that would prove, one way or another, whether this tour was going to be a success.

My son Tommy was just about to turn fourteen years old. And up until now he really didn't know what the "Stompin' Tom" thing was all about. All he knew was that, because his old man was called Stompin' Tom, the kids he went to school with would often mock him in the corridors and outside the building by stomping their feet in front of him and calling him names. This, of course, wasn't too easy for a child to take. He would often ask himself why he alone, among so many other kids, had to be born as the son of a dad who was known everywhere as Stompin' Tom. He didn't understand why, through no fault of his own, he would have

494

to be labelled for the rest of his life as "just that kid whose father wouldn't know how to make an honourable living if he wasn't making a spectacle of himself, by the mere pounding of his foot on a piece of plywood."

But tonight, at long last, this was all going to change. Tommy was about to take in his first Stompin' Tom concert. He and his mom were sitting in the middle about ten rows back, and when I entered the stage to a standing ovation he didn't know what to think.

The people remained standing while I sang "Sudbury Saturday Night" and about thirty young people, just a bit older than Tommy, paraded up and down the aisles and across in front of the stage a couple of times carrying a huge Canadian flag.

The flag was made out of two or three bed sheets sewn together and whoever drew the large maple leaf was quite the artist.

Pretty soon another group came marching and bearing another huge banner which read "Stompin' Tom for Prime Minister." There seemed to be no end to the enthusiasm of these young people and poor Tommy didn't know what to make of it all. He was bewildered. Was that really his dad up there who had all these people leaning on every word instead of poking fun? He was now seeing his dad in a new light. Someone he could feel proud of instead of ashamed of.

The backdrop for the stage was itself the largest maple leaf flag we could buy anywhere, and we spread it out behind us everywhere we went.

Television cameras from different networks were moving about before and after the show and everyone was looking for an interview. Newspaper people from as far away as Toronto wanted to do an article on the Stompin' Tom "Return." The *Sudbury Star* dedicated four full pages of their paper to the "comeback." These pages were printed on the fourth and fifth of May 1990. As well as a huge write-up and interview done by John Farrington, the pages also included a contest whereby people were asked to write another verse to "Sudbury Saturday Night." The winners would receive an assortment of Stompin' Tom T-shirts, pictures, cassettes and albums.

Again, the representatives from radio were conspicuously missing.

Lena and Tommy had driven up to Sudbury with Dave and Pat Newlands, a couple of good friends of ours. All four stayed overnight and went back home the next day, while the crew and I continued on to Sault Ste. Marie, Thunder Bay and all points west.

In Sault Ste. Marie, Don Ramsay came out to the show and we had a good talk in the dressing room after the show. Don was one guy in radio who never had any qualms about playing Stompin' Tom. (One of the rare ones. And for this I was always grateful.)

The "Soo" was the fourth packed show of the tour and by now I had gained back some of the old confidence I might have lost after being away for so long. All the crowds seemed to be more like a welcoming committee of old friends than just a plain audience. And the autograph lines were quite lengthy.

After Brandon and Regina, we played Saskatoon. It was here that I met David Orchard for the first time. David was the head of an organization known as Citizens Concerned About Free Trade (CCAFT) and was well versed in all the arguments, pro and con, about the Free Trade Agreement being proposed by the Mulroney government at the time. Although David was only a Saskatchewan farmer, he certainly knew his beans about Canadian political history and I enjoyed the couple of hours we were able to spend discussing it.

The reader may also remember how some eight years later, David Orchard ran against Joe Clark for the leadership of the Conservative Party. Joe of course won that one, but David certainly showed himself as being a great debater and a worthy opponent even though he wasn't nearly as well known. David also has a great book out called *The Fight for Canada* (Stoddart) that I personally feel should be read by every Canadian.

We then played Calgary, Alberta, and Trail and Penticton, B.C. (where I called my old friend Wiz Bryant up on stage to do a couple of numbers in front of his hometown fans. We later had dinner together).

I believe Tom Gallant was the only member of this tour who had ever been out west before. All the rest were in awe of the prairie provinces and the beautiful mountains of British Columbia.

The names of everyone on Tour '90 once again were (and I hope I don't forget anybody) Tom Gallant and J.P. Cormier, both from Nova Scotia; Ray Keating, from Ontario; Mickey Andrews and Mary MacIntyre, also from Nova Scotia. These were members of the band The Merry-Mick-Ray.

Our lighting and sound guys were Alex Golota and Andy White, both from Ontario. Brian Edwards booked this huge tour (and was not now having nearly as many headaches). Brian's sister Ella Page and her friend, Fern, both sold T-shirts, records, etc., at the concession stand. (Ella also looked after other things, such as hotel-room arrangements.) They were all from Peterborough, Ontario.

Art Hawes, who lived close to me in Ontario, was my personal road manager and assistant. And among the "extras" who joined us for brief periods on the tour were Duncan Fremlin, from the band Whiskey Jack in Ontario; Darren Walters, from the band The Walters Family in Ontario; and a security man named Jerry, who was with us for two or three shows. (My son Tommy also worked with us for a couple of months during his summer vacation from school.)

By May 28, 1990, we were in Vancouver, where a short break of about four days had been planned for everybody. This enabled Lena and a couple of the other guys' wives to fly out and pay us a visit. We took them up the lift to Grouse Mountain for dinner one evening and went for a nice boat cruise one afternoon. The weather was excellent and we had a great time. After taking in the Vancouver show, the wives flew home again and we proceeded on to Nanaimo and Victoria, on Vancouver Island.

Back on the mainland again, we played Kamloops and Prince George, B.C., and then Edmonton, Red Deer, Lethbridge and Medicine Hat, Alberta.

In Manitoba once again, we did Flin Flon and Winnipeg before re-entering Ontario to play Dryden, Barrie, Timmins, Englehart and North Bay.

On July 1, Canada Day, 1990, we were playing in

Hamilton. This is where Tommy and Lena joined the tour
and remained until August 30.

In Tillsonburg (my back still aches when I hear that
word) I was given a nice plaque for writing the song and
"putting the town on the musical map," which I thought was
very nice of them. It was presented by Matt Scholtz, the sec-
retary/treasurer of the Chamber of Commerce.

About 60 per cent of the audience were young people
waving flags and singing right along to the words of the
song. Among the older people I even met a couple of guys I
primed tobacco with many years previously.

After Welland, Belleville, Coldwater, Petawawa, Huntsville, Watford and London came Leamington. This was the
ketchup song town and also the home of Tim Trombley, one
of the vice-presidents and the A&R man for Capitol Records
EMI. It just so happened that Tim was home on vacation at
the time and he brought a lot of his friends and relatives out
to the show. Although Leamington is not that large a town,
the venue was packed and Tim was able to get a restaurant
owner whom he knew to stay open after hours so the crew
and I could have something to eat. (This is not always an
option when you're on tour.)

The next town was Kitchener, where we played the very
famous night club known as Lulu's, which had the longest
bar in the world. We packed it out that night, breaking all
previous records. And that included some very big name
acts from the States. One of the guys from the radio station
CKGL was also there that night as a witness to the scene. His
name was Randy Owen, and he said he played my records
occasionally. (Kudos for another radio rarity.)

On the weekend of August 4 we played the Gatineau
Clog, which took place about thirty miles north of Ottawa in
the province of Quebec. Other artists featured on the same
show that weekend were Loretta Lynn, Ray Price, Porter
Wagoner and Wayne Rostad.

During the next long drive to Summerside, P.E.I., one of
our stopovers was at a motel in Magnetic Hill, New
Brunswick. It was here that Tom Gallant and I had a pretty
serious disagreement concerning the tour. We held a long
meeting in the boardroom of the motel at which everyone

was present. As nothing could be resolved at this meeting, I invited Tom over to my room in a last-ditch effort to try and see if we could reach a private agreement. I waited for Tom to show up, but he decided against it, and the following day we split company. The trouble was, he also took J.P. Cormier with him.

It seems that because J.P. had joined the tour with Tom Gallant, he felt his allegiance should remain with Tom instead of with me and the tour, so they left together. The Merry-Mick-Ray and I continued on alone.

After Summerside and Charlottetown, we sailed to the Magdalene Islands and played a show for the first time in Grindstone. This was the smallest venue of Tour '90. And although we lost our shirts on this one, I felt I just had to play this gig for Lena and the people from Entry Island who had often asked me to do a show somewhere in the Mags so that they would be able to attend.

From here we went to Halifax and Sydney, in Nova Scotia, and then on to Newfoundland, where we played St. John's, Grand Falls, Corner Brook and Stephenville. I did get to see my old pal "Lucky" Jim Frost again. In Stephenville, Lena and Tommy had to fly back to Ontario, as Tommy would have to go back to school in a few days.

In the next day or so we took the ferry back to Cape Breton Island, Nova Scotia. And on the mainland we played Antigonish and Kentville before arriving in Bridgewater, where I received a writ informing me that Tom Gallant was suing me for wrongful dismissal from the tour. (A number of months later, I was prepared to fight the claims in court but the whole thing was mysteriously dropped. J.P. Cormier had not taken part in any of this.)

Digby and Truro were next in Nova Scotia and then Sackville and Saint John, New Brunswick. It was here that I had Stevedore Steve come up on stage and sing two or three songs. I was surprised he didn't have the guitar I had given him the money to buy, but nonetheless, I invited him to come on the rest of the tour with me. He remained through Fredericton and Bathurst and then decided to go back home to Saint John.

Campbellton was the last town we played in New

Brunswick before going on to Lennoxville and Montreal.
With only nine more shows to do in Ontario, Tour '90 was
beginning to wind down. Cornwall and Kingston would be
first and then on to Brian's home town of Peterborough.

Once again the flags and banners came out as if the
prodigal had returned. This, after all, was the town where I
was first named Stompin' Tom, and all my old friends
weren't going to let me forget it.

You could even hear Stompin' Tom records on the radio
in this town. Especially when "Sunshine" Sean Eyre was at
the station. Sean was not only a very popular DJ in the area,
but also somewhat of a local celebrity whose presence was
required at every function and fund-raiser. It was Sean that
Brian got to help promote the show and he even got me up
to the station for an interview.

My guests on the show that night of October 13 were
Kent Brockwell and "Washboard" Hank Fisher, both popular
entertainers in the area. And both helped to make the show
a tremendous success. A huge party was held after the show
in the large boardroom of the building. It was here that
Hank and Kent entertained us all once more.

Rubbing shoulders with Brian a couple of times, I
noticed he was smiling from ear to ear. "How's the
headache?" I asked him. "What headache?" he replied.
"I haven't had one of them for a week now."

The next three towns were Ottawa, Brockville and
Oshawa. And then we played the Molson Park in Barrie at
the Mariposa Folk Festival. Unfortunately, this turned out to
be a nasty cold and rainy day. And while lots of people
turned out for the concert, they either had to hide under
tarps and blankets or just get up off the cold ground and
leave. The date was October 22, and when you leave it that
late in the year to hold an outside show you can never really
know what to expect, weather-wise.

The last two concerts of Tour '90 were held on the
twenty-fourth and twenty-fifth of October, at Massey Hall
in Toronto.

The place was packed both nights and the young people
once again paraded around with the huge maple leaf flags.

The grand finale of the last show of the tour was when

Brian Edwards got up on the stage and auctioned off my autographed stompin' board. The bids were furious, and it finally went for $1,050. Proceeds went to Sick Kids Hospital. (Not bad for an old kicked-in piece of plywood.)

By this time Capitol Records EMI were trying to convince the major radio stations in the country to play Stompin' Tom. Although for some reason they were late getting the *Phenomenon* album on the market (it arrived after Tour '90 was over), I was singing songs from it all across the country. And especially "Margo's Cargo," which was proving to be very popular with my audiences. The people were asking for the record but we had none.

EMI, by now, had a single out to the stations of "Margo's Cargo" but it was getting thumbs down as usual. The excuse EMI was getting was that they couldn't play it "because Stompin' Tom was only known regionally in a few pockets of the country and was relatively unknown elsewhere. Especially in the major cities."

At this stage EMI paid to have a Canada-wide survey done throughout the major cities. Although I forget the name of the polling company that conducted the survey, it was the same one the Canadian government was using at the time, and considered to be highly reliable.

The survey was taken in every major city from Victoria, British Columbia, to St. John's, Newfoundland. The results were that three out of every four people in this country not only knew of Stompin' Tom, but knew what he did for a living, where he was from, and what he stood for. The results of the survey, which ran to approximately a hundred pages, proved that Stompin' Tom was one of the most well-known people in Canada.

Faced with this evidence, which contradicted their own beliefs, the radio people merely found other excuses to suit their purposes, and with the exception of a handful of stations, Stompin' Tom still went unplayed.

It was kind of comical, at the time, how one of the major country radio stations out of Hamilton, Ontario, which would never play Stompin' Tom, was running a song popularity contest among their listeners. It was suggested by EMI that, even though they refused to play Stompin' Tom, why not enter the single "Margo's Cargo" in the contest to see what happened.

Reluctantly, the station agreed, figuring it would shut EMI up about Stompin' Tom forever. But in the event that Stompin' Tom should win, defying all the odds, they agreed to play his record on "regular rotation."

The American Paul Overstreet had what was termed a huge hit at the time, and had been receiving all the listeners' votes in this song popularity contest. And immediately, when they entered "Margo's Cargo" at the bottom of the list, within twenty-four hours of it being heard, it zoomed from the bottom to the top, bumping Overstreet and many others completely off the list.

So what did the station do?

While "Margo's Cargo" refused to leave the top of the list, the contest was declared to be of little import or consequence, so it was soon discontinued. They played "Margo's Cargo" for a week or so after that on a very light rotation, and Stompin' Tom just quietly and subtly disappeared forever. (Just as if there wasn't even one more song worth playing on the whole sixteen albums I currently had on the market.) And what listeners don't hear, they don't request. And even if they did request something radio didn't want to play, they'd be given the run-around and told to request something else, anyway.

Have you ever heard this one? "Oh, yes. I really like that song, too. But because we don't have it, do you have a second choice?" And then they suggest a song they were already going to play anyway, making you think your request was granted. After hanging up the phone, have you ever felt you've been duped?

Awards, Tours and Videos

OUR CHRISTMAS HOLIDAYS THAT year, 1990, were spent enjoying a visit from Pauline and Bill Hawes, who flew up to Ontario from Prince Edward Island. Gaet and Jean Lepine were also with us, and Gaet and I wrote a couple of songs together.

By the time Bill and Pauline got home, they found that they had a buyer for the house they had up for sale in P.E.I., so they sold and moved to Halifax.

And in the meantime, Rob Cohn, the founder of the East Coast Music Awards, was wanting me to go down to Halifax to be there for this year's award presentations, which were to take place on February 17, 1991. I was nominated in four categories and it looked like I might be a winner in one or two. But to me, this presented an age-old problem. I had given my Juno Awards back a long time ago; I had refused to join ACME which was now the CCMA (or Canadian Country Music Association, which also presented awards every year), and when Rob and his people formed the East Coast Music Awards (ECMA) a few years previous, I told them I didn't want any part of it.

My reasons once more had been because they were planning to give radio people important positions among the executive. (The "fox in the hen house" scenario, as previously explained.)

I knew that Rob and his people meant well, but there

503

were none of them who had been in the position that I had been in all these years. As far as I was concerned, they were all as green as grass. Once again, another organization was going to let radio determine what was good music in this country and what was not. Radio would determine the rules of the game, and everybody else would have to play accordingly.

I tried to bow out of this as gracefully as I could. I knew I would have to "write a book," never mind make a number of phone calls and send out letters, to make these people and all others understand once and for all that an artist who is liked by the people receives his rewards from the people. And those who try to stand between what the people want and those who try to fulfil that want can only stand in the doorway so long. Inevitably, they'll have to be replaced.

This is no threat. It's the democratic way. Once people are informed about what's going on, they change things themselves. The key word here is "informed." And to the extent that people are not informed, they can be duped. And all I ask in this book is that people be totally informed about why radio prefers to play American music, foreign music, and the imitators thereof, instead of playing our own distinctive, identifiable, Atlantic, Pacific, northern and central good old-fashioned Canadian "hoopla." If that's what they want to call it. At least it's ours. And there's a hell of a lot of people in this country who would prefer to hear it, instead of being told, "It doesn't fit the format."

Back to Rob Cohn and the ECMA.

They were just nicely getting started and were hoping to get some TV coverage this year. I had just finished a tremendously successful Canadian comeback tour. I knew this would mean a lot in the way of enticing television to come on side. So I didn't say I wasn't going to be there. If TV didn't show up because of my absence, a lot of the other acts might not get the exposure they might have gotten otherwise.

So instead of turning down all nominations, I just sat on it, allowing things to happen as they may.

As it turned out, on February 17, I wasn't there. But it was announced that first I had won the ECMA Award for Country Artist of the Year, and then I had won Entertainer of the

Year. Lena's sister Pauline, who was now living in Halifax, had decided to attend, and she made the two trips to the podium to collect on my behalf.

Did I compromise my principles? And if I did, was it for a worthy enough cause? To me, at the time, it was a catch-22. I could be damned if I did, and damned if I didn't. So again, let the reader be the judge.

In March of 1991, Brian Edwards and I were planning another summer tour. Art Hawes was kind of dragging his feet a little because he didn't like the hours that road musicians had to keep. The more I insisted that, as my road manager, he would have to stay up as long every night as I would have to, the more he decided he didn't want to be a part of the next tour. He began complaining about how it would ruin his health. So by the end of March, I had to say that I would give him another month to decide whether he was coming or not, and if not I would have to get someone else.

In the meantime, I had another video to film. EMI wanted a video on "Margo's Cargo" before I left on another tour.

I must say this was a fun video to make. If you can imagine doing a video that had all to do with a couple coming from Newfoundland with a cow and a pick-up truck full of cow dung, with intentions of selling it in Toronto to make cow dung clocks, and actually unloading it near the corner of Yonge and Queen streets, downtown, you know exactly what I mean.

The only time the video company could get a licence from the city to do such a thing was early on a Sunday morning.

Just west of Yonge Street, where the Eaton Centre faced The Bay store, on Queen Street, the traffic was blocked off, except for streetcars taking people to and from church.

Now, if you can also imagine the looks of the conductor and the faces of the people on each streetcar that came passing through, when they saw a guy in a black cowboy hat standing laughing his ass off, as a "Newfie" husband and wife unloaded a truckful of cow shit on the downtown Toronto city sidewalk, with a big Holstein cow wandering around by the front door of The Bay, you might have an inkling of what a good laugh is. And that was nothing. We even had a large pig there.

The people on the streetcar, who took this same trip every Sunday morning, must have thought the conductor got lost and took a detour through some old farmer's barnyard. Some of the streetcar windows were up and you could smell the beautiful aroma everywhere. Even the cops, who were supposed to be controlling traffic, couldn't control themselves from laughing. Nobody had ever seen the likes of this on the main intersection of Toronto for over 150 years.

I can just imagine the talk when little old grandma finally got back home that day. "You'll never guess what I saw on the way to church this morning?"

MARGO'S CARGO

1.

Have you heard the news in Newfoundland, goin'
   around the "Rock"?
How Reggie brought for Margie home, a "Cowsy
   Dungsy Clock"?
With Margo being' a farm girl, she almost took a fit,
To find the "Cowsy Dungsy Clock" was really made
   of "IT."

2.

The Clock was from Toronto and her mind was soon
   made up.
She said to Reggie, "Get the Cow, and load 'er on the
   truck;
We're headin' for Ontario and we're off to Make 'er
   big";
'Cause MARGO'S GOT THE CARGO, B'ye, and Reggie's
   got the Rig.—sing REFRAIN

REFRAIN—Reggie's got the Rig; Reggie's got the Rig;
MARGO'S GOT THE CARGO, B'ye, and Reggie's got the
   Rig.

3.

Now, they're rollin' through the Maritimes, the truck
   was nearly full;

*The cow began to bawl, she was lonesome for the
    bull.*
*The Mountie pulled them over, "Is there something I
    can do?"*
*"Go right ahead, Sir," Margie said, "Climb in the
    back and moo."*

4.

*Now, when they got to Montreal, they missed the
    "Auto Route"*
*But they found that everyone in town was glad to
    "help them out";*
*"The sooner you hit Toronto," they said, "the sooner
    you'll make 'er big";*
*'Cause MARGO'S GOT THE CARGO, B'ye, and Reggie's
    got the Rig.——sing REFRAIN*

5.

*The truck was overflowin' when Toronto hit their
    eyes;*
*The 401 was full of dung and the cab was full of
    flies.*
*"We're losin' lots of money, Reg, we can't afford to
    stop;*
*We gotta find the place that makes the Cowsy
    Dungsy Clock."*

6.

*Well, I wish you could have been there, on the corner
    of Queen and Yonge*
*When Margo found the "Company" and she
    dumped her load of dung;*
*And when she found the "office" she was singin'
    and doin' a jig;*
*MARGO'S GOT THE CARGO, B'ye, and Reggie's got the
    Rig. ——sing REFRAIN*

7.

*It was later in the evenin' when they heard from "Mr.
    Judge,"*

"I don't know what to give ye, but I'll never hold a grudge;
I think a thousand dollars would be fair to hand you down,
And thirty days of 'lodging' will be free upon the town."

8.

Well Margo says to Reggie, "What a hell of a deal we struck;
We might have lost the cow, B'ye, but still we got the truck."
And now they're back in Newfoundland, they're loadin' up the pig;
'Cause MARGO'S GOT THE CARGO, B'ye, and Reggie's got the Rig.——sing REFRAIN.

On the first of May, I asked Art again if he was going to come on the road under the agreement that he would have to keep the same hours as myself. Again he remained non-committal.

By this time I began to think that he might be playing a little game. If he kept me waiting long enough for his definite answer on the hours, he wouldn't have to commit to them and I would have to take him anyway, due to the fact that there wouldn't be enough time left before the tour to find and train a replacement.

Around about the middle of the third week in May, I asked him again. After another noncommittal answer, I said I'd have to know for sure in a couple of days or I'd be looking for someone else, starting Monday the twentieth.

At this, he threw a box of papers all over my hall floor and stormed out the door, and I've never seen him since. I certainly heard from him, though.

For more than a year afterwards he continually phoned and wrote letters to practically every company I had dealings with, alleging that I not only owed him money, but had coerced him out of a couple of songs five years ago, back in 1986.

Although these companies finally saw through it all, it

did put me in a bad light with them for a while. One or two of them even held up some royalty payments for six months or so, until I was able to show documentation that these allegations were false.

I personally received letters and bills from him for another while after that, until I told him I'd take him to court to prove all these allegations false, and finally the hassling stopped.

By the last week in May of '91, a new guy became my assistant. I had not made him quite so privy to all my business as Art had become, mainly because I was now in a big hurry to get somebody for the job, and I had never met this guy before.

By now, I also knew the Merry-Mick-Ray band were committed to come on tour with me, but I was having a hard time finding a fiddle player. Each one I contacted was busy. Then I thought of Sam Leitch, my furnace man, who played on weekends with Marion's Country Band. I didn't know whether he would come or not, but there was no harm asking.

As it turned out Sam was delighted to come, and during the second and third weeks of June we had rehearsals.

The tour began on June 25. And because we had done such an extensive tour the year before, most all the dates were confined to Ontario, so as to pick up some of the towns we previously missed. Although we did fifteen or twenty towns, the new ones we picked up were Matheson, St. Catharines, Gravenhurst, Parry Sound, Bobcaygeon, Ontario Place in Toronto and Wiarton.

My son Tommy worked with us all through this tour. And the rest of the help remained pretty much the same as the previous tour, except for the addition of Barry Herr (stage manager) and Jerry Ambromowicz (security).

While playing St. Catharines, after the autograph session that night, I met my daughter Karma, whom I hadn't seen in almost thirty years. With a girlfriend whom she brought to the concert, she waited around until everything was over and then surprised me by telling me who she was. We couldn't talk very long, but exchanged addresses and got in touch later on that year.

In Kitchener, we played Lulu's again. And I don't know how it was possible, but we broke our previous record by jamming in a few more people.

Our last concert took place in Wiarton, Ontario (the home of the famous groundhog known as Wiarton Willy, the Wonderful Wizard of Weather).

I'm not sure whether Willy had anything to do with it, but my stompin' board was autographed and auctioned off again and fetched a price of $2,300, with proceeds going to the Cancer Society. The guy who got the board was Donald Bumstead, a car dealer from Meaford, Ontario.

On August 24 we held one of our "Camp-n-Jams" for everyone who had been on the tour, something we try to do every summer.

This is where we have a corn boil along with hamburgers and hot dogs, and beverages of all varieties. People can bring their own campers and small trailers and stay on the grounds overnight if they wish.

Everyone who plays an instrument is invited to do so. We often set up an old hay wagon as a stage and have a campfire at night. Everyone just sits around pickin' and grinnin'.

We have a small boat and a raft in the pond that the kids quite often like to play on, as well as an assortment of lawn games for both kids and adults. One of the most popular games we play is croquet. But with a slight difference. Our rules require a three-hundred-pound referee. (Almost.)

On this particular occasion, our guests included Dean Cameron and all the people we knew from Capitol Records EMI, including one of their new guys, David MacMillan (whose only purpose with the company was to always keep Stompin' Tom in a good humour. And don't you ever forget it, Dave).

Other guests were Mark Altman, my old partner in the Morning Music Publishing Company, Brian "No Headache" Edwards and his sister Ella, and a whole clan of friends too numerous to mention.

After the Camp-n-Jam I decided to keep my new assistant working for me on a part-time basis. He knew something about computers so I thought if I bought a real good one, with laser printer, scanner and the whole bit, he could learn it while I was paying him, and as soon as I could afford the time, he could teach me what he had learned.

To this he readily agreed. But to cut a long story short, I paid him for another six months, and when the day came that I was ready to sit down and be taught what he had learned, he quit. Without notice, he just up and walked out.

As I didn't have the time to sit down and go through all these manuals by myself, I just took the damn computer back to the store and forgot the whole thing. Not counting his wages, I lost about eight grand on that deal. As they say, you got to live and learn.

In January of 1992, I was again nominated for an ECMA Award on the east coast, but I didn't bother going down. Besides, I was heavy into songwriting, and preparing to record an album at the end of the month.

By now, I had also received a letter or two from Karma, and she and I and Lena were preparing to meet and have dinner together sometime in the middle of February, as soon as the new album was out of the way.

On January 28 I recorded my seventeenth album of all original songs. It would be called *Believe in Your Country*, and it contained two songs co-written with Gaet Lepine, "Alberta Rose" and "My Sleeping Carmello." The most popular song eventually turned out to be the one the album was named after.

Among other musicians on this album were the accordionist Walter Ostanek, and fiddle champion Graham Townsend, with his son, Gray, doing some piano and drums.

I believe it was on Sunday the sixteenth of February that Lena and I met Karma. Then after having dinner together we all came to the house for a long chat. We found out Karma had a young daughter by the name of Sky, and her husband's name was Mike. We continued with a long personal conversation, and then it was time for her to go. She lived down near St. Catharines, so she had a long drive.

In Sixteen Overseas Countries

AROUND THE FIRST OF MAY, LENA and I were
wondering what we were going to do for the summer.
For the last two years I had been on tour, which wasn't all that
great for her, having to stay at home for a lot of the time.

"Why don't we just pack our duds and take a trip to
Europe?" I said. "After all, we haven't been outside Canada
since our honeymoon, and that was almost nineteen
years ago."

"That's a great idea," she said. "What do they do over
there, anyway?" "Well, you just let me do a little planning,
and before you know it, we'll both be finding out," I told her.
Then, after deciding to take another couple along for company, we gave Gaet and Jean Lepine a call.

"How would you like to go to Europe for a month or so?"
I asked Gaet on the phone.

"No, I don't think so," he said. "It's too damn far to walk.
Now, what's the gag?"

"There's no gag," I said. "I'm dead serious. Lena and I
are planning a trip to Europe in about three weeks' time.
And I know this is very short notice. But if you and Jean can
scrounge up enough money to pay for your meals, Lena and
I will pay for the accommodations and all travel expenses.
Besides, I might need you to help me with my French while
we're in France."

Gaet knows I can be a practical joker sometimes, and it

took over half an hour to convince him that I meant everything I was saying.

Finally, he said, "Of course we'd like to go. But of all the people you could have chosen to take on a trip like this, why did you pick me and Jean?"

"Because I owe you a lot of money," I said. "Remember back in October of 1964 when I walked into the Maple Leaf Hotel in Timmins? And remember how you added that nickel to the thirty-five cents I had, so I could afford a beer? Well, just consider this offer to be the interest on the loan of the nickel."

(This "nickel scene" was described in *Before the Fame*.)

A couple of weeks before we left, I got a call from a John Brunton, who represented a company called Insight Productions. They were doing a documentary film for television about the history of Canadian country music, and they wanted me to be a part of it.

A day or two later, I had John and his crew out to the house where they filmed an interview and a segment of me singing my new song, "Believe in Your Country."

This was the last thing I did before heading out on our trip to Europe.

On July 7, 1992, Lena, Tommy, Gaet, Jean and I were all assembled at the airport, nervously waiting to board the plane for Shannon, Ireland.

Arriving at Shannon airport, we all had jet lag. So we picked up our rented car, threw in our luggage, and drove the short distance to Limerick. It was only early in the day, but there was no sense trying to see Ireland while we all felt so beat. So we booked ourselves into a hotel and slept for the rest of the day and night, awaking only to have something to eat and then going back to bed again. But bright and early the following morning we struck out for Tralee and Kilarney.

As I was the only one who had been to Ireland before, I was the guide and did all the driving. Everyone else admired all the beautiful scenery as we went.

I told them the stories about the tour that Bill Lewis, Gary Empey and I had taken twenty years before, what places we played and the things we did. Then we came to the town called Blarney, just outside the city of Cork.

As we drove into town I was telling them about how Bill, Gary and I had kissed the famous Blarney Stone the last time I was here, and now, twenty years later, I intended to kiss it again. Within a few minutes we had parked the car and made our way on foot up to Blarney Castle. (There are many old castles in Ireland and the British Isles. Almost every town has got one.)

As the Blarney Stone itself is at the very top of the castle, I had a hard time getting Gaet, who was afraid of heights, to go up. After a little arm twisting I got him up there. But then when he saw how you had to bend over backwards down into a hole over a precipice to kiss the Blarney, he wanted no part of it. From then on I had to keep my eye on him. Every chance he got, he was trying to sneak back down.

Pretty soon, after he watched the rest of us bend over into the hole and kiss the stone, he didn't want to be called chicken for the rest of the trip. So, reluctantly, he took his turn.

When he got back up and on his feet again, I said, "There now. That wasn't so bad, was it?"

Looking a little pale, he said, "No, that wasn't so bad. Now let's get the hell down out of here and into that little pub we passed on the way up."

Fortunately, there was a little souvenir shop at the bottom of the castle which also sold beer. And after he got a couple of pints into him, as we stood listening to a group of musicians playing harps and other traditional Irish instruments, he looked like he might want to go back up and kiss the Blarney Stone again.

That evening, while the girls and Tommy did a little sight-seeing, Gaet and I sampled the beer in all the Blarney pubs, and the next day we headed out for . . . well, you know the song "It's a Long Way to Tipperary."

It was funny, because we no sooner got to the sign on the outskirts of Tipperary when everyone wanted to get out and kiss that, too. As motorists drove by they must have thought we were nuts. We were standing there taking pictures of each other singing, "It's *not* a long way to Tipperary, 'cause our heart is right here."

Next, we wanted to sing "Galway Bay" right in Galway, so

after driving another eighty miles that's just what we did. Then about twenty miles farther, on the north shore of Galway Bay, we found a hotel in a little place called Spiddal. And there, again, as the song says, we "watched the sun go down on Galway Bay."

The reader must remember that no accommodations were ever booked ahead. The only things pre-arranged on this trip were the car rentals. This enabled us to come and go whenever and wherever we wished. With no schedules, we just took our chances as we went. Seventy-five per cent of the plans we made were usually based on local information gained in hotels, bars, restaurants and service stations. We were on a holiday. We wanted to see lots but also take our good old time doing it.

Next day we drove across the central part of Ireland, coast to coast, from Galway to Dublin, the capital, a distance of about 130 miles. (Ireland is much longer than it is wide.)

After a day of sightseeing around Dublin, we took the ferry over to Holyhead, Wales, then on to Liverpool, England. Instead of a car, we now had a van which we picked up in Holyhead. And of course the steering wheel was on the opposite side of the vehicle and you had to drive on the left-hand side of the road.

This got me into more jackpots than one, especially with Gaet being the co-pilot.

We'd come to these damnable traffic circles which had four or five lanes going around them and six or seven highways shooting off from them. And with everybody knowing exactly where they were going but us, the traffic was insane.

I'd wind up getting myself on the inside lane just spinning around this thing, not being able to look up at signs or anything else, while these maniacs darted in front of me, around me, and practically on top of me, as they kept switching from lane to lane as if they actually knew where they were going.

After two or three times around the circle, with Gaet sitting beside me holding the road map, I asked him, "Haven't you found which highway we're supposed to take yet?"

With mustard from his hamburger dripping on the map, he says, "Yeah, I got it now, Tom. It's M6."

"I know it's M6. But look at the signs and tell me when I'm coming to it. I can't take my eyes off these insane drivers." By now we're already around the circle again.

"Okay, Tom, go. No, no. Don't go now. There's a car coming in right beside you." Another time around the circle.

"Right here. Put your signals on, Tom. Quick!"

I grab for the windshield washers, which are on the side of the wheel the signals would be on if it was a North American car. And now I got water spewing all over the glass with the wipers going full tilt. I can't shut them off until they run their course. Another two turns around the circle, now Jean is getting dizzy.

"When are we going to stop going around and around, Tom?" she asks.

"Just as soon as Gaet tells me it's safe, and when it's the right time to get over," I reply.

Gaet now drops the map on the floor along with the remains of his hamburger. And while he's down scrounging around trying to pick everything up, I'm able to cross over two lanes.

One more time around the circle and I finally manage to get off the damn thing.

Gaet's now got the map straightened out and I'm just heaving a big sigh, when he tells me, "Tom, Tom, we're on the wrong road. I think we have to go back to the circle and take another one."

Screeech! Stop. "Here," I say. "Let me see that goddamn map."

One glance, and I say, "You still got the goddamn map of Ireland. We're in England now, for chrissake." At this point I just throw up my hands. "Oh, me friggin' nerves." Gaet now digs out the map of England and passes it to me.

As it turned out we were on the right road after all. But that wasn't the last merry-go-round we'd be on! Those damn traffic circles were all over the place.

Heading straight to the north of England now, we passed Hadrian's Wall, built by the Romans in Hadrian's time, and then crossed into Scotland. We spent the night in Stirling, visiting its famous Stirling Castle and taking in other sights. And because we were no more than ten miles from a little town called Braco, we decided to take a little detour and pay it a visit.

Braco is the home town of Dave Newlands, whose wife Pat often helped me with my fan mail back in Canada. Although Dave hadn't been home in a great many years, he often mentioned growing up around Braco when he was young. So a beer or two in the Braco Hotel wasn't at all out of order on a hot July afternoon. Again, driving around some of the back roads we came to a couple little towns called Muthill and Auchterarder, also mentioned by Dave. And then we doubled back to Stirling and across to Loch Lomond.

Once again, we sang about "the bonny, bonny banks of Loch Lomond" all the way up the west side of the loch, a distance of twenty miles or so.

Scotland is indeed a very pretty country. As a matter of fact, by the time we were ready to come home, we had all agreed that out of all sixteen countries we had visited, Scotland and Ireland had been the prettiest.

We spent that night in Glencoe. The following day was very windy when we drove up to Loch Ness. Here we visited an old castle, now in ruins, and walked around a lot with our binoculars trained on the loch, in hopes of catching a glimpse of Nessie, the famous but very elusive sea monster.

Unfortunately, Nessie was nasty that day and didn't bother to show up for the photo session. After driving so far to see her, we felt very disappointed. In fact, we felt downright insulted by nasty old Nessie, so we drove on and spent the night in the town of Inverness, at the head of the loch.

The next day as we were heading south towards Perth, we stopped for something to eat, and Gaet bought a newspaper. Nessie had been spotted early that morning. "Are we going back to see her, Dad?" Tommy wanted to know. "Yeah, maybe," I said, as we all got in the van but I just kept on heading south instead of north.

Passing Edinburgh, the home of Prince Philip, we again crossed the Scotland/England border and stayed the night in some little town not too far from Newcastle Upon Tyne.

Leeds, Manchester, Birmingham and Oxford soon passed by and a couple of nights later we decided to get a hotel for two or three days near Salisbury. We would use this as our temporary home to come back and forth from, as we wanted to see the world-famous Stonehenge, and a number of other oddities, such as crop circles.

On the day we went to Stonehenge, I was just getting interested in these massive stones when a whole class of school kids came running up with their teacher.

"Stompin' Tom! It's Stompin' Tom!" they were shouting. "Can we take a picture with you and get your autograph?"

It was a class of 4th or 5th graders from Manitoba who had won a trip to England, and they were now all of a sudden a lot more interested in Stompin' Tom than they were in studying some old funny-looking rocks.

After obliging them and listening to them sing a verse or two of a couple of my songs, I wandered around for a few more minutes and headed down to the concession pavilion where Lena was busy looking at knick-knacks.

It was now time to go, and though I planned to go back the following day for a better look, something else came up and I never went. (My main interest here had been a personal one. I knew that Stonehenge had been some sort of an ancient calendar, and calendars had always been one of my secret preoccupations.)

The next day we went hunting for crop circles, those mysterious circular designs that appear overnight in large grain fields. While they have been known to appear in many parts of the world, the countryside we were now in seemed to be the centre for most of this strange phenomenon.

Driving around the back roads for a couple of hours by ourselves didn't bring us any luck. We came across many places where hundreds of massive stones had been strangely aligned in ancient times. Enough to make anybody stop and wonder. And we, along with many other people, were doing just that. But crop circles? We found none.

Then about three o'clock in the afternoon we were driving through this little town which had a small pub. As the day was hot, Gaet and I decided we'd stop in for a cold beer, while the girls and Tommy had a bottle of pop.

There were a couple of guys standing at the bar talking as we walked in. As soon as we ordered our drinks, Gaet asked one of the fellows where all these crop circles were around here that everybody kept talking about.

"There's all kinds of those," he said. "You people are just not looking in the right places."

The other fellow interrupted, "Yeah! As a matter of fact, there's another huge one over on [some road] that just happened last night. There's a bunch of scientists and other people over there already, trying to make heads or tails of it."

After getting directions and drinking our beer, we piled in the van and headed down the road, making the turns the fellow had indicated. And just when we thought we'd been sent on a wild goose chase, we came over the brow of a hill, and there it was. Close to the centre of a huge field of grain that I would estimate to contain nearly a hundred acres was this massive and strange-looking crop circle.

A few cars were parked along the narrow paved road, but more were parked in a little scrubby field on the left-hand side of the road. The crop circle was on the right.

We parked in the little field, and armed only with binoculars, a camera and a pocket compass, we walked across the road and down through the grain field.

We stopped to talk to several people coming back from the circle, and after we asked them what their impression was, they said they didn't know what to make of it.

Upon arriving at the circle, having once been a farm boy, I immediately estimated that at least an acre of grain had been flattened down like a pancake. And looking around at the lay of the land, the entire field itself was in a valley with the nearest hill at least a quarter of a mile away. The other hills were farther away, and there were several houses within plain vision of where I was standing at the centre of the circle.

As I looked with my fairly wide-range eight-power binoculars I could plainly see some people walking around beside a couple of the houses. I therefore deduced that if any of them had a similar pair of binoculars, they would be able to see me quite plainly as well. And if I could see their house, which was a hell of a lot smaller than this crop circle, with the naked eye, I was certain they could see the circle.

I considered all these things to check the feasibility of the claim of a couple of pranksters who got themselves interviewed on television, that it was they who had made all the circles with a wooden roller in the middle of the night.

"Well," I thought to myself as I looked around, "if these two guys are capable of making this beautiful crop circle in just a few hours in the dead of night, undetected, I'd hate to see what they could do if there were ten more of them. They just better not allow them into Egypt. Because some morning the world just may awaken to discover another Great Pyramid on the Giza Plateau we'll all have to ponder."

The stalks of grain had been bent over at ground level and all perfectly lay side by side, pointing in the same circular direction. Under the flattened stalks, when they were gently lifted in different places, there were no signs in the clay whatever to indicate that a man, beast or machine had ever even been there.

Out from either end of this one massive circle there were perfectly straight lines which led to several other smaller circles. And everywhere at the edges of the downed grain the stalks that were still standing and growing had not even been touched, not even bent a little. This work, without any doubt, had been done with the greatest precision, almost as if someone had decided this stalk must continue to stand and grow and the one beside it must be flattened.

The needle on my pocket compass remained normal. And when I asked one of the guys (scientists?) who came with a lot of boxes and fancy-looking equipment what his instruments were telling him, he just looked at me blankly and said, "Nothing."

We spent over two hours around there, talking to locals and people from as far away as the United States. Some said it was space aliens, some said it was miniature whirlwinds, and some said it was a sign the end of the world was at hand. From leprechauns to the work of midnight pranksters, we heard it all. (And did I have a theory? Yes! It was Gaet Lepine having a dream the night before. Slipping through the fourth dimension, he doodled on a piece of ethereal paper. And in the morning? Behold! Crop circles!)

Back on the road the next day, we skirted around

London, going to Southampton, Portsmouth, Brighton and Hastings. In Hastings we went to a museum where we saw a lot of miniature depictions of the battles fought against King Harold during the invasion of William the Conqueror from Normandy in 1066. Harold was eventually killed with an arrow through the eye.

We spent the next couple of days sightseeing around the White Cliffs of Dover, and of course we had to sing that song a few times.

We often discussed how nice it would be if people from other lands could come to Canada and drive all around singing the famous songs about our country. The sad truth of it all, however, is that there is a terrible drought of songs written about our country. And a worse drought when it comes to promoting the ones that are written. Especially on the radio.

(Of all the countries I've ever been to—all of Western Europe, South America, the United States and Mexico—Canada is the only place in the world that people come to for a visit, turn on the radio, and never hear songs that are truly and distinctively our own. All other countries do, so why can't we? Although I've never, as yet, been to Japan, Russia, China, Israel, Australia, and many more, the people from these lands assure me that when they turn on the radio in their countries they do hear a lot of their own music. So what the hell is the matter with us? Do we really love the Yankees that much that we have to play their music all the time?)

Before leaving Dover we visited some very interesting smugglers' caves, went to the beach, and Gaet and I and Tommy played some snooker. We also had to take our vehicle back to the car rental depot because in the morning we would be taking the hovercraft over the English Channel to Calais, France, where we would be picking up another van.

When morning came we were all ready with our luggage at the hotel, but the taxi we called was late. And when it finally did arrive it was only a small car. There were five of us and ten or twelve pieces of luggage and the trunk of the car would hold no more than three.

It was too late to order another taxi, so we all piled in the best way we could. After everybody got in and sat on some of the luggage, I stood outside and passed the rest in to them. Finally it was my turn to force myself in the back door with my guitar case. But only being able to get half-way in, I told the driver to proceed. We may have already been too late to catch the hovercraft, but we had to try.

Nobody could see each other, let alone where we were going. And I was expending a lot of energy trying to hold myself in the car, and at the same time keep the door closed as tight as I could up against my right leg which was still dragging outside, near the ground.

It was a good thing the drive was only a couple of miles, because the moment the driver stopped, I fell out.

I hurt my knee a little, but I had to hurry up and pull out some of the luggage so everybody else could get out. After paying the cabbie, it was just a mad scramble. Everybody grabbed as much as he could carry and, all stumbling over one another, we hurried through the turnstiles, fumbled for ticket money, leaving huge amounts of change, and ran like hell for . . . for . . . for what? The goddamn hovercraft was going to be twenty minutes late.

I felt too embarrassed to go back and ask for my change. And though it was still early in the morning, I said to Gaet, "Let's go have a beer."

When the hovercraft finally came in, it was a sight to behold. She just skimmed in across the water and didn't stop for land at all. She just eased her way right on up the concrete slip and plunked herself down near the gateway to the pavilion.

This thing was huge. She carried cars, trucks and transports in her hold, and while there were only about a hundred passengers on this particular trip, I figured she could have taken a couple hundred more.

The distance was about forty miles and we made the trip in about twenty minutes. We passed a couple of ferry boats going the same way, and it looked like they were standing still. The water was a little rough that day, and we were told that on a good day the trip could be made in twelve minutes.

Once in France, we picked up our new vehicle, a Volks-wagen van, in Calais, and headed south. The first place we visited was Dieppe. And here we went to the Canadian War Cemetery. This made us all quite emotional to see so many graves bearing the names of so many French- and English-speaking Canadian boys who fought side by side and never got to come home.

It also made us angry to stand in this reverend spot and realize that back home Quebec was planning to separate from the rest of Canada. While Gaet had been born in Quebec and I had been born in New Brunswick, he had some Irish-Canadian blood and I had some French. And the question we were asking each other was this: If English and French Canadians could fight and die together to free the French-speaking people of France from the clutches of Hitler's Germany, how did France's General DeGaulle ever have the nerve to come across the ocean and declare that from Canada, Quebec should be free? ("Vive le Québec, libre.")

If that's not total ingratitude, I don't know what is. And now, in Quebec, the separatists have erected a monument to this man. What are we going to see next? A monument to Hitler in Ottawa?

After Dieppe, we went to visit the very famous Roman Catholic church and monastery that is built on a mountain on a small island just off the coast. You have to drive there over a small causeway, and it's really quite a spectacular sight. It is called the Church on the Mont Saint Michel. And because the rest of the land around there is so flat you can see this church on the mount for miles.

The next day we pulled into a small city where I decided I'd better get some gas. As I stopped at the pumps, a young fellow about eighteen years old came up to my side window and I signalled with my hands that I wanted him to "fill 'er up."

Three or four blocks later, after leaving the service station, I came to a set of lights. As I waited to make a left-hand turn, the motor in the van started chugging badly.

As the light turned green and I pressed on the accelerator, the van started to hop. And I do mean hop. We jumped, hopped and bounced through the intersection and there the motor just quit.

After putting the shift into neutral, we all got out and pushed. With traffic going everywhere, we finally got the van into a bus lane and a half block later, we stopped it in a bus parking lot.

After Gaet and I checked everything that either one of us knew about motors, I decided to take off the gas tank cover. And there in plain view was a little sign in both French and English which read: This Vehicle Takes Diesel Fuel (*gazzoil* in French).

They hadn't told me this when I picked the van up in Calais, and this was the first tank of fuel I had stopped for. I naturally pulled up to the gas pump, and the kid, without looking, just shoved the hose in and let 'er go. Now I had a diesel motor full of gas. What to do?

Leaving Tommy with Lena and Jean at the van, Gaet and I walked up the busy street looking for someone who could help us. We stopped several people, but we weren't long finding out that, although this was France, Gaet couldn't understand their dialect and neither could they understand his.

Soon we came to a store where we found a guy who understood enough to make a phone call for us and get a tow truck to come to where our van was located.

Back at the van we waited for another hour and a half until a tow truck came. After checking the motor out to see what was wrong he just shook his head and hooked onto the front of the van with us in it. As I did the steering, he took us for about a ten-mile drive out of town to an old junkyard. Here we unhooked and a couple of guys started pumping the gas out of our tank and flushing the motor.

Every time Gaet would talk to the guy for five minutes or so, I'd ask him, "What's wrong? What did the guy say?"

The only answer I ever got was a shrug of the shoulders and "I don't know. Don't ask me."

While all this was going on, there was an old ugly-looking, flea-bitten, overly friendly German shepherd dog who was scratching himself continuously, and for some reason had taken a shine to me.

As I kept trying to walk away from him, he just kept following me and brushing himself against my leg, wanting me to pet him. I felt more like giving him a good bat in the nose, but I figured if I did, the guy might get mad and not fix my van. So for two hours I had to put up with this mutt. I don't know if I caught the fleas or not, but after a while I was scratching more than he was.

Finally, the van was fixed. I paid the guy. And while I was trying to listen to him explain to me that he couldn't guarantee the job, the goddamn dog was trying to jump into the van.

"Oui, oui," I said, as I slammed the door, threw 'er in gear and left the guy standing there talking to himself.

A minute later, Gaet says, "What's the matter, Tom? Don't you like dogs?" I never even answered. I just kept driving.

As it turned out, the van was good enough for the rest of the tour, although she lost a lot of the pep she had before.

The next evening after the mishap, we drove into Lourdes, in southern France. This, of course, is where the young woman, Bernadette Soubirous, now known as Saint Bernadette by the Catholics, saw "The Lady," since proclaimed by all Christians to be the Virgin Mary, the Mother of Jesus.

According to a plaque I read on the magnificent church built on top of the grotto where this miracle was said to have taken place, the event occurred in the year 1858.

It's just too hard to imagine how many people from every country in the world come to visit this spot. And most seem to be there looking for a miraculous healing of one sort or another. There are people in wheelchairs, people on crutches, some coughing, limping, weeping, and some without limbs being carried down to the grotto where the first miracle is believed to have happened. There were other people, of course, with cancer and other maladies not readily perceived by people such as us, who were only there as curious tourists.

As I can be no judge as to whether the claimed healings are authentic, and being there as a mere spectator, I must say I felt extremely odd when a certain bell rang throughout the town around six o'clock in the evening.

During the afternoon, we had been through the church, we had seen the grotto, and on our way back, we had passed all the sleazy-looking rip-off shops that sold everything from switch-blade jack knives to Madonna-shaped bottles which held the "real authentic holy water," gathered each year on the anniversary of the day when Bernadette saw the vision.

As we began to walk up this narrow street, picking our way through the hundreds of mingling people (there were no automobiles), all of a sudden the bells rang.

We were on our way back to our hotel when these seemingly docile people became electrified. They all started heading in the direction of the church from which we had just come.

Without warning, we found ourselves going in the wrong direction, facing hundreds of people bent on nothing but racing as fast as they could towards the sound of the bells. We were almost trampled.

Hollering to the rest to "Follow me!" I grabbed Lena by the hand and dragged her off to the wall of one of the buildings. Gaet had done the same with Jean, and Tommy had fended for himself.

As we lined up holding hands with our backs hugging the wall, this stampede of frenzied people would have trampled or crushed anybody unlucky enough to be standing in their way.

This wall-to-wall street full of people were brushing by us like we weren't even there. They didn't even see us. It was all we could do to keep ourselves from falling into this crowd.

Up ahead of me I saw where the next building jutted out towards the street about a foot farther than the one we were standing against, so hand in hand I gently tugged everybody up along the wall until we reached a spot that provided a little more safety.

I had seen people in concerts before, but I had never seen anything like this. And to say the truth, I don't care to see anything like it again.

I have no disrespect for what other people believe, but when their single-mindedness allows them to ignore the safety and even the lives of other human beings, that's when I draw the line.

For all I know, there might have been another unsuspecting tourist on that street, or on any other street that day, who didn't make it back home because thousands of others were rushing to get healed.

After about fifteen or twenty minutes the entire street was completely empty. We then stepped down from our perch and slowly and silently walked back to our hotel, each thinking his own thoughts.

Getting ready to leave Lourdes the following day, Gaet came to me with a map and a route all figured out, as to how we were going to get from Lourdes to Barcelona, Spain. His route was 400 miles and the one I was proposing was about 175 miles straight through some pretty rugged mountains. Gaet wanted to avoid all these because he was afraid of heights. Thus the huge difference in mileage.

I told him I wasn't going to drive 225 miles more than I had to, so like it or not, we were going through the mountains.

Passing through canyons, over summits, through long tunnels and over narrow bridges, we came to a little town about half-way to our destination. This was the first town we came to in Spain so we decided to stop and have lunch and a couple of beers (if you want to call it beer. France, Spain and Italy make some of the worst beer in the world. And the climate is very hot).

While sitting at a table outside on the sidewalk where it wasn't any cooler than it was inside, we were just having a chat when, all of a sudden, Gaet took on somewhat of a strange look. He mumbled something, got up from his chair, and wandered down the street.

Jean turned white and said she had never seen him like that before. I told her I hadn't either, but not to worry, I'd follow him and try to find out what was going on.

Down the little street about half a block or so, he stopped to lean against an old building for three or four minutes, and by the time I got there he started walking back towards me.

I was going to say something but, seeing that same strange look on his face, I thought I'd better not. Still mumbling something to himself, he walked right past me as if I wasn't there. There wasn't the slightest hint of recognition. So I just turned around and followed him back.

When he got to the table he ignored everybody and walked by. At this point, Jean shouted, "Gaetan! What the hell is wrong with you, anyway?"

At the sound of his name, he stopped dead in his tracks for five or ten seconds, as if thinking, then turned around and walked back to the table and sat down. What looked to me like some kind of a sleepwalk was now over. And he didn't remember a thing about it, except for seeing himself on horseback being chased by a number of other horsemen. All were dressed much the same as himself, in some kind of ancient military armour.

The chase was taking place on a very high precipitous roadway, and rather than be captured, he and his horse went tumbling over the cliff to their deaths.

During the rest of the conversation at the table, he told us how, when he was a kid, his mother would often wake him up from some recurring nightmare, where he was always screaming something about horses chasing him.

I then told everybody that I had read about very similar experiences in my studies on reincarnation. And if they wanted to accept my answer, the vision that Gaet just had was merely a throwback to one of his past lives. For all we knew, the incident might have taken place right here, somewhere in these very hills.

About twenty minutes later, while we were driving through an especially high and dangerous mountain pass, Gaet shouted, "Tom! I can't believe it. I'm not afraid of heights anymore! Seriously, Tom. The fear I've always felt is gone. Completely gone."

As I looked over at him, I could see he was laughing like a little kid. This was something he never did in high places. And remembering how he sweated that day and kept wringing his hands on the top of Blarney Castle, I said, "Jeez, that's great, Gaet. I hope things stay that way."

"Oh, they will," he said, still laughing. "They will." And from that day till this, I've never heard Gaet Lepine complain about heights again. Was it the nightmares? Was it the midafternoon vision in the heat? Was it the explanation and/or realization that he might have lived before? Or was it the result of his visit to the grotto at Lourdes? Again, I leave it up to the reader.

The places we stayed in Spain were Lerida and Barcelona

and then we drove along the Mediterranean Sea back into France. Passing Marseille, we drove to Monaco. And here we stayed for a couple of days' rest.

Our hotel was down near the water, just below Prince Rainier and Princess Grace's palace. We were going to go up and see it closer a couple of times but we kept missing the little train that takes people there.

We didn't "break the bank" at Monte Carlo, but we at least gambled there one evening, with none of us coming up a winner. It was all quite interesting. A sort of a once-in-a-lifetime thing.

There was a little shop owner right near our hotel, and every time I walked by he wanted to buy my cowboy hat. He wanted it so bad that all I had to do was name my price and he would have given it to me. If it had not been the only one I had with me on the trip, I might have made myself a little fortune. Cowboy hats are a real rare commodity in that neck of the woods.

Leaving Monaco, we crossed into Italy. And passing Genoa, we spent the night in Verona. Early the next day we arrived in Venice.

You of course don't go to Venice without taking a gondola ride through the canals. This we did. But it's a shame how much pollution there is in these canals. Other than that, you might say the late evening ride was quite romantic.

Another evening we took a ferry from where our hotel was and went to see the old part of Venice with all its magnificent buildings. The ancient architecture was exquisite. It made you want to just stand there and study each building in wonderment at the ingenious craftsmanship of these ancient builders. You don't see anything being built today that even comes close.

From Venice we headed straight north through a lot more rugged mountain country until we crossed the border from Italy into Austria. And here, in a small town, we got a hotel for the night.

It was here that we had our first great meal since we hit Europe a couple of weeks earlier. And was the beer ever good. We hadn't tasted anything this good since we left Canada.

From Innsbruck, Austria, we headed west into Liechten-stein. This is a little country of hardly more than sixty square miles. Here we stayed the night and drove through Switzer-land the next day, and found a hotel in Zurich.

During the next three or four days we drank some more great beer in Stuttgart and Karlsruhe, Germany, and sang all the German songs we knew, such as "Lili Marlene," "Wooden Heart" and, of course, "Fraulein," as we crossed the River Rhine. All these countries have some great traditional and modern songs. After Belgium and Luxembourg we arrived in Holland, the Netherlands, and here we spent a couple of days on the beaches of the North Sea. This would be north of Utrecht in a little town called Wijk Aan Zee. We were call-ing it "We Can See" because we could see everything on these beaches. Everybody but us was nude. They looked at us like we were the freaks of the beach.

Our last day in Holland, Gaet and I alone took a long drive still farther north to see the dikes that span the Zuyder Zee, now called Lake Ijssel. The longest of these dikes had to be over forty miles long. In the very middle there's a tower which we climbed, and even from up there we couldn't see either end.

After crossing over the longest one and coming back over a shorter one we drove back to Wijk Aan Zee. This would be our last sightseeing tour as we'd be going to Amsterdam the following day and flying back home the next.

The night I drove everybody to the airport in Amster-dam, I dropped them off with the luggage and said I'd be back in five minutes. I was going to drop the van off at the car rental depot, not more than a hundred yards from where we were, and I'd be right back.

Somehow I made a wrong turn and wound up back on the highway driving away from the airport. I drove some thirty miles before I found a place to turn around and get myself on the other highway going back. My gas needle was now showing empty and the panic was setting in.

I don't know how I made it, but I did. The five minutes I said it would take me turned into almost an hour. And this time I just left the van and the keys at the airport door and ran like hell to catch the plane. Everyone else had waited for me, and they were running, too. If we hadn't caught the plane, all our luggage would have gone to Canada without us.

It's a good thing we were able to book one of the smoking seats at the back of the plane because, once we were aloft, I started smoking like a Sudbury stack.

Due to the lack of space and time, there's a lot more I haven't told about this overseas trip. But to quickly sum up, we saw a lot of great countryside, including the big grape-growing valleys in the wine provinces of both France and Germany, we sampled the foods, both good and bad, in sixteen countries, we had some parties in pubs with people of strange languages and customs who sang us their songs and we sang them ours (I often took my guitar into these places), and we drank, talked, made friends and had a lot of fun with people who said, "If the rest of the folks in Canada are anything like you people, we'll be over to visit the first time we get a chance."

You may have noticed that we didn't go to the very large and more famous cities, such as London and Paris. There were several reasons for this. It's hectic enough to drive through the smaller cities and towns of a strange country where you don't know the laws or the customs, without trying to tackle the larger ones. Secondly, if one really wants to learn something about people of a strange land, you go out into the countryside where folks are friendlier and more apt to talk and tell you things, without first looking upon you with a great deal of mistrust and suspicion. And thirdly, if you just want to go to a country to see what their large and polluted cities are all about, you're better off to just fly there and taxi around.

In total, we had been gone five and a half weeks. But there's still one last word to say. "There's still no place like Canada."

Arriving back home from Europe about the sixteenth of August 1992, I was bushed from all that driving (almost five thousand miles), so I didn't do a hell of a lot for a week. Then I got into writing some more songs.

"The Hockey Song" Reborn

I N SEPTEMBER, THE CHARLOTTETOWN Accord was on everybody's mind and a lot of people wanted to know which way I was going to vote in the referendum. Yes or No.

At the end of September, Joe Ghiz, the premier of P.E.I., invited me down to take part in a rally he was holding for the Yes side. But I declined on the grounds that I hadn't been able to make up my mind yet. (Actually, I was taking my time to read the Accord and try to study it comparatively with the Canadian Constitution.)

The more I read and studied the more my answer became No. And this was firmly my position when Premier Frank McKenna of New Brunswick called me to try and sway me to the Yes side. He didn't succeed and I also told him that even though all the polls were saying the Yes side was going to win, the No side would overtake them and defeat the Accord.

I became active for the No side by writing letters to the newspapers, magazines, members of parliament and anybody who would listen. And as history would tell, on Referendum Day the No side won, and the Accord went down.

Another interesting thing happened in the fall of '92. Randy Burgess, the guy responsible for playing the taped music during the Ottawa Senators' hockey games, opened the season with a brand-new twist. Instead of playing the usual high-powered rock songs during the commercial breaks, he popped on an old country song by Stompin' Tom "just to see how it would go with the fans." And wonders never cease. The old song became an instant hit with everybody, and "The Hockey Song" was reborn.

The next thing you know, Pat Burns, coach of the Toronto Maple Leafs, heard the song while the Leafs were playing the Senators and decided to try it at the Gardens. The fans took to it right away.

Now a lot more teams were hearing it and taking it back to their home rinks, and pretty soon "The Hockey Song" had become the main theme at every hockey game throughout the NHL. And not only in Canada and the States, but a lot of European countries were playing it as well. The fans were taking to it everywhere, and this prompted other groups to record it.

So what was really happening here? That was the question that was on my mind. I had written and recorded "The Hockey Song" some twenty years before all this took place. And had it been played on radio twenty years before? No. And like all other Stompin' Tom songs, radio completely ignored it. And if others had recorded it twenty years ago, would radio have played it? No. Because it was written by Stompin' Tom Connors. That's why. And if that's not out-and-out discrimination against an artist for merely exercising his democratic right to speak up about injustices no matter where he finds them, then I don't know what is.

As radio stations, by the "formats" they follow, have set themselves up to be the judge of what songs their listeners would like to hear, how come they missed this one for twenty long years? Are they totally out of touch with the people's likes and dislikes of music? Or is it just because they don't like Stompin' Tom?

No matter which way you look at it, for twenty years they have deprived the Canadian public of hearing a song that would have been liked equally well back then as it is now. And you know what? Now that it's well known that "The Hockey Song" has finally become popular with the people, they still won't play it.

Isn't this proof that radio only plays those artists who speak out on behalf of radio or those who don't speak at all?

No matter how good your music is, or how well the public likes it, we will penalize you and the public by not playing your records because you have dared to speak out against some of our policies.

Is that the kind of attitude our government is granting radio licences to perpetuate? How can the same people who claim to be so unbiased while disseminating the news and other important messages be so prejudiced when it comes to the artists and the music they play?

As far as I'm concerned, the merits and the choices of all music played on the airwaves should be determined in a democratic fashion by the listening public. As they are the ultimate owners of the airwaves and the ultimate buyers of the products advertised, they should be the ultimate judges of the kinds of music they wish to hear. And it seems the only ones in disagreement with this observation are the radio stations themselves.

I'm speaking about what happened in 1992. And a lot of hockey has been played since then. There's a lot of new hockey players, a lot of new fans, and a lot of new coaches and general managers.

And as times have changed, we now see Ken Dryden as the general manager of the Toronto Maple Leafs. He happens to be another Stompin' Tom fan. And although Ken, or anybody else, still can't hear this twenty-eight-year-old "Hockey Song" on the radio, he and another few million can get to hear and enjoy it around the world wherever hockey is played. (Kudos for hockey and kicks for radio.)

Back to 1992. Gaet and Jean showed up for Christmas, Gaet and I wrote a couple of songs together, talked and laughed about our European trip, and went out to a big New Year's party with a bunch of friends.

Then January of 1993 came in with a hell of a bang. A sports writer for the *Ottawa Sun*, by the name of Earl McRae, who apparently views himself as being the judge of all human pedigree as well as of the kind of music people should listen to, wrote something in his column on January 19.

It seems that during the hockey game of the previous night, when the Senators were playing against one of the

American teams, Earl was trying to impress his American colleagues who were also there to report the highlights of the game. And because he didn't personally like "The Hockey Song," which was playing that night, he felt embarrassed that his friends from the States would have to listen to it. (Another American kowtow-er.)

So the next day, on the nineteenth, instead of reporting on the hockey game as it was his job to do, he wrote an apology, of sorts, to his American counterparts.

Describing "The Hockey Song" and its singer, Stompin' Tom, in the most degrading of words, he wrote:

> I was embarrassed to be a Canadian last night when the media sophisticates of [American city names] were suddenly subjected to the horrendous caterwauling of that all-Canadian rube, Stompin' Tom Connors. [This] big, steaming yob . . . makes Dylan sound like Pavarotti. And . . .
>
> As if that wasn't humiliating enough for those of us with taste and class, entire sections of hayseeds in the stands began undulating, clapping and singing along at the top of their lungs.
>
> They actually cheered the big, talentless galoot when [the song] was finished.
>
> I wanted to turn and apologize to my American colleagues. I wanted to say, look, you don't understand.
>
> Please don't judge us [Canadians] on the reaction of these people.
>
> These people are from the God-forsaken [Ottawa] Valley. These people are from bastions of yokeldom. These people are from places like Embrun, Arnprior, Renfrew and Pembroke, where inbreeding, wood-burning stoves, moonshine stills, out-houses, human manure on their boots, and baying hounds in the night reign supreme.
>
> These bindlestiffs [tramps or bums] don't

STOMPIN' TOM

eat with spoons, they play them on their kneecaps.

Stompin' Tom and the Hockey Song will have to go. And the sooner the better. And if those hicks in the stands don't like it, let them eat catfish.

There was a lot more in the column, but I think this much says it all. This article made headlines in papers across the country the following day. And my thoughts, at the time, on the matter? If the Earl McRaes of this country can get away with saying this kind of crap to the entire nation, while the music of Stompin' Tom doesn't fit the radio formats, either Earl McRae or Stompin' Tom should be kicked the hell out of Canada.

And what were the thoughts of the people of the Ottawa Valley? They were enraged. They wanted to tar and feather this guy. For months after, they tried to sue both him and the newspaper. But for some reason it was tossed out of court.

For weeks, the *Ottawa Sun* sold tons of newspapers because of the uproar, but at least some of their profits must have gone to their lawyers to have the case thrown out.

As a public figure, I might have been fair game for this "small c canadian." But there should be some law in this country to protect the good name of hardworking, innocent people, who did nothing but go to a hockey game and spend their hard-earned money to lend support to a home-town team, whose predecessors failed for lack of the same kind of interest. (And maybe the same kind of journalism.) And if these same people happen to get off on the music that is being played, that's a small plus for the money they paid. And it's no damn business of any newspaper columnist to run them down and insult them just because they happened to be having a good time.

My own rebuttal to this column of trash was released to the Canadian Press a few days later. Part of my letter went this way:

The next time I play Ottawa, there's going to be a big picture of Squirrelly Earl McRae

glued to my stompin' board. I'll borrow a cowboy boot from one of the boys in "The Valley."
And when this so-called Yankee lover gets to
feel the full weight of each cosmic Canadian
cultural crunch, there won't be much left to
the face of Squirrelly Earl when the show is
done.

(And on my first opportunity to do a show in the Valley,
on August 31, '93, that's exactly what I did.)

Lifetime Award for the Doctor?

O N FEBRUARY 14, 1993, Valentine's Day, Lena and I flew
to Halifax with a group of others from Capitol Records
EMI. And that night would be the first time I attended an
awards show in fifteen years.

After swearing off from award shows for so long, how did
all this come about?

Well, back two and a half years previous to this, an artist
by the name of Bill Wrigley was looking for a spot in Toronto
to paint a huge sixty-foot by thirty-foot mural on the side of
somebody's building. And when Sam Sniderman (Sam the
Record Man) heard what the subject of the mural was going
to be, he donated the outside wall of his building on the
northwest corner of the Dundas and Church Street intersection for the massive project.

It took this dedicated artist, Bill Wrigley (whom I didn't
know, by the way), seven solid weeks in the hot summer sun
to complete a giant picture of Canada with a colossal
Stompin' Tom playing his guitar and stompin' on a piece of
plywood. It was all in magnificent colour. And to give the
reader some perspective about its size, the distance between
the toe and the heel on the sole of my cowboy boot was more
than the height of an average man. This was some piece of
work. And the newspapers flaunted pictures of it everywhere. And indeed they should. Not so much for the subject
matter, but for the wonderful work that went into its

accomplishment. (And thank you so much, Bill, for choosing me for your subject.)

Now, when the East Coast Music Awards wanted to present me with the Helen Creighton Award for Lifetime Achievement, on the fourteenth of February, I didn't want to go down to accept it. (Remember, I had refused the same offer two years before.)

This time Rob Cohn of the ECMA enlisted a couple of heavyweights to help pressure me to go down. One was Dean Cameron, president of Capitol Records EMI, and the other was Sam the Record Man. Talking to these guys on the phone every second day I finally agreed to accept the award on one condition.

And that was that, upon receiving the award, I would be allowed to re-dedicate it and have it given out every year by the ECMA as "The Stompin' Tom Award" to several east-coast musicians who, in the past, had never won an award but had been a great inspiration to the present award winners by the great music they played and the perseverance they had shown when there were no awards to be obtained. I felt these people deserved recognition for their efforts even though there might not be a category in the present system in which they could be nominated.

Once this condition was met, I agreed to go. And on the night of February 14, 1993, I was presented with my Lifetime Achievement Award by Sam the Record Man, and immediately called Rob Cohn onto the stage to receive it back as I publicly re-dedicated it in the manner described above. You might say it was a Valentine's gift.

And although it actually took them three more years to make the Stompin' Tom Award a reality in 1996, during the ECMAs in Charlottetown, P.E.I., it was a great moment for about a dozen of the old-time unsung heroes. The award has been given out to several others each year ever since.

Lena's brother Ted was now living in Halifax. He had recently split up with his wife, Cathy, and we spent some time with him and his new ladyfriend, Eileen, before flying back to Ontario.

In March, EMI Records (they had dropped the name Capitol by now) wanted to put out a new compilation album featuring "The Hockey Song" and they arranged to have a photo-shoot with me in the penalty box at Maple Leaf Gardens. Tommy, who was still playing hockey at the time, got a great charge going up and down the ice that afternoon while the photo-shoot was going on. I'm sure he must have had some interesting stories to tell the other kids when he got home. Pat Burns was there and gave Tommy a tour of the Maple Leafs' dressing room and a couple of autographed hockey sticks that had been used in the game the night before by Wendel Clark and Peter Zezel.

Also in late March '93, I received word from St. Thomas University, in Fredericton, New Brunswick, that they wished to confer an honorary Doctorate of Laws, honoris causa, on Stompin' Tom Connors.

This came as quite a surprise. So I called the president of the university, Dr. Dan O'Brien, to make sure this wasn't some kind of a prank. When Dan confirmed its legitimacy, I told him I'd readily accept the honour, but as Stompin' Tom, I would have to wear my black hat during the ceremony, instead of one of those square ones.

To this he agreed. And on May 17, 1993, Lena and I, along with Brian Edwards and his sister Ella, flew down to Fredericton, where they outfitted me with my robe and I joined the procession into the Aitkens Centre to receive my doctorate.

In a line of about 150 students, I was about three-quarters of the way back. And when I entered the arena, the symphony orchestra, which, up until now had been playing fairly sombre music, broke into "Bud the Spud."

At the sight of the guy in the big black cowboy hat, all the people in the bleachers gave me a standing ovation. And the orchestra continued to play "Bud the Spud" until I took my seat on the podium, along with other dignitaries.

When my turn came to receive my Doctorate of Laws, Dr. Stan Atherton read a glowing citation over the PA and the orchestra again struck up with a chorus or two of "Bud the Spud." After receiving my diploma, they placed a coronation robe around my neck and I gave a big wave to everybody. The reaction to this was about thirty seconds of stomping by all the university students in attendance. Soon we all marched out again, and there in the parking lot about twenty minutes of autograph signing began. Everyone wanted to be first to have his paper signed by "Dr. Stompin' Tom Connors."

That night we were invited to the home of friends of ours, Bob and Joan Kenny. We had a big party where I sang a few songs. And before the evening was through, the premier of New Brunswick, Frank McKenna, who was a great friend of Bob's, dropped in with his wife, Julie, to say hello. During lunch, Bob, Frank and I had a chance to chat for a while, without getting into too much politics, and a great time was had by all.

Back in Ontario a week later, on the twenty-fifth, Lena and I and Tommy and Dave MacMillan of EMI attended a hockey game at the Gardens where the Leafs were playing the L.A. Kings. During the second break in the game, I was called up to the broadcast booth where I met Canada's favourite coach, Don Cherry, for the first time. The meeting was only brief but we got along famously. Then I had to go for a short interview with Ron McLean. The Leafs won that night, three to two over the Kings in overtime. I don't know whether "The Hockey Song" or "Sudbury Saturday Night" had anything to do with the win, but they played both several times.

The Cup, the Flag and the Key

B Y NOW, BRIAN EDWARDS and I were planning another cross-Canada tour, and I was looking for a band to do both the tour and also cut a new album.

Duncan Fremlin, who had played banjo on my last album, was also the leader of a band called Whiskey Jack, who had played backup for Tommy Hunter for a couple of seasons on television. So after I called Duncan and found out that he and his band would be available, we began rehearsals and recorded my eighteenth self-penned album in the month of June 1993. Three songs on this album were co-written with Gaet Lepine. One of them, called "Suzanne De Lafayette," was half French and half English. The album was called *Dr. Stompin' Tom . . . Eh?*

This album also contained a song called "The Blue Berets." I wrote this mainly because I had received so many letters from the Blue Berets overseas, who told me that my songs about Canada were being played constantly by all the boys in the army camps. These songs always kept them "in touch" as they often thought of friends and relatives back home and so far away. A video was also made for this song a year later at Petawawa and Camp Borden, where I personally met some of the guys I had written to while they were overseas. One or two of the guys I especially remember were Captain Rob Kearney and Corporal Carl Dinsdale. The latter presented me with a nice plaque while I was at the

Canadian Forces Base in Petawawa on May 26, 1994. We also got to have a couple of beers together. In co-operation with EMI Records, the co-ordinator of this project to do "The Blue Berets" video, on behalf of the CFB, was Lieutenant Kent Page.

The members of the band Whiskey Jack were Duncan Fremlin, Bob McNiven, Greg "Chip" Street, Rob Duffus and Conrad Kipping. These were the boys who went on Tour '93 with me. But joining them on the album *Dr. Stompin' Tom . . . Eh?* were Graham Townsend on fiddle, his son, Gray, on piano, Dennis Keldie and Freddie Northcotte on accordions and Chris Whiteley on steel, dobro and harmonica.

Our first public performance on Tour '93 was on Canada Day, on Parliament Hill, in Ottawa. Duncan played the banjo, Bob played acoustic rhythm, Chip played stand-up bass, Rob played drums, Conrad played lead and mandolin, and our fiddle player was the master himself, Graham Townsend.

To an audience of thousands, and a couple of million on television, I sang "Canada Day, Up Canada Way," and behind my back, while I was singing "The Hockey Song," a group of people from the NHL wheeled in a little table on stage which contained nothing less than the Stanley Cup itself.

As I made a half turn before going into the last verse of the song, I caught the view of the Cup in the corner of my eye, and stopped singing. I signalled to the boys to keep on playing the tune as I went over and grabbed the Cup and held 'er high. I made two or three turns, bowing and gesturing to the crowd with the Cup well over my head. And then placing it back on the little table, I continued with the last verse of "The Hockey Song" to thunderous applause.

After the boys and I got off the stage we had the honour of meeting Kurt Browning, Canada's gold medalist that year in figure skating. I congratulated him later as we all had a beer together back in the dressing room.

Our sound and lighting for Tour '93 was provided by Westbury. And our man on the control board was Chris Quilliam, and our lighting man was Matt Rice. Security was provided by the Hewitt brothers, Frank and Randy. The concession stand was run by Ella Page, Brian's sister, and her daughter, Krista. Tommy was also on this tour until he had to go back to school.

By August 3, we'd played Kenora, Ontario, and without mentioning all the western towns previously named on other tours, we were back playing Thunder Bay on the seventeenth.

On August 25, we were playing Ontario Place in Toronto, when one of the fans was removed from the audience for waving a Canadian flag during the concert by one of the security guards who was certainly not hired by us. Brian Edwards and myself were outraged because of this. And the next day, in the Toronto papers we placed an apology for this act even though we had nothing to do with it. As far as we're concerned, waving the flag during a Stompin' Tom concert is encouraged. And any venue, large or small, who wants to book Stompin' Tom to play a concert should know that.

Before heading out for the east coast we played Carleton Place, in the Ottawa Valley. When I walked on the stage showing the picture of Earl McRae's face glued to my stompin' board, the audience went ballistic. And even more so when I threw it on the floor and proceeded to kick the livin' shit out of it. This was the only concert in history where an entertainer got more applause for every time he stomped his foot down than he did for each song he sang.

During the intermission, some of the players from the Senators hockey club gave me one of their jerseys, which I wore during my next set. And the "Stompin' on Earl McRae Show" continued for the next hour. And it sure wasn't hard to get three or four curtain calls that night after picking my board up off the stage and letting the sawdust drop to the floor, intermingled with whatever paper particles were left of Mr. McRae's portrait. (Gee, thanks, Earl.)

While playing the eastern provinces I got a chance, in Charlottetown, P.E.I., to go and see Cora, my stepmother, who was now in the Alberton Hospital. While I was there, I took the boys up to Skinners Pond for a short visit. As time was pressing, we moved on to the rest of our Maritime leg of the tour.

By September 22, we were back in Ontario, playing

Niagara Falls, and then Lulu's in Kitchener for the second time during this tour.

On October 2, we were in Peterborough, where Mr. Doris, the mayor, presented me with the key to the city, which to me was really something special. (Those who have read my previous book may remember how I first arrived in this town as a hitch-hiker, and later played at the King George Hotel where the waiter, Boyd MacDonald, gave me the name of Stompin' Tom. The role that Fate plays in the lives of individuals can be amazing when one takes the time to make the observation.)

The tour finally wound up in Ottawa on the fourth of October, where we all expected some kind of a retaliation by Earl McRae for the Carleton Place "humiliation," but it never came. (Again, gee, thanks, Earl.)

THE HOCKEY SONG
1.

Hello out there, we're on the air,
It's hockey night tonight;
Tension grows, the whistle blows
And the puck goes down the ice.
The goalie jumps, the players bump,
And the fans all go insane,
Someone roars, Bobby scores,
At the good old hockey game.

CHORUS:
Oh the good old hockey game,
Is the best game you can name,
And the best game you can name,
Is the good old hockey game.

2.

Speak: Second period . . .
Where players dash with skates aflash,
The home team trails behind;
But they grab the puck and go bursting up,
And they're down across the line.
They storm the crease like bumble bees,

They travel like a burning flame.
We see them slide the puck inside,
It's a one, one hockey game.

REPEAT CHORUS

3.

Speak: *Third period . . . Last game in the playoffs too . . .*
Oh take me where the hockey players
Face off down the rink,
And the Stanley Cup is all filled up,
For the champs who win the drink.
Now the final flick of a hockey stick
And one gigantic scream;
The puck is in, the home team wins,
The good old hockey game.

REPEAT CHORUS THREE TIMES

Books, "Whacks" and Awards

As soon as Tour '93 was over we held another big "Camp-n-Jam" party on our property at which seventy or more people were in attendance.

Just some of the names besides the Whiskey Jack boys were Graham and Eleanor Townsend, Brian Baron, John Prince, Lynn and Shirley Russworm, Freddy White, with a couple more of the boys from the Carleton Show Band, Clare Adlam, Reg and Muriel Chapman, Gaet and Jean Lepine, Dean Cameron and most of the guys and gals from EMI, Jim and Kim McKinley, Ron Jones, Mark Altman, Sam Leitch, Bruce Eaton . . . Bruce who? Bruce Eaton. He's the guy who brought the kegs of draft out from Upper Canada.

Everyone sang or played an instrument around the campfire and a lot more just listened. And other than the fact that Chip Street got the head broken off the neck of his stand-up bass, and Clare Adlam got his fiddle bow snapped in two when somebody walked on it, everybody had a good time.

Around the middle of October, I got Muriel Chapman to help me answer some of the vast amounts of fan mail that always seems to be the heaviest just after a tour. I always try to answer these letters personally, but there's just no way I can handle them all. Because if I did, I wouldn't have any time to get anything else done. I just hope the folks out there will try to understand this.

Near the end of October, I received a letter from Floyd Keefe, who lives in Skinners Pond. He told me he would like to re-open the school to the tourist trade. At first I thought he was crazy or something. And I told him I wanted no part of it. "Don't you realize how much money I've wasted on that project?" I asked him.

But as it turned out, all he wanted was permission to use the school and school property to give it a try. If he had that permission to show the government, he felt certain he could obtain a grant to fix the old place up.

Under these conditions I gave the permission but told him to make damn sure that because of the grant the government wouldn't be trying to get a lien on the place. And furthermore, if he was smart, he wouldn't connect my name to the place at all, for fear the old "unknown" enemies would turn up again to burn the place down.

As it turned out, Floyd and his wife, Karen, formed the Skinners Pond Improvement Council, with committee members being Karen Keefe, Pauline Arsenault, Brenda Doyle and Charlene Shields. They obtained the grant and had their official opening of the school on July 1, 1994. (So far there's been no problems and I hope it stays that way. And it probably will, as long as there's no involvement by someone on whom certain people may once again start exercising their jealous animosity.)

Also, near the end of October '93, I received a letter and was later paid a visit by a Mr. Allan Evans, who runs the Royal Atlantic Wax Museum in Cavendish, Prince Edward Island.

The purpose of his visit was to ask my permission to have a wax figure of Stompin' Tom added to the museum collection. And if I agreed, could I donate some clothes that I had worn during one of my concerts?

After I supplied him with everything but the guitar, he went home quite happy. And the following year, 1994, there I was in the museum for all to see, as they listened to a tape recording of "Bud the Spud" every time they pressed a button.

It was several years before I got to see this mannequin myself. And then it was all too briefly, as I had to talk with people and sign autographs at the same time. Maybe the next time I go there, there'll be fewer people around.

Something else I failed to mention up until now is the subject of songbooks. In 1970, Canadian Music Sales published *Stompin' Tom Connors' Song Folio No. 1.* Then in 1975, Crown-Vetch Music Ltd. published, *Stompin' Tom, Story and Song.* This contained 125 songs with a short story written by Stevedore Steve. (Both of these are currently out of print.)

In 1993, Doubleday published a five-song children's book called *My Stompin' Grounds.* This was illustrated by Kurt Swinghammer. (I'm unsure of its current availability.)

And in 1994, Ragweed Press of Charlottetown published a one-song children's book called *Bud the Spud* and a second one-song children's book in 1995 called *Hockey Night Tonight,* featuring "The Hockey Song." Both these books were illustrated by Brenda Jones. (Both are still available.)

Now, because of these songs, both in books and on records, the Periodical Marketers of Canada and the Foundation for the Advancement of Canadian Letters, in November of 1993, saw fit to present me with their special Author's Award for Leadership. (This particular award had only been presented to two Canadians prior to this time. They were Pierre Elliott Trudeau and Pierre Berton.)

The award, which now hangs on my wall, reads: "This Author's Award for Leadership is presented in Appreciation and Admiration to Stompin' Tom Connors—Balladeer, Patriot and Composer—Who has entertained, and inspired Canadians through his music and his love for Canada. By the Periodical Marketers of Canada and the Foundation for the Advancement of Canadian Letters. On November 15th, 1993."

The award was presented in the Sheraton Centre in Montreal. Accompanying Lena and myself that evening was my promoter, Brian Edwards. And while this awards show was not too much different than others, something very comical happened that night, though it wasn't intended to be so.

Among other authors who were there to receive awards and citations was Farley Mowat, who was sitting at a table at the opposite end of the large room, away from where we were sitting.

There were paper placemats on each table, and we were

all served drinks and snack food as we sat in the semi-lighted room to watch the presentations.

Farley Mowat was called up to the podium about half an hour before I was. I had never met him before, and as he made his acceptance speech he laughed and told a few risqué jokes. He was much shorter than I had expected. But he looked very Scotch, crusty, and well used to banking the cabin woodstove for a long winter night.

After I accepted my award, there were one or two others, and the show was over. Or was it?

As Lena and I and Brian sat at our table wondering what was supposed to happen next, who should come walking across the room but Farley, with several people following him.

Although the room was dimly lit, I could make out that he was looking and heading straight for me. And when he shouted "Stompin' Tom" from about ten feet away, I stood up to welcome his approach.

"Farley Mowat," I said, as I offered my hand. "It's a pleasure meeting you."

"No way! Stompin' Tom," he said, "The pleasure is all mine. I've been wanting to meet you for a long time. And now that the time has come, I want your autograph. And I want it right on here." And as he passed me the paper placemat he was holding in his hand, he said, "And make it a damn good one."

As I grabbed the paper out of his hand, I said, "Okay, Buddy. If it's a good one you're after, here you go." I then tossed the paper on the floor and gave it three or four stomps and picked it up all ripped in a couple of places.

As I passed it back to him, I thought he'd appreciate the humour. But instead, he just held it in his hands. And with a very sober, non-smiling face, he just stood there looking up at me for about five seconds, as if he was trying to catch his breath or something.

Then, finally, he blurted out, "You son-of-a-bitch, Stompin' Tom, you stomped on my goddamn award."

In the semi-darkness the piece of paper had looked liked a placemat, so I just grabbed it and stomped on it.

"Holy jeezes, Farley," I said. "I didn't mean to stomp on your award." But then seeing the humour of it all, I started

laughing and couldn't stop. As soon as everyone else realized what had happened, they were all laughing as well. And
poor Farley had to take his award home in two or three
pieces. I often wonder today what it must look like hanging
on his wall with all the rest of his awards. With a little glue
and Scotch tape, though, it might not look all that bad.
(Seriously, though, I know it's hard to believe, but I was sorry
about that, Farley.)

A Book Launch for the Record

ONE DAY AROUND LATE NOVEMBER, after we got home from Montreal, I got a phone call from my old friend John Farrington. I met John while I played the Maple Leaf Hotel in Timmins when he was a young reporter for the *Timmins Press*. Through the years, he'd been transferred all over the place, filling different positions with different newspapers. And now he was back in Timmins, as the paper's publisher.

On the phone, John said he was in Toronto for a couple of days on business, so I asked him to come out to the house if he had a little time to spare. During the conversation at the house he happened to mention that someday I should write a book.

I told him I had already started one back in 1978, but after writing 130 pages, I got discouraged and quit. He then asked me if I would let him read what I had written so far, so I let him take a copy of the pages back to Timmins with him.

Several days later he called me again, saying he had read the pages and thought the book had a lot of merit. And the next time he was in Toronto, just after the New Year, he'd like to come out to the house and talk to me again about doing something with it.

When January came, John was back. This time that's all we talked about. The book. "You've just got to do something about finishing it," he said. "And if you want, I'll come down

periodically with a tape recorder and get a bunch of interviews on tape and have them typed up for you on the
computer."

At first, this sounded like a good idea. But we found out
pretty soon it wasn't going to work. The stories John was writing from the tapes were all out of chronological order, so I
decided I'd have to sit down and type them myself on the
typewriter.

While doing this, I found out that it was just a nuisance
going back and forth to the tape, when I could remember all
the stuff anyway. So I was now back to the situation I'd been
in when I abandoned the book in 1978.

But there was one difference. John had sparked my interest again, and I decided to keep at it. Writing a few pages of
notes at a time with a pencil, I would then do them over
more neatly on the typewriter.

John helped me for a while longer, by bringing his laptop
computer down to the house where I would sit and dictate
what I had written while he typed it into the laptop. He
would then take it back to Timmins to make copies.

As this became more and more awkward and incon-
venient, it was decided that I'd just finish the rest of the
book by myself. I guess the thing that bothered me the most
about the computer was when I received copies back from
Timmins, they contained a lot of spelling mistakes that were
not in the originals. And though it was explained to me that
all the words had been "spell-checked," there were typo-
graphical errors the spell check could not correct. Such as,
if the word "at" is typed into the computer instead of the
word "ate," it does not automatically correct it.

So once again, I just decided to go back to the old way of
doing things. That's the way *Before the Fame* was written. And
that's the way this book was written, also. It may be long and
tedious work, but when it's done, it's done. And the spelling,
etc., is all checked page by page as I go.

So with the 130 pages I did in 1978, plus 390 I wrote in
the twenty months from November 1993 until June of 1995,
the total number of pages in *Before the Fame* were 521, counting the Introduction. And by the way this book is proceeding, there will be a good many more than the last one.

So with nothing much happening while you're writing a book (and indeed, you don't want much to happen, as it throws you off your train of thought), it doesn't give you much to say for the time spent while trying to account for it in the next book.

Sometime in July of 1994 we had another Camp-n-Jam. This brought me out of hibernation for a few days and gave me a welcome break after sitting in front of a typewriter for some eight or nine months.

Again a lot of friends were at the party. Among others were Dennis and Eleanor Plata, Brian and Barb Hewson, Dr. Mike and Luba Pryszlak, Dave and Pat Newlands, Lynn and Shirley Russworm, some of the folks from EMI, Mark and Pnina Altman from Morning Music, and along with a host of other musicians, the boys from Whiskey Jack also attended. They were Duncan Fremlin, Bob McNiven, Conrad Kipping, Rob Duffus, and their new bass player, David Thompson.

Everybody, of course, wanted to know if I had my book done yet. The only answer I could give them was, "You gotta be kidding. I've got at least another whole year to go. If you think I've got a 'pool-room tan' this summer, wait till you see me next July."

In August of '94, my grind behind the typewriter was perked up one day when Lena passed me a letter from Jean Chrétien, the prime minister of Canada. In some very nice words he thanked me for writing the tribute song to Canada's Blue Berets, our United Nations Peacekeepers, overseas. One of the slogans within the lyrics of the song "The Blue Berets" that was quickly picked up and used by the troops was, "We stand between the mighty and the frail." (There was also a video done of this song which got a lot of play overseas, but hardly any back home, except on the Canadian Forces Bases.)

I think it was in September of that year that I took some time out to give Bill Welychka, of MuchMusic, an interview for their TV program "Outlaws and Heroes." And I also received a visit from my friend, Randy J. Martin,

Randy was now making records in P.E.I. and had begun to make quite a name for himself on the east coast. He left me one of his CDs before he went back home.

Among other letters being received at the time, which I

couldn't always answer, were letters from school teachers, who complimented me for the geographical and historical content within my songs. They found the playing of these songs to the children during class to be a great help as a memory aid to the lessons they were being taught. One song in particular cropped up in almost every letter. "Name the Capitals," which is on the albums *My Stompin' Grounds* and the children's compilation *Once Upon a Stompin' Tom*.

One teacher told me it was a real treat to hear the kids going around one day singing the names of the provinces and their capitals after only playing the song several times during class the day before. What would normally have taken the students a couple of weeks to learn, they now knew in the span of only one day. (It's a pity the school boards across the country wouldn't pick up on this fast way of learning things. Maybe the students could learn twice as much in half the time, thereby making the lessons of life more enjoyable. Especially for the parents, when they find out their school taxes for the year could be cut in half.)

Dean Cameron and Eddy Colero came out from EMI to spend an evening before Christmas that year, and Gaet and Jean Lepine were there to spend two or three weeks. I had promised Gaet now for some time that I would take a look at some of the many songs he had written and advise him as to which ones he should send out to be looked at by other publishing companies.

After listening to some of these songs, I realized that they needed a lot of serious work. So after about three weeks or so, we had not only cleaned up eight or ten of these, but we decided to co-write a few others besides. Altogether, we must have worked on or co-written over twenty songs. A lot of these, I myself decided to record on the album I was planning to do the following summer.

Gaet and Jean left for home around the middle of January 1995, and I went back to writing *Before the Fame*.

At the end of April, Cynthia Good, publisher of Penguin Books Canada, asked me if I could make a contribution to a book she was putting out, entitled *If You Love This Country: Fifteen Voices for a Unified Canada*.

The Quebec Referendum of '95 was coming up that fall,

and she wanted fifteen dissenting voices to speak their piece against the separation of Quebec.

Although I was still working day and night to finish my own book for a June deadline, I took a day or so to write my contribution. After all, it was for the cause of Canada. And it was called "The Liberation of Quebec?"

Some of the other contributors to *If You Love This Country* were Lewis Mackenzie, Roberta Bondar, Laurier LaPierre, Bob White, Matthew Coon Come, Peter C. Newman and Joe Clark.

During the month of May '95, Lena couldn't even talk to me. I had to get this damn book done by the end of the first week in June or else it would have to wait for another year.

I also had the Escarpment Sound Studio booked on June 7, and Brian Hewson was preparing to record another Stompin' Tom album.

I finally passed the finished book on to one of Penguin's editors, David Kilgour, on the second of June, and called on the musicians to have rehearsals for the album on the following day. These musicians were Chris Whiteley, Denis Keldie, David Thompson, Rob Duffus, Conrad Kipping and Ike Kelneck.

Gaet Lepine showed up for the recording, and it was he who had contacted Ike Kelneck to play some of the instruments his father, Henry Kelneck, used to play in Timmins when he led the Henry Kelneck Orchestra. And all this came about because Gaet and I had written a tribute song, called "Polka Playin' Henry," and we thought it only appropriate that Ike, his son, should be playing on the album. (It was unfortunate, however, that on the day Ike showed up to perform, he was only able to play some of the instruments his dad used to play, these being the trombone, sax and tuba. And when he came to play the trumpet, which was the main instrument his dad was noted for, he didn't have "the lip" for it. The trumpet part in the song was later done by Chris Whiteley. But those things can happen in a recording session.)

This was my nineteenth album, and it contained seventeen original songs, most of them co-written with Gaet Lepine back in January of that year, 1995. The title song which gave the new album its name was "Long Gone to the

Yukon." And its official release by EMI Records would take place at the same time as Penguin released *Before the Fame*, in late October.

Shortly after the album was recorded, I received an invitation to attend the Classic Country Music Reunion by Bill Oja, the southwestern Ontario column contributor for *Country Music News*.

This event occurred each year, and in 1995 it would be held in Lindsay, Ontario, on August 4, 5 and 6. So Lena and I decided to go.

Upon arriving at the grounds we met John Lester (who now works with Brian Edwards of Rocklands Talent) and he took us to a large trailer parked behind the outside stage. Here we spoke for a while with friends I hadn't seen in a long time. Among others there were Chef Adams, Al Hooper, Johnny Burke, Al Brisco, Larry Mercey, Gary Hooper and Lorne Hachey.

After having a beer or two with some of the old gang, Lena and I went out in the stands for an hour and watched some of the acts.

We also took in their record and instrument museum, which was mainly donated for the occasion by one of Canada's great country music historians, Dan Foster. And then we made our way back to the trailer behind the stage.

Here I struck up a conversation with the CRTC's Sjef Frenken (which was very interesting, to say the least), while Terry Sumsion, Anita Perras, Diana Leigh, Washboard Hank and Larry Mercey were either performing on stage or preparing to do so.

Then, while in a conversation with Murray Hunt, one of the country DJs who *does* play Stompin' Tom when he gets the chance, I was asked if I might like to go on the stage and sing a couple of numbers. If I wanted to go, I was told that Larry Mercey would be good enough to donate some of his allotted time to me, and a good flat-top guitar would also be provided.

Accepting the offer, I waited behind the curtains until Larry sang several songs, and then he gave the introduction.

As I wasn't even on the bill, the audience seemed to take all this as some kind of a joke until I walked out and shouted into the mike, "It's Bud the Spud, from the bright red mud, rollin' down the highway smilin'. . ."

In surprise, the audience came to their feet with applause. I then sang the "Gumboot Cloggeroo" and "Sudbury Saturday Night." And while the crowd were still applauding, I turned to thank the guys who had backed me up. They were known as the Mark LaForme Band. (And you'll hear a lot more about these guys later.)

Back at the hotel that night, Lena and I paid a short visit to another couple of parties, and then we turned in. We came home the next day promising ourselves that we would attend the Canadian Country Music Reunion again the following year. But as always, something else came up. Still, we had a great time, and we'll no doubt go back again some day.

Johnny and Judy Reid were up from Charlottetown that fall. Johnny had to take some kind of treatment at one of the hospitals in Toronto, and while they were up they stayed with their daughter Alice Anne and her husband Arian. They all came out to our place one night and another night we all went out to dinner.

Also that fall, in 1995, the first Henry Kelneck Award was instituted in Timmins by the city, in co-operation with the *Timmins Press*. This was given to present and past residents for special achievements in music and as an entertainer of the year award. I became its first recipient and my award read, in part: "To Stompin' Tom Connors . . . who has put Timmins on the map by his unique songwriting and music." As the great Timmins bandleader, Henry Kelneck, is now deceased the award was presented by his son, Ike.

On October 26, '95, the famous Ann Dunn's Matador Club, in Toronto, once again became the scene of a party for Stompin' Tom. This time it was to be not only a new album launch of *Long Gone to the Yukon*, by EMI Records, but also the book launch of *Before the Fame* by Penguin Books. Both these companies had gotten together to create one huge gala celebration.

Everyone was given small Canadian flags to wave. (And this, of course, was all the more appropriate, given the fact the Quebec Referendum was due to take place in just four days, on October 30.)

Along with Dean Cameron of EMI and Cynthia Good of Penguin, there were scads of business types from both the record and the book-publishing industry. TV cameras from the CBC and MuchMusic, and people from the press were everywhere. Steve Fruitman from CIUT and other campus radio DJs all got interviews, along with Denise Donlon and other people from the TV networks.

In anticipation of all this, instead of arriving late as the guest of honour, I arrived early and chatted with a lot of people as they came in the door. One of these was good old Sam the Record Man, who had always been instrumental in selling my records over the years whether the big radio stations played them or not. (Again, big radio was conspicuous by their absence.)

The live music was provided by all the boys of Whiskey Jack, who were joined by Chris Whiteley and Denis Keldie. And during each of their breaks, the songs on the new album, *Long Gone to the Yukon,* were played continually.

Again there were many young people there, as well as other EMI recording artists. Some of these were Kim Stockwood, Susan Aglukark and John McDermott. (John sang "O Canada" to start the evening off.)

Throughout the evening, there were numerous speeches given, and I even got up and sang a few songs.

Among our personal friends present were Lena's sister, Pauline; Mr. and Mrs. John Farrington; Mr. and Mrs. Dennis Plata; Mr. and Mrs. Mike O'Brien; Mr. and Mrs. Gaet Lepine; Mrs. Muriel Chapman; Mr. Jim McKinley; and my son Tommy and his lady friend. Mr. and Mrs. Brian Edwards were also in attendance.

The fare that night was "all you could eat" lobsters, brought in from P.E.I., and for those who may not have a taste for lobster, there was a beautiful roast of beef with all the trimmings. There was also lots of Moosehead beer along with Upper Canada draft. And what a party this was.

By the time the night was over, it seemed like everyone was going home with a new Stompin' Tom record or a new book under his arm. Even Bruce Eaton . . . Bruce who? Oh, . . . you know. The guy who brought the beer.

My Sixtieth Birthday Award

O N OCTOBER 30, 1995: I guess nobody hardly wants to be reminded how the results of the Quebec Referendum almost brought the heartbeat of Canada to a stop. And I'll bet my boots that, had the squeaker gone the other way, the separatist government of Quebec would have never again allowed another referendum to see if the "sovereign Quebec people" would care to rejoin Canada. (This very Canadian democratic mechanism which would allow a province to separate in the first place would have been denied to the people of Quebec forever.)

Another footnote to this referendum was that EMI Records (Canada) sent hundreds of packages of the pro-Canadian songs of Stompin' Tom on CD to the radio stations in hopes they might play some of them to help incite Canadians everywhere to be a little more Canadian during our nation's hour of dire need. All this happened months before the referendum. And did radio play them . . . ? No! (They were probably too busy playing foreign/American music to even notice.)

In November that year, Tommy graduated from high school. And while Lena was up and about, flashing smiles everywhere, I was sitting in the back row of the audience thinking how proud and glad I was that Tommy had been able to accomplish something that I never could. Like a big baboon with tears in his eyes, all I could do was sit there and not talk to anyone. Even after, when we took pictures and I shook his hand and hugged him, I had to get the hell out of there before I broke up. But then, how could Tommy or Lena ever understand all the pictures of life that were running through my mind during what was, to them, a time to celebrate?

The boys from EMI were out to the house again for an evening before Christmas. We had a few beers and exchanged gifts, while Gaet entertained us with a few songs and impressions of people that only he can do. (Some impressionists can imitate movie stars, politicians, animals, etc. But only Gaet can do ice cream, Jell-O, porridge and bacon.)

After a New Year's party at the house with a few close friends—Clare Adlam, Brian and Barb Hewson, Bonnie Brigant and a few others, including Gaet and Jean Lepine—we said goodbye to the old year, and I immediately started the new one, 1996, by commencing to write this book.

During the month of January *Before the Fame* went to number one on most of the bestseller lists and stayed in the top ten for another few months. To everyone's surprise, and especially mine *Before the Fame* had beaten out such heavyweights as Bill Gates, Ellen DeGeneres, Pierre Berton, Peter C. Newman, Colin Powell and a book on Prime Minister Chrétien, by Lawrence Martin. (Those in the know were telling me this was quite an accomplishment for a Canadian author, and especially with his very first book.)

All through January 1996, with the incentive of having a number one bestseller, I just kept writing. And then by the first of February I got another call to go down to Charlottetown, P.E.I., to attend the East Coast Music Awards which were being held there that year.

"I can't go. I'm writing," was my reply, "and besides, I don't want to go. Because they haven't done a damn thing about the Lifetime Achievement Award that I re-dedicated in 1993 to all the Unsung Heroes of Music on the east coast. That was the reason I went down there three years ago, and for no other. So to get me down there, what kind of a promise they can't live up to are they willing to make this time? Award shows, they're all the same, and I just don't want any part of them. So don't bother me."

Now they enlisted the help of Sam the Record Man again. "No, Sam," I told him. "You were there onstage when I re-dedicated my award and gave it back to Rob Cohn in 1993. And that was the condition I set for even going down there. So without a guarantee that this new award to unsung heroes has become a reality, I don't even want to talk about it."

"I remember very well," Sam said, "and you are absolutely right. Let me look into it."

I don't know what Sam did, but a day or so later, word came through to me that if I came down to attend the ECMA in Charlottetown, there would definitely be a new Stompin' Tom Award presented to a number of east coast unsung musical heroes, and I would have the honour of unveiling the special award myself. It would, thereafter, become a yearly presentation.

I was still quite leery of the whole thing, but I accepted. I couldn't figure out why they hadn't done all this before. And if this was just another scheme to get me down there, I'd never attend another award's show as long as I live.

Then I found out they also wanted me to open the awards show by singing "Bud the Spud." And because it was being broadcast live on the CBC television network from Charlottetown, I wondered if there wasn't some other motive behind all this.

"Well, whether there is or whether there isn't," I thought, "I can't let the unveiling of this new award interfere with the fee I would have to charge for performing on television." And once this was all properly negotiated, Lena and I flew down to Charlottetown.

We arrived on the seventh of February, and on the evening of the eighth we attended a reception held by the premier of Prince Edward Island, Catherine Callbeck.

After listening to several citations and speeches delivered by certain dignitaries, including that of the premier, the orchestra struck up the music of "Bud the Spud." And from the floor above us, down a long flight of stairs, came a huge choir of children singing all the words. It was indeed an emotional moment.

After shaking hands and thanking the kids, I was led over

to one side of the room where a large object stood concealed behind a shroud. "This can't be the award," I
thought. "It's much too large." (It must have stood seven
feet tall.)

Then Ms. Callbeck, the premier, said a few words, shook
my hand and signalled for me to pull down the veil.

And there, for all to see, was a huge wood carving of
Stompin' Tom, in silhouette. And engraved down one side
were the names of the first recipients of the Stompin' Tom
Award to the east coast unsung musical heroes. Their names
were Lem Jay, Lyman Dunsford, George Chappell, Helen
Byrne, Dot MacAulay, Collin Boyd, Russell Downe, Pius
Blackett, Wilmot MacDonald, Aubrey Hanson and Jimmy
Linegar. And all had been thanked and given certificates for
the outstanding music they had performed for so many
years without recognition, and for the great inspiration they
had been to the young ECMA trophy winners of today. (It was
about time they knew we were all grateful. There were many
of them present, and I got to shake their hands and thank
them personally, because I had been one of those whom
they had inspired.)

The carving had been done by Jeff Scott, whom I later
met and thanked for doing such a great job. And in suc-
ceeding years more names of other great people were added
to this carving, which I will mention in this book before its
completion.

Later that evening, after the reception, Pauline and Bill,
Ted and Eileen, and Amy and Foster followed us back to our
motel room where they had a little family party for me, as
tomorrow, the ninth of February, would be my sixtieth
birthday.

They waited till midnight and then came out with a little
cake with six candles on it, one for every decade, and gave
me a few little presents and a number of funny cards. A few
beers and laughs later we called it a night.

The following afternoon of the ninth, Lena and I took a
drive down to Borden, P.E.I., where we stopped at a restaurant for lunch. After I signed a few autographs for the staff,
the owner called some friends of his and arranged for us to
get a private tour of the grounds where all the massive piers

and girders were being made for the now world-famous Confederation Bridge. I was soon to write a song about this bridge which I will speak about later.

That evening, we were informed that the EMI Records people and Johnny Reid were holding a lobster supper over at Johnny Reid's dining room, and that Lena and I were expected to be there. (Just mention lobsters and I'm there anyway.)

We arrived around 8:30 and a number of people were already there. As soon as everybody was assembled, out came the lobsters, and did we ever have a great feed.

After the lobsters, everybody gave me a birthday card and some even went to the bother of getting me a present. I especially remember the beautiful camcorder the boys from EMI got me. Of course, Lena snaffled onto that pretty fast. Johnny and Judy gave me a nice silver mug with my name engraved on it, wishing me a happy sixtieth birthday. There was also a glass mug in the shape of a cowboy boot and a few other nice things. There was also a lovely birthday cake.

The people present were Johnny and Judy Reid; Dean Cameron, Peter Diemer, Steve MacAulay, Eddie Colero, Tim Trombley, Dave MacMillan, Eric and Nancy McEwen; and among personal friends and family were Ted and Eileen, Foster and Amy, and Bill and Pauline. Guests who just dropped in to say hello and wish me happy birthday were "Awesome" J.P. Cormier, and the "godfather" of Canadian Celtic music himself, John Allan Cameron.

After having a great chat with everyone, and especially Eric McEwen, who quite often played a Stompin' Tom selection on his weekly radio program, I was in for another surprise.

Next door, in Johnny's Prince Edward Lounge, a large array of entertainers had been assembling for about an hour. And when everything was ready, Johnny and the gang ushered me in to a special table, and the real party began. (Forgive me if I don't mention everybody. I was pretty much under the weather when I went in.)

The Irish Descendants had written a Stompin' Tom tribute especially for the occasion, and most other artists sang one or two of my songs. And this room, which normally holds about three hundred, was packed like sardines. EMI and Johnny had certainly gone out of their way to provide a wonderful surprise. It seemed like the whole east coast was there.

Kim Stockwood sang; Ashley MacIsaac showed he could stomp even better than I could; Joey Kitson and the Rawlins Cross were there, with Richard Wood, and Sandbox; and God knows how many others.

At one point, they got me up on the stage to say a few words. I guess I mumbled something to get a laugh and a round of applause, and then staggered back to my seat. And that was the signal for Lena to get me the hell out of there. (That was one of the only times she could ever get me to leave somewhere while the party was still going on. But thanks, gang. It was GREAT!)

After coming to and looking in the mirror the next afternoon, I was sure glad the award show wasn't taking place that night. It kind of reminded me of an old saying that Peter, Lena's dad, used to say all the time: "Wow! What a great party I went to last night. I can't remember a damn thing."

That evening we spent over at Bill and Pauline's house, where he and Foster took advantage of my condition and beat me at a few games of darts. After a few more beers, it was back to the motel, where I quickly hit the sack.

Two or three hours later, I got up out of bed to go to the washroom. On the way back I tripped in the dark and fell against one of the chairs and knocked one of my front teeth out.

Lena woke up and turned on the light asking, "Who the hell hit you? You're missing a tooth." "Thanks for telling me," I said. "I didn't know. I'll have to get the damn thing fixed before I go on television tomorrow night." (Tomorrow was Sunday, and "Awards Day.")

Early the next day we spent a couple of hours trying to get an available dentist. Finding one, I rushed right over and sat down in the chair like I was glad to be there. I wish I could remember his name, 'cause he sure saved me a lot of embarrassment.

With the tooth fixed, I rushed to the rehearsals, and

smiled at the first person I met to see if they noticed anything different. Then realizing it didn't matter 'cause I didn't know the guy in the first place, I headed for the dressing room.

There they had a rented guitar waiting for me because I hadn't brought my own with me on the plane. And after trying it, I liked it so much I later bought it and took it home with me.

After the rehearsal, I went back to the dressing room and just hung by waiting for the show to start. A couple of hours later the knock came on my dressing-room door. And in about five minutes' time they had ushered me onto the darkened stage to take my place in front of the mike to wait for my cue.

Although I could see the audience, they couldn't see me. And when the announcer said, "Ladies and gentlemen, from Charlottetown, Prince Edward Island, we now present to you the 1996 East Coast Country Music Awards," I started stompin' my boot. And as the lights slowly came up, I appeared out of the darkness with a bellow that almost sunk the Island, "It's Bud the SPUD! FROM THE BRIGHT RED MUD!" Then I finished the song with "Because he's got another big LOAD . . . of the Best Doggone TALENT that's Ever Been GROWED!!! . . . And it's from PRINCE EDWARD ISLAND . . . It's from PRINCE EDWARD ISLAND!!!"

Well, I shouldn't have to say what happened after that. The tone and the pace was set for the rest of the show. And thanks to all the other performers, they kept 'er rollin' throughout every performance. And it turned out to be the greatest awards night the ECMA had put on up until that time.

As soon as my portion was over and I left the stage, I was escorted from behind the curtains around to a seat beside Lena near the front of the audience, where a three-song tribute to Gene MacLellan was now being sung by Lennie Gallant, Marty Reno and his daughter, Tara MacLean. Gene had recently passed away, and the Helen Creighton Lifetime Achievement Award was being presented to him, posthumously. It was a very touching but appropriate scene to see his son and two daughters, Phillip, Rachel and Catherine, go up to the podium to accept it for him.

After watching such great talent perform that night, I was again surprised when I was called to the stage to proudly accept the ECMA's Male Country Artist Award. (Just a little more frosting on the sixtieth birthday cake.)

Another big celebration took place after the show that night in a large suite in one of the hotels. This was all again provided for by those great people from EMI Records. And their contribution to these things should never go unnoticed. (Many thanks.)

Another guy who worked his butt off during all this hoopla, and may not have received his due recognition, was Eric McEwen. Eric was the P.E.I. chairman for the ECMAS that year, and without him it never could have been the success it was. ('Way to go, Eric.)

The Order of Canada Medal

ARRIVING HOME FROM THE ECMAS on February 12, 1996, I thought I'd go right back into writing this book. But it wasn't so easy. Too many things had happened to take away my concentration. I guess it took about a week or so. And then David MacMillan from EMI called and said that Ron Hynes was in town and he wanted to know if he could bring him out to the house.

I always wanted to meet Ron, and never got a chance, even though we had both been in Charlottetown during the awards. A couple of nights later, Ron and Dave arrived at the house, and also brought Connie, Ron's wife, along.

We mainly talked about writing songs, and of course, we sang a few together. As Ron is the writer of that great song "Sonny's Dream," I had to get him to sing it a couple of times.

Before he left, he gave Lena and me a copy of his new CD *Cryer's Paradise*. The song we both liked the best on this record was "If I Left You Alone with My Heart." (It should have been a single.)

At any rate, we had a few beers and a midnight lunch, and promised to get together again sometime. (It's funny, though, how that word "sometime" can often turn out to be a "long time." Too bad.)

Two or three days later I got back to writing. And this time I stuck with it for about three months. Then I got a letter informing me that I had been selected as one of a large group of people that year to be received by the governor general, in Ottawa, to be presented with the Order of Canada Medal. (I goddamn near fell off my chair.)

I called Lena. "Look at this," I said. "Those crazy people in Ottawa got me mixed up with somebody else. The only people that get a medal are those who have done something outstanding for their country. And what the hell have I ever done? Write a few songs that no radio station in the country wants to play?"

After contacting the secretary to the governor general and finding out that this was all on the up-and-up, and that they wanted me to appear before His Excellency, the Right Honourable Romeo LeBlanc, to receive the medal in November, I could only think of one question. "Can I wear my hat?"

When they told me I could, I said to myself, "Now, that's the kind of country I'm proud to live in. A country where even the governor general can make allowances once in a while for a down-to-earth country boy whose only contribution to this great land so far has been a mere handful of songs." (As the summer wore on, I could hardly wait to get there. I think I wanted to meet the governor general and the rest of these nice people even more than I wanted the medal.)

By now it was the first of June '96, the weather was getting warm, and it became extremely hard to stay indoors to write the book. Lena had been talking for a few years now about moving to another location where we could find a bigger house, or build an extension onto the one we had.

So with only about a hundred and sixty some pages of the book completed, I was sitting outside one day looking at our house, and decided to draw some plans on how our house could be extended. The more I drew, the more I liked what I saw. About a week later, I had almost exactly what Lena wanted and also what I wanted, all planned into the house we were now living in. The next thing to do was to talk to some contractors. So I started looking around.

On July 13, Lena and I went to Brian and Barb Hewson's wedding reception, which took place in Brian's recording studio, which was very interesting and rather unique. Through the course of the evening we met a lot of nice people, and one of them said he was a building contractor. After a few beers I told him my plans for adding an extension onto my house, and we planned to meet in a day or so to discuss it.

While I discussed the business of building with the contractor, Lena decided to fly down to the east coast to visit her relatives and then go home to Entry Island for a week or so.

It just so happened that while Lena was visiting her sister Amy in Nova Scotia, who should drop by but Brian and Barb Hewson, while on their honeymoon. They all decided to have lunch together in Pictou.

By this time the contractor had a draftsman draw up a blueprint from my original drawings and I was told the addition could be started by the middle of August, and be finished in three months by the last week in November.

Lena flew home on August 9 and I told her the addition would commence in another week. Unfortunately, one week dragged into two, and two dragged into three. The excuse given was that the guy who issued the building permits for the area was away on vacation. (Seems everything stops in our county when one person goes on holidays.)

Finally, the clearing of a few trees and the first excavation began on August 30, 1996.

Then my old friend Reg Chapman, who had been in and out of the hospital during this time, passed away. I believe the date was September 5. Lena and I went up to pay our respects and help Muriel out as much as we could during her bereavement. Of course, most of the family was there to console one another and this helped a great deal.

Meanwhile the work at the house seemed to drag along at a snail's pace. Lots of work seemed to be done while there was someone on the job. But with two days this week and three the next, I began to have serious doubts about whether it would be finished by January of '97. But then, who was I to judge, when the contractor just smiled and assured me all would be done on time.

On the thirteenth of November 1996, Lena and I and Brian Edwards stepped out of the limousine and walked up the steps of Rideau Hall and entered the reception area. Here we joined about fifty other people who had also arrived for the purpose of receiving the Order of Canada Medal.

Everyone wore gowns, suits and ties, including Lena and Brian, while I wore the normal black clothes not unbefitting the role of Stompin' Tom. Complete with cowboy boots and hat.

In just a few moments a couple of important-looking gentlemen came out and separated all those who were to receive the Order from their escorts and invited us into another room. Here we received instructions and information on how the ceremony would be conducted.

From here we were taken to another large room where we rejoined our escorts to have a small libation and get acquainted with the others. ("Libation" is a fancy word I learned in Skinners Pond University. It means, "Let's all have a drink." And what do you know, they had beer there, too, which they served in little glasses.)

Among other interesting people, I met Beryl Potter. She was there in her motorized wheelchair to receive the Order for having been such a strong advocate for the rights of the physically disabled.

Then we were all ushered into the special room where we were given our designated seats while we waited for the arrival of His Excellency, the Right Honourable Romeo LeBlanc.

In the first seat of the front row sat a lady who would be the only person this year to receive the Order's highest medal. This is called "Companion of the Order of Canada (C.C.)." It's actually a "promotion" within the Order, and was given to Huguette Oligny, the world-famous actress.

The next twelve seats were reserved for those receiving the second-highest medal. This is called "Officer of the Order of Canada (O.C.)." And this is the medal I was about to receive. The next thirty-five or so seats were reserved for those receiving the third-highest medal. This is called "Member of the Order of Canada (C.M.)." I think there were forty-nine people in all who received medals that day.

The entire wall to the right of the room was reserved for TV, radio and the press. And to the far left at the front of the room was a small podium from where a brief citation was given on behalf of each person receiving a medal.

In the front centre of the room, facing everybody, were

two large plush chairs, one reserved for the governor general and the other for his wife, Diana Fowler LeBlanc. And just to the right of the two big chairs was a large table which held all the medals. There were also two or three people seated at this table to help sort out the medals and pass them to His Excellency as each recipient's name was being called out.

As your name was called out, you got up from your seat and walked down the centre aisle and stopped at a special spot until the person on the podium explained to everyone why you were receiving your medal and being inducted into the Order of Canada.

As my name was called, and I walked down and stood on the spot, a part of the citation given from the podium was the following:

"Known across the country, this singer-songwriter, fiddler and guitarist is a staunch supporter of Canada, its music and its musicians. A modern minstrel, he has criss-crossed the country chronicling our times and capturing our heritage in song. Mindful of his humble roots, he has spent a lifetime championing the 'common' folk. His songs have given a voice to the indomitable spirit of working Canadians and have become woven into our national fabric. . . . Your Excellency, may I present Stompin' Tom Connors."

At this point, the governor general was handed the medal. And walking up to me, he placed the medal, which hung from a long wide ribbon, around my neck. Then, calling mc Tom, and pronouncing me to be an "Officer of the Order of Canada," he shook my hand and said, "I'm one of your fans, too, Tom. Keep up the good work."

After everyone else got their medals, we were all ushered into another large room where more libations were supplied, and where everyone could get a chance to congratulate each other and sort of let their hair down.

After a little glass of beer or two, and a chit-chat with several people, I spotted Beryl Potter sitting in her wheelchair over against one wall. As there didn't seem to be anybody talking to her, I grabbed two of these little glasses of beer off the table and headed over her way. I offered her one of the glasses, and we began to have a little talk. First, we told each

other a few jokes, and then we got talking about her motorized wheelchair.

"Did you ever get a speeding ticket, driving that rig?" I
asked. "What kind of speed will it do?"

"Well, why don't you just sit on the arm of it there," she
said, "and I'll take you for a little ride around the room so
you can see what it will do?"

Thinking we might go for eight or ten feet and then stop,
I obliged. But was I ever in for a surprise.

As I plunked myself down on the arm of her chair, she
turned on a switch, gave a long blast of the horn, and we
were off.

With the attention of the whole room, everybody just
scattered. I'll bet she had that wheelchair doing at least ten
miles an hour. I was all arms and legs just trying to stay on
the damn thing. And the more she leaned on the throttle
and blew that screechy horn, the more I kept hollering, "Hi
Ho Silver, and . . . Awaayyyy!"

It was like a couple of kids trying out a new dirt bike. We
must have bobbed and weaved and zig-zagged two or three
times around the room with all those nicely dressed people
ducking, dodging and backing up everywhere.

After almost falling off a couple of times, I finally had to
beg her to stop.

As she finally pulled back into her stall, where she started
from, you could hear a big sigh of relief go up from the
crowd. That's when we both started to laugh.

As other people now started to gather around to talk to
her, I gave her a big kiss, and said, "That's one hell of a
wheelchair you got there, Beryl, and one of these days
you're gonna get caught for 'dangerous driving.'"

As I left to join Lena and Brian, I could hear her asking
somebody else if they wanted a ride. And the answer was an
emphatic "No thanks."

After two or three more of these little glasses of beer (it
probably took about four to make a pint), a fellow named
Kevin, one of the governor general's young aides, came up to
us and asked if we'd like to take a little tour of Rideau Hall.

Slipping away from the crowd, we were soon by ourselves
walking up and down these huge halls lined with all the

portraits of past prime ministers and everybody who had ever been somebody in the history of Canada.

Room after room, we saw the offices, living rooms, libraries, boardrooms, and even some of the private haunts of not only the present governor general, but all those before him. This was a real guided tour, with answers given to each and every question we could ask. And I kid you not, this place is a real palace.

Then this gentleman took us into the adjacent glassed-in garden which has a little stream running through it everywhere. The stream contains all kinds of exotic fish where the temperature is controlled and adjusted to suit their own natural habitat. And the floral gardens are something out of this world. Walking through this place is like a short visit to the tropics. It was just abundantly luxurious.

We thanked our guide for this wonderful tour as he quietly slipped us back into the crowd just in time to meet the governor general and his elegant wife, Diana, in a little less formal setting than we had before.

I don't know what Lena and Brian chatted about when they met this illustrious couple, but I didn't think that a good yarn or two about fishing in New Brunswick would be out of place. This was with no disrespect, mind you. For I knew that this great and honourable man had come from humble beginnings, had known what it was like to get his hands dirty, and worked his way up the ladder to where the respect of his title was now deserved.

Then came the beautiful dinner they spread out for all of us. And although I'm just an ordinary meat and potatoes sort of a guy, when I saw this magnificent buffet of just about every kind of food in the world I'd ever heard of, I just had to try a little bit of everything. And "sumptuous" is only an inadequate word for the message I was getting from my taste buds.

(It's a damn good thing I didn't know before how well they treat a fella up there in Rideau Hall, or I would have had ten or fifteen more medals before receiving this one. But seriously, I met a lot of good people. You might say the more humane side of government. And while I would like to congratulate all recipients of the Order of Canada Medal, and encourage others to be next in line, I would also like to express many thanks to all those people who, in confidentiality, nominated me to receive this wonderful Medal of Canada. You've all said to me, in your own way, "Tom, it's no crime to be a proud Canadian.")

After this great dinner, and a couple more little glasses of beer, Lena and I and Brian headed over to see Larry Delaney, of *Country Music News*. There I walked in with a case of 24 Moosehead, with the full intention of starting some very serious libations.

I'm not sure now whether Larry had a beer with us or not. But the camera came out almost immediately, and we took a bunch of pictures. The medal, of course, had to be conspicuously visible. (The pictures appeared in the next issue of *Country Music News*.)

We then said "So long" to Larry and his wife, Joanne, and headed out to our hotel suite where Gaet and Jean Lepine and a few other friends were waiting to hear the news.

They wanted to know what it felt like to be kicked out of Rideau Hall. They looked rather disappointed when I told them the opposite had occurred, and that I now actually owned the place after winning it in a crap game. (Just kidding, of course.) Everybody was ecstatic when they saw the medal. They wanted to touch it and put it around their necks, if only for an instant.

Even the night-man of the hotel came over to the door to say hello. And when he did, we just brought him in, gave him a beer, and made his year by quickly putting the medal around his neck and snapping a picture. His name was Paul Kit. And as it turned out, he was a great Stompin' Tom fan. And this was the greatest thing that had ever happened to him. As he left, I said, "Paul, this medal actually belongs to everyone in this country who ever bought a Stompin' Tom record. And me? I just get to carry it around for everybody."

After a few more libations (gee, I like that word; the folks back home'll think I gave up drinkin'), we played and sang a few more songs about Canada, and finally turned in. This had really been one hell of a day in the life of Stompin' Tom. I dreamt about that medal all night. (Sorry, Lena.)

A New Bridge for Bud the Spud

THAT YEAR, IN DECEMBER 1996, I got word that my hero had died. Yep! The great Canadian grand-daddy of country music had finally passed away. Wilf Carter, the greatest yodelling cowboy of them all, rode into that beautiful western sunset that he always sang about, just a couple of weeks before his ninety-second birthday. Upon hearing about this I had to get my guitar, go down in the basement by myself, and sing the song I had written about Wilf a whole lot of years ago. My "Tribute to Wilf Carter." (He used to carry the single of this song around with him in his guitar case.)

As I had suspected, the extension to my house was not completed by the end of November. And while the snow was flying, I was assured that the roof would be boarded up and the windows would be set into place before Christmas. The rest of the work would all be finished up by the third week in January.

"But what about the promise that the whole thing would be completed before the end of November?" I demanded.

"Well, you know, Tom, it's the suppliers. They didn't get the material to me in time. And that has really been the problem."

"Okay," I said, "but remember, I've got songs to write, a book to complete, an album to record, and a cross-Canada tour to plan for this coming summer; and the end of January is about all the time I can spare. If you take longer than that, you're cutting into my way of making a living. And I can't do the things I need to do while all this hammering, banging and sawing is going on everywhere in the house."

"Don't worry, Tom, I know what you mean. And I promise you the whole thing will be completed in January." I told him I'd take his word on it, wished him a Merry Christmas, and said I'd see him first thing in January.

On December 20, '96, David Orchard, of Citizens Concerned About Free Trade, CCAFT, headquartered in Saskatchewan, paid us a visit. He had been to the house once or twice before. This time he brought along one of his co-workers, Marjalena Repo. David had brought me a very nice red cowboy shirt with white fringe that a friend of his from out west had given him to give to me. His friend had also given him another shirt which was identical to the one he gave me. Of course, we had to put them on and take some pictures.

Gaet and Jean had also arrived, and all of us went out to supper on the twentieth. And the next day we all helped Lena celebrate her birthday. David and Marjalena stayed for one more night, and then they were off again to Saskatchewan. As they were leaving I told David he'd better spruce up on his pool, checkers and chess before he came back the next time. He never won a game. (But then again, he didn't do too bad for a guy from 'round Borden, Saskatchewan.)

Soon after New Year's, I heard that Smiley Bates had passed away. Here was another one of Canada's best talents who never got played on radio. He sang country songs the way they should really be sung. And I would dare say that Smiley would have to be ranked right up there with the best flat-top acoustic guitar players in North America. He also played great banjo and fiddle. (Too bad your music couldn't have been known right across Canada, Smiley. You tried for forty-five years, but you had one flaw. You didn't go to the States. Too bad. You should have done what Canadian radio advises all Canadian talent to do. "Play it like the Americans do. And maybe someday when you get it all down right, we'll play your records." Well, Smiley, like I told you one time, when we played for three weeks together at the Wawa Motor

Hotel, in northern Ontario, circa 1966, "It doesn't matter how good you are; in this country, if you wait for Canadian radio to give you the needed exposure, you'll wait forever." And I'm just sorry that Smiley and a whole lot of others couldn't wait that long.)

Also in January of 1997, the word was out that the Confederation Bridge between Prince Edward Island and New Brunswick would be completed by the end of May that year. So I immediately sat down and wrote a song called "The Confederation Bridge." I sang it for some of the guys still working on the extension to my house, and a few hours later they were still whistling the melody. When I asked a couple of guys what it was they were whistling, they said, "It's that damn 'bridge song' you just wrote. I can't get it out of my mind."

That was the sign I needed. I had to record it right away. (I have always tested my songs on others to see what the long-term reaction would be before wasting my time and money to record it.)

Once I had the necessary musicians together, and knowing a couple of them could sing backup vocals, I called Brian Hewson and booked the Escarpment Studio. All I was missing was a female voice to help in the backup vocals.

I heard that Kim Stockwood, famous for the song "You Jerk," was in Toronto, so I got Lena to find out where she was staying and ask her if she would come out and do voices on the recording. She not only agreed but rented a car, and through a blinding snowstorm found her way from the 401 highway through back-country roads until she found the studio. She was all alone, and the only help she had was the use of her cellular phone by which we directed her to the exact location. Now, here's a plucky lady. Of course, her being from Newfoundland, could anyone expect less?

At any rate, "The Confederation Bridge" was recorded and immediately sent to EMI Records by the end of January '97.

After that, I really don't know what happened. They had the master of the only song dedicated to the first crossing of this world-famous bridge, and didn't get the recording out until just two days before the bridge was officially opened. I felt extremely disappointed.

I harkened back to the days when I wrote "The Marten Hartwell Story" in 1972. And Boot Records had the single recording of the song out to the radio stations and into the marketplace in less than three weeks from the day it was written.

I mean, this wasn't 1972. This was twenty-five years later, in 1997. This was the computer age, where the boast is that we can now do everything faster and more efficiently than it could ever be done before.

Well, I don't know who got raked over the coals over that one, but I know that somebody should have. When you have the completed master of a song which describes an event four months before the event occurs, common sense will tell anybody, whether you're in the record business or not, you don't wait to get it into people's hands after the event is over, when everybody's gone home. You make it available now, while there's still people around who might like to buy it.

A couple of east coast radio stations played "Confederation Bridge" for a few days as a "novelty" and then dropped it. And as far as I know, that's about all the play it ever got.

The winners of the Stompin' Tom Award at the ECMAs that year, 1997, were Dan R. MacDonald, Stevedore Steve Foote, Eloi LeBlanc, George Hector, Raymond Sellick, Marg Osburne, Gerald Mitchell, Helen Doucette, Billy Whelan, Wilf Doyle, Lillian C. Walsh, Tex Cochrane and Michael T. Wall.

The official opening and "drive over" of the Confederation Bridge took place on June 1, '97. The ribbon cutting and all the celebrations were known as "The Bridgefest." Lena and I had been invited to attend and to also be among the first to cross the bridge. The invitation had been personally given more than a year previously by Prince Edward Island Premier Catherine Callbeck herself. And as the Bridgefest drew near I was asked to sing a few songs for the occasion, to which I readily agreed. Unfortunately, the whole deal went down when the artistic director for the Bridgefest entered the picture.

Negotiations between him and my promoter, Brian Edwards, were going nowhere. Finally, it came down to the wire, and still no deal was firmed up. I couldn't even be sure now if I could be a part of the bridge drive-over or not. Then a fax was received by Brian from a Mr. Jacques Lemay, clearing everything up once and for all. It read, in part: "I will ask that Tom's name be removed from the guest list at the inaugural dinner and that the vehicle reserved for him and his wife Lena be removed from the inaugural drive fleet." So that was that.

What started out as a verbal invitation by the premier to cross the bridge, with no strings attached, turned out to mean I could only cross the bridge on the condition that I accept the amount of money they were willing to pay me for singing the songs they wanted me to sing. (As part of the deal, I had initially wanted to sing the new song "The Confederation Bridge," but they would have no part of it.)

When it was learned I wasn't going to be there, a couple of newspaper articles came out about the fiasco and then nothing more was said about it.

I guess it really all boils down to this: When somebody offers to do you a big favour, don't count on it before you know exactly what you're obliged to do before you receive it.

And now at this point, I'd like to talk a little bit about the song "Bud the Spud." The term, "Bud the Spud" did not exist in the English vocabulary before the year 1967, whether in Prince Edward Island or any other part of the world. As explained in a previous chapter of this autobiography, it was I who coined the term and originated the character of "Bud the Spud" and associated him with "the best doggone potatoes that's ever been growed, and they're from Prince Edward Island."

Now, most people in the world would say, "Yeah, okay. We know all that, Tom. So why are you bothering to even tell us it all again?"

Well, it seems that the owners of a potato packing company in Elmsdale, P.E.I., not fifteen miles from Skinners Pond, didn't know these facts in the 1960s, the 1970s and the 1980s and '90s. And it looks like they'll go on denying these facts right into the next millennium.

Why? Because the W.P. Griffin Company realized after the song "Bud the Spud" had become popularized for some ten or fifteen years, due to the efforts and the expense of

Stompin' Tom, that this magic phrase could sell a lot of potatoes. So they put the name "Bud the Spud" on their potato
bags. (After all, with the popularity of the song "Bud the
Spud," they had a free and ready-made commercial.)

So what is wrong with that? Well, it's using someone else's
idea in a commercial venture to make money without paying
anything to the person who originated the idea. That's
what's wrong with it. And every time I sing my own song
"Bud the Spud," I'm being used to promote the products of
the W.P. Griffin Company.

Now, in today's world, companies hire specialists to come
up with ideas on how to better market their products. And
they also hire advertising agencies to come up with jingles
that will be sung on TV and radio commercials which will
also help to sell their products. And do these specialists and
advertising agencies give their ideas and sing these commercial jingles for *free*? Well, ahem! I guess not. All companies pay dearly for these services. Except, in this case, the
company pays nothing.

Now, as if this was not enough, this potato packing company then goes ahead and designs a logo depicting a potato-
man walking along the beach with a cap on his head which
tells you his name is Bud. And what does he carry in his
hand? Just a small ghetto blaster with musical notes coming
out from it. And what song would you suppose this Spud-
man called Bud would be listening to from the cassette tape
in his ghetto blaster? Somehow, I don't think it's "An American in Paris" or even "Jingle Bells."

Even more blatant, this company now applies to the
Canadian government for a copyright and a trademark to
use this whole idea, not only on potato bags, but they want
to sell caps, T-shirts and other items of clothing, along with
key chains, wallets, drinking mugs and another list of things
as long as your arm. And of course, near the bottom of this
list was children's books, and wouldn't you just believe it—
cassette tapes!???

I wondered why a potato packing company wanted to get
into selling all these things. As a matter of fact, so did the
giant Anheuser-Busch Brewing Company, from the States,
which brews Budweiser beer. (Remember the slogan, "This

Bud's for you"?)

Well, unknown to me, while I had a lawyer trying to see if I could get this company to stop taking further advantage of me, my song and my ideas, Anheuser-Busch had all their lawyers going after the company for a somewhat similar reason. And a big thanks to this coincidence, W.P. Griffin Inc. backed off.

I know this company will probably say, Oh, we didn't mean any harm. All we wanted to do was provide a few ballcaps and T-shirts for our employees to wear. But there's a big difference between doing just that and taking out a national copyright and/or a trademark that says that they, and only they, can market a long list of goods, including books and cassettes, that contain the name Bud the Spud.

In the beginning, I was well aware that the name and character that I was creating, namely Bud the Spud, would no doubt promote the Prince Edward Island potato. And I have a citation from the Island's minister of agriculture, Dan MacDonald, thanking me in 1970 for the tremendous boost in sales that year that my song Bud the Spud gave to the P.E.I. potato industry.

This song was for the Island and everybody on the Island, so that everybody could benefit equally. And as far as I'm concerned, that's the way it should stay. The character and name of "Bud the Spud" was my gift to all the people of Prince Edward Island. It was not meant to be a gift to the W.P. Griffin potato packing company. So to the extent that this company has asserted their encroachment upon the name and character of "Bud the Spud" for the purpose of making money for themselves, I will always feel that they are using me and my work without payment or compensation.

"Man of the Land" Tour '98

SOMETIME IN JUNE OF 1997, Lena received some good news. She had had a daughter some three or four years before we were married and due to some very trying circumstances had to give her up for adoption. She had always wondered what had happened to her and had always been trying in one way or another to find out where she was.

Through a mutual friend and a few coincidences over the Internet, the daughter was found in Saint John, New Brunswick. Within the next month a meeting was arranged and Lena flew down to P.E.I. where the reunion was held in Summerside. Though Lena had named her daughter Eva, her name had been changed at the time of adoption and was now Trudy. She has since come to visit us in Ontario and they get along famously.

Another coincidence about all this is that Trudy was brought up in Elmsdale, Prince Edward Island. And in the hundreds of times that Lena and I drove back and forth to Skinners Pond we passed right by the house where she lived.

I had wanted to go on a concert tour this summer, since I hadn't done one now in four years. But due to the extension on my house not being finished, I had to cancel it. It was now August, a full year since they started it, and most of the electrical and other inside work was still not done. I wouldn't see the contractor for two weeks at a time, sometimes, and when he did come he'd fiddle around at something for a day or two, and I wouldn't see him again for another week. Several times I heard he had taken on some other jobs and just left me hanging. The excuse I always got was that he couldn't find any help. But I wondered, if that were true, how was he getting the other jobs done?

At the end of August, we were paid a weekend visit by the poet Judith Fitzgerald. Judith, who often signs her name as just plain "Fitz," has authored many books, including *River* (ECW Press) and *Walkin' Wounded* (Black Moss Press), to name just a couple. She's been a columnist for the *Toronto Star* and for several magazines as well as writer in residence at the University of Windsor.

She happens to be a staunch Canadian as well as a Stompin' Tom fan, so while a lot of her poetry is away over my head, we still had plenty of things in common to talk about. That is, our two styles of writing, free trade, her book review of *Before the Fame* and a whole raft of things Canadian. (There's something odd about good conversation. The time just seems to slip away while there's still so much more to talk about. The two days seemed like only two hours, and she was off again to her little house in the bush, somewhere near Sundridge, Ontario.)

Just after Fitz left, we had a short visit from J.P. and Hilda Cormier, otherwise known as "Awesome and Wic." They were doing a couple of folk festivals in Ontario, and decided to drop by with their bass player. We had a few jars, of course, and jammed through most of the night. They left for Nova Scotia the following afternoon.

It took four more months to finally get the extension on my house completed. And that was around the twentieth of January in 1998. It had taken almost a year and a half, seventeen months to be exact, to complete a project that was supposed to be done in three months. Six times longer than promised, and double the cost originally estimated.

By this time I hadn't even seen the contractor for several months. And if it hadn't been for the reliability of one of the carpenters, Karl Kothe, coming back on his own whenever he could, the place might still not be finished.

(So if any of my enemies out there would like to build a

house, just write me a letter and I'll recommend a good contractor.)

It was now February 1998, and as part of the East Coast Music Awards, the Stompin' Tom Award was presented to Fred Reddon, Kevin Broderick, James Banks and to two groups, the Ranch Boys and the Bunk House Boys.

In March, Brian Edwards was glad to hear that my house was finally done and that I was available to go on tour again. It would be five years since he started booking the last one.

Calling the boys from the Whiskey Jack band, I found that they weren't interested in going on tour this time, so I went looking for another band.

After contacting a few people and trying to put a band together by patchwork, I was talking to Lynn Russworm, who gave me Larry Mercey's phone number. Larry told me that I should contact a guy by the name of Mark LaForme. Maybe he would be interested.

I asked him where I had heard that name before. It sounded familiar. He reminded me that it was the Mark LaForme band that had backed him up at the Canadian Country Music Reunion the night I went onstage as a guest up in Lindsay, Ontario. That brought it all together for me and I called Mark.

After negotiating back and forth for a couple of weeks a road band was finally put together. They included Mark LaForme as leader, playing electric lead and harmonica, and singing; Larry Murphy on bass; Steve Petrie on steel, dobro and fiddle; and Steve Sennick on drums.

By the middle of June we had our rehearsals complete and everybody was ready to hit the road. For the sake of the tour the band would now be called Mark LaForme and the Formula, and on June 28 we headed out for our first gig in Lindsay, Ontario. Lena and Tommy and I drove in our own van.

Our sound and lighting people would be Chris Quilliam, Matt Rice, Trevor Nash and Jeremy Purdy. Brian's road manager would be Larry Fitzpatrick, and handling concessions was Damon Deszegheo. All security was handled by Frank Hewitt and his helper, Eddie Grey. (Any secondary help would of course be hired as needed, from town to town.)

The first leg of the tour in '98 was only in Ontario, and took us from Lindsay to Ottawa, on Canada Day, and from there to Brantford, Coldwater, London, Wiarton and Blyth.

It was around here that we had a change in drummers. Danny Lockwood was our drummer for the rest of the tour. Chris Quilliam had also left the tour by now, as he had only agreed to stay long enough to familiarize Trevor Nash with the board and the type of sound I usually expected.

After about ten days off towards the end of July, we were on our way again, driving to the east coast, where we arrived in Sackville, New Brunswick, a couple of days before our scheduled show in that town.

With nothing much to do around the motel, we set up the croquet set and that's all we did for the next couple of days and nights. Play some vicious croquet. How do you play croquet all night till the sun comes up? You open up the sound and lighting truck, set up the stage lights, plug them in, and point them towards the croquet field. Next question.

Of course, the first night, the police came around wondering what all the lights were doing shining in the field. When they were told it was just Stompin' Tom and the boys having a little game of croquet, they watched for a moment, shook their heads and drove away. (I don't know what the sergeant said to these guys when they turned in their nightly report.) Around 3 A.M., in the middle of the second game, the fog set in. But we kept on playing anyway. The next day we bought two more sets of croquet mallets and balls in preparation for an earlier start the second night. (I think, during the whole tour, we went through about ten sets of those damn things. They sure don't make 'em like they used to.)

After Sackville, we finally got to drive over the Confederation Bridge to Prince Edward Island. First we stopped to take pictures, and once back in our vehicles it seemed like no time, and we were there on the Island. For those of us who had taken the old Abegweit ferry so many times, the whole thing just didn't quite seem the same. (I really think they should have left one of the ferries on for those travellers who have lots of time and who would have enjoyed the romance of the one-hour sail.)

Arriving in Summerside, we had another day off and managed to get a big feed of lobsters. Some of the boys on this trip had never tried them before. But never worry. The guys who tried them and didn't like them just left more for the guys who did. (I also took the boys up to Skinners Pond.)

After two concerts on two different nights in Summerside, we played Charlottetown, and then went on to Pictou and Halifax.

While in Pictou, we went out to the beach near the lighthouse on Caribou Island, which used to be run by Lena's brother-in-law Foster. (The lighthouse has since been automated.) Once the boys had a swim, and we were about ready to go, Tommy dug up a very large clam along the beach and brought it up to show the green horns who had never seen one up close before. While one of the boys was examining it, I said, "Here, let me see that."

With jackknife in hand, I opened it up for all the boys to have a better look at what was inside. Someone said, "You people from the east coast don't really eat them things, do you?" As I gulped it down, raw from the shell, and said, "Nope. Not cooked, anyway," I thought they were about to head back to Ontario. They ran to their van and never looked back until we met them again up at Foster's house. The other boys, of course, just laughed and took it all in stride.

Amy and the girls cooked up a nice big supper for us that night and the next day we were off to Halifax.

On August the fifteenth, we played Fredericton, New Brunswick, where I did a television interview with Carmen Kilburn right after the show. Carmen also has a weekly radio program and quite often gives my records a spin. We talked about our mutual hero, Wilf Carter, and why they don't play any real Canadian music on regular radio anymore. (Seems like everybody's mystified about that one, except the owners of big radio stations themselves. And they're not telling anyone.)

We then did a show in Moncton, and on to Saint John, where I took the boys on a tour of some of the places where I used to live as a little kid. Especially the site in Silver Falls, on the Loch Lomond Road, where the old St. Patrick's

Orphanage used to be. Most of the boys had read the first half of my autobiography by now, and taking them out to this location gave them a lot greater perspective into the chapters I wrote about my years in the orphanage.

After playing our show in Saint John in the very same theatre where I had once worked as an usher, I signed a lot of autographs and met a lot of people I once knew from years ago. I was expecting to see my cousin, the famous fiddler Ned Landry, that night, but Ned apparently wasn't feeling too good and wasn't able to make it. I had, however, met his brother Tony, in Fredericton, a few days before.

Gerry Taylor, the country music columnist for the *Telegraph Journal*, and *Country Music News*, was also at the show that night and we got a chance to have a short conversation together. Too bad it couldn't have been longer, as we'd both been looking forward to meeting each other for years.

Stevedore Steve didn't make it to the show that night due to a sore back. Gerry Taylor informed me of this, so I called Steve the next day, on my way to playing the Miramichi, to wish him well and say hello to Gini.

Lena left the tour in Saint John, where her daughter Trudy was now living, and the two of them went to Nova Scotia to meet some more of Trudy's relatives that she had not known before. I didn't see Lena again until the tour took us to Alberta.

After the Miramichi, we played Montreal, and then back into Ontario to play Carleton Place, Pembroke and North Bay. It was at this time that Doug McKenric joined the show as our new lighting man, replacing Jeremy Purdy. Matt Rice also left at this time, due to some commitments he had previously engaged.

On the rainy days, when the weather was too bad to play croquet, we played a number of board games indoors, such as chess, checkers and Scrabble. Scrabble? Now, there's a nice, quiet, friendly, sociable game that any adult male could sit down and go to sleep at. Well, think again. This game, after a while, got to be almost as competitive as croquet. Some guys will try anything to win. Even to go so far as to palm the "Q," when he knows he's gonna be stuck with it. And then slip it back into the bag for someone else to get.

Now, we all agreed that anyone who would stoop that low to try and win such a simple game as Scrabble was not really fit to join with decent people in the playing of any game. The trouble was, we all knew someone did it but we didn't know who. But there's one thing for sure. The guy that did it kept on playing Scrabble with us till the end of the tour. And guys like me, and three or four others, had to continually be on the alert from that time on, to make sure that someone didn't slip us the "Q."

Driving now to Manitoba, we played Brandon and Yorkton, where I was able to have a nice chat with my friend Ron Waddell, who still remembered Jury and all the difficulties we encountered on my very first concert tour out west. And then on the twelfth of September 1998, we arrived in Calgary, Alberta.

Now, it just so happened through a sheer quirk of Fate that in Calgary, the Canadian Country Music Association (CCMA) was holding its Country Music Awards Night on Sunday, September 13—the very same night I was due to play the big Jack Singer's Auditorium.

As described earlier in this book, the CCMA was an outgrowth of ACME, the Association of Canadian Musical Entertainers, whose board of directors was, and still is, dominated by members associated with radio and some of the very same people that stand in the way of "distinctive and identifiably Canadian music" being played over Canadian airwaves. (Remember the fox in the hen house?)

As far as I had always been concerned, I could not, in all good conscience, become a part of the CCMA or any other musical organization which did not fairly represent all the interests of all Canadian country entertainers, everywhere. And I know there's a lot of these singers, songwriters, recording companies and publishers who agree with this point of view, that the CCMA does not represent. On the contrary, they ignore them, in hopes they'll just go away.

And so, on Sunday, September 13, 1998, the battle lines were unnoticeably being drawn. In one camp, the CCMA had amassed all their heavyweights. All the Canadian entertainers who had been convinced to go south to seek their musical fortunes were standing in line to receive their awards for doing so. This army of philistines was very impressive. Then they called out their horn blowers (TV, radio, newspapers, etc.) to announce that their giant Goliath had duly arrived.

And where was the opposing army to all this might?

Oh, they were just out picking up sticks and stones off the street, on their way to Jack Singer's. Or was it David the Slinger's place? I just forget which. But, anyway, they were going there to cheer for one of their own. Somebody they could "identify" with. Somebody who cared more about blowing their horn than he cared about blowing his own.

Now, given the fact that modern society has changed a lot since the biblical days, when the great Goliath, with armour, sword and javelin, was decapitated by David, the slingshot-bearing shepherd boy, and that we now live in a democracy where battles are won by votes and not weapons, when the dust finally settled on the battlefield of Calgary, the CCMA Goliath was not decapitated. But he sure wound up with one hell of a big black eye.

When the votes were finally counted, the CCMA awards show, which was broadcast all across the country, had drawn a mere six hundred people, while the Stompin' Tom show, just up the street, drew three times as many, with a total of 1,800. Again, Goliath, with all his army, and all his great and illustrious parade of "stars," went down to bite the dust. (So much for the CCMA and the southerly direction in which they're moving. And again I say, let's get the "foxy" radio out of the hen house. For while we listen to the crap they feed us, they listen to the sweet cackles of their next chicken dinner. We have allowed them to control and determine what music they want us to hear. And to the extent they control the CCMA or any other musical organization, they leave the people of Canada with a country its young talent are becoming progressively more ashamed to sing about.)

From Calgary, the tour took us into Banff for a show, and then on to Vancouver. We played Mission, Victoria and Richmond, and then headed out for the long drive to Fort St. John. I had wanted to go up and play Whitehorse, Yukon, on this trip, but somehow negotiations between them and Brian had broken off and the show got cancelled.

While playing Edmonton, I met David Orchard again.

David had now thrown his hat in to run for the leadership of the national P.C. party. Believing David to be a good man, as I do, I gave him a few plugs from the stage once in a while to help him in his cause.

Lena flew out to join us in Edmonton and only stayed on the tour for our two concert dates in Red Deer and in Saskatoon, Saskatchewan.

It was here that Old Man Winter paid an early visit and dumped two or three feet of snow just after we finished our concert on the night of October 10.

Lena was at the airport next day trying to fly out, but the planes were all delayed. While she waited there, we waited back at the motel until we knew for sure whether she was going to get away, as we didn't want to hit the road and leave her stranded.

When we heard she got off all right, we decided to strike out for Regina. The whole works of us, including the sound truck, got stuck two or three times before we got out of town. And when we hit the highway, there was no one on it but us and all the cars and trucks that had gone in the ditch the night before.

Although the distance to Regina was only about 150 miles, for the first three hours we could only crawl along doing thirty or forty miles an hour. As we neared Regina, the roads got better, and after stopping for gas and something to eat, we pulled into our motel at about 6 P.M. We had left Saskatoon just around noon.

After Regina, we played Winnipeg, where we paid a visit to the Boulet Boot Company and bought a bunch of western gear before driving back into Ontario. The Boulet Company are the people who make the short style of cowboy boot that I have always worn, even before my career as Stompin' Tom began. They have another name for the style of boots that I wear, but I call them My Stompin' Boots. So there, Boulet. You'll have to change the name of your boots, 'cause I won't change mine.

By the twenty-first of October we played Sarnia, Ontario, and two nights later we were back at Lulu's in Kitchener. (As the reader may recall, I used to play a lot of bars in the old days. And to tell you the truth, I miss playing them today. But unfortunately, there's not too many bars in Canada that have the seating capacity of a place like Lulu's, where they seat over 3,000.)

Our third-last show of the "Man of the Land" Tour, as it came to be called, was in good old Peterborough, Ontario. This, of course, is the home of my promoter, Brian (no more headaches) Edwards, and the city where the name Stompin' Tom was born. There's always a huge turnout in Peterborough, and this time would be no exception. The Memorial Centre was once again coming apart at the seams. This time they had a beer licence at the back of the centre and there just seems to be something about drinking beer and listening to Stompin' Tom songs.

After the show, Brian's brother-in-law, Joe Page, was good enough to keep his little restaurant open for a few hours and served us up a very nice meal.

Two days later we played Hamilton, where most of the boys in the band were now living, and I think that almost everyone who came out to the show was either related to one of these guys or at least knew them.

The final date of Tour '98 was on October 29 at Massey Hall in Toronto. Gaet and Jean came down from Ottawa for this one and decided to stay and visit us for a couple of weeks.

Massey Hall was packed again that night, and during intermission something spectacular happened.

Once or twice during each tour Brian usually auctions off my Stompin' Board. And during intermission at the Massey Hall concert he auctioned it off again. This time the proceeds were going to Project Warmth, an organization that provides meals and sleeping bags for street people during the winter months in Toronto. (To these people I can relate, having been one myself many years ago.)

What happened during this auction was incredible. The most money the board had brought in up until now was a whopping $2,300. But tonight was going to be phenomenal. If you can believe it, the autographed Stompin' Board went for (brace yourself) $10,000. Yep! Ten thousand smackeroos!

Who would ever believe that an old piece of plywood

with a hole stomped through it by ol' Stompin' Tom from Skinners Pond would someday be worth $10,000? But there it was, for the world to see. While people held their breath, the bidding just went up in leaps of five hundred and bounds of a thousand. It was like something you would read in the *Guinness Book of World Records* or *Ripley's Believe It or Not*. But it happened, folks. And Project Warmth was overwhelmingly pleased to receive the money. (And I hope it was able to prevent one or two old fellas from freezing to death that winter.)

When the show was over that night, EMI Records held a big party in the basement of Massey Hall at which they announced I had received yet another Gold record for the sales of *Bud the Spud*. This meant that it had sold another 50,000 copies.

Now, to try and put the real significance of all this in the right perspective for the reader: it is very difficult for a record company to sell 50,000 copies of an album when the artist has twenty-three other albums that are currently available on the market (counting nineteen original albums and four compilations). And one must remember that this album, *Bud the Spud*, had gone Gold four times already before EMI Records had begun to handle it in 1990. This is the equivalent of two platinums and one gold in today's way of tabulating. (Not too bad, I would say, for an album of songs that never got played on the major radio stations.)

With Tour '98 now over, it had been a great experience for Tommy. Not only did he learn a lot about co-ordinating every aspect of the shows themselves, but Brian and Larry Fitzpatrick also taught him a great deal about the box office and other details about the touring business in general.

Everyone Sang at
Maple Leaf Gardens

O N OCTOBER 30, '98, WE arrived home. And knowing that Lena and I would be celebrating our twenty-fifth, or Silver Wedding Anniversary, on the second of November, I only had a couple of days to scramble around to buy her some gifts of silver for the occasion. But I already had another, much bigger surprise gift for her that I'd been planning for months.

While the tour had been in progress, I had been scheming with Brian Edwards to make arrangements for me to make Lena's anniversary surprise become a reality. And in Georgetown, where Lena does a lot of her shopping, the surprise plan began to unfold in the late afternoon of November 1, the day before our anniversary.

On the evening of November 2, Lena and I, with Gaet and Jean and Tommy, all headed out to a dining room in Georgetown. As I drove fairly slow past a certain location, Lena was talking to Jean and therefore missed the big surprise. So I made some excuse for driving around the block so I could come back and pass the special location again. Only this time, as I made my approach to the location, I pulled over and stopped.

All of a sudden there was a big scream. "Oh, my God, Tom, it's beautiful. Pull in so I can really get up close to it."

That's all we heard from Lena as she got out of the van and walked up to a huge billboard, all lit up with hearts and flowers. The text read: To Lena With Love From Tom, On Our Silver Anniversary. X X O X O. Nov. 2nd, 1973 / Nov. 2nd, 1998.

All we could hear from Lena was, "My camera, my camera. Why didn't you tell me? I could have brought my camera."

"Don't worry about it, dear," I said "You'll have plenty of time to take pictures. The billboard is going to be there every day and every night for the next month. So, come on, let's go and celebrate with a couple of drinks and a nice candlelight dinner."

Around the middle of November we threw a party for all those who had been on tour. I had gotten some nice plaques made up for each of the boys in the band which recognized them for having been a part of the "Most Successful Stompin' Tom Tour to Date" and along with the plaques, I presented each of them with a little cash bonus. I thought it might help to pay for a few croquet lessons to get them in shape for the next big match.

This was the night that poor Tommy learned why he could never win a coin toss against Larry Murphy. Larry finally showed him his two-headed nickel.

Before the boys and their wives left that night, they presented me with a nice native stone carving of a turtle. I think the message here was that they were hoping I'd slow down a little, and maybe let them win a game of something once in a while.

Another party was held just before Christmas which was attended by most of the people we know from EMI. Gaet Lepine, again, was the bartender. (I just can't seem to get rid of that guy. Don't ever owe him a nickel or he'll hound you till the day you die. If he doesn't get it out of you one way, he'll get it another. When he comes to visit me now, he just walks in, throws his baggage in the bedroom he wants to sleep in, walks over to the fridge, cracks a beer, and only after he plunks his ass down on my favourite chair does he ever say, "Hi, have I ever told you about the time me and my cousin, Rolly Brazzo, were playin' snooker . . . and . . . blah, blah,

blah, blah, blah. And by the way, . . . blah, blah, blah . . . what time is Lena gonna have supper?" Oh, me nerves! What did I ever do to deserve this?)

It was while Gaet and Jean were at the house that we were all very saddened to hear that Graham Townsend, the great fiddler, had passed away. And then, about three weeks later, we heard that his wife, Eleanor, died when a fire destroyed their house. It was rumoured that Eleanor was so distraught that she may have unintentionally set the house on fire herself. Whatever happened, it was a terrible tragedy that left their son, Gray, in such a shock he had to be hospitalized for a period of time. Graham and Eleanor will be gravely missed by all. And especially the music world.

Just before Gaet and Jean left for home, I picked up some kind of a flu bug. And although I rarely get sick, I was in for a good one this time. The flu didn't actually keep me off my feet, but it made me feel like I didn't want to do anything but mope around. I knew that I had to get back at finishing the book you are presently reading, but I just couldn't. The damn flu had sapped all my strength. I felt more tired when I got up in the morning than I did before I went to bed. And this lasted all through the months of January and February 1999. I don't know what kind of a flu it was, but it was the worst one I ever remember having.

Throughout the month of January, Tom Jr. was expressing some strong interests in starting a recording company. And with my old record company, ACT Records, still sitting on the back burner just waiting for someone to come along and run it, I decided to let Tommy try his hand at it.

His first artist would be Mark LaForme, and the Escarpment Sound Studio was booked for the second and third weeks of February. While I was present, helping Tommy to produce, I wasn't feeling very well so my help was rather limited. Besides, Mark had recorded a couple of albums before and was quite familiar with the importance of creating a good sound.

Most of the songs on the album would be Mark's own compositions, although he did include several of mine. I especially liked the way he sang "I Am the Wind," "Hey, Hey, Loretta" and "Old Flat-Top Guitar."

On the evening of February 9, Lena walked in to the studio with a birthday cake and a nice card. This of course prompted the boys to go out to their vehicles and bring in some of the cards and other little things they had brought as a surprise at the end of the session. Brian Hewson's wife, Barb, then came down to the studio and introduced us all to their baby daughter, Hannah. And after a small celebration, it was back to the business of recording.

As everyone now knows, the last NHL game of hockey to ever be played in Toronto's Maple Leaf Gardens took place on the thirteenth of February 1999, and was played between the Maple Leafs and the Chicago Blackhawks. The final score of the game was six to two for the Hawks, and the last goal of that game was scored by the Hawks' player, number 24, Bob Probert.

Well, several weeks before this game was played, the Gardens were negotiating with my promoter, Brian Edwards, to have Stompin' Tom appear live at the Gardens to sing "The Hockey Song" right after the game and just before the huge closing celebrations got under way.

During this whole evening, the Molson's Brewing Company were also going to have a massive beer tent set up all along the street on one side of Maple Leaf Gardens. Here they would have a stage erected where different bands would play music, continuously, while the celebrations were going on. The Molson's people were also negotiating with Brian to have Stompin' Tom and his band appear as the featured act.

So while we were in the middle of recording Mark LaForme's album, we got word from Brian that both contracts had been finalized. This meant that we had to forget about finishing the album for two or three days and prepare ourselves for the Gardens' big spectacular.

On February 12, the night before the gig, we moved in close to Toronto at a motel within easy access of the Gardens, and there waited for further instructions.

The next afternoon we were chauffeured to the Gardens where we were quickly directed to our dressing room to await the call for camera rehearsal.

John Brunton and Joan Tosoni of Insight Productions would handle our portion of the filming and it was very thoughtful of them to set a nice arrangement of flowers in our dressing room for Lena when we arrived.

Although we knew that the Gardens would have lots of security floating around everywhere, we brought Frank and Randy Hewitt along with us just in case. These boys were a lot more familiar with our needs, and could instruct the others accordingly.

The members of "The Formula" band again were Mark LaForme, Larry Murphy, Steve Petrie and Danny Lockwood. And for Brian Edwards, who was now taking all these big shows in stride, it was really no more than a "one-Tylenol night."

After Ken Dryden and a few others dropped by the dressing room to say hi, we headed out to one end of the rink to do our rehearsal in front of the cameras. Here they adjusted their angles and sound levels and we returned to our dressing room to wait for the final call.

When the call came at around 10:30 the boys took their places on the ice in the semi-darkness and I waited until an old film flick of Foster Hewitt was quickly run with a modern-day "Foster imitator" welcoming listeners everywhere to the game. With a shot of Foster now looking down towards one end of the ice, the voice-over said, "And now, ladies and gentlemen, let's go down to where the action begins with Stompin' Tom Connors."

This was my cue to walk out through a pre-arranged puff of smoke, and with a big wave to the audience of about 17,000, I stepped up to the microphone and blasted out with the now familiar words, "Hello, out there. We're on the air. It's Hockey Night tonight," etc. And by the time I got to the first chorus, everyone in the Gardens was singing, "Oh! The good ol' hockey game, is the best game you can name. And the best game you can name, is the good ol' hockey game."

I didn't know how the song was received by the two or three million TV viewers that night, but in truth, by the time the song was over, I was too emotional to care. This was my first time playing at "The Gardens," and what a moment of pride and honour it had been. (And back in the dressing room, the boys expressed the same feelings.)

But, not to get caught up in one's personal feelings, we

had other work to do. While the great parade of old hockey heroes presented themselves to the world audience, and the stirring music of Canada's 48th Highlanders piped them in, we were on our way to the Molson's beer tent, outside.

The show was running late. John Allan Cameron had just come off the stage. And about the time I was supposed to be going on, Tom Cochrane was beginning his set.

As the hour was now very late, by the time the boys and I finally hit the stage, it was almost time to wave goodbye to everybody. With buses waiting to take the people home at a given time, we were only left with about twenty minutes to play (hardly time to warm up), and then it was over.

Although we would liked to have entertained more for the beer tent audience, the real charge of our night was, without question, having the opportunity to play Maple Leaf Gardens on the very last night of its glorious era. (Now, for an orphan guy out of Skinners Pond, P.E.I., this was a real accomplishment. But with no time to bask in the sunlight, me, Tommy and the boys were back in the studio the following week to finish the recording and mixing of the album we had started before the big event occurred.)

By the end of the third week in February, Tommy had the master of his first ACT Records album in his hand. But this was only the beginning. From now on he would have to learn through the process of hard knocks how to spend money wisely in the next five or six months; the time it would take to finally have a finished product on the shelves of stores that people might or might not like to buy. And if they don't buy it, he will, of course, have lost the money it took to produce the album in the first place.

This is where Canadian radio becomes a major player in the success or downfall of many a Canadian record company and the artists they believe in. Because we have allowed radio to decide what is good or bad for the public to hear, a lot of good artists and fledgling companies bite the dust for lack of exposure. And it's a fact, unfortunately, that thousands of good artists with great songs get really discouraged when radio refuses to play their best efforts. It becomes very difficult to go on writing songs and spending more money to record them when you know in your heart that some of the best songs you'll ever write were on your first album that never got played.

At any rate, I wish Tommy much success with ACT Records and his very first album, entitled *Mark LaForme . . . True to Form.* Mark is an excellent singer, songwriter and musician. And believe me, this opinion does not come clouded or tainted with prejudice. I have listened to the work on this album very objectively and I recommend it highly to any buyer of records, whether it ever gets played on the air or not. I hope it does.

I also hope that, just because I have exercised my democratic right to voice my opinions in this book about what I consider to be bad about radio, they won't now take it out on two innocent people and refuse to play this excellent album on such flimsy grounds.

Just because there may be radio stations out there who hate Stompin' Tom and everything he stands for is no reason for them to discriminate against someone else just because they may, in some way, be associated with him.

Besides, why should radio or anyone else be surprised, or think it so strange, for a man who is widely known to be a Canadian patriot to get his back up against some organization he feels is not doing enough to serve the best interests of their country?

You would think that, as a Canadian institution, they would welcome the suggestions of such a person instead of trying to annihilate him and everything he stands for.

I personally can't understand how anyone can feel justified, let alone contented, to make his living under licence provided by one country while performing his duties and kowtowing to the formats and dictates of another.

If any radio station in the United States went to the American government in Washington, demanding the right to play less than 30 per cent American music, they'd be branded a communist, lose their licence, and be thrown in jail for treason. Why? Because it would be deemed that they had no intention of serving the best interests of their country.

Winding Down for
Another Start

B Y THE FIRST WEEK OF MARCH 1999, I was getting a
little panicky about writing this book. The damn flu, or
whatever it was, still had a hold of me, and no matter what I
did I just couldn't seem to shake it.

I only had 163 pages written since the last book came out
and it seemed like I'd never get back to writing.

Then on Sunday, the seventh day of March, I felt just a little bit better and decided to put the 164th page in the typewriter. I only wrote one page the first day. And from then on
till the first week of June it was non-stop. With an average of
fifteen hours a day just to get three or four pages, it's been a
long haul. And as I write these words on June 13, I don't
have far to go now to wind it all down.

The Stompin' Tom Award to the unsung musical heroes
of the east coast was presented earlier in 1999 to Archie
Dixon, Rudy Pace, Joan Morrissey, Eddie Arsenault and
Gilles Losier. It's so nice to know that so many of our former
Canadian entertainers who have been such an inspiration to
our present-day award winners are finally receiving some
due recognition themselves. If I had my way, this type of
award would be presented each year to the unsung musical
heroes right across Canada. Not only by CARAS and the
CCMA, but by all provincial music associations everywhere.

These people may not like me or what I stand for, so they could take my name off the award altogether. But at least keep the idea living, because where would our present-day talented musicians be if it wasn't for those who came ahead of us to show us the way? Let their music and inspiration forever be appreciated and never forgotten. (Hear me, radio.)

Also as I write today, I hear the chainsaw going down behind my house. Tommy and one of our good neighbours from Newfoundland, Wallie Williams, are out there cutting and splitting a bit of fireplace wood for the oncoming winter. Wallie's wife, Charlene, is around somewhere talking to Lena. And their son, Trevor, is due to arrive at any time. As soon as the splitting is done, I'll have to quit writing for the evening and have a few beers with the boys.

I expect to have this book into the publisher in a couple of days, now, and then get into some serious songwriting. I must try to write and record an album before the end of July. Brian Edwards is planning a concert tour around the first of August and the album has to be done by then.

Now, there's a coincidence for you. I just this minute received a fax from Brian. My first concert date will be in Tignish, Prince Edward Island, on August 1, 1999, and I'll also be playing Lulu's in Kitchener, Ontario, on New Year's Eve, 1999. Now that should be a big one. The place seats about 3,200 and I'll bet she'll be packed like sardines. So when the big "double zeros" roll in, old Bud the Spud will be rollin' down the highway smilin', and singin' "Sudbury Saturday Night." (And by the way, rumour has it that this might be the "last hurrah" for Lulu's. They may be closing down to make way for the construction of something much bigger. Such as a mall of some kind. This is not the gospel, just a rumour.)

This year, incidentally, is Lena's twentieth year with the Lioness Club. As everyone knows, they have done some remarkable work towards raising funds for the needy. And their contributions over the years to so many worthy causes have just been phenomenal. They not only donate a considerable amount of time to this cause, but on a good many occasions they dig into their purses and donate a lot of their own money as well. So whenever you happen to see these gals in their little blue uniforms, give generously. Your money will always find its way to someone a lot less fortunate than yourself.

Well, I had a few beers with Wallie and the boys last night, and today is Tom Jr.'s birthday, June 14. He just turned twenty-three. He's going out somewhere tonight. I suspect that his pal Matt Anderson will take him to a surprise party somewhere. Anyway, happy birthday, Tom, from me and Mom.

My Last Twentieth-Century Tour

WELL, HELLO AGAIN EVERYBODY. Since I wrote that last paragraph on June 14, 1999, I learned from my publisher that the release of this book would be delayed until the year 2000. So with my deadline extended, I thought it would be appropriate to add some more information as soon as I got the chance, and try to at least bring the data of this book up to the millennium.

So here I am in late January in the year 2000 recounting the events of the last six or seven months.

Upon finalizing the contract to play Lulu's, in June, I wrote a few more songs and called Mark LaForme and his band to rehearse for the new album, *Move Along with Stompin' Tom*. This we recorded during the first half of July 1999, and then started making our plans for the forth-coming concert tour of the Maritimes and Ontario.

The east coast towns on our agenda were Tignish, P.E.I.; Glace Bay, N.S.; Halifax and Kentville, N.S.; then Campbell-ton and Woodstock, N.B.

The show in Tignish, near my home in Skinners Pond, promised to be a big one. Tignish was holding its bicenten-nial celebrations on the first of August and I was to be their headline performer at the huge concert that night. In fact the concert was called the "Welcome Home Stompin' Tom" concert. Other performers on the bill were Jason McCoy, Slainte Mhath, Randy J. Martin and the band Acadilac from

Prince Edward Island.

Although it was supposed to be a big secret, someone leaked it to the media that the road from the Skinners Pond School to the harbour was to be renamed the "Stompin' Tom Road," and I read about it in the papers even before I left Ontario. This was all to take place at a homecoming celebration at the school on the afternoon after the concert. This, of course, dampened the surprise but I was nevertheless truly elated.

By noon on July 28, with all our vehicles well serviced, we headed out for the east coast.

By the time we reached Oshawa, the "service motor" light came on in my G.M. Suburban and we all pulled in to the next service centre we came to. After the mechanic checked everything he assured me there didn't seem to be anything wrong and we proceeded down the highway.

About an hour later the light came on again. And once again I stopped in to have it cheked out. After finding nothing wrong, the mechanic suggested I might have developed a short in the wires leading to the light and said he didn't think I had anything to worry about.

After driving to Cornwall with the light still on, we pulled into our designated motel, and after unloading the things I would need for the night I had one of the boys check the vehicle once more.

The next morning with the mystery of the light still unsolved, we proceeded down the highway towards Montreal.

About five miles on this side of Dorion, Quebec, I heard a big bang. My motor began to lose compression fast and I was just able to hobble into a G.M. dealer about five seconds before she conked altogether.

With only 90,000 kilometres on the motor, the mechanic informed me that it was finished and I would have to have it replaced.

With no time to spend muckin' around, I told them to go ahead and put in a new motor while I went to a car rental to find myself another vehicle.

With a long holiday weekend coming up, to find a vehicle that was suitable for such a long drive was nearly impossible. All the good ones were taken. So after trying several places I finally had to settle for an old beat-up panel truck. The whole thing was painted a very bright yellow with very large black letters all over it which read: RENT-A-WRECK. These letters were everywhere. And of course the boys all had to have pictures of this thing and me driving it down the highway.

I told them at the G.M. dealer that I would pick up my Suburban with its new motor when I came back from touring the east coast. When they looked at me with the wreck I was driving, they just shook their heads and smiled.

I wasn't smiling, though, when I got this thing out on the road. Especially driving through Montreal. It had absolutely no guts and I had to tramp the accelerator right to the floor in order to keep up with the rest of the troupe. There was even three or four inches of play in the steering wheel. And every time I had to weave in and out of traffic I did so with more of a wobble than with anything that looked like a controlled manoeuvre. "Boy!" I thought, "this is sure going to be some tour. The folks back home are going to feel some proud when they see me driving up in this old rattle-trap." In one place I could look out through the floor boards and see the ground. And try to keep my rear-view mirrors straight? Forget it. Even the gas tank acted like it must have had a hole in it.

Anyway, that night we pulled into Montmagny, Quebec, and I headed straight for the bar.

After a couple of beers I went back to my motel room where I saw our new security man, Roger Bal, walking around with the appearance of being bored with not haveing much to do.

I had first met Roger the previous night in Cornwall, Ontario, where he joined our troupe along with Frank Hewitt, who had been one of our security people during the last couple of tours. As Roger was the new man on our tour, I struck up a conversation with him and found out that he liked to play checkers. So, after telling him that I just happened to have a checker board on the road with me, we decided to have a few games. And being the "gentleman" that I am, after playing twenty games or more, I didn't let him win even one game. So tonight he was determined to get me back for the terrible humiliation.

After losing another thirty games or so, he just shook his head and left the room. "I'll get you back for this, Stompin' Tom," he said. "I'm going to practise up by playing some of the other boys on the tour and the next time we play I'm going to beat your ass." Well, to cut a long story short, although we played more than a hundred games after that, poor Roger never won one. But I must say that his determination was indefatigable, because all the other boys had long since quit trying to beat me at checkers, and even chess, for that matter. As far as I'm concerned, I probably just lucked out. But I never lost one checker or chess game throughout the whole tour. (So much for those amateurs who never had the privilege of going to Skinners Pond University where they might have learned sump'n'.)

The next day we drove to Woodstock, N.B., and the night of July 31, we stayed at the Lewis Motel just outside of O'Leary, P.E.I. Lena had just flown into Charlottetown from Toronto and one of the boys had driven down to meet her at the airport. He also picked up a good feed of lobsters. And after a game or two of croquet we all hit the sack fairly early to rest up for the following big day in Tignish.

Although it rained hard all the next day, it cleared up towards evening and a huge rainbow appeared in the sky just before showtime. Brian Edwards and most of the gang had arrived in Tignish earlier in the afternoon to make contact with Judy Morrisey, one of the co-ordinators of the bicentennial celebrations. And while Judy was very worried about the rain she nevertheless showed a great deal of kindness in her co-operation and made sure all our requirements were met.

While I didn't have to arrive till seven-thirty or eight o'clock, Brian kept me informed by telephone about everything that was going on. And when Frank Hewitt and I drove up in his van there were more people in Tignish than I had ever seen there before.

The show was being held at Perry's Campgrounds and as we made our way to the dressing-room trailer behind the stage, Jason McCoy was just about half-way through his performance. The bands, Slainte Mhath, Acadilac and Randy J. Martin, had all performed a little earlier in the evening.

Around about nine o'clock it was our turn to go on stage. And after Mark and the boys did a few numbers, they called me on. And so did the audience. I hadn't played in Tignish for well over twenty years and they certainly let me know it. There must have been at least three thousand people standing in front of the stage shouting "Welcome home, Stompin' Tom," and these were joined by dozens of people sitting on the rooftops of all the houses that circled the campground. This was truly a sight to behold. All that was required now to make the place go ballistic was the first verse of "Bud the Spud." The rest of the show can only be explained by describing it as one continuous round of applause. And all this was being prompted, of course, by songs like "The Confederation Bridge," "Home on the Island," "Song of the Irish Moss," "My Home Cradled Out in the Waves," and many more about Prince Edward Island and the people who knew just what I was talking about.

Unfortunately, and upon the advice of my management and security, I wasn't able to give autographs after the show. It was felt that with such a large and volatile crowd they would not be able to get me out of there for several hours. It was nevertheless announced, before and after the show, that I would make an appearance at the Skinners Pond school grounds on the following afternoon and there I would sign autographs and take pictures with all and everyone.

The next day at the motel we were informed that the show had been a huge success and the co-ordinating committee were planning to have a similar concert every year from now on as a result.

And what about the old RENT-A-WRECK van that nobody had seen yet? Well, the plans for its first appearance were soon to unfold.

Brian Edwards and a few of the boys took off for Skinners Pond just after noon to prepare for my arrival and me and the rest of the gang left about an hour later.

In hopes of making the best of first impresions, I decided that Lena and I should arrive at the school first in the RENT-A-WRECK, followed by Tommy and the band. And instead of coming in by the main highway as expected, we approached by one of the old dirt roads and came in through a cloud of dust from the back.

As Lena and I drove through the waiting crowd and into the schoolyard, the surprised look on some of the people's faces was something to behold. But the expressions soon turned to laughter as we emerged from the RENT-A-WRECK with a very loud and hearty "Hi, everybody! How ya doin' anyway?"

It couldn't have been more appropriate. Everyone immediately loosened up and the tone was set for the rest of the afternoon. Instead of arriving home as one who had gone away, become "a somebody," and then come back to show it off, I was being readily accepted as one who had never lost his roots. Just one of the boys who never changed and never forgot. The rest of the day was just wonderful, and the old RENT-A-WRECK couldn't have served a better purpose.

While TV and other cameras surveyed the scene, I went to work immediately to sign autographs for young and old alike, as they presented their Stompin' Tom T-shirts, records and other souvenirs they had bought during the concert in Tignish the night before.

Soon a microphone was set up in the front schoolyard and before hundreds of people many speeches were made on my behalf by such persons as the Honourable Kevin MacAdam, P.E.I.'s minister of Fisheries and Tourism, and Karen Keefe, the leader of the committee for promoting the Skinners Pond School as a tourist attraction. There were others who said some very nice words and then it was my turn.

I kind of choked up a couple of times as I recounted some of my earlier years living in Skinners Pond and called out some of the names of the older people in the audience I recognized as having known me since I was a child. I told them it had been a long hard road and how it had all paid off in the end. And to the kids I gave a word of encouragement: "If you wish to accomplish something, stick to your guns and never give up. For to persevere is the only way to win against all odds." Then, after thanking everybody for coming, I followed Kevin MacAdam across Lady Slipper Drive to where a cloth-covered signpost stood on the northwest corner of the crossroads. And here I was asked to pull down the cloth that revealed a nice brand-new green and white sign which said, "STOMPIN' TOM ROAD." It was an emotional moment.

The audience applauded as I reached up and patted the sign and explained to everybody how wonderful it felt to have a road named after you. Expecially one that you had driven many a team of horses over while hauling Irish moss from the shore as a kid. And for some reason, it reminded me of a line of verse I had once learned in the very same school I was now looking at: "A boy's will is the wind's will, and the thoughts of youth are long, long thoughts."

Then, after thanking the people once more, I made my way back to the schoolyard where many branches of the media were waiting to ask about the impressions I had throughout the day. There were TV, radio, magazine and newspaper people from both near and far, and one newspaperman, George Bently, had been sent all the way to P.E.I. from the Cornwall, Ontario, *Standard Freeholder*, to take in the events and get an interview. Both inside and outside of the school, George and all the others got what they came for; then it was time to sign more autographs. This I did for about another hour and a half, and then it was time to go.

I had spoken to practically everybody who was there that day and so did Tommy and Lena and the boys. We then said goodbye, jumped into the old RENT-A-WRECK and the rest of the vehicles, and headed back out over the old dirt road from whence we came, in a cloud of dust.

We were now headed for Glace Bay, on Cape Breton Island, Nova Scotia, where we had to do our second concert of the tour on August 4.

That evening we crossed the Confederation Bridge and drove as far as Pictou, Nova Scotia, where we were visited in our motel room by Lena's sister, Amy, and her husband, Foster. Later that night, when they were leaving for home, on Caribou Island, Lena decided to go with them and catch up with us later on in Halifax.

The next evening we pulled into Glace Bay. We had not played anywhere in Cape Breton the previous year and even though my promoter told me the word was out that the economy here was really bad and people had no money to spend, especially on such things as concerts, I decided against his better judgment and insisted that we do at least one show in Cape Breton to prove to the people that I hadn't forgotten them. After lowering our ticket prices from the usual, we had the old Savoy theatre just a-hoppin', even though she wasn't quite full. We didn't do much better than to just break even but the folks really enjoyed themselves and the whole thing was really well worth it.

We also had a lot of problems trying to do a Newfoundland date, just as we had had the year before in 1998. It wasn't just the economy problem, but with the prices the way they were, just to get our troupe and equipment to the island and back would have meant a loss of a few thousand dollars instead of a profit. And after all, everyone has to still get paid. So once again we had to move on, even though we were almost on the doorstep. Sorry, Newfoundland. Maybe next time.

The following day, after leaving Glace Bay, we drove to Halifax. Here we met Lena again, who had driven up from Caribou Island with Foster, and also her brother Ted and Eilene, who brought along Ted's daughter, Lisa, and her boyfriend. Lena's sister, Pauline, and her husband, Bill, also arrived. So needless to say, out motel room was packed for a few hours while we talked and joked and enjoyed as good a family reunion as could be expected during any one night in the life of a travelling musician.

The rest of the boys had been given the night off and most of them went downtown to take in the entertainment that was playing at some of the local bars. And although a few of them came back to the motel as very late morning arrivals, they all made sure they were available for the huge seafood supper they were invited to on the following evening.

On August 7 we played the Rebecca Cohn Auditorium for the second time in a year and the place was almost packed. And although one of the newspaper articles complained about tickets being on the steep side, they were nowhere near the prices most of the Americans charge to play the same venue. And besides, not one word of complaint was heard from the people in attendance, not for the 1999 show or the previous show in 1998. We always try to set our prices to make them affordable for the people living and working in the towns we play. And you really can't compare a city the size of Halifax with one the size of Glace Bay. I also learned later that the very person who had done the complaining in the article had previoiusly received his ticket to the show for free. Now that's gratitude for you.

The next afternoon, on Sunday, I said goodbye to Lena once more. The boys and I would drive down to Kentville, Nova Scotia, and she would continue to visit with her family and meet us later in Ottawa.

The Kentville show took place on Monday night and I was surprised to find that one of Lena's young cousins, Kevin Hubert, from the Magdalene Islands, was now working for the local newspaper. I hadn't seen him since he was a little kid so I promptly obliged him with an interview. I also made sure he received a special pass and this enabled him to come backstage and see just how everything was being organized. As Kevin and his wife had never seen a live Stompin' Tom show before, his article in the *Advertiser* on the following day reflected just how greatly they had been impressed by hearing so many songs being sung about Canada. The article also praised Mark LaForme and the boys for being the great musicians that they are. I believe the turnout was somewhere between seven and eight hundred that night. Pretty darn good for a small town.

On Tuesday we drove to Campbellton, New Brunswick, took Wednesday off, and played the Civic Centre on Thursday. Then it was off to Woodstock where we played our last gig in the Maritimes before returning to Ontario.

On our way through Montreal, we had to stop at the G.M. dealers in Dorion to pick up my Suburban, complete with its brand-new motor. I can't tell you how glad I was to see it after driving that damn old RENT-A-WRECK all through the Maritimes and back. The total cost for all this inconvenience was a cool $6,500: $5,100 for the motor and another $1,400 for the truck rental.

And now, in the midst of all my excitement and the hurry to get back on the road, I found out as soon as I hit the highway that my cruise control was not working.

After a few phone calls back to the G.M. dealer, I was

informed that they would not take any responsibility for the cruise control and said it must have been broken long before I dropped off the vehicle. This, of course, was insane, as I had several witnesses who knew the cruise was working right up to the time the motor blew just outside of Dorion.

Subsequent letters and phone calls to the General Motors' head offices gave me absolutely no satisfaction, either for the cruise control or the motor. And with only 90,000 kilometres on the vehicle, I felt they were certainly not standing up for the quality of their products. And needless to say, I won't be in any big hurry to buy another vehicle from General Motors. And my wife and my son and the others who witnessed all this feel exactly the same way.

Later that day, on August 16, we arrived in Cornwall, Ontario, to find that John Farrington and all the great guys and gals who work for the local newspaper, the *Standard Freeholder*, had done one very excellent job at promoting our show at the Aultsville Hall. They had run a big songwriting contest which covered more than ten newspaper pages over the course of several days, with many prizes going out to all the winners. The words had to be written to the melody of "The Hockey Song" and many of them were very good. The prizes ranged from autographed T-shirts, CDs and pictures to a number of free tickets to the show.

The show took place on August 17, and the place was packed. The boys and I signed autographs for at least two hours after the show and we got to meet with John and all the gang immediately thereafter.

It was also a pleasant surprise to meet Bill McIntyre and his wife, France, after the show that night. Bill had been one of the reporters at the *Timmins Press* back in 1965 when I was just getting started at the old Maple Leaf Hotel. It was Bill and John Farrington and a group of other reporters who went out of their way at times to see that I got some ink in the paper. They were also instrumental in getting me in to meet Prime Minister Lester B. Pearson when he visited Timmins. That was how Mr. Pearson got to be one of the earliest members of the old Stompin' Tom Fan Club. As Bill and John and I reminisced about all the shenanigans we used to pull back in the "good old days" we certainly had a lot of laughs about some of the things that we would never try now. John was now the publisher of the *Standard Freeholder*, and I believe Bill told me he was now with the *Glengarry News*.

On August 18, we drove to Ottawa where Lena again joined the tour. We were visited at the motel by Gaet and Jean Lepine and the following night we played the Straits Dance Hall and Saloon. The place holds about a thousand people and again it was packed.

Our next stop was Havelock, Ontario, where, on August 21, I was honoured to have the privilege of headlining the Havelock Jamboree. This was an outside event where the crowd was estimated to be between 65,000 and 70,000 people. Some of the other entertainers appearing on the extravaganza were Billy Ray Cyrus, Charlie Daniels, Freddy Fender, Hank Williams the Third, The Wilkinsons, Julian Austin, Myrna Lorrie, Kitty Wells, the Good Brothers, Terry Sumsion, Jamie Warren, Rick Tippe, Duane Steele, Stephanie Beaumont, Johnny Burke and the East Wind, Jimmy Flynn, Lost & Found, Celtic Pride, Harold McIntyre, Stu McCue, Marc Ekins, the Swamp Band, Bobby Lalonde, Violet Ray, Printer's Alley, Robyn Scott, Matt Minglewood, and, of course, Mark LaForme and the Formula.

The next day we drove to Delhi, Ontario, and on August 23, we took a day off. Some of us went to the Delhi Tobacco Museum where I again recounted my days of priming tobacco to the boys, while some of the other guys just drove home to Hamilton to visit their families.

As Tillsonburg has always been such a great town for me to play ever since those words were written, "My back still aches when I hear that word," it was a good thing we had the previous day off. We were going to need the extra energy to face the great excitement that Tillsonburg generates when they know Stompin' Tom is coming back to perform and sing about the realism and reality that will forever be the proud history of hard-working people. Although the job may not be as hard today as it was at one time, the memories will always be there.

(I've often thought how unfortunate it has been that the big shots of Sudbury have never been able to get with it the way the people of Tillsonburg have, because both songs, "Sudbury Saturday Night" and "Tillsonburg," quite accurately describe the history of both areas. While the ordinary people from Sudbury acknowledge their history with pride, the upper crust would rather sweep it under the rug and deny it. Perhaps some day, like the people of Tillsonburg, they too may realize that any song about any place can only live and last and maintain its popularity to the extent that it is able to capture that one great true and fleeting moment with complete accuracy. And I believe my songs have always matched this prescribed standard.)

At any rate, Tillsonburg was a huge success. I met a lot of old friends and someone even trounced out an old stompin' board that I had once autographed and left there many years ago. But again, as all good things must come to a close, the following day we were heading north to do a concert in Sault Ste. Marie on August 28.

The show was at the Memorial Gardens and among the people in attendance were Mr. and Mrs. Don Ramsay. You'll probably remember Don as one of the first DJs to ever play a Stompin' Tom record. This was shortly after I left Timmins in 1966. The Ramsays came backstage after the autograph signing and while the boys were taking down the equipment, we were able to do some reminiscing about the old Royal Hotel and how we "drank 'er dry" of champagne on more than one or two occasions. Mr. and Mrs. Ramsay, by the way, are the proud parents of country singer Donna Ramsay.

August 29, 1999, saw us driving to Timmins, Ontario, where it all began back in 1964 at the Maple Leaf Hotel. We had the next day off, so a bunch of us went down to the Maple Leaf where we had a few beers while we waited for the arrival of the owner, Roger Richard. After we signed a few autographs for some of the patrons in the small bar downstairs, Roger came in and took us up to the now famous lounge. Here we had a few more beers while I described to everyone how it was back in the "old days."

We took some pictures in front of the Stompin' Tom mural and Roger wanted one or two for himself and, of course, one for the *Timmins Press*. I also met a couple of the boys from the band that would be playing there that night and autographed a couple of their guitars for them. It was such an impromptu meeting that I hope they'll forgive me for not remembering their names. These things do happen.

Before we left, Roger offered to sell me the old Maple Leaf but I declined on the grounds that I'd probably drink up all the profits. (I don't think either one of us knew for sure whether the other was joking or not.)

On August 31, we performed at the Archie Dillon Sportsplex Arena where I sang all my old Timmins songs to a large and very enthusiastic audience. It seemed like everyone could remember the many nights they spent at the old Maple Leaf requesting some of the 2,300 songs I used to sing by heart at the time. I even saw the odd hankie come out once or twice as some of the people recalled the days when they and Timmins were quite a bit younger.

The following afternoon, the mayor of Timmins invited me to city hall where I signed autographs both inside and outside for about fifty people. I got to sign the guest book, took a lot of pictures and was given a nice plaque as "an expression of gratitude and good will from all the people of Timmins." I was very touched. And God love 'em all, when they saw me fidget a little, they even allowed me to have a cigarette or two. Now, that was making a fellow feel right at home. Thanks, gang, it was much appreciated.

Now, with so much more to tell, and with time and pages running short on me again, I'm afraid I'll just have to run through the rest of this last tour of the twentieth century with only a mention of the towns we played or just give a brief comment.

On September 2 we played Englehart, Ontario, and then it was on to St. Catharines, London and Kingsville. Oshawa and Barrie were next, and by September 16 we were playing Hamilton.

All these shows had excellent turnouts and in a couple of places we even broke previous records. The show in Hamilton was especially memorable because Mark LaForme and the rest of the band lived there and a lot of people turned out to see them playing a big concert in their own home town. It's always nice to see people lending support for this kind of thing. Mark's new CD, *True to Form,* was also for sale at the concert and a great many people were buying it.

On September 18, we again wound up our tour by playing Toronto's Massey Hall. And although 1998's Massey Hall gig saw my stompin' board being auctioned off for the amazing sum of $10,000 for the benefit of Project Warmth, an organization that provides sleeping bags, etc., for the homeless in the winter time, this year it went for the very respectable sum of $5,000 to aid the Daily Bread Food Bank. It's so nice to know that so much money can be generated by an old worn-out piece of plywood. And for such worthy causes. I only wished the media had picked up on the great generosity of these people, as it might have prompted others to make donations for similar causes.

After the show that night my record company, EMI of Canada, threw another great party in the downstairs part of Massey Hall which was attended by many of my friends as well as a lot of people from the industry. As this was the last show of our tour, it was an excellent way for everyone to say farewell for the time being.

That night most of us stayed in a motel outside of Toronto and the next day we all headed home. It had been a great tour and with the exception of only one or two incidents, such as Steve Petrie having his guitar stolen after one of the shows and a couple of the other boys playing hookie from the troupe one day when they were close to home, everything had gone pretty well according to plan.

In Steve's case, as soon as he got to a town where he could buy another guitar he did so, with Brian Edwards, Steve and myself sharing the cost in a three-way split. In the event the stolen guitar shows up somewhere, Steve has of course agreed that Brian and I will be reimbursed.

Anyhow, now that the tour was over, it was good to get home again and try to relax for a while. There was still other business to attend to, with bills to pay, etc., but at least the pace was not nearly as demanding as being on the road.

SOCAN Awards and Gretzky Scores

ONE PROBLEM WAS BEGINNING to develop, however, and that was the fact that the owner of Lulu's in Kitchener, Ontario, was beginning to drag his feet about paying half the sum promised for me to play a New Year's concert at his venue which had already been booked since the previous June.

As I had not done a New Year's gig in over twenty-five years, Brian and I thought the turning of the millennium would be an excellent time to do one. And with several options at our disposal we decided to do Lulu's Roadhouse if we could get the same money we could expect elsewhere. Lulu's could seat over three thousand people and its bar scene was thought to be ideal. I had packed the place four or five times in the past and on such a special occasion we figured the whole thing to be a natural shoo-in.

So, with a signed contract for the appropriate amount, the conditions and terms of payment all in place, I began to advertise through newspaper interviews and on every date of my concert tour that I would be playing Lulu's on December 31, 1999.

With tickets now being advertised and available everywhere for all the other millennium shows, at least since the first of September, Brian and I kept wondering what was happening to Lulu's. And by October 29, the date the first half of our contract was to be paid, the money was just not forthcoming. Indeed, it took Brian another month through fax, phone calls and letters before we finally got it. By now it was the end of November and the owner was trying his level best to get us to re-open the contract and to drastically reduce the amount of payment.

Our answer, of course, had to be "No." It was only a month away from the millennium and way too late to change plans now. Had we agreed to re-open the contract we felt there was no telling what price he might want to reduce it to. And any reduction at all would have been less than we could have gotten had we exercised our options in the first place way back in June. So, as there was just no way for us to book or advertise another venue in time for the millennium we had to stand pat. The gig was eventually cancelled, but I'll have to come back to these details a little later on as there were a couple of other important happenings that occurred during the month of November 1999.

On Monday, November 8, SOCAN, the Society of Composers, Authors and Music Publishers of Canada, was holding its annual Awards Night at Toronto's Sheraton Centre Hotel. And because I belong to this society, I was invited and decided to attend.

I was accompanied by Lena, Tommy, and Brian Edwards, along with his wife, Barb.

As we stepped out of our limousine and were escorted to the huge ballroom, it was already about half full. And as soon as our coats were looked after and we had our drinks, we began to mingle and chat with some of the celebrities and many of the other people who contribute to the music business in one way or another.

There were publishers, composers, administrators, entertainers, producers and arrangers of just about any kind of music you might like to name. Store outlets, distributors, record companies, magazines, radio and television—they were all represented. And by the time the place was full, practically everybody you might read, see or hear about was there.

Soon it was announced that the award show would begin and everybody took their seats. Our table was just up to the right of the stage so we all had a very good view. And for others way back, who might not have been able to see so well, there were huge television screens mounted on the walls.

Between the announcing and presenting of awards, we were all treated to some great music from various entertainers and acts of comedy as well as your regular speech making and joke telling.

About three-quarters of the way through the show, after applauding so many winners for their creation of so much great music, the one and only Gordon Lightfoot was called to the stage.

As Gordie approached the mike, he began to speak rather earnestly on behalf of the person to whom he was about to present the next award. He explained that it was SOCAN's National Achievement Award and was being presented to a person who had achieved outstanding success in the Canadian music industry and virtually on his own, with little or no Canadian radio airplay.

At this point I really perked up and began to look around. And when he said he was honoured to be presenting the award to Stompin' Tom Connors, I quickly gave Lena's hand a squeeze and headed for the podium.

As I shook hands and told Gordie we should get together for a good chat sometime, I accepted the award and approached the microphone.

I then held up the award and told everybody how surprised I was to receive it. With SOCAN Awards mainly given out to those whose music receives the most airplay, I had long given up on the idea of ever receiving one. "I really don't know what a guy like me is even doing here," I said, "but if you people honestly think I deserve this then I thank you all very much." I congratulated all the other winners and went down to my table to show Lena, Tommy and all the gang my new and unexpected treasure.

The biggest winners that night were Sarah McLachlan and Shania Twain, while Gordon Lightfoot, Oskar Morawetz, Loreena McKennitt, Bryan Adams, Jim Vallance, Chantal Kreviazuk, Bruce Guthro, Dan Deviller, Sean Hosein, Jim Brickman and Oliver Jones were also winner of various other awards.

Another thing that happened during the first part of November was the EMI Music (Canada) release of the forty-fifth album of my career. It is titled *Move Along with Stompin' Tom* and marks the twentieth album which contains my own self-penned songs. It also contains a few covers that I had always previously wanted to record. Of the sixteen songs on the album, eleven of them are my own, with three from other artists, and two traditional.

I even wrote a song for this album about a Canadian Sasquatch (the Americans call him Big Foot), and while the word is a hard one to find anything to rhyme with, you may get a kick out of how this was accomplished. At any rate, I hope you'll all like the album.

Now, by the middle of November Brian Edwards called and said, "Guess what, Tom? You have been asked to sing your Hockey Song at the induction of Wayne Gretzky into the Hockey Hall of Fame. I'll fax you the terms and you can tell me whether you want to accept."

Well, it didn't take more than a few minutes for the faxes to be exchanged and within the next couple of days the deal was on. The induction would take place on November 22, 1999, and I was going to be there in flying colours.

We contacted Mark LaForme and the Formula and needless to say, they just couldn't wait for the opportunity.

On the night of the twenty-first of November, we all took up residence in a motel just outside of Toronto and waited for word from Brian as to what our next instructions would be.

Around four o'clock the next afternoon we went into town and upon arriving at BCE Place, which houses the Hockey Hall of Fame, we went straight away to the stage where we had to set up for a TV and sound check. When that was over we were led to a very large restaurant where one whole secluded section was designated to be our private dressing room. Lots of food and beer was brought and here we stayed until further notice.

Jim Cuddy and his band were also given a dressing room next to ours and we were able to get together for a while and have a couple of beers. I was to sing "The Hockey Song" just before the inductions and Jim was to play right after.

The whole thing was to be televised that night on the TSN

and ESPN networks and the two other inductees, besides Wayne Gretzky, were to be Scotty Morrison and Andy Van Hellemond, two more great names in the history of hockey.

Soon Mark and the boys were given their signal to hit the stage and as soon as they had their instruments ready to play, it was my turn to appear. I entered from backstage and as soon as I walked to the microphone and dropped my board the lights came on and the cameras were rolling.

In the midst of thunderous applause I bellered out, "Hello out there, we're on the air; it's Hockey Night tonight. Tension grows, the whistle blows, and the puck goes down the ice. The goalie jumps, and the players bump, and the fans all go insane. Someone roars, 'Gretzky scores,' at the good ol' Hockey Game."

Although Gretzky was in a different room than I was at the time, the cameras caught a glimpse of his surprised expression as he looked towards the monitor when he heard the sound of his name. As everyone knows, the name "Gretzky" is not in the recorded version of the song, but I thought I would just throw it in for him on this very special night.

When I came to the third line of the second verse, something distracted me and I paused for a couple of seconds while trying to think of the words. This was soon remedied, however, when I merely went back two lines to the beginning of the verse and started it over again. After that, everything went perfect without a hitch. Everyone thought I had done it on purpose, and even the media hadn't noticed a thing until I told them about it later.

After the song, more applause, and then we went back to our dressing room for another beer until we got the signal that we were going to be escorted downstairs to the Bell Great Hall where we could mingle and have a drink with all the greats of hockey.

This is the moment that all hockey fans, and especially the kids, would give their eye teeth for. And us guys weren't really any different.

Once we entered the Hall, which was massive, everyone was pretty well on his own. You more or less picked out the hockey player or sports personality you wanted to see most and headed in that general direction.

Lena and I and Tommy, along with Brian Edwards, stayed in one group most of the time, while the boys and the others just went wherever their fancy took them.

The room was like a who's who of hockey, from the current players to the old-timers. Some of the ones we met were names like Howie Meeker, Frank Mahovlich, Bobby Hull, Glen Sather, Ken Dryden, Scotty Bowman, Daryl Sittler, and of course, Lena's favourite hocker player of all, Lanny McDonald, who gave her a great big hug. Then we had the pleasure of meeting and chatting with inductees, Scotty Morrison and Andy Van Hellemond, two of hockey's greatest referees, and then it was time to meet the "Great One" himself, Wayne Gretzky.

Wayne, of course, was swamped with people and flanked by three or four red-coated Mounties. I did manage to shake his hand in congratulations and chat with him long enough to hear him say he has always been a Stompin' Tom fan. This really made my night. Lena snapped a couple of pictures and we moved away, allowing others to shake his hand and obtain his autograph.

Just then from out of nowhere came Wayne's little daughter, Paulina, to obtain my autograph. I thought this was one of the nicest things that ever happened to me, especially in such a star-studded place as this. Lena and I both gave her a big hug and took a picture or two. She then ran back to where her mother must have been standing in the crowd next to her daddy, while further introductions forced us to move on.

As we now began to move slowly back towards the door we'd come in, we spoke to many other players and personalities way too numerous to mention. We heard that Gordie Howe, Jean Beliveau and many others were in the crowd but, unfortunately, we never got to meet them. And as all good things must come to an end sooner or later, it was now time for us to leave. But needless to say, it had been one very great night. We talked about it all the way home and for many days after. And we still do. It was certainly a very memorable occasion.

Lights Out at Lulu's

NOW THAT I'M BACK TO THE END of November, I'll pick up the story about how my millennium show at Lulu's Roadhouse in Kitchener, Ontario, was cancelled.

While the owner of Lulu's did have his tickets for this show for sale sometime in August, he did little or no advertising of this fact. We were telling concert audiences about this show in places as far away as Prince Edward Island and Nova Scotia, but the owner of Lulu's did not even begin his advertising campaign until mid-October. And then only because he was coaxed into it by Brian Edwards, who couldn't understand why he was waiting so long.

As a matter of fact, whoever was advertising the tickets for the Tragically Hip show in Toronto had sixty thousand sold by the first day of September. And while not slighting the Hip in any way, we know a lot of their fans might have bought a ticket to the Lulu's show, had they only known they were available. As both these shows had to draw people from the same general area, waiting until October to advertise tickets was a big mistake. It was a case of "too little, too late." And now, at the end of November, the owner of Lulu's was crying for us to re-open our contract and play for a lot less money. The reason, he said, was because he didn't think he could sell enough tickets to make it pay.

By the middle of December 1999, we were told that if we didn't renegotiate our contract and accept a lower pay-off the show would be cancelled altogether. And to this we answered that if he cancelled the show we would have to sue him for the rest of our money. This was for several reasons.

First, it was way too late now for us to book another show for the millennium, and especially for the same money. Had this happened back in July or even August it might have been a different story.

Second, we felt he was bailing out too soon. Ticket sales are always slow for New Year's concerts in the middle of December due to a lot of last-minute Christmas shopping and people can't be sure of exactly how it's going to affect their budgets. By the time their after-Christmas adjustments were made, we felt the ticket sales would pick up.

Third, because we packed Lulu's every time we played there before and a great portion of the Stompin' Tom fans always buy tickets at the last minute, we felt that a wait-and-see approach would have been the best policy.

Some other thinking between Brian and me at the time was that we only had the owner's word by phone that he wasn't selling very many tickets. We had no way of knowing how many were sold or even whether he was telling the truth. And judging by all precedents we believed that we would pack the place. And if we had agreed to take less money just to satisfy the owner's fears, would he have come to us on the night the place was packed and be man enough to compensate us for our losses by giving us back the money we had first contracted for?

This we doubted very much. So instead we chose to stick to the contract and wait until the concert happened. If we saw by the number of people and the count of tickets that the owner was losing his shirt, we could offer to give him some money back.

This, of course, was all hypothetical. But we reasoned, and I think rightly so, that if the owner was looking for us to give him a break, why should we first have to trust him up front instead of him trusting us on the night of the show? He was looking for the favour, not us.

One more point in all of this began while Brian was negotiating with the owner of Lulu's in the first place, and that was back in May of 1999. When Brian was told the price of the tickets for Lulu's would be $100 per person it wasn't hard to figure out that in a facility that would seat over three thousand the take for the door could be over $300,000. And that was not counting the amount of money that would have been made on the sale of all those drinks and souvenirs that would have been sold on such an important occasion.

So, based on our track record for always packing the house, we insisted that our take should be roughly one-third of the gate, which would come to $100,000, and this figure was right in line with the other options we were considering at the time.

Now, it wasn't our fault the owner chose to charge $100 per person. That was his decision to make. And based on his own decision he felt comfortable about signing the contract and paying us the same sum of money we could have gotten by playing elsewhere. If this had not been the case he would not have signed it. And if this had not been the case, we would not have signed it either.

So the contract was signed on June 10. We agreed to do the show and he agreed to pay us $50,000 by the end of October, and the other $50,000 upon our arrival at Lulu's on December 31, 1999.

And now, at last, my reason for taking the time to explain all these details. It's so my readers may understand why my promoter and I were so upset when Mr. Spiegel from Lulu's Roadhouse issued a press release on or about December 21 to announce that the Stompin' Tom Show had been cancelled because I would not renegotiate my contract for a lesser fee. He said it was all just a "cash grab" on my part. "Just business." And because I would not now "revisit it" (the contract) "in some fashion" I somehow didn't care about my fans.

Well, for Mr. Spiegel's information, I could never count on radio to help my career, and if I didn't care about my fans I wouldn't have any career at all. I'm sure my fans would have taken care of that a long time ago. On the contrary, had the show not been cancelled, I knew of some fans who were going to travel all the way up from New Brunswick just to see it. Now, if that's not dedication, I don't know what is.

So no, Mr. Spiegel, you've got it all wrong. The reason I

wouldn't renegotiate for a lot less money was to make sure that you wouldn't get a whole lot more, and the so-called "cash grab" wouldn't be yours at my expense.

As far as I'm concerned, the owner of any club should know his clientele far better than the people he hires to entertain. And he should also be a much better judge as to just what price they might be willing and able to pay for a ticket. Then, in that case, he won't be going over his head by signing contracts with higher-priced bands when he knows his ticket sales and other revenue just won't allow it.

But if and when he does make such a boo-boo, he should take it like a man and not go crying to the entertainment, demanding his money back, and threatening to ruin their reputation by splattering innuendoes all over the newspapers.

In my case, just one article alone came out with the headline, "Stompin' Tom Quits Lulu's." Brian and I had to immediately get them to print a retraction. It was Lulu's who cancelled the show at least ten days before it happened, while Brian and I were urging them to at least wait until after Christmas when things were expected to pick up a little. But as the reader already knows, it's always the person whose name is the most well known that gets the biggest headline, even if they're only involved in the story indirectly.

Eventually, we had to issue our own press release to try to correct some of the things that were said in the one from Lulu's. In the first place, I had never quit or even missed one publicized performance in over thirty-five years. I was always there, winter and summer, rain or shine. And this article was making it look like I was not only irresponsible, with a "lack of interest," but that I was also "more concerned about my wallet than I was about my fans."

This simply isn't true, as any one of my fans will attest. And the only purpose for this kind of talk is to mar a person's good record and try to ruin one's career and a good reputation.

I expect the lawyers will iron all this out one day, but all I can say for now is that all our accommodations, rentals, musicians, security, sound and lighting personnel, office and other expenses have all been paid, even though our show was unexpectedly cancelled. After all, these people expected

to work on New Year's Eve and when the job never material-
ized it was too late for them to obtain other employment, so
Brian and I decided to do the only thing we considered to
be fair under the circumstances.

It would have been nice, especially at Christmas time, if
Mr. Spiegel and/or Lulu's Roadhouse would have had the
same consideration.

Oh well, Fate has a job to do, too, I suppose. What will
be will be; because if it wasn't meant to be, it never could
have happened. It's only the Purpose with which I sometimes wrestle.

The Doctor Concludes

WITH OUR MILLENNIUM SHOW AT Lulu's now gone bust, Lena and I didn't have any plans made to celebrate the advent of the twenty-first century, so we just spent a quiet night at home with our friends, Gaet and Jean Lepine, who had come down to visit us from Ottawa. Their intention had been to come out to the big show in Kitchener, but instead we just had a few drinks, played some cards and listened to records.

Tom Jr. fared a little better as he joined a few of his friends who rented a limousine and went bar-hoppin' all over the city of Toronto. He finally came home late the next afternoon looking somewhat dishevelled after sleeping at a friend's place with his clothes on. He said he had a great time, though, so I guess that's all that matters.

As we sat down to have our New Year's supper that evening (they always call it "dinner" in Ontario), we chatted about the Apocalypse, the Y2K threat and all the other scary things we heard about that never happened. It seemed to us like the year 2000 came in more like a lamb than a lion. And probably a good thing, too. It may be a sign of better things ahead for all of us. God knows we've had enough wars, crimes and other disasters in the twentieth century to almost last us for another whole millennium.

The damned ole flu bug didn't let up, though. As soon as Gaet and Jean went home on January 2, I came down with it, and it just knocked the crap out of me for about a month. I didn't feel like doing anything, including writing this book, until February.

By then, Tommy had gotten EMI Music (Canada) to distribute his new ACT Records CD and cassette by Mark LaForme and he also got a new web site on "Stompin' Tom" set up for his computer.

The site was set up by a couple of Tommy's friends he calls "The Two Mikes": Mike Helms, from Cambridge, Ontario, did the discography and the other technical work, while Mike Dunlop, from Ajax, did all the graphic designing. There's really a ton of information here about me that a lot of people may not have known before. And if you'd like to check it out, the letters www.StompinTom.com or just Stompintom.com will get you there.

Around February 4, Lena's brother, Ted, who had just gotten laid off from his job in Kitchener, Ontario, came to visit us for a few days before making a trip to Halifax. While he was here, Lena talked him into doing some painting for her in the old part of our house. As soon as one job was finished she got him to do another, and before you knew it, she had the whole house redecorated, and the "few days" turned into over three weeks. She also had our old carpenter friend Karl Kothe over for a while to do some patch work and build her a couple of cabinets. Soon she had the house looking brand new again and poor Ted finally got to make his long-awaited trip to Halifax. I don't expect he'll be back for another visit in the very near future. Lena might want some more painting done.

Also, at the beginning of February 2000, the East Coast Music Awards took place in Sydney, Nova Scotia. And it was at this time that another five "unsung heroes of the east coast music industry" received a Stompin' Tom Award for the contribution they have made and the inspiration they have given to the music, the industry and the artists of today's Atlantic Canada.

Along with the other names already mentioned in this book, the five new recipients are: for Newfoundland, Omar Blondahl; for Mainland Nova Scotia, Carol Fredericks-Frank; for Cape Breton Island, Nova Scotia, Gib Whitney; for New

Brunswick, Eddie Poirier; and for Prince Edward Island, Gordon Gallant. Congratulations to these, and to those who have and those who will have received the Stompin' Tom Award, whether now, or in the past, or in the future.

And now, friends, on this twenty-ninth day of February, in the year 2000, it looks like I'm finally going to finish this, the second part of my autobiography. The day is very mild, there's no snow on the ground, and the sun is shining through my window. A very rare thing for this time of year, to say the least. But then again, so is the fact of there being twenty-nine days in the month of February, especially in a year that ends with at least two zeroes. It only happens once in every four hundred years. The last time was in the year 1600 and the next time won't be until the year 2400. So for anyone who might have a penchant for strange days and odd occurrences, somewhere in this little coincidence they may find an omen.

Also, at twelve o'clock, midnight, on the ninth of this month, I turned sixty-four. And on the following day a very important announcement was being made to the Governing Council of the University of Toronto by the president, J. Robert S. Prichard.

I say the announcement was important (especially to me) because Mr. Prichard was conveying to the Council my affirmative answer to the following letter he sent me, dated February 1, 2000.

> Dear Mr. Connors:
> It is my great pleasure to write on behalf of the Governing Council of the University of Toronto to invite you to accept the degree of Doctor of Laws, honoris causa. The degree would be awarded at Convocation on a mutually convenient date in the month of June, 2000.
>
> This degree is offered to you in recognition of your outstanding contributions to the musical and cultural identity of Canada and the Canadian people.
>
> In your long career, you have given voice to

the common people of Canada in a way unmatched by any other composer or performer of your generation. Your songs tell the stories of working Canadians who form the backbone of this country. Our prosperity is owed to the millions of Canadians who have seen themselves in your songs that have created heroic portraits of ordinary people, from truck drivers to farm workers. In each song, people can see themselves, their friends, or their neighbours. Each is an accurate rendering of Canadian life in the latter half of the twentieth century.

Few performers have garnered the fond respect and legendary status the Canadian people have bestowed on you through numerous awards, and general public approval. Therefore the University of Toronto would be proud and grateful if you would now agree to add our highest honour to your list of awards.

Should you agree to accept our invitation I would appreciate your keeping it in confidence until February 10th, 2000, when I can inform the Governing Council of your acceptance. I would be grateful if you would provide me with your response as soon as you can.

I look forward to your reply . . .

Warm regards,

(Signed) J. Robert S. Prichard

Wow! What a great letter, eh? I must have read that one over about ten times. And did I accept the offer? You bet your boots I did. When a university as large and as well known as the U. of T. offers you their highest honour you've got to sit up and take notice.

And how would you like to have one of these honours, boys and girls? Well, you can someday, you know. And this is how you do it. First, you find out by asking yourself what it is you would like to accomplish in your life. Then keep your mind on that picture you see of yourself and always work towards your goal no matter how many people try to distract you or keep you away from it. Try to do a little something every day to bring your goal a little closer to you. And if it's something you can't bring to you, then you must go to it.

Sometimes when you see others getting rewards for the things they do, and you don't seem to be getting anywhere, don't be discouraged and don't give up. A whole lot of little awards are never as good as the one big one you will get when you have reached your own goal and accomplished what you set out to do. Besides, winning awards that other people want you to win is not nearly as good or as satisfying as that one big award you know you won all by yourself.

And here's something else. Always keep your mind and your eyes only on your goal and never on the award. To think of the award will only distract you from accomplishing your goal. So don't be distracted by anything and you'll be sure to succeed. And when you succeed you won't even have to think about receiving your award because everybody will be reminding you that you deserve it, and they'll hardly be able to wait to give it to you.

And just one more thing. Once you've set your goal, there's really no need to discuss it with anybody, because nobody can see your goal as good or as clear as you can. And discussing it with people who don't understand only causes them to laugh at you and say you're crazy for trying to do something they believe to be impossible. Just stick to your goal and don't give them a chance to discourage you. And you can do that best by keeping it to yourself.

Now, I'm not just preaching about something I read somewhere is a book. I've been there and done that. I've been down that road before. And sometimes my road has been pretty rocky and bumpy. And sometimes it's been very dark and dismal. But through it all, I've never lost sight of my goal. And that's why I sometimes receive letters just like the one you've just read. They come as a surprise when you're not even looking for them. So just pursue your goal and don't listen to the smart alecks, the tough guys and the trouble makers, because they have no goal to pursue. And if you do this, I guarantee that someday you too will receive a very nice letter just like mine. So don't give up.

Well, I guess that's just about it folks. And by the time most of you read this, I suppose the year 2000 will already have come and gone. It will take a number of months from the time these pages leave my typewriter until they're actually manufactured in book form and placed on the market. I'm expecting this to happen sometime in late summer or early fall.

In the meantime, lots of people have been asking me if and when I plan to retire; if and when I'll be going on tour again; and if and when I think Canadian radio will ever play Stompin' Tom songs on the hit parade, or at least with any consistency.

The answer to the first two questions is, simply, I just don't know. I'll just take one day at a time and accomplish whatever I'm capable of. At this moment I really have no specific plans, but whatever comes up, I'm sure you'll all be reading about it in the newspapers. And the answer to the third question about radio is simply that I don't believe they'll ever play Stompin' Tom songs, on the hit parade, consistently or any other way. Their minds have been made up to boycott my music right from the very beginning in hopes that I would just go away and quit altogether. Perhaps go back to being just another one of the homeless on the streets of one of our fair Canadian cities.

While I say this I want to make it very clear that the brush with which I paint does not cover or include those small and/or independent radio stations, nor those at a number of Canadian universities, whose power may not have been very strong. For it is they, and they alone, who have played some of my music from time to time on special programs. And for this I have always been grateful.

I have travelled my country from coast to coast and I have considered it from top to bottom. And not through rose-coloured glasses. I've seen our good points and I've seen some bad. We have our strengths and we have our weaknesses. But when all is said and done, we have been blessed with one great big young and beautiful country of which we can all be proud. And I'm talking about the kind of pride that we should all be writing and singing about. And not the kind of shame and embarrassment that big radio stations feel when they refuse to play the music that should always be encouraged to flow freely from the hearts of all true Canadians.

And to all these big radio stations I would like to ask just one final question before concluding this book.

If I've made a mistake by staying home here in Canada and writing songs about the people I'm proud to live with, and if, as you've claimed for so many years, my lifetime's work of forty-five albums and three hundred songs does not contain even one song that fits your Canadian radio format, will somebody please be kind enough to stand up and tell me in front of this nation and the people I sing about, just what other country they would advise me to go to? Where else in this world could I expect a more sympathetic radio system to play the Canadian songs of Stompin' Tom? If not here, then where?

Well, finally that's it. I'm done. I don't know how the publisher will number the pages in this book, but counting the 521 manuscript pages in *Before the Fame*, and the 641st page of *The Connors Tone* that I'm about to take out of my typewriter, this makes a grand total of a 1,162-page autobiography.

To some, this may seem like a lot. But I also left out a lot. Especially the deeper and more penetrating questions and answers that have bothered people since the beginning of time. Such as who and what is God? Who and what are we? What are we doing here and what is our purpose? And did those who came thousands of years before us leave all the answers hidden to those unable to use them wisely, and yet glaringly obvious to the sincere seeker and the humble of heart? Maybe someday I'll be afforded the time and pages to tackle some of these issues. but until then, may we all ponder Gen: ch. 5, v. 24, which reads: And Enoch walked with God: and he was not; for God took him.

Stompin' Tom Connors, O.C., LL.D.
February 29th, 2000

Appendix

To my readers who may be interested in perpetual calendars, I now print here, free of charge, a calendar that is truly perpetual and complete with instructions for immediate use. In reality, what you get here is exactly what was advertised in the *National Enquirer* and is totally accurate for all practical day and date calculations. But as extensive as it may seem, it is merely a very small segment of the much larger "Everdate Perpetual Calendar" which calculates millions of years. This little one is only operative from the time of Christ to A.D. 3100, but quite adequate for the needs of most people. The larger one is more adapted to archaeologists and people with like interests.

First off, in calculating any dates, it's always important to remember how many days there are in each month of the year. So here is a simple poem I've composed that will tell you just that. It is an adaptation of a much older poem which was considerably harder to memorize.

DAYS IN A MONTH POEM

30 days in September, April, June and November;
The rest have 31 like January.
But the month with the fate of only having 28,
And in Leap Year, 29, is February.

INSTRUCTIONS: To find the name of the day any given date falls on, you must first, of course, have a date. So let's pick the year of 1895, on July 22. The number of centuries that have gone by is 18, and the number of years is 95. Now look for 18 in the Century Box on the calendar and move to the right along the row it's situated on, until you come to the column in which the 95 is situated in the Years Chart A. Your finger should now be resting on a "3" which is your key number for going to the next chart, called the Month Chart B.

You will now notice that Chart B has a left side composed of all letters which represent Leap Years, and a right side composed of all numbers which represent Regular Years.

We now look for your key number "3" in the January Column of Regular Years in Chart B and from the "3" we follow the row to the right until we come to the column which contains July, and here we find a "2."

The "2" now is your key number for going to the Day Chart C and there on the far left we find a column of letters and numbers called the Day Code.

We now find your key number "2" in the Day Code and we move along this row to the right until we come to the number 22. And there at the top of the column which contains the number 22 is "M" for Monday.

We have just found out that July 22 of 1895 was a Monday. Now, that wasn't too hard, was it? So let's find out now what day Christmas fell on in the year 1976.

STOMPIN' TOM'S 3000 YEAR CALENDAR

EVERDATE © 1978
BY T.C. CONNORS

DAY CODE

J-7

Sn	M	T	W	T	F	S
						1
2	3	4	5	6	7	8
9	10	11	12	13	14	15
16	17	18	19	20	21	22
23	24	25	26	27	28	29
30	31					

K-6

Sn	M	T	W	T	F	S
					1	2
3	4	5	6	7	8	9
10	11	12	13	14	15	16
17	18	19	20	21	22	23
24	25	26	27	28	29	30
31						

V-5

Sn	M	T	W	T	F	S
				1	2	3
4	5	6	7	8	9	10
11	12	13	14	15	16	17
18	19	20	21	22	23	24
25	26	27	28	29	30	31

R-4

Sn	M	T	W	T	F	S
			1	2	3	4
5	6	7	8	9	10	11
12	13	14	15	16	17	18
19	20	21	22	23	24	25
26	27	28	29	30	31	

M-3

Sn	M	T	W	T	F	S
		1	2	3	4	5
6	7	8	9	10	11	12
13	14	15	16	17	18	19
20	21	22	23	24	25	26
27	28	29	30	31		

S-2

Sn	M	T	W	T	F	S
	1	2	3	4	5	6
7	8	9	10	11	12	13
14	15	16	17	18	19	20
21	22	23	24	25	26	27
28	29	30	31			

T-1

Sn	M	T	W	T	F	S
1	2	3	4	5	6	7
8	9	10	11	12	13	14
15	16	17	18	19	20	21
22	23	24	25	26	27	28
29	30	31				

DAY CHART C

MONTH

	Ja	Fb Mr	Ap My Jn	Jl Au Sp	Oc Nv Dc
7	J	M R	J S V	J M T	T R K
6	K	S M	K T R	K S V	J M V
5	V	T S	V J M	V T F	K S R
4	R	J T	R K S	R J M	V T M
3	M	K J	M V T	M K E	R J S
2	S	V K	S R J	S V T	M K T
1	T	R V	T M K	T R J	S V J

CHART B

YEARS CHART A

00	01	02	03	04	05	06	07	08	09	10	11	12	13	14	15
28	29	30	31	32	33	34	35	36	37	38	39	40	41	42	43
56	57	58	59	60	61	62	63	64	65	66	67	68	69	70	71
84	85	86	87	88	89	90	91	92	93	94	95	96	97	98	99

16	17	18	19	20	21	22	23	24	25	26	27	28
44	45	46	47	48	49	50	51	52	53	54	55	
72	73	74	75	76	77	78	79	80	81	82	83	

LY	K	R	S	J	V	T	M			J	R	S	V	T	K

CENTURY BOX

	00	J
0 4 8 12 16 20 24 28		J
1 5 9 13 17 21 25 29		6
2 6 10 14 18 22 26 30		4
3 7 11 15 19 23 27 31		2

*LY— Stands for Leap Year

First we take the 19 from the 1976 and go to the Century Box. With our finger on the 19 we follow the row to the right until we stop at the bottom of the column which contains the number 76 in the Years Chart A. This time our finger has stopped on the letter "V" instead of a number. This means that 1976 was a Leap Year as indicated by the letters LY in the middle of the column.

We now take our key letter "V" and go to the January Column on the Leap Year side of the Month Chart B and from the "V" we follow the row to the right until we come to the last column under December and our finger should now be resting on an "R."

We now look for the "R" in the Day Code Column at the far left of the Day Chart C. And if we follow the row to the right which contains the "R" we pass all the days in December until we stop at 25, which is Christmas Day, and at the top of the column we see that Christmas, on the twenty-fifth of December in 1976, fell on a Saturday.

Now, there's only one more thing you need to know. If you look at the Years Chart A you will see that the numbers only go from 01 to 99. So what happened to all the years that end in 00, such as 1400, 1900, 2000, 2300, etc.? Well, just to the immediate right of the Century Box you will see a small column with two zeros (00) on the top. So if you wanted to find out what day March 1 fell on in the year 2000, you would go to the 20 in the Century Box and follow this row to the right and immediately stop at the small column directly under the two zeros (00), and there you would find a "J." And because "J" is a letter and not a number, you know the year 2000 is a Leap Year.

You now go to the January Column on the Leap Year side of the Month Chart B and in the row that starts with "J" you go across to the March Column and find that your finger now rests on an "R." Now, in the Day Code Column of the Day Chart A you will find that "R" will lead you directly to the number one (1) right under the "W" for Wednesday. So March 1 in the year 2000 was a Wednesday.

Always remember that Key Letters represent Leap Years and you go to the left side of the Month Chart B, and Key Numbers represent Regular Years and you go to the right side of the Month Chart B. And one more little thing that you'll no doubt find out for yourself: once you have found your Key Letter or Key Number in the Years Chart A and the date you're looking for is in January of any year, you can bypass the Month Chart B altogether, and go directly to the Day Code in the Day Chart C. (This quick method is only good for January and no other months.)

Well, there it is. And with a little bit of practice you will be able to operate the calendar at a glance. And here's a few names of some famous people, along with their birthdates and the day of the week on which they were born, so you can look them up and check your accuracy. This will give you enough practice to go ahead and reveal to all your friends the actual day they were born on. Happy Dating.

Neil Armstrong was born August 5, 1930, on a Tuesday.

Albert Einstein was born March 14, 1879, on a Friday.

Martin Luther King was born January 15, 1929, on a Tuesday.

Sophia Loren was born September 20, 1934, on a Thursday.

Pierre Trudeau was born October 18, 1919, on a Saturday.

Wayne Gretzky was born January 26, 1961, on a Thursday.

George Washington was born February 22, 1732, on a Friday.

Stompin' Tom Connors was born February 9, 1936, on a _____?

Selected Discography

Northlands' Own (1967)
(re-released as Northlands Zone on Boot Records and EMI)
The World Goes Round
The Maritime Waltz
The Northern Gentleman
Movin' On to Rouyn
May, the Millwright's Daughter
Algoma Central No. 69
Emily the Maple Leaf
Goin' Back Up North
Streets of Toronto
My Home Cradled Out in the
Waves
The Peterborough Postman
Carolyne
Sudbury Saturday Night
Little Wawa
My Swisha Miss
The Flying C.P.R.

Bud the Spud (1969)
Bud the Spud
The Ketchup Song
Ben, In the Pen
Rubberhead
Luke's Guitar (Twang, Twang)
My Brother Paul
The Old Atlantic Shore
My Little Eskimo
Reversing Falls Darling
She Don't Speak English
The Canadian Lumber Jack
Sudbury Saturday Night
T.T.C. Skidaddler
(I'll Be) Gone with the
Wind

On Tragedy Trail (1968)
Tragedy Trail
How the Mountain Came Down
Shanty Town Sharon
Fire in the Mine
Somewhere There's Sorrow
Don Valley Jail
Benny the Bum
Black Donnelly's Massacre
Battle of Despair
Reesor Crossing Tragedy
Little Boy's Prayer
Around the Bay and Back Again

Merry Christmas Everybody (1970)
Merry Christmas Everybody
Merry Bells
Christmas Angel
Down On Christmas
Jingle Jangle Aeroplane
Kiss Me the New Year In
Mr. Snowflake
Story of Jesus
An Orphan's Christmas
One Blue Light
Gloria
Our Father

Stompin' Tom Connors Meets Big Joe Mufferaw (1970)
Big Joe Mufferaw
Sable Island
Don't Overlove Your Baby
Log Train
Roll On Saskatchewan
Jenny Donnelly
The Coal Boat Song
Algoma Central No. 69
The Night That I Cremated Sam McGee
Poor, Poor Farmer
My Last Farewell
Rocky Mountain Love
Around the Bay and Back Again

My Stompin' Grounds (1971)
My Stompin' Grounds
The Bridge Came Tumblin' Down
Snowmobile Song
"Wop" May
Cross Canada
Tillsonburg
Tribute to Wilf Carter
Song of the Irish Moss
Song of the Peddler
Bonnie Belinda
Name the Capital
Song of the Cohoe

Live at the Horseshoe (1971)
Happy Rovin' Cowboy
Big Joe Mufferaw
Come Where We're At
The Green, Green Grass of Home No. 2
Spin, Spin
Muleskinner Blues
Horseshoe Hotel Song
I've Been Everywhere
Sudbury Saturday Night
Bus Tour to Nashville
Luke's Guitar
Bud the Spud

Stompin' Tom and the Hockey Song (1972)
The Consumer
The Last Fatal Duel
The Curse of the Marc Guylaine
Blue Spell
Singin' Away My Blues
The Hockey Song
The Maritime Waltz
Gaspe Belle Faye
Where Would I Be?
True, True Love
The Piggy Back Race
Your Loving Smile
Mr. Engineer

Stompin' Tom and the Moon Man Newfie (1973)

Oh Laura
Isles of Magdalene
Fire in the Mine
I Can Still Face the Moon
The Bug Song
The Moon Man Newfie
Roving All Over the Land
Movin' In (From Montreal by Train)
Benny the Bum
Twice as Blue
Little Wawa
Rubberhead

Stompin' Tom Meets Muk Tuk Annie (1974)

Streaker's Dream
My Home by the Fraser
Bibles and Rifles
Paddle Wheeler
Unfaithful Heart
Ballad of Muk Tuk Annie
We're Trading Hearts
Oh Chihuahua
Zakuska Polka
I Saw the Teardrop
Wishful Hummin'
Renfrew Valley
My Old Canadian Home

To It and At It (1973)

Prince Edward Island, Happy Birthday
To It and At It
Keepin' Nora Waitin'
Marten Hartwell Story
New Brunswick and Mary
Moonlight Lady
Muk Luk Shoo
Manitoba
Don Messer Story
Alcan Run
Pizza Pie Love
Golden Gone Bye
Cornflakes

The North Atlantic Squadron and Other Favourites (1975)

The North Atlantic Squadron
Red River Jane
High, Dry and Blue
Blue Nose
Back Yardin'
Jack of Many Trades
Unity
Fleur De Lis
I'll Love You All Over Again
(Too Late to Hurry) When the Snow Flurries Fall
Take Me Down the River
Gypsy Chant

The Unpopular Stompin' Tom
(1976)
Good Morning Mr. Sunshine
Where the Chinooks Blow
Zephyrs in the Maple
My Door Is Always Open to You
Blue Misery
The Pole and the Hole
Damn Good Song for a Miner
(aka Muckin' Slushers)
Cowboy Johnny Ware
Ghost of Bras D'Or
Don Valley Jail
Big and Friendly Waiter John
Olympic Song

Fiddle and Song (1989)
Lady, k.d. lang
Fiddler's Folly
It's All Over Now, Anyhow
The French Song
I Never Want to See the World
Again
Hillside Hayride
Morning & Evening & Always
Return of the Sea Queen
Canada Day, Up Canada Way
Jolly Joe MacFarland
Skinner's Pond Teapot
Teardrop Waltz
Entry Island Home
I Am the Wind
Wreck of the Tammy Anne

At the Gumboot Cloggeroo
(1977)
Legend of Marty & Joe
Jaqueline
Handy Man Blues
Man from the Land
Farewell to Nova Scotia
Ripped Off Winkle
Gumboot Cloggeroo
The Happy Hooker
We Doubt Each Other's Love
Old Forgetful Me
The Singer
Isle of Newfoundland
Roses in the Snow
Home on the Island

A Proud Canadian—
Compilation—(1990)
Bud the Spud
Snowmobile Song
Roll on Saskatchewan
Manitoba
Sudbury Saturday Night
Tillsonburg
Roving All Over the Land
New Brunswick and Mary
Big Joe Mufferaw
Gumboot Cloggeroo
The Old Atlantic Shore
Blue Nose
Fleur De Lis
The Moon Man Newfie
The Ketchup Song
Lady, k.d. lang
The Bridge Came Tumblin' Down
Marten Hartwell Story
I Am the Wind
The Singer (The Voice of the
People)

More of the Stompin' Tom Phenomenon (1991)

Margo's Cargo
Flyin' C.P.R.
Rita MacNeil (A Tribute)
Brown Eyes for the Blues
J.R.'s Bar
Loser's Island
St. Anne's Song and Reel
Made in the Shade
Love's Not the Only Thing
Land of the Maple Tree
A Real Canadian Girl
Okanagan Okee
No Canadian Dream
(I'll Be) Gone with the Wind

Believe In Your Country (1992)

Johnny Maple
My Home Cradled Out in the Waves
Prairie Moon
She Called from Montreal
Lover's Lake
Lena Kathleen
Believe In Your Country
Alberta Rose
Sunshine & Teardrops
My Sleeping Carmello
Lookin' for Someone to Hold
Paper Smile
Smile Away Your Memory
The Ballinafad Ball

Once Upon a Stompin' Tom— Compilation—(1991)

Canada Day, Up Canada Way
The Ketchup Song
Zephyrs in the Maple
The Piggy Back Race
The Hockey Song
Cornflakes
Song of the Cohoe
C-A-N-A-D-A (Cross Canada)
Name the Capitals
Little Wawa
Moon-Man Newfie
The Olympic Song
"Wop" May
Unity

Dr. Stompin' Tom Eh? (1993)

Football Song
Horse Called Farmer
Road to Thunder Bay
Your Someone Lonesome
Just a Blue Moon Away
Old Flat-Top Guitar
Honeymoon Is Over, Poochie Pie
Canada Day, Up Canada Way
Blue Berets
Let's Smile Again
Suzanne De Lafayette
(aka Girl from Lafayette)
Gumboot Cloggeroo
Shakin' the Blues

KIC* Along with Stompin'
Tom—*Compilation*—(1993)
The Hockey Song
To It and At It
The Coal Boat Song
Margo's Cargo
Luke's Guitar
Muckin' Slushers (A Damn Good
Song for a Miner)
Handy-Man Blues
Song of the Irish Moss
Wreck of the Tammy Anne
Black Donnelly's Massacre
Jenny Donnelly
Tribute To Wilf Carter
Zakuska Polka
Red River Jane
The Consumer
Muk Luk Shoo
Okanagan Okee
Rita MacNeil (A Tribute)
Don Messer Story
Believe In Your Country

Long Gone to the Yukon
(1995)
Long Gone to the Yukon
Al Sass and Dee John
Case Closed
How Do You Like It Now?
Country Jack (aka Wino of Skid
Row)
Kitchen Show
Maple Leaf Waltz
Polka Playin' Henry
Broken Wings
I'll Dream You Back
My Home's in Newfoundland
Song Bird Valley
All Night Cafe Blues
No, No, No
Hey, Hey, Loretta
I'll Do It for You
Mrs. Blue Guitar

25 of the Best Stompin' Tom
Souvenirs—*Compilation*—
(1998)
Blue Berets
Cross Canada
Believe in Your Country
Rubberhead
The Ketchup Song
Gumboot Cloggeroo
Tillsonburg
Red River Jane
The Hockey Song
Suzanne De Lafayette
Canada Day, Up Canada Way
Alberta Rose
Bud the Spud
Old Flat-Top Guitar
Prairie Moon
Long Gone to the Yukon
Polka Playin' Henry
My Home's in Newfoundland
I Am the Wind
A Real Canadian Girl
Blue Nose
Okanagan Okee
Sudbury Saturday Night
Shakin' the Blues
To It and At It

Move Along with
Stompin' Tom (1999)
Move Along
Songwriter's Wife
Excuse Me
If a Memory Was a Melody
A Brand New Love Affair
Stop Me
Confederation Bridge
Silver Sea
Wildwood Flower
Meadows of My Mind
Sammy Morgan's Gin
Dominoes & Dice
Long Gone to the Yukon
Big Joe Mufferaw
Sasquatch Song
Waltzing Matilda